Frommer's®
Chicago

My Chicago

by Elizabeth Canning Blackwell

FOR ME, CHICAGO IS ALL ABOUT ATTITUDE—AND NOT THE IN-YOUR-FACE

kind. The city and many of its citizens buzz with positive energy. It's easy to define Chicago by what it's not—not high-pressure like New York, not edgy like San Francisco or Seattle; not blessed with beautiful weather like L.A. But what Chicago does have is all the adrenaline rush and diverse charms of a big city without the accompanying pressure.

I can stroll through the Loop and feel sufficiently awed by the towering high-rises; then a few minutes later I can get a nature fix by walking along the shores of Lake Michigan. There's enough culture to keep my mind sharp, but no one's competitive about snagging tickets to the latest exhibit or theater performance. I can find pretty much any designer look I covet, but most people aren't caught up in fashion and fads.

Chicago may be big and bustling, but it still has a self-effacing, Midwestern reticence. It's the kind of place that seduces you with comfort rather than flashiness. When I came here for college, I didn't plan on staying. But Chicago sucked me in. I was drawn to the down-to-earth people, the bike paths along the lakefront, the great restaurants, and most of all the welcoming aura the city exudes that made me feel I belonged. I hope you have the same experience. These photos offer a glimpse of the Chicago I love.

© Tim Turner/Charlie Trotter's

Chicago restaurants run the gamut from gourmet showplaces to neighborhood dives to virtually every ethnic cuisine you can imagine. If you want to splurge, **CHARLIE TROTTER'S (left)** is the place to do it. The food (such as this turbot ceviche wrapped in smoked salmon with razor clam vinaigrette) is beautifully presented, painstakingly prepared, and always dazzlingly original.

Though Chicago has more than its fair share of fancy, pricey restaurants, on an average evening, I'm more likely to head to **LOU MALNATI'S (above)** for deep-dish pizza. There are plenty of other pizza joints in this town known for its pizza—all of them fine—but Malnati's is my favorite: not too much cheese, generous toppings, and a fantastic cornmeal crust.

Serious shoppers can spend days scouting for deals around Chicago. But the massive **MARSHALL FIELD'S DEPARTMENT STORE (above)** on State Street has a special place in most Chicagoans' hearts. Built in the mid-19th century, the grand building harks back to a time when shopping downtown was an event; highlights include the massive **TIFFANY GLASS DOME (right)** that towers over a multi-story atrium. Just as impressive is the way Field's has managed to keep up with the times, offering a range of mini-designer boutiques along with more affordable brands.

Opposite page: © Richard Cummins/Lonely Planet Images

Walk through downtown Chicago and you'll get a capsule history of modern urban architecture. One of the city's earliest high-rises, **THE ROOKERY** (designed by some of Chicago's best-known architects: Burnham & Root and Frank Lloyd Wright), looks gloomy and imposing from the outside, with thick, fortress-like walls. But step inside, and you'll find yourself entering a bright, two-story atrium filled with natural light and artfully-twisting staircases curving overhead (far more open and welcoming than your standard office lobby). Take an architectural walking tour around Chicago to glimpse more of the city's hidden treasures.

© Michael Brosilow/Lookingglass Theatre Company

What I love most about Chicago's theater scene is the variety: You can see everything from flashy, Broadway-bound musicals to in-your-face storefront shows where the performers on stage outnumber the people in the audience. Two of the best theater companies in town are particularly visitor-friendly, since they're within easy reach of downtown hotels. The **LOOKINGGLASS THEATRE COMPANY** **(above)** usually takes inspiration from works of literature to create thought-provoking and visually-arresting shows (this photo is from a performance of George Orwell's *1984*). On Navy Pier, the **CHICAGO SHAKESPEARE THEATRE** **(right)** presents the classics in a lovely courtyard-style theater that brings the actors up close and personal.

© Kim Karpeles/Alamy

It seems like every movie set in Chicago features an elevated train zipping along in the background of a crucial scene. **THE EL (right)** is more than just a symbol of the city; it's also a great way to experience the town. Take a ride on my favorite route, the Brown Line, to see what I mean.

Whether you're headed to the monkey house, the polar bear pool, or the elaborate African habitat, the **LINCOLN PARK ZOO (below)** takes you worlds away. Because it's free, families wander in and out, stopping to watch whatever catches their fancy or take a break on the zoo's welcoming lawns; this zoo feels like an extension of the park rather than a special excursion.

Millennium Park covers only a few blocks in the northwest corner of downtown's Grant Park, but that compact space is home to some stunning works of art—pieces meant to be experienced up close rather than admired from afar. The **CROWN FOUNTAIN (left)** projects massive photos of ordinary Chicagoans; water pours out of their mouths every few minutes, splashing giggling children below.

Another highlight of Millennium Park is sculptor Anish Kapoor's ***CLOUD GATE*** **(above, at left)**, which reflects the city skyline and the figures of people walking around and underneath it. A few steps away, dramatic curves of steel seem to billow over the **PRITZKER MUSIC PAVILION (above, at right)**, designed by Frank Gehry, where the Grant Park Music Festival performs free summer concerts.

The **FIELD MUSEUM OF NATURAL HISTORY (left)** is one of those massive institutions that seem to have everything: mummies, precious gems, dusty dioramas, and modern interactive exhibits. But it's "Sue," the most complete *Tyrannosaurus rex* fossil ever discovered, that makes a dramatic first impression.

If you've only got time for one trip out of Chicago, head to Oak Park. Home to Frank Lloyd Wright in the years he began transforming American architecture, the town's juxtaposition of traditional wood-frame Victorian houses and low-slung, Prairie-style homes show exactly why Wright's work was so revolutionary. One of Wright's Oak Park masterpieces is **UNITY TEMPLE (below)**, a building that subverts traditional church architecture to create a new kind of sacred space.

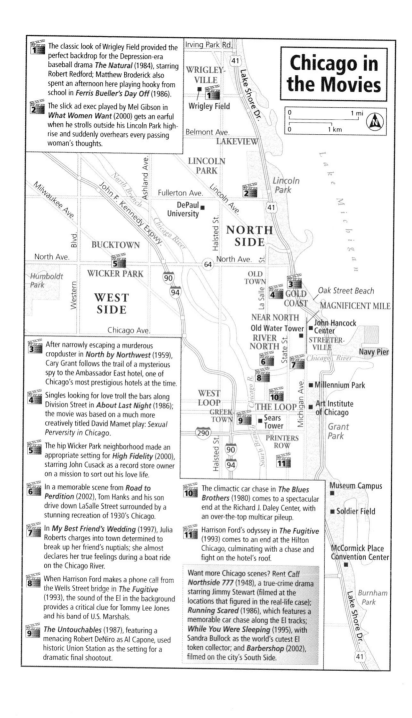

Chicago in the Movies

0 — 1 mi
0 — 1 km

1 The classic look of Wrigley Field provided the perfect backdrop for the Depression-era baseball drama *The Natural* (1984), starring Robert Redford; Matthew Broderick also spent an afternoon here playing hooky from school in *Ferris Bueller's Day Off* (1986).

2 The slick ad exec played by Mel Gibson in *What Women Want* (2000) gets an earful when he strolls outside his Lincoln Park highrise and suddenly overhears every passing woman's thoughts.

3 After narrowly escaping a murderous cropduster in *North by Northwest* (1959), Cary Grant follows the trail of a mysterious spy to the Ambassador East hotel, one of Chicago's most prestigious hotels at the time.

4 Singles looking for love troll the bars along Division Street in *About Last Night* (1986); the movie was based on a much more creatively titled David Mamet play: *Sexual Perversity in Chicago*.

5 The hip Wicker Park neighborhood made an appropriate setting for *High Fidelity* (2000), starring John Cusack as a record store owner on a mission to sort out his love life.

6 In a memorable scene from *Road to Perdition* (2002), Tom Hanks and his son drive down LaSalle Street surrounded by a stunning recreation of 1930's Chicago.

7 In *My Best Friend's Wedding* (1997), Julia Roberts charges into town determined to break up her friend's nuptials; she almost declares her true feelings during a boat ride on the Chicago River.

8 When Harrison Ford makes a phone call from the Wells Street bridge in *The Fugitive* (1993), the sound of the El in the background provides a critical clue for Tommy Lee Jones and his band of U.S. Marshals.

9 *The Untouchables* (1987), featuring a menacing Robert DeNiro as Al Capone, used historic Union Station as the setting for a dramatic final shootout.

10 The climactic car chase in *The Blues Brothers* (1980) comes to a spectacular end at the Richard J. Daley Center, with an over-the-top multicar pileup.

11 Harrison Ford's odyssey in *The Fugitive* (1993) comes to an end at the Hilton Chicago, culminating with a chase and fight on the hotel's roof.

Want more Chicago scenes? Rent *Call Northside 777* (1948), a true-crime drama starring Jimmy Stewart (filmed at the locations that figured in the real-life case); *Running Scared* (1986), which features a memorable car chase along the El tracks; *While You Were Sleeping* (1995), with Sandra Bullock as the world's cutest El token collector; and *Barbershop* (2002), filmed on the city's South Side.

Irving Park Rd.
WRIGLEY-VILLE
Wrigley Field
Belmont Ave.
LAKEVIEW
LINCOLN PARK
Fullerton Ave.
DePaul University
NORTH SIDE
Lincoln Park
Milwaukee Ave.
Ashland Ave.
John F. Kennedy Expwy
North Branch
Chicago River
Halsted St.
Lincoln Ave.
BUCKTOWN
North Ave.
Blvd.
Humboldt Park
WICKER PARK
WEST SIDE
Western
Chicago Ave.
North Ave.
OLD TOWN
GOLD COAST
Oak Street Beach
MAGNIFICENT MILE
La Salle
NEAR NORTH
Old Water Tower
RIVER NORTH
John Hancock Center
STREETER-VILLE
Navy Pier
State St.
Chicago River
WEST LOOP
GREEK TOWN
THE LOOP
Sears Tower
PRINTERS ROW
Halsted St.
South Branch
Michigan Ave.
Millennium Park
Art Institute of Chicago
Grant Park
Museum Campus
Soldier Field
McCormick Place Convention Center
Burnham Park
Lake Shore Dr.
Lake Michigan

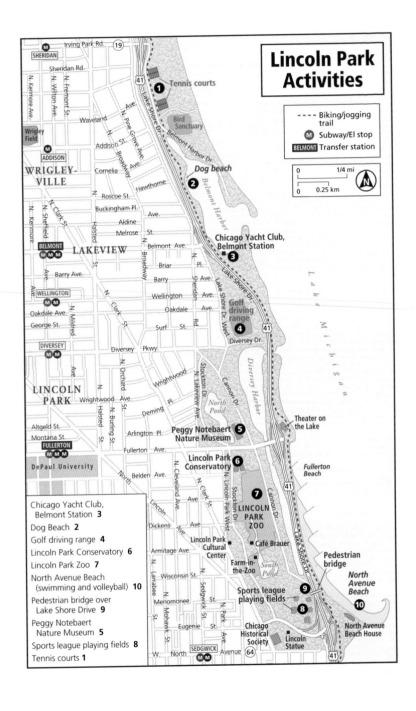

Lincoln Park Activities

- - - - Biking/jogging trail
Ⓜ Subway/El stop
BELMONT Transfer station

Chicago Yacht Club, Belmont Station **3**
Dog Beach **2**
Golf driving range **4**
Lincoln Park Conservatory **6**
Lincoln Park Zoo **7**
North Avenue Beach (swimming and volleyball) **10**
Pedestrian bridge over Lake Shore Drive **9**
Peggy Notebaert Nature Museum **5**
Sports league playing fields **8**
Tennis courts **1**

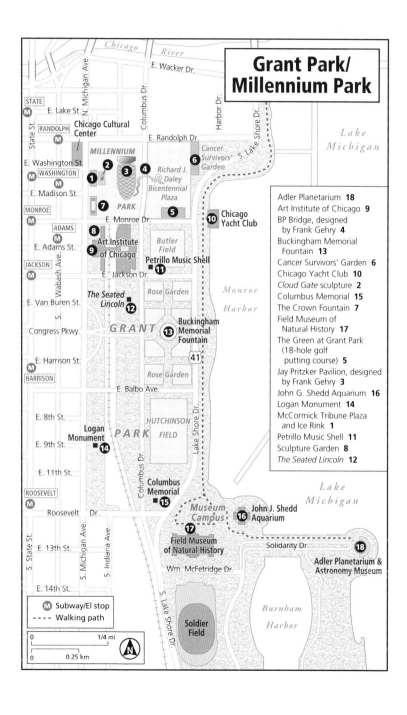

Grant Park/
Millennium Park

STATE
M E. Lake St.

RANDOLPH
M

Chicago Cultural
Center

MILLENNIUM

E. Washington St.
M WASHINGTON

E. Madison St.

MONROE
M

ADAMS
M

E. Adams St.

JACKSON
M

Art Institute
of Chicago

PARK

Richard J.
Daley
Bicentennial
Plaza

E. Randolph Dr.

Cancer
Survivors'
Garden

E. Monroe Dr.

Butler
Field

Petrillo Music Shell

E. Jackson Dr.

Chicago
Yacht Club

Chicago River

E. Wacker Dr.

*Lake
Michigan*

E. Van Buren St.

Congress Pkwy.

The Seated
Lincoln

GRANT

Rose Garden

Buckingham
Memorial
Fountain

41

Rose Garden

*Monroe

Harbor*

E. Harrison St.
HARRISON

E. Balbo Ave.

E. 8th St.

Logan
Monument

E. 9th St.

PARK

HUTCHINSON
FIELD

E. 11th St.

ROOSEVELT
M

Roosevelt Dr.

E. 13th St.

Columbus
Memorial

*Museum
Campus*

John J. Shedd
Aquarium

Field Museum
of Natural History

*Lake
Michigan*

Solidarity Dr.

E. 14th St.

M Subway/El stop
- - - - Walking path

0   1/4 mi

0   0.25 km

N

Wm. McFetridge Dr.

Soldier
Field

*Burnham

Harbor*

Adler Planetarium &
Astronomy Museum

Adler Planetarium **18**
Art Institute of Chicago **9**
BP Bridge, designed
  by Frank Gehry **4**
Buckingham Memorial
  Fountain **13**
Cancer Survivors' Garden **6**
Chicago Yacht Club **10**
Cloud Gate sculpture **2**
Columbus Memorial **15**
The Crown Fountain **7**
Field Museum of
  Natural History **17**
The Green at Grant Park
  (18-hole golf
  putting course) **5**
Jay Pritzker Pavilion, designed
  by Frank Gehry **3**
John G. Shedd Aquarium **16**
Logan Monument **14**
McCormick Tribune Plaza
  and Ice Rink **1**
Petrillo Music Shell **11**
Sculpture Garden **8**
The Seated Lincoln **12**

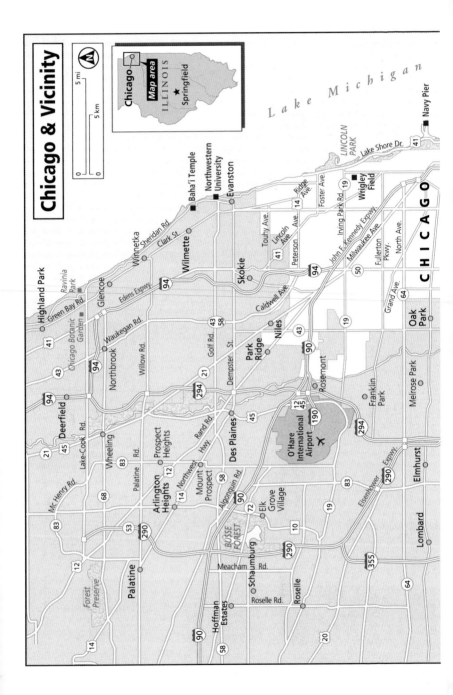

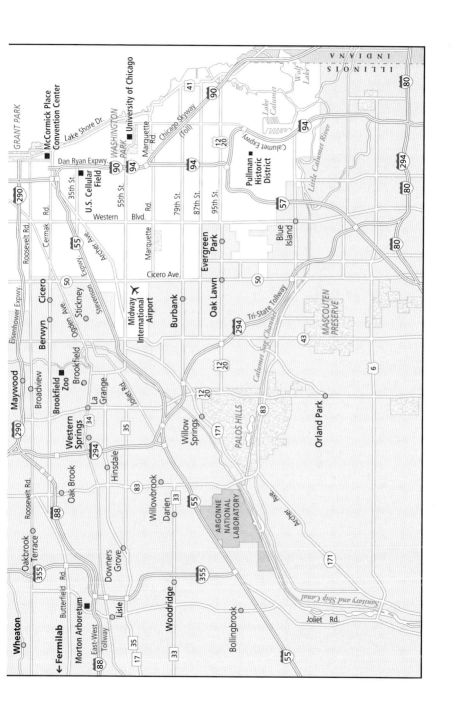

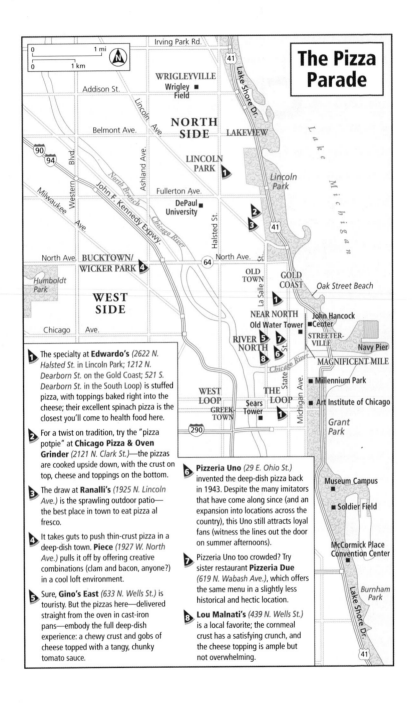

The Pizza Parade

0 —— 1 mi
0 —— 1 km

Irving Park Rd.

41

WRIGLEYVILLE
Wrigley ■ Field

Addison St.

Belmont Ave.

NORTH SIDE **LAKEVIEW**

90
94

Lincoln Ave.

Ashland Ave.

Blvd.

Milwaukee Ave.

Western

North Branch

John F. Kennedy Expwy.

Chicago River

LINCOLN PARK ❶

Fullerton Ave.

DePaul ■ University

Halsted St.

Lincoln Park

❷
❸
41

Lake Michigan

North Ave. **BUCKTOWN/ WICKER PARK** ❹

Humboldt Park

WEST SIDE

Chicago Ave.

64 North Ave.

La Salle St.

OLD TOWN

GOLD COAST Oak Street Beach

❶

NEAR NORTH
Old Water Tower

John Hancock ■ Center

RIVER NORTH ❺ ❼
❽ ❻

Chicago River

STREETER- VILLE

Navy Pier

MAGNIFICENT MILE

WEST LOOP

GREEK TOWN

Sears Tower ■

THE LOOP

State Ave.

Michigan Ave.

■ Millennium Park

■ Art Institute of Chicago

290

❶

Grant Park

Museum Campus

■ Soldier Field

❶ The specialty at **Edwardo's** *(2622 N. Halsted St.* in Lincoln Park; *1212 N. Dearborn St.* on the Gold Coast; *521 S. Dearborn St.* in the South Loop) is stuffed pizza, with toppings baked right into the cheese; their excellent spinach pizza is the closest you'll come to health food here.

❷ For a twist on tradition, try the "pizza potpie" at **Chicago Pizza & Oven Grinder** *(2121 N. Clark St.)*—the pizzas are cooked upside down, with the crust on top, cheese and toppings on the bottom.

❸ The draw at **Ranalli's** *(1925 N. Lincoln Ave.)* is the sprawling outdoor patio— the best place in town to eat pizza al fresco.

❹ It takes guts to push thin-crust pizza in a deep-dish town. **Piece** *(1927 W. North Ave.)* pulls it off by offering creative combinations (clam and bacon, anyone?) in a cool loft environment.

❺ Sure, **Gino's East** *(633 N. Wells St.)* is touristy. But the pizzas here—delivered straight from the oven in cast-iron pans—embody the full deep-dish experience: a chewy crust and gobs of cheese topped with a tangy, chunky tomato sauce.

❻ **Pizzeria Uno** *(29 E. Ohio St.)* invented the deep-dish pizza back in 1943. Despite the many imitators that have come along since (and an expansion into locations across the country), this Uno still attracts loyal fans (witness the lines out the door on summer afternoons).

❼ Pizzeria Uno too crowded? Try sister restaurant **Pizzeria Due** *(619 N. Wabash Ave.)*, which offers the same menu in a slightly less historical and hectic location.

❽ **Lou Malnati's** *(439 N. Wells St.)* is a local favorite; the cornmeal crust has a satisfying crunch, and the cheese topping is ample but not overwhelming.

McCormick Place Convention Center

Burnham Park

Lake Shore Dr.

41

Frommer's®

Chicago

2008

by Elizabeth Canning Blackwell & Michael Austin

917.731
F92c
2008

Here's what the critics say about Frommer's:

"Amazingly easy to use. Very portable, very complete."

—*Booklist*

"Detailed, accurate, and easy-to-read information for all price ranges."
—*Glamour Magazine*

"Hotel information is close to encyclopedic."

—*Des Moines Sunday Register*

"Frommer's Guides have a way of giving you a real feel for a place."
—*Knight Ridder Newspapers*

BICENTENNIAL
1807
WILEY
2007
BICENTENNIAL

Wiley Publishing, Inc.

Published by:

Wiley Publishing, Inc.

111 River St.
Hoboken, NJ 07030-5774

ISBN: 978-0-470-16537-9
Editor: Anuja Madar
Production Editor: Eric T. Schroeder
Cartographer: Anton Crane
Photo Editor: Richard Fox
Wiley Bicentennial Logo: Richard J. Pacifico
Production by Wiley Indianapolis Composition Services

Front cover photo: Wrigley Building in clear light
Back cover photo: Blue Chicago Club, musicians performing on stage

For information on our other products and services or to obtain technical support, please contact our Customer Care Department within the U.S. at 800/762-2974, outside the U.S. at 317/572-3993 or fax 317/572-4002.

Wiley also publishes its books in a variety of electronic formats. Some content that appears in print may not be available in electronic formats.

Manufactured in the United States of America

5   4   3   2   1

Contents

9 Shopping   224

10 Chicago After Dark   251

Appendix: Chicago in Depth   293

Index   300

List of Maps

An Invitation to the Reader

In researching this book, we discovered many wonderful places—hotels, restaurants, shops, and more. We're sure you'll find others. Please tell us about them so we can share the information with your fellow travelers in upcoming editions. If you were disappointed with a recommendation, we'd love to know that, too. Please write to:

Frommer's Chicago 2008
Wiley Publishing, Inc. • 111 River St. • Hoboken, NJ 07030-5774

An Additional Note

Please be advised that travel information is subject to change at any time—and this is especially true of prices. We therefore suggest that you write or call ahead for confirmation when making your travel plans. The authors, editors, and publisher cannot be held responsible for the experiences of readers while traveling. Your safety is important to us, however, so we encourage you to stay alert and be aware of your surroundings. Keep a close eye on cameras, purses, and wallets, all favorite targets of thieves and pickpockets.

About the Authors

Elizabeth Canning Blackwell began life on the East Coast, but 4 years at Northwestern University transformed her into a Midwesterner. She has worked as a writer and editor at *Encyclopedia Brittanica,* Northwestern University Medical School, the *Chicago Tribune,* and *North Shore,* a lifestyle magazine for the Chicago suburbs. She also has written for national magazines on everything from planning the perfect wedding to fighting a duel. She lives just outside the city with her husband, daughter, and an extensive collection of long underwear.

A Chicago-area native and the son of a Trans World Airlines employee, **Michael Austin** caught the travel bug at a profoundly young age (around about 9, he guesses). Today he is a freelance writer specializing in food, wine, and, naturally, travel. His stories and personal essays have appeared in *Esquire, GQ, Outside,* and the *Chicago Tribune Magazine.* Most recently he collaborated with Oprah Winfrey's personal chef, Art Smith, on *Back to the Family,* a cookbook featuring reflections on sharing meals with loved ones. A James Beard Award finalist for feature writing, Michael lives in his favorite city, Chicago.

Other Great Guides for Your Trip:

Frommer's Memorable Walks in Chicago
Frommer's Chicago with Kids
Chicago For Dummies
Frommer's Chicago Day by Day
The Unofficial Guide to Chicago
Frommer's Irreverent Guide to Chicago
Frommer's Portable Chicago

Frommer's Star Ratings, Icons & Abbreviations

Every hotel, restaurant, and attraction listing in this guide has been ranked for quality, value, service, amenities, and special features using a **star-rating system.** In country, state, and regional guides, we also rate towns and regions to help you narrow down your choices and budget your time accordingly. Hotels and restaurants are rated on a scale of zero (recommended) to three stars (exceptional). Attractions, shopping, nightlife, towns, and regions are rated according to the following scale: zero stars (recommended), one star (highly recommended), two stars (very highly recommended), and three stars (must-see).

In addition to the star-rating system, we also use **seven feature icons** that point you to the great deals, in-the-know advice, and unique experiences that separate travelers from tourists. Throughout the book, look for:

Finds	Special finds—those places only insiders know about
Fun Fact	Fun facts—details that make travelers more informed and their trips more fun
Kids	Best bets for kids and advice for the whole family
Moments	Special moments—those experiences that memories are made of
Overrated	Places or experiences not worth your time or money
Tips	Insider tips—great ways to save time and money
Value	Great values—where to get the best deals

The following **abbreviations** are used for credit cards:

AE	American Express	DISC	Discover	V	Visa
DC	Diners Club	MC	MasterCard		

Frommers.com

Now that you have this guidebook to help you plan a great trip, visit our website at **www.frommers.com** for additional travel information on more than 3,600 destinations. We update features regularly to give you instant access to the most current trip-planning information available. At Frommers.com, you'll find scoops on the best airfares, lodging rates, and car rental bargains. You can even book your travel online through our reliable travel booking partners. Other popular features include:

- Online updates of our most popular guidebooks
- Vacation sweepstakes and contest giveaways
- Newsletters highlighting the hottest travel trends
- Online travel message boards with featured travel discussions

What's New in Chicago

WHERE TO STAY The **James Hotel,** 55 E. Ontario St. (© 877/ JAMES-55 or 312/337-1000), attracts a stylish, design-conscious clientele with its sleek, contemporary look. Located just off bustling Michigan Avenue, its J Bar has already become a top see-and-be-seen spot for trendy young Chicagoans; it's also home to David Burke's Primehouse, a modern interpretation of the traditional steakhouse. Rooms feature dark wood platform beds, contemporary artwork, and the usual high-tech amenities (plasma-screen TVs, iPod docks, etc.). With guest rooms averaging $300 and up, you'd expect no less.

The former House of Blues Hotel has been transformed into the **Hotel Sax** (© 877/569-3742 or 312/245-0333), which bills itself as "bohemian boutique." That means eclectic room decor (such as snakeskin-covered chairs) and a cool lobby lounge, done up in a vaguely *Arabian Nights* theme. What hasn't changed is the hotel's great location, steps from the Chicago River and some of the city's best restaurants and nightlife.

WHERE TO DINE Attention smokers! By order of the Chicago City Council, smoking is banned in all restaurant dining rooms. Restaurants with a separate bar area can choose to allow smoking there, but only if they install an air filtration system. If you want to light up when you go out, call first to see if there's a bar where smoking is permitted.

The restaurant drawing the most attention lately is **De La Costa,** in the River East Arts Center, 465 E. Illinois St. (© 312/464-1700), the first Chicago restaurant from Chef Douglas Rodriguez (who got raves for his Latin cuisine at restaurants such as Patria in New York and Alma de Cuba in Philadelphia). The sprawling, dramatic space does not disappoint: with everything from a DJ booth to a ceviche bar (a Latin take on the sushi bar), the loftlike setting oozes urban cool. The must-order drink: the "Poptails," which come with mini (alcoholic) popsicles. The menu offers a minitour of Latin America and Spain, with everything from tapas to Uruguayan steaks.

A few blocks away, hidden inside a high-rise condo building, **Copperblue,** 580 E. Illinois St. (© 312/527-1200), draws diners with a creative take on Mediterranean cuisine. Chef Michael Tsonton has a whimsical sense of humor (Pacific snapper comes with a "mustard spice and everything nice" butter broth), but it never upstages the flavorful food. Feeling adventurous? Try the "Fifth Quarter" tasting menu to sample meat cuts that normally don't get cooked in fine restaurants, let alone eaten.

EXPLORING CHICAGO Michigan Avenue added another example of eye-catching architecture with the opening of the new **Spertus Museum,** 610 S. Michigan Ave. (© 312/322-1747), in fall 2007. Unlike the museum's previous, undistinguished-looking home next door, the new building is airy and inviting. It also has space for expanded exhibits, an interactive learning center for children, and a kosher cafe run by Wolfgang Puck's catering company.

In other museum news, the **National Museum of Mexican Art,** formerly the Mexican Fine Arts Museum, 1852 W. 19th St. (© 312/738-1503), was accredited by the American Association of Museums in 2007. It's the first—and so far, the only—Latino museum in the country to receive accreditation. As part of the museum's outreach program, the name was changed to better reflect its mission.

Before visiting any Chicago museum, it pays to check out the museum's website first; more and more cultural institutions now offer downloadable tours and interactive trip planners. For example, the website for the **Field Museum of Natural History** (www.fieldmuseum.org) has mp3 audiotours of the museum's permanent collection; you can also print out a Family Adventure Tour, which sends kids on a scavenger hunt throughout the museum. The **Millennium Park** mp3 audiotour (available at www.millenniumpark.org) includes interviews with the artists who created the park's eye-catching artwork.

SHOPPING   To find out what's new on the Chicago shopping scene, head to West Division street, where trendy new boutiques continue to spring up on the blocks between Milwaukee and Damen avenues. Emblematic of Division Street's focus on modern style is the ecofriendly baby boutique **Grow,** 1943 W. Division St. (© 773/489-0009). The bright, open space showcases streamlined kids' furniture, as well as clothing made of organic fabrics.

This is a great time to visit Chicago if you've got a sweet tooth, now that outposts of **Ethel's Chocolate Lounge** seem to be opening up around town. (The most convenient locations for visitors are inside Westfield North Bridge mall, 520 N. Michigan Ave. (© 312/464-9330), and inside the 900 N. Michigan Avenue mall (© 312/440-9747). A celebration of all things chocolate, these bright, candy-colored cafes have a distinctly feminine vibe and offer a mouth-watering array of tasty (if pricey) candies; flavors range from espresso-flavored truffles to the "Etheltini" (a dark chocolate square spiked with vodka and dry vermouth). Ethel's also has a location along the Armitage Avenue shopping strip, 819 W. Armitage Ave. (© 773/281-0029).

Need to stock up on supplies for a lakefront picnic lunch? A new upscale deli, **Goddess & Grocer,** 25 E. Delaware St. (© 312/896-2600), stocks everything from specialty sandwiches to chicken and pasta dishes to freshly baked cookies and brownies. The prepared foods are a few notches above the standard takeout spot (wild Alaskan salmon, wild mushroom risotto), and the staff can put together meals for any occasion (including "to go" meals for you to take on your next flight out of O'Hare airport).

CHICAGO   AFTER   DARK   At Chicago's upscale lounges, the drinks keep getting more expensive and the bottle service trend shows no signs of slowing down. In Lincoln Park, a neighborhood filled mostly with sports bars, **Krem,** 1750 N. Clark St. (© 312/932-1750), attracts scenesters with its 33-foot "bed" and white furniture that glows under the blue light. You can order off a small-plates menu, or simply pose with everyone else.

Still, the Chicago nightlife scene isn't all about attitude. At the new West Loop hot spot **Lumen,** 839 W. Fulton Market (© 312/733-2222), there's no VIP section and no list to get in. Instead, all eyes turn toward the massive LED light display, which runs along the ceiling and changes color throughout the night. Otherwise, the look at this bar is sleek and spare, with concrete walls and low-slung minimalist banquette seating.

The environmentally friendly **Butter-fly Social Club,** 722 W. Grand Ave. (© **312/666-1695**), features treehouse-like nooks, organic juices in drinks, and is smoke-free (fittingly, it opened on Earth Day in 2007). It uses solar power for some of its electrical needs and incorporates recycled and natural materials into its design, such as "trees" made from mud, sand, clay, and straw. DJs spin upbeat world music that thumps through speakers made of recycled wood.

1

The Best of Chicago

Like any great city, Chicago's got something for everyone, whether your tastes run toward world-famous museums and blow-your-budget luxury hotels or family-friendly lodgings and low-key neighborhood restaurants. Narrowing down your choices may seem daunting, but never fear: Here's your cheat sheet to the very best of the city, the places to which I send out-of-town friends and relatives when they want to experience the "real" Chicago. Some are well-known tourist attractions, others are insider secrets, but all are places and experiences that truly sum up this town. Happy exploring!

1 The Most Unforgettable Travel Experiences

- **Studying the Skyline:** The birthplace of the modern skyscraper, Chicago is the perfect place to learn about—and appreciate—these dramatic buildings. If you're only in town for a short time, get a quick skyscraper fix by strolling through the heart of downtown, known as the Loop, where you'll be surrounded by canyons of stone, concrete, and glass. (To get the full urban experience, visit on a weekday, when the streets are bustling.) If you have more time, take an architectural tour by foot, bus, bike, or boat. See "Sightseeing Tours," p. 212.

- **Chilling Out on the Lakefront:** It really is cooler—meteorologically and metaphorically—by the lake, and we Chicagoans treat the Lake Michigan waterfront as our personal playground. Miles of parkland hug the shoreline; walk to Monroe Harbor for picture-perfect views of the downtown or join active Lincoln Park singles for biking or jogging farther north. For an even better look at the city, get out on the water. At Navy Pier, you can board a vessel that's just

your speed, from a powerboat to a tall-masted schooner. See "Staying Active," p. 218.

- **Riding the Rails:** Find out why the Loop is so named by hopping a Brown Line elevated train (or "the El," for short). Watch the city unfold as the train crosses the Chicago River and screeches past downtown high-rises. Half the fun is peeping into the windows of offices and homes as you speed by (don't feel guilty—we all do it). See "Getting Around," p. 73, and "Sightseeing Tours," p. 212.

- **Escaping Downtown:** Local politicians like to refer to Chicago as "a city of neighborhoods"—and in this case, they're telling the truth. You won't really experience Chicago unless you leave downtown and explore some residential areas, whether it's the historic wood-framed homes in Old Town or the eclectic boutiques of Wicker Park. It's one of the best ways to get a feeling for how the people here actually live, from Hispanic families in Pilsen to gay couples on Halsted Street. See "Neighborhoods in Brief," p. 70.

2 The Best Splurge Hotels

- The **Four Seasons** (120 E. Delaware Place; ℂ **800/332-3442;** www.four seasons.com): Appropriately enough in this skyscraper-packed city, some of the best hotels perch far above the sidewalk. The Four Seasons (as well as the Ritz-Carlton; see below) is tucked above a high-rise shopping mall on Michigan Avenue. A favorite among camera-shy celebrities who want to keep a low profile, the hotel exudes understated luxury; expect discretion, not a lively lobby scene. Where the Four Seasons really shines is its service—the concierges might be the best in town. The clubby full-service spa provides on-site pampering, for a price. See p. 92.

- The **Park Hyatt** (800 N. Michigan Ave.; ℂ **800/233-1234;** www. parkchicago.hyatt.com): If the thought of overstuffed couches and thick brocade curtains make you wince, this is the hotel for you. With its focus on modern design and clean lines, the Park Hyatt feels like one of those cool urban spaces featured in *Architectural Digest.* Reproductions of Eames and Mies furniture fill the guest rooms, and in-room electronics include flatscreen TVs and DVD players. The coolest feature? Moveable bathroom walls that allow you to soak in the view while you lounge in the tub. See p. 93.

- The **Peninsula** (108 E. Superior St.; ℂ **866/288-8889;** http://chicago. peninsula.com): Inspired by the elegance of 1920s Shanghai and Hong Kong, the Chicago outpost of this Asian chain is a seamless blend of classic and modern. The grand public spaces may be a throwback to the past, but the hotel's amenities are ultramodern. Bedrooms and bathrooms feature "command stations" that allow you to adjust lights, temperature, and TVs without getting up. The top-notch gym, spa, and indoor swimming pool (filled with natural light) make The Peninsula a must for fitness fanatics. See p. 93.

- The **Ritz-Carlton** (160 E. Pearson St.; ℂ **800/621-6906;** www.fourseasons. com): Located above the Water Tower shopping center, the Ritz has one of the most welcoming lobbies in town, with light streaming through the windows, masses of fresh flowers, and bird's-eye views of the city. The guest rooms, decorated in warm shades of yellow and blue, have European-style elegance, and the staff prides itself on granting every wish. See p. 94.

- The **W Chicago Lakeshore** (644 N. Lake Shore Dr.; ℂ **877/W-HOTELS;** www.whotels.com): The city's only hotel with a lakefront address may try a little too hard to be hip, but it offers a nightclubby vibe that sets it apart from the many cookie-cutter convention-friendly hotels in town. (The rates are substantially lower than those at the hotels listed above, but the W is

Impressions

We were on one of the most glamorous corners of Chicago. I dwelt on the setting. The lakeshore view was stupendous. I couldn't see it but I knew it well and felt its effect—the shining road beside the shining gold vacancy of Lake Michigan. Man had overcome the emptiness of this land. But the emptiness had given him a few good licks in return.

—Saul Bellow, *Humboldt's Gift,* 1975

still a splurge for thrifty travelers.) The rooms' color scheme—shades of gray, black, and deep red—are a refreshing change from the chain-hotel look (although they won't appeal to guests who like things light and airy). The top-floor Whiskey Sky bar is cramped, but good for people-watching, and the outpost of New York's trendy Bliss spa is a must-visit for beauty junkies. See p. 97.

3 The Best Moderately Priced Hotels

- **Chicago City Centre** (300 E. Ohio St.; ℂ **800/HOLIDAY;** www.chicc.com): A real find for budget-conscious families, the City Centre scores big for its amenities: two pools (indoor and outdoor), free access to the Lake Shore Athletic Club next door, and free meals for children 11 and under at the hotel's restaurants. The location is great, too—just a few blocks from kid-friendly Navy Pier. See p. 98.

- **Hampton Inn & Suites Chicago Downtown** (33 W. Illinois St.; ℂ **800/HAMPTON;** www.hamptoninn.com): Located in a busy neighborhood full of restaurants and nightlife, the Hampton Inn feels more expensive than it is. The rooms have an upscale urban look, and the indoor pool is a draw for families. The hotel's hot breakfast buffet, included in the room rates and served in an attractive second-floor lounge, puts the standard coffee-and-doughnut spread at other motels to shame. See p. 102.

- **Red Roof Inn** (162 E. Ontario St.; ℂ **800/733-7663;** www.redroof-chicago-downtown.com): This high-rise version of the roadside motel is your best bet for the cheapest rates downtown. The rooms don't have much in the way of style (or natural light), and the bathrooms, though spotless, are a little cramped, but it fits the bill if you want a central location and plan on using your hotel as a place to sleep rather than hang out. See p. 100.

- **Majestic Hotel** (528 W. Brompton St.; ℂ **800/727-5108;** www.cityinns.com): A bit off the beaten path, this neighborhood hotel is tucked away on a residential street just a short walk from Wrigley Field and the lakefront. You won't find lots of fancy amenities, but the atmosphere here has the personal touch of a B&B. Rates include continental breakfast and afternoon tea in the lobby. See p. 106.

4 The Most Unforgettable Dining Experiences

- **Charlie Trotter's** (816 W. Armitage Ave.; ℂ **773/248-6228**): Charlie Trotter is the city's original celebrity chef, and his intimate restaurant, inside a town house, is the first place I steer foodie visitors. The formula may be rigid (tasting menus only), but the food is anything but: fresh-as-can-be ingredients in dazzling combinations. The service lives up to Trotter's legendary perfectionism; the chef himself has been known to come out of the kitchen and ask diners why they didn't finish a certain dish. See p. 156.

- **Alinea** (1723 N. Halsted St.; ℂ **312/867-0110**): Widely considered the town's top restaurant of the moment, Alinea has gotten national press for chef Grant Achatz's revolutionary twist on contemporary dining. Each course of the ever-changing prix-fixe menu showcases Achatz's creativity, whether it's duck served on a scented "pillow" of juniper or a complete reinvention of "wine and cheese" (frozen grape juice rolled in grated bleu cheese and served with red-wine gelée). An added bonus: service that's friendly, not snobby. See p. 153.

- **Gibsons Bar & Steakhouse** (1028 N. Rush St.; ℂ **312/266-8999**): Chicago has no shortage of great steakhouses, but Gibsons has a great scene, too—a mix of moneyed Gold Coast singles, expense-account-fueled business travelers, and the occasional celebrity. This is the kind of place to live large (literally): The portions are enormous, so you're encouraged to share, which adds to the party atmosphere. See p. 130.
- **foodlife** (Water Tower Place, 835 N. Michigan Ave.; ℂ **312/335-3663**): This is my top pick for a quick, affordable, family-friendly meal downtown. Leaps and bounds beyond the standard mall food court, foodlife offers a wide range of non-chain food stations at affordable prices. Get everything from Asian noodles and vegetarian fare to more standard options such as pizza and burgers. See p. 137.
- **The Italian Village** (71 W. Monroe St.; ℂ **312/332-7005**): The old-school fettuccine alfredo won't win any culinary awards, but eating at this Chicago landmark is like taking a trip back in time, from the so-tacky-they're-cool twinkling "stars" embedded in the ceiling to the vintage waiters (some of whom look like they've been working here since the place opened in 1927). See p. 120.

5 The Best Museums

- **Art Institute of Chicago** (111 S. Michigan Ave.; ℂ **312/443-3600**): A must-see for art lovers, the Art Institute manages to combine blockbuster exhibits with smaller, uncrowded spaces for private meditation. Internationally known for its French Impressionist collection, the Art Institute can also transport you to Renaissance Italy, ancient China, or any number of other worlds. See p. 171.
- **Field Museum of Natural History** (Roosevelt Rd. and Lake Shore Dr.; ℂ **312/922-9410**): Its grand neoclassical entrance hall will make you feel you've entered somewhere important (the towering figure of Sue, the largest T-rex skeleton ever uncovered, enhances the sense of drama). The Field can easily entertain for an entire day. Exhibits include ancient Egyptian mummies, a full-size Maori meetinghouse, and stuffed figures of the notorious man-eating lions of Tsavo. See p. 183.
- **John G. Shedd Aquarium** (1200 S. Lake Shore Dr.; ℂ **312/939-2438**): Sure, you'll find plenty of tanks filled with exotic fish, but the Shedd is also home to some wonderful large-scale re-creations of natural habitats. Stroll through Wild Reef, and you'll see sharks swim overhead. The lovely Oceanarium, where you can watch a dolphin show, features floor-to-ceiling windows; you'll feel as if you're sitting outdoors, even on the chilliest Chicago day. See p. 184.
- **Museum of Science and Industry** (57th St. and Lake Shore Dr.; ℂ **800/468-6674**): I've been coming here for years, and I still haven't seen it all. Although the exhibits promote scientific knowledge, most have an interactive element that makes them especially fun for families. But it's not all computers and technology. Some of the classic exhibits—the underground re-creation of the coal mine and the World War II German

U-boat—have been attracting crowds for generations. See p. 194.

- **Frank Lloyd Wright Home and Studio** (951 Chicago Ave., Oak Park; ⓒ **708/848-1976**): The Midwest's greatest architect started out in the Chicago suburb of Oak Park, and his house—now a museum with guided tours—gives a firsthand look at his genius and his influence. The surrounding neighborhood, where Wright's Prairie-style homes sit side by side with rambling Victorian villas, is an eye-opening lesson in architectural history. See p. 204.

6 The Best Nightlife Experiences

- **Getting the Blues:** Here, in the world capital of the blues, you've got your pick of places to feel them, from the touristy but lively atmosphere of Kingston Mines in Lincoln Park, where musicians perform continuously on two stages, to the roadhouse feel of Buddy Guy's Legends, where musicians in town on tour have been known to play impromptu sets. See "The Music Scene," p. 267.

- **Taking in a Show:** The stage lights rarely go dark on one of the country's busiest theater scenes. Chicago is home to a downtown Broadway-style district anchored by beautifully restored historic theaters, the nationally known Goodman Theatre company, and the city's resident Shakespeare troupe. Beyond downtown, you'll find a number of innovative independent companies, where future stars get their big breaks and the pure love of theater makes up for the low budgets. See "The Performing Arts," p. 251.

- **Taking in Some Cool Jazz at the Green Mill:** This atmospheric Uptown jazz club is the place to go to soak up smooth sounds from some of the hottest up-and-coming performers on the jazz scene, while the club itself is a living museum of 1930s Chicago. The Sunday night "Poetry Slam" is a big crowd-pleaser. See p. 267.

- **Watching Improv Come Alive:** Chicago is a comedy breeding ground, having launched the careers of John Belushi, Bill Murray, Mike Myers, and Tina Fey through improv hot spots such as Second City and ImprovOlympic. The shows may soar or crash, but you just might catch one of comedy's future stars. See p. 264.

7 The Best Places to Hang with the Locals

- **Shopping the Town:** Michigan Avenue is often touted as a shopper's paradise, and I'll admit it has a great lineup of big-name designer boutiques and multilevel high-end shopping malls. But that's all stuff you can find in any other big city. For more distinctive items, head to the city's residential districts, where trendy independent clothing boutiques sit next to eclectic home-design stores filled with one-of-a-kind treasures. The home decor shops along Armitage Avenue cater to stylish young families with plenty of spending money, while Wicker Park and Bucktown attract edgy fashionistas with a range of funky clothing shops. Southport Avenue (near Wrigley Field) and West Division Street (south of Wicker Park) are the newest up-and-coming shopping meccas—with no nametag-wearing conventioneers in sight. See chapter 9.

- **Soaking Up Sun at Wrigley Field:** It's a Chicago tradition to play hooky for an afternoon, sit in the bleachers at this historic baseball park, and watch the Cubbies try to hit 'em onto Waveland Avenue. Despite being perennial losers, the Cubs sell out almost every game; your best bet is to buy tickets for a weekday afternoon (although you'll often find season ticket holders selling seats at face value in front of Wrigley right before a game). Even if you can't get in, you can still soak in the atmosphere at one of the neighborhood's many watering holes. See "In the Grandstand: Watching Chicago's Athletic Events," p. 221.

• **Playing in the Sand:** If you're staying at a downtown hotel, you can hit the sands of Chicago's urban beaches almost as quickly as your elevator gets you to the lobby. Oak Street Beach (at Michigan Ave. and Lake Shore Dr.) is mostly for posing; North Avenue Beach, a little farther north along the lakefront path, is home to weekend volleyball games, family beach outings, and a whole lot of eye candy. You probably won't do any swimming (even in the middle of summer, the water's frigid), but either

beach makes a great place to hang out with a picnic and a book on a warm afternoon. See "Beaches," p. 218.

• **Raising a Glass (or a Coffee Cup):** Chicago has its share of trendy lounges that serve overpriced specialty martinis, but the heart of the city's nightlife remains the neighborhood taverns. Here you'll get a convivial spirit without the attitude and flashy decor. Plus, you can have a conversation without being drowned out by the hoots and hollers of drunken frat boys (although there are plenty of bars catering to that particular demographic). My favorites include the **Red Lion Pub** (2446 N. Lincoln Ave.; ℭ 773/348-2695) in Lincoln Park, **Miller's Pub** (134 S. Wabash Ave.; ℭ 312/645-5377) in the Loop, and the **Map Room** (1949 N. Hoyne Ave.; ℭ 773/252-7636) in Bucktown. If you prefer to keep things nonalcoholic, grab coffee and dessert at either of my two favorite cafes: **Third Coast** (1260 N. Dearborn St.; ℭ 312/649-0730), on the Gold Coast, or **Uncommon Ground** (1214 W. Grace St.; ℭ 773/929-3680) in Wrigleyville. See chapter 10.

8 The Best Free (or Almost Free) Things to Do

• **Bonding with the Animals at Lincoln Park Zoo:** You have no excuse not to visit: Lincoln Park Zoo is open 365 days a year and—astonishingly—remains completely free, despite many recent upgrades. Occupying a prime spot of Lincoln Park close to the lakefront, the zoo is small enough to explore in an afternoon, and varied enough to make you feel as though you've traveled around the world. Most of the exhibits have been renovated in the past few years, making the place look better than ever. For families, this is a don't-miss stop. See p. 190.

• **Listening to Music Under the Stars:** Summer is prime time for live music— and often you won't have to pay a dime. The Grant Park Music Festival presents free classical concerts from June through August in Millennium Park. A few blocks south, you'll find the outdoor dance floor that's home to Chicago SummerDance, where you can learn new dance moves and swing to a variety of live acts on Thursday through Sunday nights. The summer also brings a range of large-scale music festivals—from Blues Fest to a rock-'n'-roll-themed Fourth of July concert— but the Grant Park classical concerts are considerably less crowded (and far more civilized). See "Classical Music," p. 254.

- **Discovering Future Masterpieces:** Chicago's vibrant contemporary art scene is divided between two different neighborhoods. The original, River North, is still home to many of the city's best-known galleries and is within walking distance from downtown hotels. The West Loop houses newer galleries—with, overall, a younger perspective—in freshly renovated lofts. You don't need to be a serious collector to browse; just bring an open mind. See "Art Galleries" in chapter 9.

- **Exploring Millennium Park:** This downtown park, carved out of the northwest corner of Grant Park, is Chicago's newest great showcase (and it's an easy walk from downtown hotels). While the Pritzker Music Pavilion, designed by Frank Gehry, is the highest-profile attraction, the park's two main sculptures have quickly become local favorites. *Cloud Gate,* by British sculptor Anish Kapoor, looks like a giant silver kidney bean; watch your reflection bend and distort as you walk around and underneath. The *Crown Fountain,* designed by Spanish sculptor Jaume Plensa, is framed by two giant video screens that project faces of ordinary Chicagoans; it looks a little creepy at first, but watch the kids splashing in the shallow water and you'll soon realize that this is public art at its best. See p. 176.

9 The Best One-of-a-Kind Shops

- **ArchiCenter Shop** (224 S. Michigan Ave.; C 312/922-3432): Looking for unique, well-designed souvenirs? This store, run by the Chicago Architecture Foundation, should be your first stop. You'll find Frank Lloyd Wright bookmarks, puzzles of the Chicago skyline, picture frames with patterns designed by famed local architect Louis Sullivan, and a great selection of Chicago history books. See p. 247.

- **Uncle Fun** (1338 W. Belmont Ave.; C 773/477-8223): No other place lives up to its name like Uncle Fun, one of the quirkiest shops in town. This old-fashioned storefront is crammed with a random assortment of classic dime-store gadgets (hand buzzers, Pez dispensers, rubber chickens), along with an equally eclectic selection of retro bargain-bin items (where else can you pick up a Mr. T keychain?). See p. 241.

- **The T-Shirt Deli** (1739 N. Damen Ave.; C 773/276-6266): Got a soft spot for those cheesy 1970s "Foxy Lady" T-shirts? Head to the T-Shirt Deli, where the staff will customize shirts while you wait. Come up with your own message, or browse the hundreds of in-stock iron-on decals (everything from Gary Coleman to Hello Kitty). And just like at a real deli, your purchase is wrapped in white paper and served with a bag of potato chips. See p. 241.

- **Architectural Artifacts, Inc.** (4325 N. Ravenswood Ave.; C 773/348-0622): This vast warehouse of material salvaged from historic buildings is a home renovator's dream. Although it's far off the usual tourist route, design buffs will find it well worth the trip—the enormous inventory includes fireplace mantels, stained-glass windows, and garden sculptures. There's even an attached museum where the owners display pieces of particular historic value. See p. 234.

Impressions

He glances at the new Civic Center, a tower of russet steel and glass, fronted by a gracious plaza with a fountain and a genuine Picasso-designed metalwork sculpture almost fifty feet high. He put it all there, the Civic Center, the plaza, the Picasso. And the judges and county officials who work in the Civic Center, he put most of them there, too.

Wherever he looks as he marches, there are new skyscrapers up or going up. The city has become an architect's delight, except when the architects see the great Louis Sullivan's landmark buildings being ripped down for parking garages or allowed to degenerate into slums.

—Mike Royko, *Boss: Richard J. Daley of Chicago,* 1971

10 The Best Chicago Websites

- **www.metromix.com**: Operated by the *Chicago Tribune,* this site features expanded versions of the newspaper's entertainment and restaurant coverage. It's a good place to check restaurant reviews and get an early look at new bars and nightclubs.

- **www.chicagoreader.com**: At the site of the *Chicago Reader,* the city's alternative weekly paper, you'll find extensive coverage of local music and lots of reviews of smaller theater productions.

- **www.cityofchicago.org/Landmarks/index.html**: This site, part of the city government's official website, includes definitions of Chicago architectural styles, tour information, and maps.

- **www.cityofchicago.org/exploringchicago**: The official site of the Chicago Office of Tourism gives a good overview of what's happening in town.

- **http://chicago.citysearch.com**: This local edition of the national Citysearch sites offers reviews of restaurants, bars, shows, and shops. Reviews tend to be fairly short, but they keep readers up-to-date on openings.

- **www.centerstage.net**: This local city guide tries to cover all the bases (restaurants, clubs, shows, and so forth) but is strongest on entertainment. Good for browsing if you want to know more about local theater.

- **www.ticketweb.com**: If you're planning on catching a play or other performance while you're in town, many of the city's performing arts groups sell tickets online through this site. Take a look if you want to reserve seats before leaving home.

- **www.chicagoist.com**: Want to see what issues have Chicagoans riled up? Check out this sounding board for local news (an offshoot of the New York-centric site Gothamist.com), which covers everything from government corruption scandals to the latest celebrity sightings.

- **www.enjoyillinois.com**: If you plan to travel beyond the Chicago city limits, this site, run by the Illinois Bureau of Tourism, can give you the scoop on many suburban options, as well as tourism throughout the state.

2

A Traveler's Guide to Chicago's Architecture

by Lisa Torrance

Although the Great Chicago Fire leveled almost 3 square miles of the downtown area in 1871, destroying lives and property, it did clear the stage for Chicago's emergence as the country's second city. Because the industrial base remained intact, local businessmen could afford to finance the massive rebuilding that ensued. Architects and engineers from around the nation addressed the city's need for immediate and generous office space by creating the first skyscrapers. Building innovations continued in Chicago well into the 20th century, as architects sought to follow in the footsteps of those pioneers. This chapter guides you to the best of the early buildings and the many that followed.

See the map "Chicago's Most Important Buildings," on p. 14 for the locations of the buildings mentioned in this chapter.

1 Richardsonian Romanesque (1870–1900)

Boston-based architect **Henry Hobson Richardson** (1838–86) explored designs and forms based on the Romanesque (a style distinguished by rounded arches, thick walls, and small windows). His structures, ranging from university and civic buildings to railroad stations and homes, were marked by a simplification of form and the elimination of extraneous ornament and historical detail—features that set his buildings apart from others of the period. The overall effect depended on mass, volume, and scale. Richardson's 1872 design for Boston's Trinity Church gained him national attention. In the 1880s he completed two commissions in Chicago, the Marshall Field Wholesale Store and the John J. Glessner House, which both had a strong influence on Chicago architects, notably Louis Sullivan. For more information on Sullivan, see the box "Master Builders: Sullivan, Wright & Mies" on p. 18.

Richardsonian Romanesque buildings share the following characteristics:

- A massive quality
- Arched entrances
- Squat towers
- Deeply recessed porches and doorways
- Heavy masonry exteriors
- Use of rough-hewn stone

Richardson's **John J. Glessner House** (see illustration), 1800 S. Prairie Ave. (1885–87), an elegant urban residence, still stands on Chicago's Near South Side. The influence of this structure is apparent in the **Carl C. Heisen House,** 1250 N. Lake

Rival Revivals: Architectural Styles in the Late 19th Century

During the latter half of the 19th century, several architectural styles—including Romanesque Revival, Gothic Revival, Italianate, Renaissance Revival, Second Empire, and even the exotic Moorish and Egyptian revivals—existed in Chicago. What these styles share is a certain eclecticism and picturesque quality. Midcentury architects reasoned that no age had produced the perfect architectural expression, so why not borrow freely from the best of the past and even mix different styles on the same building?

Although some of these styles were popular, none became dominant. In the 1870s, technological advancements and imaginative design came together in Chicago to create the world's first skyscrapers—*the* style that would one day dominate America's downtowns.

Shore Dr. (Frank B. Abbott, 1890), and the **Mason Brayman Starring House,** 1254 N. Lake Shore Dr. (L. Gustav Hallberg, 1889), two side-by-side residences on the city's North Side, and in **Excalibur,** 632 N. Dearborn St. (formerly the Chicago Historical Society; Henry Ives Cobb, 1892). The most celebrated example of Richardson's influence is the **Auditorium Building,** 430 S. Michigan Ave. (Adler & Sullivan, 1887–89), based on the now-demolished Marshall Field Wholesale Store and an important early example of the emerging Chicago skyscraper.

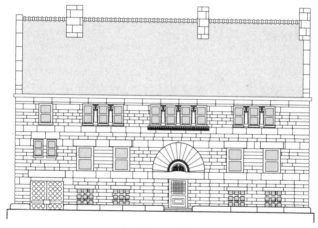

John J. Glessner House

2 Early Skyscrapers (1880–1920)

The invention of the skyscraper can be traced directly to the use of cast iron in the 1840s for storefronts, particularly in New York and later in cities such as Chicago. Experimentation with cast and wrought iron in the construction of interior skeletons eventually allowed buildings to rise higher than ever before. (Previously, the limits of load-bearing walls restricted building height.) Following the Great Chicago Fire of

Chicago's Most Important Buildings

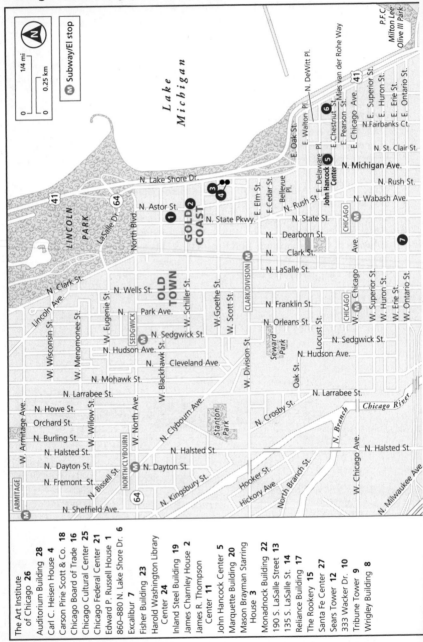

1/4 mi
0.25 km

Ⓝ

Ⓜ Subway/El stop

Lake Michigan

LINCOLN PARK

OLD TOWN

GOLD COAST

Seward Park

Stanton Park

Chicago River

N. Lake Shore Dr.

N. Astor St.
N. State Pkwy.
N. State St.
N. Dearborn St.
N. Clark St.
N. LaSalle St.
N. Franklin St.
N. Orleans St.

N. Michigan Ave.
N. Rush St.
N. Wabash Ave.

E. Oak St.
E. Walton Pl.
N. DeWitt Pl.
E. Cedar St.
E. Elm St.
Bellevue Pl.
E. Delaware Pl.
E. Chestnut St.
E. Pearson St.
E. Chicago Ave.
E. Superior St.
E. Huron St.
E. Erie St.
E. Ontario St.

N. Fairbanks Ct.
N. St. Clair St.
Mies van der Rohe Way

P.F.C. Milton Lee Olive III Park

CLARK/DIVISION Ⓜ
CHICAGO Ⓜ
CHICAGO Ⓜ
NORTH/CLYBOURN Ⓜ
ARMITAGE Ⓜ

W. Division St.
W. Goethe St.
W. Schiller St.
W. Scott St.
N. Wells St.
N. Park Ave.
N. Sedgwick St.
N. Hudson Ave.
N. Cleveland Ave.
N. Mohawk St.
N. Larrabee St.
N. Howe St.
Orchard St.
N. Burling St.
N. Halsted St.
N. Dayton St.
N. Fremont St.
N. Sheffield Ave.

W. Eugenie St.
W. Wisconsin St.
W. Menomonee St.
W. North Ave.
W. Willow St.
W. Armitage Ave.
N. Bissell St.
N. Kingsbury St.
N. Clybourn Ave.
N. Crosby St.
N. Hudson Ave.
N. Sedgwick St.
N. Larrabee St.
Locust St.
Oak St.
Hooker St.
Hickory Ave.
North Branch St.
N. Branch
W. Chicago Ave.
N. Halsted St.
N. Milwaukee Ave.
Lincoln Ave.
N. Clark St.
LaSalle Dr.
North Blvd.

SEDGWICK Ⓜ

The Art Institute of Chicago **26**
Auditorium Building **28**
Carl C. Heisen House **4**
Carson Pirie Scott & Co. **18**
Chicago Board of Trade **16**
Chicago Cultural Center **25**
Chicago Federal Center **21**
Edward P. Russell House **1**
860–880 N. Lake Shore Dr. **6**
Excalibur **7**
Fisher Building **23**
Harold Washington Library Center **24**
Inland Steel Building **19**
James Charnley House **2**
James R. Thompson Center **11**
John Hancock Center **5**
Marquette Building **20**
Mason Brayman Starring House **3**
Monadnock Building **22**
190 S. LaSalle Street **13**
135 S. LaSalle St. **14**
Reliance Building **17**
The Rookery **15**
Santa Fe Center **27**
Sears Tower **12**
333 Wacker Dr. **10**
Tribune Tower **9**
Wrigley Building **8**

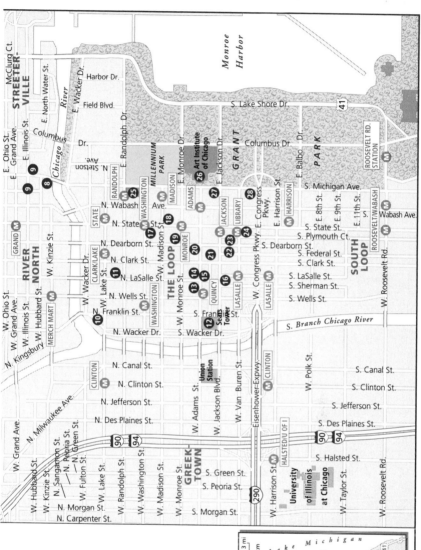

1871, important technical innovations—involving safety elevators, electricity, fire-proofing, foundations, plumbing, and telecommunications—combined with advances in skeletal construction to create a new building type: the skyscraper. These buildings were spacious, cost-effective, efficient, and quickly erected—in short, the perfect architectural solution for Chicago's growing downtown.

Solving the technical problems of the skyscraper did not resolve how the building should look. Most solutions relied on historical precedents, including decoration reminiscent of the Romanesque, with its rounded arches; Gothic, with its spires, pointy arches, and even buttresses; or Beaux Arts, with its exuberant classical details. **Louis Sullivan** (1865–1924) was the first to formalize a vision of a tall building based on the parts of a classical column. His theories inspired the **Chicago school of architecture,** examples of which still fill the city's downtown.

Features of the Chicago school include:

- A rectangular shape with a flat roof
- Tripartite divisions of the facade similar to that of a classical column (see illustration), with a *base* (usually of two stories), *shaft* (midsection with a repetitive window pattern), and *capital* (typically an elaborate, terra-cotta cornice)
- Exterior expression of the building's interior skeleton through an emphasis on horizontal and vertical elements
- Large windows made possible by the development of load-bearing interior skeletons; particularly popular are *Chicago windows* (large windows flanked by two narrow ones with double-hung sashes)
- Use of terra cotta, a light, fireproof material that could be cast in any shape and attached to the exterior, often for decoration

Reliance Building and Classical Column

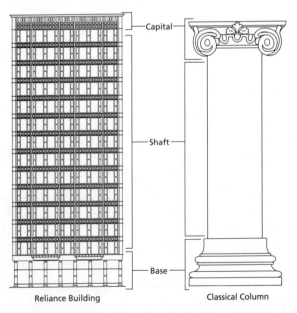

Reliance Building   Classical Column

A good example of the development of the skyscraper is the **Monadnock Building,** 53 W. Jackson Blvd. (Holabird & Root, 1889–91; Holabird & Roche, 1893). It consists of two parts: The northern section has masonry load-bearing walls, while the southern half has a steel frame clad in terra cotta. To support its 17 stories, the northern section has 6-foot-thick walls at its base. The entire building is notable for its clean, contemporary lines.

Three Chicago school examples are the **Reliance Building** (see illustration), now the Hotel Burnham (p. 86), 1 W. Washington St. (Burnham & Root and Burnham & Co., 1891–95), outstanding for its use of glass and decorative spandrels (the horizontal panel below a window); the **Fisher Building,** 343 S. Dearborn St. (D. H. Burnham & Co., 1896), similar in its use of glass, but with the addition of Gothic and aquatic-inspired details; and the **Marquette Building,** 140 S. Dearborn St. (Holabird & Roche, 1893–95), which exhibits all the style's features, although the terra-cotta cornice has been removed.

A good later example (taller and more technically sophisticated than earlier incarnations) that most visitors will pass at some point during their trip is the **Tribune Tower,** 435 N. Michigan Ave. (Howells & Hood, 1923–25). The winning entry of a major design competition, this 36-story tower has the neo-Gothic detailing (flying buttresses, spires, and a tower) popularized by New York's 1913 Woolworth Building and clearly shows the characteristics mentioned above.

3 Second Renaissance Revival (1890–1920)

Buildings in this style show a definite studied formalism. A relative faithfulness to Renaissance precedents of window and doorway treatments distinguishes it from the much looser adaptations of the Italianate, a mid-19th-century style that took its inspiration from Italian architecture. Scale and size, in turn, set the Second Renaissance Revival apart from the first, which occurred from about 1840 to 1890. The grand buildings of the Second Renaissance Revival, with their textural richness, suited the tastes of the wealthy Gilded Age well. The style was used primarily on the East Coast but also in Chicago for swank town houses, government buildings, and private clubs.

Typical features include:

- A cubelike structure with a massive, imposing quality
- Symmetrical arrangement of the facade, including distinct horizontal divisions
- A different stylistic treatment for each floor, with different column capitals, finishes, and window treatments on each level

Chicago Cultural Center

Master Builders: Sullivan, Wright & Mies

Visitors from around the world flock to Chicago to see the groundbreaking work of three major architects: Sullivan, Wright, and Mies. They all lived and worked in the Windy City, leaving behind a legacy of innovative structures that still inspire architects today. Here's the rundown on each of them:

Louis Sullivan (1865–1924)

- **Quote:** "Form ever follows function."
- **Chicago buildings:** Auditorium Building, 430 S. Michigan Ave. (Adler & Sullivan, 1887–89); James Charnley House, 1365 Astor St. (Adler & Sullivan, with Frank Lloyd Wright, 1892); and Carson Pirie Scott & Co., 1 S. State St. (1899, 1903, with later additions).
- **Innovations:** Father of the Chicago school, Sullivan was perhaps at his most original in the creation of his intricate, nature-inspired ornamentation, examples of which cover the entrance to Carson Pirie Scott & Co.

Frank Lloyd Wright (1867–1959)

- **Quote:** "Nature is my manifestation of God."
- **Chicago-area buildings:** Frank Lloyd Wright Home & Studio, 951 Chicago Ave., Oak Park (1889–1911); Unity Temple, 875 Lake St., Oak Park (1905–08); The Rookery, 209 S. LaSalle St. (interior renovation, 1907); and Frederick C. Robie House, 5757 S. Woodlawn Ave., Hyde Park (1909).
- **Innovations:** While in Chicago, Wright developed the architecture of the Prairie School, a largely residential style combining natural materials, communication between interior and exterior spaces, and the sweeping horizontals of the Midwestern landscape. (For tours of Wright's home and studio, see "Exploring the 'Burbs," p. 202.)

Ludwig Mies van der Rohe (1886–1969)

- **Quote:** "Less is more."
- **Chicago buildings:** 860–880 N. Lake Shore Dr. (1949–51); S.R. Crown Hall, 3360 S. State St. (1956); and Chicago Federal Center, Dearborn Street between Adams Street and Jackson Boulevard (1959–74).
- **Innovations:** Mies van der Rohe brought the office tower of steel and glass to the United States. His stark facades don't immediately reveal his careful attention to details and materials. (For more on Mies van der Rohe, see this chapter's section 6, "International Style.")

- Use of *rustification* (masonry in massive blocks separated from each other by deep joints) on the lowest floor
- The mixing of Greek and Roman styles on the same facade (Roman arches and arcades may appear with Greek-style windows with straight heads or *pediments,* low-pitched triangular features above a window, door, or pavilion.)
- A *cornice* (a projecting feature along the roofline) supported by large brackets
- A *balustrade* (a railing supported by a series of short posts) above the cornice

A fine example of this style is the **Chicago Cultural Center** (see illustration), 78 E. Washington St. (Shepley, Rutan & Coolidge, 1897), originally built as a public library. This tasteful edifice, with its sumptuous decor, was constructed in part to help secure Chicago's reputation as a culture-conscious city.

4 Beaux Arts (1890–1920)

This style takes its name from the Ecole des Beaux-Arts in Paris, where a number of prominent American architects (including H. H. Richardson [see section 1, "Richardsonian Romanesque (1870–1900)"] and Louis Sullivan) received their training, beginning around the mid–19th century. These architects adopted the academic principles of the Ecole des Beaux-Arts, which emphasized the study of Greek and Roman structures, composition, and symmetry, and the creation of elaborate presentation drawings. Because of the idealized origins and grandiose use of classical forms, the Beaux Arts in America was seen as the ideal style for expressing civic pride.

In 1893 Chicago played host to the **World's Columbian Exposition,** attended by 21 million people at a time when Chicago's population was just over one million. Overseen by Chicagoan **Daniel H. Burnham** (1846–1912), the fairgrounds in Hyde Park were laid out in Beaux Arts style, with broad boulevards, fountains, and temporary ornate, white buildings, mostly by New York–based architects. (One of the few permanent structures is now the Museum of Science and Industry, p. 194.) The style created somewhat of a classical revival in Chicago and led to Burnham's spearheading of a movement to beautify America's urban areas. (In 1909 he created a plan for Chicago that forever ensured public lakefront access.)

Grandiose compositions, exuberance of detail, and a variety of stone finishes typify most Beaux Arts structures. Particular features include:

- A pronounced cornice topped by a *parapet* (a low wall), balustrade, or attic story
- Projecting pavilions, often with colossal columns grouped in pairs
- Windows framed by freestanding columns, a sill with a balustrade, and pediments or decorative *keystones* (the central stone of an arch)
- Grand staircases
- Grand arched openings
- Classical decoration: freestanding statuary, ornamental panels, swags, and medallions

Chicago has several Beaux Arts buildings that exhibit the style's main features. The oldest part of the **Art Institute of Chicago,** Michigan Avenue at Adams Street (Shepley, Rutan & Coolidge, 1893), was built for the World's Columbian Exposition. The **Santa Fe Center,** 80 E. Jackson Blvd. (D. H. Burnham & Co., 1904), across the street from the museum, is an example of a Chicago school skyscraper with Beaux Arts ornamentation (the lobby also has a grand staircase). A later example of yet another skyscraper is the gleaming white **Wrigley Building,** 400–410 N. Michigan Ave. (Graham, Anderson, Probst & White, 1919–24), which serves as a gateway to North Michigan Avenue.

5 Art Deco (1925–33)

Art Deco is a decorative style that took its name from the Exposition Internationale des Arts Décoratif, held in Paris in 1925. One of the first widely accepted styles not based on historic precedents (the jazzy style embodied the idea of modernity), it influenced all areas of design, from jewelry and household goods to cars, trains, and ocean liners.

Art Deco buildings are characterized by a linear, hard edge or angular composition, often with a vertical emphasis and highlighted with stylized decoration. The Chicago zoning ordinance of 1923, which required setbacks in buildings above a certain height to ensure that light and air could reach the street, helped give Art Deco skyscrapers their distinctive profile. Other important features include:

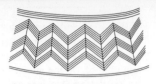

Chevron

- An emphasis on geometric form
- Strips of windows with decorated spandrels, adding to the sense of verticality
- Use of hard-edged, low-relief ornamentation around doors and windows
- Frequent use of marble and of black and silver tones
- Decorative motifs of parallel lines, zigzags, chevrons (see illustration), and stylized florals

The **Chicago Board of Trade** (see illustration), 141 W. Jackson Blvd. (Holabird & Root, 1930), punctuates LaSalle Street with its dramatic Art Deco facade. High atop the pyramidal roof, an aluminum statue of Ceres, the Roman goddess of agriculture, gazes down over the building's setbacks. **135 S. LaSalle St.** (originally the Field Building; Graham, Anderson, Probst & White, 1934), the last major construction project in Chicago before the Great Depression deepened, has a magnificent Art Deco lobby. A fine example of an Art Deco town house is the **Edward P. Russell House,** 1444 N. Astor St. (Holabird & Root, 1929), in the city's Gold Coast.

Chicago Board of Trade

6 International Style (1932–45)

In 1932 the Museum of Modern Art in New York mounted its first architecture exhibit, simply titled *Modern Architecture.* Displays included images of International Style buildings from around the world, many designed by architects from Germany's Bauhaus, a progressive design school. The structures all shared a stark simplicity and vigorous functionalism, a definite break from historically based, decorative styles.

The International Style was popularized in the United States through the teachings and designs of **Ludwig Mies van der Rohe** (1886–1969), a German émigré who taught and practiced architecture in Chicago after leaving the Bauhaus school of design. Interpretations of the "Miesian" International Style were built in most U.S. cities as late as 1980. In the 1950s, erecting an office building in this mode made companies appear progressive. After the International Style became a corporate mainstay, the style took on conservative connotations.

Fragments of Chicago's Past

For a glimpse of the city's past, head to the **Art Institute of Chicago** (p. 171), where you'll find a permanent installation of architectural fragments on the second floor. On the museum's east side, there's a reconstruction of the Trading Room from Dankmar Adler and Louis Sullivan's demolished Chicago Stock Exchange, which includes beautifully stenciled wallpaper designed by Sullivan. More architectural fragments are embedded in the base of the **Tribune Tower**, at 435 N. Michigan Ave.

Features of the International Style as popularized by Mies van der Rohe include:

- Rectangular shape
- Frequent use of glass
- Balance and regularity, but not symmetry
- Horizontal bands of windows
- Windows meeting at corners
- Absence of ornamentation
- Clear expression of the building's form and function (The interior structure of stacked office floors is clearly visible, as are the locations of mechanical systems, such as elevator shafts and air-conditioning units.)
- Placement, or cantilevering, of building on tall piers

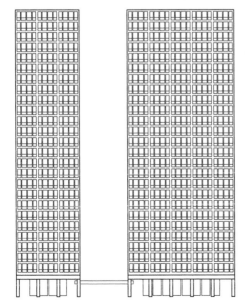

860–880 N. Lake Shore Dr.

Some famous Mies van der Rohe designs are the **Chicago Federal Center,** Dearborn Street between Adams Street and Jackson Boulevard (1959–74), and **860–880 N. Lake Shore Dr.** (1949–51; see illustration). Interesting interpretations of the style by Skidmore, Owings & Merrill, a Chicago firm that helped make the International Style a corporate staple, are the **Inland Steel Building** (1954–58), the **Sears Tower** (1968–74), and the **John Hancock Center** (1969)—the latter two impressive engineering feats that rise 110 and 100 stories, respectively.

Field Study

To learn more about Chicago's architecture, take a tour by foot, boat, or bus with the **Chicago Architecture Foundation** (p. 214).

7 Postmodern (1975–90)

After years of steel-and-glass office towers in the International Style, postmodernism burst on the scene in the 1970s with the reintroduction of historical precedents in architecture. With many feeling that the office towers of the previous style were too cold, postmodernists began to incorporate classical details and recognizable forms into their designs—often applied in outrageous proportions.

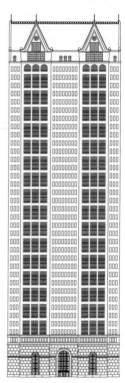

Postmodern skyscrapers tend to include:

- An overall shape (or incorporation) of a recognizable object not necessarily associated with architecture
- Classical details, such as columns, domes, or vaults, often oversize and used in inventive ways
- A distinctive profile in the skyline
- Use of stone rather than glass

190 S. LaSalle St. (John Burgee Architects with Philip Johnson, 1987; see illustration) brings the shape of a famous Chicago building back to the skyline. The overall design is that of the 1892 Masonic Temple (now razed), complete with the tripartite divisions of the Chicago school. Another amalgam of historical precedents is the **Harold Washington Library Center,** 400 S. State St. (Hammond, Beeby & Babka, 1991). An extremely modern interpretation of a three-part skyscraper—but you have to look for the divisions to find them—is **333 Wacker Dr.** (Kohn Pedersen Fox, 1979–83), an elegant green-glass structure that curves along a bend in the Chicago River. Unlike this harmonious juxtaposition, the **James R. Thompson Center,** 100 W. Randolph St. (Murphy/Jahn, 1979–85), inventively clashes with everything around it.

190 S. LaSalle St.

3

Planning Your Trip to Chicago

After choosing a destination, most prospective travelers have two fundamental questions: "What will it cost?" and "How will I get there?" This chapter answers both questions and resolves other important issues including when to go and where to obtain more information about Chicago.

1 Visitor Information & Maps

The **Chicago Office of Tourism,** Chicago Cultural Center, 78 E. Washington St., Chicago, IL 60602 (© **877/CHICAGO** or TTY 866/710-0294; www.choose chicago.com), will mail you a packet of materials with information on upcoming events and attractions. Click the "Maps & Transportation" link at the top of the home page for links to maps of Chicago neighborhoods. You can even create your own personalized map of sights you'd like to visit. The **Illinois Bureau of Tourism** (© **800/2CONNECT** or TTY 800/406-6418; www.enjoyillinois.com) will also send you information about Chicago and other Illinois destinations.

In addition to the above websites, which offer visitors a good deal of information, see chapter 1 for a list of the best Chicago websites.

2 Entry Requirements

PASSPORTS

For information on how to get a passport, go to **"Passports"** in the **"Fast Facts"** section of this chapter—the websites listed provide downloadable passport applications as well as the current fees for processing passport applications. For an up-to-date country-by-country listing of passport requirements around the world, go to the "Foreign Entry Requirement" Web page of the U.S. Department of State at **http://travel.state.gov**. International visitors can obtain a visa application at the same website. *Note:* Children are required to present a passport when entering the United States at airports. More information on obtaining a passport for a minor can be found at http://travel.state.gov.

VISAS

For information on how to get a visa, go to **"Visas"** in the **"Fast Facts"** section of this chapter.

The U.S. Department of State has a **Visa Waiver Program** allowing citizens of the following countries (at press time) to enter the U.S. without a visa for stays of up to 90 days: Andorra, Australia, Austria, Belgium, Brunei, Denmark, Finland, France, Germany, Iceland, Ireland, Italy, Japan, Liechtenstein, Luxembourg, Monaco, the Netherlands, New Zealand, Norway, Portugal, San Marino, Singapore, Slovenia, Spain, Sweden, Switzerland, and the United Kingdom. Canadian citizens may enter the U.S. without visas; they will need to show passports and proof of residence, however. *Note:* Any

U.S. Entry: Passport Required

New regulations issued by the Homeland Security Department now require virtually every air traveler entering the U.S. to show a passport—and future regulations will cover land and sea entry as well. As of January 23, 2007, all persons, including U.S. citizens, traveling by air between the United States and Canada, Mexico, Central and South America, the Caribbean, and Bermuda are required to present a valid passport. Similar regulations for those traveling by land or sea (including ferries) are expected as early as January 1, 2008.

passport issued on or after October 26, 2006, by a VWP country must be an **e-Passport** for VWP travelers to be eligible to enter the U.S. without a visa. Citizens of these nations also need to present a round-trip air or cruise ticket upon arrival. E-Passports contain computer chips capable of storing biometric information, such as the required digital photograph of the holder. (You can identify an e-Passport by the symbol on the bottom center cover of your passport.) If your passport doesn't have this feature, you can still travel without a visa if it is a valid passport issued before October 26, 2005, and includes a machine-readable zone, or between October 26, 2005, and October 25, 2006, and includes a digital photograph. For more information, go to **www.travel.state.gov/visa**.

Citizens of all other countries must have (1) a valid passport that expires at least 6 months later than the scheduled end of their visit to the United States and (2) a tourist visa, which may be obtained without charge from any U.S. consulate.

As of January 2004, many international visitors traveling on visas to the United States will be photographed and fingerprinted on arrival at Customs in airports and on cruise ships in a program created by the Department of Homeland Security called **US-VISIT.** Exempt from the extra scrutiny are visitors entering by land or those (mostly in Europe; p. 23) that don't require a visa for short-term visits. For more information, go to the Homeland Security website at **www.dhs.gov/dhspublic**.

MEDICAL REQUIREMENTS

Unless you're arriving from an area known to be suffering from an epidemic (particularly cholera or yellow fever), inoculations or vaccinations are not required for entry into the United States. If you have a medical condition that requires **syringe-administered medications,** carry a valid signed prescription from your physician; syringes in carry-on baggage will be inspected. Insulin in any form should have the proper pharmaceutical documentation. If you have a disease that requires treatment with **narcotics,** you should also carry documented proof with you—smuggling narcotics aboard a plane is a serious offense that carries severe penalties in the U.S.

For **HIV-positive visitors,** requirements for entering the United States are somewhat vague and change frequently. For up-to-the-minute information, contact **AIDSinfo** (© **800/448-0440** or 301/519-6616 outside the U.S.; www.aidsinfo.nih.gov) or the **Gay Men's Health Crisis** (© **212/367-1000;** www.gmhc.org).

CUSTOMS

For information on what you can bring into and take out of the United States, go to **"Customs"** in the **"Fast Facts"** section of this chapter.

3 When to Go

THE CLIMATE

When I tell people from more temperate climates that I live in Chicago, their first question is how I handle the winters. In reality, the winters here are no worse than in other northern cities, but it still isn't exactly prime tourist season. The ideal time to visit is summer or fall. Summer offers a nonstop selection of special events and outdoor activities, but you'll also be dealing with the biggest crowds and periods of hot, muggy weather. Autumn days are generally sunny, and the crowds at major tourist attractions grow thinner—you don't have to worry about snow until late November at the earliest. Spring is extremely unpredictable, with dramatic fluctuations of cold and warm weather, and usually lots of rain. If your top priority is indoor cultural sights, winter's not such a bad time to visit: no lines at museums, the cheapest rates at hotels, and the pride that comes with slogging through the slush with the natives.

Chicagoans like to joke that if you don't like the weather, just wait an hour—it will change. (In spring and autumn, I've been known to use my car's heat in the morning and the air-conditioning in the afternoon.) The key is to be prepared for a wide range of weather with clothing that can take you from a sunny morning to a chilly, drizzly evening. As close to your departure as possible, check the local weather forecast at the websites of the *Chicago Tribune* newspaper (www.chicagotribune.com) or the **Weather Channel** (www.weather.com).

Chicago's Average Temperatures & Precipitation

	Jan	Feb	Mar	Apr	May	June	July	Aug	Sept	Oct	Nov	Dec
High °F	20	34	44	59	70	79	85	82	76	64	48	35
Low °F	14	18	28	39	48	58	63	62	54	42	31	20
High °C	−7	1	7	15	21	26	29	28	24	18	9	2
Low °C	−10	−8	−2	4	9	14	17	17	12	6	−1	−7
Rainfall (in.)	1.6	1.3	2.6	3.7	3.2	4.1	3.6	3.5	3.4	2.3	2.1	2.1

CHICAGO CALENDAR OF EVENTS

The best way to stay on top of the city's current crop of special events is to ask the **Chicago Office of Tourism** (© 877/CHICAGO; www.choosechicago.com) or the **Illinois Bureau of Tourism** (© 800/2CONNECT; www.enjoyillinois.com) to mail you a copy of the *Chicago Visitor's Guide,* a quarterly publication that surveys special events, including parades, street festivals, concerts, theatrical productions, and museum exhibitions. Also request the latest materials produced by the **Mayor's Office of Special Events** (© 312/744-3315; or call the Special Events Hot Line at 312/744-3370, TTY 312/744-2964; www.cityofchicago.org/specialevents), which keeps current with citywide and neighborhood festivals.

Of the annual events, the most lively and unpredictable tend to revolve around the national parades and street celebrations staged by Chicago's diverse ethnic communities. In addition, food, music, art, and flower fairs have their special niches.

Remember that new events might be added every year, and occasionally special events are discontinued or rescheduled. To avoid disappointment, telephone the sponsoring organization, or check out the Mayor's Office of Special Events website in advance to verify dates, times, and locations. For an exhaustive list of events beyond those listed here, check **http://events.frommers.com**, where you'll find a searchable, up-to-the-minute roster of what's happening in cities all over the world.

January

Chicago Boat, RV & Outdoor Show, McCormick Place, 23rd Street and Lake Shore Drive (© 312/946-6200; www.chicagoboatshow.com). All the latest boats and recreational vehicles are on display, plus trout fishing, a climbing wall, boating safety seminars, and big-time entertainment. January 16 to January 20.

Winter Delights. Throughout January and February, the city's Office of Tourism (© **877/CHICAGO**; www. choosechicago.com) offers special travel deals to lure visitors during tourism's low season. Incentives include bargain-priced hotel packages, affordable prix-fixe dinners at downtown restaurants, and special music and theater performances. Early January through February.

February

Chicago Auto Show, McCormick Place, 23rd Street and Lake Shore Drive (© **630/495-2282**; www.chicagoauto show.com). More than 1,000 cars and trucks, domestic and foreign, current and futuristic, are on display. The event draws nearly a million visitors. Look for special weekend packages at area hotels that include show tickets. February 8 to February 17.

Chinese New Year Parade, Wentworth and Cermak streets (© **312/326-5320**; www.chicagochinatown.org). Join in as the sacred dragon whirls down the boulevard and restaurateurs pass out small envelopes of money to their regular customers. Call to verify the date, which varies from year to year. Depending on the lunar calendar, the actual holiday falls between January 21 and February 19. In 2008, it's on February 7.

March

St. Patrick's Day Parade. In a city with a strong Irish heritage (and a mayor of Irish descent), this holiday is a big deal. The Chicago River is even dyed green for the occasion. The parade route is along Columbus Drive from Balbo Drive to Monroe Street. A second, more neighborhoodlike parade is held on the South Side the day after the Dearborn Street parade, on Western Avenue from 103rd to 115th streets. Visit www.chicagostpatsparade.com for information. The Saturday before March 17.

April

Opening Day. For the **Cubs,** call © **773/404-CUBS** or visit **www.cubs. mlb.com**; for the **White Sox,** call © **312/674-1000** or go to **www.white sox.mlb.com**. Make your plans early to get tickets for this eagerly awaited day. The calendar may say spring, but be warned: Opening Day is usually freezing in Chi-town (the first Cubs home games have occasionally been postponed because of snow). Early April.

Chicago Improv Festival. Chicago's improv-comedy scene is known as a training ground for performers who go on to shows such as *Saturday Night Live* or *MADtv*. Big names and lesser-known (but talented) comedians converge for a celebration of silliness, with large main-stage shows and smaller, more experimental pieces. Most performances are at the Athenaeum Theater on the North Side (2936 N. Southport Ave.; © **773/935-9810**; www.chicagoimprovfestival.org). Last week of April.

May

Buckingham Fountain Color Light Show, Grant Park, Congress Parkway and Lake Shore Drive. The water and ever-changing colored lights put on a show in the landmark fountain daily from May 1 to October 1 until 11pm.

The Ferris Wheel and Carousel begin spinning again at Navy Pier, 600 E. Grand Ave. (© **312/595-PIER**; www. navypier.com). The rides operate through October. From Memorial Day through Labor Day, Navy Pier also hosts twice-weekly fireworks shows

Wednesday nights at 9:30pm and Saturday nights at 10:15 pm.

Wright Plus Tour, Frank Lloyd Wright Home and Studio, Oak Park (© **708/ 848-1976;** www.wrightplus.org). This annual tour of 10 buildings, including Frank Lloyd Wright's home and studio, the Unity Temple, and several other notable buildings in both Prairie and Victorian styles, can sell out within 6 weeks. Tickets go on sale March 1. Third Saturday in May.

June

Printers Row Book Fair, Dearborn Street from Congress Parkway to Polk Street (© **312/222-3986;** www.chicago tribune.com/about/custom/events/ printersrow). One of the largest free outdoor book fairs in the country, this weekend event celebrates the written word with everything from readings and signings by big-name authors to panel discussions on penning your first novel. Located within walking distance of the Loop, the fair also features more than 150 booksellers with new, used, and antiquarian books; a poetry tent; and special activities for children. First weekend in June.

Chicago Gospel Festival, Petrillo Music Shell, Jackson Drive and Columbus Drive, Grant Park (© **312/ 744-3315**). Blues may be the city's most famous musical export, but Chicago is also the birthplace of gospel music: Thomas Dorsey, the "father of gospel," and the greatest gospel singer, Mahalia Jackson, were Southsiders. This 3-day festival—the largest outdoor, free-admission event of its kind—offers music on three stages with more than 40 performances. First weekend in June.

Chicago Blues Festival, Petrillo Music Shell, Randolph Street and Columbus Drive, Millennium Park (© **312/744- 3315**). Muddy Waters would scratch his noggin over the sea of suburbanites

who flood into Grant Park every summer to quaff Budweisers and accompany local legends Buddy Guy and Lonnie Brooks on air guitar. Truth be told, you can hear the same great jams and wails virtually any night of the week in one of the city's many blues clubs. Still, a thousand-voice chorus of "Sweet Home Chicago" under the stars has a rousing appeal. Blues Fest is free, with dozens of acts performing over 4 days, but get there in the afternoon to get a good spot on the lawn for the evening show. Second weekend in June.

Ravinia Festival, Ravinia Park, Highland Park (© **847/266-5100;** www. ravinia.com). This suburban location is the open-air summer home of the Chicago Symphony Orchestra and the venue of many first-rate visiting orchestras, chamber ensembles, pop artists, and dance companies. See also "Exploring the 'Burbs," in chapter 8. June through September.

Puerto Rican Fest, Humboldt Park, Division Street and Sacramento Boulevard (© **773/292-1414;** www.prparade chicago.com). This festival includes 5 days of live music, theater, games, food, and beverages. It peaks with a parade that winds its way from Wacker Drive and Dearborn Street to the West Side Puerto Rican enclave of Humboldt Park. Mid-June.

Old Town Art Fair, Lincoln Park West and Wisconsin Street, Old Town (© **312/337-1938;** www.oldtown triangle.com). This juried fine arts fair has drawn crowds to this historic neighborhood for more than 50 years with the work of more than 250 painters, sculptors, and jewelry designers from the Midwest and around the country on display. It also features an art auction, garden walk, concessions, and children's art activities. Second weekend in June.

Wells Street Art Festival, Wells Street from North Avenue to Division Street (© 312/951-6106; www.oldtown chicago.org). Held on the same weekend as the more prestigious Old Town Art Fair, this event is lots of fun, with 200 arts and crafts vendors, food, music, and carnival rides. Second weekend in June.

Jammin' at the Zoo, Lincoln Park Zoo, 2200 N. Cannon Dr., at Fullerton Parkway (© 773/742-2000; www. lpzoo.com). The lovely lawn south of the zoo's Park Place Café is certainly one of the more unusual outdoor venues for rock, zydeco, and reggae music fans. The first of three summer concerts is held in late June. Ticket prices vary.

Grant Park Music Festival, Pritzker Music Pavilion, Randolph Street and Columbus Drive, Millennium Park (© 312/742-7638; www.grantpark musicfestival.com). The free outdoor musical concerts in the park begin the last week in June and continue through August.

Chicago Country Music Festival, Petrillo Music Shell, Jackson Drive and Columbus Drive, in Grant Park (© 312/744-3315). This free event features big-name entertainers of the country-and-western genre. Last weekend in June.

Taste of Chicago, Grant Park (© 312/744-3315). The city claims that this is the largest free outdoor food fest in the nation. Three and a half million rib and pizza lovers feeding at this colossal alfresco trough say they're right. Over 10 days of feasting in the streets, scores of Chicago restaurants cart their fare to food stands set up throughout the park. To avoid the heaviest crowds, try going on weekdays earlier in the day. *Claustrophobics, take note:* If you're here the evening of July 3 for the Independence Day fireworks, pick out a vantage point farther north on the lakefront—unless dodging sweaty limbs, spilled beer, and the occasional bottle rocket sounds adventurous to you. Admission is free; you pay for the sampling. June 27 through July 6.

Gay and Lesbian Pride Parade, Halsted Street, from Belmont Avenue to Broadway, south to Diversey Parkway, and east to Lincoln Park, where a rally and music festival are held (© 773/348-8243; www.chicagopridecalendar. org). This parade is the colorful culmination of a month of activities by Chicago's gay and lesbian communities. Halsted Street is usually mobbed; pick a spot on Broadway for a better view. Last Sunday in June.

July

Independence Day Celebration (© 312/744-3315). Chicago celebrates the holiday on the 3rd of July. Concerts and fireworks are the highlights of the festivities in Grant Park. Expect huge crowds. July 3.

Sheffield Garden Walk, starting at Sheffield and Webster avenues (© 773/929-9255; www.sheffieldfestivals.org). Here's your chance to snoop in the lush backyards of Lincoln Park homeowners. The walk isn't just for garden nuts; the bands, children's activities, and food and drink tents attract lots of singles and young families. July 19 and 20.

Dearborn Garden Walk & Heritage Festival, North Dearborn and Astor streets (© 312/632-1241; http://dear borngardenwalk.com). A more upscale affair than the Sheffield Garden Walk, this event allows regular folks to peer into private gardens on the Gold Coast, one of the most expensive and exclusive neighborhoods in the city. As you'd expect, many yards are the work of the best landscape architects, designers, and art world luminaries that old money can buy. There's also live music, a marketplace, and a few architectural tours. July 13.

Old St. Patrick's World's Largest Block Party, 700 W. Adams St., at Des Plaines Avenue (© 312/648-1021; www.oldstpats.org). This hugely popular blowout is hosted by the city's oldest church, an Irish Catholic landmark in the West Loop area. It can get pretty crowded, but Old St. Pat's always lands some major acts. Six bands perform over 2 nights on two stages and attract a young, lively crowd. July 12 and 13.

Chicago SummerDance, east side of South Michigan Avenue between Balbo and Harrison streets (© 312/742-4007). From July through late August, the city's Department of Cultural Affairs transforms a patch of Grant Park into a lighted outdoor dance venue on Thursday, Friday, and Saturday from 6 to 9:30pm, and Sunday from 4 to 7pm. The 4,600-square-foot dance floor provides ample room for throwing down moves while live bands play music—from ballroom and klezmer to samba and zydeco. One-hour lessons are offered from 6 to 7pm. Free admission.

Chicago Yacht Club's Race to Mackinac Island, starting line at the Monroe Street Harbor (© 312/861-7777; www.chicagoyachtclub.org). This 3-day competition is the grandest of the inland water races. The public is welcome at a Friday-night party. On Saturday, jockey for a good place to watch the boats set sail. Mid-July.

Venetian Night, Monroe Harbor to the Adler Planetarium (© 312/744-3315). This carnival of illuminated boats on the lake is complete with fireworks and synchronized music by the Grant Park Symphony Orchestra. Shoreline viewing is fine, but you'll have to get there early to snag a prime viewing spot; the best way to take it in, if you can swing it, is from another boat nearby. This is a fine time to woo your sweetie with a dinner cruise. (See "Sightseeing Tours," in chapter 8.) Last Saturday in July.

Taste of Lincoln Avenue, Lincoln Park, between Fullerton Avenue and Wellington Street (© 773/868-3010; www.wrightwoodneighbors.org). This is one of the largest and most popular of Chicago's many neighborhood street fairs; it features 50 bands performing music on five stages. Neighborhood restaurants staff the food stands, and there's also a kids' carnival. Last weekend in July.

Newberry Library Book Fair and Bughouse Square Debates, 69 W. Walton St. and Washington Square Park (© 312/255-3501; www.newberry.org). Over 4 days, the esteemed Newberry Library invites the masses to rifle through bins stuffed with tens of thousands of used books, most of which go for less than $2 a pop. Better than the book fair is what happens across the street in Washington Square Park: Soapbox orators re-create the days when left-wing agitators came here, with Pulitzer Prize-winning author Studs Terkel, oral historian nonpareil, emceeing the spirited chaos. Late July.

August

Northalsted Market Days, Halsted Street between Belmont Avenue and Addison Street (© 773/868-3010; www.northalsted.com). The largest of the city's street festivals, held in the heart of this gay neighborhood, Northalsted Market Days offers music on three stages, lots of food and offbeat merchandise, and the best people-watching of the summer. August 2 and 3.

Bud Billiken Parade and Picnic, starting at 39th Street and King Drive and ending at 55th Street and Washington Park (© **312/225-2400;** www.budbillikenparade.com). This annual African-American celebration, which celebrated its 75th anniversary in 2004, is one of the oldest parades of its kind in the nation. It's named for the mythical figure Bud Billiken, reputedly the patron saint of "the little guy," and features the standard floats, bands, marching and military units, drill teams, and glad-handing politicians. Second Saturday in August.

Chicago Air & Water Show, North Avenue Beach (© **312/744-3315**). The U.S. Air Force Thunderbirds and Navy Seals usually make an appearance at this hugely popular aquatic and aerial spectacular. (Even if you don't plan to watch it, you can't help but experience it with jets screaming overhead all weekend.) Expect huge crowds, so arrive early if you want a spot along the water, or park yourself on the grass along the east edge of Lincoln Park Zoo, where you'll get good views (and some elbow room). Free admission. August 16 and 17.

Viva! Chicago Latin Music Festival, Petrillo Music Shell, Jackson Drive and Columbus Drive, Grant Park (© **312/744-3315**). This musical celebration features salsa, mambo, and the hottest Latin rock outfits. Free admission. August 23 and 24.

September
Chicago Jazz Festival, Petrillo Music Shell, Jackson Drive and Columbus Drive, Grant Park (© **312/744-3315**). Several national headliners are always on hand at this steamy gathering, which provides a swell end-of-summer bookend opposite to the gospel and blues fests in June. The event is free; come early and stay late. First weekend in September.

The art season, in conjunction with the annual Visions series of art gallery programs for the general public, begins with galleries holding their season openers in the Loop, River North, River West, and Wicker Park/Bucktown gallery districts. Contact the **Chicago Art Dealers Association** (© **312/649-0065;** http://chicagoartdealers.org) for details. First Friday after Labor Day.

Boulevard Lakefront Bike Tour (Chicagoland Bicycle Federation; © **312/427-3325;** www.chibikefed.org). This 35-mile leisurely bicycle excursion is a great way to explore the city, from the neighborhoods to the historic link of parks and boulevards. There's also a 10-mile tour for children and families. The Sunday morning event starts and ends at the University of Chicago in Hyde Park, which plays host to vendors and entertainment at the annual Bike Expo. Mid-September.

Mexican Independence Day Parade, Dearborn Street between Wacker Drive and Van Buren Street (© **312/744-3315**). This parade is on Saturday; another takes place the next day on 26th Street in the Little Village neighborhood (© **773/521-5387**). September 13.

Celtic Fest Chicago, Petrillo Music Shell, Jackson Drive and Columbus Drive, Grant Park (© **312/744-3315**). This festival celebrates the music and dance of global Celtic traditions. September 13 and 14.

World Music Festival Chicago, various locations around the city (© **312/742-1938;** www.cityofchicago.org/worldmusic). The World Music Festival is a major undertaking by the city's Department of Cultural Affairs. Held at venues around town—notably the Chicago Cultural Center, Museum of Contemporary Art, Old Town School of Folk Music, and Hot House—the festival brings in top performers from Hungary, Sri Lanka, Zimbabwe, and more to perform traditional, contemporary, and

Major Convention Dates

Listed below are Chicago's major (30,000 visitors or more) conventions for 2008, with projected attendance figures. Plan ahead because hotel rooms and restaurant reservations can be hard to come by when the big shows are in town—and even if you snag a room, you'll be paying top price. Contact the **Chicago Convention and Tourism Bureau** (✆ **877/CHICAGO** or 877/244-2246; www.choosechicago.com) to double-check the latest info before you commit to your travel dates as convention schedules can change.

Event	2008 Dates	Expected Attendance
International Home and Housewares Show	Mar 16–18	60,000
Kitchen/Bath Industry Show	Apr 11–13	60,000
National Restaurant Association Show	May 17–20	75,000
Neo-Con—World's Trade Fair	June 9–11	40,000
International Manufacturing Technology Show	Sept 8–13	90,000
Graph Expo	Oct 26–29	40,000
Radiological Society of North America	Nov 30–Dec 5	60,000

fusion music. Shows are a mix of free and ticketed ($10 or less) events. Call for information and updates. Late September.

October

Chicago International Film Festival (✆ 312/683-0121; www.chicagofilmfestival.org). The oldest U.S. festival of its kind screens films from around the world at various theaters, over 2 weeks, beginning the first Thursday in October.

Chicago Marathon (✆ 312/904-9800; www.chicagomarathon.com). Sponsored by LaSalle Bank, Chicago's marathon is a major event on the international long-distance running circuit. It begins and ends in Grant Park, but can be viewed from any number of vantage points along the route. October 5.

November

The **Chicago Humanities Festival** takes over locations throughout downtown, from libraries to concert halls

(✆ 312/661-1028; www.chfestival.org). Over a 2-week period, the festival presents cultural performances, readings, and symposiums tied to an annual theme (recent themes included "Brains & Beauty" and "Crime & Punishment"). Expect appearances by major authors, scholars, and policymakers, all at a very reasonable cost ($5 per event). Early November.

Dance Chicago (✆ 773/989-0698; www.dancechicago.com). All of the city's best-known dance troupes (including Hubbard Street and Joffrey Ballet) and many smaller companies participate in this month-long celebration of dance, with performances and workshops at the **Athenaeum Theatre,** 2936 N. Southport Ave., on the city's North Side. It's a great chance to check out the range of local dance talent.

Magnificent Mile Lights Festival (✆ 312/642-3570; www.gnmaa.com).

Beginning at dusk, a colorful parade of Disney characters makes its way south along Michigan Avenue, from Oak Street to the Chicago River. Thousands of lights are entwined around trees, and street lights switch on as the procession passes. Carolers, elves, and minstrels appear with Santa along the avenue throughout the day and into the evening, and many retailers offer hot chocolate and other treats. Saturday before Thanksgiving.

Christmas Tree Lighting, Daley Center Plaza, in the Loop (© 312/744-3315). The switch is flipped the day after Thanksgiving, around dusk.

December

A Christmas Carol, Goodman Theatre, 170 N. Dearborn St. (© 312/443-3800; www.goodman-theatre.org). This seasonal favorite, performed for more than 2 decades, runs from about Thanksgiving to the end of December.

The *Nutcracker* **ballet,** Joffrey Ballet of Chicago, Auditorium Theatre, 50 E. Congress Pkwy. For tickets, call © 312/559-1212 (Ticketmaster), or contact the Joffrey office (© 312/739-0120; www.joffrey.com). The esteemed company performs its Victorian-American twist on the holiday classic. Late November to mid-December.

4 Getting There

BY PLANE

O'HARE INTERNATIONAL AIRPORT

Chicago's **O'Hare International Airport** (© 773/686-2200; www.flychicago.com; online airport code ORD) has long battled Atlanta's Hartsfield for the title of the world's busiest airport. O'Hare is about 15 miles northwest of the Loop. Depending on traffic, the drive to or from downtown can take anywhere from 30 minutes to more than an hour.

O'Hare has information booths in all five terminals; most are on the baggage level. The multilingual employees, who wear red jackets, can assist travelers with everything from arranging ground transportation to getting information about local hotels. The booths also offer a plethora of useful tourism brochures. The booths, labeled "Airport Information," are open daily from 9am to 8pm.

Domestic carriers that fly regularly to O'Hare include **American** (© 800/433-7300; www.aa.com), **America West** (© 800/235-9292; www.americawest.com), **Continental** (© 800/525-0280; www.continental.com), **Delta** (© 800/221-1212; www.delta.com), **Northwest** (© 800/225-2525; www.nwa.com), **United** (© 800/241-6522; www.united.com) and discount offshoot **Ted** (© 800/CALL-TED; www.flyted.com), and **US Airways** (© 800/428-4322; www.usairways.com). You'll have the most flight options with American or United, both of which have hubs in Chicago. Several regional airlines provide commuter service.

Fun Fact **O'Hare, Oh My**

Chicago's O'Hare International Airport comes in second place (after Hartsfield-Jackson Atlanta International Airport) as the busiest airport in the world. Approximately 970,000 planes take off and land at O'Hare each year, generating about 500,000 jobs for the region. O'Hare is completely self-supporting, requiring no local taxpayer dollars to keep it going.

MIDWAY INTERNATIONAL AIRPORT

On the opposite end of the city, the southwest side, is Chicago's other major airport, **Midway International Airport** (© 773/838-0600; www.flychicago.com; online airport code MDW). Although it's smaller than O'Hare and handles fewer airlines, Midway is closer to the Loop and attracts more discount airlines, so you may be able to get a cheaper fare flying into here. (Always check fares to both airports if you want to find the best deal.) A cab ride from Midway to the Loop usually takes about 20 minutes. You can find the latest information on both airports at the city's Department of Aviation website: www.flychicago.com.

Airlines that fly to Chicago's Midway International Airport are **AirTran** (© 800/247-8726; www.airtran.com), **ATA** (© 800/435-9282; www.ata.com), **Continental** (© 800/525-0280; www.continental.com), **Frontier** (© 800/432-1359; www.frontierairlines.com), **Northwest** (© 800/225-2525; www.nwa.com), and **Southwest** (© 800/435-9792; www.southwest.com). ATA and Southwest operate the most frequent flights in and out of Midway.

FLYING FOR LESS: TIPS FOR GETTING THE BEST AIRFARE

- Passengers who can book their ticket either **long in advance or at the last minute,** or who **fly midweek** or **at less-trafficked hours** may pay a fraction of the full fare. If your schedule is flexible, say so, and ask if you can secure a cheaper fare by changing your flight plans.
- Search **the Internet** for cheap fares. The most popular online travel agencies are **Travelocity.com** (www.travelocity.co.uk); **Expedia.com** (www.expedia.co.uk and www.expedia.ca); and **Orbitz.com**. In the U.K., go to **Travelsupermarket** (© 0845/345-5708; www.travelsupermarket.com),

a flight search engine that offers flight comparisons for the budget airlines whose seats often end up in bucket-shop sales. Other websites for booking airline tickets online include **Cheapflights.com**, **SmarterTravel.com**, **Priceline.com**, and **Opodo** (www.opodo.co.uk). Meta search sites (which find and then direct you to airline and hotel websites for booking) include **Sidestep.com** and **Kayak.com**—the latter includes fares for budget carriers, such as JetBlue and Spirit, as well as the major airlines. **Site59.com** is a great source for last-minute flights and getaways. In addition, most **airlines** offer online-only fares that even their phone agents know nothing about. British travelers should check **Flights International** (© 0800/0187050; www.flights-international.com) for deals on flights all over the world.

- Watch local newspapers for **promotional specials** or **fare wars,** when airlines lower prices on their most popular routes. Also keep an eye on price fluctuations and deals at websites such as **Airfarewatchdog.com** and **Farecast.com**. Try to book a ticket in its country of **origin.** If you're planning a one-way flight from Johannesburg to New York, a South Africa–based travel agent will probably have the lowest fares. For foreign travelers on multileg trips, book in the country of the first leg; for example, book New York–Chicago–Montreal–New York in the U.S.
- **Consolidators,** also known as bucket shops, are wholesale brokers in the airline-ticket game. Consolidators buy deeply discounted tickets ("distressed" inventories of unsold seats) from airlines and sell them to online ticket agencies, travel agents, tour operators, corporations, and, to a lesser degree, the general public. Consolidators advertise in Sunday

newspaper travel sections (often in small ads with tiny type), both in the U.S. and the U.K. They can be great sources for cheap international tickets. On the down side, bucket shop tickets are often rigged with restrictions, such as stiff cancellation penalties (as high as 50%–75% of the ticket price). And keep in mind that most of what you see advertised is of limited availability. Several reliable consolidators are worldwide and available online. **STA Travel** (www.statravel.com) has been the world's leading consolidator for students since purchasing Council Travel, but their fares are competitive for travelers of all ages. **Flights.com** (© **800/TRAV-800;** www.flights.com) has excellent fares worldwide, particularly to Europe. They also have "local" websites in 12 countries. **FlyCheap** (© **800/FLY-CHEAP;** www.1800 flycheap.com) has especially good fares to sunny destinations. **Air Tickets Direct** (© **800/778-3447;** www. airticketsdirect.com) is based in Montreal and leverages the currently weak Canadian dollar for low fares; they also book trips to places that U.S. travel agents won't touch, such as Cuba.

• Join **frequent-flier clubs.** Frequent-flier membership doesn't cost a cent, but it does entitle you to free tickets or upgrades when you amass the airline's required number of frequent-flier points. You don't even have to fly to earn points; **frequent-flier credit cards** can earn you thousands of miles for doing your everyday shopping. But keep in mind that award seats are limited, seats on popular routes are hard to snag, and more and more major airlines are cutting their expiration periods for mileage points—so check your airline's frequent-flier program so you don't lose your miles

before you use them. *Inside tip:* Award seats are offered almost a year in advance, but seats also open up at the last minute, so if your travel plans are flexible, you may strike gold. To play the frequent-flier game to your best advantage, consult the community bulletin boards on **FlyerTalk** (www.flyertalk.com) or go to Randy Petersen's **Inside Flyer** (www.inside flyer.com). Petersen and friends review all the programs in detail and post regular updates on changes in policies and trends.

ARRIVING AT THE AIRPORT
IMMIGRATION & CUSTOMS CLEARANCE   Foreign visitors arriving by air, no matter what the port of entry, should cultivate patience and resignation before setting foot on U.S. soil. U.S. airports have considerably beefed up security clearances in the years since the terrorist attacks of 9/11, and clearing Customs and Immigration can take as long as 2 hours.

People traveling by air from Canada, Bermuda, and certain Caribbean countries can sometimes clear Customs and Immigration at the point of departure, which is much faster.

GETTING INTO TOWN FROM O'HARE & MIDWAY
Taxis are plentiful at both O'Hare and Midway, but getting to town is easily accessed by public transportation as well. A cab ride into the city will cost about $30 to $35 from O'Hare (20 miles from downtown), and $25 to $30 from Midway (10 miles from downtown). *One warning:* Rush hour traffic can be horrendous, especially around O'Hare. If you have to get downtown in a hurry, the El can actually be faster than driving.

If you're not carting enormous amounts of luggage and want to save money, I highly recommend taking public transportation, which is convenient from both

---

Tips **Getting Through the Airport**

- Arrive at the airport at least 1 hour before domestic flights and 2 hours before an international flight. You can check the average wait times at your airport by going to the TSA **Security Checkpoint Wait Times** site (waittime/tsa.dhs.gov).
- Know what you can carry on and what you can't. For the latest updates on items you are prohibited to bring in carryon luggage, go to **www.tsa.gov/travelers/airtravel**.
- Beat the ticket-counter lines by using the self-service electronic ticket kiosks at the airport or even printing out your boarding pass at home from the airline website. Using curbside check-in is also a smart way to avoid lines.
- Bring a current, government-issued photo ID such as a driver's license or passport. Children under 18 do not need government-issued photo IDs for flights within the U.S., but they do for international flights to most countries.
- Help speed up security before you're screened. Remove jackets, shoes, belt buckles, heavy jewelry, and watches and place them either in your carry-on luggage or the security bins provided. Place keys, coins, cellphones, and pagers in a security bin. If you have metallic body parts, carry a note from your doctor. When possible, pack liquids in checked baggage.
- Use a TSA-approved lock for your checked luggage. Look for Travel Sentry certified locks at luggage or travel shops and Brookstone stores (or online at www.brookstone.com).

---

airports. For $2, you can take the El (vernacular for the elevated train) straight into downtown.

O'Hare is on the Blue Line; a trip to downtown takes about 40 minutes. Trains leave every 6 to 10 minutes during the day, and every half-hour in the evening and overnight.

Getting downtown from Midway is even faster; the ride on the Orange Line takes 20 to 30 minutes. (The Orange Line stops operating each night at about 11:30pm and resumes service by 5am.) Trains leave the station every 6 to 15 minutes. The train station is a significant walk from the terminal—without the benefit of O'Hare's moving sidewalks—so be prepared if you have heavy bags.

Both airports also have outposts for every major car rental company (see "Getting Around" in chapter 5 for details).

Continental Airport Express (*©* 888/2-THEVAN; www.airportexpress.com) serves most first-class hotels in Chicago with its blue-and-white vans; ticket counters are at both airports near baggage claim (outside Customs at the international terminal at O'Hare). For transportation to the airport, reserve a spot through one of the hotels (check with the bell captain). The cost is $25 one-way ($45 round-trip) to or from O'Hare, and $20 one-way ($36 round-trip) to or from Midway. Group rates for two or more people traveling together are less expensive than sharing a cab. The shuttles operate from 4am to 11:30pm.

For limo service from O'Hare or Midway, call **Carey Limousine of Chicago**

⌐Tips **Don't Stow It—Ship It**

Though pricey, it's sometimes worthwhile to travel luggage-free, particularly if you're toting sports equipment, meeting materials, or baby equipment. Specialists in door-to-door luggage delivery include **Virtual Bellhop** (www.virtual bellhop.com); **SkyCap International** (www.skycapinternational.com); **Luggage Express** (www.usxpluggageexpress.com); and **Sports Express** (www.sports express.com).

(© **773/763-0009;** www.ecarey.com) or **Chicago Limousine Services** (© **312/ 726-1035**). Depending on the number of passengers and whether you opt for a sedan or a stretch limo, the service will cost about $100 to $150 from Midway and $150 to $200 from O'Hare, excluding gratuity and tax.

LONG-HAUL FLIGHTS: HOW TO STAY COMFORTABLE

- Your choice of airline and airplane will definitely affect your legroom. Find more details about U.S. airlines at **www.seatguru.com**. For international airlines, the research firm Skytrax has posted a list of average seat pitches at **www.airlinequality.com**.
- Emergency exit seats and bulkhead seats typically have the most legroom. Emergency exit seats are usually left unassigned until the day of a flight (to ensure that someone able-bodied fills the seats); it's worth getting to the ticket counter early to snag one of these spots for a long flight. Many passengers find that bulkhead seating (the row facing the wall at the front of the cabin) offers more legroom, but keep in mind that bulkheads are where airlines often put baby bassinets, so you may be sitting next to an infant.
- To have two seats for yourself in a three-seat row, try for an aisle seat in a center section toward the back of coach. If you're traveling with a companion, book an aisle and a window

seat. Middle seats are usually booked last, so chances are good you'll end up with three seats to yourselves. And in the event that a third passenger is assigned the middle seat, he or she will probably be more than happy to trade for a window or an aisle.

- Ask about entertainment options. Many airlines offer seatback video systems where you get to choose your movies or play video games—but only on some of their planes. (Boeing 777s are your best bet.)
- To sleep, avoid the last row of any section or the row in front of an emergency exit, as these seats are the least likely to recline. Avoid seats near highly trafficked toilet areas. Avoid seats in the back of many jets—these can be narrower than those in the rest of coach. You also may want to reserve a window seat so you can rest your head and avoid being bumped in the aisle.
- Get up, walk around, and stretch every 60 to 90 minutes to keep your blood flowing. This helps avoid **deep vein thrombosis,** or "economy-class syndrome."
- Drink water before, during, and after your flight to combat the lack of humidity in airplane cabins. Avoid alcohol, which will dehydrate you.
- If you're flying with kids, don't forget to carry toys, books, pacifiers, and chewing gum to help them relieve ear pressure buildup during ascent and descent.

Flying with Film & Video

Never pack film—exposed or unexposed—in checked bags, because the new, more powerful scanners in U.S. airports can fog film. The film you carry with you can be damaged by scanners as well. X-ray damage is cumulative; the faster the film and the more times you put it through a scanner, the more likely it is that damage will result. Film under 800 ASA is usually safe for up to five scans. If you're taking your film through additional scans, U.S. regulations permit you to demand hand inspections. In international airports, you're at the mercy of airport officials. On international flights, store your film in transparent baggies so you can remove it easily before you go through security. Keep in mind that airports are not the only places where your camera may be scanned: Highly trafficked attractions are X-raying visitors' bags with increasing frequency.

Most photo supply stores sell protective pouches designed to block damaging X-rays. The pouches fit both film and loaded cameras. They should protect your film in checked baggage, but they also may raise alarms and result in a hand inspection.

You'll have little to worry about if you're traveling with **digital cameras**. Unlike film, which is sensitive to light, the digital camera and storage cards are not affected by airport X-rays, according to Nikon.

Carry-on scanners will not damage **videotape** in video cameras, but the magnetic fields emitted by the walk-through security gateways and hand-held inspection wands will. Always place your loaded camcorder on the screening conveyor belt or have it hand-inspected. Be sure your batteries are charged, as you may be required to turn the device on to ensure that it's what it appears to be.

BY CAR

Interstate highways from all major points on the compass serve Chicago. I-80 and I-90 approach from the east, crossing the northern sector of Illinois, with I-90 splitting off and emptying into Chicago on the Skyway and the Dan Ryan Expressway. From here, I-90 runs through Wisconsin, following a northern route to Seattle. I-55 snakes up the Mississippi Valley from the vicinity of New Orleans and enters Chicago from the west along the Stevenson Expressway; in the opposite direction, it provides an outlet to the Southwest. I-57 originates in southern Illinois and forms part of the interstate linkage to Florida and the South, connecting within Chicago on the west leg of the Dan Ryan. I-94 links Detroit with Chicago, arriving on the Calumet Expressway and leaving the city on the Kennedy Expressway en route to the Northwest.

Here are approximate driving distances in miles to Chicago: from **Milwaukee,** 92; from **St. Louis,** 297; from **Detroit,** 286; from **Denver,** 1,011; from **Atlanta,** 716; from **Washington, D.C.,** 715; from **New York City,** 821; and from **Los Angeles,** 2,034.

BY TRAIN

Traveling great distances by train is certainly not the quickest way to go, nor always the most convenient, but many travelers still prefer it to flying or driving.

For tickets, consult your travel agent or call **Amtrak** (© **800/USA-RAIL;** www.amtrak.com). Ask the reservations agent to send you Amtrak's useful travel planner, with information on train accommodations and package tours.

When you arrive in Chicago, the train will pull into **Union Station,** 210 S. Canal St., between Adams and Jackson streets (© **312/655-2385**). Bus nos. 1, 60, 125, 151, and 156 all stop at the station, which is just west across the river from the Loop. The nearest El stop is at Clinton Street and Congress Parkway (on the Blue Line), which is a fair walk away, especially when you're carrying luggage.

5 General Travel Resources

MONEY

It's always advisable to bring money in a variety of forms on a vacation: a mix of cash, credit cards, and traveler's checks. You should also exchange enough petty cash to cover airport incidentals, tipping, and transportation to your hotel before you leave home, or withdraw money upon arrival at an airport ATM.

ATMS

Nationwide, the easiest and best way to get cash away from home is from an ATM (automated teller machine), sometimes referred to as a "cash machine" or "cashpoint." The **Cirrus** (© **800/424-7787;** www.mastercard.com) and **PLUS** (© **800/843-7587;** www.visa.com) networks span the country; you can find them even in remote regions. Go to your bank card's website to find ATM locations at your destination. Be sure you know your daily withdrawal limit before you depart.

Note: Many banks impose a fee every time you use a card at another bank's ATM, and that fee can be higher for international transactions (up to $5 or more) than for domestic ones (where they're rarely more than $2). In addition, the bank from which you withdraw cash may charge its own fee. To compare banks' ATM fees within the U.S., use **www.bankrate.com**. Visitors from outside the U.S. should also find out whether their bank assesses a 1% to 3% fee on charges incurred abroad.

CREDIT CARDS & DEBIT CARDS

Credit cards are the most widely used form of payment in the United States: **Visa** (Barclaycard in Britain), **MasterCard** (EuroCard in Europe, Access in Britain, Chargex in Canada), **American Express, Diners Club,** and **Discover.** They also provide a convenient record of all your expenses, and offer relatively good exchange rates. You can withdraw cash advances from your credit cards at banks or ATMs, but high fees make credit card cash advances a pricey way to get cash.

It's highly recommended that you travel with at least one major credit card. You must have one to rent a car, and hotels and airlines usually require a credit card imprint as a deposit against expenses.

ATM cards with major credit card backing, known as **"debit cards,"** are now a commonly acceptable form of payment in most stores and restaurants. Debit cards draw money directly from your checking account. Some stores enable you to receive cash back on your debit-card purchases as well. The same is true at most U.S. post offices.

TRAVELER'S CHECKS

Though credit cards and debit cards are more often used, traveler's checks are still widely accepted in the U.S. Foreign visitors should make sure that traveler's checks are denominated in U.S. dollars; foreign-currency checks are often difficult to exchange. In Chicago, you should have no trouble using them at most hotels and downtown restaurants (places that are used to accommodating international visitors), but they may not be accepted at smaller businesses in the city's residential neighborhoods.

You can buy traveler's checks at most banks. Most are offered in denominations of $20, $50, $100, $500, and sometimes $1,000. Generally, you'll pay a service charge ranging from 1% to 4%.

The most popular traveler's checks are offered by **American Express** (© **800/ 807-6233;** 800/221-7282 for cardholders—this number accepts collect calls, offers service in several foreign languages, and exempts AmEx gold and platinum cardholders from the 1% fee); **Visa** (© **800/ 732-1322;** AAA members can obtain Visa checks for a $9.95 fee—for checks up to $1,500—at most AAA offices or by calling 866/339-3378); and **MasterCard** (© **800/223-9920**).

Be sure to keep a copy of the traveler's checks serial numbers separate from your checks in the event that they are stolen or lost. You'll get a refund faster if you know the numbers.

Another option is the new **prepaid traveler's check cards,** reloadable cards that work much like debit cards but aren't linked to your checking account. The **American Express Travelers Cheque Card,** for example, requires a minimum deposit ($300), sets a maximum balance ($2,750), and has a one-time issuance fee of $15. You can withdraw money from an ATM ($2.50 per transaction, not including bank fees), and the funds can be purchased in dollars, euros, or pounds. If you lose the card, your available funds will be refunded within 24 hours.

TRAVEL INSURANCE

The cost of travel insurance varies widely, depending on the cost and length of your trip, your age and health, and the type of trip you're taking, but expect to pay between 5% and 8% of the vacation itself. You can get estimates from various providers through **InsureMyTrip.com**. Enter your trip cost and dates, your age, and other information for prices from more than a dozen companies.

For **U.K. citizens,** insurance is always advisable when traveling in the States. Travelers or families who make more than one trip abroad per year may find an annual travel insurance policy works out cheaper. Check **www.moneysupermarket. com**, which compares prices across a wide range of providers for single- and multi-trip policies.

Most big travel agents offer their own insurance and will probably try to sell you their package when you book a holiday. Think before you sign. **Britain's Consumers' Association** recommends that you insist on seeing the policy and read the fine print before buying travel insurance. **The Association of British Insurers** (© **020/7600-3333;** www.abi.org. uk) gives advice by phone and publishes *Holiday Insurance,* a free guide to policy provisions and prices. You might also shop around for better deals: Try **Columbus Direct** (© **0870/033-9988;** www. columbusdirect.net).

TRIP-CANCELLATION INSURANCE

Trip-cancellation insurance will help retrieve your money if you have to back out of a trip or depart early, or if your travel supplier goes bankrupt. Trip cancellation traditionally covers such events as sickness, natural disasters, and Department of State advisories. The latest news in trip-cancellation insurance is the availability of **expanded hurricane coverage** and the **"any-reason"** cancellation coverage—which costs more but covers cancellations made for any reason. You won't get back 100% of your prepaid trip cost, but you'll be refunded a substantial portion. **TravelSafe** (© **888/885-7233;** www. travelsafe.com) offers both types of coverage. Expedia also offers any-reason cancellation coverage for its air-hotel packages.

Travel in the Age of Bankruptcy

Airlines go bankrupt, so protect yourself by **buying your tickets with a credit card.** The Fair Credit Billing Act guarantees that you can get your money back from the credit card company if a travel supplier goes under (and if you request the refund within 60 days of the bankruptcy). **Travel insurance** can also help, but make sure it covers against "carrier default" for your specific travel provider. And be aware that if a U.S. airline goes bust midtrip, a 2001 federal law requires other carriers to take you to your destination (albeit on a space-available basis) for a fee of no more than $25, provided you rebook within 60 days of the cancellation.

For details, contact one of the following recommended insurers: **Access America** (© 866/807-3982; www.access america.com); **Travel Guard International** (© 800/826-4919; www.travel guard.com); **Travel Insured International** (© 800/243-3174; www.travel insured.com); and **Travelex Insurance Services** (© 888/457-4602; www.travelex-insurance.com).

MEDICAL INSURANCE

Although it's not required of travelers, health insurance is highly recommended. Most health insurance policies cover you if you get sick away from home—but check your coverage before you leave.

International visitors should note that unlike many European countries, the United States does not usually offer free or low-cost medical care to its citizens or visitors. Doctors and hospitals are expensive, and in most cases will require advance payment or proof of coverage before they render their services. Good policies will cover the costs of an accident, repatriation, or death. Packages such as **Europ Assistance's "Worldwide Healthcare Plan"** are sold by European automobile clubs and travel agencies at attractive rates. **Worldwide Assistance Services, Inc.** (© 800/777-8710; www. worldwideassistance.com) is the agent for Europ Assistance in the United States.

Though lack of health insurance may prevent you from being admitted to a hospital in nonemergencies, don't worry about being left on a street corner to die: The American way is to fix you now and bill the living daylights out of you later.

If you're ever hospitalized more than 150 miles from home, **MedjetAssist** (© **800/527-7478;** www.medjetassistance. com) will pick you up and fly you to the hospital of your choice in a medically equipped and staffed aircraft 24 hours day, 7 days a week. Annual memberships are $225 individual, $350 family; you can also purchase short-term memberships.

Canadians should check with their provincial health plan offices or call **Health Canada** (© **866/225-0709;** www. hc-sc.gc.ca) to find out the extent of their coverage and what documentation and receipts they must take home in case they are treated in the United States.

LOST-LUGGAGE INSURANCE

On flights within the U.S., checked baggage is covered up to $2,500 per ticketed passenger. On flights outside the U.S. (and on U.S. portions of international trips), baggage coverage is limited to approximately $9.05 per pound, up to approximately $635 per checked bag. If you plan to check items more valuable than what's covered by the standard liability, see if your homeowner's policy covers your valuables, get baggage insurance as part of your comprehensive travel insurance package, or buy Travel Guard's "BagTrak" product.

If your luggage is lost, immediately file a lost-luggage claim at the airport, detailing the luggage contents. Most airlines require that you report delayed, damaged, or lost baggage within 4 hours of arrival. The airlines are required to deliver luggage, once found, directly to your house or destination free of charge.

HEALTH
STAYING HEALTHY
Contact the **International Association for Medical Assistance to Travelers (IAMAT)** (© 716/754-4883 or, in Canada, 416/652-0137; www.iamat.org) for tips on travel and health concerns in the countries you're visiting, and for lists of local, English-speaking doctors. The United States **Centers for Disease Control and Prevention** (© 800/311-3435; www.cdc.gov) provides up-to-date information on health hazards by region or country and offers tips on food safety. The website **www.tripprep.com**, sponsored by a consortium of travel medicine practitioners, **Travel Health Online,** may also offer helpful advice on traveling abroad. You can find listings of reliable clinics overseas at the **International Society of Travel Medicine** (www.istm.org).

WHAT TO DO IF YOU GET SICK AWAY FROM HOME
We list **hospitals** and **emergency numbers** under "Fast Facts," p. 51.

If you suffer from a chronic illness, consult your doctor before your departure. Pack **prescription medications** in your carry-on luggage, and carry them in their original containers with pharmacy labels, otherwise they won't make it through airport security. Visitors from outside the U.S. should carry generic names of prescription drugs. For U.S.

travelers, most reliable health care plans provide coverage if you get sick away from home. Foreign visitors may have to pay all medical costs up front and be reimbursed later. See "Medical Insurance" under "Travel Insurance" above.

SAFETY
STAYING SAFE
Chicago has all the crime problems of any urban center, so use your common sense and stay cautious and alert. At night, you might want to stick to well-lit streets along the Magnificent Mile, River North, Gold Coast, and Lincoln Park, which are all high-traffic areas late into the night. That said, Chicago is still a big city; muggings can—and do—happen anywhere.

Late at night, avoid wandering dark residential streets on the fringes of Hyde Park and Pilsen, which border areas with more troublesome reputations. You can also ask your hotel concierge or an agent at the tourist visitor center about the safety of a particular area.

The El is generally quite safe, even at night, although some of the downtown stations can feel eerily deserted late in the evening. Buses are a safe option, too, especially nos. 146 and 151, which pick up along North Michigan Avenue and State Street and connect to the North Side via Lincoln Park.

Blue-and-white police cars are a common sight, and officers also patrol by bicycle downtown and along the lakefront and by horseback at special events and parades. There are police stations in busy nightlife areas, such as the 18th District station at Chicago Avenue and LaSalle Street in River North and the 24th District station (known as Town Hall) at Addison and Halsted streets.

6 Specialized Travel Resources

TRAVELERS WITH DISABILITIES
Most disabilities shouldn't stop anyone from traveling in the U.S. There are more

options and resources out there than ever before. Most of Chicago's sidewalks, as well as major museums and tourist attractions, are fitted with wheelchair ramps. Many hotels provide special accommodations such as ramps and large bathrooms for visitors in wheelchairs, as well as telecommunications devices for visitors with hearing impairments; inquire when you make your reservation.

Pace, the company that runs bus routes between Chicago and its suburbs, offers paratransit services throughout the area for travelers with disabilities. Visitors must be registered with a similar program in their home city. For information, call © **800/ 606-1282** or visit **www.pacebus.com**.

Several **Chicago Transit Authority (CTA)** El stations on each line have elevators. Call the CTA at © **312/836-7000** for a list of accessible stations. All city buses are equipped to accommodate wheelchairs.

For specific information on facilities for people with disabilities, contact the **Mayor's Office for People with Disabilities,** 121 N. LaSalle St., Room 1104, Chicago, IL 60602 (© **312/744-7050** for voice, or 312/744-4964 for TTY; www.cityofchicago.org/disabilities). The office is staffed from 8:30am to 4:30pm Monday through Friday.

Horizons for the Blind, 2 N. Williams St., Crystal Lake, IL 60014 (© **815/444-8800**), is a social service agency that provides information about local hotels equipped with Braille signage and cultural attractions that offer Braille signage and special tours. The **Illinois Relay Center** enables hearing- and speech-impaired TTY callers to call individuals or businesses without TTYs 24 hours a day. Calls are confidential and billed at regular phone rates. Call TTY at © **800/526-0844** or voice 800/526-0857. The city of Chicago operates a 24-hour information service for hearing-impaired callers with TTY equipment; call © **312/744-8599.**

Organizations that offer a vast range of resources and assistance to travelers with disabilities include **MossRehab** (© **800/ CALL-MOSS;** www.mossresourcenet.org);

the **American Foundation for the Blind (AFB)** (© **800/232-5463;** www.afb.org); and **SATH (Society for Accessible Travel & Hospitality)** (© **212/447-7284;** www.sath.org). **AirAmbulanceCard.com** is now partnered with SATH and allows you to preselect top-notch hospitals in case of an emergency.

Access-Able Travel Source (© **303/ 232-2979;** www.access-able.com) offers a comprehensive database of travel agents from around the world with experience in accessible travel; destination-specific access information; and links to such resources as service animals, equipment rentals, and access guides.

Many travel agencies offer customized tours and itineraries for travelers with disabilities. Among them are **Flying Wheels Travel** (© **507/451-5005;** www.flyingwheelstravel.com) and **Accessible Journeys** (© **800/846-4537** or 610/521-0339; www.disabilitytravel.com).

Flying with Disability (www.flying-with-disability.org) is a comprehensive information source on airplane travel. **Avis Rent a Car** (© **888/879-4273**) has an "Avis Access" program that offers services for customers with special travel needs. These include specially outfitted vehicles with swivel seats, spinner knobs, and hand controls; mobility scooter rentals; and accessible bus service. Be sure to reserve well in advance.

Also check out the quarterly magazine *Emerging Horizons* (www.emerging horizons.com), available by subscription ($17 year U.S.; $22 outside U.S).

The "Accessible Travel" link at **Mobility-Advisor.com** offers a variety of travel resources for persons with disabilities.

British travelers should contact **Holiday Care** (© **0845-124-9971** in U.K. only; www.holidaycare.org.uk) to access a wide range of travel information and resources for elderly people and travelers with disabilities.

GAY & LESBIAN TRAVELERS

While it's not quite San Francisco, Chicago is a very gay-friendly city. The neighborhood commonly referred to as "Boys Town" (roughly from Belmont Ave. north to Irving Park Ave., and from Halsted St. east to the lakefront) is the center of gay nightlife—and plenty of daytime action, too. **Gay and Lesbian Pride Week** (© 773/348-8243; www.chicagopride calendar.org), highlighted by a lively parade on the North Side, is a major event each June. You might also want to stop by **Unabridged Books,** 3251 N. Broadway (© 773/883-9119), an excellent independent bookseller with a large lesbian and gay selection. Here, and elsewhere in the Lakeview neighborhood, you can pick up several gay publications, including the weekly *Chicago Free Press* (www.chicagofreepress.com) and *Windy City Times* (www.windycitymediagroup. com/index.html), which both cover local news and entertainment. **Horizon Community Services** (© 773/929-HELP; www.horizonsonline.org), a gay social service agency with counseling services, support groups, and an antiviolence project, provides referrals daily from 6 to 10pm; you can also call the main switchboard at © 773/472-6469 during the day.

The International Gay and Lesbian Travel Association (IGLTA) (© 800/448-8550 or 954/776-2626; www.iglta.org) is the trade association for the gay and lesbian travel industry, and offers an online directory of gay- and lesbian-friendly travel businesses and tour operators.

Many agencies offer tours and travel itineraries specifically for gay and lesbian travelers. **Above and Beyond Tours** (© 800/397-2681; www.abovebeyondtours.com) are Australia gay-tour specialists. San Francisco–based **Now, Voyager** (© 800/255-6951; www.nowvoyager.com) offers worldwide trips and cruises, and **Olivia** (© 800/631-6277; www.olivia.com) offers lesbian cruises and resort vacations.

Gay.com Travel (© 800/929-2268 or 415/644-8044; www.gay.com/travel or www.outandabout.com) is an excellent online successor to the popular *Out & About* print magazine. It provides regularly updated information about gay-owned, gay-oriented, and gay-friendly lodging, dining, sightseeing, nightlife, and shopping establishments in every important destination worldwide. British travelers should click on the "Travel" link at **www.uk.gay.com** for advice and gay-friendly trip ideas.

The Canadian website **GayTraveler** (http://gaytraveler.ca) offers ideas and advice for gay travel all over the world.

The following travel guides are available at many bookstores, or you can order them from any online bookseller: *Spartacus International Gay Guide, 35th Edition* (Bruno Gmünder Verlag; www.spartacus world.com/gayguide), *Odysseus: The International Gay Travel Planner, 17th Edition* (www.odyusa.com); and the *Damron* guides (www.damron.com), with separate, annual books for gay men and lesbians.

SENIOR TRAVEL

Traveling as a senior can definitely save you money in Chicago; people 60 and older qualify for reduced admission to most major museums and theaters, as well as discounted fares on public transportation.

Members of **AARP,** 601 E St. NW, Washington, DC 20049 (© 888/687-2277; www.aarp.org), get discounts on hotels, airfares, and car rentals. AARP offers members a wide range of benefits, including *AARP: The Magazine* and a monthly newsletter. Anyone over 50 can join.

Many reliable agencies and organizations target the 50-plus market. **Elderhostel**

(© **800/454-5768**; www.elderhostel.org) arranges worldwide study programs for those ages 55 and over. **ElderTreks** (© **800/741-7956** or 416/558-5000 outside North America; www.eldertreks. com) offers small-group tours to off-the-beaten-path or adventure-travel locations, restricted to travelers 50 and older.

Recommended publications offering travel resources and discounts for seniors include: the quarterly magazine *Travel 50 & Beyond* (www.travel50andbeyond. com) and the bestselling paperback *Unbelievably Good Deals and Great Adventures That You Absolutely Can't Get Unless You're Over 50 2005–2006, 16th Edition* (McGraw-Hill), by Joann Rattner Heilman.

FAMILY TRAVEL

Chicago is full of sightseeing opportunities and special activities geared toward children. To locate those accommodations, restaurants, and attractions that are particularly kid-friendly, refer to the "Kids" icon throughout this guide. Also see "Kid Stuff" in chapter 8 for information on family-oriented attractions. Chapter 6 includes a list of the best hotel deals for families, and chapter 7 lists kid-friendly restaurants. For information on finding a babysitter, see "Fast Facts: Chicago," later in this chapter. The guidebook *Frommer's Chicago with Kids* (Wiley Publishing, Inc.) highlights the many family-friendly activities available in the city.

Recommended family travel websites include **Family Travel Forum** (www. familytravelforum.com), a comprehensive site that offers customized trip planning; **Family Travel Network** (www. familytravelnetwork.com), an online magazine providing travel tips; **TravelWith YourKids.com** (www.travelwithyourkids. com), a comprehensive site written by parents for parents offering sound advice for long-distance and international travel with children.

MULTICULTURAL TRAVELERS

Chicago is a cosmopolitan city with a population that's about 36% African American, 30% white, and 26% Latino (Chicago has the second-largest Mexican population in the U.S. after Los Angeles). Visitors of all racial and ethnic groups shouldn't expect to encounter any discrimination, especially in the downtown area. We're used to welcoming tourists and businesspeople from around the world. That said, Chicago is still extremely divided residentially along racial lines. The South Side is overwhelmingly African American, the North Side is mostly white, and Latino residents tend to settle in neighborhoods such as Pilsen, just southwest of downtown.

Travelers can explore the city's rich black heritage with a specialized tour (see "Chicago & the Great Black Migration," p. 296, and "Neighborhood Tours," p. 216). Visitors with an interest in Latin-American art might want to stop by the vibrant National Museum of Mexican Art in Pilsen (p. 201).

STUDENT TRAVEL

The best resource for students in Chicago is **STA Travel** (www.statravel.com), one of the biggest student-travel agencies in the world, which can set you up with an ID card and get you discounts on plane tickets and rail travel. There is an STA office in Lincoln Park at 2570 N. Clark St., Chicago, IL 60614 (© **773/880-8051**).

Chicago also has several hostels offering students and other travelers inexpensive, no-frills lodging. The best is **Hosteling International Chicago,** 24 E. Congress Pkwy., in the Loop (© **312/ 360-0300;** fax 312/360-0313; www.hi chicago.org). Opened in 2000, it features many amenities and can help set up activities throughout the city. Other hostels open year-round include **Arlington House International Hostel,** 616 W. Arlington

Place, Chicago, IL 60614 (© **800/ HOSTEL-5** or 773/929-5380; fax 773/ 665-5485; www.arlingtonhouse.com), in Lincoln Park, and **Chicago International**

Hostel, 6318 N. Winthrop Ave., Chicago, IL 60660 (© **773/262-1011;** fax 773/ 262-3632; www.hostelinchicago.com), on the North Side.

7 Sustainable Tourism/Ecotourism

Each time you take a flight or drive a car CO_2 is released into the atmosphere. You can help neutralize this danger to our planet through "carbon offsetting"— paying someone to reduce your CO_2 emissions by the same amount you've added. Carbon offsets can be purchased in the U.S. from companies such as **Carbonfund.org** (www.carbonfund.org) and **TerraPass** (www.terrapass.org), and from **Climate Care** (www.climatecare.org) in the U.K.

Although one could argue that any vacation that includes an airplane flight can't be truly "green," you can go on holiday and still contribute positively to the environment. In addition to purchasing carbon offsets from the companies mentioned above, you can take other steps toward responsible travel. Choose forward-looking companies who embrace responsible development practices, helping preserve destinations for the future by working alongside local people. An increasing number of sustainable tourism initiatives can help you plan a family trip and leave as small a "footprint" as possible on the places you visit.

Responsible Travel (www.responsible travel.com), run by a spokesperson for responsible tourism in the travel industry, contains a great source of sustainable travel ideas.

You can find ecofriendly travel tips, statistics, and touring companies and associations—listed by destination under "Travel Choice"—at the TIES website, **www.ecotourism.org**. Also check out **Conservation International** (www. conservation.org)—which, with *National Geographic Traveler,* annually presents **World Legacy Awards** to those travel tour operators, businesses, organizations, and places that have made a significant contribution to sustainable tourism. **Ecotravel.com** is part online magazine and part ecodirectory that lets you search for touring companies in several categories (water-based, land-based, spiritually oriented, and so on).

In the U.K., **Tourism Concern** (www. tourismconcern.org.uk) works to reduce social and environmental problems connected to tourism and find ways of improving tourism so that local benefits are increased.

The **Association of British Travel Agents (ABTA)** (www.abta.com) acts as a focal point for the U.K. travel industry and is one of the leading groups spearheading responsible tourism.

The **Association of Independent Tour Operators (AITO)** (www.aito.co.uk) is a group of interesting specialist operators leading the field in making holidays sustainable.

8 Staying Connected

TELEPHONES

Generally, hotel surcharges on long-distance and local calls are astronomical, so you're better off using your **cellphone** or a **public pay telephone.** Many convenience groceries and packaging services sell **prepaid calling cards** in denominations

up to $50; for international visitors these can be the least expensive way to call home. Many public pay phones at airports now accept American Express, MasterCard, and Visa credit cards. **Local calls** made from pay phones in Chicago cost 35¢ (no pennies, please).

Frommers.com: The Complete Travel Resource

It should go without saying, but we highly recommend **Frommers.com**, voted Best Travel Site by *PC Magazine*. We think you'll find our expert advice and tips; independent reviews of hotels, restaurants, attractions, and preferred shopping and nightlife venues; vacation giveaways; and an online booking tool indispensable before, during, and after your travels. We publish the complete contents of more than 128 travel guides in our **Destinations** section covering nearly 3,600 places worldwide to help you plan your trip. Each weekday, we publish original articles reporting on **Deals and News** via our free **Frommers.com Newsletter** to help you save time and money and travel smarter. We're betting you'll find our new **Events** listings (http://events.frommers.com) an invaluable resource; it's an up-to-the-minute roster of what's happening in cities everywhere—including concerts, festivals, lectures, and more. We've also added weekly **Podcasts, interactive maps,** and hundreds of new images across the site. Check out our **Travel Talk** area, featuring **Message Boards** where you can join in conversations with thousands of fellow Frommer's travelers and post your trip report once you return.

Most long-distance and international calls can be dialed directly from any phone. **For calls within the United States and to Canada,** dial 1 followed by the area code and the seven-digit number. **For other international calls,** dial 011 followed by the country code, city code, and the number you are calling.

Calls to area codes **800, 888, 877,** and **866** are toll-free. However, calls to area codes **700** and **900** (chat lines, bulletin boards, "dating" services, and so on) can be very expensive—usually a charge of 95¢ to $3 or more per minute, and they sometimes have minimum charges that can run as high as $15 or more.

For **reversed-charge or collect calls,** and for person-to-person calls, dial the number 0 then the area code and number; an operator will come on the line, and you should specify whether you are calling collect, person-to-person, or both. If your operator-assisted call is international, ask for the overseas operator.

For **local directory assistance** ("information"), dial © 411; for long-distance information, dial 1, then the appropriate area code and 555-1212.

CELLPHONES

Just because your cellphone works at home doesn't mean it'll work everywhere in the U.S. (thanks to our nation's fragmented cellphone system). It's a good bet that your phone will work in major cities, but take a look at your wireless company's coverage map on its website before heading out; T-Mobile, Sprint, and Nextel are particularly weak in rural areas. If you need to stay in touch at a destination where you know your phone won't work, **rent** a phone that does from **InTouch USA** (© 800/872-7626; www.intouchglobal.com) or a rental car location, but beware that you'll pay $1 a minute or more for airtime.

If you're not from the U.S., you'll be appalled at the poor reach of our **GSM (Global System for Mobile Communications) wireless network,** which is used by much of the rest of the world. Your phone will probably work in most major U.S. cities; it definitely won't work in many rural areas. To see where GSM phones work in the U.S., check out www.t-mobile.com/coverage. And you may or may not be able to send SMS (text messaging) home.

VOICE-OVER INTERNET PROTOCOL (VOIP)

If you have Web access while traveling, you might consider a broadband-based telephone service (in technical terms, **Voice over Internet protocol, or VoIP**) such as Skype (www.skype.com) or Vonage (www.vonage.com), which allows you to make free international calls if you use their services from your laptop or in a cybercafe. The people you're calling must also use the service for it to work; check the sites for details.

INTERNET/E-MAIL
WITHOUT YOUR OWN COMPUTER

To find cybercafes in your destination, check **www.cybercaptive.com** and **www. cybercafe.com**. In Chicago, try **Screenz,** 2717 N. Clark St., 1 block south of Diversey Ave. in Lincoln Park (© **773/ 348-9300**), a computing center where you can check e-mail, burn CDs of your digital photos, and print out your favorite pictures.

Aside from formal cybercafes, most **youth hostels** and **public libraries** offer Internet access, and though **hotel business centers** are accessible to guests, they can be expensive.

Most major airports have **Internet kiosks** that provide basic Web access for a per-minute fee that's usually higher than cybercafe prices. Check out copy shops such as **Kinko's** (FedEx Kinko's),

which offers computer stations with fully loaded software (as well as Wi-Fi).

WITH YOUR OWN COMPUTER

More and more hotels, resorts, airports, cafes, and retailers are going Wi-Fi (wireless fidelity), becoming "hotspots" that offer free high-speed Wi-Fi access or charge a small fee for usage. Wi-Fi is even found in campgrounds, RV parks, and even entire towns. Most laptops sold today have built-in wireless capability. To find public Wi-Fi hotspots at your destination, go to **www. jiwire.com**; its Hotspot Finder holds the world's largest directory of public wireless hotspots.

In downtown Chicago, both Starbucks and the sandwich chain Cosí have numerous locations with Wi-Fi access. In the southern part of the Loop, the **Harold Washington Library Center,** 400 S. State St. (© **312/747-4300**), also has wireless access. Wireless hotspots in Lincoln Park include **Panera Bread,** 616 W. Diversey Pkwy. (© **773/528-4556**), and **Argo Tea,** 958 W. Armitage Ave. (© **773/ 388-1880**).

For dial-up access, most business-class hotels in the U.S. offer dataports for laptop modems, and a few thousand hotels in the U.S. and Europe now offer free high-speed Internet access.

Wherever you go, bring a **connection kit** of the right power and phone adapters, a spare phone cord, and a spare Ethernet network cable—or find out whether your hotel supplies them to guests.

For information on electrical currency conversions, see "Electricity," in the "Fast Facts" section at the end of this chapter.

9 Packages for the Independent Traveler

Package tours are simply a way to buy airfare, accommodations, and other elements of your trip (such as car rentals, airport transfers, and sometimes even

activities) at the same time and often at discounted prices.

One good source of package deals is the airlines themselves. Most major airlines

Online Traveler's Toolbox

Veteran travelers usually carry some essential items to make their trips easier. Following is a selection of handy online tools to bookmark and use.

- **Airplane Food** (www.airlinemeals.net)
- **Airplane Seating** (www.seatguru.com and www.airlinequality.com)
- **Chicago Cultural Events and Restaurant Reviews** (www.metromix.com)
- **Chicago Transit Authority Subway and Bus Maps** (www.transitchicago. com)
- *Chicago Tribune* **Newspaper** (www.chicagotribune.com)
- **Foreign Languages for Travelers** (www.travlang.com)
- **League of Chicago Theaters** (www.chicagoplays.com)
- **Maps** (www.mapquest.com)
- **Subway Navigator** (www.subwaynavigator.com)
- **Time and Date** (www.timeanddate.com)
- *Time Out Chicago* **Magazine** (www.timeoutchicago.com)
- **Universal Currency Converter** (www.xe.com/ucc)
- **Visa ATM Locator** (www.visa.com), **MasterCard ATM Locator** (www. mastercard.com)
- **Visas for International Travelers** (http://travel.state.gov)
- **Weather** (www.intellicast.com and www.weather.com)

offer air/land packages, including **American Airlines Vacations** (© 800/321-2121; www.aavacations.com), **Delta Vacations** (© 800/221-6666; www.deltavacations. com), **Continental Airlines Vacations** (© 800/301-3800; www.covacations. com), and **United Vacations** (© 888/ 854-3899; www.unitedvacations.com). Several big **online travel agencies**— Expedia, Travelocity, Orbitz, Site59, and Lastminute.com—also do a brisk business in packages.

Travel packages are also listed in the travel section of your local Sunday newspaper, or check ads in national travel magazines such as *Arthur Frommer's Budget Travel Magazine, Travel & Leisure, National Geographic Traveler,* and *Condé Nast Traveler.*

10 Tips on Accommodations

Most hotels in Chicago are owned by major chains, from the massive Hilton Chicago to the far-more-modest Red Roof Inn, and almost all cater overwhelmingly to business travelers during the week. Although some of the hotels here look and feel fairly interchangeable, others are set apart by their architectural style (the Sofitel Chicago Water Tower), historic charm (The Drake Hotel; Hotel Burnham), or their lavish amenities (The Peninsula Chicago; the Four Seasons). See chapter 6, "Where to Stay," for detailed descriptions.

SURFING FOR HOTELS

In addition to the online travel booking sites **Travelocity, Expedia, Orbitz, Priceline,** and **Hotwire,** you can book hotels through **Hotels.com; Quikbook** (www. quikbook.com); and **Travelaxe** (www. travelaxe.net).

Tips **Ask Before You Go**

Before you invest in a package deal or an escorted tour:

- Always ask about the **cancellation policy.** Can you get your money back? Is there a deposit required?
- Ask about the **accommodations choices and prices** for each. Then look up the hotels' reviews in a Frommer's guide and check their rates online for your specific dates of travel. Also, find out what types of rooms are offered.
- Request a complete **schedule** (escorted tours only).
- Ask about the **size** and demographics of the group (escorted tours only).
- Discuss what is included in the **price** (transportation, meals, tips, airport transfers, and so on; escorted tours only).
- Look for **hidden expenses.** Ask whether airport departure fees and taxes, for example, are included in the total cost (rarely).

HotelChatter.com is a daily webzine offering smart coverage and critiques of hotels worldwide. Go to **TripAdvisor.com** or **HotelShark.com** for helpful independent consumer reviews of hotels and resort properties.

It's a good idea to **get a confirmation number** and **make a printout** of any online booking transaction.

SAVING ON YOUR HOTEL ROOM

The **rack rate** is the maximum rate that a hotel charges for a room. Hardly anybody pays this price, however, except in high season or on holidays. To lower the cost of your room:

- **Ask about special rates or other discounts.** You may qualify for corporate, student, military, senior, frequent flier, trade union, or other discounts.
- **Dial direct.** When booking a room in a chain hotel, you'll often get a better deal by calling the individual hotel's reservation desk rather than the chain's main number.
- **Book online.** Many hotels offer Internet-only discounts, or supply rooms to Priceline, Hotwire, or

Expedia at rates much lower than the ones you can get through the hotel itself.

- **Remember the law of supply and demand.** Resort hotels are most crowded and therefore most expensive on weekends, so discounts are usually available for midweek stays. Business hotels in downtown locations are busiest during the week, so you can expect big discounts over the weekend.
- **Look into group or long-stay discounts.** If you come as part of a large group, you should be able to negotiate a bargain rate. Likewise, if you're planning a long stay (at least 5 days), you might qualify for a discount. As a general rule, expect 1 night free after a 7-night stay.
- **Sidestep excess charges and hidden costs.** Many hotels have the unpleasant practice of nickel-and-diming their guests with opaque surcharges. When you book a room, ask what is included in the room rate and what is extra. Avoid dialing direct from hotel phones, which can have exorbitant rates. And don't be tempted by the room's minibar offerings: Most hotels

Tips for Digital Travel Photography

- **Take along a spare camera—or two.** Even if you've been anointed the "official" photographer of your travel group, encourage others in your party to carry their own cameras and provide fresh perspectives—and backup. Your photographic "second unit" may include you in a few shots so you're not the invisible person of the trip.
- **Stock up on digital film cards.** At home, it's easy to copy pictures from your memory cards to your computer as they fill up. During your travels, cards seem to fill up more quickly. Take along enough digital film cards for your entire trip or, at a minimum, enough for at least a few days of shooting. At intervals, you can copy images to CDs. Many camera stores and souvenir shops offer this service, and a growing number of mass merchandisers have walk-up kiosks you can use to make prints or create CDs while you travel.
- **Share and share alike.** No need to wait until you get home to share your photos. You can upload a gallery's worth to an online photo sharing service. Just find an Internet cafe where the computers have card readers, or connect your camera to the computer with a cable. You can find online photo sharing services that cost little or nothing at **www.clickherefree. com**. You can also use America Online's Your Pictures service or commercial enterprises that give you free or low-cost photo sharing: Kodak's EasyShare gallery (www.kodak.com), Snapfish (www.snapfish.com), or Shutterfly (www.shutterfly.com).
- **Add voice annotations to your photos.** Many digital cameras allow you to add voice annotations to your shots after they're taken. These serve as excellent reminders and documentation. One castle or cathedral may look like another after a long tour; your voice notes will help you distinguish them.
- **Experiment!** Travel is a great time to try out new techniques. Take photos at night, resting your camera on a handy wall or other support as your self-timer trips the shutter for a long exposure. Try close-ups of flowers, crafts, wildlife, or maybe the exotic cuisine you're about to consume. Discover action photography—shoot the countryside from trains, buses, or cars. With a digital camera, you can experiment and then erase your mistakes.

—From *Travel Photography Digital Field Guide*, 1st edition
(*John Wiley & Sons, 2006*)

charge through the nose for water, soda, and snacks. Finally, ask about local taxes and service charges, which can increase the cost of a room by 15% or more.

- **Book an efficiency.** A room with a kitchenette allows you to shop for groceries and cook your own meals. This is a big money saver, especially for families on long stays.
- **Consider enrolling in hotel "frequent-stay" programs,** which are upping the ante lately to win the loyalty of repeat customers. Frequent

guests can now accumulate points or credits to earn free hotel nights, airline miles, in-room amenities, merchandise, tickets to concerts and events, discounts on sporting facilities, and even credit toward stock in the participating hotel (in the case of the Jameson Inn hotel group). Perks are awarded not only by many chain hotels and motels (Hilton HHonors, Marriott Rewards, Wyndham ByRequest, to name a few), but also by individual inns and B&Bs. Many chain hotels partner with other hotel chains, car rental firms, airlines, and credit card companies to give consumers additional incentive to do repeat business.

LANDING THE BEST ROOM

Somebody has to get the best room in the house, so it might as well be you. You can start by joining the hotel's frequent-guest program, which may make you eligible for upgrades. A hotel-branded credit card usually gives its owner "silver" or "gold" status in frequent-guest programs for free. Always ask about a corner room. They're often larger and quieter, with more windows and light, and they often cost the same as standard rooms. When you make your reservation, ask if the hotel is renovating; if it is, request a room away from the construction. Ask about nonsmoking rooms, rooms with views, and rooms with twin, queen- or king-size beds. If you're a light sleeper, request a quiet room away from vending machines, elevators, restaurants, bars, and discos. Ask for a room that has been most recently renovated or redecorated.

If you aren't happy with your room when you arrive, ask for another one. Most lodgings will be willing to accommodate you.

FAST FACTS: Chicago

American Express Travel-service offices are located in the Loop at 55 W. Monroe St. (© **312/541-5440**) and just north of the Tribune Tower at 605 N. Michigan Ave.

Area Codes The 312 area code applies to the Loop and the neighborhoods closest to it, including River North, North Michigan Avenue, and the Gold Coast. The code for the rest of the city is 773. Suburban area codes are 847 (north), 708 (west and southwest), and 630 (far west). You must dial "1" plus the area code for all telephone numbers, even if you are making a call within the same area code.

ATM Networks See "Money," p. 38.

Automobile Organizations Auto clubs will supply maps, suggested routes, guidebooks, accident and bail-bond insurance, and emergency road service. The **American Automobile Association (AAA)** is the major auto club in the U.S. If you belong to an auto club in your home country, inquire about AAA reciprocity before you leave. You may be able to join AAA even if you're not a member of a reciprocal club; to inquire, call © **800/222-4357**. AAA is actually an organization of regional auto clubs, so look under "AAA Automobile Club" in the White Pages of the telephone directory. AAA has a nationwide emergency road service telephone number (© **800/AAA-HELP**).

Babysitters Check with the concierge or desk staff at your hotel; they likely maintain a list of reliable sitters who they have worked with in the past. Many of the top hotels work with **American ChildCare Service** (✆ **312/644-7300;** www.americanchildcare.com), a state-licensed and insured babysitting service that can match you with a sitter. The sitters are required to pass background checks, provide multiple child-care references, and be trained in infant and child CPR. It's best to make a reservation 24 hours in advance; the office is open from 9am to 5pm weekdays. Rates are $19 per hour, with a 4-hour minimum, and a $20 agency fee (you're also expected to give the sitter a cash tip).

Business Hours Shops generally keep normal business hours, 10am to 6pm Monday through Saturday. Most stores stay open late at least 1 evening a week. Certain businesses, such as bookstores, are almost always open during the evening hours all week. Most shops (other than in the Loop) are now open on Sundays, usually from noon to 5pm. Malls are generally open until 7pm and on Sunday as well. Banking hours in Chicago are normally from 9am (8am in some cases) to 5pm Monday through Friday, with select banks remaining open later on specified afternoons and evenings.

Car Rentals See "Getting Around," p. 73.

Cashpoints See "ATM Networks," above.

Currency The most common bills are the $1 (a "buck"), $5, $10, and $20 denominations. There are also $2 bills (seldom encountered), $50 bills, and $100 bills (the last two are usually not welcome as payment for small purchases).

Coins come in seven denominations: 1¢ (1 cent, or a penny); 5¢ (5 cents, or a nickel); 10¢ (10 cents, or a dime); 25¢ (25 cents, or a quarter); 50¢ (50 cents, or a half dollar); the gold-colored Sacagawea coin, worth $1; and the rare silver dollar.

For additional information see "Money," p. 38.

Customs **What You Can Bring into the United States** Every visitor more than 21 years of age may bring in, free of duty, the following: (1) 1 liter of wine or hard liquor; (2) 200 cigarettes, 100 cigars (but not from Cuba), or 3 pounds of smoking tobacco; and (3) $100 worth of gifts. These exemptions are offered to travelers who spend at least 72 hours in the United States and who have not claimed them within the preceding 6 months. It is altogether forbidden to bring into the country foodstuffs (particularly fruit, cooked meats, and canned goods) and plants (vegetables, seeds, tropical plants, and the like). Foreign tourists may carry in or out up to $10,000 in U.S. or foreign currency with no formalities; larger sums must be declared to U.S. Customs on entering or leaving, which includes filing form CM 4790. For details regarding U.S. Customs and Border Protection, consult your nearest U.S. embassy or consulate, or **U.S. Customs** (✆ **202/927-1770;** www.customs.ustreas.gov).

What You Can Take Home from the United States:

Canadian Citizens: For a clear summary of Canadian rules, write for the booklet *I Declare,* issued by the **Canada Border Services Agency** (✆ **800/461-9999** in Canada, or 204/983-3500; www.cbsa-asfc.gc.ca).

U.K. Citizens: For information, contact **HM Customs & Excise** at ✆ **0845/010-9000** (from outside the U.K., 020/8929-0152), or consult their website at **www.hmce.gov.uk.**

Australian Citizens: A helpful brochure available from Australian consulates or Customs offices is *Know Before You Go.* For more information, call the **Australian Customs Service** at ✆ **1300/363-263,** or log on to **www.customs.gov.au.**

New Zealand Citizens: Most questions are answered in a free pamphlet available at New Zealand consulates and Customs offices: *New Zealand Customs Guide for Travellers, Notice no. 4.* For more information, contact **New Zealand Customs,** The Customhouse, 17–21 Whitmore St., Box 2218, Wellington (✆ **04/473-6099** or 0800/428-786; www.customs.govt.nz).

Dentists The referral service of the **Chicago Dental Society** (✆ **312/836-7300;** www.cds.org) can help you find an area dentist; you can also get a referral online through their website. Your hotel concierge or desk staff may also keep a list of dentists.

Doctors In the event of a medical emergency, your best bet—unless you have friends who can recommend a doctor—is to rely on your hotel physician or go to the nearest hospital emergency room. **Northwestern Memorial Hospital** also has a **Physician Referral Service** (✆ **877/926-4664**). Also see "Hospitals" below.

Drinking Laws The legal age for the purchase and consumption of alcoholic beverages is 21; proof of age is required and often requested at bars, nightclubs, and restaurants, so it's always a good idea to bring ID when you go out. In Chicago, beer, wine, and other alcoholic beverages are sold at liquor stores and supermarkets. Bars may sell alcohol until 2am, although some nightclubs have special licenses that allow alcohol sales until 4am. Do not carry open containers of alcohol in your car or any public area that isn't zoned for alcohol consumption. The police can fine you on the spot. And nothing will ruin your trip faster than getting a citation for DUI (driving under the influence), so don't even think about driving while intoxicated.

Driving Rules See "Getting Around," p. 73.

Electricity Like Canada, the United States uses 110 to 120 volts AC (60 cycles), compared to 220 to 240 volts AC (50 cycles) in most of Europe, Australia, and New Zealand. Downward converters that change 220 to 240 volts to 110 to 120 volts are difficult to find in the United States, so bring one with you.

Embassies & Consulates All embassies are located in the nation's capital, Washington, D.C. Some consulates are located in major U.S. cities, and most nations have a mission to the United Nations in New York City. If your country isn't listed below, call for directory information in Washington, D.C. (✆ **202/555-1212**), or log on to **www.embassy.org/embassies.**

The embassy of **Australia** is at 1601 Massachusetts Ave. NW, Washington, DC 20036 (✆ **202/797-3000;** www.austemb.org). There are consulates in New York, Honolulu, Houston, Los Angeles, and San Francisco.

The embassy of **Canada** is at 501 Pennsylvania Ave. NW, Washington, DC 20001 (✆ **202/682-1740;** http://geo.international.gc.ca/can-am/washington). Other Canadian consulates are in Buffalo (New York), Detroit, Los Angeles, New York, and Seattle.

The embassy of **Ireland** is at 2234 Massachusetts Ave. NW, Washington, DC 20008 (✆ **202/462-3939;** www.irelandemb.org). Irish consulates are in Boston,

Chicago, New York, San Francisco, and other cities. See website for complete listing.

The embassy of **New Zealand** is at 37 Observatory Circle NW, Washington, DC 20008 (© **202/328-4800;** www.nzemb.org). New Zealand consulates are in Los Angeles, Salt Lake City, San Francisco, and Seattle.

The embassy of the **United Kingdom** is at 3100 Massachusetts Ave. NW, Washington, DC 20008 (© **202/588-7800;** www.britainusa.com). Other British consulates are in Atlanta, Boston, Chicago, Cleveland, Houston, Los Angeles, New York, San Francisco, and Seattle.

Emergencies For fire or police emergencies, call © **911.** This is a free call. If it is a medical emergency, a city ambulance will take the patient to the nearest hospital emergency room. The nonemergency phone number for the Chicago Police Department is © **311.** If you desire a specific, nonpublic ambulance, call **Vandenberg Ambulance** (© **773/521-7777).**

Gasoline (Petrol) At press time, cost of gasoline (also known as gas, but never petrol), is fluctuating around $3 per gallon in Chicago. Taxes are already included in the printed price. You will pay more within the Chicago city limits than you will in the suburbs (the city adds an extra tax into the price), so if you're planning a day trip, it pays to fill up once you're out of town. One U.S. gallon equals 3.8 liters or .85 imperial gallons. Fill-up locations are known as gas or service stations.

Holidays Banks, government offices, post offices, and many stores, restaurants, and museums are closed on the following legal national holidays: January 1 (New Year's Day), the third Monday in January (Martin Luther King, Jr., Day), the third Monday in February (Presidents' Day), the last Monday in May (Memorial Day), July 4 (Independence Day), the first Monday in September (Labor Day), the second Monday in October (Columbus Day), November 11 (Veterans' Day/Armistice Day), the fourth Thursday in November (Thanksgiving Day), and December 25 (Christmas). The Tuesday after the first Monday in November is Election Day, a federal government holiday in presidential-election years (held every 4 years, and next in 2008).

For more information on holidays, see "Calendar of Events," earlier in this chapter.

Hospitals The best hospital emergency room in downtown Chicago is, by consensus, at **Northwestern Memorial Hospital,** 251 E. Huron St. (© **312/926-2000;** www.nmh.org), a state-of-the-art medical center right off North Michigan Avenue. The emergency department (© **312/926-5188** or 312/944-2358 for TDD access) is located at 251 E. Erie St., near Fairbanks Court. For an ambulance, dial © **911,** which is a free call.

Internet Access Many Chicago **hotels** have business centers with computers available for guests' use. Computers with Internet access are also available to the public at the **Harold Washington Library Center,** 400 S. State St. (© **312/ 747-4300),** and at the Internet cafe inside the **Apple** computer store, 679 N. Michigan Ave. (© **312/981-4104).** Most Starbucks coffee shops and McDonald's restaurants in downtown Chicago also have wireless Internet access available. See "Internet/E-Mail" under "Staying Connected," p. 47.

Laundry The closest laundromat to downtown is **Sudz Coin Laundry,** 1246 N. Ashland Ave. (© **773/218-9630;** www.sudzlaundry.com), about a block north of Division Street. Rates are 90¢ per pound for drop-off service and $2 per wash at self-service machines. It's open daily from 5am to midnight (last wash at 10:30pm). You can also arrange to have your laundry picked up and delivered.

Legal Aid If you are "pulled over" for a minor infraction (such as speeding), never attempt to pay the fine directly to a police officer; this could be construed as attempted bribery, a much more serious crime. Pay fines by mail or directly into the hands of the clerk of the court. If accused of a more serious offense, say and do nothing before consulting a lawyer. Here the burden is on the state to prove a person's guilt beyond a reasonable doubt, and everyone has the right to remain silent, whether he or she is suspected of a crime or actually arrested. Once arrested, a person can make one telephone call to a party of his or her choice. International visitors should call your embassy or consulate.

Lost & Found Be sure to tell all of your credit card companies the minute you discover your wallet has been lost or stolen, and file a report at the nearest police precinct. Your credit card company or insurer may require a police report number or record of the loss. Most credit card companies have an emergency toll-free number to call if your card is lost or stolen; they may be able to wire you a cash advance immediately or deliver an emergency credit card in a day or two. Visa's U.S. emergency number is © **800/847-2911** or 410/581-9994. American Express cardholders and traveler's check holders should call © **800/221-7282.** MasterCard holders should call © **800/307-7309** or 636/722-7111. For other credit cards, call the toll-free number directory at © **800/555-1212.**

If you need emergency cash over the weekend when all banks and American Express offices are closed, you can have money wired to you via **Western Union** (© **800/325-6000;** www.westernunion.com).

Mail At press time, domestic postage rates were 26¢ for a postcard and 41¢ for a letter. For international mail, a first-class letter of up to 1 ounce costs 90¢ (69¢ to Canada and Mexico); a first-class postcard costs the same as a letter. For more information, go to **www.usps.com**, and click on "Calculate Postage."

If you aren't sure what your address will be in the United States, mail can be sent to you, in your name, c/o General Delivery at the main post office of the city or region where you expect to be. (Call © **800/275-8777** for information on the nearest post office.) The addressee must pick up mail in person and must produce proof of identity (driver's license, passport, and so on). Most post offices will hold your mail for up to 1 month, and are open Monday to Friday from 8am to 6pm, and Saturday from 9am to 3pm.

Always include zip codes when mailing items in the U.S. If you don't know your zip code, visit **www.usps.com/zip4**.

Newspapers & Magazines The *Chicago Tribune* (© **312/222-3232;** www.chicagotribune.com) and the *Chicago Sun-Times* (© **312/321-3000;** www.suntimes.com) are the two major dailies. *Time Out Chicago* (© **312/924-9555;** www.timeoutchicago.com) is a weekly magazine that includes comprehensive roundups of the week's special events and performances. The *Chicago Reader* (© **312/828-0350;** www.chicagoreader.com) is a free weekly that appears each

Thursday, with all the current entertainment and cultural listings. *Chicago Magazine* (www.chicagomag.com) is a monthly that is widely read for its restaurant reviews. *CS* is a free lifestyle monthly that covers nightlife, dining, fashion, shopping, and other cultural pursuits. The *Chicago Defender* covers local and national news of interest to the African-American community. The Spanish-language *La Raza* (www.laraza.com) reports on stories from a Latino point of view. The *Chicago Free Press* (www.chicagofreepress.com) and *Windy City Times* (www.windycitytimes.com) publish both news and feature articles about gay and lesbian issues.

Passports **For Residents of Australia:** You can pick up an application from your local post office or any branch of Passports Australia, but you must schedule an interview at the passport office to present your application materials. Call the **Australian Passport Information Service** at ✆ **131-232,** or visit the government website at **www.passports.gov.au**.

For Residents of Canada: Passport applications are available at travel agencies throughout Canada or from the central **Passport Office,** Department of Foreign Affairs and International Trade, Ottawa, ON K1A 0G3 (✆ **800/567-6868;** www.ppt.gc.ca). *Note:* Canadian children who travel must have their own passport. However, if you hold a valid Canadian passport issued before December 11, 2001, that bears the name of your child, the passport remains valid for you and your child until it expires.

For Residents of Ireland: You can apply for a 10-year passport at the **Passport Office,** Setanta Centre, Molesworth Street, Dublin 2 (✆ **01/671-1633;** www.irl gov.ie/iveagh). Those under age 18 and over 65 must apply for a 3-year passport. You can also apply at 1A South Mall, Cork (✆ **021/272-525**) or at most main post offices.

For Residents of New Zealand: You can pick up a passport application at any New Zealand Passports Office or download it from their website. Contact the **Passports Office** at ✆ **0800/225-050** in New Zealand or 04/474-8100, or log on to **www.passports.govt.nz**.

For Residents of the United Kingdom: To pick up an application for a standard 10-year passport (5-yr. passport for children under 16), visit your nearest passport office, major post office, or travel agency, or contact the **United Kingdom Passport Service** at ✆ **0870/521-0410** or search its website at **www.ukpa. gov.uk**.

Pharmacies **Walgreens,** 757 N. Michigan Ave. (✆ **312/664-4000**), is open 24 hours. Both Walgreens and **CVS,** another major chain, have a number of downtown locations.

Police For emergencies, call ✆ **911.** This is a free call (no coins required). For nonemergencies, call ✆ **311.**

Post Office The main post office is at 433 W. Harrison St. (✆ **312/983-8182**); free parking is available. You'll also find convenient branches in the Sears Tower, the Federal Center Plaza at 211 S. Clark St., the James R. Thompson Center at 100 W. Randolph St., and a couple of blocks off the Magnificent Mile at 227 E. Ontario St.

Safety See "Safety," earlier in this chapter.

Taxes The U.S. has no value-added tax (VAT) or other indirect tax at the national level. Every state, county, and city may levy its own local tax on all purchases, including hotel and restaurant checks and airline tickets. These taxes will not appear on price tags. In Chicago, the local sales tax is 9%. Restaurants in the central part of the city, roughly the 312 area code, are taxed an additional 1%, for a total of 10%. The hotel room tax is a steep 14.9%.

Telephone, Telegraph, Telex & Fax **Telegraph and telex services** are provided primarily by Western Union. You can telegraph money, or have it telegraphed to you, very quickly over the Western Union system, but this service can cost as much as 15% to 20% of the amount sent.

Most hotels have **fax machines** available for guest use (be sure to ask about the charge to use it). Many hotel rooms are even wired for guests' fax machines. A less expensive way to send and receive faxes may be at stores such as **The UPS Store** (formerly Mail Boxes Etc.).

Time The continental United States is divided into **four time zones:** eastern standard time (EST), central standard time (CST), mountain standard time (MST), and Pacific standard time (PST); Chicago is in the central time zone. Alaska and Hawaii have their own zones. For example, when it's 9am in Los Angeles (PST), it's 7am in Honolulu (HST), 10am in Denver (MST), 11am in Chicago (CST), noon in New York City (EST), 5pm in London (GMT), and 2am the next day in Sydney.

Daylight saving time is in effect from 1am on the second Sunday in March to 1am on the first Sunday in November, except in Arizona, Hawaii, the U.S. Virgin Islands, and Puerto Rico. Daylight saving time moves the clock 1 hour ahead of standard time.

Tipping Tips are a very important part of certain workers' income, and gratuities are the standard way of showing appreciation for services provided. (Tipping is certainly not compulsory if the service is poor!) In hotels, tip **bellhops** at least $1 per bag ($2–$3 if you have a lot of luggage), and tip the **chamber staff** $1 to $2 per day (more if you've left a disaster area for him or her to clean up). Tip the **doorman** or **concierge** only if he or she has provided you with some specific service (for example, calling a cab for you or obtaining difficult-to-get theater tickets). Tip the **valet-parking attendant** $1 every time you get your car.

In restaurants, bars, and nightclubs, tip **service staff** 15% to 20% of the check, **bartenders** 10% to 15%, **checkroom attendants** $1 per garment, and **valet-parking attendants** $1 per vehicle.

As for other service personnel, tip **cab drivers** 15% of the fare; **skycaps** at airports at least $1 per bag ($2–$3 if you have a lot of luggage); and **hairdressers** and **barbers** 15% to 20%.

Toilets You won't find public toilets or "restrooms" on the streets in Chicago, but they can be found in hotel lobbies, bars, restaurants, museums, department stores, railway and bus stations, and service stations. Large hotels and fast-food restaurants are often the best bet for clean facilities. The toilets at parks and beaches are okay if you're desperate, but they're usually not too clean.

Transit Info The **CTA** has a useful number to find out which bus or El train will get you to your destination: ℂ **836-7000** (from any area code in the city or suburbs) or TTY 836-4949.

Visas For information about U.S. Visas, go to **http://travel.state.gov** and click on "Visas." Or go to the websites of the following countries:

Australian citizens can obtain up-to-date visa information from the **U.S. Embassy Canberra,** Moonah Place, Yarralumla, ACT 2600 (ℂ **02/6214-5600**), or by checking the U.S. Diplomatic Mission's website at **http://usembassy-australia.state.gov/consular**.

British subjects can obtain up-to-date visa information by calling the **U.S. Embassy Visa Information Line** (ℂ **0891/200-290**) or by visiting the "Visas to the U.S." section of the American Embassy London's website at **www.us embassy.org.uk**.

Irish citizens can obtain up-to-date visa information through the **Embassy of the USA Dublin,** 42 Elgin Rd., Dublin 4, Ireland (ℂ **353/1-668-8777**), or by checking the "Consular Services" section of the website at **http://dublin.us embassy.gov**.

Citizens of **New Zealand** can obtain up-to-date visa information by contacting the **U.S. Embassy New Zealand,** 29 Fitzherbert Terrace, Thorndon, Wellington (ℂ **644/472-2068**), or get the information directly from the website at **http://wellington.usembassy.gov**.

4

Suggested Chicago Itineraries

Downtown Chicago is relatively compact, so it's possible to get a general sense of the city in 1 day (although, of course, I highly recommend spending more than 24 hours here). How you spend your time depends in part on your interests and the weather; you could easily spend 3 days exploring Chicago's museums, and if you're here in the winter, that's probably a lot more appealing than a daylong walking tour. On a sunny summer day, though, you might be tempted to spend an afternoon wandering along the lakefront without any particular destination. Ideally, you should experience both indoors *and* outdoors, so the following itineraries contain a mix of cultural institutions and scenic walks.

1 The Best of Chicago in 1 Day

The day begins with a walking tour of the Loop, which I think is the best way to get your bearings (and understand why Chicago's architecture is world-famous). Then you can squeeze in a quick visit to one of the city's preeminent museums before strolling along Michigan Avenue, Chicago's most famous thoroughfare, which takes you to the ritzy Gold Coast neighborhood. If possible, I'd recommend following this itinerary on a weekday, when downtown offices are open and the sidewalks buzz with energy. This route works fine on weekends as well, but you won't experience quite the same big-city rush. *Start: Green, Orange, Brown, or Purple line to Adams, or Red Line to Jackson.*

❶ Chicago ArchiCenter

Start your day with the Chicago Architecture Foundation's "Historic Skyscrapers" tour, which begins daily at 10am year-round. The 2-hour walking tour takes you to the oldest high-rises in the Loop, and the docents explain why these early office buildings were revolutionary. Sure, you'll get a basic architecture education, but this is also a great way to get a sense of the Loop's layout and dramatic vistas. (Another popular tour, "Modern Skyscrapers," starts daily at 1pm). See p. 178.

❷ The Art Institute ✸✸✸

Across the street from the Chicago Architecture Foundation stands one of the city's most prestigious cultural institutions; if you have time for only one museum while you're here, this is the one to visit. Head right for the must-see exhibits: the Impressionist collection and the galleries of European and American contemporary art (home to iconic pictures such as Edward Hopper's *Nighthawks*). See p. 171.

❸ Millennium Park ✸✸✸

Just north of the Art Institute is one of the city's most popular gathering spots. Check out the massive video-screen faces on the Crown Fountain, then take a walk around (and under) Anish Kapoor's bean-shaped sculpture *Cloud Gate*. The Pritzker Music Pavilion, designed by Frank Gehry, features the architect's signature ribbons

Suggested Chicago Itineraries

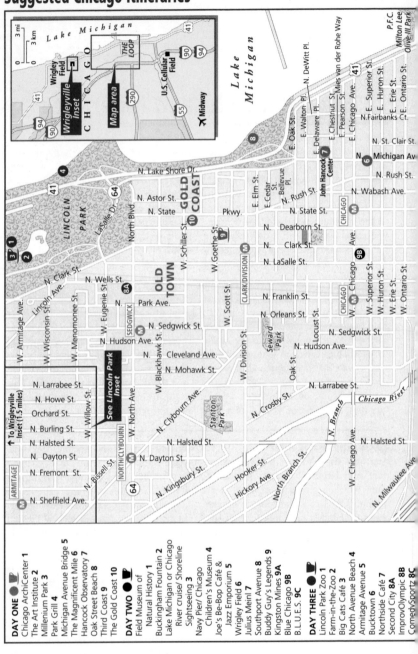

DAY ONE ●🚶
Chicago ArchiCenter **1**
The Art Institute **2**
Millenium Park **3**
Park Grill **4**
Michigan Avenue Bridge **5**
The Magnificent Mile **6**
Hancock Observatory **7**
Oak Street Beach **8**
Third Coast **9**
The Gold Coast **10**

DAY TWO ●🚶🚗
Field Museum of
  Natural History **1**
Buckingham Fountain **2**
Lake Michigan or Chicago
  River cruise/ Shoreline
  Sightseeing **3**
Navy Pier/ Chicago
  Children's Museum **4**
Joe's Be-Bop Café &
  Jazz Emporium **5**
Wrigley Field **6**
Julius Meinl **7**
Southport Avenue **8**
Buddy Guy's Legends **9**
Kingston Mines **9A**
Blue Chicago **9B**
B.L.U.E.S. **9C**

DAY THREE ●🚶🚗
Lincoln Park Zoo **1**
Farm-in-the-Zoo **2**
Big Cats Café **3**
North Avenue Beach **4**
Armitage Avenue **5**
Bucktown **6**
Northside Café **7**
Second City **8A**
ImprovOlympic **8B**
ComedySportz **8C**

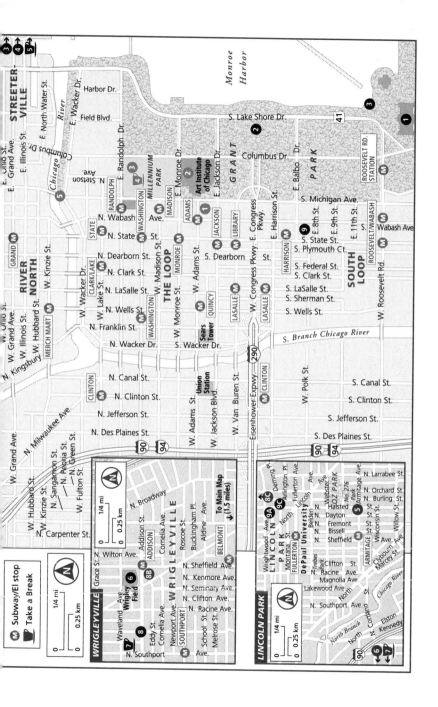

of silver steel; Gehry also designed the adjoining serpentine bridge. See p. 176.

4️⃣ PARK GRILL 😊😊
In the winter, this restaurant overlooks Millennium Park's ice-skating rink; come summer, the rink transforms into an outdoor cafe, perfect for sipping a drink and admiring the skyline. 11 N. Michigan Ave. ℭ **312/521-PARK.** See p. 118.

5️⃣ Michigan Avenue Bridge

Walk north along Michigan Avenue and you'll come to this bridge, which spans the Chicago River. Stop here for a great photo op—on a nice day, you'll be joined by plenty of other visitors doing the exact same thing.

6️⃣ The Magnificent Mile

The 14-block stretch of Michigan Avenue from the river to Oak Street, known as the "Magnificent Mile," is shopping central, a dense concentration of high-rise malls, designer boutiques, and practically every mass-market clothing brand. Even if you're not a shopper, it's worth a stroll; busy at almost all hours, it's great for people-watching. Some Chicagoans dismiss the Mag Mile as too touristy, but I think walking here makes you feel like you're part of a vibrant metropolis. See p. 186.

7️⃣ Hancock Observatory 😊😊

This may only be Chicago's third-tallest building, but the view from the top is spectacular: In the right weather conditions, you can see all the way to three

other states (Wisconsin, Indiana, and Michigan). The "talking telescopes" help you get your bearings. See p. 186.

8️⃣ Oak Street Beach

Where Michigan Avenue merges into Lake Shore Drive at Oak Street, head down the underpass to get to Oak Street Beach, a curved stretch of sand that's a summertime hot spot. Bikers, skaters, and joggers fill the paths, while kids play in the sand. Think of it as Chicago's own miniresort getaway—just don't plan on swimming in the frigid water. See p. 218.

9️⃣ THIRD COAST 😊
If you're tired of generic chain coffeehouses (of which Chicago has plenty), stop by this somewhat shabby, lower-level cafe that welcomes both well-heeled locals and the occasional starving artist. In addition to the usual lattes and muffins, there's a full lunch and dinner menu, and wine and beer are available. 1260 N. Dearborn St. ℭ **312/649-0730.** See p. 290.

🔟 The Gold Coast

To get an idea of how Chicago's wealthiest live, take a stroll through this neighborhood of historic town homes (including the original Playboy Mansion, at 1340 N. State Pkwy.). The tranquil, tree-lined streets are only a few blocks away from Michigan Avenue, but they feel like a different city. Finish up the night with dinner at one of the many restaurants in River North, or catch a show and discover Chicago's vibrant theater scene. See p. 257.

---

2 The Best of Chicago in 2 Days

After Day 1, you should be oriented to the city. Now it's time to explore at least part of the city's Museum Campus, home to three major museums. Although I recommend the Field Museum for this itinerary, you could certainly substitute the nearby Shedd Aquarium (p. 184) or Adler Planetarium (p. 182). The first part of this day keeps you firmly in tourist territory, but you'll journey off the beaten track later in the day when you wander through Wrigleyville and get a sense of how real Chicagoans live. ***Start:*** *Bus no. 6, 10, 12, 130, or 146 to Roosevelt Road and Lake Shore Drive.*

❶ Field Museum of Natural History ⋆⋆⋆

You'll feel as though you've entered a truly grand place when you walk into the museum's massive Stanley Field Hall. Indeed, the Field Museum is one of those classic, something-for-everyone institutions, with everything from animal dioramas to Sue, the largest Tyrannosaurus rex fossil ever discovered. The *Inside Ancient Egypt* exhibit is more than just mummies: It's a complete re-creation of ancient daily life, including a marketplace, royal barge, and religious shrines (with lots of hands-on activities for kids). The second-floor African and South Pacific exhibits are also worth a stop, with beautifully designed interactive displays that feel like movie sets. See p. 183.

❷ Buckingham Fountain ⋆

This grand, stone fountain is one of the city's iconic structures. (If you're a sitcom fan, you might recognize it from the opening credits of *Married with Children*.) Try to get here on the hour, when jets of water spurt dramatically into the sky. The fountain blazes with colored lights at night, so if you're staying downtown, it's also worth a stop after dark. (*Note:* The fountain is closed Nov–Mar.) See p. 177.

❸ Lake Michigan or Chicago River cruise

Departing from a dock at the nearby Shedd Aquarium, **Shoreline Sightseeing** ⋆ runs water taxis that cruise north to Navy Pier (daily from Memorial Day to Labor Day). From the pier, you can also catch boats that cruise along the Chicago River all the way to the Sears Tower. See p. 214.

❹ Navy Pier ⋆

Yes, it's touristy and crowded, but Navy Pier is also full of energy—and if you stroll all the way to the end, you'll be rewarded with great views of downtown. If you're traveling with kids, stopping at

Navy Pier is pretty much mandatory; it has a carousel and other carnival-type rides, lots of boats to admire, and the **Chicago Children's Museum.** See p. 187.

---

❺ JOE'S BE-BOP CAFE & JAZZ EMPORIUM
Owned by the same family that runs Jazz Showcase, one of the best jazz clubs in town, this Navy Pier cafe offers a fun atmosphere (with plenty of outdoor seating), Southern barbecue, and a great soundtrack. 600 E. Grand Ave. ✆ 312/595-5299. See p. 188.

From Navy Pier, take the free Navy Pier shuttle to the Grand El station (Red Line), and ride north to the Addison stop.

❻ Wrigley Field ⋆⋆

If you're a baseball fan, Wrigley is hallowed ground: the second-oldest stadium in the major leagues, home to the perennially jinxed **Chicago Cubs.** The surrounding blocks are a good place to stock up on Cubs souvenirs. If you want to catch a game, tickets can be tough to come by (the entire season tends to be sold out by Opening Day). Show up an hour or so before a game, and you can sometimes find a season-ticket holder trying to sell unused seats (and ticket brokers always have seats available—for a price). See p. 221.

---

❼ JULIUS MEINL ⋆
Run by an Austrian coffee company, this cafe is a mix of Old World and New. Large picture windows make it feel bright and inviting, while the European pastries and coffee (served elegantly on silver trays) are a welcome change from standard chain coffeehouses. 3601 N. Southport Ave. ✆ 773/868-1857. See p. 290.

---

❽ Southport Avenue

This residential area is well into the gentrified stage (witness the number of trendy clothing boutiques), but it's still very much a neighborhood. Stroll along Southport between Belmont Avenue and Grace Street, and you'll see young moms pushing designer strollers, singles walking their dogs, and hardly any other tourists. If you're here in the early evening, you'll find plenty of low-key, affordable restaurants for dinner. See p. 232.

❾ Buddy Guy's Legends ⭐⭐

Chicago is the birthplace of "electric blues," that rocking blend of soulful singing and wailing electric guitars. To experience the city's most famous form of music, my top pick is Buddy Guy's Legends in the South Loop, which has the honky-tonk feel of a Southern roadhouse. The owner, blues guitarist and Rock and Roll Hall of Famer Buddy Guy, makes regular appearances; even if he's not on the bill, the talent level is always top-notch. (If you're staying on the North Side of the city and would rather stick close to home, try **Kingston Mines, Blue Chicago,** or **B.L.U.E.S.**) See p. 270.

3 The Best of Chicago in 3 Days

For this itinerary, it's time to escape downtown completely and spend the day on the North Side of the city. You'll start out in Lincoln Park, which is both an actual park and the name of a popular residential neighborhood, where singles and young families can be seen strolling or jogging along the lakefront paths during nice weather. You'll also visit two major cultural institutions, both suitable for kids, and then head into a residential neighborhood for some shopping. *Start: Bus no. 151 or 156 to North Cannon Drive and Fullerton Parkway.*

❶ Lincoln Park Zoo ⭐⭐⭐

A beloved local institution, this zoo won't dazzle you a la San Diego, but it does a good job of covering all the bases, with a mix of indoor habitats and naturalistic outdoor environments (plus, did I mention it's *free?*). Don't miss the *Regenstein African Journey* exhibit (which re-creates both a tropical jungle and a dusty African savanna), and the internationally renowned Great Ape House. If you have kids, stop at the **Children's Zoo,** where a unique climbing structure gives little ones 2 and older a chance to release some energy. See p. 212.

❷ Farm-in-the-Zoo ⭐

Just south of the zoo, this re-creation of a working farm gets children in touch (literally) with animals. The highlight for many little ones is the giant John Deere tractor; you'll usually find a line of kids waiting for their turn to sit behind the massive steering wheel. See p. 212.

> **▣ BIG CATS CAFÉ**
> This cafe, on the roof of the zoo's gift shop, has outdoor seating and panoramic views over the zoo. 2200 N. Cannon Dr. ✆ 312/742-2000.

❹ North Avenue Beach

Come summer, this is Lincoln Park's prime playground—a place to jog, play volleyball, build sandcastles, or simply pose. Even in August, the water is usually icy, but if you want to at least dip your feet in Lake Michigan, this wide stretch of sand is the place to do it. See p. 218.

Take a taxi or walk about a mile to the corner of Halsted Street and Armitage Avenue.

❺ Armitage Avenue

To call this the city's chicest shopping strip isn't meant as a put-down to Michigan Avenue; while the Mag Mile goes for big and showy, the boutiques along

Armitage tend to be smaller and more personal (that is, fewer chains). You'll find an especially appealing selection of home decor stores and gift shops with eclectic selections of well-designed merchandise. See p. 231.

Take a taxi to the corner of North Avenue and Damen Avenue, then walk north along Damen.

⑥ Bucktown

If you're not shopped out yet, finish up the day with a walk through Bucktown, home to the city's highest concentration of edgy clothing boutiques. It feels grittier than Armitage Avenue, and that's part of the appeal for the cool kids who live here. See p. 233.

☕ NORTHSIDE CAFÉ

Bucktown's unofficial neighborhood hangout, this low-key cafe is a sandwich spot by day and a bustling bar by night. When the weather's nice, grab a seat on the outdoor patio and people-watch with everyone else. 1635 N. Damen Ave. ✆ 773/384-3555. See p. 168.

⑧ Improv Comedy

Although it's best known for **Second City,** Chicago is home to a number of excellent improv comedy troupes. You can catch rising stars before they land their own sitcom deals. Second City is the big man on campus, while **iO** is the slightly scrappier and more creative bunch. If you're here with older kids or teens, catch the family-friendly **ComedySportz.** See p. 264.

5

Getting to Know the Windy City

The orderly configuration of Chicago's streets and the excellent public transportation system make the city quite easy to get around—once you identify and locate a few basic landmarks.

This chapter provides an overview of the city's layout, as well as some suggestions for how to maneuver within it. You'll also get an introduction to Chicago's many distinctive neighborhoods.

1 Orientation

VISITOR INFORMATION

The **Chicago Office of Tourism** runs a toll-free visitor hot line (© 877/CHICAGO or TTY 866/710-0294; www.choosechicago.com) and operates two visitor information centers staffed with people who can answer questions. Stop here to stock up on brochures of area attractions, including materials on everything from museums and city landmarks to lakefront biking maps and even fishing spots. The main visitor center, located in the Loop and convenient to many places that you'll likely be visiting, is on the first floor of the **Chicago Cultural Center,** 77 E. Randolph St. (at Michigan Ave.). The center has a phone that you can use to make hotel reservations, and several couches and a cafe where you can study maps and plan your itinerary. The center is open Monday through Friday from 8am to 6pm, Saturday from 9am to 6pm, and Sunday from 10am to 6pm; it's closed on holidays.

A second, smaller center, the **Chicago Water Works Visitor Center,** is in the old pumping station at Michigan and Chicago avenues in the heart of the city's shopping district. The entrance is on the Pearson Street side of the building, across from the Water Tower Place mall. It's open daily from 7:30am to 7pm. This location has the added draw of housing a location of **Hot Tix,** which offers both half-price day-of-performance and full-price tickets to many theater productions around the city, as well as a gift shop. Part of the building has been converted into a theater, including a small cabaret space for tourist-oriented shows and a larger playhouse for the acclaimed Lookingglass Theatre Company.

The **Illinois Bureau of Tourism** (© 800/2CONNECT or TTY 800/406-6418; www.enjoyillinois.com) can provide general and specific information 24 hours a day. Many of the bureau's brochures can be ordered online or picked up at the Water Works Visitor Center (see above).

INFORMATION BY TELEPHONE   The **Mayor's Office of Special Events** operates a recorded hot line and website (© 312/744-3370 or TTY 312/744-2964; www.cityofchicago.org/specialevents) listing current special events, festivals, and parades occurring throughout the city.

⌐ *Fun Fact* __A River Runs Through It__

The Chicago River remains one of the most visible of the city's physical features. It's spanned by more movable bridges within the city limits (52 at last count) than any other city in the world. An almost-mystical moment occurs downtown when all the bridges spanning the main and south branches—connecting the Loop to both the Near West Side and the Near North Side—are raised, allowing for the passage of some ship, barge, or contingent of high-masted sailboats. The Chicago River has long outlived the critical commercial function that it once performed. Most of the remaining millworks that occupy its banks no longer depend on the river alone for the transport of their materials, raw and finished. The river's main function today is to serve as a fluvial conduit for sewage, which, owing to an engineering feat that reversed its flow inland in 1900, no longer pollutes the waters of Lake Michigan. Recently, Chicagoans have begun to discover another role for the river, including water cruises, park areas, cafes, public art installations, and a riverside bike path that connects to the lakefront route near Wacker Drive. Actually, today's developers aren't the first to wonder why the river couldn't be Chicago's Seine. A look at the early-20th-century Beaux Arts balustrades lining the river along Wacker Drive, complete with comfortably spaced benches and Parisian-style bridge houses, shows that Chicago architect and urban planner Daniel Burnham knew full well what a treasure the city had.

PUBLICATIONS   Chicago's major daily newspapers are the *Tribune* and the *Sun-Times*. Both have cultural listings, including movies, theaters, and live music, not to mention reviews of the latest restaurants that have opened since this guidebook went to press. The Friday edition of both papers contains a special pullout section with more detailed, up-to-date information on special events happening over the weekend. The *Tribune* also publishes *Red Eye,* a weekday tabloid aimed at younger readers with a mix of "lite" news items, entertainment news, and quirky features.

Chicago magazine is an upscale monthly with good restaurant listings. Even better for short-term visitors is the weekly magazine *Time Out Chicago,* which lists just about everything going on around town during the week, from art openings to theater performances. For a look at the city's beautiful people, pick up *CS* (formerly *Chicago Social*), a glossy, monthly magazine filled with photos from charity galas and ads for high-priced local boutiques.

Two free weeklies with good event listings are widely available in newspaper boxes downtown. The *Chicago Reader* is an invaluable source of entertainment reviews, classifieds, and well-written articles on contemporary issues of interest in Chicago. *New City* appeals to a slightly younger audience than the earnest *Reader,* with an editorial tone that tends toward the edgy and irreverent.

Most Chicago hotels stock their rooms or lobbies with at least one informational magazine, such as *Where Chicago,* that lists some of the city's entertainment, shopping, and dining locales.

CITY LAYOUT

The **Chicago River** forms a Y that divides the city into its three geographic zones: North Side, South Side, and West Side (Lake Michigan is where the East Side would be). The downtown financial district is called **the Loop.** The city's key shopping street is **North Michigan Avenue,** also known as the **Magnificent Mile.** In addition to department stores and vertical malls, this stretch of property north of the river houses many of the city's most elegant hotels. North and south of this downtown zone, Chicago stretches along 29 miles of Lake Michigan shoreline that is, by and large, free of commercial development, reserved for public use as green space and parkland from one end of town to the other.

Today, Chicago proper has about three million inhabitants living in an area about two-thirds the size of New York City; another five million make the suburbs their home. The towns north of Chicago now stretch in an unbroken mass nearly to the Wisconsin border; the city's western suburbs extend 30 miles to Naperville, one of the fastest-growing towns in the nation over the past 2 decades. (Lake Michigan is to the city's east, while, a few miles to the south, you've got economically depressed former steel towns such as Gary, IN) The real signature of Chicago, however, is found between the suburbs and the Loop, where a colorful patchwork quilt of residential neighborhoods gives the city a character all its own.

FINDING AN ADDRESS   Chicago is laid out in a **grid system,** with the streets neatly lined up as if on a giant piece of graph paper. Because the city itself isn't rectangular (it's rather elongated), the shape is a bit irregular, but the perpendicular pattern remains. Easing movement through the city are a half-dozen or so major diagonal thoroughfares.

Point zero is located at the downtown intersection of State and Madison streets. **State Street** divides east and west addresses, and **Madison Street** divides north and south addresses. From here, Chicago's highly predictable addressing system begins. Making use of this grid, it's relatively easy to plot the distance in miles between any two points in the city.

Virtually all of Chicago's principal north-south and east-west arteries are spaced by increments of 400 in the addressing system—regardless of the number of smaller streets nestled between them—and each addition or subtraction of 400 numbers to an address is equivalent to a half-mile. Thus, starting at point zero on Madison Street and traveling north along State Street for 1 mile, you will come to 800 N. State St., which intersects Chicago Avenue. Continue uptown for another half-mile and you arrive at the 1200 block of North State Street at Division Street. And so it goes, right to the city line, with suburban Evanston located at the 7600 block north, 9½ miles from point zero.

The same rule applies when you're traveling south, or east to west. Thus, heading west from State Street along Madison Street, Halsted Street—at 800 W. Madison St.—is a mile's distance, while Racine Avenue, at the 1200 block of West Madison Street, is 1½ miles from the center. Madison Street then continues westward to Chicago's boundary with the nearby suburb of Oak Park along Austin Avenue, which, at 6000 W. Madison, is approximately 7½ miles from point zero.

The key to understanding the grid is that the side of any square formed by the principal avenues (noted in dark or red ink on most maps) represents a distance of half a mile in any direction. Understanding how Chicago's grid system works is of particular importance to those visitors who want to do a lot of walking in the city's many

Chicago Neighborhoods

To:
Baha'i Temple
Evanston
Northwestern University
Skokie
Wilmette
Winnetka

0   1 mi
0   1 km

LINCOLNWOOD

Touhy Ave.

ROGERS PARK

Devon Ave.

Loyola University/
Mundelein College

Peterson   Ave.

Northeastern
Illinois University

Foster Ave.

ANDERSONVILLE

Lawrence Ave.

LINCOLN SQUARE

UPTOWN

NORTH SIDE

To
O'Hare
Airport

Irving   Park   Rd.

IRVING PARK

John F. Kennedy Expwy.

WRIGLEYVILLE

Addison St.

Wrigley Field

Belmont   Ave.

LAKEVIEW

Milwaukee   Ave.

North Branch

LINCOLN PARK

DePaul University

Lincoln Park

Fullerton   Ave.

LOGAN SQUARE

Chicago River

Humboldt Park

North   Ave.

BUCKTOWN/
WICKER PARK

OLD TOWN

GOLD COAST

Oak Street Beach

Grand Ave.

NEAR NORTH

John Hancock Center

Chicago   Ave.

WEST SIDE

Old Water Tower

RIVER NORTH

STREETERVILLE

Navy Pier

Garfield Park

United Center

Washington   St.

MAGNIFICENT MILE

To Oak Park

WEST LOOP

GREEK TOWN

THE LOOP

Millennium Park

Art Institute of Chicago

Eisenhower Expwy.

Sears Tower

PRINTERS ROW

Grant Park

Roosevelt Rd.

LITTLE ITALY

SOUTH LOOP

Museum Campus

Soldier Field

Ogden Ave.

Douglas Park

Cermak Rd.

PILSEN

CHINA-TOWN

South Branch Chicago River

McCormick Place
Convention Center

31st St.

31st St.

31st Street Beach

Sanitary and Ship Canal

35th St.

BRIDGEPORT

U.S. Cellular Field

Burnham Park

Stevenson   Expwy.

CANARYVILLE

Pershing Rd.

Oakwood Blvd.

Dr. Martin Luther King Jr. Dr.

SOUTH SIDE

47th St.

Midway Airport

55th St.

Archer   Ave.

Kedzie Ave.

Western   Ave.

Damen   Ave.

Ashland   Ave.

Halsted St.

Garfield   Blvd.

51st St.

55th St.

Washington Park

University of Chicago

HYDE PARK

Museum of Science & Industry

Lake   Michigan

Lake Shore Dr.

Broadway

Ashland   Ave.

Lincoln   Ave.

Halsted   St.

Clark St.

LaSalle St.

State   St.

Michigan   Ave.

Cicero   Ave.

Pulaski   Rd.

Grand   Ave.

CICERO

(Value) Insider Tours—Free!

Want a personalized view of the city—aside from your trusted Frommer's guidebook? A program called **Chicago Greeter** matches tourists with local Chicagoans who serve as volunteer guides. Visitors can request a specific neighborhood or theme (everything from Polish heritage sites to Chicago movie locations), and a greeter gives them a free 2- to 4-hour tour. (Greeters won't escort groups of more than six people.) Specific requests should be made at least a week in advance, but "InstaGreeters" are also available on a first-come, first-served basis at the Chicago Cultural Center, 77 E. Randolph St., from Friday through Sunday. For details, call (C) **312/744-8000**, or visit **www.chicago greeter.com**.

neighborhoods and who want to plot in advance the distances involved in trekking from one locale to another.

The other convenient aspect of the grid is that every major road uses the same numerical system. In other words, the cross street (Division St.) at 1200 N. Lake Shore Dr. is the same as at 1200 N. Clark St. and 1200 N. LaSalle St.

STREET MAPS   Maps are available at the city's visitor information centers at the **Chicago Cultural Center** and the **Chicago Water Works Visitor Center** (see "Visitor Information," p. 66). You can also print out maps from the Chicago Convention and Tourism Bureau website, **www.choosechicago.com**.

NEIGHBORHOODS IN BRIEF

The Loop & Vicinity

Downtown In the case of Chicago, downtown means the Loop. The Loop refers literally to a core of high-rise buildings contained within a rectangular loop of elevated train tracks. Greater downtown Chicago overflows these confines and is bounded by the Chicago River to the north and west, by Michigan Avenue to the east, and by Roosevelt Avenue to the south.

The North Side

Near North/Magnificent Mile North Michigan Avenue from the bridge spanning the Chicago River to its northern tip at Oak Street is known as the Magnificent Mile. Many of the city's best hotels and shops are to be found on and around elegant North Michigan Avenue. The area stretching east of Michigan Avenue to the lake is sometimes referred to as "Streeterville"—the

legacy of George Wellington "Cap" Streeter. Streeter was an eccentric, bankrupt showman who staked out 200 acres of self-created landfill here about a century ago after his steamship ran aground, and then declared himself "governor" of the "District of Lake Michigan." True story.

River North Just to the west of the Mag Mile is an old warehouse district called River North. These formerly industrial buildings have been transformed into one of the city's most vital commercial districts, with many of the city's hottest restaurants, nightspots, and art galleries. Large-scale residential loft-conversion developments have also sprouted on its western and southwestern fringes.

The Gold Coast Some of Chicago's most desirable real estate and historic architecture are found along Lake

Shore Drive, between Oak Street and North Avenue and along the adjacent side streets. Despite trendy little pockets of real estate popping up elsewhere, the moneyed class still prefers to live by the lake. On the neighborhood's southwestern edge, around Division and Rush streets, a string of raucous bars and late-night eateries contrasts sharply with the rest of the area's sedate mood.

Old Town West of LaSalle Street, principally on North Wells Street between Division Street and North Avenue, is the residential district of Old Town, which boasts some of the city's best-preserved historic homes. This area was a hippie haven in the 1960s and '70s; now the neighborhood is one of the most expensive residential areas in the city. A major transformation is taking place just southwest of Old Town, as Cabrini Green, a massive and once-notorious housing project, is gradually demolished to make way for mixed-income housing. Old Town's biggest claim to fame, the legendary Second City comedy club, has served up the lighter side of life to Chicagoans for more than 30 years.

Lincoln Park Chicago's most popular residential neighborhood for young singles and urban-minded families is Lincoln Park. Stretching from North Avenue to Diversey Parkway, it's bordered on the east by the huge park of the same name, which is home to two major museums and one of the nation's oldest zoos (established in 1868). The trapezoid formed by Clark Street, Armitage Avenue, Halsted Street, and Diversey Parkway also contains many of Chicago's most happening bars, restaurants, retail stores, music clubs, and off-Loop theaters—including the nationally acclaimed Steppenwolf Theatre Company.

Lakeview & Wrigleyville Midway up the city's North Side is a one-time blue-collar, now mainstream middle-class quarter called Lakeview. It has become the neighborhood of choice for many gays and lesbians, recent college graduates, and residents priced out of Lincoln Park. The main thoroughfare is Belmont Avenue, between Broadway and Sheffield Avenue. Wrigleyville is the name given to the neighborhood in the vicinity of Wrigley Field—home of the Chicago Cubs—at Sheffield Avenue and Addison Street. Not surprisingly, the ball field is surrounded by sports bars and memorabilia shops.

Uptown & Andersonville Uptown, which runs along the lakefront as far north as Foster Avenue, has traditionally attracted waves of immigrants. While crime was a major problem for decades, the area has stabilized, with formerly decrepit buildings being converted into—you guessed it—condominiums. Vietnamese and Chinese immigrants have transformed Argyle Street between Broadway and Sheridan Road into a teeming market for fresh meat, fish, and all kinds of exotic vegetables. Slightly to the north and west is the old Scandinavian neighborhood of Andersonville, whose main drag is Clark Street, between Foster and Bryn Mawr avenues. The area has an eclectic mix of Middle Eastern restaurants, a distinct cluster of women-owned businesses, and a burgeoning colony of gays and lesbians.

Lincoln Square West of Andersonville and slightly to the south, where Lincoln, Western, and Lawrence avenues intersect, is Lincoln Square, the only identifiable remains of Chicago's once-vast German-American community. The surrounding leafy residential streets have attracted many families, who flock to the Old Town School of Folk Music's theater and education center, a beautiful restoration of a former library building.

Rogers Park Rogers Park, which begins at Devon Avenue, is located on the northern fringes of the city bordering suburban Evanston. Its western half has been a Jewish neighborhood for decades. The eastern half, dominated by Loyola University's lakefront campus, has become the most cosmopolitan enclave in the entire city: African Americans, Asians, East Indians, German Americans, and Russian Jews live side by side with the ethnically mixed student population drawn to the Catholic university. Much of Rogers Park has a neohippie ambience, but the western stretch of Devon Avenue is a Midwestern slice of Calcutta, colonized by Indians who've transformed the street into a veritable restaurant row serving tandoori chicken and curry-flavored dishes.

The West Side

West Loop Also known as the Near West Side, the neighborhood just across the Chicago River from the Loop is the city's newest gentrification target, as old warehouses and once-vacant lots are transformed into trendy condos. The stretch of Randolph Street just west of Highway 90/94 and the surrounding blocks are known as "Restaurant Row" for the many dining spots that cluster there. Chicago's old Greektown, still the Greek culinary center of the city, runs along Halsted Street between Adams and Monroe streets. Much of the old Italian neighborhood in this vicinity was the victim of urban renewal, but remnants still survive on Taylor Street; the same is true for a few old delis and shops on Maxwell Street, dating from the turn of the 20th century when a large Jewish community lived in the area.

Bucktown/Wicker Park Centered near the confluence of North, Damen,

and Milwaukee avenues, where the Art Deco Northwest Tower is the tallest thing for miles, this resurgent area has hosted waves of German, Polish, and, most recently, Spanish-speaking immigrants (not to mention writer Nelson Algren). In recent years, it has morphed into a bastion of hot new restaurants, alternative culture, and loft-dwelling yuppies surfing the gentrification wave that's washing over this still-somewhat-gritty neighborhood. Although the terms Bucktown and Wicker Park are often used interchangeably, Bucktown is technically the neighborhood north of North Avenue, while Wicker Park is to the south.

The South Side

South Loop The generically rechristened South Loop area was Chicago's original "Gold Coast" in the late 19th century, with Prairie Avenue (now a historic district) as its most exclusive address. But in the wake of the 1893 World's Columbian Exposition in Hyde Park, and continuing through the Prohibition era of the 1920s, the area was infamous for its Levee vice district, home to gambling and prostitution, some of the most corrupt politicians in Chicago history, and Al Capone's headquarters at the old Lexington Hotel. However, in recent years, its prospects have turned around. The South Loop—stretching from Harrison Street's historic Printers Row south to Cermak Road (where Chinatown begins), and from Lake Shore Drive west to the south branch of the Chicago River—is now one of the fastest-growing residential neighborhoods in the city.

Pilsen Originally home to the nation's largest settlement of Bohemian-Americans, Pilsen (which derives its name from a city in Bohemia, the Czech Republic) was for decades the principal entry point in Chicago for immigrants of every ethnic background. Centered at Halsted and 18th streets just southwest of the Loop, Pilsen now contains the second-largest Mexican-American community in the U.S. This vibrant and colorful neighborhood, which was happily invaded by the outdoor mural movement launched years earlier in Mexico, boasts a profusion of authentic *taquerias* and bakeries. The neighborhood's annual Day of the Dead celebration, which begins in September, is an elaborate festival that runs for 8 weeks. The artistic spirit that permeates the community isn't confined to Latin American art. In recent years, artists of every stripe, drawn partly by the availability of loft space in Pilsen, have nurtured a small but thriving artists' colony here.

Hyde Park Hyde Park is like an independent village within the confines of Chicago, right off Lake Michigan and roughly a 30-minute train ride from the Loop. Fifty-seventh Street is the main drag, and the University of Chicago—with all its attendant shops and restaurants—is the neighborhood's principal tenant. The most successful racially integrated community in the city, Hyde Park is an oasis of furious intellectual activity and liberalism that, ironically, is hemmed in on all sides by neighborhoods suffering some of the highest crime rates in Chicago. Its main attraction is the world-famous Museum of Science and Industry.

2 Getting Around

The best way to savor Chicago is by walking its streets. Walking isn't always practical, however, particularly when moving between distant neighborhoods and on harsh winter days. In those situations, Chicago's public train and bus systems can get you almost anywhere you want to go.

BY PUBLIC TRANSPORTATION

The **Chicago Transit Authority (CTA)** operates an extensive system of trains and buses throughout the city of Chicago. The sturdy system carries about 1.5 million passengers a day. Subways and elevated trains (known as the El) are generally safe and reliable, although it's advisable to avoid long rides through unfamiliar neighborhoods late at night.

Fares for the bus, subway, and El are $2, with an additional 25¢ for a transfer that allows CTA riders to make two transfers on the bus or El within 2 hours of receipt. Children 6 and under ride free, and those between the ages of 7 and 11 pay $1.

Tips **Free Ride**

During the summer, the city of Chicago operates free trolleys daily between Michigan Avenue and the Museum Campus (site of the Adler Planetarium, the Field Museum of Natural History, and the Shedd Aquarium); the trolleys run only on weekends in the fall and spring. Free trolleys also run year-round between Navy Pier and the Grand/State El station on the Red Line. While the trolleys are supposed to make stops every 30 minutes, waits can be longer during peak tourist season—and the trolleys aren't air-conditioned. If you get tired of waiting, remember that CTA public buses travel the same routes for only $2 per person.

Seniors can also receive the reduced fare if they have the appropriate reduced-fare permit (call © **312/836-7000** for details on how to obtain one, although this is probably not a realistic option for a short-term visitor).

The CTA uses credit card–size fare cards that automatically deduct the exact fare each time you take a ride. The reusable cards can be purchased with a preset value already stored, or riders can obtain cards at vending machines located at all CTA train stations and charge them with whatever amount they choose (a minimum of $2 and up to $100). If within 2 hours of your first ride you transfer to a bus or the El, the turnstiles at the El stations and the fare boxes on buses will automatically deduct from your card just the cost of a transfer (25¢). If you make a second transfer within 2 hours, it's free. The same card can be recharged continuously.

Fare cards can be used on buses, but you can't buy a card on the bus. If you get on the bus without a fare card, you'll have to pay $2 cash (either in coins or in dollar bills); the bus drivers cannot make change, so make sure that you've got the right amount before hopping on board.

CTA INFORMATION The CTA operates a useful telephone information service (© **836-7000** or TTY 836-4949 from any area code in the city and suburbs) that functions daily from 5am to 1am. When you want to know how to get from where you are to where you want to go, call the CTA. Make sure that you specify any conditions you might require—the fastest route, for example, or the simplest (the route with the fewest transfers or the least amount of walking), and so forth. You can also check out the CTA's website at **www.transitchicago.com**. Excellent CTA comprehensive maps, which include both El and bus routes, are usually available at subway or El stations, or by calling the CTA. The CTA has also added a toll-free customer service hot line (© **888/YOUR-CTA** or TTY 888/CTA-TTY1; Mon–Fri 7am–8pm, with voice mail operating after hours) to field questions and feedback. Ticket agents are available at some of the busiest El stations to offer customer assistance.

BY THE EL & THE SUBWAY The rapid-transit system operates five major lines, which the CTA identifies by color: The **Red Line** runs north-south; the **Green Line** runs west-south; the **Blue Line** runs through Wicker Park/Bucktown west-northwest to O'Hare Airport; the **Brown Line** runs in a northern zigzag route; and the **Orange Line** runs southwest, serving Midway airport. The **Purple Line,** which runs on the same Loop elevated tracks as the Orange and Green lines, serves north-suburban Evanston and runs only during rush hour.

Tips **Ticket to Ride**

Visitors may consider buying a **Visitor Pass,** which works like a fare card and allows individual users unlimited rides on the El and CTA buses over a 24-hour period. The cards cost $5 and are sold at airports, hotels, museums, Hot Tix outlets, transportation hubs, and Chicago Office of Tourism visitor information centers (you can also buy them in advance online at www.transitchicago.com or by calling © 888/YOUR-CTA). You can also buy 2-, 3-, and 5-day passes. While the passes save you the trouble of feeding the fare machines yourself, they're economical only if you plan to make at least three distinct trips at least 2 or more hours apart (remember that you get two additional transfers within 2 hrs. for an additional 25¢ on a regular fare).

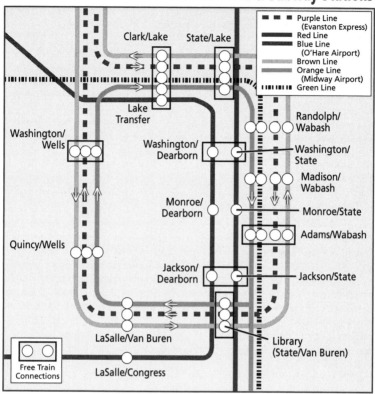

I highly recommend taking at least one El ride while you're here—you'll get a whole different perspective on the city (not to mention fascinating views inside downtown office buildings and North Side homes as you zip past their windows). While the Red Line is the most efficient for traveling between the Magnificent Mile and points south, your only views along this underground stretch will be of dingy stations. For sightseers, I recommend taking the aboveground Brown Line, which runs around the downtown Loop and then north through residential neighborhoods. You can ride all the way to the end of the line at Kimball (about a 45-min. ride from downtown), or hop off at Belmont to wander the Lakeview neighborhood. Avoid this scenic ride during rush hour (before about 9am and between 3:30 and 6:30pm), when your only view will be of tired commuters.

Study your CTA map carefully (there's one printed on the inside back cover of this guide) before boarding any train. While most trains run every 5 to 20 minutes, decreasing in frequency in the off-peak and overnight hours, some stations close after work hours (as early as 8:30pm) and remain closed on Saturday, Sunday, and holidays. The Orange Line train does not operate from about 11:30pm to 5am, the Brown Line operates only north of Belmont after about 9:30pm, the Blue Line's Cermak branch has ceased operating overnight and on weekends, and the Purple Line does not run overnight.

(*Fun Fact* **Sky Train: Chicago's El**

Watch any Hollywood film or TV series set in Chicago, and chances are they'll feature at least one scene set against our screeching elevated train system, more commonly known as the **"El"** (witness *The Fugitive, ER,* and others). The trains symbolize Chicago's gritty, "city-that-works" attitude, but they actually began as cutting-edge technology.

After the Great Fire of 1871, Chicago made a remarkable recovery; within 20 years, the downtown district was swarming with people, streetcars, and horses (but no stoplights). To help relieve congestion, the city took to the sky, building a system of elevated trains 15 feet above all the madness. The first El trains were steam-powered, but by the end of the century, all the lines—run by separate companies—used electricity. In 1895, the three El companies collaborated to build a set of tracks into and around the central business district that all the lines would then share. By 1897, the "Loop" was up and running.

Chicago's El wasn't the nation's first. That honor belongs to New York City, which started running its elevated trains in 1867, 25 years before Chicago. But the New York El has almost disappeared, moving underground and turning into a subway early last century. With 289 miles of track, Chicago has the biggest El and the second-largest public transportation system in the country.

BY BUS   Add to Chicago's gridlike layout a comprehensive system of public buses, and virtually every place in the city is within close walking distance of a bus stop. Other than on foot or bicycle, the best way to get around Chicago's warren of neighborhoods—the best way to actually see what's around you—is by riding a public bus, especially if you're staying near the lakefront, where the trains don't run. Look for the **blue-and-white signs to locate bus stops,** which are spaced about 2 blocks apart. Each bus route is identified by a number and the name of the main street it runs along; the bus that follows Grand Avenue, for example, is the no. 65 Grand.

A few buses that are particularly handy for many visitors are the **no. 146 Marine/Michigan,** an express bus from Belmont Avenue on the North Side that cruises down North Lake Shore Drive (and through Lincoln Park during nonpeak times) to North Michigan Avenue, State Street, and the Grant Park museum campus; the **no. 151 Sheridan,** which passes through Lincoln Park en route to inner Lake Shore Drive and then travels along Michigan Avenue as far south as Adams Street, where it turns west into the Loop (and stops at Union Station); and the **no. 156 LaSalle,** which goes through Lincoln Park and then into the Loop's financial district on LaSalle Street.

PACE buses (© **836-7000** from any Chicago area code or 847/364-7223; Mon–Fri 8am–5pm; www.pacebus.com) cover the suburban zones that surround Chicago. They run every 20 to 30 minutes during rush hour, operating until midevening Monday through Friday and early evening on weekends. Suburban bus routes are marked with nos. 208 and above, and vehicles may be flagged down at intersections where stops aren't marked.

BY COMMUTER TRAIN

The **Metra** commuter railroad (© **312/322-6777** or TTY 312/322-6774; Mon–Fri 8am–5pm; at other times call the **Transit Information Center** at © **312/836-7000** or TTY 312/836-4949; www.metrarail.com) serves the six-county suburban area around Chicago with 12 train lines. Several terminals are located downtown, including **Union Station** at Adams and Canal streets, **LaSalle Street Station** at LaSalle and Van Buren streets, **North Western Station** at Madison and Canal streets, and **Randolph Street Station** at Randolph Street and Michigan Avenue.

To view the leafy streets of Chicago's northern suburbs, take the **Union Pacific North Line,** which departs from the North Western Station, and get off at one of the following scenic towns: Kenilworth, Winnetka, Glencoe, Highland Park, and Lake Forest.

The **Metra Electric** (once known as the Illinois Central–Gulf Railroad, or the IC), running close to Lake Michigan on a track that occupies some of the most valuable real estate in Chicago, will take you to Hyde Park (see "Exploring Hyde Park: The Museum of Science and Industry & More," in chapter 8). You can catch the Metra Electric in the Loop at the Randolph Street Station and at the Van Buren Street Station at Van Buren Street and Michigan Avenue (both these stations are underground, so they're not immediately obvious to visitors).

Commuter trains have graduated fare schedules based on the distance you ride. On weekends and holidays and during the summer, Metra offers a family discount that allows up to three children under age 12 to ride free when accompanying a paid adult. The commuter railroad also offers a $5 weekend pass for unlimited rides on Saturday and Sunday.

BY TAXI

Taxis are a convenient way to get around the Loop and to get to the dining, shopping, and entertainment options found beyond downtown, such as on the Near North Side, in Old Town and Lincoln Park, and in Bucktown/Wicker Park.

Taxis are easy to hail in the Loop, on the Magnificent Mile and the Gold Coast, in River North, and in Lincoln Park, but if you go far beyond these key areas, you might need to call. Cab companies include **Flash Cab** (© 773/561-4444), **Yellow Cab** (© **312/TAXI-CAB**), and **Checker Cab** (© **312/CHECKER**).

The meter in Chicago cabs currently starts at $2.25 for the first mile and costs $1.80 for each additional mile, with a $1 surcharge for the first additional rider and 50¢ for each person after that.

BY CAR

One of the great things about visiting Chicago is that you don't need to rent a car to get around: Public transportation and taxis are plentiful, and most of the main tourist attractions are within walking distance of downtown hotels. If you do drive here, Chicago is laid out so logically that it's relatively easy for visitors to get around the city by car. Although rush-hour traffic jams are just as frustrating as they are in other large cities, traffic runs fairly smoothly at most times of the day. Chicagoans have learned to be prepared for unexpected delays; it seems that at least one major highway and several downtown streets are under repair throughout the spring and summer months (some say we have two seasons: winter and construction).

Great diagonal corridors—such as Lincoln Avenue, Clark Street, and Milwaukee Avenue—slice through the grid pattern at key points in the city and shorten many a trip that would otherwise be tedious on the checkerboard surface of the Chicago streets. On scenic **Lake Shore Drive** (also known as Outer Dr.), you can travel the length of the city (and beyond), never far from the great lake that is Chicago's most awesome natural feature. If you're driving here, make sure you take one spin along what we call LSD; the stretch between the Museum Campus and North Avenue is especially stunning.

DRIVING RULES   Unless otherwise posted, a right turn on red is allowed after stopping and signaling. As in any big city with its share of frustrating rush-hour traffic, be prepared for aggressive drivers and the occasional taxi to cut in front of you or make sudden, unexpected turns without signaling. Chicago drivers almost universally speed up at the sight of a yellow light; you'll most likely hear some honking if you don't make that mad dash before the light turns red.

PARKING   Parking regulations are vigorously enforced throughout the city. Read signs carefully: The streets around Michigan Avenue have parking restrictions during rush hour—and I know from bitter firsthand experience that your car will be towed immediately. Many neighborhoods have adopted resident-only parking that prohibits others from parking on their streets, usually after 6pm each day (even all day in a few areas, such as Old Town). The neighborhood around Wrigley Field is off-limits during Cubs night games, so look for yellow sidewalk signs alerting drivers about the dozen-and-a-half times the Cubs play under lights. You can park in permit zones if you're visiting a friend who can provide you with a pass to stick on your windshield. Beware of tow zones, and, if visiting in winter, make note of curbside warnings regarding snow plowing.

A safe bet is valet parking, which most restaurants provide for $7 to $10. Downtown you might also opt for a public garage, but you'll have to pay premium prices. Several garages connected with malls or other major attractions offer discounted parking with a validated ticket.

If you'll be spending an entire day downtown, the best parking deal in the Loop is the city-run **Millennium Park** garage (© 312/742-7644), which charges $17 for up to 8 hours (enter on Columbus Dr., 1 block east of Michigan Ave., between Monroe and Randolph sts.). A little farther south are two municipal lots underneath **Grant Park,** with one entrance at Michigan Avenue and Van Buren Street and the other at Michigan Avenue and Madison Street (© 312/616-0600). Parking costs $14 for the first hour and $22 for 2 to 8 hours. Other downtown lots (where prices are comparable or even higher) include **Midcontinental Plaza Garage,** 55 E. Monroe St. (© 312/986-6821), and **Navy Pier Parking,** 600 E. Grand Ave. (© 312/595-7437). There's also a large lot next to the **McCormick Place Convention Center,** 2301 S. Lake Shore Dr. (© 312/791-7000).

CAR RENTAL   Hertz (© 800/654-3131), Avis (© 800/831-2847), **National** (© 800/227-7368), and **Budget** (© 800/527-0700) all have offices at O'Hare and Midway airports. Each company also has at least one office downtown: Hertz at 401 N. State St., Avis at 214 N. Clark St., National at 203 N. LaSalle St., and Budget at 65 E. Lake St.

BY BOAT

During the summer, boat traffic booms along the Lake Michigan shoreline and the Chicago River. The water taxi service offered by **Shoreline Sightseeing** (© 312/222-9328; www.shorelinesightseeing.com) ferries passengers on the lake between Navy

Pier and the Shedd Aquarium, and on the Chicago River between Navy Pier and the Sears Tower (Adams St. and the river). The rides take about 15 to 20 minutes. The boats run daily Memorial Day to Labor Day every half-hour from 10am to 6pm, and single rides cost $6 for adults, $5 for seniors, and $3 for children.

The "RiverBus," operated by **Wendella Commuter Boats** (© **312/337-1446;** www.wendellaboats.com), floats daily April through October between a dock at Madison Street (near Union Station and the Sears Tower) and River East Plaza, near the lake (the boats also make stops at LaSalle St. and Michigan Ave.). The ride, which costs $2 each way (or $3 round-trip) and takes about 10 minutes, is popular with both visitors and commuters.

BY BICYCLE

The city of Chicago has earned kudos for its efforts to improve conditions for bicycling (designated bike lanes have been installed on stretches of Wells St., Roosevelt Rd., Elston Ave., and Halsted St.), but it can still be a tough prospect trying to compete with cars and their drivers, who aren't always so willing to share the road. Make sure that you wear a helmet at all times, and stick to the lakefront path or area parks if you're nervous about veering into traffic.

The **Chicagoland Bicycle Federation** (© **312/427-3325;** www.chibikefed.org), a nonprofit advocacy group, is a good resource for bicyclists. The group publishes several bicycling maps with tips on recommended on-street routes and parkland routes, as well as a guide to safe cycling in the city.

Bike Chicago rents all sorts of bikes, including tandems and four-seater "quadcycles," as well as in-line skates, from three locations: North Avenue Beach, Millennium Park, and Navy Pier (© **888/BIKE-WAY;** www.bikechicago.com). Bike rentals start at $8.75 an hour or $30 a day. Helmets, pads, and locks are provided free of charge. The shops are open daily from 9am to 7pm, weather permitting.

6

Where to Stay

Downtown Chicago is packed with hotels, thanks to the city's booming convention trade. The competition among luxury hotels is especially intense, with the Ritz-Carlton and Four Seasons winning international awards even as newer properties (such as the James and the Hard Rock) get in on the action. The bad news: low-price lodgings have become even harder to find. Steadily increasing room rates (especially during peak convention season in late spring and during the busy summer months) mean that Chicago is not exactly a budget destination; all the more reason to do some research before booking.

Many Chicago hotels offer a quintessential urban experience: Rooms come with views of surrounding skyscrapers, and the bustle of city life hits you as soon as you step outside the lobby doors. Although every property listed here caters to business travelers, Chicago attracts lots of tourists as well, and you won't have a problem finding family-friendly hotels in the most convenient neighborhoods; this is not a city where luxury hotels have dibs on all the prime real estate.

Although Chicago has its share of places that tout themselves as "boutique" hotels (Hotel Burnham, Hotel Monaco, W Chicago Lakeshore), these aren't quite the same as their New York, Miami, or Los Angeles counterparts—the so-called beautiful people who frequent these spots on the coasts aren't likely to stop off in Chicago. No matter where you stay in town, you'll likely find that your fellow guests are business travelers or vacationing families, but the boutiques usually attract business travelers who are a little more adventurous.

Hotel rates can vary enormously throughout the year, but I've divided hotels into four categories based on their average rates. "Very Expensive" hotels are luxury properties where rooms cost an average of $400 and up (and are seldom discounted). At "Expensive" hotels, rooms are at least $200 per night, with an upper price limit of $350 to $400. At a "Moderate" hotel, you can usually find a room for less than $200 per night; "Inexpensive" hotels are usually $150 or less per night. The rates given in this chapter are per night and do not include taxes, which are quite steep at 14.9%, nor do they take into account corporate or other discounts. Prices are always subject to availability and vary according to the time of week and season.

Note: For information on getting good room rates and the best rooms in hotels, see "Tips on Accommodations," in chapter 3, on p. 48. See the "Neighborhoods in Brief" section of chapter 5 for descriptions of the areas mentioned in this chapter.

Because Chicago's hospitality industry caters first and foremost to the business traveler, rates tend to be higher during the week. The city's slow season is from January to March, when outsiders steer clear of the cold and the threat of being snowed in at O'Hare. (If you'd like to watch your pennies but don't want to sightsee in a heavy down coat, another option is to stay in an outlying neighborhood during the week and then move into downtown for the weekend.)

You never know when some huge convention will gobble up all the desirable rooms in the city (even on the weekends), so it pays to book a room well in advance at any time of year. To find out if an upcoming convention coincides with your trip, check the "Major Convention Dates" calendar in chapter 3 (p. 31). You can also contact the **Chicago Convention & Tourism Bureau** (© 312/ 567-8500; www.choosechicago.com; click on "Meeting Professionals," and then click on "Convention Calendar").

RESERVATIONS   While our listings give the national toll-free numbers for most of the hotels in this book (as well as their local numbers), the best rates tend to show up on the hotels' websites, which often tout special deals. If you book online, follow up with a call to the hotel to discuss the type of room you want—otherwise you might get stuck with a view of an alley rather than the Sears Tower.

Most hotels have check-in times between 3 and 6pm; if you are going to be delayed, call ahead and reconfirm your reservation to prevent cancellation.

CORPORATE DISCOUNTS   Most hotels offer discounts of roughly 10% to individuals who are visiting Chicago on business. To qualify for this rate, your company usually must have an account on file at the hotel. In some cases, however, you may be required only to present some perfunctory proof of your commercial status, such as a business card or an official letterhead, to receive the discount. It never hurts to ask.

RESERVATION SERVICES   For discounted rooms at more than 30 downtown hotels, try **Hot Rooms** (© 800/ 468-3500 or 773/468-7666; www.hot rooms.com). Expect to get anywhere from 25% to 50% off standard rates (the rates here aren't always cheaper than the hotels' own websites, but it's worth

checking out). The 24-hour service is free, but if you cancel a reservation, you're assessed a $25 fee. For a free copy of the annual *Illinois Hotel-Motel Directory,* which also provides information about weekend packages, call the **Illinois Bureau of Tourism** at © 800/2-CONNECT.

The **Chicago Convention & Tourism Bureau**'s website (www.choosechicago. com) allows you to book hotels as well as complete travel packages. Check out the "Immersion Weekends," trips planned around a particular theme (such as fashion or museums) that include behind-the-scenes tours and meals at distinctive local restaurants.

BED & BREAKFAST RESERVATIONS A centralized reservations service called **At Home Inn Chicago,** P.O. Box 14088, Chicago, IL 60614 (© 800/375-7084 or 312/640-1050; fax 312/640-1012; www. athomeinnchicago.com), lists more than 70 accommodations in Chicago. Options range from high-rise and loft apartments to guest rooms carved from a former private club on the 40th floor of a Loop office building. Most lie within 3 miles of downtown (many are located in the Gold Coast, Old Town, and Lincoln Park neighborhoods) and will run you $150 to $300 for apartments, and as low as $105 for guest rooms in private homes. Most require a minimum stay of 2 or 3 nights.

A group of local B&B owners has formed the **Chicago Bed and Breakfast Association,** with a website that links to various properties throughout the city: **www.chicago-bed-breakfast.com.**

ACCESSIBILITY   Most hotels are prepared to accommodate travelers with physical disabilities, but you should always inquire when making reservations to make sure that the hotel can meet your particular needs. Older properties, in particular, may not meet current requirements or may only have limited numbers of specially equipped rooms.

A WORD ABOUT SMOKING   Most hotels offer rooms or entire floors for nonsmokers. If it's important to you, be sure to specify whether you want a smoking or nonsmoking room when you make your reservation.

1 The Best Hotel Bets

- **Best Historic Hotel: The Drake Hotel,** 140 E. Walton Place (© **800/55-DRAKE**), is a master at combining the decorous charm of yesteryear with every modern convenience. See p. 95.
- **Best Rehab of a Historic Structure:** The Loop's revered Reliance Building, one of the world's first glass-walled skyscrapers, has regained its dignity thanks to a thrilling reincarnation as the tony **Hotel Burnham,** 1 W. Washington St. (© **877/294-9712**). See p. 86.
- **Best for Business Travelers:** Virtually every hotel in Chicago qualifies, but the **Swissôtel Chicago,** 323 E. Wacker Dr. (© **888/737-9477**), combines extensive business services with stunning city views from all rooms. See p. 89.
- **Best Hotel Dining Experience:** Almost every luxury hotel in town has a first-class restaurant—usually with eye-popping prices. To give your wallet a break, try the Atwood Café at the **Hotel Burnham,** 1 W. Washington St. (© **877/294-9712**), which offers accessible, modern American dishes in a dining room with real character. See p. 86.
- **Best Service:** The attention to detail, regal pampering, and well-connected concierges at both the ultraluxe **Ritz-Carlton,** 160 E. Pearson St. (© **800/621-6906**), and the **Four Seasons,** 120 E. Delaware Place (© **800/332-3442**), make them the hotels of choice for travelers who want to feel like royalty. See p. 94 and 92, respectively.
- **Best for a Romantic Getaway:** For a splurge, **The Peninsula,** 108 E. Superior St. (© **866/288-8889**), or the **Park Hyatt,** 800 N. Michigan Ave. (© **800/233-1234**), will pamper you with luxurious rooms and top-notch amenities (p. 93 and 93, respectively). For a cozier getaway, try the **Talbott Hotel,** 20 E. Delaware Place (© **800/TALBOTT**), which is centrally located but tucked away from the crowds. See p. 96.
- **Best Trendy Hotel:** The **W Chicago Lakeshore,** 644 N. Lake Shore Dr. (© **877/W-HOTELS**), brings the hip W sensibility to a prime location overlooking Lake Michigan (p. 97).
- **Best Views:** This isn't an easy call. Consider several hotels for their mix of lake and city views: the **Swissôtel;** the **Four Seasons; The Drake Hotel;** the **Ritz-Carlton;** the **Park Hyatt Chicago;** and the **Chicago City Centre** (p. 89, 92, 95, 94, 93, and 98, respectively). Peering over the elevated tracks, **The Silversmith Hotel & Suites,** 10 S. Wabash Ave. (© **312/372-7696**), in the Loop, offers a distinctly urban vista (p. 89).
- **Best for Families:** With every room a suite, the **Embassy Suites,** 600 N. State St. (© **800/362-2779**), and **Homewood Suites,** 40 E. Grand Ave. (© **800/CALL-HOME**), are ideal for families looking for a little more space than the typical hotel room provides (p. 102 and 99, respectively). The **Chicago City Centre,** 300 E. Ohio St. (© **800/HOLIDAY**), not only has a great outdoor pool, but guests also get free access to an indoor pool, so you can go swimming no matter what the weather (p. 98).

- **Best Off-the-Beaten-Path Hotels:** The **City Suites Hotel,** 933 W. Belmont Ave. (✆ **800/248-9108**), the **Majestic Hotel,** 528 W. Brompton St. (✆ **800/727-5108**), and the **Best Western Hawthorne Terrace,** 3434 N. Broadway Ave. (✆ **888/401-8781**), located in residential North Side neighborhoods, have a more personal feel than many downtown hotels. They're also convenient to public transportation. See p. 105, 106, and 105, respectively.
- **Best Location:** Most visitors will be more than happy with the location of any hotel on the Magnificent Mile of North Michigan Avenue. See the "Near North & the Magnificent Mile" section beginning on p. 91.
- **Best Health Club:** The fitness center and spa at **The Peninsula,** 108 E. Superior St. (✆ **866/288-8889**), offer the latest workout equipment and skin treatments in a sparkling, airy setting. Plus, afterward, you can relax on the outdoor sun deck or take a dip in the pool with stunning city views. See p. 93.
- **Best Hotel Pool:** With its dazzling all-tile, junior Olympic-size pool constructed in 1929, the **InterContinental Chicago,** 505 N. Michigan Ave. (✆ **800/327-0200**), takes this title easily. See p. 95.
- **Best for Travelers with Disabilities:** The **Four Seasons,** 120 E. Delaware Place (✆ **800/332-3442**), and the **Fairmont Hotel,** 200 N. Columbus Dr. (✆ **800/526-2008**), go the extra mile for guests with special needs, also providing high-tech accessories for those who are hearing- or vision-impaired. See p. 92 and see below, respectively.

2 The Loop

Strictly speaking, "downtown" in Chicago means the Loop—the central business district, a 6×8-block rectangle enveloped by elevated tracks on all four sides. Within these confines are the city's financial institutions, trading markets, and municipal government buildings, making for a lot of hustle and bustle Monday through Friday. The Art Institute of Chicago sits on the Loop's edge, and the Museum Campus, home to the Field Museum of Natural History and John G. Shedd Aquarium, is an easy walk to the south on a nice day. For visitors who want a real "city" experience, the Loop offers dramatic urban vistas of skyscrapers and the feeling that you're at the heart of the action—on weekdays. Come Saturday and Sunday, however, the Loop is pretty dead; on Sunday, almost all the stores are closed. If nightlife is a priority, you won't find much here, but you do have some good dining options.

EXPENSIVE

Fairmont Hotel ⟪⟪   The Fairmont ranks right up there with the city's most luxurious hotels, offering an array of deluxe amenities and services and regularly hosting high-level politicians and high-profile fundraisers. The only downside is the hotel's location; although it's only a short walk from bustling Millennium Park, the Art Institute, and Michigan Avenue, it's tucked among anonymous office towers, which makes it feel cut off from the life of the city. The grand circular lobby sets the hotel's tone: upscale and lavish rather than cozy and personal (you might wander awhile before finding the check-in desk). Still, the rooms are large and inviting, with plush bedding and comfortable chairs (ask for one with a lake view, although city-view rooms aren't bad either). The posh bathrooms feature extra-large tubs, separate vanity areas, and swivel TVs. The windows open (a rarity in high-rise hotels), so you can enjoy the breeze drifting off Lake Michigan. Suites have one or two bedrooms, a living room, a

Where to Stay in Chicago

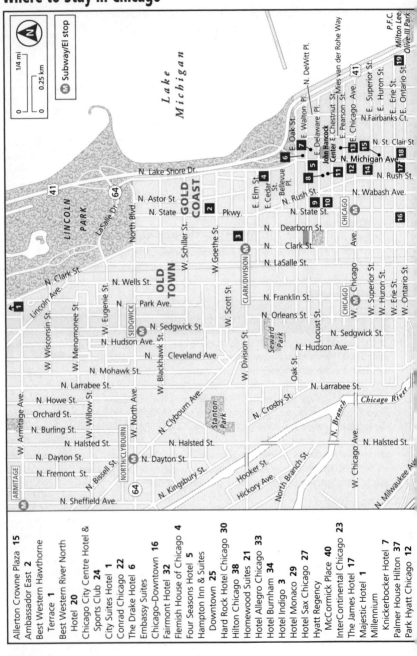

Allerton Crowne Plaza **15**
Ambassador East **2**
Best Western Hawthorne
   Terrace **1**
Best Western River North
   Hotel **20**
Chicago City Centre Hotel &
   Sports Club **24**
City Suites Hotel **1**
Conrad Chicago **22**
The Drake Hotel **6**
Embassy Suites
Chicago–Downtown **16**
Fairmont Hotel **32**
Flemish House of Chicago **4**
Four Seasons Hotel **5**
Hampton Inn & Suites
   Downtown **25**
Hard Rock Hotel Chicago **30**
Hilton Chicago **38**
Homewood Suites **21**
Hotel Allegro Chicago **33**
Hotel Burnham **34**
Hotel Indigo **3**
Hotel Monaco **29**
Hotel Sax Chicago **27**
Hyatt Regency
McCormick Place **40**
InterContinental Chicago **23**
The James Hotel **17**
Majestic Hotel **1**
Millennium
Knickerbocker Hotel **7**
Palmer House Hilton **37**
Park Hyatt Chicago **12**

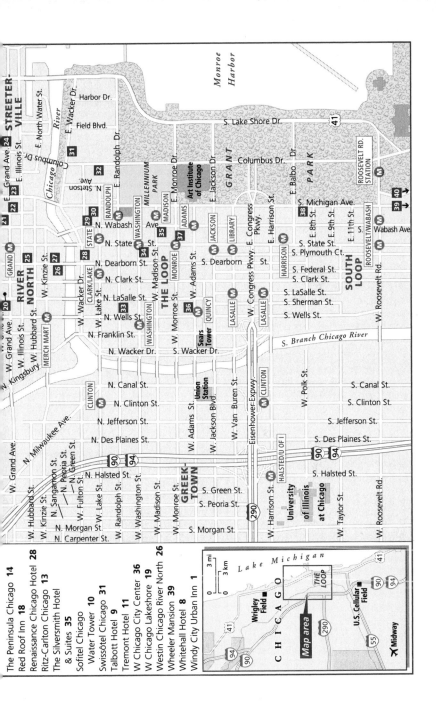

The Peninsula Chicago **14**
Red Roof Inn **18**
Renaissance Chicago Hotel **28**
Ritz-Carlton Chicago **13**
The Silversmith Hotel
  & Suites **35**
Sofitel Chicago
  Water Tower **10**
SwissÔtel Chicago **31**
Talbott Hotel **9**
Tremont Hotel **11**
W Chicago City Center **36**
W Chicago Lakeshore **19**
Westin Chicago River North **26**
Wheeler Mansion **39**
Whitehall Hotel **8**
Windy City Urban Inn **1**

dining area, and a built-in bar—and all come with lake views. For $20 a day, guests get access to the Lakeshore Athletic Club, one of the best health clubs in the city (with full-court basketball, climbing wall, pool, and spa). Aria, the hotel's restaurant, is worth a visit for its creative, internationally inspired comfort food. Visiting in winter? The Fairmont is connected to the city's underground "pedway" system, through which you can walk all the way to Macy's on State Street (a florist, pharmacy, and salon are conveniently located in an adjoining building).

200 N. Columbus Dr. (at Lake St.), Chicago, IL 60601. © 800/526-2008 or 312/565-8000. Fax 312/856-1032. www.fairmont.com. 692 units. $129–$389 double; $229–$539 suite. AE, DC, DISC, MC, V. Valet parking $41 w/in-out privileges. Subway/El: Red, Green, Orange, Brown, or Blue line to State/Lake. Small pets accepted for a $25 fee. **Amenities:** Restaurant (eclectic); lounge; access to nearby health club; concierge; business center; 24-hr. room service; babysitting; laundry service; 24-hr. dry cleaning. In room: A/C, TV w/pay movies, high-speed Internet access, minibar, hair dryer, iron.

Hard Rock Hotel Chicago 𝕲 The good news: This hotel is not located on top of the super-touristy Hard Rock Cafe (which is about a mile or so away in River North). In fact, it is a relatively restrained rehab of one of the city's historic skyscrapers, the 40-story Carbide and Carbon Building. The overall theme here is music: Pop tunes echo throughout the lobby, TV monitors show videos, and glass cases display pop-star memorabilia. But the mix of old and new can be somewhat jarring—the black-and-gray lobby feels like a nightclub, while the marble-and-gold-trimmed elevator bank still feels like an office building. Don't expect too much in the way of rock-star attitudes or personalities here; like most Chicago hotels, the Hard Rock attracts plenty of business travelers and families. The guest rooms are neutral, with modern furniture; the building's larger-than-average windows let in plenty of natural light. The so-called Hard Rock Rooms on the corners of each floor are larger than the standard double rooms and feature chaise lounges for stretching out. The suites, located in the tower at the top of the building, come in various one- and two-bedroom configurations and allow an added layer of privacy (with only one or two suites per floor, you're separated from the masses).

The lobby starts swinging after dark, when the music gets going at the street-level bar, Base (open 'til 4am, it hosts live music and DJs most nights). The hotel's restaurant, China Bar & Grill, serves up Asian fusion cuisine in a high-energy setting. And because the hotel actively courts rock bands who come through town on tour, you never know who you'll see stopping in for a drink.

230 N. Michigan Ave. (at Lake St.), Chicago, IL 60601. © 866/966-5166 or 312/345-1000. Fax 312/345-1012. www.hardrockhotelchicago.com. 387 units. $169–$349 double; from $1,500 suite. AE, DC, DISC, MC, V. Valet parking $39 w/in-out privileges. Subway/El: Red or Blue line to State/Lake. **Amenities:** Restaurant (Asian fusion); bar; exercise room; concierge; business services; 24-hr. room service; same-day laundry service; dry cleaning. In room: A/C, TV w/DVD player and video games, free high-speed Internet access, minibar, coffeemaker, hair dryer, iron, safe, CD player.

Hotel Burnham 𝕲𝕲𝕲 If you're looking for a spot with a sense of history, this is it. The historic Reliance Building—one of the first skyscrapers ever built and a highly significant architectural treasure—has been brilliantly restored as an intimate boutique hotel named for Daniel Burnham, whose firm designed the building in 1895. The prime State Street location is across from the massive downtown Macy's department store and a few blocks away from the historic Cadillac Palace Theater and Ford Center for the Performing Arts/Oriental Theater. The Burnham is a must for architecture buffs: Wherever possible, the restoration retained period elements—most obviously in the hallways, with their terrazzo tile floors, white marble wainscoting, mahogany door and window frames, and room numbers painted on the translucent glass doors. Rooms are clubby but glamorous, with plush beds, mahogany writing desks, and chaise lounges. The hotel's 19 suites feature a separate living-room area and CD stereo systems. Don't come to the Burnham if you're looking for extensive amenities—the lobby is tiny, as is the exercise room. But the Burnham is one of Chicago's most distinctive hotels, and it's highly recommended for visitors who want a historic location jazzed up with a dash of colorful modern style. Ask for a room on a high floor in the northeast corner—the views north and east are dazzling. The on-site Atwood Café (p. 116) serves creative comfort food against a Gilded Age backdrop. There's also complimentary Starbucks coffee in the lobby every morning and a wine reception each afternoon from 5 to 6pm.

A bonus for animal lovers: Pets are positively welcome here. The hotel provides beds, treats, and dog-walking services, among other amenities (they'll even clean out your in-room kitty-litter box!). The Hotel Monaco (see below) and the Hotel Allegro (p. 90), owned by the same company, offer similar pet perks.

1 W. Washington St. (at State St.), Chicago, IL 60602. ℂ **866/690-1986** or 312/782-1111. Fax 312/782-0899. www.burnhamhotel.com. 122 units. $299 double; $229–$399 suite. AE, DC, DISC, MC, V. Valet parking $40 w/in-out privileges. Subway/El: Red or Blue line to Washington. Pets allowed. **Amenities:** Restaurant (contemporary American); access to nearby health club; concierge; business services; meeting space; 24-hr. room service; laundry service; dry cleaning. *In room:* A/C, TV, free high-speed Internet access, minibar, coffeemaker, hair dryer, iron, safe.

Hotel Monaco 🟊🟊🟊   This 14-story boutique hotel deftly manages to straddle the line between fun and conservative. The stylish decor is a fresh alternative to Chicago's many cookie-cutter business hotels: The rooms feature dramatic deep-red headboards and green-striped walls, while the lobby—with its gold decorative accents and zebra-striped chairs—looks like a 1930s-era salon. Despite the funky feel, the Monaco is rather subdued; it's a place to relax, not pose. The eclectic furniture includes mahogany writing desks and ergonomic chairs; suites come with a two-person whirlpool spa and pull-out queen-size sofa bed. (If you're taller than average, you can request a Tall Room, with longer beds.) All rooms include "meditation stations"—comfy seats tucked into the larger-than-average windows, which are perfect for taking in the cityscape outside (ask for a river view). Along with its sister hotels—the Burnham and the Allegro—the Monaco also offers an in-room yoga program and offers special packages for visitors traveling with pets. Given the hotel's playful spirit, it attracts a younger clientele, with an overall vibe that is laid-back and friendly rather than so-hip-it-hurts (this is Chicago, after all, not New York).

225 N. Wabash Ave. (at Wacker Dr.), Chicago, IL 60601. ℂ **800/397-7661** or 312/960-8500. Fax 312/960-1883. www.monaco-chicago.com. 192 units. $169–$329 double; $279–$429 suite. AE, DC, DISC, MC, V. Valet parking $38 w/in-out privileges. Subway/El: Brown, Green, or Orange line to Randolph, or Red Line to Washington. Small pets allowed. **Amenities:** Restaurant (American); small fitness room (and access to nearby health club for $10/day); concierge; business center; 24-hr. room service; in-room massage; babysitting; laundry service; dry cleaning. *In room:* A/C, TV w/pay movies, fax, high-speed Internet access, minibar, coffeemaker, hair dryer, iron, safe.

Palmer House Hilton   The longest continually operating hotel in North America (since 1871), the Palmer House was named for legendary State Street merchant prince Potter Palmer. The building's grand Italianate lobby retains a Gilded Age aura (it's worth a look even if you're not staying here), but don't come here expecting to be swept back in time. The massive complex depends heavily on large business groups, so the hotel often feels like an extension of the McCormick Place Convention Center. The good news: Rooms that were previously decorated in drab, motel-worthy colors

---

Fun Fact **Did You Know?**

Merriel Abbott, the dance choreographer who booked all the acts at the Palmer House's famed Empire Room—one of the nation's leading supper clubs from the 1930s to the 1950s—gave Liberace and Bob Fosse their first breaks. Liberace, a cocktail pianist at the club, was "discovered" in Milwaukee by Abbott, who is credited with dressing up the flamboyant entertainer's piano with a candelabra to lend his act some pizzazz. Fosse, a native Chicagoan, made his debut at age 18 as part of a dance team. He and his partner made $500 a month in 1947; Liberace was paid $1,100 for 5 weeks in 1946.

---

have been upgraded in the past few years with new, cheerier bedding and carpets. Standard double rooms are quite spacious, with plenty of room to spread out. The bad news: Rooms also feel somewhat spartan, with only two fairly uncomfortable chairs to sit in. Bathrooms are small but serviceable (some rooms come with two bathrooms, a plus for families). Executive Level rooms on the top two floors come with DVD players, thick robes, and complimentary breakfast and afternoon hors d'oeuvres; guests on those floors have use of a lounge and their own concierge. No matter where your room is located, don't expect grand views of surrounding skyscrapers; most rooms look out into offices across the street. Kids might appreciate the sheer size of the place, with plenty of room to wander (and an indoor pool), and the location is good for access to the Museum Campus.

17 E. Monroe St. (at State St.), Chicago, IL 60603. ⓒ 800/HILTONS or 312/726-7500. Fax 312/917-1797. www.hiltonchicagosales.com. 1,639 units. $129–$350 double; $450–$1,500 suite. AE, DC, DISC, MC, V. Valet parking $35 w/in-out privileges; self-parking across the street $25. Subway/El: Red Line to Monroe. **Amenities:** 3 restaurants (the legendary but dated Trader Vic's and 2 American bar and grills); 2 lounges; health club w/indoor pool, Jacuzzi, and sauna for $10/day or $20/entire stay; children's programs; concierge; business center; shopping arcade; room service until 2am; babysitting referrals; laundry service; overnight dry cleaning; executive rooms. *In room:* A/C, TV w/pay movies, high-speed Internet access, minibar, coffeemaker, hair dryer, iron.

Renaissance Chicago Hotel 🌟🌟   A hotel without much of a personality, the Renaissance Chicago is tasteful and understated—perfectly suited to the business travelers who are the hotel's bread and butter. This large operation offers all your standard high-end amenities but is indistinguishable from any number of executive-style hotels elsewhere in the country. Still, this is a good bet for high-end service if you want a Loop location, and the hotel's bay windows provide stunning views of the Chicago River and the towers of North Michigan Avenue. Standard double rooms include a small sitting area with an armchair and desk; Club-level rooms, located on the top four floors, are half a room larger and have their own concierge and private lounge, where complimentary continental breakfast and evening hors d'oeuvres are served. The rooms are decorated stylishly, with deep yellow and blue bedding and silver decorative accents; suites include a sitting room with couches, meeting table, and wet bar and separate bedrooms. Request a river view for the best cityscape (corner suites also have excellent views of both the Chicago River and Lake Michigan).

1 W. Wacker Dr. (at State St.), Chicago, IL 60601. ⓒ 800/HOTELS-1 or 312/372-7200. Fax 312/372-0093. www.marriott. com. 553 units. $199–$399 double; $249–$399 club-level double; suites from $500. AE, DC, DISC, MC, V. Valet parking $40 w/in-out privileges. Subway/El: Brown Line to State/Lake or Red Line to Washington. Small pets accepted.

Amenities: Restaurant (American); lounge; indoor pool w/skylights; health club w/whirlpool and steam room; concierge; FedEx Kinko's in lobby; 24-hr. room service; babysitting; same-day laundry service and dry cleaning; club-level rooms. *In room:* A/C, TV w/pay movies, high-speed Internet access, minibar, coffeemaker, hair dryer, iron, CD player.

The Silversmith Hotel & Suites 🗝🗝 *(Finds)*   This landmark building was built in 1897 to serve the jewelry and silver trade on Wabash Avenue, still known as Jeweler's Row. Fittingly, the hotel is a hidden gem (often, even the Loop office workers who pass by it daily don't know it's there), so rooms don't book up as quickly as other, hotter spots, which is good news for anyone traveling during the busy convention season. Rooms come in varying configurations, with 12-foot-high ceilings, 10-foot picture windows, Frank Lloyd Wright–inspired wrought-iron fixtures, armoires, homey bedding, and generous-size bathrooms. (Suites have bedrooms that can be closed off behind glass-paned doors.) Because buildings surround this very urban hotel, natural light is unfortunately limited in the rooms, and those along the hotel's main corridor tend to be quite dark. Rooms at the front on the fifth floor or higher have a quintessentially Chicago view: the El tracks along Wabash Avenue. Yes, the windows are extra thick to muffle the noise of the rumbling trains, but you'll want to avoid the lower-level floors if you like things quiet. For the best combination of natural light and views, request a Wabash Avenue room on the 9th or 10th floor. Guest-friendly touches include complimentary desserts available Monday through Thursday nights from 9 to 10pm (including the city's famous Eli's cheesecake).

10 S. Wabash Ave. (at Madison St.), Chicago, IL 60603. ⓒ 312/372-7696. Fax 312/372-7320. www.silver smithchicagohotel.com. 143 units. $179–$359 double; from $289 suite; weekend rates available. AE, DC, DISC, MC, V. Valet parking $30 w/in-out privileges. Subway/El: Brown, Green, or Orange line to Madison, or Red Line to Washington. **Amenities:** Restaurant (deli); lounge; fitness room (w/access to nearby health club for $10/day); concierge; business center and secretarial services; limited room service; laundry service; dry cleaning; club-level rooms. *In room:* A/C, TV w/pay movies, high-speed Internet access, minibar, coffeemaker, fridge, hair dryer, iron, safe.

Swissôtel Chicago 🗝🗝   This sleek, modern hotel is all business and may therefore feel a bit icy to some visitors, but its no-nonsense aura makes it especially attractive to business travelers in search of tranquillity. The hotel's triangular design gives every room a panoramic vista of Lake Michigan, Grant Park, and/or the Chicago River. The spacious rooms have separate sitting areas and warm contemporary furnishings. Business travelers will appreciate the oversize desks (convertible to dining tables), ergonomic chairs, and—in upgraded Business Advantage rooms—CD players and high-speed and Wi-Fi Internet access. All Executive Level guests also receive complimentary breakfast and hors d'oeuvres and have access to a lounge with Internet connections, a library, and a personal concierge. Executive suites, with wonderful 180-degree views, have separate sleeping areas.

Active travelers will want to break a sweat in the lofty environs of the Penthouse Health Club and Spa, perched on the 42nd floor. And those who just want to indulge themselves can enjoy the ultimate steak-and-lobster expense-account restaurant, the on-site outpost of New York's The Palm.

323 E. Wacker Dr., Chicago, IL 60601. ⓒ **888/737-9477** or 312/565-0565. Fax 312/565-0540. www.swissotel chicago.com. 632 units. $159–$409 double; $395–$2,500 suite. AE, DC, DISC, MC, V. Valet parking $45 w/in-out privileges. Subway/El: Red, Brown, Orange, or Green line to Randolph. **Amenities:** 2 restaurants (steakhouse, American); lounge; penthouse fitness center w/indoor pool, spa, Jacuzzi, and sauna; concierge; business center w/extensive meeting services; 24-hr. room service; massage; babysitting; laundry service; 24-hr. dry cleaning; executive-level rooms. *In room:* A/C, TV w/pay movies, dataport, minibar, coffeemaker, hair dryer, iron.

W Chicago City Center ⭐   One of two Chicago properties in the hip W hotel chain (the other is the W Chicago Lakeshore, p. 97), this is an oasis of cool in the button-down Loop. Unfortunately, the rooms tend toward the small and dark (most look out into a central courtyard), and the W color scheme—dark purple and gray—doesn't do much to brighten the spaces. Don't stay here if you crave lots of natural light. All W properties pride themselves on their "whatever, whenever" service: Whatever you want, whenever you want it (the modern version of a 24-hr. on-call concierge). If you're the loll-around-in-bed type, this is a great place to do it; the super-comfy beds feature cushiony pillow-top mattresses, soft duvets, and mounds of pillows.

The bar, designed by nightlife wunderkind Rande Gerber (Mr. Cindy Crawford), gives hotel guests a stylish spot to sit and pose amid dance music and cocktail waitresses who look like models. Given its location, this W is foremost a business hotel—although one that's definitely geared toward younger workers rather than crusty old executives.

172 W. Adams St. (at LaSalle St.), Chicago, IL 60603. © **877/W-HOTELS** or 312/332-1200. Fax 312/332-5909. www.whotels.com. 368 units. $219–$569 double; $399–$1,500 suite. AE, DC, DISC, MC, V. Valet parking $42 w/in-out privileges. Subway/El: Brown Line to Quincy. Pets allowed. **Amenities:** Restaurant (European); bar; exercise room; concierge; business services; 24-hr. room service; in-room massage; babysitting; same-day laundry service; dry cleaning. *In room:* A/C, TV/VCR/DVD w/pay movies, fax, high-speed Internet access, minibar, hair dryer, iron, safe, CD player.

MODERATE

Hotel Allegro Chicago ⭐ *Value*   Owned by the same company as the Hotel Monaco and the Hotel Burnham (both listed above), the Allegro is my top pick in the Loop for families in search of a fun vibe. Although its published rates are about the same as those of its sister properties, the Allegro is far larger than the Monaco or the Burnham and consequently is more likely to offer special rates to fill space (especially on weekends and in the winter). Guests enter a lobby with plush, boldly colored furnishings ("Art Deco with punch" is the way one hotel employee described it to me). That whimsical first impression segues into the cheery, pink-walled guest rooms. Most rooms are small (without much space beyond the bed, an armoire, and one chair) but manage to feel cozy rather than cramped; the compact bathrooms, annoyingly, have only pedestal sinks—meaning minimal storage for beauty-product junkies. Suites have separate bedrooms and foldout couches and come with robes, VCRs, and two-person Jacuzzi tubs.

Befitting a place where the doorman hums along to the tunes playing on speakers out front, the Allegro appeals to younger travelers. There's plenty of opportunity for socializing at Encore, the cafe that hosts DJs at night, or at the complimentary evening wine reception in the lobby. The hotel's restaurant, 312 Chicago (p. 120), attracts nonguests in search of excellent Italian cuisine. *A note to theater fans:* The Allegro has access to exclusive seats for many high-profile downtown shows and often promotes special theater packages.

171 W. Randolph St. (at LaSalle St.), Chicago, IL 60601. © **800/643-1500** or 312/236-0123. Fax 312/236-0917. www.allegrochicago.com. 483 units. $149–$299 double; $225–$399 suite. AE, DC, DISC, MC, V. Valet parking $30 w/in-out privileges. Subway/El: All lines to Washington. Pets allowed. **Amenities:** Restaurant (northern Italian); lounge; exercise room (and access to nearby health club w/indoor pool for $10/day); concierge; business center; salon; limited room service; same-day laundry service; dry cleaning. *In room:* A/C, TV w/pay movies, free high-speed Internet access, minibar, coffeemaker, hair dryer, iron.

3 South Loop

EXPENSIVE

Hilton Chicago ★★ (Kids)   When it opened in 1927, this massive brick-and-stone edifice billed itself as the largest hotel in the world. Today the Hilton still runs like a small city, with numerous restaurants and shops and a steady stream of conventioneers. Its colorful history includes visits by Queen Elizabeth, Emperor Hirohito, and every president since FDR—and riots outside its front door during the 1968 Democratic Convention. The classical-rococo public spaces—including the Versailles-inspired Grand Ballroom and Grand Stair Lobby—are magnificent, but the rest of the hotel falls into the chain-hotel mold: comfortable and well-run but fairly impersonal.

Some rooms are on the small side, but all feel homey thanks to the warm cherry furniture, and many of the standard rooms have two bathrooms (great for families). Rooms facing Michigan Avenue offer sweeping views of Grant Park and the lake. The hotel's Executive Level rooms (you'll pay about $75 above the standard rate for these) have a separate registration area, upgraded amenities (including robes), and a lounge serving complimentary continental breakfast and evening hors d'oeuvres.

The Hilton is a great choice for families thanks to its vast public spaces, proximity to major museums and Grant Park (where kids can run around), and policy of children 17 and under staying free in their parent's room. Because the Hilton depends heavily on convention traffic, however, those seeking a cozy, romantic getaway should head elsewhere.

720 S. Michigan Ave. (at Balbo Dr.), Chicago, IL 60605. © **800/HILTONS** or 312/922-4400. Fax 312/922-5240. www.hilton.com. 1,544 units. $129–$399 double; $179–$7,000 suite. AE, DC, DISC, MC, V. Valet parking $45; self-parking $41. Subway/El: Red Line to Harrison. **Amenities:** 4 restaurants (cafe, American, steakhouse, Irish pub w/live music); 2 lounges; indoor pool; health club w/indoor track, hot tubs, sauna, and steam room; concierge; business center; 24hr. room service; massage; babysitting; laundry service; 24-hr. dry cleaning. *In room:* A/C, TV w/pay movies, high-speed and Wi-Fi Internet access, minibar, coffeemaker, hair dryer, iron.

Wheeler Mansion ★★ (Finds)   Want to feel like you've gone back in time without giving up modern amenities such as cable TV? This grand Italianate building has been restored and transformed into a bed-and-breakfast that combines the best of old and new. The mosaic tile floor in the vestibule and some of the dark walnut woodwork and fixtures are original to the house; welcome additions include good-sized private bathrooms (some have only shower stalls rather than bathtubs). The rooms—which are spacious enough to include armoires and armchairs—feel even larger than they are, thanks to the high ceilings. The four suites come with gas fireplaces. Antique European furniture fills the house, and guests sleep on goose-down feather beds with high-end linens. Adding to the homey ambience is the courtyard garden, where you can relax with a glass of wine after a day of sightseeing. A full gourmet breakfast—served on elegant bone china—is included in the daily room rate.

2020 S. Calumet Ave., Chicago, IL 60616. © **312/945-2020.** Fax 312/945-2021. www.wheelermansion.com. 11 units. $230–$285 double; $265–$365 suite. AE, DC, DISC, MC, V. Free parking. Bus: 62 from State St. downtown. **Amenities:** Laundry service; computer rental available. *In room:* A/C, TV w/digital cable, Wi-Fi, hair dryer, iron.

4 Near North & the Magnificent Mile

VERY EXPENSIVE

Conrad Chicago ★   Tucked into the Westfield North Bridge mall, the Conrad Chicago maintains a low profile. But this property—part of the Hilton hotel group's

(Kids) Family-Friendly Hotels

Chicago has plenty of options for families on the go. The **Hampton Inn & Suites** (p. 102) keeps the kids in a good mood with a pool, Nintendo, and proximity to the Hard Rock Cafe and the Rainforest Cafe. Children 17 and under stay free in their parent's room. Kiddies also stay free at the **Chicago City Centre Hotel & Sports Club** (p. 98), which has a large outdoor pool, access to an indoor pool at an adjoining health club, and is near Navy Pier and the beach. The **Best Western River North Hotel** (p. 102) won't win any prizes for its no-frills decor, but it's one of the best values in River North and lies within walking distance of many family restaurants. The indoor pool and outdoor deck—with great city views—are another big draw.

When you want a little extra room to spread out, both **Homewood Suites** (p. 99) and **Embassy Suites** (p. 102) make traveling en masse a little easier with separate bedrooms and kitchenettes (so you can save money on food). The **Hilton Chicago** (p. 91) has lots of public space for wandering, and many of the rooms come with two bathrooms.

Of course, luxury hotels can afford to be friendly to all of their guests. At the **Four Seasons Hotel** (see below), kids are indulged with little robes, balloon animals, Nintendo, and milk and cookies; the hotel also has a wonderful pool. The concierge at the **Ritz-Carlton Chicago** (p. 94) keeps a stash of toys and games for younger guests to borrow, and kids' menu items are available 24 hours; the hotel even provides a special gift pack just for teenage guests. The upscale **Westin Chicago River North** (p. 101) also caters to families with baby accessories and programs for older kids, respectively.

upscale "boutique" brand—is determined to compete with the city's more established luxury properties (with room rates to match). The overall vibe here is old-money classiness rather than new-money flashiness, from the lobby, filled with dark wood furniture, to the deep brown curtains in the tranquil guest rooms. Rooms are a bit small (especially the least expensive ones on the north side), but the amenities are top-of-the-line: flatscreen TVs and Bose sound systems. High rollers will want to book one of the suites overlooking Michigan Avenue; a few even come with private terraces, something very few hotels in the city offer. The Conrad can't compete with the Park Hyatt or The Peninsula in the glamour department, but its cozy style should appeal to travelers looking for someplace a little more personal. It also makes a good base for anyone visiting during frigid winter weather; with a mall just a few steps away, you can get out without even putting on your coat.

521 N. Rush St. (at Grand St.), Chicago, IL 60611. © 800/HILTONS or 312/645-1500. Fax 312/645-1550. http://conradhotels1.hilton.com. 311 units. $325–$530 double; from $500 suite. AE, DC, DISC, MC, V. Valet parking $41 w/in-out privileges. Subway/El: Red Line to Chicago. **Amenities:** Restaurant (European bistro); bar; health club; concierge; business center; 24-hr. room service; in-room massage; babysitting; laundry service; same-day dry cleaning. *In room:* A/C, flatscreen TV w/pay movies and video games, high-speed Internet access, minibar, fridge, coffeemaker, hair dryer, iron, safe, CD player w/Bose sound system, turndown service.

Four Seasons Hotel ⟨⟨⟨ (Kids)   Consistently voted one of the top hotels in the world by frequent travelers, the Four Seasons offers an understated luxury that appeals to publicity-shy Hollywood stars and wealthy families. The hotel has every conceivable luxury amenity, and in 2007 it underwent a $30-million renovation that changed its look from that of a subdued English country manor to that of a sleek and elegant modern getaway. The hotel's location—hidden between the 30th and 46th floors of the Mag Mile's most upscale vertical mall—epitomizes the hotel's discretion. This is not a place you wander into casually to gawk or people-watch. The elegant rooms feature contemporary furnishings, subdued colors, and modern artworks, and each has windows that open to let in the fresh air. Bathrooms boast a lighted makeup mirror, oversize towels and robes, scales, and L'Occitane toiletries. Kid-friendly services include child-size robes, tub amenities, board and video games, and a special room service menu. The hotel's elegant fitness center exudes upscale exclusivity (the pool, surrounded by Roman columns, looks like it could be part of an aristocratic private club). The on-site spa is small but luxurious, with a wide range of treatments. An 18-foot-high white marble fountain marks the entrance to the opulent Seasons Restaurant, and the lobby lounge is a cozy spot for afternoon tea.

120 E. Delaware Place (at Michigan Ave.), Chicago, IL 60611. ⓒ **800/332-3442** or 312/280-8800. Fax 312/280-1748. www.fourseasons.com. 343 units. $495–$695 double; $735–$3,700 suite; weekend rates from $385. AE, DC, DISC, MC, V. Valet parking $36 w/in-out privileges; self-parking $30. Subway/El: Red Line to Chicago. Pets accepted. **Amenities:** 2 restaurants (New American, cafe); lounge; indoor pool; fitness center and spa; concierge; business center; 24-hr. room service; babysitting; laundry service; 24-hr. dry cleaning. *In room:* A/C, TV/DVD w/pay movies and video games, free high-speed Internet access, minibar, coffeemaker, hair dryer, iron, safe, CD player.

Park Hyatt Chicago 🟊🟊🟊   For those in search of chic modern luxury, the Park Hyatt is the coolest hotel in town (as long as money is no object). The building occupies one of the most desirable spots on North Michigan Avenue and the best rooms are those that face east, overlooking the bustle of the Mag Mile and the lake in the distance.

Luxury might be the watchword here, but the look is anything but stuffy: The lobby feels like a sleek modern art gallery. German painter Gerhard Richter's *Piazza del Duomo Milan* masterpiece is the visual centerpiece of the space, providing ample evidence of what visual treats lie in store for guests. Rooms feature Eames and Mies van der Rohe reproduction furniture and window banquettes with stunning city views (another plus: the windows actually open). The comfortable beds are well appointed with several plush pillows. While some hotels might provide a TV and VCR, this is the kind of place where you get a DVD player and flatscreen TV. The spalike bathrooms are especially wonderful: Slide back the cherrywood wall for views of the city while you soak in the tub.

NoMI, a restaurant nestled on the seventh floor overlooking Water Tower Square and the Museum of Contemporary Art, serves French-inspired cuisine and features an *Architectural Digest*–worthy interior by New York–based designer Tony Chi. In the summer, you can sample appetizers and sip cocktails while checking out the skyline from an outdoor terrace.

800 N. Michigan Ave., Chicago, IL 60611. ⓒ **800/233-1234** or 312/335-1234. Fax 312/239-4000. www.parkchicago.hyatt.com. 198 units. $385–$525 double; $695–$3,000 suite. AE, DC, DISC, MC, V. Valet parking $42 w/in-out privileges. Subway/El: Red Line to Chicago. **Amenities:** Restaurant (French/American); lounge; indoor pool; health club w/Jacuzzi and spa; concierge; business center w/computer technical support; 24-hr. room service; massage; babysitting; laundry service; 24-hr. dry cleaning. *In room:* A/C, TV/DVD w/pay movies, free high-speed Internet access, minibar, coffeemaker, hair dryer, iron, safe, CD player, iPod connectivity.

The Peninsula Chicago 🟊🟊🟊   Taking design cues from the chain's flagship Hong Kong hotel, The Peninsula Chicago mixes Art Deco sensibility with modern, top-of-the-line amenities. Service is practically a religion; when I visit, every staff member I pass makes a point of greeting me. Although the lobby is impressively grand, rooms are average in size (the "junior suites" are fairly small, with living rooms that can comfortably seat only about four people). But the hotel's in-room technology is cutting edge: A small "command station" by every bed allows guests to control all the lights, the TV, and room temperature without getting out from under the covers. The marble-filled bathrooms have separate shower stalls and tubs, vanities with plenty of room to sit, and another "command station" by the bathtub. Add in the flatscreen TVs, and you have a classic hotel that's very much attuned to the present. The business center features a private office for guests' use.

The sultry hotel bar is one of the city's top spots for romantic assignations (or confidential late-night business negotiations). The hotel's four full-service restaurants include Shanghai Terrace, with cuisine reflecting the Peninsula Group's Asian properties (if you're here in nice weather, snag a table on the outdoor terrace overlooking Michigan Ave., but be prepared to get dizzy when you see the bill). The bright, airy spa and fitness center fill the top two floors and make a lovely retreat (especially the outdoor deck).

108 E. Superior St. (at Michigan Ave.), Chicago, IL 60611. ☎ **866/288-8889** or 312/337-2888. Fax 312/751-2888. http://chicago.peninsula.com. 339 units. $525–$650 double; $795–$7,500 suite. AE, DC, DISC, MC, V. Valet parking $45 w/in-out privileges. Subway/El: Red Line to Chicago. Pets accepted. **Amenities:** 4 restaurants (contemporary, Asian, eclectic, and European bakery); bar; indoor pool w/outdoor deck; fitness center; spa; hot tub; sauna; children's amenities; concierge; business center; 24-hr. room service; in-room massage; babysitting; laundry service; same-day dry cleaning. *In room:* A/C, TV/DVD w/pay movies, fax, free high-speed and Wi-Fi Internet access, minibar, fridge (upon request), coffeemaker, hair dryer, iron, safe.

Ritz-Carlton Chicago ★★★ (Kids) Top-notch service and an open, airy setting make this one of Chicago's most welcoming hotels. Perched high atop the Water Tower Place mall, the Ritz-Carlton's lobby is on the 12th floor, with a large bank of windows to admire the city below. Not surprisingly, the quality of the accommodations is of the highest caliber, although the standard rooms aren't very large. Doubles have space for a loveseat and desk but not much more; the bathrooms are elegant but not huge (for extra-large, lavish bathrooms, request a "Premier" room or suite on the 30th floor). Guests staying in any of the hotel's suites are treated to a gratis wardrobe pressing upon arrival, personalized stationery, and fresh flowers. Service is the Ritz-Carlton's selling point, whether it's the "compcierge" who helps guests with computer problems, or the "allergy-sensitive" rooms that are cleaned with special nonirritating products and come stocked with nonfeather duvets and pillows and hypoallergenic bath products on request. Lake views cost more but are spectacular (although in all the rooms, you're up high enough that you're not staring into surrounding apartment buildings).

Families will find this luxury crash pad quite welcoming. Every child receives a gift and can borrow toys and games from a stash kept by the concierge. PlayStation and Nintendo are also available, and kids' food is available from room service 24 hours a day.

Whether or not you stay here, the Ritz-Carlton is an elegant place for afternoon tea, served at 2:30 and 4:30pm in the lobby. The hotel's excellent Sunday brunch in The Dining Room includes a special buffet for children replete with M&Ms, macaroni and cheese, and pizza.

160 E. Pearson St., Chicago, IL 60611. ☎ **800/621-6906** or 312/266-1000. Fax 312/266-1194. www.fourseasons. com. 435 units. $495–$635 double; $710–$4,000 suite; weekend rates from $385. AE, DC, DISC, MC, V. Valet parking $40 w/in-out privileges; self-parking $32 w/no in-out privileges. Subway/El: Red Line to Chicago. Pets accepted. **Amenities:** 2 restaurants (French, American); 2 lounges; indoor pool; health club w/spa, Jacuzzi, and sauna; children's

programs; concierge; business center; 24-hr. room service; in-room massage; babysitting; laundry service; same-day dry cleaning; premier suites. *In room:* A/C, TV/VCR w/pay movies, high-speed Internet access, minibar, hair dryer, iron, safe, CD player.

EXPENSIVE

The Drake Hotel ✿✿✿   If ever the term "grande dame" fit a hotel, it's The Drake, which opened in 1920. Fronting East Lake Shore Drive, this landmark building is Chicago's version of New York's Plaza or Paris's Ritz. Despite a massive renovation in the 1990s, The Drake feels dated compared to places such as the glitzy Peninsula— but for many, that's part of its charm.

The Drake's public spaces still maintain the regal grandeur of days gone by, but the guest rooms have been modernized with new furniture and linens. Most rooms include a small sitting area with couch and chairs; some have two bathrooms. The lakeview rooms are lovely, and—no surprise—you'll pay more for them. Be forewarned that "city view" rooms on the lower floors look out onto another building, so you'll probably be keeping your drapes shut. Rooms and suites on the Executive Level provide such additional amenities as a generous continental breakfast in a private lounge, free evening hors d'oeuvres, plus a daily newspaper and private concierge assistance.

The hotel's restaurants include Drake Bros., an upscale steakhouse with great views of the lake and Michigan Avenue; the Cape Cod Room (p. 130), an old-timey seafood spot; and the Coq d'Or (p. 275), one of Chicago's most atmospheric piano bars.

140 E. Walton Place (at Michigan Ave.), Chicago, IL 60611. 🕐 **800/55-DRAKE** or 312/787-2200. Fax 312/787-1431. www.thedrakehotel.com. 535 units. $199–$425 double; $279–$495 executive floor; from $545 suite. AE, DC, DISC, MC, V. Valet parking $41 w/in-out privileges. Subway/El: Red Line to Chicago. **Amenities:** 3 restaurants (American, steakhouse, seafood); 2 lounges; fitness center; concierge; business center; shopping arcade (including a Chanel boutique); 24-hr. room service; in-room massage; laundry service; 24-hr. dry cleaning; executive-level rooms. *In room:* A/C, TV w/pay movies, high-speed Internet access, minibar, coffeemaker, hair dryer, iron.

InterContinental Chicago ✿✿   Newer hotels might get all the attention, but the InterContinental remains a sentimental favorite for many Chicagoans. Built as the Medinah Athletic Club in 1929, the building features truly grand details: marble columns, hand-stenciled ceilings, and historic tapestries (for a peek, go in the southern entrance on the corner of Illinois St.). An unfortunate 1960s addition made no attempt to blend with the original building's character, but a complete renovation in 2002 gave the public spaces a more unified, upscale look.

The guest rooms have two distinct identities, depending on location. Rooms in what's called the Main Building (the '60s addition) have an elegant, urban style, with lots of dark wood, deep yellow walls, and red velvet banquettes. The bathrooms feel brand-new but aren't particularly spacious, with small tubs. Rooms in the Historic Tower (the original building) have a more old-world feel: elaborately carved headboards, gold accents, and deep-red-and-cream drapes and bedding. The bathrooms, however, are completely modern; most come with both a tub and separate, large shower stall. (You'll pay about $50 more for rooms in the Historic Tower).

The hotel's restaurant, Zest, is the only street-level restaurant on Michigan Avenue (try to grab a table by the front windows to enjoy the never-ending street scene), and Eno, a cozy corner of the Historic Tower's lobby, is a popular place for wine, cheese, and chocolate. The InterContinental's main claim to fame is its junior Olympic-size pool on the top floor, a beautiful 1920s gem surrounded by elegant mosaics (residents of nearby high-rises buy memberships to the hotel's fitness center just so they can swim here). Architecture buffs can pick up an audio tour of the hotel at the concierge desk; the lavishly decorated meeting rooms and ballrooms (with themes such as Camelot or Renaissance Italy) are definitely worth a peek.

505 N. Michigan Ave. (at Grand Ave.), Chicago, IL 60611. © 800/327-0200 or 312/944-4100. Fax 312/944-1320. http://chicago.intercontinental.com. 790 units. $235–$350 double; from $500 suite. AE, DC, DISC, MC, V. Valet parking $43 w/in-out privileges. Subway/El: Red Line to Grand. **Amenities:** Restaurant (American); 2 lounges; indoor pool; 24-hr. fitness center w/sauna; concierge; 24-hr. business center; 24-hr. room service; massage; babysitting; laundry service; same-day dry cleaning. *In room:* A/C, TV w/pay movies, high-speed and Wi-Fi Internet access, minibar, coffeemaker, hair dryer, iron, safe.

Sofitel Chicago Water Tower 🌟🌟 The Sofitel aims to impress by drawing on the city's tradition of great architecture. French architect Jean-Paul Viguier created a building that's impossible to pass without taking a second look: a soaring, triangular white tower that sparkles in the sun. But the place doesn't take itself too seriously, as you'll see when you walk in the airy lobby and check out the luminescent floor tiles that change color in a never-ending light show. The overall feel of the hotel is European modern; you'll hear French accents from the front-desk staff, and foreign-language magazines are scattered on tables throughout the lobby. The hotel's bright, stylish Café des Architects has become a favorite business lunch spot for locals.

The guest rooms feature contemporary decor with natural beechwood walls and chrome hardware. All the rooms enjoy good views of the city (but the privacy-conscious will want to stay on the upper floors, where they won't be on display to surrounding apartment buildings). The standard doubles are fairly compact—but thanks to large picture windows, the spaces don't feel cramped. The luxurious marble bathrooms are quite spacious. Recognizing that business travelers are the bread and butter of Chicago hotel profits, ample support services exist for working visitors. But this doesn't mean that Sofitel doesn't welcome families; in fact, they'll even roll in a portable bed for kids.

20 E. Chestnut St. (at Wabash St.), Chicago, IL 60611. © 800/SOFITEL or 312/324-4000. Fax 312/324-4026. www.sofitel.com. 415 units. $240–$555 double; $370–$685 suite. AE, DC, DISC, MC, V. Valet parking $40. Subway/El: Red Line to Chicago. Small pets accepted. **Amenities:** Restaurant (French cafe); bar; fitness center; concierge; business center; 24-hr. room service; babysitting; laundry service; same-day dry cleaning. *In room:* A/C, TV w/pay movies, high-speed Internet access, minibar, hair dryer, iron, safe.

Talbott Hotel 🌟🌟 *(Finds* With the feel of an upscale European inn—and service that competes with upscale properties such as the Ritz-Carlton—the Talbott is one of the city's best small, independent hotels. The cozy, wood-lined lobby has the secluded, intimate feel of a private English club, with roaring fireplaces in the winter and leather couches perfect for curling up with a cup of tea. Proprietor Basil Kromelow takes a keen personal interest in the hotel's decor: Most of the gorgeous antiques strewn throughout are purchases from Kromelow's European shopping trips.

The larger-than-average rooms—which were completely renovated in 2006—are decorated in soothing neutral tones, with furniture chosen for its residential feel (such as carved-wood desks), European linens, and plasma TVs. The upscale bathrooms vary in size; some have separate shower stalls and bathtubs and others only tubs, so ask when making your reservation. Suites have separate bedrooms and sitting areas as well as Jacuzzi tubs. Perhaps surprising for a property that feels so traditional, the Talbott is also at the forefront of guest-service technology; the lights turn on automatically when guests enter their rooms, and a high-tech sensor system shows housekeeping when a room is occupied—so no one will barge in to make up your room while you're enjoying a late-morning sleep-in.

20 E. Delaware Place (between Rush and State sts.), Chicago, IL 60611. ℂ 800/TALBOTT or 312/944-4970. Fax 312/944-7241. www.talbotthotel.com. 149 units. $169–$449 standard kings; $260–$671 suites. AE, DC, DISC, MC, V. Valet parking $40 w/in-out privileges; self-parking $30. Subway/El: Red Line to Chicago. **Amenities:** Restaurant (Italian), lounge; complimentary access to nearby health club; concierge; business services; 24-hr. room service; laundry service; dry cleaning. *In room:* A/C, TV, high-speed and Wi-Fi Internet access, minibar, coffeemaker, hair dryer, iron, safe.

W Chicago Lakeshore 🏨🏨   This property prides itself on being a hip boutique hotel—although sophisticated travelers might feel like it's trying way too hard with dance music playing in the lobby and the black-clad staff members doing their best to be eye candy. But if you've had your fill of cookie-cutter chain hotels, the W has a fun, relaxed vibe that appeals to younger travelers. The compact rooms are decorated in deep red, black, and gray—some visitors have told me they find the color scheme gloomy, while others think it's a welcome change from the sterile, neutral decor that fills so many other hotels. Although the Asian-inspired bathrooms are stylish, the wooden shades that separate them from the bedroom don't make for much privacy. In W-speak, rooms and suites are designated "wonderful" (meaning standard, with a city view) or "spectacular" (meaning a lake view, for which you'll pay more). I actually prefer the "wonderful" rooms with their dramatic city views. Although the W boasts of being the only hotel in Chicago with a location on the lake, it is separated from the water by busy Lake Shore Drive, so don't expect to step onto a sandy beach from the lobby. Still, the hotel is within easy reach of the lakefront walking paths and tourist magnet Navy Pier.

In the lobby, you'll find Wave, a stylish "small plates" restaurant and popular bar that rocks into the wee hours on weekends. Whiskey Sky, the hotel's see-and-be-seen spot, designed by Rande Gerber, is on the top floor. If you need to recover the next day, book a massage or facial at the hotel's outpost of New York's popular Bliss Spa.

644 N. Lake Shore Dr. (at Ontario St.), Chicago, IL 60611. ℂ 877/W-HOTELS or 312/943-9200. Fax 312/255-4411. www.whotels.com. 520 units. $219–$429 double; from $399 suite. AE, DC, DISC, MC, V. Valet parking $44 w/in-out privileges. Subway/El: Red Line to Grand. Pets accepted. **Amenities:** Restaurant (Mediterranean); bar; pool; exercise room; spa; concierge; business center; 24-hr. room service; in-room massage; babysitting; same-day laundry service; dry cleaning. *In room:* A/C, TV/VCR/DVD w/pay movies, high-speed and Wi-Fi Internet access, minibar, coffeemaker (on request), hair dryer, iron, safe, CD player.

Whitehall Hotel 🏨🏨   Staying here is like visiting a wealthy, sophisticated aunt's town house: elegant but understated, welcoming but not effusive. Before the Four Seasons and Ritz-Carlton entered the picture, the patrician Whitehall reigned as Chicago's most exclusive luxury hotel, with rock stars and Hollywood royalty dropping by when in town. Although those glory days have passed, the independently owned Whitehall still attracts a devoted clientele who relish its subdued ambience and highly personalized service.

Since this is an older property, the hallways are quite narrow and the bathrooms are small. But the rooms are spacious and bright, with immaculate furniture. Rooms on the north side of the building come with a wonderful straight-on view of the Hancock Building, with Lake Michigan sparkling in the background. "Pinnacle Level" rooms are the same size as standard rooms, but come with extra amenities, including four-poster beds (with luxury linens), irons and ironing boards, and umbrellas; Pinnacle guests also receive complimentary breakfasts.

The hotel's restaurant, Fornetto Mei, offers an eclectic Pan-Italian menu; the covered, heated sun porch attracts outdoor diners year-round. And don't miss the hotel's dimly lit, clubby bar, which hasn't changed since the hotel opened in 1928 (ask the staff to point out Katharine Hepburn's favorite seat).

105 E. Delaware Place (west of Michigan Ave.), Chicago, IL 60611. © **800/948-4255** or 312/944-6300. Fax 312/944-8552. www.thewhitehallhotel.com. 222 units. $199–$379 double; from $700 suite; weekend packages from $199. AE, DC, DISC, MC, V. Valet parking $39 w/in-out privileges. Subway/El: Red Line to Chicago. **Amenities:** Restaurant (Italian); lounge; exercise room (and access to nearby health club for $20/day); concierge; business center (for upper floors); 24-hr. room service; babysitting; laundry service; dry cleaning. *In room:* A/C, TV w/pay movies, dataport, high-speed Internet access, minibar, hair dryer, safe.

MODERATE

Allerton Crowne Plaza ⟨★⟩   A historic hotel that received a fairly bland makeover, the Allerton's main appeal is its central location and relatively reasonable rates. Built in 1924 as a "club hotel," providing permanent residences for single men and women, the Allerton is now one of the flagship hotels of the Crowne Plaza chain. The Italian Renaissance–inspired exterior has been painstakingly restored to its original dark-red brickwork, stone carvings, and limestone base. Too bad the distinctive exterior style wasn't replicated inside. The rooms have a generic chain-hotel feel, and because the hotel was originally built for single men and women, the rooms are fairly small (the "Petite Classic" rooms are—surprise, surprise—tiny). Still, all the rooms and public areas have a warm and homey feel. Snag one overlooking Michigan Avenue to get the best views (or at least stop by the hotel's Renaissance Ballroom for a peek at the Mag Mile).

701 N. Michigan Ave. (at Huron St.), Chicago, IL 60611. © **800/621-8311** outside Illinois or 312/440-1500. Fax 312/440-1819. www.ichotelsgroup.com. 443 units. $109–$299 double; $159–$449 suite. AE, DC, DISC, MC, V. Valet parking $40 w/in-out privileges. Subway/El: Red Line to Chicago. **Amenities:** Restaurant (American); lounge; fitness center (w/excellent city views); concierge; business center; 24-hr. room service; laundry service; same-day dry cleaning. *In room:* A/C, TV w/pay movies, high-speed Internet access, minibar, coffeemaker, hair dryer, iron.

Chicago City Centre Hotel & Sports Club ⟨★★⟩ ⟨*Kids*⟩ ⟨*Value*⟩   The soaring modern atrium lobby is impressive, as is the location east of the Magnificent Mile and close to the Ohio Street Beach and Navy Pier. Although the public spaces have the impersonal feel of a conference center, the rooms are cheerily decorated, and the large windows allow sweeping city views from the upper floors. (I recommend the rooms on the north side of the building, which look toward the Hancock Building.) But it's the amenities that help this hotel stand out, making it one of the best values in the city.

Fitness devotees will delight in the fact that the hotel adjoins the Lakeshore Athletic Club, where guests may enjoy the extensive facilities free of charge (including an indoor pool, fitness classes, and sauna); you don't even have to go outside to get there. The hotel also has its own spacious outdoor pool and sun deck; in the summer you can sit back and enjoy a drink at the outdoor bar, Breezes. (Be forewarned, however, that the hotel fills up during summer vacation; book as far in advance as possible for July–Aug). Rooms on the two Priority Floors include upgraded amenities, a daily newspaper, and feather pillows.

The City Centre is a good bet for the budget-conscious family, as kids 17 and under stay free in their parent's room. Leave the pay-per-view movies one night and head to the massive AMC theaters next door, where all 21 screens offer stadium seating.

300 E. Ohio St. (at Fairbanks Court), Chicago, IL 60611. © **800/HOLIDAY** or 312/787-6100. Fax 312/787-6259. www.chicc.com. 500 units. $109–$270 double. AE, DC, DISC, MC, V. Self-parking $38. Subway/El: Red Line to Grand. **Amenities:** 3 restaurants (American, cafe); bar; outdoor and indoor pools; complimentary access to nearby health club w/whirlpool and sauna; concierge; business center; 24-hr. room service; babysitting; laundry room; dry cleaning;

executive-level rooms. *In room:* A/C, TV w/pay movies and video games, high-speed Internet access, coffeemaker, hair dryer, iron, safe.

Homewood Suites 🅡 *Value* *Kids*   An excellent choice for families, this hotel offers some nice little extras. Because all of the rooms are suites with full kitchens, you can prepare your own meals (a real money saver) and there's plenty of space for everyone to spread out at the end of the day. Housed just off the Mag Mile in a sleek tower above retail shops, offices, and a health club—and adjacent to ESPN Zone—the hotel's decor is described as "Italian Renaissance meets Crate & Barrel." Distressed-leather sofas, Mediterranean stone tile, wrought-iron chandeliers, and beaded lamp-shades adorn its sixth-floor lobby. Rooms—one- and two-bedroom suites and a handful of double-double suites, which can connect to king suites—feature velvet sofas that are all sleepers, and the beds have big, thick mattresses. Each comes with a full kitchen, a dining-room table that doubles as a workspace, and decent-size bathrooms. The hotel provides a complimentary hot breakfast buffet as well as beverages and hors d'oeuvres on weekday evenings; there's also a free grocery-shopping service and free access to an excellent health club next door.

40 E. Grand Ave. (at Wabash Ave.), Chicago, IL 60611. ✆ **800/CALL-HOME** or 312/644-2222. Fax 312/644-7777. www.homewoodsuiteschicago.com. 233 units. $109–$449 2-room suite. AE, DC, DISC, MC, V. Valet parking $35 w/in-out privileges. Subway/El: Red Line to Grand. **Amenities:** Fitness room w/small pool and nice views of the city; business center; laundry machines; dry cleaning. *In room:* A/C, TV w/pay movies, high-speed Internet access, fully equipped kitchen, coffeemaker, hair dryer, iron, safe.

Millennium Knickerbocker Hotel 🅡   Another historic hotel that has undergone a major face-lift, the Knickerbocker looks spiffy from the lobby but still retains a shabby-chic feel on the guest floors. The epitome of Jazz Age indulgence when built in 1927, the hotel was rumored to have shady underworld connections during the Capone era. In the 1970s, Hugh Hefner turned it into the gaudy Playboy Towers and invited the leisure-suit set to a perpetual disco inferno on the hotel's famed illuminated ballroom floor. By the time the 1980s rolled around, the Knickerbocker had been through the ringer. A multimillion-dollar renovation in 2000 brought the hotel back to life, even if its past glamour has long since faded.

Despite the renovation, the Knickerbocker remains a vintage property, with rooms that don't have space for much more than a bed, desk, and chair. (The "business center," for example, is a cramped alcove off the lobby with two computers, where you're charged $5 for 15 minutes of Internet access.) But the beds are soft and comfy, and the bathrooms, tiny though they are, at least look new and clean. The Knickerbocker's real draw is its superb location, a block from the Oak Street Beach and across the street from the more-expensive Drake. ***One caveat:*** Views are often rather dismal, but you can catch a glimpse of the lake in all rooms ending in 14, and corner rooms (ending in 28) look onto Michigan Avenue. Executive-level rooms include separate sitting areas with sofa beds, larger bathrooms, and upgraded bath amenities, including robes and slippers.

163 E. Walton Place (half-block east of Michigan Ave.), Chicago, IL 60611. ✆ **800/621-8140** or 312/751-8100. Fax 312/751-9663. www.millenniumhotels.com. 305 units. $169–$299 double; $285–$1,000 suite. AE, DC, DISC, MC, V. Valet parking $40 w/in-out privileges. Subway/El: Red Line to Chicago. **Amenities:** Restaurant (American); bar; exercise room; concierge; business center; 24-hr. room service; babysitting; laundry service; dry cleaning. *In room:* A/C, TV w/pay movies, high-speed Internet access, minibar, coffeemaker, hair dryer, iron, safe, turndown service.

Tremont Hotel 🅡   The Tremont won't dazzle you with style or amenities, but it fits the bill for anyone looking for a small, European-style hotel. The cozy lobby (complete with fireplace) makes a fine space to hang out and plan your itinerary for the day. The guest rooms aren't too big—there's space for a bed, a desk, and either a sofa or two chairs—but they are bright, with yellow walls and large windows. Ask for a room facing Delaware Street if you crave natural light (rooms in other parts of the hotel look into neighboring buildings). The furniture shows signs of wear, and the bathrooms are fairly basic, but the Tremont will appeal to anyone who likes their hotels homey rather than slick. The steak-and-chops restaurant off the lobby, the memorabilia-filled Mike Ditka's Restaurant (p. 135), is co-owned by the Chicago Bears' legendary former football coach.

100 E. Chestnut St. (1 block west of Michigan Ave.), Chicago, IL 60611. © 800/621-8133 or 312/751-1900. Fax 312/751-8650. www.tremontchicago.com. 130 units. $119–$279 double; $199–$350 suite. AE, DC, DISC, MC, V. Valet parking $40. Subway/El: Red Line to Chicago. **Amenities:** Restaurant (American); small exercise room (and access to nearby health club); concierge; secretarial services; massage; babysitting; dry cleaning; high-speed Internet access in lobby. *In room:* A/C, TV, hair dryer, iron, safe.

INEXPENSIVE

Red Roof Inn ⭐ *(Value)*   This is your best bet for low-price lodgings in downtown Chicago. The location is the main selling point: right off the Magnificent Mile (and within blocks of the Ritz-Carlton and The Peninsula, where rooms will cost you at least three times as much). The guest rooms are stark and small, but the linens and carpeting are clean and relatively new. Ask for a room facing Ontario Street, where at least you'll get western exposure and some natural light (rooms in other parts of the hotel look right into neighboring office buildings). The bathrooms are tiny but spotless. You're not going to find much in the way of style or amenities here—but then you don't stay at a place like this to hang out in the lobby (except, maybe, to sip the free coffee that's available there 24 hrs.).

162 E. Ontario St. (half-block east of Michigan Ave.), Chicago, IL 60611. © 800/733-7663 or 312/787-3580. Fax 312/787-1299. www.redroof-chicago-downtown.com. 195 units. $100–$140 double. AE, DC, DISC, MC, V. Valet parking $33 w/in-out privileges. Subway/El: Red Line to Grand. *In room:* A/C, TV w/pay movies and video games, dataport, hair dryer, iron.

5 River North

EXPENSIVE

Hotel Sax Chicago ⭐⭐   In 2007, a $17-million renovation transformed the former House of Blues Hotel into the new Hotel Sax Chicago, a luxury property with a bohemian boutique feel. While the lobby is certainly grand—with Italian marble floors and *trompe l'oeil* candelabras—the adjoining lounge, Crimson, goes for a Middle-Eastern vibe, with exotic rugs, jewel tone colors, and floor-to-ceiling screens and mirrors. This eclectic sensibility carries over to the guest rooms, which feature wingback chairs covered in snakeskin and side tables constructed entirely of mirrored panels. Despite the eye-catching decor, one of the hotel's biggest selling points remains its location in the entertainment-packed Marina Towers complex. Within steps of the hotel, you've got a bowling alley, a marina with boat rentals, the riverside Smith & Wollensky steakhouse (an outpost of the New York restaurant), the innovative Bin 36 wine bar and restaurant (p. 141), and the House of Blues music hall and restaurant (p. 148; don't miss its gospel brunch on Sun).

333 N. Dearborn St. (at the river), Chicago, IL 60610. © 877/569-3742 or 312/245-0333. Fax 312/923-2444. www.hotelsaxchicago.com. 353 units. $269–$449 double; $629–$849 suite. AE, DC, DISC, MC, V. Valet parking $40 w/in-out privileges. Subway/El: Brown Line to Clark/Lake, or Red Line to Grand. Pets accepted. **Amenities:** Lounge;

access to Crunch fitness center for $15 per day; concierge; business center; 24-hr. room service; babysitting; laundry service; same-day dry cleaning. *In room:* A/C, TV w/pay movies and video games, Wi-Fi, minibar, coffeemaker, hair dryer, iron, safe, multiline telephone.

The James Hotel   One of the city's newest hotels (opened in 2006), The James blurs the line between upscale luxury and stylish boutique, as ever-earnest doormen move comfortably among quirky art installations (such as the pile of used suitcases that was featured recently in the lobby). Because of its close proximity to North Michigan Avenue shopping, River North nightlife, and the Loop theater district, The James attracts even locals to its sleek, secluded J Bar. Guest rooms get a modern treatment, with private dining niches, reproductions of Mies Van der Rohe chairs and Saaranen tables, plasma TVs, and an iPod/mp3-player docking station. If your view is an interior one, don't fret; what looks like a dismal wall during the day becomes a giant screen for a delightfully frantic black and white animated film when the sun goes down. Bathrooms are well appointed with slate and marble accents and thick robes for lounging. A spa and gym offer a full range of treatments, and there's traditional tea service in the lobby, where large windows offer sidewalk views of the River North hustle.

The hotel's restaurant, David Burke's Primehouse, mixes a classic steakhouse feel with modern touches, including stylish red leather tablecloths. The restaurant even has its own bull that lives and breeds in Kentucky.

55 E. Ontario St. (at Rush St.), Chicago, IL 60611. (C) **877/526-3755** or 312/337-1000 www.jameshotels.com. 297 units (including 52 studios). $189–$529 double; $229–$569 studio; $289–$629 loft; $329–$669 apartment; $1,400–$2,000 penthouse loft. AE, DISC, MC, V. Valet parking $42. Subway/El: Red Line to Grand. Pets welcome. **Amenities:** Restaurant (steakhouse); fitness room; concierge; business center; 24-hr. room service; laundry; dry cleaning. *In room:* AC, TV w/pay movies, fax, high-speed Internet access, minibar, coffeemaker, hair dryer, iron, safe, stereo with iPod/mp3-player dock.

Westin Chicago River North 🍴🍴 *(Kids*   Geared to upscale business travelers, the Westin Chicago River North has an understated, modern feel that will appeal to those looking for a quiet retreat. The hotel still retains traces of its previous incarnation as the Japanese-owned Hotel Nikko, with a Zen rock garden at the rear of the lobby and bamboo growing beside one of the lobby's staircases; the lobby's Hana Lounge also offers a sushi menu.

Rooms are handsome, with furniture and artwork that give them a residential look. For the best view, get a room facing south, overlooking the Chicago River. For those who feel like splurging, a suite on the 19th floor more than satisfies, with three enormous rooms, including a huge bathroom and a large window offering a side view of the river.

If you like to sleep in, the Westin chain is known for its "Heavenly Beds," which have soft pillow-top mattresses and piles of pillows (believe me, it's more than just a marketing ploy—the beds are *really* comfortable). Although the Westin River North has the personality of a business hotel, it has made an effort to be family-friendly; especially notable are the many baby and toddler accessories available to guests, from bottle warmers and cribs to night lights and electrical-outlet covers. Older kids can while away the hours with an in-room PlayStation.

320 N. Dearborn St. (on the river), Chicago, IL 60610. (C) **800/WESTIN1** or 312/744-1900. Fax 312/527-2650. www.westinchicago.com. 424 units. $199–$350 double; $400–$2,800 suite. AE, DC, DISC, MC, V. Valet parking $39 w/in-out privileges; self-parking $16. Subway/El: Brown, Orange, or Green line to State/Lake. **Amenities:** Restaurant (contemporary American); lounge; fitness center; concierge; business center; 24-hr. room service; babysitting; laundry service; same-day dry cleaning. *In room:* A/C, TV w/pay movies and video games, fax, high-speed Internet access, minibar, coffeemaker, hair dryer, iron, safe.

MODERATE

Embassy Suites Chicago–Downtown 🐾🐾 *Kids*   Although this hotel does a healthy convention business, its vaguely Floridian ambience—with a gushing waterfall and palm-lined ponds at the bottom of a huge central atrium—makes the place very family-friendly (there's plenty of room for the kids to run around). The guest rooms (all suites) have a generic chain-hotel feel but are spacious enough for both parents and kids, with two rooms, consisting of a living room with a sleeper sofa, a round table, and four chairs; and a bedroom with either a king-size bed or two double beds; there's also a minifridge and microwave. Guests staying on the VIP floor get nightly turndown service and in-room fax machines and robes. At one end of the atrium, the hotel serves a complimentary cooked-to-order breakfast in the morning and, in the other end, supplies complimentary cocktails and snacks in the evening.

Off the lobby is an excellent restaurant, Osteria Via Stato (p. 144), and next door is a Starbucks outlet with outdoor seating.

600 N. State St. (at West Ohio St.), Chicago, IL 60610. ℂ **800/EMBASSY** or 312/943-3800. Fax 312/943-7629. www. embassysuiteschicago.com. 366 units. $139–$279 king suite; $169–$319 double suite. AE, DC, DISC, MC, V. Valet parking $38 w/in-out privileges. Subway/El: Red Line to Grand. **Amenities:** Restaurant (Italian); coffee bar; indoor pool; exercise room w/whirlpool; concierge; business center; limited room service; babysitting; laundry machines; dry cleaning. *In room:* A/C, TV w/pay movies and video games, high-speed Internet access, kitchenette, coffeemaker, hair dryer, iron.

INEXPENSIVE

Best Western River North Hotel *Value* *Kids*   This former motor lodge isn't going to win any design prizes, but it's got some of the most affordable rates to be found in this busy neighborhood, within easy walking distance of Chicago's art-gallery district and numerous restaurants. Rooms are spacious if rather generic (with comfortable bedding and down pillows); the bathrooms, though no-frills, are spotless. One-room suites have a separate sitting area, while other suites have a separate bedroom; all suites come with a sleeper sofa (the Family Suite has two separate bedrooms and two bathrooms). A big selling point for families is the indoor pool, with an adjoining outdoor roof deck (a smallish fitness room looks out onto the pool, for parents who want to work out while the kids splash around). The almost unheard-of free parking in the hotel's parking lot can add up to significant savings for anyone who drives here for a visit. There's a 2-night minimum for weekend stays May through October.

125 W. Ohio St. (at LaSalle St.), Chicago, IL 60610. ℂ **800/528-1234** or 312/467-0800. Fax 312/467-1665. www.rivernorthhotel.com. 150 units. $159–$199 double; $225–$295 suite. AE, DC, DISC, MC, V. Free parking for guests (1 car per room) w/in-out privileges. Subway/El: Red Line to Grand. **Amenities:** Restaurant (pizzeria); lounge; indoor pool; exercise room; room service; laundry service; same-day dry cleaning. *In room:* A/C, TV w/pay movies and video games, high-speed and Wi-Fi Internet access, coffeemaker, hair dryer, iron, safe.

Hampton Inn & Suites Chicago Downtown 🐾 *Value* *Kids*   This family-friendly hotel manages to appeal to both adults and kids—the Prairie-style lobby and breakfast lounge give the place a tranquil feel, while the indoor pool and free hot breakfast are a plus for families. Built in 1998, the hotel still feels brand-new; the rooms have an urban look, with dark wood furniture and plush duvets. You can book a standard room, which includes a desk, armchair, and ottoman; a studio, which has a microwave, sink, and minifridge along one wall; or a suite, which includes a kitchenette, separate bedroom, and VCR. Request a room overlooking Illinois or Dearborn streets if you crave natural light. Nice, user-friendly touches include a nightlight in the bathroom and clock radios with guides to local radio stations. An Italian restaurant is located off the lobby, and a second-floor skywalk connects to Ruth's Chris Steak House next door. The complimentary continental breakfast with two hot items per day, served in an attractive second-floor lounge, can save families money on food; you won't need much lunch if you fill up here each morning.

33 W. Illinois St. (at Dearborn St.), Chicago, IL 60610. ℂ 800/HAMPTON or 312/832-0330. Fax 312/832-0333. www. hamptoninn.com. 230 units. $159–$299 double; $199–$309 suite. Children 17 and under stay free in parent's room. AE, DC, DISC, MC, V. Valet parking $38 w/in-out privileges. Subway/El: Red Line to Grand. **Amenities:** Restaurant (Italian); indoor pool w/Jacuzzi and sun deck; exercise room w/sauna; business center; room service; laundry and dry-cleaning service. *In room:* A/C, TV w/pay movies and video games, high-speed Internet access, coffeemaker, hair dryer, iron, safe.

6 The Gold Coast

EXPENSIVE

Ambassador East ★★ *(Kids)*   The glory days of the Ambassador East, when stars including Frank Sinatra, Humphrey Bogart, and Liza Minnelli shacked up here during layovers or touring stops in Chicago, are ancient history. Though today's celebs tend to ensconce themselves at the Ritz-Carlton or Four Seasons these days, the Ambassador name still evokes images of glamour in these parts.

Although it's now more low profile than in the past, the Ambassador still retains a sense of elegance, from the large floral arrangements in the lobby to the mahogany four-poster beds in the king-size rooms. Executive suites have separate sitting areas; celebrity suites (named for the stars who've crashed in them) come with a separate bedroom, two bathrooms, a small kitchen, and a dining room. Most extravagant is the Presidential Suite, which boasts a canopied terrace, marble fireplace, oval dining room, and full-size refrigerator. One nod to modern times are the "Get Fit" rooms, which come with treadmills and a minibar stocked with healthy snacks.

The hotel's ritzy Pump Room restaurant (p. 132), like the hotel itself, no longer attracts big names, but it remains an elegant spot for drinks and dinner.

1301 N. State Pkwy. (1 block north of Division St.), Chicago, IL 60610. ℂ 888/506-3471 or 312/787-7200. Fax 312/ 787-4760. www.theambassadoreasthotel.com. 285 units. $189–$299 double; from $400 suite. AE, DC, DISC, MC, V. Valet parking $34 w/in-out privileges. Subway/El: Red Line to Clark/Division. **Amenities:** Restaurant (contemporary American); small fitness room; concierge; business center; 24-hr. room service; babysitting; 24-hr. laundry service; dry cleaning. *In room:* A/C, TV w/pay movies, high-speed Internet access, minibar, coffeemaker, hair dryer, iron, safe.

MODERATE

Flemish House of Chicago ★★ *(Finds)*   Want to pretend you live in a grand historic mansion? Book a room at this B&B, tucked away on one of the Gold Coast's most picturesque (and expensive) streets. The entire building—including the Flemish Revival facade that inspired its name—was renovated in the late 1990s by innkeepers Tom Warnke (an architect) and Mike Maczka (a real-estate appraiser). Their architecture experience is evident in the rooms' tasteful decor: a mix of Victorian and Arts and Crafts furniture and decorative details that respect the home's late-19th-century design—along with all the necessary modern amenities. The rooms are a mix of spacious studios and one-bedroom suites; all have full kitchen facilities, including stoves, fridges, and microwaves. This isn't the kind of B&B that promotes socializing; there are no common rooms, and breakfast is strictly self-serve (all the fixings are stocked in the fridge). But for independent travelers looking for a quiet, personal getaway, the location and setting are truly unique.

68 E. Cedar St. (at Lake Shore Dr.), Chicago, IL 60611. (🕿 312/664-9981. Fax 312/664-0387. www.innchicago.com. 7 units. $145–$225 double. AE, MC, V. Valet parking in nearby lot $25/day. Subway/El: Red Line to Clark/Division. *In room:* A/C, TV/VCR/DVD, Wi-Fi, full kitchen.

Hotel Indigo (🕿   An accessible version of the boutique hotel concept, the Indigo is perfect for anyone looking for a cool (but not too edgy) alternative to the cookie-cutter business hotel. The bright, beachy decor makes the place feel more like a tropical resort than an urban hotel; the small lobby has oversize Adirondack chairs and walls painted in shades of blue, peach, and green, while pineapple-shaped chairs line the bar.

But it's the guest rooms that really make an impact. Rather than the dark wood furniture and generic carpeting found in so many chain hotels, rooms here are light and bright with blonde hardwood floors and white wood furniture. Walls have splashes of bright color and giant photomurals of seashells, fruit, and other "relaxing" images. Because this is a conversion of an older property, room sizes vary. The king rooms on the north side of the building tend to be larger (with separate entry halls and sitting areas), but they also look out on neighboring buildings (and, in some cases, the fire escape). If you don't need a lot of room to spread out, the queen rooms (on the south side of the building) are small but have lovely views of downtown and plenty of natural light. Bathrooms have glass-walled shower stalls (no tubs) and spa-style showerheads; they're fairly small, but have lots of storage space (multiple wall hooks and a granite storage ledge above the sink). There are also three suites, which have separate sitting rooms and working fireplaces.

Hotel Indigo won't overwhelm you with facilities; the hotel's restaurant and bar are both quite small, but there's a decent-size fitness room and—very unusual in a hotel of this size—a salon/spa with separate facial and massage treatment rooms. Though the hotel is tucked on a residential street, it's close to restaurants and shopping, and within walking distance of Michigan Avenue, Division Street, Old Town's nightlife, and Lincoln Park's many attractions. The surrounding neighborhood of elegant town houses makes a great place for a stroll—without the traffic and noise of other downtown neighborhoods.

1244 N. Dearborn St. (1 block north of Division St.), Chicago, IL 60610. (🕿 **866/2-INDIGO** or 312/787-4980. Fax 312/787-4069. www.goldcoastchicagohotel.com. 165 units. $169–$269 double. AE, DC, DISC, MC, V. Valet parking $35 w/in-out privileges. Subway/El: Red Line to Clark/Division. Pets accepted. **Amenities:** Restaurant (American); lounge; exercise room; spa services; concierge; business center; room service; same-day dry cleaning. *In room:* A/C, TV w/pay movies and video games, high-speed and Wi-Fi Internet access, coffeemaker, hair dryer, iron, safe.

7 Lincoln Park & the North Side

MODERATE

Windy City Urban Inn (🕿🕿 *(Finds*   This grand 1886 home is located on a tranquil side street just blocks from busy Clark Street and Lincoln Avenue—both chock-full of shops, restaurants, and bars. While the inn is charming enough, the true selling point is its hosts, Andy and Mary Shaw. He's a well-known local television reporter, while she has more than 20 years of experience in the Chicago bed-and-breakfast business. Together, they are excellent resources for anyone who wants to get beyond the usual tourist sites. Plus, their subtle touches give guests a distinctive Chicago experience: Blues and jazz play during the buffet breakfast, and local food favorites offered to guests include the famous cinnamon buns from Ann Sather's restaurant, and beer from Goose Island Brewery.

The more-open-than-typical remodeled Victorian home has five rooms in the main house and three apartment suites in a coach house; all are named after Chicago writers. Lovebirds should request the Nelson Algren and Simone De Beauvoir Suite, which has a large bathroom with a Jacuzzi tub and a view of the Sears Tower. Two of the coach-house apartments can sleep four: two in an upstairs bedroom and two on a bed that folds up against the wall (custom-made for the Shaws, these feature top-quality mattresses, making them much more comfortable than the Murphy beds of old). In good weather, guests are invited to eat breakfast on the back porch or in the garden between the main house and the coach house.

607 W. Deming Place, Chicago, IL 60614. © 877/897-7091 or 773/248-7091. Fax 773/529-4183. www.windycity inn.com. 8 units. $125–$255 double; $175–$325 coach-house apts. Rates include buffet breakfast. AE, DISC, MC, V. Parking $6 in nearby lot w/in-out privileges. Subway/El: Red Line to Fullerton. **Amenities:** Laundry machines. *In room:* A/C, TV, Wi-Fi, kitchenettes, coffeemaker, hair dryer and iron available for guest use upon request.

INEXPENSIVE

Best Western Hawthorne Terrace ⚑ *Value*   If you're looking for a neighborhood inn away from the tourist hordes, this independently-owned spot fits the bill. Located in Lakeview—within walking distance of Wrigley Field, Lake Michigan, and the Lincoln Park walking and bike paths—the hotel is set back from busy Broadway Avenue, thanks to a charmingly landscaped terrace (a good spot to enjoy your complimentary continental breakfast when the weather's nice). Inside, the relatively large rooms—decorated in standard motel decor—won't win extra style points, but most are bright and cheery, with spotless bathrooms (another plus: many rooms have two windows, a bonus if you crave natural light). The spacious "Whirlpool King" rooms come with whirlpool bathtubs, DVD players, pay-per-view movies, and great views out onto the street. Junior suites include a separate sitting area and come with a sleeper sofa. The ground-level exercise room is especially welcoming, with large windows to let light in and a glass-enclosed hot tub. The hotel's extremely varied clientele—from business travelers in search of a homey environment, to diehard baseball fans, to gay travelers in town for the annual Gay Pride Parade—is part of its charm.

3434 N. Broadway Ave. (at Hawthorne Place), Chicago, IL 60657. © 888/401-8781 or 773/244-3434. Fax 773/244-3435. www.hawthorneterrace.com. 59 units. $149–$229 double and suites. Rates include continental breakfast. AE, DC, DISC, MC, V. Valet parking $20 w/in-out privileges. Subway/El: Red Line to Addison. **Amenities:** Exercise room w/hot tub and sauna; business services; concierge; same-day dry cleaning. *In room:* A/C, TV w/pay movies, free Wi-Fi, fridge, microwave, coffeemaker, hair dryer, iron.

City Suites Hotel ⚑ *Value*   A few doors down from the El stop on Belmont Avenue, this former transient dive has been transformed into a charming small hotel. Most rooms are suites, with separate sitting rooms and bedrooms, all furnished with first-rate pieces and decorated in a homey and comfortable style. The overall feel is that of a bed-and-breakfast, with added amenities such as plush robes and complimentary continental breakfast. A bonus—or drawback, depending on your point of view—is the hotel's neighborhood setting. Most rooms can be fairly noisy; those facing north overlook Belmont Avenue, where the nightlife continues into the early morning hours, and those facing west look right out over the rumbling El tracks. On your way in and out of the hotel, you'll be able to mingle with plenty of locals, everybody from young professional families to gay couples to punks in full regalia. Blues bars, nightclubs, and restaurants abound in the area, making the City Suites a find for the bargain-minded and adventurous. Suites have both fridges and microwaves on request.

Room service is available from Ann Sather, a Swedish diner and neighborhood institution (p. 163).

933 W. Belmont Ave. (at Sheffield Ave.), Chicago, IL 60657. © 800/248-9108 or 773/404-3400. Fax 773/404-3405. www.cityinns.com. 45 units. $149–$249 double; $199–$409 suite. Rates include continental breakfast. AE, DC, DISC, MC, V. Parking $22 in nearby lot w/in-out privileges. Subway/El: Red Line to Belmont. **Amenities:** Free access to Bally's health club 5 blocks away; concierge; limited room service; laundry service; same-day dry cleaning. *In room:* A/C, TV, free Wi-Fi, hair dryer, iron.

Majestic Hotel *⭐⭐ (Finds*   Owned by the same group as the City Suites Hotel (above), the Majestic blends seamlessly into its residential neighborhood. Located on a charming tree-lined street—but convenient to the many restaurants and shops of Lincoln Park—this is a good choice for anyone who wants a quiet retreat rather than a see-and-be-seen spot. Guests receive a complimentary continental breakfast, 24-hour coffee and tea service, and afternoon cookies in the lobby. Some of the larger suites—the most appealing are those with sun porches—offer butler's pantries with a fridge, microwave, and wet bar. Most of the other rooms are fairly dark (since you're surrounded by apartment buildings on almost all sides), and you should avoid the claustrophobic single rooms with alley views. Ideally suited for enjoying the North Side, the Majestic is only a short walk from both Wrigley Field and the lake.

528 W. Brompton St. (at Lake Shore Dr.), Chicago, IL 60657. © 800/727-5108 or 773/404-3499. Fax 773/404-3495. www.cityinns.com. 52 units. $99–$179 double; $129–$219 suite. Rates include continental breakfast. AE, DC, DISC, MC, V. Self-parking $22 in nearby garage w/no in-out privileges. Subway/El: Red Line to Addison; walk several blocks east to Lake Shore Dr. and then 1 block south. **Amenities:** Free passes to nearby Bally's health club; secretarial services; limited room service; laundry service; same-day dry cleaning. *In room:* A/C, TV w/pay movies, dataport, free Wi-Fi, minibar, hair dryer, iron.

8 Near McCormick Place

MODERATE

Hyatt Regency McCormick Place *⭐*   The Hyatt Regency rises 33 stories from Chicago's ever-sprawling convention center. While the hotel is often solidly booked during trade shows and meetings, it has rooms to spare during convention lulls in the winter and late summer, so vacationers might find bargains if they're willing to sacrifice the convenience of staying downtown. (A recent promotion offered free breakfast for families of up to four people on weekends.) Although the hotel is only minutes from the Museum Campus, the lakefront, and the Loop, getting around is a little tricky without a car or a cab (though cabs are plentiful at the hotel), and the hotel does offer a complimentary shuttle to downtown shopping areas, the main museums, and Navy Pier. The average-size rooms have contemporary furnishings, including blue-green checkerboard-patterned comforters. Bathrooms are small, with the sink and vanity outside the bathroom. Business-plan rooms ($20 extra) include a workstation with a fax/copier/printer and complimentary continental breakfast. Most north-facing rooms feature scenic views of the city skyline and lakefront.

2233 S. Martin Luther King Dr. (at 22nd St.), Chicago, IL 60616. © 800/233-1234 or 312/567-1234. Fax 312/528-4000. www.hyattregencymccormickplace.com. 800 units. $149–$449 double; $650–$2,500 suites; weekend rates from $99. AE, DC, DISC, MC, V. Valet parking $29 w/in-out privileges; self-parking $24. Bus: 3 or 4. **Amenities:** Restaurant (American); bar; indoor lap pool; exercise room; sauna; concierge; business center; 24-hr. room service; laundry service; same-day dry cleaning. *In room:* A/C, TV w/pay movies, high-speed Internet access, hair dryer, iron.

7

Where to Dine

Joke all you want about bratwurst and deep-dish pizza; Chicago is a genuine culinary hot spot. One of the city's most creative dining spots, Alinea, was even named the top restaurant in the United States by *Gourmet* magazine in 2007 (take that, New York and San Francisco!). The city's top chefs consistently win national awards and make appearances on the Food Network, while we locals try to keep up with all the new restaurant openings.

What makes eating out in Chicago fun is the variety. We've got it all: stylish see-and-be-seen spots, an amazing array of steakhouses, chef-owned temples to fine dining, and every kind of ethnic cuisine you could possibly crave. Plus—yes—some not-to-be-missed deep-dish pizza places.

It's not easy to narrow down the list of impressive restaurants in this city. The competition among high-end establishments is especially intense. A few well-regarded chefs—Jean Joho at Everest, Arun Sampanthavivat at Arun's, Charlie Trotter at his namesake place—still reign supreme, but relatively new spots, including Alinea, Moto, and Tru, have upped the stakes (and the average check price) considerably.

But if a budget-busting, one-of-a-kind meal isn't your style, there's also been a recent resurgence in comfort food. From the wine bar Avec (which has attracted a loyal following of local foodies) to River North's Osteria Via Stato to Bucktown's homey Hot Chocolate, some of the most popular new spots attract diners by focusing on simple, straightforward preparations and a low-key, welcoming ambience.

Chicago's many ethnic restaurants—in all price ranges—are highlights of the city's dining scene. Funky fusion concepts include the Japan-meets–South America theme at SushiSamba Rio and the Indian/Latin American combos at Vermilion. You'll find upscale versions of ethnic cuisine at places such as Frontera Grill (Mexican), Arun's (Thai), and Spiaggia (which might be the country's most elegant Italian restaurant). But affordable (and attitude-free) restaurants still thrive in the city's original immigrant neighborhoods—Greektown, Little Italy, and Chinatown. For more on ethnic food, see the "Ethnic Dining near the Loop" box on p. 126.

Unfortunately, Chicago is no longer the budget-dining destination it once was. (Hipness doesn't come cheap.) But just because prices have risen doesn't mean that attitudes have. Restaurants in Chicago might have become trendy, but they're still friendly.

I've divided restaurants in this chapter into four price categories: "Very Expensive" means that most entrees cost $25 to $30 (and sometimes more); "Expensive" indicates that most entrees run from $18 to $25; "Moderate" means that most entrees are $20 or less; and at an "Inexpensive" place, they cost $15 or less.

Whether you're looking for a restaurant to impress a business colleague or simply a no-frills spot to dig in, these are the places the locals go when they want to eat well. To find out more about restaurants that have opened since this book went to press, check out the *Chicago Tribune*'s entertainment website (**www.metromix.com**), the websites for the monthly magazine *Chicago* (**www.chicagomag.com**) and the weekly *Time Out Chicago* (**www.timeout chicago.com**), and the entertainment/ nightlife website **http://chicago.city search.com**.

Note to smokers: The Chicago City Council has banned smoking in all restaurants; those with a separate bar area can choose to allow smoking there, but only if they have installed an air filtration system. If you want to light up when you go out, call first to see if smoking is permitted.

1 The Best Dining Bets

- **Best View:** Forty stories above Chicago, **Everest,** 440 S. LaSalle St. (© **312/663-8920**), astounds with a spectacular view—and food to match. Closer to earth, diners on the patio at Greektown's **Athena,** 212 S. Halsted St., between Adams and Jackson sts. (© **312/655-0000**), get a panoramic view of the city skyline. See p. #116 and 127, respectively.

- **Best Spot for a Romantic Dinner:** Secluded **North Pond,** 2610 N. Cannon Dr. (© **773/477-5845**), is an Arts and Crafts–style retreat with a postcard-perfect setting in Lincoln Park. Not only does it boast a dramatic vista of the Gold Coast skyline, but the restaurant's out-of-the-way locale also requires diners to begin and end their meals with an idyllic stroll through the park. For charm at a much more affordable price, try **Cyrano's Bistrot & Wine Bar,** 526 N. Wells St. (© **312/467-0546**), a cozy spot with warm, personal service and an eclectic Parisian bistro decor that will make you feel like you've jetted off to the romantic City of Love. See p. 157 and 146, respectively.

- **Best Spot for a Business Lunch:** A millennial take on the classic American steakhouse, stylish **Nine,** 440 W. Randolph St. (© **312/575-9900**), offers superslick environs, prime steaks, fresh seafood, a champagne-and-caviar bar, and—most importantly—tiny TV sets above the men's-room urinals for those who can't bear to miss the latest from CNBC. See p. 117.

- **Best Spot for a Celebration:** Not only does **Nacional 27,** 325 W. Huron St. (© **312/664-2727**), offer a grand setting and a menu of creative Latin American dishes, it also turns into a party on Friday and Saturday nights, when a DJ spins salsa tunes and center tables are cleared for dancing. See p. 144.

- **Best Value:** At longtime city favorite **Carson's,** 612 N. Wells St. (© **312/280-9200**), $20 gets you a full slab of incredible baby back ribs accompanied by a bowl of Carson's almost-as-famous coleslaw and a choice of potatoes. Lincoln Park residents swarm to **RoseAngelis,** 1314 W. Wrightwood Ave. (© **773/296-0081**), where you can get a glass of wine, a generous serving of pasta, and a slice of the city's best bread pudding for around $20. See p. 146 and 161, respectively.

- **Best for Kids:** Visiting families often limit themselves to the many chain restaurants in the River North neighborhood (Rainforest Cafe, Hard Rock Cafe, and the like), but for something different, try **Wishbone,** 1001 Washington St. (© **312/850-2663**), a family-owned spot specializing in Southern food with a casual vibe and plenty of mix-and-match menu options for fussy eaters. See p. 129.

- **Best American Cuisine:** It's no longer the see-and-be-seen spot it was when it first opened, but **mk,** 868 N. Franklin St. (© **312/482-9179**), is actually better now that the crowds have moved on, serving up accessible twists on classic American dishes in a space that is both comfortable and sophisticated. **Crofton on Wells,** 535 N. Wells St. (© **312/755-1790**), is a true labor of love for Chef Suzy

Crofton—and her devoted local fans keep coming back for more. See p. 140 and 142, respectively.

- **Best French Cuisine:** For a Parisian bistro experience, few places delight quite like Bucktown's charming **Le Bouchon,** 1958 N. Damen Ave. (© **773/862-6600**). Convivial **Mon Ami Gabi,** 2300 N. Lincoln Park West (© **773/348-8886**), re-creates the look and feel of a Parisian cafe, just steps from Lincoln Park Zoo. See p. 168 and 158, respectively.

- **Best Italian Cuisine:** Even without the glamorous view of the Magnificent Mile, **Spiaggia,** 980 N. Michigan Ave. (© **312/280-2750**), would draw diners in droves with its gourmet takes on classic Italian cuisine. For a more casual, old-world experience, it's hard to beat **Rosebud on Taylor,** 1500 W. Taylor St. (© **312/942-1117**), which has reigned supreme in Chicago's Little Italy neighborhood for as long as anyone can remember. See p. 132 and 126, respectively.

- **Best Steakhouse:** Legendary Chicago restaurateur Arnie Morton no longer prowls the dining room, but **Morton's,** 1050 N. State St. (© **312/266-4820**), remains the king of the city's old-guard steakhouses, serving up gargantuan wet-aged steaks and baked potatoes. See p. 130.

- **Best Pizza:** In the town where deep-dish pies were born, Chicagoans take their out-of-town relatives to either **Gino's East,** 633 N. Wells St. (© **312/943-1124**), or **Lou Malnati's,** 439 N. Wells St. (© **312/828-9800**), to taste the real thing: mouthwatering slabs of pizza loaded with fresh ingredients atop delectably sweet crusts. See p. 147 and 138, respectively.

- **Best Pretheater Dinner:** A longtime local favorite, **The Italian Village,** 71 W. Monroe St. (© **312/332-7005**)—three restaurants run by one family under one roof—knows how to get its clientele seated and (well) fed in time for a show. For Chicago Symphony Orchestra audiences, **Rhapsody,** 65 E. Adams St. (© **312/786-9911**), is conveniently located in the Symphony Center building. If you're seeing a play in Lincoln Park, go for tasty tapas at **Café Ba-Ba-Reeba!,** 2024 N. Halsted St. (© **773/935-5000**). See p. 120, 119, and 159, respectively.

- **Best Wine List:** Two spots take their food and drink pairings especially seriously: Try **Zealous,** 419 W. Superior St. (© **312/475-9112**), if money is no object, and **Bin 36,** 339 N. Dearborn St. (© **312/755-9463**), if you're looking for a more casual vibe. See p. 141 and 141, respectively.

- **Best Brunch:** The luxury hotels along Michigan Avenue offer all-you-can-eat gourmet spreads, but the locals prefer the sinfully rich cinnamon rolls at **Ann Sather,** 929 W. Belmont Ave. (© **773/348-2378**). See p. 163.

2 Restaurants by Cuisine

ALSATIAN
Brasserie Jo ★ (River North, $$$, p. 142)
Everest ★★★ (the Loop, $$$$, p. 116)

AMERICAN
Ann Sather ★★ (Wrigleyville/North Side, $, p. 163)

Atwood Café ★★ (the Loop, $$$, p. 116)
Bin 36 ★★ (River North, $$$, p. 141)
Blackbird ★★ (West Loop, $$$$, p. 122)
Boka ★ (Lincoln Park, $$$, p. 157)
Bongo Room (Wicker Park/ Bucktown, $, p. 149)

Key to Abbreviations: $$$$ = Very Expensive $$$ = Expensive $$ = Moderate $ = Inexpensive

Carson's ★ (River North, $$, p. 146)

Charlie's Ale House (Lincoln Park, $, p. 151)

Charlie's Ale House at Navy Pier (Magnificent Mile/Gold Coast, $, p. 150)

Crofton on Wells ★★ (River North, $$$, p. 142)

Custom House ★★ (the Loop, $$$$, p. 114)

Dave & Buster's (Magnificent Mile/ Gold Coast, $, p. 123)

ESPN Zone (Magnificent Mile/Gold Coast, $, p. 123)

Goose Island Brewing Company (Lincoln Park, $, p. 159)

Harry Caray's (River North, $$, p. 147)

Hot Chocolate ★ (Wicker Park/ Bucktown, $, p. 168)

Hot Doug's (Wrigleyville, $, p. 139)

Lou Mitchell's (the Loop, $, p. 148)

Meritage Café and Wine Bar ★★ (Wicker Park/Bucktown, $$$, p. 164)

Mike Ditka's Restaurant ★ (Magnificent Mile/Gold Coast, $$$, p. 135)

mk ★★★ (River North, $$$$, p. 140)

Moody's (Wrigleyville, $, p. 151)

Mr. Beef ★ (River North, $, p. 153)

Naha ★★ (River North, $$$$, p. 140)

Nine ★★ (the Loop, $$$, p. 117)

North Pond ★★★ (Lincoln Park, $$$$, p. 157)

Northside Café (Wicker Park/ Bucktown, $, p. 168)

Oak Street Beachstro (Magnificent Mile/Gold Coast, $$, p. 150)

Oak Tree ★ (Magnificent Mile/ Gold Coast, $, p. 137)

O'Brien's Restaurant (Lincoln Park, $, p. 151)

Orange (Lincoln Park, $, p. 149)

Park Grill ★★ (the Loop, $$$, p. 118)

Petterino's ★★ (the Loop, $$$, p. 118)

Piece ★ (Wicker Park/Bucktown, $, p. 169)

Pump Room (Magnificent Mile/ Gold Coast, $$$$, p. 132)

Rainforest Cafe (River North, $$, p. 123)

Rhapsody ★★ (the Loop, $$$, p. 119)

Rockit Bar & Grill ★ (River North, $$, p. 148)

Silver Cloud ★★ (Wicker Park/ Bucktown, $, p. 169)

South Water Kitchen ★ (the Loop, $$$, p. 119)

Spring ★★★ (Wicker Park/ Bucktown, $$$, p. 166)

Superdawg Drive-In (Northwest Side, $, p. 139)

312 Chicago ★ (the Loop, $$, p. 120)

Toast (Lincoln Park, $, p. 123)

Tru ★★★ (Magnificent Mile/Gold Coast, $$$$, p. 133)

Zealous ★★★ (River North, $$$$, p. 141)

ASIAN

Kevin ★★ (River North, $$$$, p. 139)

Opera ★★ (the Loop, $$$, p. 118)

Penny's Noodle Shop ★ (Wrigleyville/North Side, $, p. 163)

Red Light ★ (West Loop, $$$, p. 125)

Vong's Thai Kitchen–VTK ★ (River North, $$, p. 152)

BARBECUE

Carson's ★ (River North, $$, p. 146)

Twin Anchors ★ (Lincoln Park, $$, p. 159)

BISTRO

Bistrot Margot ★★ (Lincoln Park, $$, p. 158)

Cyrano's Bistrot & Wine Bar ★ (River North, $$, p. 146)

La Sardine ★ (West Loop, $$, p. 128)

Le Bouchon ★★ (Wicker Park/ Bucktown, $$, p. 168)

Marché ★ (West Loop, $$$, p. 125)

Mon Ami Gabi ★ (Lincoln Park, $$$, p. 158)

Yoshi's Café (Wrigleyville/North Side, $$$, p. 162)

BREAKFAST & BRUNCH

Ann Sather ✹✹ (Wrigleyville/North Side, $, p. 163)

Billy Goat Tavern ✹ (Magnificent Mile/Gold Coast, $, p. 136)

Bongo Room (Wicker Park/Bucktown, $, p. 149)

The Café, Four Seasons Hotel (Magnificent Mile/Gold Coast, $$$, p. 148)

Drake Bros. Restaurant, The Drake Hotel (Magnificent Mile/Gold Coast, $$, p. 148)

Heaven on Seven ✹✹ (the Loop, $, p. 121)

House of Blues (River North, $$, p. 273)

Lou Mitchell's (the Loop, $, p. 148)

Nookies (Lincoln Park, $, p. 148)

Orange (Lincoln Park, $, p. 149)

Room 12 (the Loop, $$, p. 149)

Toast (Lincoln Park, $, p. 123)

Wishbone ✹✹ (West Loop, $, p. 129)

BURGERS

Billy Goat Tavern ✹ (Magnificent Mile/Gold Coast, $, p. 136)

Northside Café (Wicker Park/Bucktown, $, p. 168)

CAJUN & CREOLE

Heaven on Seven ✹✹ (the Loop, $, p. 121)

House of Blues (River North, $$, p. 273)

Wishbone ✹✹ (West Loop, $, p. 108)

CALIFORNIAN

Puck's at the MCA (Magnificent Mile/Gold Coast, $, p. 150)

CHINESE

Phoenix (Chinatown, $$, p. 126)

Saint's Alp Teahouse (Chinatown, $, p. 126)

Won Kow (Chinatown, $, p. 126)

CONTINENTAL

Bistro 110 (Magnificent Mile/Gold Coast, $$$, p. 134)

DINER

Ed Debevic's (River North, $, p. 123)

Heaven on Seven ✹✹ (the Loop, $, p. 121)

Lou Mitchell's (the Loop, $, p. 148)

Nookies (Lincoln Park, $, p. 148)

ECLECTIC

Alinea ✹✹✹ (Lincoln Park, $$$$, p. 153)

Charlie Trotter's ✹✹✹ (Lincoln Park, $$$$, p. 156)

foodlife ✹✹ (Magnificent Mile/Gold Coast, $, p. 137)

Green Zebra ✹ (River North, $$$, p. 144)

Jane's ✹ (Wicker Park/Bucktown, $$, p. 167)

Moto ✹✹✹ (West Loop, $$$$, p. 124)

Yoshi's Café (Wrigleyville/North Side, $$$, p. 162)

FONDUE

Geja's Cafe ✹ (Lincoln Park, $$$$, p. 156)

FRENCH

Bistrot Margot ✹✹ (Lincoln Park, $$, p. 158)

Brasserie Jo ✹ (River North, $$$, p. 142)

Cyrano's Bistrot & Wine Bar ✹ (River North, $$, p. 146)

Everest ✹✹✹ (the Loop, $$$$, p. 116)

La Creperie ✹✹ (Lincoln Park, $, p. 160)

La Sardine ✹ (West Loop, $$, p. 128)

Le Bouchon ✹✹ (Wicker Park/Bucktown, $$, p. 168)

Le Colonial ✹✹ (Magnificent Mile/Gold Coast, $$, p. 136)

Marché ✹ (West Loop, $$$, p. 125)

Mon Ami Gabi ✹ (Lincoln Park, $$$, p. 158)

one sixtyblue ★★★ (West Loop, $$$$, p. 124)

Pump Room (Magnificent Mile/
Gold Coast, $$$$, p. 132)

Tizi Melloul ★ (River North, $$$,
p. 145)

Yoshi's Café (Wrigleyville/North Side,
$$$, p. 162)

FUSION

Kevin ★★ (River North, $$$$,
p. 139)

GREEK

Artopolis (Greektown, $, p. 127)

Athena ★ (Greektown, $$, p. 127)

Costas (Greektown, $$, p. 127)

Greek Islands (Greektown, $$,
p. 127)

Parthenon (Greektown, $$, p. 127)

Pegasus (Greektown, $$, p. 127)

Santorini (Greektown, $$, p. 127)

HOT DOGS

Fluky's (Magnificent Mile/
Gold Coast, $, p. 139)

Gold Coast Dogs (Magnificent
Mile/Gold Coast, $, p. 139)

Murphy's Red Hots (Wrigleyville, $,
p. 139)

Portillo's (River North, $, p. 139)

Superdawg Drive-In (Northwest Side,
$, p. 139)

The Wieners Circle (Lincoln Park, $,
p. 139)

INDIAN

Vermilion ★ (River North, $$,
p. 152)

ITALIAN

Buca di Beppo (Magnificent
Mile/Gold Coast, $$, p. 123)

Club Lucky ★ (Wicker Park/
Bucktown, $$, p. 167)

Il Covo ★ (Wicker Park/Bucktown,
$$, p. 167)

Francesca's on Taylor (Little Italy, $$,
p. 123)

Gene & Georgetti ★ (River North,
$$$, p. 143)

Gioco ★ (the Loop, $$$, p. 117)

Harry Caray's (River North, $$,
p. 147)

La Cantina Enoteca (the Loop, $$,
p. 121)

Maggiano's (River North, $, p. 123)

Mia Francesca (Wrigleyville/
North Side, $$, p. 163)

Osteria Via Stato ★★ (River North,
$$$, p. 144)

Ranalli and Ryan's (Lincoln Park, $,
p. 138)

RoseAngelis ★★ (Lincoln Park, $,
p. 161)

Rosebud on Taylor ★ (Little Italy, $$,
p. 126)

Spiaggia ★★★ (Magnificent
Mile/Gold Coast, $$$$, p. 132)

312 Chicago ★ (the Loop, $$,
p. 120)

Trattoria No. 10 (the Loop, $$$,
p. 120)

Tuscany (Little Italy, $$, p. 127)

The Village ★ (the Loop, $$, p. 121)

Vivere ★ (the Loop, $$, p. 121)

JAPANESE

Mirai Sushi ★★ (Wicker Park/
Bucktown, $$$, p. 166)

Sushi Wabi ★ (West Loop, $$$,
p. 128)

LATIN AMERICAN

Café Mestizo (Pilsen, $, p. 127)

Carnivale ★ (West Loop, $$$, p. 124)

De La Costa ★ (Magnificent Mile/
Gold Coast, $$$, p. 134)

Mas ★★ (Wicker Park/Bucktown,
$$$, p. 164)

Nacional 27 ★★ (River North, $$$,
p. 144)

SushiSamba Rio ★★ (River North,
$$$, p. 145)

Vermilion ★ (River North, $$,
p. 152)

MALAYSIAN

Penang (near the Loop, $$, p. 126)

MEDITERRANEAN
Avec ⚜ (West Loop, $$, p. 128)
Copperblue ⚜ (Magnificent Mile/
Gold Coast, $$$, p. 134)

MEXICAN
Adobo Grill (Lincoln Park, $$,
p. 158)
Café Jumping Bean (Pilsen, $, p. 127)
Frontera Grill & Topolobampo ⚜⚜⚜
(River North, $$$, p. 143)
Nuevo Leon (Pilsen, $, p. 127)
Playa Azul (Pilsen, $, p. 127)

MIDDLE EASTERN
Reza's ⚜⚜ (River North, $$, p. 147)
Tizi Melloul ⚜ (River North, $$$,
p. 145)

PIZZA
Chicago Pizza & Oven Grinder
(Lincoln Park, $, p. 138)
Edwardo's (Magnificent Mile/Gold
Coast, South Loop, and Lincoln
Park, $, p. 138)
Gino's East ⚜⚜ (River North, $$,
p. 147)
Leona's Pizzeria (Wrigleyville, $,
p. 138)
Lou Malnati's Pizzeria ⚜ (River
North, $, p. 138)
Piece ⚜ (Wicker Park/Bucktown, $,
p. 169)
Pizzeria Due (River North, $, p. 153)
Pizzeria Uno ⚜ (River North, $,
p. 153)
Ranalli and Ryan's (Lincoln Park, $,
p. 138)

POLISH
Red Apple (Northwest Side, $, p. 129)

RUSSIAN
Russian Tea Time ⚜⚜ (the Loop,
$$$, p. 119)

SANDWICHES
Potbelly Sandwich Works (Lincoln
Park, $, p. 160)

SEAFOOD
Cape Cod Room (Magnificent
Mile/Gold Coast, $$$$, p. 130)
La Cantina Enoteca (the Loop, $$,
p. 121)
Nick's Fishmarket ⚜⚜ (the Loop,
$$$$, p. 116)
Shaw's Crab House and Blue Crab
Lounge ⚜ (Magnificent Mile/
Gold Coast, $$, p. 136)

SOUTHERN
House of Blues (River North, $$,
p. 273)
Wishbone ⚜⚜ (West Loop, $,
p. 129)

SPANISH & TAPAS
Arco de Cuchilleros ⚜ (Wrigleyville,
$$, p. 151)
Café Ba-Ba-Reeba! ⚜ (Lincoln Park,
$$, p. 159)
Café Iberico ⚜⚜ (River North, $,
p. 152)

STEAK & CHOPS
Gene & Georgetti ⚜ (River North,
$$$, p. 143)
Gibsons Bar & Steakhouse ⚜⚜
(Magnificent Mile/Gold
Coast, $$$$, p. 130)
Mike Ditka's Restaurant ⚜ (Magnifi-
cent Mile/Gold Coast, $$$, p. 135)
Morton's ⚜⚜⚜ (Magnificent Mile/
Gold Coast, $$$$, p. 130)
Petterino's ⚜⚜ (the Loop, $$$,
p. 118)

SUSHI
Mirai Sushi ⚜⚜ (Wicker Park/
Bucktown, $$$, p. 166)
Sushi Wabi ⚜ (West Loop, $$$,
p. 128)
SushiSamba Rio ⚜⚜ (River North,
$$$, p. 145)

SWEDISH
Ann Sather ⚜⚜ (Wrigleyville/
North Side, $, p. 163)

TEA

The Greenhouse, Ritz-Carlton Hotel (Magnificent Mile/Gold Coast, $$$, p. 133)

Palm Court, The Drake Hotel (Magnificent Mile/Gold Coast, $$$, p. 133)

Russian Tea Time ✷✷ (the Loop, $$$, p. 119)

Seasons Lounge, Four Seasons Hotel (Magnificent Mile/Gold Coast, $$$, p. 133)

THAI

Arun's ✷✷✷ (Wrigleyville/North Side, $$$$, p. 162)

Bamee Noodle Shop (Wrigleyville, $, p. 161)

Penny's Noodle Shop ✷ (Wrigleyville/ North Side, $, p. 163)

Star of Siam (Magnificent Mile/Gold Coast, $, p. 161)

Thai Classic (Wrigleyville, $, p. 161)

Tiparos (Lincoln Park, $, p. 161)

VEGETARIAN

Green Zebra ✷ (River North, $$$, p. 144)

VIETNAMESE

Le Colonial ✷✷ (Magnificent Mile/Gold Coast, $$, p. 136)

3 The Loop

In keeping with their proximity to the towers of power, many of the restaurants in the Loop and its environs feature expense-account-style prices, but it's still possible to dine here for less than the cost of your hotel room. The South Loop—a neighborhood just west of the lake and south of Congress Parkway—has seen a miniboom in restaurants in the past few years, accompanying a rash of condo conversions and new construction in the area. *Note:* Keep in mind that several of the best downtown spots are closed on Sunday.

VERY EXPENSIVE

Custom House ✷✷ AMERICAN   Chef Shawn McClain won raves for his seafood at Spring (see p. 166), and then proved Chicagoans would flock to an off-the-beaten-path, mostly vegetarian restaurant with Green Zebra (p. 144). Given that track record, it's no surprise that his next venture, Custom House, had local foodies lining up almost immediately when it opened in 2005.

This time around, McClain seems determined to prove that he can cook red meat, too. Although the menu has a decent seafood section, the highlights here are strictly carnivore, from the rich, almost buttery short rib (served with horseradish-flavored cream puffs) to the pork chop accompanied by pork-stuffed cannelloni and wild mushrooms. There are no gimmicks; you won't be dazzled with flavored foams or other culinary tricks. The draw here is McClain's sure touch with ingredients, his knack for mixing unexpected flavors simply but perfectly. (Take, for example, the seemingly straightforward spinach salad, which is livened up with thick chunks of bacon, roasted shiitake mushrooms and hazelnuts). The prices strike me as fairly high for such simplicity, but the service is top-notch and the setting sophisticated, with velvet-upholstered booths that allow for quiet conversation.

Because Custom House is located in a hotel, the restaurant serves breakfast daily, weekday lunch, and a Sunday brunch.

500 S. Dearborn St. (at Congress Pkwy.), in the Hotel Blake. ✆ 312/523-0200. www.customhouse.cc. Reservations recommended on weekends. Main courses $24–$38. AE, DC, DISC, MC, V. Mon–Fri 7:30–10am, 11:30am–2pm, and 5–10pm; Sat 7:30–10:30am and 5–10pm; Sun 7:30am–2pm and 5–9pm. Subway/El: Brown Line to Library.

Dining in the Loop & West Loop

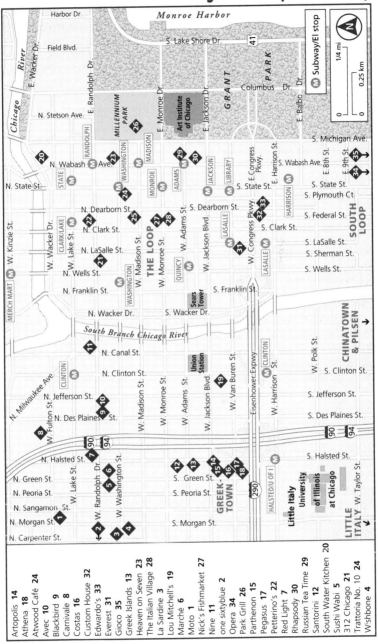

Everest ⭐⭐⭐ ALSATIAN/FRENCH   Towering high above the Chicago Stock Exchange, Everest is an oasis of fine-dining civility, a place where you can taste the creations of one of Chicago's top chefs while enjoying one of the city's top views. The space is nothing dramatic (it looks like a high-end corporate dining room), but the focus here is the view, the food, and you (the service team seamlessly anticipates your every need). Chef Jean Joho draws inspiration from the earthy cuisine of his native Alsace, and mixes what he calls "noble" and "simple" ingredients, such as caviar or foie gras, with potatoes or turnips. While the menu changes frequently, the salmon soufflé and cream-of-Alsace-cabbage soup with smoked sturgeon and caviar are popular appetizers; signature entrees include roasted Maine lobster in Alsace Gewürztraminer butter and ginger, and poached tenderloin of beef cooked *pot-au-feu* style and served with horseradish cream. Desserts are suitably sumptuous, and the wine list offers some wonderful American and Alsatian selections.

440 S. LaSalle St., 40th floor (at Congress Pkwy.). ⓒ **312/663-8920.** www.everestrestaurant.com. Reservations required. Main courses $27–$46; menu degustation $89; 3-course pretheater dinner $49. AE, DC, DISC, MC, V. Tues–Thurs 5:30–9pm; Fri 5:30–9:30pm; Sat 5–10pm. Complimentary valet parking. Subway/El: Brown Line to LaSalle/Van Buren, or Red Line to Adams.

Nick's Fishmarket ⭐⭐ SEAFOOD   Taking the elevator down below street level to Nick's feels a little like plunging underwater in a submarine. Once submerged, you'll find yourself in one of the best seafood restaurants in the city. This is definitely special-occasion dining that attracts an older, power-elite crowd, as well as business travelers with generous expense accounts (jackets are recommended, and shorts are a no-no).

The dining room is a spacious, open affair overlooking an outdoor plaza with an illuminated fountain and Chagall mosaic. Plush booths and loveseats (with individual light dimmers, no less) attract cuddly couples, while the generous space between tables allows you to whisper sweet nothings—or hammer out a business contract—without being overheard. Fresh seafood is the focus of the menu, which highlights the specials that are flown in daily. Most of the preparations are straightforward, although some dishes include French or Asian accents (citrus-ginger salmon served with black-sesame-seed-dotted rice). The menu also offers a decent selection for non–seafood eaters, including steak, veal Marsala, and roasted free-range chicken.

The street-level Nick's Grill serves more casual fare, including sandwiches and flat-bread pizzas. It's an appealing option for a late-afternoon light meal or for theater patrons in a hurry to catch a show.

Bank One Plaza at Monroe and Clark sts. ⓒ **312/621-0200.** www.nicksfishmarketchicago.com. Reservations recommended. Main courses $25–$47. AE, DC, DISC, MC, V. Mon–Fri 11:30am–2pm; Mon–Thurs 5:30–10pm; Fri–Sat 5–11pm. Subway/El: Blue or Red Line to Monroe.

EXPENSIVE

Atwood Café ⭐⭐ *Finds* AMERICAN   If you're tired of the exotic menus at trendy restaurants, Atwood Café will come as a welcome relief. Located in the historic Hotel Burnham, this place combines a gracious, 1900-era feel with a fresh take on American comfort food. The dining room—one of my favorites in the city—mixes elegance and humor with soaring ceilings; lush velvet curtains; and whimsical, colorful china and silverware.

Executive Chef Heather Terhune dabbles in global influences (most notably Asian and Southwestern) here, but the vast majority of the dishes are straightforward American. Appetizers include calamari with graham-cracker coating; ahi tuna and salmon tartar; and warm pistachio-crusted goat cheese salad with roasted beets, honey, and orange zest vinaigrette. Recent entree selections included maple-grilled pork chops with three-cheese macaroni; braised lamb shank with lemon zest-mint pesto; and spinach tagliatelle with bacon, peas, and shrimp in a garlic cream sauce. In the winter, try one of the signature potpies. Terhune began as a pastry chef, so desserts are a high point of Atwood Café's menu. Seasonal fruit is the basis for cobblers, trifles, and pies; for a decadently rich experience, tackle the banana-and-white-chocolate bread pudding.

1 W. Washington St. (at State St.). ℂ 312/368-1900. www.atwoodcafe.com. Main courses $18–$26. AE, DC, DISC, MC, V. Mon–Fri 7–10am; Sat 8–10am; Sun 8am–3pm; Mon–Sat 11:30am–3:45pm; Sun–Thurs 4:30–10pm; Fri–Sat 5–11pm. Subway/El: Red Line to Washington.

Gioco ⓐ ITALIAN   The South Loop was officially gentrified with the opening of this funky Italian restaurant. The cozy, convivial ambience—with exposed brick, mahogany accents, an open kitchen, stacks of wine bottles, and hip music—is par for the course in other restaurant-rich neighborhoods, but it's a welcome oasis of good food in this area. While Gioco's nouveau Italian dishes include a few standard appetizers (such as fried calamari), you'll also find some creative new options: octopus carpaccio, steamed mussels with white wine, and truffle-scented scallops with white polenta and wild mushroom sauce. The fine selection of pastas includes ricotta and spinach tortelloni and pappardelle with braised wild boar. Seafood shows up in various preparations, along with heartier dishes such as filet of beef in Barolo wine sauce, or the massive *Bistecca all Fiorentina,* a porterhouse steak served in a portion for two. Even if you're loath to order tiramisu for the umpteenth time, try this heavenly version—light as air and easy on the rum. The lunch menu also has a few panini and pizza selections.

1312 S. Wabash Ave. (at 13th St.). ℂ 312/939-3870. www.gioco-chicago.com. Reservations recommended on weekend evenings. Main courses $13–$22 lunch, $15–$36 dinner. AE, DC, MC, V. Mon–Fri 11:30am–2pm; Mon–Thurs 5–10pm; Fri–Sat 5pm–midnight; Sun 9am–2pm and 5–10pm. Subway/El: Red Line to Roosevelt.

Nine ⓐⓐ AMERICAN   The sizzle isn't all on the grill at this contemporary Chicago steakhouse-meets-Vegas dining palace. You'll feel like you're making a grand entrance from the moment you walk in the front door and step down an open staircase into the high-ceilinged, white and silver dining room, where the dramatic central champagne-and-caviar bar and glittering crowd all vie for your immediate attention.

Begin with something from the caviar appetizers or "crustacea" station (clams, oysters, crab, shrimp, and crawfish). The signature starter is the "two cones" appetizer, one overflowing with tuna tartare, another with chunks of lobster and avocado. For a splurge, try the Kobe beef burger or the prime, dry-aged steaks, particularly the 24-ounce bone-in rib-eye and 22-ounce porterhouse. The menu wisely accommodates a variety of tastes; non-red-meat options include a generous veggie chopped salad, roast chicken with chipotle marinade, and a few seafood selections such as the delicious miso-marinated black cod. For dessert, grill your own s'mores on a hibachi grill at your table. The lunch menu adds some burgers, flatbread pizzas, sandwiches, and entree salads. If you want to keep hanging with the beautiful people after dinner, head upstairs to the sleek, futuristic Ghost Bar.

440 W. Randolph St. (at Canal St.). ℂ 312/575-9900. www.n9ne.com. Reservations recommended. Main courses $9–$22 lunch, $21–$43 dinner. AE, DC, MC, V. Mon–Fri 11:30am–2pm; Mon–Thurs 5:30–10pm; Fri–Sat 5pm–midnight. Subway/El: Blue, Orange, Brown, or Green line to Clark/Lake.

Opera 🎭🎭 ASIAN   This place has nothing to do with *Aida* or *La Bohème,* but the mood is certainly theatrical at the South Loop's most eye-catching restaurant. The folks behind Red Light (p. 125) take classic Chinese dishes to the next level at Opera. You'll know you're in for something far beyond Chinatown when you walk past the dramatic velvet curtains and take in the bold red-and-orange decor, not to mention the grand staircase leading up to the private dining room. Signature East-meets-West dishes include a spicy crab cake served with "chopsticks" (skinny crab-stuffed spring rolls) and peppered filet mignon served over a brandied beurre blanc with a side of broccoli in black-bean sauce. Duck is not for everyone, but the signature Peking duck service (three preparations) should not be missed; there is a reason it is the chef's specialty. Do save room for dessert, whether it's one of the light homemade sorbets (the caramel is out of this world) or the more decadent Tao of Chocolate (a liquid-center flourless chocolate cake with sticks of frozen chocolate mousse). This building used to house a film warehouse, and the storage vaults in the back have been converted into cozy dining nooks—the best tables in the house for romantic couples.

1301 S. Wabash Ave. (at 13th St.). ✆ 312/461-0161. www.opera-chicago.com. Reservations recommended. Main courses $17–$32. AE, DC, MC, V. Sun–Thurs 5–10pm; Fri–Sat 5pm–midnight. Subway/El: Red Line to Roosevelt.

Park Grill 🎭🎭 AMERICAN   Location, location, location—it's what sets Park Grill apart from all the other upscale comfort-food restaurants in town. Set in the middle of Millennium Park, a hugely popular gathering spot along Michigan Avenue and Randolph Street, Park Grill makes a great stop after a late-afternoon stroll or before a summer concert at the Pritzker Music Pavilion (since this is a popular preshow dinner spot, definitely make a reservation). The dining room itself is simple but welcoming, with floor-to-ceiling windows along one wall that look out onto the Michigan Avenue skyline (you won't, alas, get a view of the park). The menu highlights American favorites, some prepared simply (grilled leg of lamb and rotisserie chicken), others featuring a more international twist, such as pappardelle pasta with littleneck clams, chorizo sausage, leeks, and basil; and braised rabbit. For lighter appetites, there are a number of fish dishes, salads, and some thin-crust pizzas. Lunch selections include a good mix of sandwiches—everything from Cajun chicken breast and barbecue beef to a smoked-salmon club and BLT with truffle mayonnaise. There's also a kids' menu.

11 N. Michigan Ave. (at Madison St.). ✆ 312/521-PARK. Reservations recommended. Main courses $10–$21 lunch, $17–$41 dinner. AE, DC, MC, V. Sun–Thurs 11am–9:30pm; Fri–Sat 11am–10:30pm. Subway/El: Red Line to Washington or Brown, Orange, Purple, or Green line to Madison.

Petterino's 🎭🎭 AMERICAN/STEAK & CHOPS   Named for Arturo Petterino, maitre d' at the Pump Room (p. 132) in the days when it swarmed with celebrities, this restaurant re-creates the feeling of downtown dining in the 1940s and '50s. Located in the Goodman Theatre building, Petterino's is a popular pretheater option, so book a table in advance if you have to catch a show. The dimly lit dining room is decorated in dark wood with red leather booths, and the overall feel is relaxed rather than hyped-up. The straightforward menu is filled with classic American big-night-out favorites: veal chops, New York strip steak, slow-cooked beef brisket, and some fresh fish selections. Pastas include baked ravioli and fettuccine Alberto (a version of Alfredo with peas and prosciutto). Among the old-time appetizers, you'll find shrimp *de jonghe,* coated with garlic and bread crumbs, and an excellent tomato bisque soup. In keeping with the restaurant's entertainment connection, some dishes are named after local celebrities—a nicely done salad of chopped mixed greens and blue cheese is named for longtime *Sun-Times* columnist Irv Kupcinet. The lunch menu offers smaller versions of the dinner entrees, along with a good mix of salads and sandwiches.

150 N. Dearborn St. (at Randolph St.). ② 312/422-0150. www.leye.com. Reservations recommended. Main courses $8.95–$25 lunch, $10–$40 dinner. AE, DC, DISC, MC, V. Mon–Thurs 11am–9pm; Fri 11am–11pm; Sat 11:30am–11pm; Sun 3–7pm. Subway/El: Red Line to Washington, or Brown Line to State/Lake.

Rhapsody *✿✿* AMERICAN   This fine-dining restaurant inside Symphony Center (with floor-to-ceiling windows overlooking an outdoor dining area and a small park) is a hit with the concert-going crowd, as much for the setting as for the food. In the summer the restaurant's outdoor garden is a mini oasis of flowers and greenery, definitely the most charming outdoor dining spot in the Loop.

The menu emphasizes contemporary American dining with European influences. Escargot and carpaccio show up on the appetizer list, as do crab cakes and seasonal soups (asparagus in the spring, mushroom in the fall). Entrees include grilled pork tenderloin with sage jus and date chutney; pan-seared wallet pike; and a sirloin filet with truffle spaetzle. There is also always at least one vegetarian option, in addition to the chef's daily risotto, which is often meat-free. The lunch menu features mostly salads and sandwiches (brie, tomato, and pesto served on a baguette), as well as casual bistro entrees such as steak frites.

65 E. Adams St. (at Wabash Ave.). ② 312/786-9911. www.rhapsodychicago.com. Reservations recommended before symphony concerts. Main courses $11–$15 lunch, $21–$29 dinner. AE, DC, DISC, MC, V. Mon–Fri 11:30am–2pm; Mon–Thurs 5–9pm; Fri–Sat 5–10pm. Closed Sun mid-June to mid-Sept. During symphony season, mid-Sept to mid-June, the restaurant is also open Sun 4:30–9pm; Thurs–Sat until 10:30pm. Subway/El: Brown, Purple, Green, or Orange line to Adams; or Red Line to Monroe or Jackson.

Russian Tea Time *✿✿* (Finds) RUSSIAN/TEA   Another spot very popular with Chicago Symphony Orchestra patrons and musicians, Russian Tea Time is far from being the simple tea cafe that its name implies. Reading through this family-owned restaurant's extensive menu is like taking a tour through the cuisine of czarist Russia and the former Soviet republics (for Russian neophytes, all the dishes are well described). The atmosphere is old-world and cozy, with lots of woodwork and a friendly staff. Start off a meal with potato pancakes, blini with Russian caviar, or chilled smoked sturgeon; if you can't decide, there are a number of mixed appetizer platters to share. For the best sampling of old Russia, try the beef stroganoff; *kulebiaka* (meat pie with ground beef, cabbage, and onions); or roast pheasant served with a brandy, walnut, and pomegranate sauce and brandied prunes.

77 E. Adams St. (between Michigan and Wabash aves.). ② 312/360-0000. www.russianteatime.com. Reservations recommended. Main courses $15–$27. AE, DC, DISC, MC, V. Sun–Thurs 11am–9pm; Fri–Sat 11am–midnight (the restaurant sometimes closes earlier during the summer months). Tea service daily 2:30–4:30pm. Subway/El: Brown, Purple, Green, or Orange line to Adams; or Red Line to Monroe or Jackson.

South Water Kitchen *✿* (Kids) AMERICAN   Because Loop restaurants cater to office workers and business travelers, there aren't a lot of family-friendly options other than fast food. So while South Water Kitchen isn't breaking any new culinary ground, it deserves a mention as one of the few places in the area that welcomes kids—while featuring food sophisticated enough for discerning moms and dads. The dining room evokes the spirit of an old-fashioned city saloon, and the menu goes the retro route as well. Entrees include modern twists on familiar favorites, including pork chops, pot roast, macaroni and cheese, and a "TV Dinner" with meatloaf, mashed potatoes, green beans, and a mini fruit crisp. The restaurant provides not only kids' menus but also games to keep the little ones occupied. Best of all, half the proceeds of all children's meals go to the Chicago Coalition for the Homeless.

In the Hotel Monaco, 225 N. Wabash Ave. (at Wacker Dr.). ⓒ 312/236-9300. www.southwaterkitchen.com. Main courses $9–$19 lunch, $16–$26 dinner. AE, DC, MC, V. Mon–Fri 7–10:30am and 11am–3pm; Sat–Sun 7am–2:30pm; daily 5–10pm. Subway/El: Red Line to State/Lake.

Trattoria No. 10 ITALIAN   Elegant but not pretentious, Trattoria No. 10 is a favorite with Chicagoans who work in the Loop. A professional restaurant designer once told me he considers this one of the best-looking restaurants in the city: the burnt-orange tones, ceramic floor tiles, and gracefully arched ceilings set a dining-in-Italy mood. The house specialty is ravioli, which can be ordered as an appetizer or main course (recent fillings included butternut and acorn squash topped with walnut sauce, and homemade Italian sausage and mozzarella served with spicy Arrabbiatta sauce). If you're not in the mood for ravioli, there are plenty of other worthwhile pasta dishes to choose from such as farfalle with duck confit, asparagus, caramelized onions, and pine nuts, or the linguine with roasted eggplant, grilled tomatoes, and smoked mozzarella; there's also a daily risotto special. While Trattoria No. 10 serves beef, veal, and a decent variety of seafood dishes, the restaurant's strength is clearly pasta. For a lighter (and cheaper) meal, stop by between 5 and 8pm on weekdays for an all-you-can-eat buffet at the bar; $12 (with a $6 drink minimum) gets you tastes of beef tenderloin, shrimp, and various pasta specials.

10 N. Dearborn St. (between Madison and Washington sts.). ⓒ 312/984-1718. Reservations recommended. Main courses $15–$33. AE, DC, DISC, MC, V. Mon–Fri 11:30am–2pm; Mon–Fri 5:30–9pm; Sat 5:30–10pm. Subway/El: Red line to Madison.

MODERATE

312 Chicago ⓐ AMERICAN/ITALIAN   This in-house restaurant of the flashy Hotel Allegro has proven itself by serving the Italian-inspired specialties of chef Dean Zanella. The restaurant has a clubby Jazz Age feel, with mahogany, antiques, and an earthy color scheme. Because this is a hotel restaurant, the hours are more extensive than those of other dining spots in the area (including breakfast and lunch every day of the week), and the crowd is as eclectic as the guests who patronize the Allegro. 312 Chicago isn't the sort of place that sends food critics into a frenzy, but it serves consistently dependable meals at prices that are quite reasonable for downtown.

The seared day-boat scallops appetizer with wild mushrooms and truffle oil is one of the restaurant's signature dishes. The entree list is filled with familiar pasta and meat favorites, plus there are always at least a couple seafood dishes, but most dishes have subtly creative touches (*bucatini* filled with ahi tuna or roasted pheasant with chestnut purée). Zanella draws on his family heritage for dishes such as Grandma Anna's veal meatballs, which are topped with tomato sauce and ricotta. On weekends the restaurant has simple brunch offerings distinguished by home-baked breads.

136 N. LaSalle St. (at Randolph St.). ⓒ 312/696-2420. www.312chicago.com. Reservations recommended. Main courses $20–$23. AE, DC, DISC, MC, V. Mon–Fri 7–10am and 11am–3pm; Sat 8–11am; Mon–Thurs 5–10pm; Fri–Sat 5–11pm; Sun 8am–2pm and 5–9pm. Subway/El: Red Line to Washington.

THE ITALIAN VILLAGE

Open since 1927, this downtown dining landmark houses three separate Italian restaurants that are popular with pre- and posttheater crowds. Each has its own menu and ambience, but they share an exemplary wine cellar and fresh produce from the

I don't speak sign language.

A hotel can close for all kinds of reasons.

Our Guarantee ensures that if your hotel's undergoing construction, we'll let you know in advance. In fact, we cover your entire travel experience. See www.travelocity.com/guarantee for details.

family garden. Since each restaurant in the Italian Village is distinct, they are listed separately below.

La Cantina Enoteca ITALIAN/SEAFOOD   La Cantina, the most casual of the three restaurants in the Italian Village, makes the most of its basement location by creating the feel of a wine cellar. Focusing on seafood, La Cantina offers at least five fresh varieties daily, along with dishes such as macaroni with scallops and shrimp in a garlic-pesto cream sauce, and *cacciucco*, a Tuscan seafood stew with scallops, squid, and clams. There's also a small selection of nonseafood items (your basic pasta favorites and some beef and veal dishes).

71 W. Monroe St. (between Clark and Dearborn sts.). © **312/332-7005.** www.italianvillage-chicago.com. Reservations recommended. Main courses $11–$25 lunch, $13–$32 dinner. AE, DC, DISC, MC, V. Mon–Fri 11:30am–4pm; Mon–Sat 5pm–midnight. Subway/El: Red Line to Monroe.

The Village *Finds* ITALIAN   Upstairs in the Italian Village is The Village, with its charming interpretation of alfresco dining in a small Italian town, complete with a midnight-blue ceiling, twinkling "stars," and banquettes tucked into private, cavelike rooms. It's the kind of Pan-Chicago place where you might see one man in a tux and another in shorts. This is old-school Italian: eggplant parmigiana, a heavy fettuccine Alfredo that would send your cardiologist into fits, veal scaloppini, and even calves' liver. The food is good rather than great, but what sets The Village apart is the bordering-on-corny faux-Italian atmosphere. The service is outstanding, from the Italian maitre d' who flirts with all the ladies to the ancient waiters who manage somehow to keep up with the nonstop flow. The staff here are pros at handling pretheater dining.

71 W. Monroe St. (between Clark and Dearborn sts.). © **312/332-7005.** www.italianvillage-chicago.com. Reservations recommended (accepted for parties of 3 or more). Main courses (including salad) $9–$23 lunch, $13–$24 dinner. AE, DISC, MC, V. Mon–Thurs 11am–1am; Fri–Sat 11am–2am; Sun noon–midnight. Subway/El: Red Line to Monroe.

Vivere *Finds* ITALIAN   On the main floor of the Italian Village is Vivere, the Italian Village's take on gourmet cooking—and eye-catching design. The bold interior, with rich, textured walls, spiraling bronze sculptures, and fragmented mosaic floors, makes dinner a theatrical experience. No spaghetti and meatballs here; the pasta dishes feature upscale ingredients, from the pappardelle with braised duck to the *agnolottini* filled with pheasant. Fresh fish is always on the menu (a recent entree selection was salmon with spiced carrot broth), along with a good selection of meats and game. Grilled venison medallions are served with foie gras ravioli, while roasted duck is accompanied by a potato terrine and sautéed spinach.

71 W. Monroe St. (between Clark and Dearborn sts.). © **312/332-7005.** www.italianvillage-chicago.com. Reservations recommended. Main courses $13–$24 lunch, $16–$34 dinner. AE, DC, DISC, MC, V. Mon–Fri 11:30am–2:30pm; Mon–Thurs 5:30–10pm; Fri–Sat 5–11pm. Subway/El: Red Line to Monroe.

INEXPENSIVE

Heaven on Seven *Finds* BREAKFAST & BRUNCH/CAJUN & CREOLE/ DINER   Hidden on the seventh floor of an office building opposite Macy's, this is truly an insider's spot (you'll find it by following the office workers who line up for lunch during the week). Loud, crowded, and casual, it's a no-frills spot that buzzes with energy. Chef/owner Jimmy Bannos's Cajun and Creole specialties come with a cup of soup and include such Louisiana staples as red beans and rice, a catfish po' boy sandwich, and jambalaya. If you don't have a taste for Tabasco, the extensive coffee-shop-style menu covers all the traditional essentials: grilled-cheese sandwiches, omelets, tuna—the works. Indulge in chocolate peanut butter pie or homemade rice pudding for dessert. Although Heaven on Seven is usually open only for breakfast and lunch, they do serve dinner on the third Friday of the month from 5:30 to 9pm.

Heaven also has another downtown location just off the Mag Mile at **600 N. Michigan Ave.** (© 312/280-7774); unlike the original location, they accept reservations and credit cards and are open for dinner. The ambience is more lively than gritty, making it a popular spot for families.

111 N. Wabash Ave. (at Washington St.), 7th floor. © **312/263-6443.** www.heavenonseven.com. Reservations not accepted. Sandwiches $8–$12; main courses $10–$14. No credit cards. Mon–Fri 8:30am–5pm; Sat 10am–3pm; 3rd Fri of each month 5:30–9pm. Subway/El: Red Line to Washington.

4 The West Loop

For restaurants listed in this section, see the map "Dining in the Loop & West Loop" on p. 115.

The stretch of Randolph Street just west of the Chicago River—once known as the Market District—used to be filled with produce trucks and warehouses that shut down tight after nightfall. In the 1990s, in an echo of New York's Meatpacking District, a few bold restaurant pioneers moved in, bringing their super-hip clientele with them. It wasn't long before industrial buildings began their transformation into condos, and now it seems like there's a construction zone on every corner. Despite the upheaval, the West Loop still feels like a neighborhood in transition; it's home to some of the city's coolest restaurants and clubs, but not much else.

Transportation to the West Loop is easy—it's about a $5 cab ride from Michigan Avenue or a slightly longer trek by bus (no. 8 or 9) or El, with stops at Halsted and Lake, a block from the Randolph Street's "restaurant row." The walk from the Loop is pleasant and secure in the daytime, but at night I'd take a taxi.

VERY EXPENSIVE

Blackbird 𝕮𝕮 AMERICAN   Stylishly spare, Chef Paul Kahan's Blackbird exudes a smart urban chic that could blend into the dining scene of any major city. The white, narrow room is dense with close-packed tables, and the floor-to-ceiling windows in front frame the urban landscape outside. As in many newer restaurants, the noise level can get high (and the tables are crammed much too close together). Nevertheless, Blackbird is fun for people who like a scene (everyone pretends not to be looking around too much), but I'd recommend somewhere else if you're looking for a romantic dinner.

The seasonal menu here features creative fare, from a charcuterie plate to braised octopus with hummus. Kahan is a big proponent of local, organic ingredients, so expect top-notch quality—but you'll pay for it (a plate of two melt-in-your-mouth Maine diver scallops goes for $14). Artfully prepared dishes make up the entree list: pan-roasted monkfish with Parmesan, crispy prosciutto, ruby grapefruit and salsify; grilled organic veal rib-eye with cornbread porridge, rapini, bittersweet chocolate, black truffle, and rosemary; and crispy buckwheat crepes with hazelnut "cassoulet," fresh ricotta, pickled baby carrots, and grilled abalone mushrooms. Recent desserts included bittersweet chocolate brioche with smoked banana, Manjari chocolate ice cream, and aged rum.

619 W. Randolph St. © **312/715-0708.** www.blackbirdrestaurant.com. Reservations recommended. Main courses $8–$19 lunch, $25–$36 dinner. AE, DC, DISC, MC, V. Mon–Fri 11:30am–2pm and 5:30–10:30pm; Fri–Sat 5:30–11:30pm.

Kids Family-Friendly Restaurants

One of the city's first "theme" restaurants, **Ed Debevic's,** 640 N. Wells St., at Ontario Street (© 312/664-1707), is a temple to America's hometown lunch-counter culture. The burgers-and-milkshakes menu is kid-friendly, but it's the staff shtick that makes this place memorable. The waitresses play the parts of gum-chewing toughies who make wisecracks, toss out good-natured insults, and even sit right down at your table. It's all a perform-ance—but it works.

Two national chain spots in River North that do big family business are **Rainforest Cafe,** 605 N. Clark St., at Ohio Street (© 312/787-1501), and **ESPN Zone,** 43 E. Ohio St., at Wabash Avenue (© 312/644-3776). Rainforest Cafe creates a jungle feel with the sounds of waterfalls, thunder, and wild ani-mals. Sports-loving older kids will find plenty of entertainment at ESPN Zone, including a game room and an endless array of TVs flashing the lat-est scores.

One of the best all-around options, and a homegrown place as well, the Southern-style restaurant **Wishbone** ★★ (p. 129) has much to recommend it. Children can be kept busy looking at the large and surrealistic farm-life paintings on the walls or reading a picture book, *Floop the Fly,* loaned to diners (written and illustrated by the parents of the owners). The food is diverse enough that both adults and kids can find something to their liking, but there's also a menu geared just toward children. Another all-American choice in the Loop is **South Water Kitchen** ★ (p. 119), which offers a kids' menu and coloring books.

A fun breakfast-and-lunch spot in Lincoln Park, **Toast,** 746 W. Webster St., at Halsted Street (© 773/935-5600), serves up all-American favorites (pan-cakes, eggs, sandwiches) and employs an age-old restaurateur's device for keeping idle hands and minds occupied: Tables at this neighborhood spot are covered with blank canvases of butcher-block paper on which kids of all ages can doodle away with crayons. But be forewarned: this is a very popu-lar spot for weekend brunch, so showing up with ravenous kids at 11am on Saturday—only to be told there's an hour wait—is not the best idea.

At **Gino's East** ★★ (p. 147), the famous Chicago pizzeria, long waits can also be an issue during the prime summer tourist season. But once you get your table, the kids can let loose: patrons are invited to scrawl all over the graffiti-strewn walls and furniture. For fun and games of the coin-operated and basement-rec-room variety, seek out **Dave & Buster's,** 1024 N. Clark St. (© 312/943-5151), the Chicago location of the Dallas-based mega enter-tainment/dining chain.

With heaping plates of pasta served up family style, **Maggiano's,** 516 N. Clark St. (© 312/644-7700), in River North, and **Buca di Beppo,** 521 N. Rush St., right off Michigan Avenue (© 312/396-0001), are good choices for budget-conscious families. These Italian-American restaurants (both parts of national chains) serve up huge portions of pasta and meat to be passed and shared.

Moto ✰✰✰ ECLECTIC   If you think food is meant to be experienced with all the senses, book a table at Moto, home to Chicago's most jaw-droppingly original dishes. Chef Homaro Cantu, who worked with Chicago celebrity chef Charlie Trotter for 4 years, calls his cuisine "avant-garde with Asian influences"—but what he's really interested in is taking dining beyond just eating. Dishes here are interactive experiences. For example, he entwines fresh herbs in custom-designed corkscrew-handled spoons, which allows the scent of the herbs to waft toward diners as they eat. For the ultimate made-to-order dish, an insulated box cooks a piece of fish right at the table. Cantu's got a sense of humor, too—during a raw food course, he uses a "virtual aroma device" to emit a subtle smoky scent, and sometimes the menu itself is edible. Dining here is strictly degustation, with a five-course, seven-course, and "gastronomic tasting menu" of up to 18 courses. Courses are creative but not necessarily filling, so be prepared to snack later if you choose the five-course option. The restaurant itself has a minimalist Zen feel—here, all the drama is at your table.

945 W. Fulton Market Ave. (at Sangamon St.). ☎ 312/491-0058. www.motorestaurant.com. Reservations recommended. Prix-fixe dinners $70–$165. AE, DC, DISC, MC, V. Tues–Sat 5–11pm.

one sixtyblue ✰✰✰ FRENCH   Once considered one of the very best restaurants in town, one sixtyblue has been eclipsed in recent years by newer, flashier places. But if you're looking for a dining experience that is refined without being stuffy—and you prefer reading menus that don't require a thesaurus—then you'll have a memorable meal here. (Basketball legend Michael Jordan, one of the owners, has been known to mix margaritas at the bar.) While I found the prices high for the fairly straightforward food, the restaurant's tranquil dining room and stellar service are worth the splurge for serious diners.

Designed by Adam Tihany (Le Cirque 2000, Jean Georges), the setting is sophisticated and modern: high ceilings, upholstered banquettes, and carpeting that keeps down the noise level. The restaurant's relative quiet is one of its biggest assets (there's also plenty of space between tables, making this a good spot for business discussions or romantic whispers). Also, the service is top-notch but unobtrusive.

Chef Martial Noguier brings a French influence to the preparation of the contemporary dishes, but he draws on practically every world cuisine for inspiration. The must-have appetizer, if it is offered, is the duck confit, which is fall-off-the-bone tender; an orange glaze and slice of Grand Marnier–soaked French toast provide the perfect complementary flavor. Entrees include a wide range of meats and fish: the signature delmonico steak with potato puree, thyme, and roasted shallot sauce; guinea hen with glazed baby turnips, dried raisins, and prosciutto; and blue nose grouper with bell peppers, quail egg, capers, pine nuts, and Niçoise olives. The extensive dessert menu includes a selection of homemade truffles; or you might skip the liqueurs and treat yourself to the hot chocolate sampler.

1400 W. Randolph St. (at Loomis St.). ☎ 312/850-0303. www.onesixtyblue.com. Reservations recommended on weekends. Main courses $29–$38. AE, DC, MC, V. Mon–Thurs 5:30–10pm; Fri–Sat 5:30–11pm.

EXPENSIVE

Carnivale ✰ LATIN AMERICAN   Another entry in the dinner-as-theater category, this sprawling, Pan-Latin spot is housed a former nightclub—and judging from the dance music that played throughout a recent meal there, the stereo system remains intact. Head for the cavernous, two-story central dining room if you want to be at the center of the action; request a table in one of the more intimate side rooms if you prefer not to shout through your meal. For the best view of the action, try snagging one of the tables just off the central staircase, which overlook the scene below.

Carnivale's menu takes inspiration from Central and South America, covering everything from rum-glazed pork shoulder with Puerto Rican rice and beans to Argentine-style steaks. (While there is a decent selection of seafood, I found the portions rather small; go with a meat dish if you want to fill up.) Befitting its clubby vibe, there's also an extensive selection of tropical drinks. Overall, the food is good rather than great; Carnivale's main selling point is its bright, buzzy atmosphere, not the cuisine. It attracts lots of groups in search of a lively night out (I saw two different bachelorette parties dining here one Saturday night), so plan your romantic date night elsewhere. The large bar area has ample room for hanging out if you want to linger after dinner.

702 W. Fulton St. (between Clinton St. and the Kennedy Expressway/I-94). ⓒ 312/850-5005. www.carnivalechicago. com. Reservations recommended on weekends. Main courses $8–$15 lunch; $16–$38 dinner. AE, DISC, MC, V. Mon–Fri 11:30am–2:30pm; Mon–Thurs 5–10:30pm; Fri–Sat 5–11:30pm; Sun 5–10pm. Bar open Mon–Thurs till midnight; Fri–Sat 1:30am; Sun till 10pm. Subway/El: Green Line to Clinton.

Marché ⚝ BISTRO/FRENCH   If you've ever longed to run away and join Cirque du Soleil, spend an evening at Marché. An Americanized, oversize take on the French bistro, Marché offers a convivial (though noisy) dining experience, enhanced by the phantasmagoric decor and bustling bar scene that blends into the dining room. Although the hipsters who thronged here when it opened a decade ago have long since moved on, the restaurant still retains a certain theatrical flair; multilevel seating, brightly colored umbrellas that hang from the ceiling, and velvet seats in shades of red and yellow add to the circus atmosphere, as does the clang of the open kitchen and enticing scents from the rotisserie. The food—a mix of bistro favorites—is fine, but the decor is the real draw here. The spit-roasted chicken is quite popular, and you can't miss with the New York strip au poivre partnered with a mound of shoestring frites. Chops and creative seafood entrees round out the menu. Simple, classic desserts and a cheese plate provide a refreshingly light finale to the meal.

833 W. Randolph St. (1 block west of Halsted St.). ⓒ 312/226-8399. www.marche-chicago.com. Reservations accepted. Main courses $12–$18 lunch, $17–$35 dinner. AE, DC, MC, V. Mon–Fri 11:30am–4pm; Sun–Thurs 5:30–10pm; Fri–Sat 5:30–midnight.

Red Light ⚝ ASIAN   One of the "theatrical" restaurants (along with Marché, Nine, and others) that wowed Chicago when it opened in the mid-1990s, Red Light isn't quite the scene it once was. But the setting is still stunning: two dramatic dining rooms with deep-red walls, colorful lanterns, gently waving palm fronds, sensuously curved windows and ceilings, and chairs that could be mistaken for metal sculptures. (They're not very comfortable, but they do look cool.) Even more spectacular is the food. Chef Jackie Shen incorporates Chinese, French, Thai, and other Asian ingredients and cooking techniques. Curries and seafood entrees are the highlights, from a traditional Japanese *tatsu* curry to the crispy Shanghai-style whole catfish in red-vinegar-sweet-and-sour sauce. It's not on the menu, but the delicious "Hong Kong Jerry," named for the restaurant's owner, should not be missed: pepper-crusted beef chunks with mushrooms and vegetables in oyster sauce. You can also dig into traditional dishes such as pad thai or a modern version of kung pao chicken. And as befits a restaurant that's big on style, there's a fine selection of (expensive) specialty cocktails.

820 W. Randolph St. ⓒ 312/733-8880. www.redlight-chicago.com. Reservations recommended on weekends. Main courses $13–$16 lunch, $19–$31 dinner; chef's tasting menu $70. AE, DC, MC, V. Mon–Fri 11:30am–2pm; Sun–Thurs 5:30–10pm; Fri–Sat 5:30pm–midnight.

Fun Fact   Ethnic Dining near the Loop

CHINATOWN

Chicago's Chinatown is about 20 blocks south of the Loop. The district is strung along two thoroughfares, Cermak Road and Wentworth Avenue as far south as 24th Place. Hailing a cab from the Loop is the easiest way to get here, but you can also drive and leave your car in the validated lot near the entrance to Chinatown, or take the Orange Line of the El to the Cermak stop, a well-lit station on the edge of the Chinatown commercial district.

The spacious, fairly elegant **Phoenix,** 2131 S. Archer Ave. (between Wentworth Ave. and Cermak Rd.; © **312/328-0848**), has plenty of room for big tables of family or friends to enjoy the Cantonese (and some Szechuan) cuisine. A good sign: The place attracts lots of Chinatown locals. It's especially popular for dim sum brunch, so come early to avoid the wait. Late night, stop by the more casual **Saint's Alp Teahouse** downstairs (© **312/842-1886**), an outpost of the Hong Kong chain, which is open until midnight daily.

Penang, 2201 S. Wentworth Ave. (at Cermak Rd.; © **312/326-6888**), serves mostly Malaysian dishes, but some lean toward Indian and Chinese (they've even added a sushi bar to complete the Pan-Asian experience). Sink your teeth into the *kambing rendang* (lamb curry in 11 spices) or the barbecued stingray wrapped in a banana leaf.

Open since 1927, **Won Kow,** 2237 S. Wentworth Ave. (between 22nd Place and Alexander St.; © **312/842-7500**), is the oldest continually operating restaurant in Chinatown. You can enjoy dim sum in the mezzanine-level dining room from 9am to 3pm daily. Most of the items cost around $2. Other house specialties include Mongolian chicken and duck with seafood.

LITTLE ITALY

Convenient to most downtown locations, a few blocks' stretch of Taylor Street is home to a host of time-honored, traditional, hearty Italian restaurants. If you're staying in the Loop (an easy cab ride away), the area makes a good destination for dinner (I don't think it's worth a special trip if you're staying farther north—there are plenty of great Italian places elsewhere in the city).

Regulars return for the straightforward Italian favorites livened up with some adventurous specials at **Francesca's on Taylor,** 1400 W. Taylor St. (at Loomis St.; © **312/829-2828**). I recommend the fish specials above the standard meat dishes. Other standouts include eggplant ravioli in a four-cheese sauce with a touch of tomato sauce and shaved parmigiano, as well as sautéed veal medallions with porcini mushrooms in cream sauce. (This is part of a local chain that includes the popular Mia Francesca, p. 163.)

Expect to wait well beyond the time of your reservation at **Rosebud on Taylor** ⊛, 1500 W. Taylor St. (at Laflin St.; © **312/942-1117**), but fear not—your hunger will be satisfied. Rosebud is known for enormous helpings of pasta, most of which lean toward heavy Italian-American favorites: deep-dish lasagna and a fettuccine Alfredo that defines the word "rich." I highly recommend any of the pastas served with vodka sauce. Another location is near the Mag Mile at 720 N. Rush St. (© **312/266-6444**).

Tuscany, 1014 W. Taylor St. (between Morgan and Miller sts.; ℂ **312/829-1990**), is one of the most reliable Italian restaurants on Taylor Street. In contrast to the city's more fashionable Italian spots, family-owned Tuscany has the comfortable feel of a neighborhood restaurant. The menu features large portions of Tuscan pastas, pizzas, veal, chicken, and a risotto of the day. Specialties include anything cooked on the wood-burning grill and Tuscan sausage dishes. A second location is across from Wrigley Field at 3700 N. Clark St. (at Waveland Ave.; ℂ **773/404-7700**).

GREEKTOWN

A short cab ride across the south branch of the Chicago River will take you to the city's Greektown, a row of moderately priced and inexpensive Greek restaurants clustered on Halsted Street between Van Buren and Washington streets.

To be honest, there's not much here to distinguish one restaurant from the other: They're all standard Greek restaurants with similar looks and similar menus. That said, **Greek Islands,** 200 S. Halsted St. (at Adams St.; ℂ **312/782-9855**); **Santorini,** 800 W. Adams St. (at Halsted St.; ℂ **312/829-8820**); **Parthenon,** 314 S. Halsted St. (between Jackson and Van Buren sts.; ℂ **312/726-2407**); and **Costas,** 340 S. Halsted St. (between Jackson and Van Buren sts.; ℂ **312/263-0767**), are all good bets for gyros, Greek salads, shish kabobs, and the classic moussaka. On warm summer nights, opt for either **Athena** ⍟, 212 S. Halsted St. (between Adams and Jackson sts.; ℂ **312/655-0000**), which has a huge outdoor seating area, or **Pegasus,** 130 S. Halsted St. (between Monroe and Adams sts.; ℂ **312/226-3377**), with its rooftop patio serving drinks, appetizers, and desserts. Both have wonderful views of the Loop's skyline. **Artopolis,** 306 S. Halsted St. (at Jackson St.; ℂ **312/559-9000**), a more recent addition to the neighborhood, is a casual option offering up Greek and Mediterranean specialties, wood-oven pizzas, breads, and French pastries, all of them tasty.

PILSEN

Just south of the Loop and convenient to McCormick Place and Chinatown, Pilsen is a colorful blend of Mexican culture, artists and bohemians, and pricey new residential developments. The area's nascent restaurant scene is showing signs of life, but, for now, the local fare is decidedly casual.

Nuevo Leon, 1515 W. 18th St. (at Laflin St.; ℂ **312/421-1517**), is a popular Mexican restaurant serving the standard offerings. Across the street, **Playa Azul,** 1514 W. 18th St. (at Laflin St.; ℂ **312/421-2552**), serves authentic Mexican seafood dishes, salads, and soups.

On the more bohemian side, linger over a salad, sandwich, or refreshing fruit milkshake *(liquado)* at **Café Jumping Bean,** 1439 W. 18th St. (at Bishop St.; ℂ **312/455-0019**), or kick back with a cup of coffee at artsy **Café Mestizo,** 2123 S. Ashland Ave. (between 21st St. and Cermak Rd.; ℂ **312/942-0095**).

Sushi Wabi ⟨R⟩ JAPANESE/SUSHI   Artfully presented sushi and chic crowds are the order of the day at Sushi Wabi, Randolph Street's Japanese jewel. The minimal-chic decor is industrial and raw, and the lighting is dark and seductive—giving the restaurant the feel of a nightclub rather than a casual sushi bar (weekend DJ music adds to the clubby feel).

Choose from dozens of nigiri sushi (fish and various eggs perched on vinegared rice), maki (rolls of seafood, veggies, and rice in seaweed), a chef's selection sashimi plate, and a smattering of appetizers, entrees, and sides. Sushi highlights include the sea-scallop roll with smelt roe, mayonnaise, avocado, and sesame seeds; the dragon roll of shrimp tempura, eel, and avocado; and the spiky, crunchy spider roll of soft-shell crab, smelt roe, mayonnaise, and pepper-vinegar sauce. Simple entrees such as seared tuna, grilled salmon, teriyaki beef, and sesame-crusted chicken breast will satisfy landlubbers who are accommodating their sushi-loving companions. An intriguing side is the Japanese whipped potato salad with ginger, cucumber, carrots, and scallions. Make a reservation or expect quite a wait, even on school nights. A selection of teas in cast-iron pots and chilled sakes is offered; or try a martini with a ginger-stuffed olive.

842 W. Randolph St. ⓒ 312/563-1224. www.sushiwabi.com. Reservations recommended. Main courses $12–$30. AE, DC, DISC, MC, V. Mon–Fri 11:30am–2pm; Sun–Tues 5–11pm; Wed–Sat 5pm–midnight.

MODERATE

Avec ⟨R⟩ MEDITERRANEAN   A casual wine bar owned by Chef Paul Kahan of neighboring Blackbird (p. 122), Avec keeps things simple: top-quality ingredients in simple preparations that take inspiration from Italian, French, and Spanish cuisines. The menu focuses on a variety of "small plates" meant for sharing (although there are always five or six entree-size offerings as well). This focus on communal dining is reflected in the restaurant's design; the long, narrow dining room, with its wood walls and floors, will strike you as either cramped or cozy, and tables sit so close together you can't help overhearing your neighbors' conversations. I know many people who love Avec's convivial spirit; others find it annoyingly crowded and loud.

The small plates include salads and upscale appetizer-style dishes such as smoked lamb and quail brochettes; dates stuffed with chorizo sausage; and spicy meatballs with Spanish rice and chickpeas. Large plates feature seasonal ingredients and tend to be heartier (pork shoulder or pappardelle with wild mushrooms, for example). There's also a good selection of specialty cheeses. The wine list—focused on the Mediterranean region—is broad but not overwhelming; don't be intimidated if you're not a wine buff because the waitstaff offers plenty of guidance. Whether you like the tight quarters or not, Avec has become a late-night hangout for local chefs and sommeliers—so they must be doing something right.

615 W. Randolph St. ⓒ 312/377-2002. Reservations not accepted. Small plates $5–$12; large plates $15–$20. AE, DC, DISC, MC, V. Mon–Thurs 3:30pm–midnight; Fri–Sat 3:30pm–1am; Sun 3:30pm–10pm.

La Sardine ⟨R⟩ (Finds) BISTRO/FRENCH   Sister to Jean-Claude Poilevey's popular Le Bouchon (and named after a critic's description of that tiny Bucktown bistro; p. 168), this more spacious and gracious destination is bathed in a honeyed glow and is filled with sensual aromas from the open kitchen and rotisserie. La Sardine has a classic bistro look and the warm, friendly service that make this the Randolph Street version of a neighborhood restaurant.

Well-prepared versions of bistro standards include the delicate bouillabaisse in a lobster-saffron broth; ragout of super-tender rabbit, onions, and mashed potatoes;

steak frites; sensational escargots bourguignon; onion soup; and *salade Lyonnaise* (greens, bacon lardons, croutons, and poached egg). The dessert menu boasts traditional soufflés (with Grand Marnier or chocolate). At lunch choose from an abbreviated menu of appetizers and salads, soups, sandwiches, and entrees, or opt for a hearty *plat du jour,* perhaps tuna Niçoise on Monday, or duck legs braised in red wine with mushrooms and potato purée on Thursday. There's also a daily $22 three-course lunch featuring soup or salad and your choice of entree and dessert.

111 N. Carpenter St. ℂ 312/421-2800. http://frenchrestaurantschicago.com. Reservations recommended. Main courses $13–$15 lunch, $16–$20 dinner. AE, DC, DISC, MC, V. Mon–Fri 11:30am–2:30pm; Mon–Thurs 5–10pm; Fri–Sat 5–11pm.

INEXPENSIVE

Wishbone 𝕣𝕣 𝑲𝒊𝒅𝒔 BREAKFAST & BRUNCH/CAJUN & CREOLE/SOUTHERN One of my best friends—a transplanted Chicagoan who now lives in New York— always has one request when she comes back to town: dinner at Wishbone. It's that kind of place, a down-home, casual spot that inspires intense loyalty (even if the food is only good rather than outstanding).

Known for Southern food and big-appetite breakfasts, Wishbone's extensive, reasonably priced menu blends hearty, home-style choices with healthy and vegetarian items. Brunch is the 'Bone's claim to fame, when an eclectic crowd of bedheads pack in for the plump and tasty salmon cakes, omelets, and red eggs (a lovely mess of tortillas, black beans, cheese, scallions, chile-ancho sauce, salsa, and sour cream). However, brunch at Wishbone can be a mob scene, so I suggest lunch or dinner; offerings include "yardbird" (charbroiled chicken with sweet red-pepper sauce), blackened catfish, and hoppin' John, the classic Southern dish of brown rice, black-eyed peas, and ham (there's also a vegetarian version, hoppin' Jack). The tart Key lime pie is one of my favorite desserts in the city. The casual ambience is a good bet for families (plus a children's menu is available).

There's a newer location at 3300 N. Lincoln Ave. (at W. School St.; ℂ 773/549-2663), but the original location has more character.

1001 Washington St. (at Morgan St). ℂ 312/850-2663. www.wishbonechicago.com. Reservations accepted, except for weekend brunch. Main courses $5–$10 breakfast and lunch, $6–$15 dinner. AE, DC, DISC, MC, V. Mon–Fri 7am–3pm; Tues–Thurs 5–9pm; Fri–Sat 5–10pm; brunch Sat–Sun 8am–3pm.

A Taste of Poland

Chicago has long been a popular destination for Polish immigrants (currently, about one million Chicagoans claim Polish ancestry). It's somewhat mystifying, then, why they haven't made much of an impact on the city's dining scene. There are Polish restaurants here, but they tend to be small, casual, family-run affairs in residential neighborhoods far removed from the usual tourist attractions. If you'd like to try some hearty, stick-to-your-ribs Polish food, the best-known restaurant is **Red Apple** (Czerwone Jabluszko), 3121 N. Milwaukee Ave. (ℂ 773/588-5781; http://redapplebuffet.com). Dining here is strictly buffet, and the lineup includes Polish specialties such as pierogi (meat- or cheese-stuffed dumplings) and blintzes, as well as a huge selection of roast meats, salads, and bread (there's even fruit, should you feel nutrient-starved). Best of all is the price: $8.50 on weekdays and $9.50 on weekends for all you can eat.

5 The Magnificent Mile & the Gold Coast

Many tourists who visit Chicago never stray far from the Magnificent Mile and the adjoining Gold Coast area. From the array of restaurants, shops, and pretty streets, it's not hard to see why. The Gold Coast is home to some of the city's wealthiest, most tradition-bound families, people who have been frequenting the same restaurants for years. But newer places, such as Tru, have carved out their own culinary niches here as well. Restaurants here are some of the best in the city—and their prices are right in line with Michigan Avenue's designer boutiques.

VERY EXPENSIVE

Cape Cod Room *(Overrated)* SEAFOOD   A venerable old restaurant in a venerable old hotel, the Cape Cod Room is the kind of place where waiters debone the Dover sole tableside while businessmen work out their next deal. There's nothing nouvelle about the Cape Cod Room, which is part of the draw for old-timers; the restaurant, located on the lower level of The Drake Hotel, is dimly lit and hasn't changed much since it opened in the 1930s. Although the food is fine, I think the prices are far too steep for what you get. But that doesn't stop Cape Cod loyalists—many of whom have been coming here for decades—from filling up the place.

For starters, the hearty Bookbinder red snapper soup is a signature dish. It's flavored to taste with dry sherry brought to the table. Or, you might order a mixed seafood appetizer of shrimp, crab fingers, clams, and oysters. Main-course offerings include Chilean sea bass served with truffle mashed potatoes, red snapper, or bouillabaisse. (If seafood's not your thing, you can order steaks and chops off the menu of Drake Bros., the hotel's steakhouse). I wouldn't call the Cape Cod Room a 'good value, but the people-watching can be priceless.

In The Drake Hotel, 140 E. Walton Place (at Michigan Ave.). ✆ 312/932-4615. Reservations recommended. Main courses $25–$42. AE, DC, DISC, MC, V. Daily 11:30am–2pm and 5:30–10pm. Subway/El: Red Line to Chicago.

Gibsons Bar & Steakhouse *(★★)* STEAK & CHOPS   Popular with its Gold Coast neighbors, Gibsons is the steakhouse you visit when you want to take in a scene. There are sporty cars idling at the valet stand, photos of celebs and near-celebs who've appeared here, and overdressed denizens mingling and noshing in the bar, which has a life all its own. The dining rooms evoke a more romantic feel, from the sleek Art Deco decor to the bow-tied bartenders. The portions are notoriously enormous, so Gibsons is best for groups who are happy to share dishes (I wouldn't recommend it, however, for a romantic dinner *a deux*). If huge portions aren't your thing, you can also order from the bar menu. The namesake martinis are served in 10-ounce glasses, and the entrees are outlandishly scaled, from the six-piece shrimp cocktail so huge you swore you downed a dozen, to the turtle pie that comes with a steak knife (and could easily serve eight people). Yes, Gibsons has a clubby atmosphere, but considering the crowds who show up nightly, the food deserves some credit.

1028 N. Rush St. (at Bellevue Place). ✆ 312/266-8999. www.gibsonssteakhouse.com. Reservations strongly recommended. Main courses $25–$80. AE, DC, DISC, MC, V. Daily 11am–midnight (bar open later). Subway/El: Red Line to Clark/Division.

Morton's *(★★★)* STEAK & CHOPS   Morton's is a well-known chain with a couple dozen locations nationwide, but it's Chicago born and bred, and many people still consider it the king of Chicago-style steakhouses. Named for its founding father, renowned Chicago restaurateur Arnie Morton, Morton's is hidden on the lower level

Magnificent Mile, Gold Coast & River North Dining

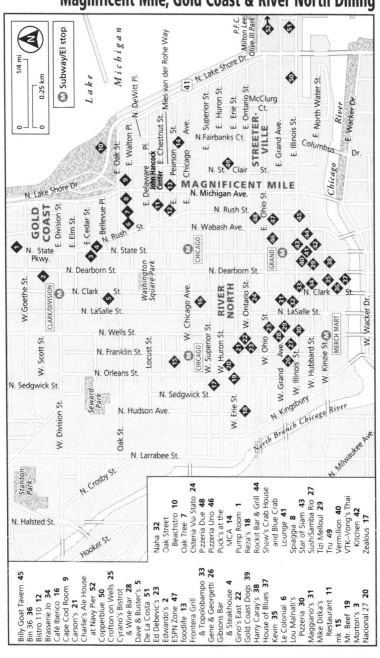

Billy Goat Tavern **45**
Bin 36 **36**
Bistro 110 **12**
Brasserie Jo **34**
Café Iberico **16**
Cape Cod Room **9**
Carson's **21**
Charlie's Ale House
  at Navy Pier **52**
Copperblue **50**
Crofton on Wells **25**
Cyrano's Bistrot
  & Wine Bar **28**
Dave & Buster's **5**
De La Costa **51**
Ed Debevic's **23**
Edwardo's **2**
ESPN Zone **47**
foodlife **13**
Frontera Grill
  & Topolobampo **33**
Gene & Georgetti **26**
Gibsons Bar
  & Steakhouse **4**
Gino's East **22**
Gold Coast Dogs **39**
Harry Caray's **38**
House of Blues **37**
Kevin **35**
Le Colonial **6**
Lou Malnati's
  Pizzeria **30**
Maggiano's **31**
Mike Ditka's
  Restaurant **11**
mk **15**
Mr. Beef **19**
Morton's **3**
Nacional 27 **20**

Naha **32**
Oak Street
  Beachstro **10**
Oak Tree **7**
Osteria Via Stato **24**
Pizzeria Due **48**
Pizzeria Uno **46**
Puck's at the
  MCA **14**
Pump Room **1**
Reza's **18**
Rockit Bar & Grill **44**
Shaw's Crab House
  and Blue Crab
  Lounge **29**
Spiaggia **8**
Star of Siam **43**
SushiSamba Rio **27**
Tizi Melloul **29**
Tru **49**
Vermillion **40**
VTK–Vong's Thai
  Kitchen **42**
Zealous **17**

of an undistinguished high-rise (look for a discreet sign on the closed door in the lobby), and the decor hasn't changed in decades: stucco walls, a line of semicircular booths, and black-and-white photos of retro celebs (Jack Lemmon, Bob Hope, and so on). Most of the menu has stayed the same for years, too. Starters include lobster bisque, Caesar salad, shrimp, or jumbo lump-crabmeat cocktail, but meat is the main event. House specialties include the double filet mignon with béarnaise sauce, and classic cuts of porterhouse, New York strip, and rib-eye, with the usual array of a la carte sides. (There are a few nods to health-conscious diners: The sautéed fresh-spinach-and-mushrooms combo is a tasty, lighter alternative to the traditional creamed spinach.) Massive two-person soufflés are a signature dessert, but after stuffing myself with steak, I prefer the Key lime pie. Overall, Morton's steaks are dependable rather than awe-inspiring, but the place has a relaxed, welcoming ambience that attracts a wide range of customers (I've seen everyone from power-suited businessmen to 20-somethings in jeans chowing down here).

Morton's also has a Loop location at 65 E. Wacker Place, between Michigan and Wabash avenues (© 312/201-0410), with the same menu and a slightly more upscale, clubby decor; unlike the original location, it's open for lunch.

1050 N. State St. (at Rush St.). © 312/266-4820. www.mortons.com. Reservations recommended. Main courses $26–$44. AE, DC, DISC, MC, V. Mon–Sat 5:30–11pm; Sun 5–10pm. Subway/El: Red Line to Chicago.

Pump Room (Overrated) AMERICAN/FRENCH   The Pump Room is definitely an iconic Chicago restaurant, but these days its main draw is nostalgia—not the food. Back when celebrities journeyed by train between Hollywood and New York, stopping in Chicago to court the press, they always had a meal at the Pump Room, located inside the Ambassador East hotel. Diners at Booth One inevitably showed up in the morning papers. Today, the only celebrities you're likely to see here are the photographs of movie stars lining the walls. It's the kind of place that's thought of fondly as a local institution, but a recent turnover of chefs (they've changed chefs almost every year for the past 5 years) has made the cuisine inconsistent.

Like the interior, the menu has had a few makeovers over the years; today the focus is on classic American dishes with a sophisticated twist. Appetizers range from a simple beef tartare or stuffed pumpkin gnocchi to a salad of poached pear, Roquefort, candied hazelnut, and zinfandel dressing. The entrees are upscale but fairly straightforward, including filet mignon with fava-bean puree, truffled carrots, and shiitake mushrooms; braised bison short ribs with white bean cassoulet; and wild Alaskan salmon with artichoke puree, charred red onions, crispy bacon, and olive oil emulsion. There's a live band and dancing every Friday and Saturday night from 8pm to midnight. Because it is located in the Ambassador East hotel, the Pump Room also serves breakfast.

In the Ambassador East Hotel, 1301 N. State Pkwy. (at Goethe St.). © 312/266-0360. www.pumproom.com. Reservations required. No jeans allowed. Main courses $20–$37. AE, DC, DISC, MC, V. Mon–Fri 6:30am–2pm; Sat–Sun 7am–2pm; daily 6–10pm. Subway/El: Red Line to Clark/Division.

Spiaggia (stars) ITALIAN   *Spiaggia* means "beach" in Italian, and the restaurant's name is a tribute to its spectacular view of Lake Michigan and Oak Street Beach. But this is no casual beach cafe. Spiaggia is widely acknowledged as the best fine-dining Italian restaurant in the city (and maybe the entire U.S.). The dining room is bright, airy, and sophisticated, an atmosphere far removed from your neighborhood trattoria—so dress to impress (gentlemen, wear your jackets).

> **Tips A Spot of Tea**
>
> If you're shopping on the Magnificent Mile and feel like having an elegant afternoon tea complete with finger sandwiches, scones, and pastries, head for the stately **Palm Court** at The Drake Hotel, 140 E. Walton Place (© 312/787-2200); the cozy **Seasons Lounge** of the Four Seasons Hotel, 120 E. Delaware Place (© 312/280-8800); or **The Greenhouse** in the Ritz-Carlton, 160 E. Pearson St. (© 312/266-1000), in the sunny 12th-floor lobby above the Water Tower Place mall. In the Loop, the appropriately named **Russian Tea Time** ★★, 77 E. Adams St. (© 312/360-0000), serves tea from 2:30 to 4:30pm daily.

You can order a la carte or a seven-course degustation menu; entree choices change often and emphasize seasonal ingredients. Recent starters included carpaccio of smoked Sicilian swordfish or pork loin wrapped in pancetta, served with sautéed artichoke hearts in a balsamic vinegar dressing. This ain't your mama's pasta, either: Recent offerings have included pheasant-stuffed ravioli, pumpkin risotto, and gnocchi with black-truffle sauce. Entree examples include products of the restaurant's wood-burning oven, including monkfish; salmon; duck breast with Ligurian black olives, tomatoes, fennel, and baby artichokes; and grilled squab over lentils with foie gras. You're encouraged to order Italian-style (appetizer, pasta, meat), which means the bill can add up pretty quickly. But if you're a cheese lover, this is the place to splurge on a cheese course: They'll roll out a cart filled with rare varieties and give you extensive descriptions of each one.

Adjacent to the restaurant in a narrow, window-lined space is the informal, lower-priced **Café Spiaggia** (© 312/280-2755), which has the same dinner hours as the main restaurant but is also open for lunch every day.

980 N. Michigan Ave. (at Oak St.). © 312/280-2750. www.levyrestaurants.com. Reservations strongly suggested on weekends. Main courses $34–$41; menu degustation $95–$135. AE, DC, DISC, MC, V. Sun–Thurs 6–9:30pm; Fri–Sat 5:30–10:30pm. Subway/El: Red Line to Chicago.

Tru ★★★ AMERICAN Chefs Rick Tramonto and Gale Gand have made Tru a top dining destination, thanks to its sophisticated-but-not-snobbish cuisine and atmosphere. The menu shines with appetizers such as grilled diver sea scallops with red pepper essence, chorizo, and avocado dumplings; and entrees such as Colorado lamb rib-eye with white turnips, grapefruit, and bergamot. The three-course menu is prix fixe ($95), with all items on the menu available a la carte. If your wallet and stomach permit, go for the nine-course Chef Tramonto's Market Collection ($145), featuring selections inspired by what was available at that day's markets. For a conspicuous splurge, order the visually sensational caviar staircase (caviars and fixin's climbing a glass spiral staircase), which goes for $250. Gand is one of the city's best pastry chefs, and her desserts perfectly echo Tramonto's savory menus. Sate your sweet tooth with her pineapple rum soup or sticky toffee pudding. Service is generally polished but not pompous. The expansive wine list is a treat for oenophiles, with 1,200 selections.

676 N. St. Clair St. (at Huron St.). © 312/202-0001. www.trurestaurant.com. Reservations required. Prix-fixe menu $80–$150. AE, DC, DISC, MC, V. Mon–Thurs 5:30–10pm; Fri–Sat 5:30–11pm. Subway/El: Red Line to Chicago.

EXPENSIVE

Bistro 110 CONTINENTAL   Bistro 110 enjoys a prime location just a half-block west of North Michigan Avenue. Although a harbinger of the now-booming bistro trend, it's really too large and pricey to be considered an authentic bistro, but it does have a bustling energy that I find invigorating. The menu covers a broad price range and includes several bistro classics such as escargots in puff pastry, mussels in white-wine sauce, French onion soup, cassoulet, and steak au poivre. While other restaurants chase the latest foodie trends, Bistro 110 keeps certain dishes on the menu year after year—such as the decadently hearty Beef Wellington with a rich port demi glaze—and that's just how the regulars like it. The wood-roasted items, including a savory half chicken and a bountiful roast vegetable plate, are consistently good. Although the menu touts *"la fameuse"* crème brûlée, there's nothing that really distinguishes it from its many cousins. Other desserts include chocolate mousse, lemon and apple tarts, and a massive *Gâteau Paradis au Chocolat,* a decadent mix of chocolate cake, caramel, and toffee (which satisfies chocoholics like me far more than the crème brûlée). On Sunday the restaurant hosts a popular brunch with live jazz music.

110 E. Pearson St. (just west of Michigan Ave.). © **312/266-3110.** www.levyrestaurants.com. Main courses $16–$30. AE, DC, DISC, MC, V. Mon–Thurs 11:30am–10pm; Fri–Sat 11:30am–11pm; Sun 10:30am–10pm. Subway/El: Red Line to Chicago.

Copperblue ☆ MEDITERRANEAN   Chef Michael Tsonton (known around here for his role in opposing the city's ban on foie gras in 2006), has created a wonderful restaurant that is truly a hidden gem. Its inconspicuous location (occupying a ground-floor corner of the curvy black Lake Point Tower in front of Navy Pier) does not allow for a lot of walk-by recognition, but Copperblue probably would have become a "destination" restaurant no matter where it chose to set up shop. The dining room is warm, with ancient mural scenes on the walls, but it is also bright, with shades of gold and deep blue. That same serious-yet-whimsical sensibility carries over to the menu. Recent offerings included snails in white wine with fresh hearts of palm and green garlic; and crispy saffron and Spanish ham rice croquettes called "ham & these." Entrees featured roasted Berkshire pork loin and crispy belly with wild ramps and dandelion greens; and Pacific snapper with fava beans and watercress in mustard spice "and everything nice" butter broth. There are three tasting menus, one of which is called "the fifth quarter," which refers not to the five courses in it ($60) but to the fact that the offerings come from the parts of the animal that normally do not get cooked in fine restaurants, let alone eaten. Traditional five- and seven-course chef's tastings cost $65 and $80, respectively. The wine list, like the food, sticks close to the Mediterranean, too, with French varietals broken down by region.

580 E. Illinois St. (between Lake Shore Dr. and Navy Pier). © **312/527-1200.** www.copperbluechicago.com. Reservations recommended. Main courses $19–$45. AE, DC, DISC, MC, V. Tues–Thurs 5:30–10:30pm; Fri–Sat 5:30–11:30pm; Sun 5–9pm. Subway/El: Red Line to Grand, then a short cab ride.

De La Costa ☆ LATIN AMERICAN   The name means "of the coast," but don't come here expecting shoreline views; Lake Michigan is a few blocks away. Executive chef Douglas Rodriguez (of New York's Patria and Philadelphia's Alma de Cuba) says the menu was inspired by the coastal cuisines of Spain, the Caribbean, and South America—which means plenty of fresh fish and some bold flavor combinations. The overall vibe (and price tag) is Miami-chic rather than beachcomber casual, with a long, gleaming white bar, artfully draped curtains, and a buzzing, boisterous clientele.

(*Finds* Dessert Tour

Eli's cheesecake is a Chicago icon—the rich, creamy cakes have been served at presidential inaugurations and numerous other high-profile events. For a behind-the-scenes peek at Chicago's most famous dessert, take a tour of Eli's bakery on the northwest side of the city. After watching the cooking and decorating processes, you get to enjoy a full-size slice of your favorite flavor. Tours are given Monday through Friday at 1pm (although reservations aren't necessary, call to make sure the bakery isn't closed for periodic maintenance). The 40-minute tour costs $3 for adults and $2 for children 11 and under; special packages are available for groups of 10 or more. Eli's bakery is at 6701 Forest Preserve Dr., at the corner of Montrose Avenue (© 800/ELI-CAKE; www.elischeesecake.com).

Whether you graze tapas-style (appetizers and small plates make up a substantial part of the menu) or want to fill up with a hearty meat entree, you should definitely start with one of the house specialty ceviches, such as the "Fire and Ice" (which mixes tuna, calamari, chiles, coconut, and lime for a unique spicy-yet-cool experience). Tapas include specialty cheeses, mussels, empanadas stuffed with porcini mushrooms, and marlin tacos. Among the entrees, the Churrasco De La Costa—a tender beef tenderloin topped with a tasty, mildly spicy chimichurri sauce—lives up to its billing as a house signature dish. The Brazilian-inspired Xim Xim (chicken and giant shrimp in a coconut sauce with roasted cashews) is flavorful and ideal for smaller appetites. If you're in the mood for a lighter meal, settle down at the ceviche bar that extends along one side of the restaurant.

465 E. Illinois St. (between McClurg Ct. and Lake Shore Dr.). © 312/464-1700. http://delacostachicago.com. Reservations recommended. Main courses $21–$38. AE, DC, DISC, MC, V. Mon–Fri 11:30am–2pm; Sun–Thurs 5–10pm; Fri–Sat 5–11pm; bar open until 1am Fri–Sat. Subway/El: Red Line to Grand, then a short cab ride.

Mike Ditka's Restaurant ✿ AMERICAN/STEAK & CHOPS   In this city, nobody refers to him by name. He is simply "Da Coach." Immortalized as such in the classic "Super Fans" sketch on *Saturday Night Live,* "Iron" Mike Ditka remains the quintessential cigar-chomping, hard-nosed Chicagoan—despite the fact that it's been more than 2 decades since he led the Chicago Bears to victory in Super Bowl XX in 1986. Flooded with dim, amber light and filled with dark wood, leather banquettes, and walls lined with Ditka memorabilia and artful tributes to the coach's own sports heroes, this is man country—and the food is a good step up from your average sports bar. Appetizers here are called "Kickoffs" and include a "Duck Cigar," a hand-rolled pastry with a hearty duck-and-mushroom filling, and a "Souper Bowl" of corn chowder ("the Coach's favorite"). There are lots of salads, pastas, and seafood dishes to choose from, but why be a wimp? Go for the "Fullback Size" filet mignon with spinach and homemade onion rings or "Da Pork Chop," surrounded by warm cinnamon apples and a green-peppercorn sauce. When you're finished, light up a stogie in the second-floor cigar lounge and who knows? You might be joined by Da Coach himself, who makes regular appearances here.

100 E. Chestnut St. (in the Tremont Hotel, between Michigan Ave. and Rush St.). *©* 312/587-8989. www.mike ditkaschicago.com. Main courses $10–$16 lunch, $15–$40 dinner. AE, DC, DISC, MC, V. Mon–Thurs 7am–10pm; Fri–Sun 7am–11pm. Subway/El: Red Line to Chicago.

MODERATE

Le Colonial *(★★ Finds* FRENCH/VIETNAMESE Appropriately enough for its tony Oak Street environs, Le Colonial has one of the loveliest dining rooms in the city—and the second-floor lounge is a sultry, seductive cocktail destination. An escapist's paradise, the restaurant is a cleverly crafted re-creation of the civilized yet exotic world of 1920s Saigon: bamboo shutters, rattan chairs, potted palms and banana trees, fringed lampshades and ceiling fans, and evocative period photography.

While the ambience certainly merits a visit, the flavorful cuisine is a draw on its own. Start with the hearty oxtail soup or the light and refreshing beef-and-watercress salad. Entrees include grilled lime-glazed sea scallops with garlic noodle salad; sautéed jumbo shrimp in curried coconut sauce; and roasted chicken with lemon-grass-and-lime dipping sauce. Refresh with the orange-mint iced tea, and finish with banana tapioca pudding, a gooey Le Colonial macaroon, or an after-dinner drink upstairs. Le Colonial offers outdoor seating in warm weather; try to reserve one of the coveted, romantic mezzanine terrace tables.

937 N. Rush St. (just south of Oak St.). *©* 312/255-0088. www.lecolonialchicago.com. Reservations recommended. Main courses $15–$22 lunch, $17–$28 dinner. AE, DC, MC, V. Daily 11:30am–2:30pm; Mon–Wed 5–11pm; Thurs–Sat 5pm–midnight; Sun 5–10pm. Subway/El: Red Line to Chicago.

Shaw's Crab House and Blue Crab Lounge *★* SEAFOOD Shaw's is a local institution—if you ask average Chicagoans where to go for seafood, chances are they'll point you here. The bright, busy room has a lively vibe, and the extensive menu should suit all tastes (the appetizers, for example, run the gamut from popcorn shrimp and fried calamari to crab cakes and exotic sushi combinations). And lest you wonder about ordering seafood when you're so far from an ocean, Shaw's does fly in seasonal seafood daily. You can even order fresh oysters according to their provenance (Nova Scotia, British Columbia, and so on). Main courses include Alaskan king crab, sautéed scallops, Texas stone-crab claws, crab cakes, and french-fried shrimp; you can also take advantage of various (expensive) surf-and-turf combinations. Shaw's trademark dessert, Key lime pie, suggests the restaurant's subtle Key West/Papa Hemingway theme, as do the suave strains of such 1930s tunes as "Begin the Beguine" playing in the background. On Sunday, Tuesday, and Thursday nights, there's live jazz and blues in the lounge.

21 E. Hubbard St. (between State St. and Wabash Ave.). *©* 312/527-2722. www.shawscrabhouse.com. Reservations accepted only for the main dining room. Main courses $14–$35. AE, DC, DISC, MC, V. Mon–Fri 11:30am–2pm; Mon–Thurs 5:30–10pm; Fri–Sat 5–11pm; Sun 5–10pm. Subway/El: Red Line to Grand.

INEXPENSIVE

Billy Goat Tavern *★ Value* BREAKFAST & BRUNCH/BURGERS "Cheeze-borger, Cheezeborger—No Coke . . . Pepsi." Viewers of the original *Saturday Night Live* will certainly remember the classic John Belushi routine, a moment in the life of a crabby Greek short-order cook. The comic got his material from the Billy Goat Tavern, located under North Michigan Avenue near the bridge that crosses to the Loop (you'll find it by walking down the steps across the street from the Chicago Tribune building). Just BUTT IN ANYTIME, says the sign on the red door. The tavern is a classic dive: dark, seedy, and no-frills. But unlike the *Saturday Night Live* skit, the guys behind the counter are friendly ("Double cheezeborger is the best!" one shouted out cheerfully to me when I couldn't decide what to order on my last visit). The menu is pretty basic (mostly hamburgers and hot dogs), but yes, the cheeseburgers are pretty good. Billy Goat is a hangout for newspaper workers and writers, so you might over-hear the latest media buzz. After work this is a good place to watch a game, chitchat at the bar, and down a few beers.

For the same "cheezeborgers" in less grungy (and more kid-friendly) surroundings, head to the Billy Goat's outpost on Navy Pier (© **312/670-8789**).

430 N. Michigan Ave. © **312/222-1525**. www.billygoattavern.com. Reservations not accepted. Menu items $4–$7. No credit cards. Mon–Fri 6am–2am; Sat 10am–2am; Sun 11am–2am. Subway/El: Red Line to Chicago.

foodlife ✦✦ *(Finds* ECLECTIC   Taking the standard food court up a few notches, foodlife consists of a dozen or so kiosks offering both ordinary and exotic specialties on the mezzanine of Water Tower Place mall. Seats are spread out cafe style in a pleas-ant environment under realistic boughs of artificial trees festooned with strings of lights. A hostess will seat you, give you an electronic card, and then it's up to you to stroll around and get whatever food strikes your fancy (each purchase is recorded on your card, and you pay on the way out).

The beauty of a food court, of course, is that it offers something for everybody. At foodlife, diners can choose from burgers, pizza, south-of-the-border dishes, an assort-ment of Asian fare, and veggie-oriented, low-fat offerings. A lunch or snack is basically inexpensive, but the payment method makes it easy to build up a big tab while hold-ing a personal taste-testing session at each kiosk.

In Water Tower Place, 835 N. Michigan Ave. © **312/335-3663**. Reservations not accepted. Most items $8–$15. AE, DC, DISC, MC, V. Breakfast kiosk daily 7:30–10:30am. All other kiosks Mon–Thurs 11am–8pm; Fri–Sun 11am–9pm. Subway/El: Red Line to Chicago.

Oak Tree ✦ AMERICAN   Though it's located on the sixth floor of the ritzy 900 N. Michigan indoor mall (home of Bloomingdale's, Gucci, and others), Oak Tree isn't exactly high profile. But it's popular with the younger ladies-who-lunch crowd and is one of my favorite places for a meal during a day of downtown shopping. The cafe

---

Tips **Kitchens Up-Close**

Serious food fans can get a firsthand look at how some of the city's culinary stars work by booking a seat at a chef's table. You'll get a personal tour of the kitchen, a special selection of dishes, and—best of all—a front-row seat for din-ner-hour drama. At **Tru** (© **312/202-0001**), four to six people can sit in a glass-enclosed room off the kitchen, where they can check out the scene without feeling the heat. The chef's table at **Charlie Trotter's** ✦✦✦ (© **773/248-6228**) seats four to six right in the kitchen, so diners can catch Trotter's legendary per-fectionism up close. At **Zealous** ✦✦✦ (© **312/475-9112**), the chef's table seats 8 to 10 and is in the main dining room—but bamboo trees surround it, so other diners won't get jealous when chef Michael Taus stops by for some one-on-one taste tests.

Chef's tables don't come cheap ($100–$175 per person), but they're a special splurge for die-hard foodies. Just remember to reserve well in advance because these tables book fast.

Only in Chicago

PIZZA

We have three pizza styles in Chicago: Chicago style, also known as deep-dish, which is thick-crusted and often demands a knife and fork; stuffed, which is similar to a pie, with a crust on both top and bottom; and thin crust. Many pizzerias serve both thick and thin, and some make all three kinds.

Three of Chicago's best gourmet deep-dish restaurants are **Pizzeria Uno** 🖈 (p. 153), **Pizzeria Due** (p. 153), and **Gino's East** 🖈🖈 (p. 147). In River North, **Lou Malnati's Pizzeria** 🖈, 439 N. Wells St. (at Hubbard St.; ℭ 312/828-9800), bakes both deep-dish and thin-crust pizza and even has a low-fat-cheese option. **Edwardo's** is a local pizza chain that serves all three varieties, but with a wheat crust and all-natural ingredients (spinach pizza is the specialty here); locations are in the Gold Coast at 1212 N. Dearborn St. (at Division St.; ℭ 312/337-4490); in the South Loop at 521 S. Dearborn St. (between Congress Pkwy. and Harrison St.; ℭ 312/939-3366); and in Lincoln Park at 2622 N. Halsted St. (at Wrightwood Ave.; ℭ 773/871-3400). Not far from Lincoln Park Zoo is **Ranalli and Ryan's,** 1925 N. Lincoln Ave. (between Wisconsin St. and Armitage Ave.; ℭ 312/642-4700), whose biggest selling point is a large open-air patio and extensive selection of beers.

In Wrigleyville, just off Belmont Avenue, is **Leona's Pizzeria,** 3215 N. Sheffield Ave. (between Belmont Ave. and School St.; ℭ 773/327-8861), which serves all three kinds of pizza. Leona's also has a location in Little Italy at 1419 W. Taylor St. (between Bishop and Loomis sts.; ℭ 312/850-2222).

For a unique take on the deep-dish phenomenon, try the "pizza potpie" at **Chicago Pizza & Oven Grinder,** 2121 N. Clark St., steps from the Lincoln Park Zoo (between Webster and Dickens aves.; ℭ 773/248-2570). The pizzas are baked in a bowl and then turned over when served. This neighborhood spot stays popular year after year, so plan on showing up early for dinner to avoid a long wait.

decor is bright and cheery, with nature-inspired murals to help you momentarily forget that you're inside a mall. If you can, get a table along the windows that look down on Michigan Avenue—but be aware that everyone else coming to eat here wants those tables, too. Oak Tree's real draw is the enormous, varied menu. You'll find something to satisfy every taste: a large salad selection, Asian noodles, sandwiches that range from trendy (duck breast with mango chutney) to manly (meatball with roasted bell peppers), Mexican quesadillas, even blue-plate specials such as turkey hash or a patty melt. The breakfast menu is just as extensive. Oak Tree can get crowded during prime weekend lunch hours, but it's relatively calm by mid-afternoon—just about the time you've power-shopped all your energy away and need a break.

900 N. Michigan Ave. (at Delaware Place), 6th floor. ℭ 312/751-1988. Reservations not accepted. Main courses $8–$15. AE, DC, DISC, MC, V. Mon–Fri 7:30am–6:30pm; Sat–Sun 7:30am–5:30pm. Subway/El: Red Line to Chicago.

HOT DOGS

The classic Chicago hot dog includes a frankfurter by Vienna Beef (a local food processor and hallowed institution), heaps of chopped onions and green relish, a slather of yellow mustard, pickle spears, fresh tomato wedges, a dash of celery salt, and, for good measure, two or three "sport" peppers, those thumb-shaped holy terrors that turn your mouth into its own bonfire.

Chicago is home to many standout hot-dog spots but one, **Hot Doug's,** 3324 N. California Ave. (at Roscoe Street, © 773/279-9550), takes encased meats to a new level, featuring several gourmet sausages on a bun every day except Sunday (plan on standing in line no matter which day you show up—and it's always worth it). Hot Doug's also serves a great classic Chicago dog just like many other stands in town, including **Gold Coast Dogs,** 159 N. Wabash Ave., at Randolph Street (© 312/917-1677), in the Loop just a block from Michigan Avenue. **Fluky's,** in The Shops at North Bridge mall, 520 N. Michigan Ave. (© 312/245-0702), is part of a local chain that has been serving great hot dogs since the Depression (Dan Aykroyd and Jay Leno are fans). **Portillo's,** 100 W. Ontario St. (at Clark St.; © 312/587-8930), is another local chain that specializes in hot dogs but also serves tasty pastas and salads. **Murphy's Red Hots,** 1211 W. Belmont Ave. (at Racine Ave.; © 773/935-2882), is a neighborhood spot not too far from Wrigley Field, while **The Wieners Circle,** in Lincoln Park at 2622 N. Clark St. (between Wrightwood Ave. and Drummond Place; © 773/477-7444), is a late-night favorite where rude order-takers are part of the shtick.

If you've got a car, head up to **Superdawg Drive-In,** 6363 N. Milwaukee Ave. (at Devon Ave.; © 773/763-0660), on the northwest side of the city (look for the giant hot dogs dressed as Tarzan and Jane on the roof). This classic 1950s-style flashback has been run by the same family for three generations, and, yes, they still have carhops who bring out your order.

6 River North

For restaurants listed in this section, see the map "The Magnificent Mile, Gold Coast & River North Dining" on p. 131.

River North, the area north of the Loop and west of Michigan Avenue, is home to the city's most concentrated cluster of art galleries and a something-for-everyone array of restaurants—from fast food and themed restaurants to chains and some of our trendiest dining destinations. Whether you seek a quick dog or burger, contemporary American fine dining, exotic Moroccan, or world-class Mexican fare, River North has it all.

VERY EXPENSIVE

Kevin ᏬᏬ ASIAN/FUSION   Chef Kevin Shikami had been cooking up fusion dishes for years in various restaurants around town, but he was finally able to let loose when he opened his own place. The overall mood of his namesake restaurant is Zen calm (dark wood tables, chairs, and floors; recessed lights that illuminate textured paper covers). The menu emphasizes Japanese and Thai preparations and flavors;

Fun Fact **Chicago Treats**

Deep-dish pizza may be Chicago's culinary claim to fame, but the city has added to the national waistline in other ways. Twinkies and Wonder Bread were invented here; Chicago businessman James L. Kraft created the first processed cheese; and Oscar Mayer got his start as a butcher in the Old Town neighborhood.

---

almost half the entrees are seafood. Shikami's signature dish is his tuna tartare, widely acknowledged as one of the city's best versions of this now-trendy appetizer (here, it's livened up with spicy wasabi and paired with a seasonal salad). Lobster and scallops get a kick from mandarin-orange sauce, while red snapper with a pistachio crust is served with steamed crab wontons in a ginger-orange sauce. Kevin doesn't quite attain the creativity of other restaurants in this price range, but it's a reliable place to find top-quality, modern takes on Asian cuisine. The subdued setting makes it a good choice for business lunches and dinners (as long as you've got a generous expense account).

9 W. Hubbard St. (at State St.). © 312/595-0055. www.kevinrestaurant.com. Main courses $17–$18 lunch, $30–$36 dinner. AE, DISC, MC, V. Mon–Fri 11:30am–2pm; Mon–Thurs 5:30–10pm; Fri–Sat 5:30–10:30pm. Subway/El: Brown Line to Merchandise Mart.

mk ✶✶✶ AMERICAN   Even though foodies rank it one of the top American restaurants in the city, mk doesn't flaunt its pedigree. The loftlike dining room is as understated as the lowercase initials that give the restaurant its name. Chef Michael Kornick keeps the menu focused on a fairly straightforward seasonal mix of meat and seafood: Menu selections might range from hearty (roasted duck breast with baby turnips and fava beans; rack of lamb with lamb-stuffed cannelloni and fig jam) to lighter offerings, such as grilled salmon with a Chinese mustard glaze and ginger-soy vinaigrette. The presentations are tasteful rather than dazzling; Kornick wants you to concentrate on the food, and that's just what the chic, mixed-age crowd does. Service is disciplined yet agreeable, and fine table appointments signal this restaurant's commitment to quality. As for dessert, The Peanut Gallery (peanut butter mousse, crispy milk chocolate, warm brownies, pretzels, hot fudge and caramel) is worth the calories.

868 N. Franklin St. (1 block north of Chicago Ave.). © 312/482-9179. www.mkchicago.com. Reservations recommended. Main courses $27–$46; menu degustation $80 ($90 w/cheese course). AE, DC, MC, V. Sun–Thurs 5:30–10pm; Fri–Sat 5:30–10:30pm. Subway/El: Brown Line to Chicago.

Naha ✶✶ AMERICAN   Chef Carrie Nahabedian (who used her nickname for the restaurant's name) did time at four-star hotels in California before returning to her hometown, and a West Coast influence is clear in her wine list and use of seasonal ingredients. But she adds Mediterranean flavors to the mix, including dishes that reflect her Armenian heritage.

Dishes at Naha combine diverse flavors without getting fussy. The duck liver with roasted preserved quince is a delightfully rich starter, and tartare of ahi tuna topped with caviar comes garnished with a colorful mix of diced vegetables. Entrees are hearty: veal rib-eye with oven-cured tomatoes and cipollini onions; sirloin steak with a goat cheese gratin; and hot smoked salmon with lentils, cabbage, and caramelized onions. The dessert menu leans toward fruit; a highlight is the warm pear cake topped

---

Fun Fact McDonald's Gets Glitzy

I have mixed feelings about recommending a fast-food chain restaurant in this guide, but let's get real: Most visitors (especially if they're here with kids) stop for a greasy fix at some point during their stay. If you're going to go the fast-food route, head for the McDonald's at the corner of Grand Avenue and Clark Street, which was unveiled for the company's 50th anniversary in 2005. The gleaming, glass-enclosed building looks like something out of *The Jetsons,* and it's filled with stylish amenities that would look right at home in a luxury airport lounge. You can chow down while relaxing in a reproduction of Mies van der Rohe's famous Barcelona chair, check out the exhibit of collectible Happy Meal toys from inside a 1960s-style egg chair, or order a cappuccino and gelato at the upstairs cafe.

---

with almond ice cream and served with a red Bartlett pear sorbet and pear compote on the side (as my waiter described it, "Naughty, but not too naughty.").

A front lounge offers a special menu of *meze* (Mediterranean "small dishes"), including flatbread with tomatoes, goat cheese, and artichokes; lamb kabobs; and feta cheese phyllo triangles made from the chef's mother's recipe. At lunchtime, Naha's hamburger ($12) is so renowned and in demand, the restaurant sometimes runs out of them.

500 N. Clark St. (at Illinois St.). © **312/321-6242.** www.naha-chicago.com. Reservations recommended. Main courses $10–$25 lunch, $26–$46 dinner. AE, DC, DISC, MC, V. Mon–Fri 11:30am–2pm; Mon–Thurs 5:30–9:30pm; Fri–Sat 5:30–10pm. Subway/El: Red Line to Grand.

Zealous *★★★* AMERICAN   One of the most stylish contemporary restaurants in town, Zealous also has one of the most eclectic menus. Chef Michael Taus's cooking combines American ingredients with the subtle complexity of Chinese, Vietnamese, Korean, and Indian cuisines. Diners order from the a la carte menu or from one of four degustation menus; recent entrees have ranged from Asian-inspired (sesame-crusted Chilean sea bass with red coconut-curry sauce) to heartland hearty (roasted pork rack stuffed with dried peaches and served with carrot pierogi). Zealous is especially welcoming to non–meat eaters; there is always a five-course vegetarian menu available, and the kitchen will prepare vegan entrees on request. The dining room is bright and airy (thanks to a central skylight), and the purple chairs, green banquettes, and silver accents make the space feel trendy but not intimidating. The 6,000-bottle wine collection and glass-enclosed wine cellar show that Zealous takes its libations just as seriously as it takes its food (450 label selections appear on the wine list).

419 W. Superior St. © **312/475-9112.** www.zealousrestaurant.com. Reservations recommended. Main courses $18–$45; menu degustation $75–$125. AE, DISC, MC, V. Tues–Sat 5–11pm. Subway/El: Brown Line to Chicago.

EXPENSIVE

Bin 36 *★★* AMERICAN   In one lofty, airy space, this River North hot spot combines wine, food, and retail in a successful, wine-centric concept. You can swirl, sniff, and snack in the Tavern wine bar; sample artisinal cheeses at the Cheese Bar; or settle down at the Cellar for a full meal of American bistro fare (where a list of higher-end wines by the bottle is available).

Bin 36 manages to be both upscale and relaxed. The restaurant is certainly serious about wine and cheese, but you're not expected to be an expert—this is a place where you're encouraged to experiment. The menu includes two or three suggested wines for every dish, all of which are available by the glass—and you won't go wrong by following the menu's suggestions. "Small plates" available at the Tavern include shiitake spring rolls, steamed mussels, and a selection of homemade pâtés, along with a few basic full-portion entrees (hamburgers, roast chicken, ahi tuna). You can also have fun ordering creative "wine flights," small glasses organized around a theme (Italian, Australian, and so on). The Cellar menu focuses on upscale American dishes, including a variety of seafood, seared venison, and braised pork shank. The food-wine pairings continue on the dessert menu; a recommended sherry along with a slice of gingerbread-pear cake here one evening was a delight.

339 N. Dearborn St. (C) 312/755-9463. www.bin36.com. Reservations recommended. Main courses $9–$15 lunch, $17–$24 dinner. AE, DC, DISC, MC, V. Mon–Thurs 11am–midnight; Fri 11am–2am; Sat noon–2am; Sun noon–10pm. Subway/El: Red Line to Grand.

Brasserie Jo *⊛* ALSATIAN/FRENCH   Brasserie Jo showcases the casual side of chef Jean Joho, whose upscale Everest, p. 116, is one of the city's longtime gourmet destinations. The high-ceilinged dining room here is open and spacious (as compared to a cozy bistro); you'll feel as if you're dining in an Art Deco Parisian cafe. Following in the tradition of the classic Alsatian *brasserie* (meaning "brewery"), Brasserie Jo makes a malty house brew, and diners are welcome for a quick stop-in snack with a glass of wine or a full five-course meal. Since the restaurant is open relatively late on weekends, it also makes a good stop for dessert (grab a seat at the pressed-metal bar).

You can order a hearty Alsatian choucroute here, but the menu focuses more on casual French classics: Entrees are divided into seafood, steak, and a variety of bistro-style specialties (chicken coq au vin, pork tenderloin ratatouille, rack of lamb), along with tartes, the Alsatians' version of thin-crust pizza. One house specialty that's worth a try is the "shrimp bag," a phyllo pastry filled with shrimp, peas, and herb rice garnished with lobster sauce. Save room for dessert: The delightfully decadent caramel-banana coupe is served in a tall glass, and just might be the perfect sundae. I also love the rich chocolate mousse, which is served tableside from a massive silver bowl, then topped with fresh cream and shaved chocolate—just like in Paris.

59 W. Hubbard St. (between Dearborn and Clark sts.). (C) 312/595-0800. www.brasseriejo.com. Reservations recommended. Main courses $18–$30. AE, DC, DISC, MC, V. Mon–Thurs 5–10pm; Fri–Sat 5–11pm; Sun 4–9pm. Subway/El: Brown Line to Merchandise Mart or Red Line to Grand.

Crofton on Wells *⊛⊛* (Finds) AMERICAN   Chef-owner Suzy Crofton has devoted herself to this contemporary American restaurant, a 70-seat River North storefront with a loyal following and plenty of critical acclaim to its credit. Crofton's food is simply sophisticated and decidedly American, and the relatively spare dining room fits in with her no-attitude, Midwestern aesthetic.

The menu is based on seasonally available ingredients: You might start with a chilled cucumber-and-Vidalia-onion soup in the summer, or a roasted squash soup in colder weather. Entree selections always include a vegan choice and run the gamut from a simple ginger-miso broth with soba noodles and seasonal vegetables to more complex creations such as grilled venison medallions topped with peppered mascarpone and served with sweet-potato gnocchi and cherries. Crofton's signature dish is the barbecued pork tenderloin garnished with apple chutney. Close with a Granny

Smith apple tart or bittersweet chocolate cake with espresso ice cream and black-peppercorn caramel sauce. Other chefs may wow the food critics with their spectacular presentations, but Crofton has built her reputation with accessible dishes that attract a low-key crowd of satisfied regulars. A four-course prix-fixe meal is available Monday through Saturday from 5 to 6:30pm for $45 ($65 with wine).

535 N. Wells St. (between Grand Ave. and Ohio St.). ✆ **312/755-1790.** www.croftononwells.com. Reservations recommended. Main courses $12–$17 lunch, $26–$36 dinner. AE, DC, MC, V. Mon–Fri 11:30am–2pm; Mon–Sat 5–11pm. Subway/El: Brown Line to Merchandise Mart.

Frontera Grill & Topolobampo ✿✿✿ MEXICAN

Owners Rick and Deann Groen Bayless, authors of the popular *Authentic Mexican: Regional Cooking from the Heart of Mexico,* are widely credited with bringing authentic Mexican regional cuisine to a wider audience. Their restaurant is the place to taste *real* Mexican food, so don't show up expecting a plate of nachos with processed-cheese topping. The building actually houses two restaurants: the casual Frontera Grill (plain wood tables, terracotta tile floor) and the fine-dining Topolobampo (white linen tablecloths, a more hushed environment). At both restaurants, the focus is on fresh, organic ingredients supplied by local artisanal farmers.

At Frontera, the signature appetizer is the *sopes surtidos,* corn-tortilla "boats" with a sampler of fillings (chicken in red mole, black beans with homemade chorizo, and so on). The ever-changing entree list might include pork loin in a green mole sauce; smoked chicken breast smothered in a sauce of chiles, pumpkin seeds, and roasted garlic; or a classic *sopa de pan* ("bread soup" spiced up with almonds, raisins, grilled green onions, and zucchini). Yes, you can also get tacos (with fillings such as portobello mushrooms, duck, and catfish). The Baylesses up the ante at the adjacent Topolobampo, where both the ingredients and presentation are more upscale.

It can be tough to snag a table at Frontera during prime dining hours, so do what the locals do: Put your name on the list and order a few margaritas in the lively, large bar area.

445 N. Clark St. (between Illinois and Hubbard sts.). ✆ **312/661-1434.** www.fronterakitchens.com. Reservations accepted at Frontera Grill for parties of 5–10; accepted at Topolobampo for parties of 1–6. Frontera Grill main courses $21–$28. Topolobampo main courses $32–$38; chef's 5-course tasting menu $75 ($120 w/wine pairings). AE, DC, DISC, MC, V. Frontera Grill Tues–Fri 11:30am–2:30pm; Sat 10:30am–2:30pm; Tues–Thurs 5–10pm; Fri–Sat 5–11pm. Topolobampo Tues 11:45am–2pm; Wed–Fri 11:30am–2pm; Tues–Thurs 5:30–9:30pm; Fri–Sat 5:30–10:30pm. Subway/El: Red Line to Grand.

Gene & Georgetti ✿ ITALIAN/STEAK & CHOPS

A classic vestige of old Chicago, Gene & Georgetti is a family-run steakhouse that's been serving up steak and Italian fare in a wood-frame house in the shadow of the El since 1941. The restaurant is dark and clubby, and the (exclusively male) waiters seem to have worked here for decades—and they no doubt have been serving some of the same patrons all that time. Gene & Georgetti has a popular following, so expect to wait in the bar area during prime dining hours. Although the place is best known for steaks, classic Italian-American specialties are also an essential part of the menu (mostaccioli, veal parmigiana, and the like). This is not the kind of place you come to make the scene, but fans of old-time restaurants will find plenty of local character.

500 N. Franklin St. (at Illinois St.). ✆ **312/527-3718.** www.geneandgeorgetti.com. Reservations recommended. Main courses $11–$24 lunch, $24–$45 dinner. AE, DC, MC, V. Mon–Sat 11am–midnight. Subway/El: Brown Line to Merchandise Mart.

Green Zebra ⭐ ECLECTIC/VEGETARIAN   Chicago's a red-meat town, but if you need a break from all the beef, it's worth tracking down Green Zebra. It's about a 10-min. drive beyond the western boundary of the River North neighborhood, in a gentrifying area with few other restaurants, but the out-of-the-way location hasn't deterred diners—probably because of executive chef Shawn McClain, who won raves for his seafood at Spring (p. 166). It's all very restrained, from the minimalist decor to the straightforward food presentation, but McClain's flair for flavor and emphasis on fresh ingredients make this an almost gourmet experience. My only complaint is the "small plates" menu: With no distinction between appetizer and entree, it's hard to know how much food you're getting (and you'll definitely need two to three dishes to fill up). Still, vegetarians who have gotten tired of ordering plain green salads at other restaurants in town will find a wealth of choices here: fennel risotto cake with a syrah reduction; curry-and-buttermilk crepes stuffed with cauliflower and greens; and Hawaiian heart of palm with kaffir lime and Thai basil chile. The menu is not strictly vegetarian—you'll find a few chicken and fish dishes—making this a good compromise spot for groups with both meat and non-meat eaters. Green Zebra won't have the power to convert real steak lovers, but it will certainly open up a whole new world of veggie flavors.

1460 W. Chicago Ave. (at Greenview St.). ✆ 312/243-7100. www.greenzebrachicago.com. Reservations recommended on weekends. Appetizer-size courses $8–$17. AE, DC, DISC, MC, V. Mon–Thurs 5:30–10pm; Fri–Sat 5–11pm; Sun 5:30–9pm. Bus: 66 (Chicago Ave.), or take a cab.

Nacional 27 ⭐⭐ *Finds* LATIN AMERICAN   Part sleek dining room, part sultry nightclub, Nacional 27 showcases the cuisine of 27 Latin American nations including Venezuela, Argentina, Costa Rica, and Brazil. Rich walnut and bamboo woods and gauzy curtains lend a tropical air to the grand dining room, which has cozy booth seating and tables arranged around a central dance floor. The innovative drink menu will get you in the mood: You'll find classic mojitos, sangrias, and trendy martini variations. For starters, there are a variety of skewers, ceviches, and empanadas; good choices are coconut-crusted shrimp and scallop-and-shrimp ceviche with avocado. The entrees are divided into steaks, seafood, and "Latin Comfort Foods," which include stick-to-your-ribs selections such as grilled pork tenderloin with corn-mushroom flan or honey-chile glazed duck. (Some of the food can be quite spicy, so ask before you order if you've got extra-sensitive taste buds.) Nacional 27 heats up on Friday and Saturday nights after 10pm, when a DJ spins fiery Latin tunes and couples take to the dance floor.

325 W. Huron St. (between Franklin and Orleans sts.). ✆ 312/664-2727. www.leye.com. Reservations recommended. Main courses $15–$28. AE, DC, DISC, MC, V. Dining room Mon–Thurs 5:30–9:30pm; Fri–Sat 5:30–11pm. Bar Mon–Thurs 5–10pm; Fri–Sat 5pm–2am. Subway/El: Brown Line to Chicago.

Osteria Via Stato ⭐⭐ *Finds* ITALIAN   Like Italian? Like surprises? Then you'll enjoy Osteria Via Stato's twist on traditional Italian dining. A set price of $36 buys you a full, European-style meal: a range of antipasto plates (which could be anything from house-cured olives to braised veal meatballs), two pasta dishes (served family style), and a meat entree (the only dish you actually choose from the menu). Pastas are usually a mix of hearty and light; pappardelle with free-range chicken ragu might be served alongside gemelli with sage and brown butter. Entrees include halibut Milanese with lemon-herb breadcrumbs; braised pork shank with white beans and bacon; and chicken Mario, a simple chicken breast perfectly seared with butter and olive oil. If you want to keep things simple with drinks, ask for the "Just Bring Me Wine" program, which matches a glass of wine to each course at three different price levels (the most affordable level, $15, is a great deal). They'll bring you unlimited helpings of everything except the entrees, so come with an appetite. Twosomes tend to be seated at communal tables in the dining room, so ask for a private table if you value your privacy. Lunch follows the same format, but there are fewer antipasti, and the entrees include salads and panini.

620 N. State St. (at Ontario St.). © 312/642-8450. www.leye.com. Reservations recommended. Set price $20 per person lunch, $36 dinner. AE, DC, DISC, MC, V. Mon–Sat 11:30am–2pm; Mon–Thurs 5–10pm; Fri–Sat 5–11pm; Sun 4–8:30pm (bar open later). Subway/El: Red Line to Grand.

SushiSamba Rio 🐟🐟 LATIN AMERICAN/SUSHI   You can't miss this place, thanks to the huge, glowing yellow-orange sign out front. At first glimpse, the menu seems like a gimmick: Latin American ceviche paired with sushi? But it's based on a real culinary tradition. In the early 20th century, Japanese immigrants moved to Peru and Brazil in search of work, eventually combining their native cuisine with South American dishes. SushiSamba takes the concept and runs with it, creating a theatrical experience that's backed up by very solid technique.

Designed by David Rockwell (Nobu, Vong, various W hotels), SushiSamba's dramatic dining room has become an "it" scene for fashionable young Chicagoans. Tables are scattered on different levels, some in a sunken red "conversation pit," others up on a balcony along one wall. Beaded curtains hang from the ceiling in the middle of the room, and the bathrooms are set in a bamboo-filled "garden." But does the food measure up? Absolutely. There's something here for everyone, making it a good choice for groups (even those who don't eat raw fish). The most talked-about appetizer is the *sawagani,* tiny river crabs that are fried and eaten whole—shell and all. (Our waiter referred to them jokingly as "Japanese nachos.") I'd recommend trying at least one of the creative "samba rolls," which combine the traditional sticky-rice-and-seaweed wrapping with unexpected fillings. The El Topo, a mix of salmon, jalapeño pepper, fresh melted mozzarella, and crispy onions, tastes better than it sounds; also worth trying is the Samba Rio roll, with guava-glazed short ribs and sweet pepper. If you'd prefer something more straightforward, Surf & Turf matches seared rare tuna and a tender beef filet on a bed of carrot-and-ginger purée. The red snapper, served whole (but deboned), is livened up with an aromatic red-curry sauce and coconut rice.

Special sampler plates, offered from noon to 5pm for $20, are a good option if you're looking for a nontraditional business lunch. There's also a Brazilian-themed brunch on Sunday, complete with samba music, and an outdoor terrace on the second floor that's a popular late-night posing spot in the summer.

504 N. Wells St. (at Illinois St.). © 312/595-2300. www.sushisamba.com. Reservations recommended. Main courses $8–$17 lunch, $12–$29 dinner. AE, MC, V. Sun–Tues 11:30am–11pm; Wed–Fri 11:30am–1am; Sat 11:30am–2am; Sun brunch 11:30am–3:30pm. Subway/El: Brown Line to Merchandise Mart or Red Line to Grand.

Tizi Melloul 🐟 FRENCH/MIDDLE EASTERN   An exotic haven in a neighborhood rife with raucous theme restaurants, Tizi Melloul creates an *Arabian Nights* fantasy world of rich reds, deep blues, and sparkling metallics. The food is good rather than spectacular, but the real draw here is the decor. In the vibrantly colored, circular Crescent Room, you'll be seated on low banquettes with floor pillows and encouraged to eat with your hands (although they'll bring silverware if you request it). The sultry, red-hued main dining room offers more traditional service, while the stark white Lounge is a hangout for the hipster set.

For the full experience, order the five-course Crescent Room menu ($35), which can include French-influenced dishes such as mussels and bouillabaisse, along with tabbouleh and other familiar Mediterranean fare. *Tagines* (traditional Moroccan stews) are a specialty of the house and are served in glazed earthenware crocks, with choices of lamb shank, a seafood medley, or *poussin* (a small chicken). Other eclectic entrees include braised lamb shank with lentils and olives; pan-roasted cod with grilled calamari and salsa verde; and crispy roast duck flavored with cardamom. For an added dose of exotica, catch a belly-dancing performance on Sunday night.

531 N. Wells St. (at Grand St.). ℭ 312/670-4338. www.tizimelloul.com. Reservations recommended. Main courses $16–$29. AE, MC, V. Sun–Thurs 5–10pm; Fri–Sat 5–11pm. Subway/El: Brown Line to Merchandise Mart or Red Line to Grand.

MODERATE

Carson's ⍟ AMERICAN/BARBECUE   A true Chicago institution, Carson's calls itself "The Place for Ribs," and, boy, is it ever. The barbecue sauce here is sweet and tangy, and the ribs are meaty. Included in the $22 price for a full slab of baby backs are coleslaw and one of four types of potatoes (the most decadent are au gratin), plus right-out-of-the-oven rolls.

For dinner, there's often a wait, but don't despair: In the bar area, you'll find a heaping mound of some of the best chopped liver around and plenty of cocktail rye to go with it. When you're seated at your table, tie on your plastic bib and indulge. In case you don't eat ribs, Carson's also barbecues chicken, pork chops, and (in a nod to health-consciousness) salmon. But let's be honest, you don't come to a place like this for the seafood, and the waitstaff will be shocked if no one in your group orders the famous ribs. If by some remarkable feat you have room left after dinner, the candy-bar sundaes are a scrumptious finale to the meal. Carson's popularity has led to something of a factory mentality among management, which evidently feels the need to herd diners in and out, but the servers are responsive to requests not to be hurried through the meal.

612 N. Wells St. (at Ontario St.). ℭ 312/280-9200. www.ribs.com. Reservations accepted for groups of 6 or more. Main courses $13–$34. AE, DC, DISC, MC, V. Mon–Thurs 11:30am–10:30pm; Fri 11:30am–11:30pm; Sat noon– 11:30pm; Sun noon–10:30pm. Subway/El: Red Line to Grand.

Cyrano's Bistrot & Wine Bar ⍟ *Value* BISTRO/FRENCH   Warm and welcoming, Cyrano's represents a haven of authentic bistro charm in the congested River North restaurant scene, due in no small part to the friendly presence of chef Didier Durand and his wife, Jamie. The cheery blue-and-red wood exterior, eclectic artwork, and charming personal asides on the menu ("Use of cellular phones may interfere with the stability of our whipped cream") all signal the owner's hands-on touch. The dining room is cozy but not overly noisy; still, Cyrano's works best for smaller groups (or romantic couples). The house specialties are the rotisserie duck and chicken served with your choice of sauce and classics such as steak frites, roasted rabbit with mustard sauce, and cassoulet. There are also a variety of salads to choose from (and some vegetarian options), but overall this is a place to eat hearty. Be sure to start with one of Durand's sensationally flavorful soups (the lobster bisque is a highlight) or the *pommes frites,* served with three condiments (Dijon mustard, homemade ketchup, and mayonnaise). Service is knowledgeable and friendly; on a recent visit, my group said we were too full for dessert, but the waiter brought us a plate of sorbet on the house. "You can't eat at a French restaurant and not have *some* kind of dessert," he admonished (good philosophy, I think). The restaurant's lower-level cabaret has live entertainment most nights of the week, and in warmer months, a sidewalk cafe is open all day.

546 N. Wells St. (between Ohio St. and Grand Ave.). ⓒ 312/467-0546. www.cyranosbistrot.com. Main courses $14–$28; 3-course prix-fixe dinner $29. AE, DC, DISC, MC, V. Mon–Fri 11:30am–2:30pm; Mon–Sat 5:30–10:30pm. Subway/El: Brown Line to Merchandise Mart.

Gino's East 𝕒𝕒 (Kids) PIZZA   Gino's—once the quintessential dive restaurant— now occupies a cavernous space that's a testament to its enduring popularity with both Chicago natives and tourists. (The original restaurant's graffiti-covered booths were brought along to keep the "authentic" flavor.) Despite the restaurant's size, be pre- pared to wait for a table during peak hours, because Gino's pizza—with good reason— is still a major draw.

Many Chicagoans consider Gino's the quintessential deep-dish Chicago-style pizza (I know transplanted Midwesterners who come here for their cheesy fix whenever they're back in town). True to its reputation, the pizza is heavy (a small cheese pizza is enough for two), so work up an appetite before chowing down. Specialty pizzas include the supreme, with layers of cheese, sausage, onions, green pepper, and mush- rooms; and the vegetarian, with cheese, onions, peppers, asparagus, summer squash, zucchini, and eggplant. Gino's also offers salads, sandwiches, and pastas—but I've never seen anyone order them. A warning for hungry families: Pizzas are cooked to order, so you'll have to wait about 45 minutes for your food (I highly recommend call- ing ahead to preorder, which will save you about a half-hour of waiting time, but pre- orders aren't accepted Fri–Sat).

If you want to take a pizza home on the plane, call a day in advance and Gino's will pack a special frozen pie for the trip.

633 N. Wells St. (at Ontario St.). ⓒ 312/943-1124. www.ginoseast.com. Reservations not accepted. Pizza $12–$29. AE, DC, DISC, MC, V. Mon–Thurs 11am–10pm; Fri–Sat 11am–11pm; Sun noon–9pm. Subway/El: Red Line to Grand.

Harry Caray's AMERICAN/ITALIAN   A shrine to the legendary Cubs play-by- play announcer, this landmark building is a repository for Harry's staggering collec- tion of baseball memorabilia. But you don't have to be a baseball lover to appreciate Harry's.

The dining rooms have an old-Chicago feel that is comfortable and familiar, with high tin ceilings, exposed brick walls, and red-checked tablecloths. It would be easy to lump Harry's with other celebrity restaurants, but as one reviewer pointed out, the food is better than it has to be. The portions are enormous here; you'll have enough left over to eat for days. Main-course offerings run from traditional items such as pas- tas with red sauce to chicken Vesuvio, veal, and a variety of seafood choices. Harry's is also a good place to order big plates of meat: dry-aged steaks, lamb, veal, and pork chops. From the list of side dishes, be sure to order the signature Vesuvio potatoes. The restaurant also has a (surprisingly) extensive and well-chosen wine list. If you don't want a full-service meal, the bar is a lively place for watching a game and grabbing some munchies—and, incidentally, the bar is 60 feet, 6 inches long, the same distance from the pitcher's mound to home plate.

33 W. Kinzie St. (at Dearborn St.). ⓒ 312/828-0966. www.harrycarays.com. Main courses $15–$40. AE, DC, DISC, MC, V. Mon–Sat 11:30am–3pm; Mon–Thurs 5–10:30pm; Fri–Sat 5–11pm; Sun 11:30am–4pm (lunch bar only) and 4–10pm. Subway/El: Brown Line to Merchandise Mart or Red Line to Grand.

Reza's 𝕒𝕒 (Value) MIDDLE EASTERN   Reza's doesn't look like the typical Middle Eastern restaurant. Housed in a former microbrewery, it has high ceilings and expan- sive, loftlike dining rooms. But the Persian-inspired menu will soon make you forget all about pints of ale. Specialties include a deliciously rich chicken in pomegranate

Breakfast & Brunch

NEAR THE LOOP & MAGNIFICENT MILE

You can get a good (and upscale) breakfast at one of the hotels near the Loop or Magnificent Mile. Favorites include **The Café** at the Four Seasons Hotel, 120 E. Delaware Place (⊘ **312/280-8800**), and **Drake Bros. Restaurant** at The Drake Hotel, 140 E. Walton Place at Michigan Avenue (⊘ **312/787-2200**).

A more informal choice in the Loop, overlooking the El tracks, is **Heaven on Seven** ⊛⊛ (p. 121, where the Cajun and Creole specialties supplement an enormous diner-style menu that has anything you could possibly desire.

For brunch with some soul, head to **House of Blues,** 329 N. Dearborn St., at Kinzie Street (⊘ **312/527-2583**; p. 273), for its popular Sunday gospel brunch. To guarantee seating, it's a good idea to book a spot 2 weeks in advance.

A local breakfast favorite since 1923 is **Lou Mitchell's,** 565 W. Jackson Blvd. (⊘ **312/939-3111**), across the south branch of the Chicago River from the Loop, a block farther west than Union Station. You'll be greeted at the door with a basket of doughnut holes and milk duds so that you can nibble while waiting for a table.

For a Southern-style breakfast of spicy red eggs, cheese grits, or biscuits and gravy, head over to **Wishbone** ⊛⊛ (p. 129), a homespun dining hall in a warehouse district west of the Loop.

LINCOLN PARK & THE NORTH SIDE

A perfect breakfast or brunch spot if you're heading up to Wrigleyville for a Cubs game or a walk through Lincoln Park is **Ann Sather** ⊛⊛ (p. 163), famous for its homemade cinnamon rolls.

The **Nookies** restaurants are Chicago favorites for all the standard morning fare. Locations include 2114 N. Halsted St., in Lincoln Park (⊘ **773/327-1400**); 1748 N. Wells St., in Old Town (⊘ **312/337-2454**); and 3334 N. Halsted St., in Lakeview (⊘ **773/248-9888**).

sauce and a variety of kabobs with heaps of dill rice (although, in a nod to carb-conscious diners, they'll substitute a salad if you want). Despite the menu's meat-heavy emphasis, there's a selection of vegetarian plates, too. If you can't decide what to order, go for an appetizer combo: a generous sampler of Middle Eastern dishes including hummus, stuffed grape leaves, tabbouleh, and other standbys, nicely presented in a red-lacquer bento box. Reza's has another location in Andersonville, at 5255 N. Clark St. (⊘ **773/561-1898**), but the River North spot is the most convenient for visitors staying downtown.

432 W. Ontario St. (at Orleans St.). ⊘ **312/664-4500.** www.rezasrestaurant.com. Main courses $13–$20. AE, DC, DISC, MC, V. Daily 11am–midnight. Subway/El: Red Line to Grand.

Rockit Bar & Grill ⊛ AMERICAN   Take your standard American burger joint, give it an upscale, urban makeover, and you've got Rockit. The current hot spot for well-heeled 20- and 30-something singles, Rockit is definitely a scene after work and on weekends, with loud music and plenty of flirting at the busy front bar. The dining

Go to **Orange,** 3231 N. Clark St., at Belmont (© **773/549-4400**), for a fun twist on breakfast foods. Try the Green Eggs and Ham—eggs scrambled with pesto, tomatoes, mozzarella, and pancetta. There's a kids' menu, too, making this a popular choice for families. But a warning to all those with hungry kids (and parents): Come early or late; the line for a table winds outside during prime weekend brunch hours.

Lincoln Park's **Toast,** 746 W. Webster St., at Halsted Street (© **773/935-5600**), is homey yet slightly funky, and kids are encouraged to scribble away on the butcher-block table coverings. Breakfast includes a twist on the usual diner fare. Pancakes come in all sorts of tempting varieties, from lemon/poppy seed drizzled with honey to the "pancake orgy," a strawberry, mango, and banana-pecan pancake topped with granola, yogurt, and honey. Come early on weekends, though; by 10:30am or so, there's guaranteed to be a lengthy wait.

WICKER PARK/BUCKTOWN

The brightly colored **Bongo Room,** 1470 N. Milwaukee Ave. (between Evergreen Ave. and Honore St.; © **773/489-0690**), is a neighborhood gathering place for the hipsters of Wicker Park/Bucktown, but the restaurant's tasty, creative breakfasts have drawn partisans from all over the city who feel right at home stretching out the morning with a late breakfast. (*A caveat:* Don't bother trekking over here for weekend brunch, when you'll have to wait an hour or more for a table; it's much more pleasant eating here during the week.) The same owners also run **Room 12,** 1152 S. Wabash Ave. (between 11th St. and Roosevelt Rd.; © **312/291-0100**), in the South Loop; the food is just as good as at the Wicker Park location, and it tends to be less crowded.

room is a trendy take on traditional tavern decor, where exposed-brick walls and distressed-wood tables combine with sleek metallic accents and chocolate-brown leather booths. The menu is fairly predictable, but a few notches above your standard bar fare. The Rockit Burger is a mix of Kobe beef and foie gras, served with french fries cooked in truffle oil; the Crispy Pork is a wonderfully tender pork medallion with a satisfyingly crunchy crust (I only wish it was served with something more exciting than kale). The Chopped Salad—a signature dish—is a hearty mix of salami, olives, tomatoes, provolone, hot cherry peppers, corn, and egg with balsamic dressing. Rockit is no gourmet destination, but if you're looking to chow down on better-than-decent food in a high-energy setting, Rockit fits the bill. (Bonus: The waitstaff range from good-looking to gorgeous.)

22 W. Hubbard St. (between Wabash and State sts.). © **312/645-6000.** www.rockitbarandgrill.com. Reservations accepted for parties of 6 or more. Main courses $9–$19 lunch; $12–$29 dinner. AE, DC, DISC, MC, V. Sun–Fri 11:30am–1:30am; Sat 11:30am–2:30am. Subway/El: Red Line to Grand.

Dining Alfresco

Cocooned for 6 months of the year, with furnaces and electric blankets blazing, Chicagoans revel in the warm months of late spring, summer, and early autumn. For locals and visitors alike, dining alfresco is an ideal way to experience the sights, sounds, smells, and social fabric of this multifaceted city. Just be prepared to wait on a nice night, because you'll be fighting a lot of other diners for a coveted outdoor table.

LOOP & VICINITY

Athena ⊛ This Greektown mainstay offers a stunning three-level outdoor seating area. It's paved with brick and landscaped with 30-foot trees, flower gardens, and even a waterfall. Best of all: an incredible view of the downtown skyline with the Sears Tower right in the middle. It's located at 212 S. Halsted St., between Adams and Jackson streets (℅ **312/655-0000**).

Park Grill ⊛⊛ Millennium Park's restaurant serves upscale versions of American comfort food with panoramic views of Michigan Avenue. In the summer, you can pick up a sandwich and grab a seat on the large patio (converted into an ice-skating rink come winter). For a review, see p. 118. It's at 11 N. Michigan Ave., at Madison Street (℅ **312/521-PARK**).

Rhapsody ⊛⊛ A tranquil oasis amid the Loop high-rises, Rhapsody's outdoor garden is my top pick for a romantic meal downtown. For more info, see p. 119. 65 E. Adams St., at Wabash Avenue; ℅ **312/786-9911.**

MAGNIFICENT MILE & GOLD COAST

Charlie's Ale House at Navy Pier One of several outdoor dining options along Navy Pier, this outpost of the Lincoln Park restaurant has lip-smacking pub fare and a great location on the southern promenade overlooking the lakefront and Loop skyline. It's located at 700 E. Grand Ave., near the entrance to the Pier (℅ **312/595-1440**).

Le Colonial ⊛⊛ This lovely French-Vietnamese restaurant, located in a vintage Gold Coast town house and evocative of 1920s Saigon, *does* have a sidewalk cafe, but you'd do better to reserve a table on the tiny second-floor porch, overlooking the street. For a full review, see p. 136. It's located at 937 N. Rush St., just south of Oak Street (℅ **312/255-0088**).

Oak Street Beachstro Suit up and head for this warm-weather-only beachfront cafe—literally on the sands of popular Oak Street Beach—which serves inventive cafe fare (fresh seafood, sandwiches, and pastas). Beer and wine are available. The address is 1000 N. Lake Shore Dr., at Oak Street Beach (℅ **312/915-4100**).

Puck's at the MCA This cafe—run by celebrity chef Wolfgang Puck—is tucked in the back of the Museum of Contemporary Art, where, from the terrace, you'll get a view of the museum's sculpture garden. Take in the art, the fresh air, and a shrimp club sandwich, Chinois salad, or wood-grilled pizza. (Restaurant-only patrons can bypass museum admission.) The address is 220 E. Chicago Ave., at Fairbanks Court (℅ **312/397-4034**).

RIVER NORTH

SushiSamba Rio ⟨★★⟩ For stunning nighttime views of the skyline—accompanied by views of some pretty stunning people—head to the rooftop deck of this Latin-Asian fusion spot. Canopied banquettes and flickering tea lights create a sultry atmosphere, along with a menu of specialty cocktails. You'll find it at 504 N. Wells St., at Illinois St. (© **312/595-2300**).

LINCOLN PARK

Charlie's Ale House A true neighborhood hangout, this Lincoln Park pub's wonderful beer garden—surrounded by tall, ivy-covered brick walls—is spacious and buzzing with activity and good vibes. It's located at 1224 W. Webster Ave., at Magnolia Avenue (© **773/871-1440**).

North Pond ⟨★★★⟩ Set on the banks of one of Lincoln Park's beautiful lagoons, the excellent North Pond serves upscale, fresh-as-can-be American cuisine in a romantic and sylvan setting. *One caveat:* Alcohol is not permitted on the outdoor patio. Also see p. 157. The address is 2610 N. Cannon Dr., halfway between Diversey Parkway and Fullerton Avenue (© **773/477-5845**).

O'Brien's Restaurant Wells Street in Old Town is lined with several alfresco options, but the best belongs to O'Brien's. The outdoor patio has teakwood furniture, a gazebo bar, and a mural of the owners' country club on a brick wall. Order the dressed-up chips, a house specialty. Located at 1528 N. Wells St., 2 blocks south of North Avenue (© **312/787-3131**).

WRIGLEYVILLE & VICINITY

Arco de Cuchilleros ⟨★⟩ The tapas and sangria at this cozy Wrigleyville restaurant can compete with other, better-known Spanish spots, and the intimate, leafy terrace out back glows with lantern light. Located at 3445 N. Halsted St., at Newport Avenue (© **773/296-6046**).

Moody's For 30 years, Moody's has been grilling some of the best burgers in Chicago. It's ideal in winter for its dark, cozy dining room (warmed by a fireplace), but it's better still in summer for its awesome outdoor patio, a real hidden treasure. The address is 5910 N. Broadway Ave., between Rosedale and Thorndale avenues (© **773/275-2696**).

WICKER PARK/BUCKTOWN

Meritage Café and Wine Bar ⟨★★⟩ Meritage wins my vote for most romantic outdoor nighttime seating. The food (American cuisine with Pacific Northwest influences) is top-notch, but it's the outdoor patio, twinkling with overhead lights, that makes for a magical experience. Best of all, the patio is covered and heated in the winter. For a full review, see p. 164. It's located at 2118 N. Damen Ave., at Charleston Street (© **773/235-6434**).

Northside Café On a sunny summer day, Northside seems like Wicker Park's town square, packed with an eclectic mix of locals catching up and checking out the scene. The entire front of the restaurant opens onto the street, making it relatively easy to get an "outdoor" table. For more info, see p. 168. Located at 1635 N. Damen Ave., just north of North Avenue (© **773/384-3555**).

Vermilion ✵ INDIAN/LATIN AMERICAN Another seemingly wacky fusion concept? Yes, but the food here is more than just a novelty. Owner Rohini Dey and chef Maneet Chauhan—both women, both originally from India—have found a common thread between Indian and Latin American cooking: Both feature similar ingredients (rice and chiles), use some of the same seasonings (cumin and coriander), and even share similar preparations (the variety of Latin salsas is comparable to the different Indian chutneys). The result is a menu that mixes flavors in new ways that still seem somewhat familiar, whether it's empanadas with mango-coconut chutney, ceviche with Indian spices, or tandoori skirt steak served on sautéed garlic spinach with fried plantain. This isn't your usual Taj Mahal–meets-Bollywood Indian decor, either—the mostly white dining room is brightened with red decorative accents and large black-and-white fashion photographs. The front lounge is open late for drinks and dessert, served to a soundtrack of Indian and Latin American dance music.

10 W. Hubbard St. (at State St.). ⓒ 312/527-4060. Reservations recommended on weekends. Main courses $15–$25. AE, DC, DISC, MC, V. Mon–Fri 11:30am–2:30pm; Sun–Thurs 5–10pm; Fri–Sat 5–11pm. Lounge open until 3am Fri–Sat. Subway/El: Red Line to Grand.

Vong's Thai Kitchen–VTK ✵ ASIAN Chef Jean-Georges Vongerichten's Vong concept was a huge hit in New York and London, so hopes were high when the trendy Thai/French restaurant hit Chicago a few years ago. But it didn't take long for the buzz to die down. Both the decor and menu were eventually overhauled; the result is a new name and more Chicago-friendly atmosphere—with only one menu item costing more than $20 (grilled tamarind beef tenderloin, $23).

Though it bills itself as a Thai kitchen, the menu offers a broad range of Asian and fusion dishes (tuna wasabi pizza, anyone?). There are a few holdovers from the original Vong menu, including the signature Black Plate of appetizers (shrimp satay, tuna sashimi roll, chicken-scallion satay, Peking duck roll, and crab roll). Traditional Thai curry dishes get a kick from nontraditional ingredients (halibut and duck), and there's always at least one seafood dish that's been wok-seared for extra flavor and texture. The wine list is adequate, but the emphasis is on specialty cocktails, including the best-selling Red Passion (raspberry-flavored vodka, cranberry, champagne, and pineapple). The lunch menu offers an appealing selection of Asian-inspired salads and noodle dishes, as well as various combination plates that let you sample two or three different dishes. There's also a kids' menu—besides the usual fish sticks and chicken fingers, Junior can order his or her very own "Pink Elephant" cocktail (Sprite, grenadine, and pineapple juice).

6 W. Hubbard St. (at State St.). ⓒ 312/644-8664. www.vongsthaikitchen.com. Main courses $8–$15 lunch, $14–$20 dinner. AE, DC, DISC, MC, V. Mon–Fri 11:30am–2pm; Mon–Thurs 5:30–10pm; Fri 5:30–11pm; Sat noon–11pm; Sun 5–9pm. Subway/El: Red Line to Grand.

INEXPENSIVE

Café Iberico ✵✵ SPANISH & TAPAS This no-frills tapas spot won't win any points for style, but the consistently good food and festive atmosphere make it a long-time local favorite for singles in their 20s and 30s. Café Iberico gets very loud, especially on weekends, so it makes a fun group destination—but plan your romantic tête-à-tête elsewhere. Crowds begin pouring in at the end of the workday, so you'll probably have to wait for a table. Not to worry: Order a pitcher of fruit-filled sangria at the bar with everyone else. When you get a table, I'd suggest starting with the *queso de cabra* (baked goat cheese with fresh tomato-basil sauce), then continue ordering rounds of hot and cold tapas as your hunger demands. A few standout dishes are the vegetarian Spanish omelet, spicy potatoes with tomato sauce, chicken brochette with caramelized onions and rice, and grilled octopus with potatoes and olive oil. There are a handful of entrees on the menu, and a few desserts if you're still not sated.

739 N. LaSalle St. (between Chicago Ave. and Superior St.). © 312/573-1510. www.cafe-iberico.com. Reservations accepted for parties of 6 or more; no reservations for Fri–Sat dinner. Tapas $4–$7; main courses $7–$10. DC, DISC, MC, V. Mon–Thurs 11am–11:30pm; Fri 11am–1:30am; Sat noon–1:30am; Sun noon–11pm. Subway/El: Red Line to Chicago or Brown Line to Chicago.

Mr. Beef ⊛ *(Finds* AMERICAN   Calling Mr. Beef a restaurant may be a stretch: The place is basically a fast-food stand, without much atmosphere or room for seating. Despite these drawbacks, Mr. Beef is a much-loved Chicago institution. Its claim to fame is the classic Italian beef sandwich, the Chicago version of a Philly cheese steak. The Mr. Beef variety is made of sliced beef dipped in *jus,* piled high on a chewy bun, and topped with sweet or hot peppers. Heavy, filling, and *very* Chicago, Mr. Beef really hops during lunchtime, when dusty construction workers and suit-clad businessmen crowd in for their meaty fix. While you're chowing, check out the celebrity photos and newspaper clippings covering the walls, and you'll see why this place is considered a local monument.

666 N. Orleans St. (at Erie St.). © 312/337-8500. Sandwiches $6–$8.50. No credit cards. Mon–Thurs 8am–9pm; Fri 8am–5am; Sat 10:30am–3:30pm and 10:30pm–5:30am. Subway/El: Red Line to Grand.

Pizzeria Uno ⊛ *(Value* PIZZA   Pizzeria Uno invented Chicago-style pizza, and many deep-dish aficionados still refuse to accept any imitations. Uno's is now a chain of restaurants throughout the country, but this location is the original. You can eat in the restaurant itself on the basement level or, weather permitting, on the outdoor patio right off the sidewalk. Salads, sandwiches, and a house minestrone are also available, but let's be honest—the only reason to come here is for the pizza. As with Gino's East (see above), pizzas take about 45 minutes to make, so if you're starving, order an appetizer or salad.

Uno was so successful that the owners opened **Pizzeria Due** in a lovely gray-brick Victorian town house nearby at 619 N. Wabash Ave., at Ontario Street (© 312/943-2400). The menu is exactly the same; the atmosphere just a tad nicer (with more outdoor seating).

29 E. Ohio St. (at Wabash Ave.). © 312/321-1000. www.unos.com. Reservations not accepted Fri–Sat. Pizza $7–$22. AE, DC, DISC, MC, V. Mon–Fri 11am–1am; Sat 11:30am–2am; Sun 11:30am–11:30pm. Subway/El: Red Line to Grand.

7 Lincoln Park & Old Town

Singles and upwardly mobile young families inhabit Lincoln Park, the neighborhood roughly defined by North Avenue on the south, Diversey Parkway on the north, the park on the east, and Clybourn Avenue on the west. In the southeast corner of this area is Old Town, a neighborhood of historic town houses that stretches out from the intersection of North Avenue and Wells Street. You'll find a few fine-dining spots, but most restaurants here are more casual, with average prices lower than you'll find in River North or along the Magnificent Mile.

VERY EXPENSIVE

Alinea ⊛⊛⊛ ECLECTIC   Alinea—anointed the best restaurant in the country by *Gourmet* magazine in 2006—is a place no serious foodie should miss. Like Homaro Cantu at Moto (p. 124), Chef Grant Achatz wants to revolutionize the way we eat,

Dining in Lincoln Park, Old Town & Wrigleyville

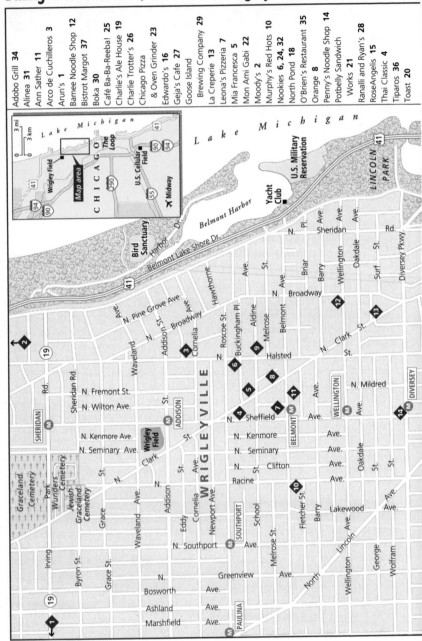

Adobo Grill **34**
Alinea **31**
Ann Sather **11**
Arco de Cuchilleros **3**
Arun's **1**
Bamee Noodle Shop **12**
Bistrot Margot **37**
Boka **30**
Café Ba-Ba-Reeba! **25**
Charlie's Ale House **19**
Charlie Trotter's **26**
Chicago Pizza
  & Oven Grinder **23**
Edwardo's **16**
Geja's Cafe **27**
Goose Island
  Brewing Company **29**
La Creperie **13**
Leona's Pizzeria **7**
Mia Francesca **5**
Mon Ami Gabi **22**
Moody's **2**
Murphy's Red Hots **10**
Nookies **6, 24, 32**
North Pond **18**
O'Brien's Restaurant **35**
Orange **8**
Penny's Noodle Shop **14**
Potbelly Sandwich
  Works **21**
Ranalli and Ryan's **28**
RoseAngelis **15**
Thai Classic **4**
Tiparos **36**
Toast **20**

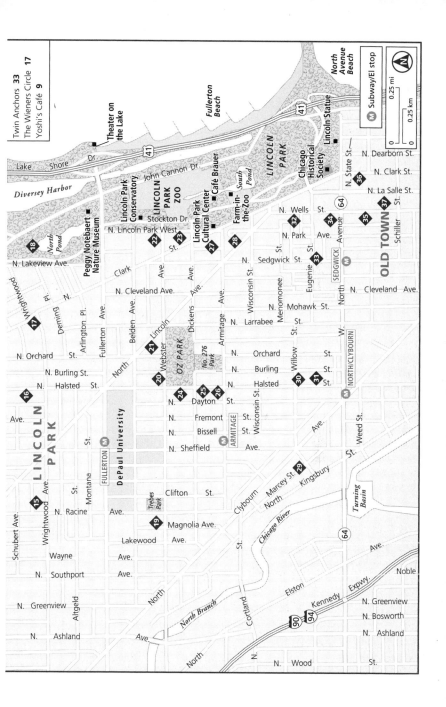

Twin Anchors **33**
The Wieners Circle **17**
Yoshi's Café **9**

Theater on
the Lake

Lake Shore Dr.

Diversey Harbor

Fullerton
Beach

North
Avenue
Beach

LINCOLN PARK

Lincoln Statue

John Cannon Dr.

LINCOLN
PARK
ZOO

Lincoln Park Conservatory

Stockton Dr.

N. Lincoln Park West

Café Brauer

Lincoln Park Cultural Center

South
Pond

Farm-in-the-Zoo

Chicago Historical Society

N. Dearborn St.

N. Clark St.

N. La Salle St.

N. Wells St.

N. Park Ave.

Schiller

OLD TOWN

N. Sedgwick St.

SEDGWICK

N. Cleveland Ave.

Eugenie St.

Peggy Notebaert Nature Museum

North Pond

N. Lakeview Ave.

Clark

Ave.

N. Cleveland Ave.

Belden Ave.

Ave.

Ave.

Dickens

Armitage Ave.

N. Larrabee St.

Wisconsin St.

Menomonee

Mohawk St.

Wrightwood

Pl.

N.

Arlington Pl.

Deming

Fullerton Ave.

Lincoln

OZ PARK

Webster

No. 276 Park

N. Orchard St.

N. Burling St.

Willow St.

N. Orchard St.

N. Burling St.

N. Halsted St.

N. Halsted St.

NORTH/CLYBOURN

W.

N. Burling St.

N. Halsted St.

N. Dayton St.

Armitage

Wisconsin St.

N. Fremont St.

N. Bissell St.

N. Sheffield Ave.

Weed St.

DePaul University

FULLERTON

Montana

St.

N. Racine Ave.

Wrightwood Ave.

Schubert Ave.

Wayne

Ave.

N. Southport Ave.

N. Greenview

Altgeld

N. Ashland

Trebes Park

Clifton St.

Magnolia Ave.

Lakewood Ave.

North

North

N. Branch

Clybourn

Marcey St.

Kingsbury

Chicago River

Turning Basin

Cortland

Elston

Kennedy Expwy.

N. Greenview

N. Bosworth

N. Ashland

N. Wood St.

LINCOLN PARK

Ave.

Noble

Ave.

Subway/El stop

0.25 mi
0.25 km

which he does by presenting familiar foods in new contexts and unexpected forms. (He's been known, for example, to serve dishes on lavender-scented pillows, so the floral scent wafts up as you eat). The menu changes constantly, but you're guaranteed to taste something new here, whether it's ravioli with a liquid-truffle filling or bites of bison tenderloin wrapped in crispy potatoes and seasoned with cinnamon. Achatz, who has worked with Spain's Ferran Adrià (the master of food deconstruction), as well as French Laundry's Thomas Keller, says he wants diners to feel like they're taking a journey, "zigzagging between challenge and comfort." The restaurant itself is certainly comfortable, with shoulder-high chairs you can sink into and soft, flattering lighting sparkling off the sharp angles of the grand staircase. But you'll only be comfortable dining here if you're willing to go along for the ride. Eat with an open mind (and a full wallet), and you'll be well rewarded.

1723 N. Halsted St. (between North Ave. and Willow St.). © 312/867-0110. www.alinea-restaurant.com. Reservations strongly recommended. Fixed-price menus $135 and $175. AE, DC, DISC, MC, V. Wed–Sun 5:30–9:30pm. Subway/El: Red Line to North/Clybourn.

Charlie Trotter's ✿✿✿ ECLECTIC   Foodies flock to the namesake restaurant of chef Charlie Trotter, Chicago's first celebrity chef. Yes, he's done TV shows and authored a series of cookbooks (with almost impossible-to-follow recipes), but Trotter's focus is this restaurant, a shrine to creative fine dining.

There is no a la carte menu, so this is not the place to come if you're a picky eater. Your only choice is to decide between the vegetable ($135) or grand ($155) degustation menu. Trotter delights in presenting diners with unfamiliar ingredients and presentations, and prides himself on using only organic or free-range products (so you can feel good about indulging). The entree descriptions signal Trotter's attention to detail; sample dishes from a recent menu include steamed Casco Bay cod with cockles, picholine olives, artichokes, and stinging nettles; and roasted saddle of rabbit with fingerling potatoes, turnips, and mustard greens. Be prepared to linger: dinner here can take up to 3 hours. The dining room may be formal, but the overall attitude is not intimidating. The wine list is extensive, and a sommelier is on hand to help match wines with each course.

For a taste of Trotter's gourmet fare without the high price tag, check out **Trotter's to Go,** his gourmet food store in Lincoln Park at 1337 W. Fullerton Ave. (between Lakewood and Wayne aves.; © 773/868-6510).

816 W. Armitage Ave. (at Halsted St.). © 773/248-6228. www.charlietrotters.com. Reservations required. Jackets required, ties requested. Fixed-price menus $135 and $155. AE, DC, DISC, MC, V. Tues–Thurs at 6 and 9pm; Fri–Sat at 5:30 and 9pm. Subway/El: Brown Line to Armitage.

Geja's Cafe ✿ FONDUE   A dark, subterranean hideaway, Geja's (pronounced gay-*haz*) regularly shows up on lists of the most romantic restaurants in Chicago (cozy couples should request a booth off the main dining room). However, the interior might strike some as too gloomy, and the cook-it-yourself technique won't appeal to anyone who wants to be pampered. If there are at least two in your party (all main courses are served for two or more), choose the Prince Geja's combination dinner, the best Geja's has to offer. The meal begins with a Gruyère cheese fondue appetizer with apple wedges and chunks of dark bread. Next, a huge platter arrives, brimming with squares of beef tenderloin, lobster tails, jumbo shrimp, chicken breast, and scallops— all raw—and a caldron of boiling oil to cook them in. These delicacies are accompanied by a variety of raw vegetables and eight different dipping sauces. When the flaming chocolate fondue arrives for dessert, with fresh fruit and pound cake for dipping and marshmallows for roasting, you'll want to beg for mercy. *Caution:* You have to work for your fondue—keeping track of how long each piece of meat has been cooking—and the aroma of cooking oil that fills the restaurant might bother some sensitive noses.

340 W. Armitage Ave. (between Lincoln Ave. and Clark St.). © 773/281-9101. www.gejascafe.com. Reservations accepted every day except late Fri–Sat. 3-course dinners $25–$45 per person. AE, DC, DISC, MC, V. Mon–Thurs 5–10pm; Fri 5–11:30pm; Sat 5pm–midnight; Sun 4:30–9:30pm. Bus: 22. Subway/El: Brown Line to Armitage.

North Pond ✿✿✿ *Finds* AMERICAN   Tucked away in Lincoln Park, North Pond truly is a hidden treasure. You can't drive up to the restaurant's front door: You must stroll along a path to reach the building, which was formerly a warming hut for ice skaters. The building's Arts and Crafts–inspired interior blends perfectly with the park outside, and a glass-enclosed addition lets you dine "outside" all year long.

In keeping with the natural setting, chef Bruce Sherman emphasizes organic, locally grown ingredients and favors simple preparations—although the overall result is definitely upscale (at these prices, it better be). Examples of seasonal menu items include herbed Parmesan gnocchi with braised rabbit, fava beans, asparagus, Wisconsin ramps, and lovage (a celerylike green); poached farm-fresh egg with wilted baby spinach and lemon-caviar butter sauce; and grilled sea scallops with orange-Parmesan grain salad, glazed organic baby carrots, and spiced lobster sauce. For dessert, try a plate of artisinal cheeses or dark chocolate mousse with roasted apricots and a hazelnut biscuit. To enjoy the restaurant's setting with a slightly lower price tag, try the fixed-price Sunday brunch ($32). The all-American wine list of 100 or so selections focuses on boutique vintners.

2610 N. Cannon Dr. (south of Diversey Pkwy.). © 773/477-5845. www.northpondrestaurant.com. Reservations recommended. Main courses $29–$34. AE, DC, MC, V. Tues–Sat 5:30–10pm; Sun 11am–2pm and 5:30–10pm. Lunch served June–Sept Tues–Sat 11:30am–2pm. Bus: 151.

EXPENSIVE

Boka ✿ AMERICAN   In a neighborhood full of Irish pubs and casual sandwich joints, Boka is a sophisticated, grown-up alternative. The dimly lit dining room manages to be both romantic and dramatic, thanks to the fabric "sculptures" stretched across the ceiling. Noteworthy appetizers include stuffed squid with baby spinach, spicy pineapple, and black tapioca; beet salad with yuzu, frisee, black pepper walnuts, and hickory bacon; and the fresh oyster selection. Entrees cover a range of meat and seafood and taste as good as they sound: Grilled hamachi with broccoflower, kalamata olives, pickled garlic, and shrimp dumplings; and rack of lamb with sweet and sour eggplant, grilled bok choy, and fire-roasted pepper sauce. The wine list has an international feel—covering Napa to Bordeaux to South Africa—and a fair number of half-bottle selections. Boka makes a great dinner stop before a show at Steppenwolf Theatre, but make a reservation, because many fellow theatergoers will have the same idea. Aesthetically, Boka's main claim to fame is its cellphone booth, where diners are encouraged to make calls rather than share their conversation with the whole dining room. Now that's an idea I hope catches on.

1729 N. Halsted St. (between North Ave. and Willow St.). © 312/337-6070. www.bokachicago.com. Reservations recommended on weekends. Main courses $15–$25. AE, MC, V. Daily 5–11pm. Subway/El: Red Line to North/Clybourn.

Mon Ami Gabi ✿ BISTRO/FRENCH   This "French steakhouse" concept seduces with its aromatic atmosphere, tasty steak preparations, and rolling cart of wines by the glass ("Gabi" refers to executive chef Gabino Sotelino). Gabi's decor is like a movie set of a cozy, boisterous bistro. There are numerous classic bistro starters and hot seafood appetizers, such as plump mussels steamed in white ale, pâtés, and cheeses, but a pleasant departure from bistro fare recently consisted of cavatelli pasta with asparagus, snap peas, and edamame. Exquisitely simple entrees include chicken paillard (a crusty, pounded chicken breast in lemon butter) and trout Grenobloise (perfectly pan-seared trout in caper butter with a sprinkle of croutons). Steak frites can be had with maître d'hotel butter, au poivre, Roquefort, or bordelaise (with caramelized onions in mushroom-and-red-wine sauce). Numerous seafood entrees, a section of seasonal specialties (a delicious halibut with roasted tomatoes and choron sauce graced the menu recently), and sides along the lines of whipped cauliflower and ratatouille round out the menu. Did I mention the fantastic *tarte tatin?* You can also get classic French treats such as dessert crepes and profiteroles.

2300 N. Lincoln Park West (at Belden Ave.). © **773/348-8886**. www.monamigabi.com. Reservations recommended. Main courses $17–$40. AE, DC, DISC, MC, V. Mon–Thurs 5:30–10pm; Fri–Sat 5–11pm; Sun 5–9pm. Bus: 151.

MODERATE

Adobo Grill MEXICAN   Although lacking the authenticity and character of Frontera Grill and Topolobampo (p. 143), Adobo Grill is definitely a cut above your average neighborhood Mexican restaurant. If you don't mind noisy crowds, join the action on the first floor. Although at first glance this may appear to be a singles' hangout, families are a growing part of the restaurant's clientele; there's even a kids' menu.

Adobo Grill's claim to fame is the fresh guacamole prepared tableside (you choose the spice level, but be warned that even the "medium" will give your tongue quite a jolt). Less spicy starters include a refreshing jicama-and-mango salad or a tasting of ceviches including tilapia, shrimp, and tuna. For an entree, try the grilled, achiotemarinated pounded pork chop with black beans, pickled purple onions, chiltomate salsa, and avocado; or for a heartier dish, indulge in the casserole of chile guajillo-braised beef tenderloin tips with potatoes. For dessert, the chocolate tamale is a brownie-dough delight, redolent with bittersweet chocolate flavor. Before you opt for a margarita or one of the 60 sipping tequilas, consider a refreshing Michelada (your choice of beer with lime juice in a chile- and salt-dusted glass) or a bittersweet Adobopolitan (tequila, Citronage liqueur, and pomegranate juice).

There's a second location in the up-and-coming West Division shopping district, at 2005 W. Division St. (at N. Damen Ave.; © **773/252-9990**).

1610 N. Wells St. (at North Ave.). © **312/266-7999**. www.adobogrill.com. Reservations recommended. Main courses $13–$20. AE, DC, MC, V. Sat noon–2:30pm; Mon–Thurs 5:30–10pm; Fri–Sat 5:30–11:30pm; Sun 11am–9:30pm. Bus: 22, 36, or 156.

Bistrot Margot ✿✿ (Finds) BISTRO/FRENCH   Bistrot Margot is not only one of the best restaurants in Old Town, it's also one of the better French bistros in Chicago. It can get very busy and loud, and the tables are quite close together, but, for many, that only adds to its charm. This is true bistro dining—very casual and never stuffy. Starters include out-of-this-world mussels in white wine with fresh herbs; escargot in garlic butter; country-style pâté; and crab folded into seafood mousse. Don't skip the salad course, either (in warm weather, go for the light, refreshing Belgian endive with spicy walnuts, blue cheese, and apples). Specials are usually the best bet for the main course. But the usual suspects (roasted chicken with garlic, lemon, herbs, and *pommes frites;* rack of lamb with Dijon mustard and garlic bread crumbs; and a terrific steak frites) are proof that, when done right, it's hard to beat classic French cuisine. On warm summer nights, the restaurant sets about half a dozen tables on the sidewalk, which, on this colorful stretch of Wells Street, makes for a truly memorable meal.

1437 N. Wells St. (at W. Schiller St.). ℂ **312/587-3660.** www.bistrotmargot.com. Reservations recommended. Main courses $16–$26. AE, DC, MC, V. Mon 11:30am–9pm; Tues–Thurs 11:30am–10pm; Fri 11:30am–11pm; Sat 10:30am–11pm; Sun 10:30am–9pm. Subway/El: Red Line to Clark/Division, or Brown Line to Sedgwick.

Café Ba-Ba-Reeba! ⟨ SPANISH & TAPAS

One of the city's first tapas restaurants, Café Ba-Ba-Reeba! is still going strong, thanks to its location on bustling Halsted Street, near the Armitage Avenue shopping strip. The clientele tends to be young and comes to the restaurant in groups, so be prepared: Loud conversations and tipsy toasts over pitchers of sangria may surround you.

Café Ba-Ba-Reeba! isn't breaking any new ground with its menu, but tapas lovers will see plenty of favorites, including garlic potato salad, roasted eggplant salad with goat cheese, beef and chicken empanadas, and roasted dates wrapped in bacon (which have been a popular menu item for years). The menu has also been updated with miniversions of more upscale fare, including a spicy devil's lobster tail dish, a cured pork lomo with frisee salad, and a flavorful plate of seared Spanish sausages. Some dishes are available in both tapas and full-portion size, and there's a range of paellas for those who don't want to go the tapas route. The vibrantly decorated cafe makes an excellent, efficient choice for pre- or posttheater dining if you're headed to Steppenwolf Theatre, a few blocks south, for a play.

2024 N. Halsted St. (at Armitage Ave.). ℂ **773/935-5000.** www.cafebabareeba.com. Reservations recommended on weekends. Tapas $4–$13; main courses $9–$30. AE, DC, DISC, MC, V. Mon–Thurs 5–10pm; Fri 5pm–midnight; Sat 11am–midnight; Sun 11am–10pm. Subway/El: Red or Brown line to Fullerton, or Brown Line to Armitage.

Twin Anchors ⟨ BARBECUE

A landmark in Old Town since the end of Prohibition, Twin Anchors manages to maintain the flavor of old Chicago. It's a friendly, family-owned pub with Frank Sinatra songs on the jukebox and pictures of Ol' Blue Eyes on the walls (he apparently hung out here on swings through town in the 1960s). But rather than striking a self-consciously retro pose, this feels like the real deal, with a long mahogany bar up front and a modest dining room in back with red Formica-topped tables crowded close. Of course, you don't need anything fancy when the ribs—the fall-off-the-bone variety—come this good. Even non–meat eaters may be swayed if they allow themselves one bite of the enormous slabs of tender baby back pork ribs. (Go for the zesty sauce.) All of this means that you should prepare for a long wait on weekends. Ribs and other entrees come with coleslaw and dark rye bread, plus your choice of baked potato, tasty fries, and the even-better crisp onion rings. For dessert, there's a daily cheesecake selection.

1655 N. Sedgwick St. (1 block north of North Ave.). ℂ **312/266-1616.** www.twinanchorsribs.com. Reservations not accepted. Sandwiches $6–$9; main courses $11–$24. AE, DC, DISC, MC, V. Mon–Thurs 5–11pm; Fri 5pm–midnight; Sat noon–midnight; Sun noon–10:30pm. Subway/El: Brown Line to Sedgwick.

INEXPENSIVE

Goose Island Brewing Company AMERICAN

Some of the best beer in Chicago is manufactured at this comfy, award-winning microbrewery on the western edge of Old Town (an impressive cast of professional beer critics agrees). In the course of a year, Goose Island produces about 100 varieties of lagers, ales, stouts, pilsners, and porters that change with the seasons. If you don't want to commit to a full pint, order some 6-ounce sampler glasses for your very own tasting session. For a behind-the-scenes look, you can tour the brewing facility Sunday at 3pm ($5, which includes tastings afterward).

The food here is far more than an afterthought. If you prefer to chow down in a restaurant atmosphere (rather than sitting at the large bar), there's a separate, casual dining area that attracts plenty of families on the weekends. Cut-above bar food includes burgers (including a killer, dragon-breath-inducing Stilton burger with roasted garlic), sandwiches (pulled pork, blackened catfish po' boy, chicken Caesar), and some serious salads. Goose Island is also known for its addictive homemade potato chips, doughy Bavarian pretzels, fresh-brewed root beer, and orange cream soda. The zero-attitude, come-as-you-are ambience is very refreshing for a lazy afternoon pit stop or a casual lunch or dinner. A second location at 3535 N. Clark St. (near W. Eddy St.) in Wrigleyville (✆ 773/832-9040) has an enclosed beer garden.

1800 N. Clybourn Ave. (at Sheffield Ave.). ✆ 312/915-0071. www.gooseisland.com. Reservations accepted. Sandwiches $7.50–$10; main courses $11–$17. AE, DC, DISC, MC, V. Sun–Thurs 11am–1am; Fri–Sat 11am–2am; main dining room closes at 10pm daily, but a late-night menu is available in the bar. Subway/El: Red Line to North/Clybourn.

La Creperie 🎗️🎗️ *Finds* FRENCH   Germain and Sara Roignant have run this intimate gem of a cafe since 1972, never straying from the reasonably priced crepes that have won them a loyal following. The decor is heavy on '70s-era brown, but if you find the main dining room too dark, head to the back patio (enclosed in colder months), which sparkles with strings of white lights. Onion soup, pâté, and escargot are all good starters, but the highlights here are the whole-wheat crepes—each prepared on a special grill that Germain imported from his native Brittany. Single-choice fillings include cheese, tomato, egg, or ham; tasty duets feature chicken and mushroom or broccoli and cheese. Beef bourguignon, coq au vin, and curried chicken are the more adventurous crepe combinations. Non-crepe offerings are few: orange roughy and steak frites. Don't leave without sharing one of the dessert crepes, which tuck anything from apples to ice cream within their warm folds.

2845 N. Clark St. (half-block north of Diversey Pkwy.). ✆ 773/528-9050. www.lacreperieusa.com. Reservations accepted for groups of 6 or more. Main courses $5–$14. AE, DC, DISC, MC, V. Tues–Fri 11:30am–11pm; Sat 11am–11pm; Sun 11am–9:30pm. Subway/El: Brown Line to Diversey.

Potbelly Sandwich Works *Value* SANDWICHES   It doesn't seem to matter what time I stop by Potbelly; there's invariably a line of hungry 20- and 30-somethings waiting to get their sandwich fix. Yes, there's a potbelly stove inside, as well as a player piano and other Old West saloon-type memorabilia, but come here for the made-to-order grilled sub sandwiches (that's all they serve). Prepared on homemade rolls stuffed with your choice of turkey, Italian meats, veggies, pizza ingredients, and more, and layered with lettuce, tomato, onion, pickles, and Italian seasonings, they're warmed in a countertop toaster oven. Even with all the fixin's, each is under $5 (unlike the massive subs found at many other spots, Potbelly's are more the size of normal sandwiches). Tempting milkshakes keep the blender busy. And the good news about those lines: The behind-the-counter staff are experts at keeping things moving, so you never end up waiting too long. Potbelly has close to 30 locations throughout the city, including 190 N. State St. (✆ 312/683-1234) and in the Westfield North Bridge shopping center, 520 N. Michigan Ave. (✆ 312/664-1008), both of which are convenient to the Loop and Mag Mile.

(Finds) Taste of Thai

Thai restaurants are to Chicago what Chinese restaurants are to many other American cities: ubiquitous, affordable, and perfect for a quick meal that offers a taste of the exotic. If you've never tried Thai, Chicago is a great place to start. Good introductory dishes are pad thai noodles topped with minced peanuts or the coconut-based mild yellow curry.

Arun's (p. 162) is the city's reigning gourmet interpreter of Thai cuisine, but many other low-key places are scattered throughout the residential neighborhoods. Most entrees at these spots don't cost much more than $10. A staple of the River North dining scene is the bright and airy **Star of Siam,** 11 E. Illinois St., at North State Street (© **312/670-0100**). On the north end of the Gold Coast where it meets Old Town, **Tiparos,** 1540 N. Clark St. at North Avenue (© **312/712-9900**), is a very friendly place that features Thai textiles on its brick interior walls and serves delicious specialties such as mussaman curry. **Thai Classic,** 3332 N. Clark St., at Roscoe Street (© **773/404-2000**), conveniently located between the busy Belmont/Clark intersection and Wrigley Field, offers an excellent all-you-can-eat buffet on weekends if you want to try a taste of everything. While wandering the Lakeview neighborhood, a good stop is the **Bamee Noodle Shop,** 3120 N. Broadway, at Wellington Street (© **773/281-2641**), which offers a good selection of "Noodles on Plates" and "Noodles in Bowls," as well as a number of soups and fried-rice combinations.

2264 N. Lincoln Ave. (between Belden Ave. and Webster St.). © **773/528-1405.** www.potbelly.com. Reservations not accepted. Sandwiches $3.50–$5.50. MC, V. Daily 11am–11pm. Subway/El: Brown or Red line to Fullerton.

RoseAngelis (★★ (*Value* ITALIAN   What keeps me coming back to RoseAngelis when there's not exactly a shortage of Italian restaurants in this city? The reliably good food, cozy ambience, and very reasonable prices—this is neighborhood dining at its best. Hidden on a residential side street in Lincoln Park, the restaurant fills the ground floor of a former private home with a charming series of cozy rooms and a garden patio. The menu emphasizes pasta (my favorites are the rich lasagna and the ravioli al Luigi, filled with ricotta and served with a sun-dried-tomato cream sauce). The garlicky chicken Vesuvio is also excellent, but it's not offered on Friday or Saturday nights because of preparation time. While RoseAngelis is not a vegetarian restaurant per se, there's no red meat on the menu, and many of the pastas are served with vegetables rather than meat. Finish up with the deliciously decadent bread pudding with warm caramel sauce, one of my favorite desserts in the city (and big enough to share). I suggest stopping by on a weeknight to avoid fighting crowds of locals on Friday and Saturday nights (when you'll wait up to 2 hrs. for a table).

1314 W. Wrightwood Ave. (at Lakewood Ave.). © **773/296-0081.** www.roseangelis.com. Reservations accepted for parties of 8 or more. Main courses $10–$16. DISC, MC, V. Tues–Thurs 5–10pm; Fri–Sat 5–11pm; Sun 4:30–9pm. Subway/El: Brown or Red line to Fullerton.

8 Wrigleyville & the North Side

For restaurants listed in this section, see the map "Dining in Lincoln Park, Old Town & Wrigleyville" on p. 154.

The area surrounding Wrigley Field has a long history as a working-class neighborhood, and although housing prices have shot up recently (as they have everywhere else), the neighborhood still attracts hordes of recent college grads who prefer chicken wings to truffles. Overall, restaurants here are more affordable and low-key than downtown, though most aren't worth a special trip if you're staying elsewhere. Throughout the North Side—a catchall phrase encompassing the neighborhoods north of Lincoln Park—you'll find mostly casual, neighborhood restaurants and a good range of ethnic eats.

VERY EXPENSIVE

Arun's 𝄞𝄞𝄞 THAI   This is the best Thai restaurant in the city—possibly the country. Here, Chef/owner Arun Sampanthavivat prepares a refined version of traditional Thai cuisine, authentic and flavorful but not palate-scorching. The only downside is its out-of-the-way location. You can get here by public transportation, but I recommend a taxi at night when the bus schedules are less reliable.

The 12-course chef's menu is your only option here, and different tables receive different dishes on a given night. This sequential banquet begins with degustation-style appetizers followed by four family-style entrees and two desserts. You might see courses of various delicate dumplings accented with edible, carved dough flowers; an alchemist's Thai salad of bitter greens and peanuts with green papaya, tomatoes, chiles, and sticky rice; and a medley of clever curries, including a surprisingly delightful seabass-and-cabbage sour curry. When classic dishes appear, such as pad thai, they're always above the norm. What really sets Arun's apart is the extremely personal service; dishes are customized for each group's preferences, and if members of a party have different tolerances for spicy food, the staff will provide variations for all taste buds. The menu is paired with an award-winning wine list.

4156 N. Kedzie Ave. (at Irving Park Rd.). ☎ 773/539-1909. www.arunsthai.com. Reservations required w/credit card. 12-course chef's menu $85. AE, DC, DISC, MC, V. Tues–Thurs 5–10pm; Fri–Sat 5–10:30pm. Subway/El and bus: Brown Line to Irving Park, and then transfer to westbound bus 80, or take a cab.

EXPENSIVE

Yoshi's Café BISTRO/ECLECTIC/FRENCH   Yoshi Katsumura has been a familiar name in the Chicago restaurant scene for years, and this casual bistro is a neighborhood favorite (meaning you'll probably have to wait for a table during prime weekend hours). The pastel decor might bring to mind a hotel coffee shop, but the menu is an intriguing mix of Yoshi's native Japan and his French training. Spring rolls come filled with chicken, mushrooms, and goat cheese, while a leek-and-brie tart is livened up with shiitake mushrooms. Vegetable and shrimp tempura show up on the entree list side by side with steak frites au poivre and grilled duck breast. There are always a number of vegetarian options, ranging from pasta to grilled tofu with brie and basil, topped with sweet-sesame paste and miso sauce.

3257 N. Halsted St. (at Aldine St.). ☎ 773/248-6160. Reservations recommended. Main courses $15–$27. AE, DC, MC, V. Tues–Thurs 5–10:30pm; Fri–Sat 5–11pm; Sun 11am–2:30pm and 5–9:30pm. Subway/El: Brown or Red line to Belmont.

MODERATE

Mia Francesca ITALIAN Though it's been open since 1992, Mia Francesca remains a hot dining spot—one that has spawned more than 10 sister restaurants throughout the city and suburbs. Its strict no-reservations policy used to mean weekend waits of up to 3 hours, but that's eased now that the reservation policy has been changed (that said, definitely call in advance for a table). The restaurant's clean, modern take on the Italian trattoria concept attracts lots of local singles and couples, and the affordable prices keep them coming back. The food—unpretentious but never dull—includes a range of homemade pastas, thin-crust pizzas, chicken, veal, and standout seafood (even if you don't usually order fish in an Italian restaurant, it's worth trying here). Tables are packed close together, so you can't help eavesdropping on your neighbors—and checking out their food.

You'll find mostly the same menu at three other Francesca's locations in the city: **Francesca's Forno,** 1576 N. Milwaukee Ave., in Wicker Park (© **773/770-0184**); **Francesca's on Taylor,** 1400 W. Taylor St., in Little Italy (© **312/829-2828**), and **Francesca's Bryn Mawr,** 1039 W. Bryn Mawr Ave., north of Wrigleyville (© **773/506-9261**). All accept reservations, which are highly recommended on weekends.

3311 N. Clark St. (1½ blocks north of Belmont Ave.). © 773/281-3310. www.miafrancesca.com. Reservations recommended. Main courses $13–$27. AE, MC, V. Sun–Thurs 5–10pm; Fri–Sat 5–11pm; Sat–Sun 11:30am–2pm. Subway/El: Brown or Red line to Belmont.

INEXPENSIVE

Ann Sather 🕸🕸 AMERICAN/BREAKFAST & BRUNCH/SWEDISH A sign hanging by Ann Sather's door bears the following inscription: "Once one of many neighborhood Swedish restaurants, Ann Sather's is the only one that remains." This is a real Chicago institution, where you can enjoy Swedish meatballs with buttered noodles and brown gravy, or the Swedish sampler of duck breast with lingonberry glaze, meatball, potato-sausage dumpling, sauerkraut, and brown beans. All meals are full dinners, including appetizer, main course, vegetable, potato, and dessert. Sticky cinnamon rolls are a highlight of Sather's popular (and very affordable) weekend brunch menu (it can get frenzied, but you should be OK if you get here before 11am). The people-watching is priceless: a cross section of gay and straight, young and old, from club kids to elderly couples and families with toddlers.

There are smaller cafes with similar menus at 3411 N. Broadway (© **773/305-0024**) and 3416 N. Southport Ave. (© **773/404-4475**).

929 W. Belmont Ave. (between Clark St. and Sheffield Ave.). © 773/348-2378. www.annsather.com. Reservations accepted for parties of 6 or more. Main courses $6–$12. AE, DC, MC, V. Mon–Fri 7am–3pm; Sat–Sun 7am–4pm. Free parking w/validation. Subway/El: Brown or Red line to Belmont.

Penny's Noodle Shop 🕸 *(Value* ASIAN/THAI Predating many of Chicago's Pan-Asian noodle shops, Penny's has kept its loyal following even as others have joined the fray. Penny Chiamopoulous, a Thai native, has assembled a concise menu of delectable dishes, all of them fresh and made to order—and all at prices that will make you do a double take. The two dining rooms are clean and spare; single diners can usually find a seat along the bar that wraps around the grill. The Thai spring roll, filled with seasoned tofu, cucumber, bean sprouts, and strips of cooked egg, makes a refreshing starter. Of course, noodles unite everything on the menu, so your main decision is choosing among the options (crispy wide rice, rice vermicelli, Japanese udon, and so on) served in a soup or spread out on a plate. There are several barbecued pork and beef entrees, and plenty of options for vegetarians as well.

The original Penny's, tucked under the El tracks at 3400 N. Sheffield Ave., near Wrigley Field (© 773/281-8222), is small and often has long waits. You stand a better chance of scoring a table at the Diversey Avenue location or the one in Wicker Park at 1542 N. Damen Ave. (at W. Pierce Ave.; © 773/394-0100). The original location is BYOB; the Diversey Avenue and Wicker Park locations have decent beer and wine lists.

950 W. Diversey Ave. (at Sheffield St.). © 773/281-8448. Reservations not accepted. Main courses $5–$8. MC, V. Sun–Thurs 11am–10pm; Fri–Sat 11am–10:30pm. Subway/El: Brown Line to Diversey.

9 Wicker Park/Bucktown

The booming Wicker Park/Bucktown area followed closely on the heels of Lincoln Park and Wrigleyville in the race to gentrification. First came the artists and musicians, followed by armies of yuppies and young families—all attracted by cheap rents and real estate. The result is a well-established, happening scene, which includes some of the city's hippest restaurants and clubs. Get yourself to the nexus of activity at the intersection of North, Damen, and Milwaukee avenues, and you won't have to walk more than a couple of blocks in any direction to find a hot spot. Cab fares from downtown are reasonable, or you can take the El's Blue Line to Damen.

EXPENSIVE

Mas 𝕽𝕽 LATIN AMERICAN   Cozy, dimly lit Mas is almost always packed with faithful regulars who come for the Latin cocktails and modern takes on traditional Central and South American cuisine. With long waits on weekends and plenty of loud conversation, it may not be to everyone's taste. But if you haven't sampled the *nuevo Latino* dining trend yet, this is a good place to try it.

The "primero" list includes spicy lime-marinated tuna tacos with papaya, rosemary, and Dijon salsa; and a succulent ceviche of the day (such as yellowtail snapper with smoked poblano chile or blue marlin with rum and vanilla). Star entrees include chile-cured pork tenderloin over smoky white beans; achiote-roasted mako shark with crawfish-lentil salsa and avocado salad; and a traditional Honduran seafood stew of shrimp, mussels, and scallops. Out-of-the-ordinary desserts include a banana and milk chocolate-filled empanada topped with dulce de leche ice cream. At the bar, try a Brazilian *caipirinha* (made with sugar, lime, and *cachaça*, a brandy made from sugar cane), a guava *batida* (an alcoholic version of a fruit smoothie), or a Peruvian Pisco sour. The margaritas are also very good, and the wine list emphasizes selections from Spain, Argentina, and Chile.

1670 W. Division St. (at Paulina St.). © 773/276-8700. www.masrestaurant.com. Reservations recommended. Main courses $18–$28. AE, MC, V. Mon–Thurs 5:30–10pm; Fri–Sat 5:30–11:30pm; Sun 11am–3pm and 5:30–10pm. Subway/El: Blue Line to Division.

Meritage Café and Wine Bar 𝕽𝕽 AMERICAN   Meritage originally opened with an emphasis on Pacific Northwest cuisine, but in the past few years the menu selections have become more broad. Regardless, the lovely decor remains the draw for me. The front room, with tables opposite a long wood bar, has the feel of a hip wine bar. But the best place to sit is the romantic patio, which is lit by overhead lights; the entire space is covered and heated in winter, so you don't have to wait for good weather to enjoy the atmosphere.

Dining in Wicker Park/Bucktown

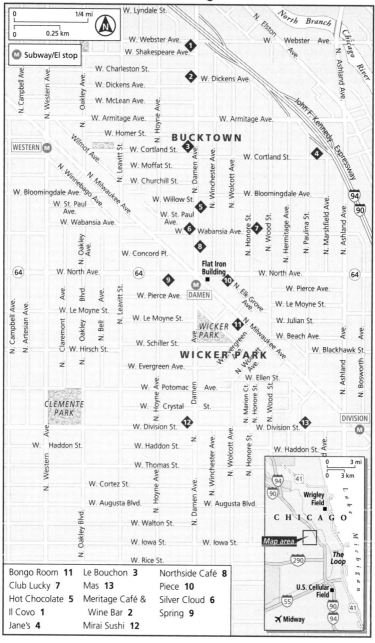

Bongo Room **11**	Le Bouchon **3**	Northside Café **8**
Club Lucky **7**	Mas **13**	Piece **10**
Hot Chocolate **5**	Meritage Café &	Silver Cloud **6**
Il Covo **1**	Wine Bar **2**	Spring **9**
Jane's **4**	Mirai Sushi **12**	

The menu offers a fair variety of seafood (king salmon, skate wing, scallops), and wild game shows up both in entrees and appetizers (the smoked pheasant and wood-land mushroom terrine appetizer, for example). Many dishes put a modern twist on the meat-starch-vegetable formula: a hearty pork chop is topped with gingered rhubarb chutney and served with goat cheese mashed potatoes and fresh asparagus. Desserts tend toward lighter, fruit-focused dishes (recent offerings included a Meyer lemon-poppy seed pound cake with warm mountain berry compote; and an apple kumquat *tarte Tatin* with caramel apple sorbet), but don't worry, there's always some-thing chocolate, too. Don't forget to try a glass of the restaurant's namesake wine; the servers can also point the way to the best food-wine pairings.

2118 N. Damen Ave. (at Charleston St.). (C) 773/235-6434. www.meritagecafe.com. Reservations recommended. Main courses $18–$34. AE, DC, MC, V. Mon 5:30–9pm; Tues–Thurs 5:30–10:30pm; Fri–Sat 5–9pm; Sun 11am–2pm. Subway/El: Blue Line to Damen, and then a short cab ride.

Mirai Sushi ★★ JAPANESE/SUSHI   Blending a serious devotion to sushi and sake with a decidedly youthful, funky-chic ambience, Mirai is a hot destination for cold raw fish (though it serves other Japanese fare as well). The futuristic second-floor sake lounge is the hippest place in town to slurp down sushi, chilled sakes, and "red ones," the house cocktail of vodka with passion fruit, lime, and cranberry juices. The bright main-floor dining room offers a comparatively traditional environment.

Fish is flown in daily for the sushi bar, where several chefs are hard at work master-crafting a lovely list of offerings—from the beginner sushi standards such as Califor-nia rolls and *ebi* (boiled shrimp) to escalating classifications of tuna, three additional shrimp varieties, five types of salmon, a half-dozen varieties of fresh oysters, and a tan-talizing list of four caviars (in addition to the four roes offered). The informative sake menu of about a dozen selections opens up a new world to diners accustomed to the generic carafe of heated sake.

2020 W. Division St. (at Damen Ave.). (C) 773/862-8500. www.miraisushi.com. Reservations recommended. Sushi $2–$6 per piece. AE, DC, DISC, MC, V. Mon–Wed 5–10pm; Thurs–Sat 5–11pm. Upstairs lounge open until 2am. Sub-way/El: Blue Line to Division.

Spring ★★★ AMERICAN   Chef Shawn McClain is one of Chicago's culinary celebrities, and Spring—his first restaurant—attracted national attention when it opened in 2001. Located in a former Russian bathhouse, the space is now an oasis of Zen tranquillity in soothing, neutral colors. Spring is not a scene: Diners step down into a dining room hidden from the street, sink into the banquettes that zigzag across the center of the room, and concentrate on the food. Unlike other chefs who feel pres-sured to keep outdoing themselves, McClain sticks to a focused menu with a heavy emphasis on seafood and Pan-Asian preparations. Appetizers include an aromatic lemon-grass red-curry broth with rice noodles, and sea-scallop-and-potato ravioli with sautéed mushrooms and truffle essence. Most of the entrees are seafood-based: New Zealand snapper with lemon couscous and fennel salad, or the braised baby monkfish and escargots with roasted eggplant in smoked tomato bouillon, for example. Among the nonfish options, beef short-rib pot stickers spiced up with Korean seasonings stand out. Desserts also go the Asian route, focusing on seasonal fruits, although the coconut mochi brûlée with warm pineapple puts a whole new twist on rice pudding.

2039 W. North Ave. (at Milwaukee Ave.). (C) 773/395-7100. www.springrestaurant.net. Reservations recommended. Main courses $22–$31. AE, DC, DISC, MC, V. Tues–Thurs 5:30–10pm; Fri–Sat 5:30–10:30pm; Sun 5:30–9pm. Subway/ El: Blue Line to Damen.

MODERATE

Club Lucky ✦ *(Value* ITALIAN   Club Lucky seems to have been carved from a local 1950s-era corner tavern with an Italian mamma cooking up family recipes in the back. The Naugahyde banquettes, Formica-topped bar and tables, and Captain Video ceiling fixtures give the place a fun retro flair. The scene here changes throughout the evening: Young families gradually give way to stylish couples posing with glasses of the restaurant's signature martinis (be prepared to wait on weekends).

You might or might not take to the scene, but the food does not disappoint. Prices overall are moderate, especially considering the generous family-style portions. The large calamari appetizer—"for two," the menu says—will almost certainly keep you in leftover land for a day or two. The menu offers real Italian home-style cooking such as *pasta e fagioli* (thick macaroni-and-bean soup—really a kind of stew). Or try the rigatoni with veal meatballs, served with steamed escarole and melted slabs of mozzarella, or the spicy grilled boneless pork chops served with peppers and roasted potatoes. The lunch menu includes about a dozen Italian sandwiches, such as scrambled eggs and pesto, meatball, and Italian sausage.

1824 W. Wabansia Ave. (1 block north of North Ave., between Damen and Ashland aves.). © **773/227-2300.** www. clubluckychicago.com. Reservations accepted for parties of 6 or more. Sandwiches $8–$11; main courses $10–$36. AE, DC, DISC, MC, V. Mon–Thurs 11:30am–11pm; Fri 11:30am–midnight; Sat 5pm–midnight; Sun 4–10pm; cocktail lounge open later. Subway/El: Blue Line to Damen.

Il Covo ✦ ITALIAN   There are no gimmicks at Il Covo, just solid Italian cooking and a cozy, low-key atmosphere—a combination that made this spot a neighborhood hangout within weeks of its 2007 opening. Appetizers include a full range of classic Italian dishes, from calamari and bruschetta to an *insalata caprese* of tomatoes, fresh mozzarella, and basil. All pasta is made in-house, and if you're looking for a dish a bit out of the ordinary, the tasty Sardinian gnocchi topped with a tomato-lamb tenderloin sauce fits the bill. Entrees are no-frills but nicely done, including a classic scaloppine al limone (veal medallions with capers in a lemon-white wine sauce) and various grilled fish specials. The wine list—not surprisingly—is heavy on Italian selections. The dining room is intimate and cozy with exposed brick walls and dark wood floors.

2152 N. Damen Ave. (at Shakespeare Ave., just south of Webster Ave.). © **773/862-5555.** www.ilcovochicago.com. Reservations accepted. Main courses $18–$27. AE, DC, DISC, MC, V. Sun–Thurs 5–10pm; Fri–Sat 5–11pm. Subway/El: Blue Line to Damen.

Jane's ✦ *(Finds* ECLECTIC   Jane's has long been ignored by dining critics on the hunt for the next big thing—all the more reason to love this inconspicuous charmer. This does not, however, mean that snagging a table at Jane's is an easy feat. On the contrary; this is a hugely popular destination among Wicker Park/Bucktown habitués, who'd prefer to keep it a secret. (Wait for your table at the friendly Bucktown Pub across the street.)

More than anything else, it may be the cozy ambience that attracts diners. Jane's is ensconced in an old house that has been gutted and rehabbed to create an open, two-story space with just 16 tables. (In summer seven more are set up on an outside patio.) The menu offers piquant, upscale comfort food prepared simply and with loving care, including both meat (duck breast pan-seared with turnips and peaches; seared sea bass with mashed potatoes, arugula, caramelized pearl onions, and mushroom coulis) and vegetarian options, such as a goat cheese, tofu, and veggie burrito. The salads are standouts, especially the mesclun greens with pear, blue cheese, pecans, and balsamic vinaigrette.

1655 W. Cortland St. (1 block west of Ashland Ave.). ✆ 773/862-5263. www.janesrestaurant.com. Reservations recommended, but only a small number are accepted for each evening. Main courses $15–$25. MC, V. Sun–Thurs 5–10pm; Fri–Sat 5–11pm; Sat–Sun 10am–2:30pm. Subway/El: Blue Line to Damen.

Le Bouchon ✰✰ (Finds) BISTRO/FRENCH   Jean-Claude Poilevey's tiny storefront restaurant, Le Bouchon, is popular for both its intimate yet boisterous atmosphere and affordable authentic bistro fare. Whatever the season, the food here is fairly heavy, although specials are lighter in warmer months. Poilevey could pack this place every night just with regulars addicted to the house specialty of roast duck for two, bathed in Grand Marnier–orange marmalade sauce. The fare covers bistro basics, with starters including steamed mussels in white wine and herbs, country pâté, onion tart, codfish *brandade* (a pounded mixture of cod, olive oil, garlic, milk, and cream), and *salade Lyonnaise* (greens with bacon lardoons, croutons, and poached egg). The authenticity continues in the entree department, with steak frites, sautéed rabbit in white wine, veal kidneys in mustard sauce, and bouillabaisse. The sounds of prominent music and voices from closely packed tables create an atmosphere that some perceive as cozy and romantic, and others as claustrophobic and noisy. There's a small bar where you can wait—something you might have to do even if you have a reservation.

1958 N. Damen Ave. (at Armitage Ave.). ✆ 773/862-6600. www.lebouchonofchicago.com. Reservations recommended. Main courses $16–$20. AE, DC, DISC, MC, V. Mon–Thurs 5:30–11pm; Fri–Sat 5pm–midnight. Subway/El: Blue Line to Damen, and then a short cab ride.

INEXPENSIVE

Hot Chocolate ✰ AMERICAN   Mindy Segal's desserts got raves when she worked at the restaurant mk (p. 140), so when she opened her own place in early 2005—with a dessert theme, no less—there were lines almost immediately. Although Segal knows her way around high-end kitchens, she's designed Hot Chocolate to be more of a casual neighborhood spot, the kind of place you can stop in for a brioche and coffee in the morning, a Kobe beef steak sandwich at lunch, or a plate of glazed pork tenderloin in the evening. However, desserts are the main event here; many use seasonal fruit (apple-cider potpie, or the banana napoleon, with layers of caramelized bananas, banana coffee cake, graham crackers, and a topping of banana ice cream), but chocoholics can get their fill, too, with dishes such as the rich chocolate soufflé with caramel ice cream. Or you can finish up with a flight of mini hot chocolates served with homemade marshmallows. The restaurant is stylish but warm, with lots of exposed wood and (not coincidentally) chocolate-brown upholstery. My only complaint is that Hot Chocolate has been a little too successful; come on a weekday (for a late lunch or early dinner) to avoid a wait.

1747 N. Damen Ave. (at Willow St.). ✆ 773/489-1747. Reservations not accepted. Main courses $10–$13 lunch, $12–$23 dinner. AE, MC, V. Tues–Fri 11am–3pm; Sat–Sun 10am–2pm; Tues–Wed and Sun 5:30–10pm; Thurs 5:30–11pm; Fri–Sat 5:30–midnight. Subway/El: Blue Line to Damen.

Northside Café AMERICAN/BURGERS   Among the best cheap eats in the neighborhood, Northside cooks up great burgers, sandwiches, and salads—all for about $15 or less. This is strictly neighborhood dining, without attitude and little in the way of decor; the back dining room looks like a rec room circa 1973, complete with a fireplace, pinball machines, and a pool table. In nice weather, Northside opens up its large front patio for dining, and a sky-lit cover keeps it in use during the winter. You're always sure to be entertained by people-watching here, as Northside attracts all sorts. During the week, the cafe is more of a neighborhood hangout, while on weekends a touristy crowd from Lincoln Park and the suburbs piles in. A limited late-night menu is available from 10pm to 1am.

1635 N. Damen Ave. (at North and Milwaukee aves.). ℂ **773/384-3555**. Reservations not accepted. Menu items $6–$15. AE, DC, DISC, MC, V. Sun–Fri 11:30am–2am; Sat 11am–3am. Subway/El: Blue Line to Damen.

Piece *ℱ* AMERICAN/PIZZA   Piece proves to deep-dish-loving Chicagoans that thin-crust pizza deserves respect. A casual, welcoming hangout, Piece makes a good lunch stop for families with older kids; at night it becomes a convivial scene full of young singles sipping one of the restaurant's seasonal microbrew beers. The large, airy dining room—a former garage that's been outfitted with dark wood tables and ceiling beams—is flooded with light from the expansive skylights overhead; even when it's crowded (as it gets on weekend evenings), the soaring space above keeps the place from feeling claustrophobic.

Piece offers a selection of salads and sandwiches on satisfyingly crusty bread, but pizza in the style of New Haven, Connecticut (hometown of one of the owners), is the house specialty. Pick from three styles—plain (tomato sauce, Parmesan cheese, and garlic), red (tomato sauce and mozzarella), or white (olive oil, garlic, and mozzarella), then add on your favorite toppings. Sausage and/or spinach work well with the plain or red, but the adventurous should sample a more offbeat choice: clam and bacon on white pizza.

1927 W. North Ave. (at Milwaukee Ave.). ℂ **773/772-4422**. www.piecechicago.com. Reservations accepted for groups of 10 or more. Pizza $11–$17. AE, DISC, MC, V. Mon–Thurs 11:30am–11pm; Fri–Sat 11:30am–12:30am; Sun 11am–10pm. Subway/El: Blue Line to Damen.

Silver Cloud *ℱℱ* AMERICAN   The motto of this casual cafe is "Food like Mom would make if she was gettin' paid." Indeed, Silver Cloud is comfort food-central, with a laid-back pub-meets-diner decor and suitably attitude-free clientele. If intimate conversation is your priority, try to snag one of the roomy red-leather booths. While the food isn't extraordinary, the restaurant does deliver consistently reliable home-style favorites: chicken potpie, grilled-cheese sandwiches, pot roast, sloppy Joes with a side of tater tots, s'mores, and root beer floats. While Silver Cloud attracts a mix of families, couples, and groups of friends during the day and early-evening hours, it becomes more of a cocktail lounge at night. A warning for those with sensitive ears: The juke-box volume gets turned up at night, too. The Sunday brunch is especially popular; the "Hangover Helpers" attract a fair amount of hip young things recovering from nightly adventures.

1700 N. Damen Ave. (at Wabansia St.). ℂ **773/489-6212**. www.silvercloudchicago.com. Main courses $6–$10 lunch, $10–$16 dinner. AE, DC, MC, V. Mon–Thurs 11:30am–11pm; Fri 11:30am–midnight; Sat–Sun 10am–midnight. Bar stays open later every night except Sun. Subway/El: Blue Line to Damen.

8

Exploring Chicago

Chicago may still be stereotyped as the home of sausage-loving, overweight guys who babble on endlessly about "da Bears" or "da Cubs," but in reality the city offers some of the most sophisticated cultural and entertainment options in the country. You'll have trouble fitting in all of Chicago's museums, which offer everything from action (the virtual-reality visit to the Milky Way galaxy at the Adler Planetarium) to quiet contemplation (the Impressionist masterpieces at the Art Institute of Chicago). Check out Sue, the biggest T. rex fossil ever discovered, at the Field Museum of Natural History, or be entranced by the colorful world of the Butterfly Haven at the Peggy Notebaert Nature Museum. Stroll through picture-perfect Lincoln Park Zoo on the Near North Side, and then enjoy the view from the top of the Ferris wheel on historic Navy Pier.

Best of all, the majority of the places you'll want to visit are in or near downtown,

making it easy to plan your day and get from place to place. And because this is a town with a thriving tourist economy, you'll have plenty of visitor-friendly options: walking tours of famous architecture; boat cruises on Lake Michigan; and even bus tours of notorious gangster sites. If you're lucky enough to visit when the weather's nice, you can join the locals at our parks and the beaches along Lake Michigan.

Extensive public transportation makes it simple to reach almost every tourist destination, but some of your best memories of Chicago may come from simply strolling along the sidewalks. Chicago's neighborhoods have their own distinct styles and looks, and you'll have a more memorable experience if you don't limit yourself solely to the prime tourist spots. And if you *really* want to talk about da Bears or da Cubs, chances are you'll find someone who's more than happy to join in.

1 In & Around the Loop: The Art Institute, the Sears Tower & Grant Park

The heart of the Loop is Chicago's business center, where you'll find the Chicago Board of Trade (the world's largest commodities, futures, and options exchange), Sears Tower, and some of the city's most famous early skyscrapers. If you're looking for an authentic big-city experience, wander the area on a weekday, when commuters are rushing to catch trains and businesspeople are hustling to get to work. The Loop is also home to one of the city's top museums, the Art Institute of Chicago, as well as a number of cultural institutions including the Symphony Center (home of the Chicago Symphony Orchestra), the Auditorium Theatre, the Civic Opera House, the Goodman Theatre, and two fabulously restored historic theaters along Randolph Street. On the eastern edge of the Loop in Grant Park, three popular museums are conveniently located within a quick stroll of each other on the landscaped Museum Campus. Busy Lake Shore Drive, which brings cars zipping past the Museum Campus, was actually rerouted a few years ago to make the area easier to navigate for pedestrians.

THE TOP ATTRACTIONS IN THE LOOP

For a map of these attractions (or this neighborhood), see p. 172.

Art Institute of Chicago ✸✸✸ *Kids*   You can't—and shouldn't—miss the Art Institute. (You really have no excuse, since it's conveniently located right on Michigan Avenue in the heart of downtown.) No matter what medium or century interests you, the Art Institute has something in its collection to fit the bill. Japanese *ukiyo-e* prints, ancient Egyptian bronzes, Greek vases, 19th-century British photography, masterpieces by most of the greatest names in 20th-century sculpture, and modern American textiles are just some of the works on display, but for a general overview of the museum's collection, take the free "Highlights of the Art Institute" tour, offered at 2pm on Tuesday, Saturday, and Sunday.

If time is limited, head straight to the museum's renowned anthology of **Impressionist art** ✸✸✸, which includes one of the world's largest collections of Monet paintings; this is one of the most popular areas of the museum, so arriving early pays off. Among the treasures, you'll find Seurat's pointillist masterpiece *Sunday Afternoon on the Island of La Grande Jatte.* The galleries of **European and American contemporary art** ✸✸ include paintings, sculptures, and mixed-media works by Pablo Picasso, Henri Matisse, Salvador Dalí, Willem de Kooning, Jackson Pollock, and Andy Warhol. Visitors are sometimes surprised when they discover many of the icons that hang here. (Grant Wood's *American Gothic* and Edward Hopper's *Nighthawks* are two that often get double takes.)

Other recommended exhibits are the collection of delicate mid–19th-century **glass paperweights** in the famous Arthur Rubloff collection, and the great hall of **European arms and armor** ✸ dating from the 15th to 19th centuries. Composed of more than 1,500 objects, including armor, horse equipment, swords and daggers, polearms, and maces, the collection is one of the most important assemblages of its kind in the country. (If you do head down here, don't miss Marc Chagall's stunning stained-glass windows at the end of the gallery.)

Children younger than 12 get in for free, and the Art Institute goes the extra mile to entertain them. The **Kraft Education Center** on the lower level features interactive exhibits and has a list of "gallery games" to make visiting the museum more fun. When I was a kid, I was entranced by the **Thorne Miniature Rooms** ✸, filled with tiny reproductions of furnished interiors from European and American history (heaven for a dollhouse fanatic).

The museum has a cafeteria and an elegant full-service restaurant, a picturesque courtyard cafe (open June–Sept), and a large shop. It offers a busy schedule of lectures, films, and other special presentations, as well as guided tours. The museum also has a research library. Allow 3 hours.

111 S. Michigan Ave. (at Adams St.). ✆ **312/443-3600.** www.artic.edu. Admission $12 adults; $7 seniors and students w/ID; free for children 11 and under. Additional cost for special exhibitions. Free admission Thurs 5–8pm. Mon–Fri 10:30am–5pm (Thurs until 8pm, until 9pm Thurs–Fri Memorial Day–Labor Day); Sat–Sun 10am–5pm. Closed Jan. 1, Thanksgiving, and Dec 25. Bus: 3, 4, 60, 145, 147, or 151. Subway/El: Green, Brown, Purple, or Orange line to Adams, or Red Line to Monroe/State or Jackson/State.

Chicago Attractions

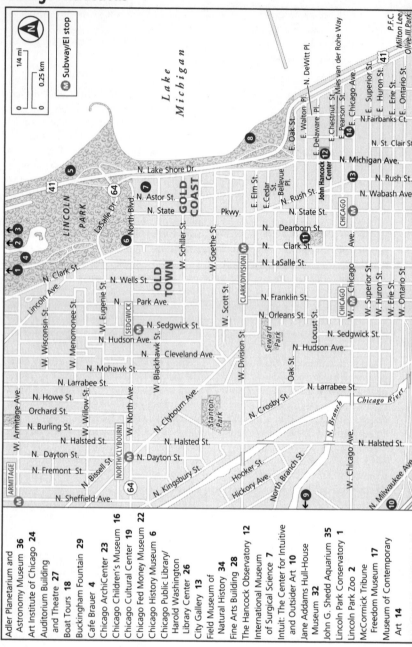

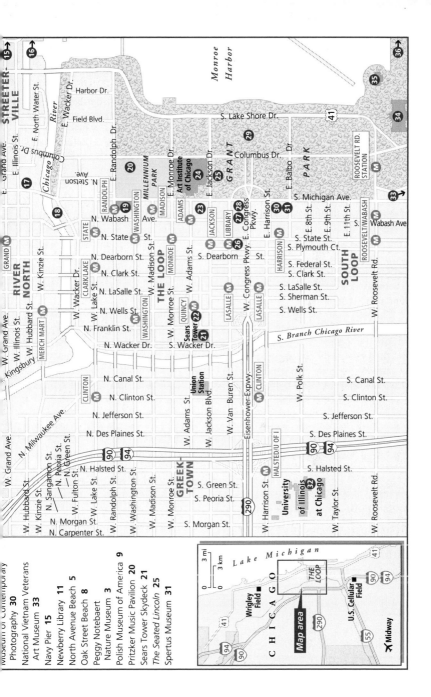

Museum of Contemporary
Photography **30**
National Vietnam Veterans
Art Museum **33**
Navy Pier **15**
Newberry Library **11**
North Avenue Beach **5**
Oak Street Beach **8**
Peggy Notebaert
Nature Museum **3**
Polish Museum of America **9**
Pritzker Music Pavilion **20**
Sears Tower Skydeck **21**
The Seated Lincoln **25**
Spertus Museum **31**

Tips **Insider Tips for Touring the Art Institute**

If you want to enjoy your favorite masterpieces in something resembling peace and quiet, put some thought into the timing of your visit to the Art Institute, a museum so popular that it draws as much traffic as our jammed expressways.

Some tips for avoiding the rush hour: Many people don't realize the museum is open on Monday; keep this secret to yourself, and visit when the galleries are relatively subdued. Also, many visitors aren't aware that the museum stays open late on Thursdays, so consider stopping by after an early dinner (another bonus: free admission).

Sears Tower Skydeck *Overrated* First Sears sold the building and moved to cheaper suburban offices in 1992. Then the skyscraper got an ego blow when the Petronas Towers in Kuala Lumpur, Malaysia, went up and laid claim to the title of world's tallest building. (The Sears Tower has since put up a 22-ft. antenna in an attempt to win back the title.) Tallest-building posturing aside, this is still a great place to orient yourself to the city, but I wouldn't put it on the top of must-see sights for anyone with limited time (and limited patience for crowds).

The view from the 103rd-floor Skydeck is everything you'd expect it to be—once you get there. Unfortunately, you're often stuck in a very long, very noisy line, so by the time you make it to the top, your patience could be as thin as the atmosphere up there. (Come in the late afternoon or early evening to avoid most of the crowds.) On a clear day, visibility extends up to 50 miles, and you can catch glimpses of four surrounding states. Despite the fact that it's called a "skydeck," you can't actually walk outside. Multimedia exhibits on Chicago history and *Knee High Chicago,* an exhibit for kids, are additional attractions. The 70-second, high-speed elevator trip will feel like a thrill ride for some, but it's a nightmare for anyone with even mild claustrophobia. Allow 1 hour, more if there's a long line.

233 S. Wacker Dr. (enter on Jackson Blvd.). © 312/875-9696. www.the-skydeck.com. Admission $13 adults; $9.50 seniors and children 3–12; free for children 2 and under. Apr–Sept daily 10am–10pm; Oct–Mar daily 10am–8pm. Bus: 1, 7, 126, 146, 151, or 156. Subway/El: Brown, Purple, or Orange line to Quincy, or Red or Blue line to Jackson; and then walk a few blocks west.

THE LOOP SCULPTURE TOUR

Monuments, statues, and contemporary sculptures are on view throughout Chicago, but the concentration of public art within the Loop and nearby Grant Park is worth noting. The best known of these works are by 20th-century artists including Picasso, Chagall, Miró, Calder, Moore, and Oldenburg. The newest addition is the massive elliptical sculpture *Cloud Gate* (known as "The Bean" because it looks like a giant silver kidney bean) by British artist Anish Kapoor. The sculpture, in Millennium Park, was Kapoor's first public commission in the U.S.

A free brochure, *The Chicago Public Art Guide* (available at the Chicago Cultural Center, 78 E. Washington St.), can help steer you toward the best examples of monumental public art. You can also conduct a self-guided tour of the city's best public sculptures by following "The Loop Sculpture Tour" (map, p. 175).

The single most famous sculpture is **Pablo Picasso's** *Untitled,* located in Daley Plaza and constructed out of Cor-Ten steel, the same gracefully rusting material used on the exterior of the Daley Center behind it. Viewed from various perspectives, its

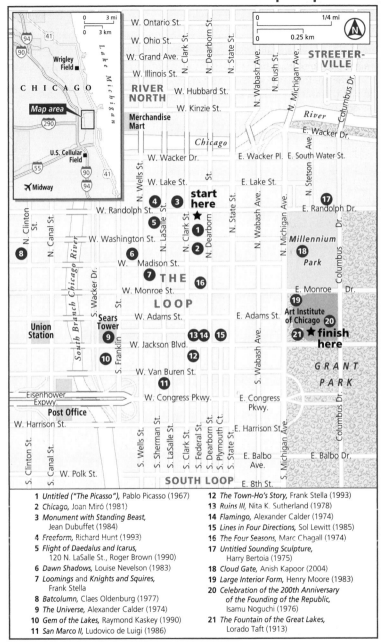

1 *Untitled ("The Picasso")*, Pablo Picasso (1967)
2 *Chicago*, Joan Miró (1981)
3 *Monument with Standing Beast*,
   Jean Dubuffet (1984)
4 *Freeform*, Richard Hunt (1993)
5 *Flight of Daedalus and Icarus*,
   120 N. LaSalle St., Roger Brown (1990)
6 *Dawn Shadows*, Louise Nevelson (1983)
7 *Loomings* and *Knights and Squires*,
   Frank Stella
8 *Batcolumn*, Claes Oldenburg (1977)
9 *The Universe*, Alexander Calder (1974)
10 *Gem of the Lakes*, Raymond Kaskey (1990)
11 *San Marco II*, Ludovico de Luigi (1986)

12 *The Town-Ho's Story*, Frank Stella (1993)
13 *Ruins III*, Nita K. Sutherland (1978)
14 *Flamingo*, Alexander Calder (1974)
15 *Lines in Four Directions*, Sol Lewitt (1985)
16 *The Four Seasons*, Marc Chagall (1974)
17 *Untitled Sounding Sculpture*,
   Harry Bertoia (1975)
18 *Cloud Gate*, Anish Kapoor (2004)
19 *Large Interior Form*, Henry Moore (1983)
20 *Celebration of the 200th Anniversary
   of the Founding of the Republic*,
   Isamu Noguchi (1976)
21 *The Fountain of the Great Lakes*,
   Lorado Taft (1913)

Oprah in Person

Oprah Winfrey tapes her phenomenally successful talk show at Harpo Studios, 1058 W. Washington Blvd., just west of the Loop. If you'd like to be in her studio audience, you'll have to plan ahead: Reservations are taken by phone only (℃ 312/591-9222), at least 1 month in advance. For information on upcoming shows, check the website (www.oprah.com); if you've got a great personal story that relates to a show being planned, you can submit it online and just might get booked as a guest.

enigmatic shape suggests a woman, bird, or dog. Perhaps because it was the button-down Loop's first monumental modern sculpture, its installation in 1967 was met with hoots and heckles, but today "The Picasso" enjoys semiofficial status as the logo of modern Chicago. It is by far the city's most popular photo opportunity among visiting tourists. At noon on weekdays during warm weather, you'll likely find a dance troupe, musical group, or visual-arts exhibition here as part of the city's long-running "Under the Picasso" multicultural program. Call ℃ 312/346-3278 for event information.

GRANT PARK & MILLENNIUM PARK

For a map of these attractions (or this neighborhood), see p. 172.

Thanks to architect Daniel Burnham and his coterie of visionary civic planners—who drafted the revolutionary 1909 Plan of Chicago—the city boasts a wide-open lake-front park system unrivaled by most major metropolises. Modeled after the gardens at Versailles, **Grant Park** (℃ 312/742-PLAY; www.chicagoparkdistrict.com) is Chicago's front yard, composed of giant lawns segmented by *allées* of trees, plantings, and paths, and pieced together by major roadways and a network of railroad tracks. Incredibly, the entire expanse was created from sandbars, landfill, and Chicago Fire debris; the original shoreline extended all the way to Michigan Avenue. A few museums are spread out inside the park, but most of the space is wide open (a legacy of mail-order magnate Aaron Montgomery Ward's *fin de siècle* campaign to limit municipal buildings).

The northwest corner of Grant Park (bordered by Michigan Ave. and Randolph St.) is the site of **Millennium Park** ℞℞℞, one of the city's grandest public-works projects. Who cares that the park cost hundreds of millions more than it was supposed to, or the fact that it finally opened a full 4 years *after* the actual millennium? It's a winning combination of beautiful landscaping, elegant architecture (the classically inspired peristyle), and public entertainment spaces (including an ice rink and theater). The park's centerpiece is the dramatic Frank Gehry–designed **Pritzker Music Pavilion,** featuring massive curved ribbons of steel. The Grant Park Symphony Orchestra and Chorus stages a popular series of free outdoor classical music concerts here most Wednesday through Sunday evenings in the summer. For a schedule of concert times and dates, contact the **Grant Park Music Festival** (℃ 312/742-7638; www.grant parkmusicfestival.com). Two public artworks well worth checking out are the kidney bean–shaped sculpture *Cloud Gate* and the **Crown Fountain,** where children splash in the shallow water between giant faces projected on video screens. Free walking tours of the park are offered daily from Memorial Day through October at 11:30am and 1pm, starting at the park's Welcome Center, 201 E. Randolph St. (℃ 312/742-1168).

> **Fun Fact Did You Know?**
> Yugoslavian sculptor Ivan Mestrovic titled his bronze sculpture of Indian war-
> riors on horseback *The Bowman and the Spearman;* however, the warriors' bow
> and arrow and spear have been removed. Mestrovic intentionally omitted
> them to make an antiwar statement.

During the summer, a variety of music and food festivals take over central Grant
Park. Annual events that draw big crowds include a blues music festival (in June) and
a jazz festival (Labor Day). The **Taste of Chicago** (© **312/744-3315;** www.cityof
chicago.org/specialevents), purportedly the largest food festival in the world (the city
estimates its annual attendance at around 3.5 million), takes place every year for 10
days around the 4th of July. Local restaurants serve up more ribs, pizza, hot dogs, and
beer than you'd ever want to see, let alone eat. (See chapter 3 for a comprehensive listing of summer events in Grant Park.)

Head south to the lake via Congress Parkway, and you'll find **Buckingham Fountain** ⊛, the baroque centerpiece of the park, composed of pink Georgia marble and
patterned after—but twice the size of—the Latona Fountain at Versailles, with adjoining esplanades beautified by rose gardens in season. From April through October, the
fountain spurts columns of water up to 150 feet in the air every hour on the hour, and
beginning at 4pm, a whirl of colored lights and dramatic music amps up the drama.
The fountain shuts down at 11pm; concession areas and bathrooms are available on
the plaza.

Sculptures and monuments stand throughout the park, including a sculpture of
two Native Americans on horseback, *The Bowman and the Spearman* (at Congress
Pkwy. and Michigan Ave.), which was installed in 1928 and has become the park's
trademark. Also here are likenesses of Copernicus, Columbus, and Lincoln, the latter
by the great American sculptor Augustus Saint-Gaudens, located on Congress Parkway between Michigan Avenue and Columbus Drive. On the western edge of the park,
at Adams Street, is the **Art Institute** (see above), and at the southern tip, in the area
known as the Museum Campus, are the **Field Museum of Natural History,** the
Adler Planetarium, and the **Shedd Aquarium** (see below for all three).

To get to Grant Park, take bus no. 3, 4, 6, 146, or 151. If you want to take the subway or the El, get off at any stop in the Loop along State or Wabash, and walk east.

ALONG SOUTH MICHIGAN AVENUE

For a map of these attractions (or this neighborhood), see p. 172.

Fashion and glamour might have moved north to the Magnificent Mile, but Chicago's
grandest stretch of boulevard is still Michigan Avenue, south of the river. From a little north of the Michigan Avenue bridge all the way down to the Field Museum,
South Michigan Avenue runs parallel to Grant Park on one side and the Loop on the
other. A stroll along this boulevard in any season offers both visual and cultural treats.
Particularly impressive is the great wall of buildings from Randolph Street south to
Congress Parkway (beginning with the Chicago Cultural Center and terminating at
the Auditorium Building) that architecture buffs refer to as the "Michigan Avenue
Cliff."

The following attractions are listed from north to south.

Chicago Cultural Center ⓐ *Finds*   The Chicago Cultural Center was built in 1897 as the city's public library, and in 1991, it was transformed into a showplace for visual and performing arts. Today, it's an overlooked civic treasure with a basic Beaux Arts exterior and a sumptuous interior of rare marble, fine hardwood, stained glass, and mosaics of Favrile glass, colored stone, and mother-of-pearl inlaid in white marble. The crowning centerpiece is Preston Bradley Hall's majestic **Tiffany dome** ⓐ, said to be the largest of its kind in the world.

The building also houses one of the **Chicago Office of Tourism** visitor centers, which makes it an ideal place to kick-start your visit. If you stop in to pick up tourist information and take a quick look around, your visit won't take longer than 15 minutes, but the Cultural Center also schedules an array of art exhibitions, concerts, films, lectures, and other special events (many free), which might convince you to extend your time here. A long-standing tradition is the 12:15pm Dame Myra Hess Memorial classical concert every Wednesday in the Preston Bradley Hall.

Guided architectural tours of the Cultural Center run at 1:15pm on Wednesday, Friday, and Saturday.

78 E. Washington St. ⓒ **312/744-6630,** or 312/FINE-ART for weekly events. www.cityofchicago.org/exploringchicago. Free admission. Mon–Thurs 10am–7pm; Fri 10am–6pm; Sat 10am–5pm; Sun 11am–5pm. Closed major holidays. Bus: 3, 4, 20, 56, 145, 146, 147, 151, or 157. Subway/El: Brown, Green, Orange, or Purple line to Randolph, or Red Line to Washington/State.

Chicago ArchiCenter   Chicago's architecture is one of the city's main claims to fame, and a quick swing through this center, run by the well-regarded **Chicago Architecture Foundation** (conveniently located across the street from the Art Institute), will help you understand why. Exhibits include a scale model of downtown Chicago, profiles of the people and buildings that shaped the city's look, and a searchable database with pictures of and information on many of Chicago's best-known skyscrapers. "Architecture ambassadors" are on hand to provide information on tours run by the foundation (see "Sightseeing Tours," p. 212). Two galleries feature changing exhibits about ongoing Chicago design projects, so you can see firsthand how local architecture continues to evolve. There's also an excellent gift shop filled with architecture-focused books, decorative accessories, and gifts. Allow a half-hour, more if you want to browse in the store.

224 S. Michigan Ave. ⓒ **312/922-3432,** ext. 241. www.architecture.org. Free admission. Exhibits Mon–Sat 9:30am–4pm. Shop and tour desk Mon–Sat 9am–6:30pm; Sun 9am–6pm. Bus: 3, 4, 145, 147, or 151. Subway/El: Brown, Green, Purple, or Orange line to Adams, or Red Line to Jackson.

Fine Arts Building   A worthwhile brief stop for architecture and history buffs, this 1885 building was originally a showroom for Studebaker carriages. In 1917 it became

---

Moments **Photo Op**

For a great photo op, walk on Randolph Street toward the lake in the morning when the sun, rising in the east over the lake, hits the cliff of buildings along South Michigan Avenue, giving you the perfect backdrop for an only-in-Chicago picture.

an arts center, with offices, shops, two theaters, and studios for musicians, artists, and writers. Its upper stories sheltered a number of well-known publications *(The Saturday Evening Post, Dial)* and provided offices for such luminaries as Frank Lloyd Wright, sculptor Lorado Taft, and L. Frank Baum, author of *The Wonderful Wizard of Oz.* Harriet Monroe published her magazine, *Poetry,* here and introduced American readers to Carl Sandburg, T. S. Eliot, and Ezra Pound. Before the literary lions prowled its halls, the building served as a rallying base for suffragettes. Located throughout the building are a number of interesting studios and musical-instrument shops. Take at least a quick walk through the marble-and-wood lobby, and ride the vintage elevator to the top floor to see the spectacular murals. Allow a half-hour.

410 S. Michigan Ave. ℂ 312/566-9800. www.fineartsbuilding.com. Free admission. Mon–Fri 7am–10pm; Sat 7am–9pm; Sun 9am–5pm. Bus: 3, 4, 145, 147, or 151. Subway/El: Brown, Green, Purple, or Orange line to Adams, or Red Line to Jackson.

Auditorium Building and Theatre 🄯🄯   A truly grand theater with historic-landmark status, the Auditorium is worth a visit to experience late-19th-century Chicago opulence. Because it's still a working theater—not a museum—it's not always open to the public during the day; to make sure you'll get in, schedule a guided tour, which are offered on Mondays at 10am and 1pm (call ℂ **312/431-2389** to confirm the date and time; reservations aren't necessary). Tours cost $8 per person.

Designed and built in 1889 by Louis Sullivan and Dankmar Adler, the 4,000-seat Auditorium was a wonder of the world: the heaviest (110,000 tons) and most massive modern edifice on earth, the most fireproof building ever constructed, and the tallest building in Chicago. It was also the first large-scale building to be lit by electricity, and its theater was the first in the country to install air-conditioning. Originally the home of the Chicago Opera Company, Sullivan and Adler's masterpiece is defined by powerful arches lit by thousands of bulbs and features Sullivan's trademark ornamentation—in this case, elaborate golden stenciling and gold plaster medallions. It's equally renowned for otherworldly acoustics and unobstructed sightlines.

During World War II, the building sheltered GIs, and its theater stage was turned into a bowling alley. The theater reopened in 1967 following a $3-million renovation made possible through the fundraising efforts of the nonprofit Auditorium Theatre Council. Remnants of the building's halcyon days remain. Don't miss the lobby fronting Michigan Avenue, with its faux-marble ornamental columns, molded ceilings, mosaic floors, and Mexican onyx walls.

An insider tip: If you can't get in for a tour, you can still get a glimpse of the Auditorium's historic past. Around the corner on Michigan Avenue, walk in the entrance that now houses Roosevelt University, and you'll get a sense of the building's grand public spaces. Take the elevator to the school's 10th-floor library reading room to see the theater's original dining room, with a barrel-vaulted ceiling and marvelous views of Grant Park.

Allow 1 hour for the guided tour.

50 E. Congress Pkwy. ℂ 312/922-2110. www.auditoriumtheatre.org. For tickets to a performance at the Auditorium, call Ticketmaster at ℂ 312/902-1500. Bus: 145, 147, or 151. Subway/El: Brown, Green, Orange, or Purple line to Library/Van Buren, or Red Line to Jackson.

Museum of Contemporary Photography   Ensconced in a ground-floor space at Columbia College—a progressive arts- and media-oriented institution that boasts the country's largest undergraduate film department and a highly respected photojournalism-slanted photography department—the Museum of Contemporary Photography is the only museum in the Midwest of its kind. As the name indicates, it exhibits, collects, and promotes modern photography, with a special focus on American works from 1959 to the present. Rotating exhibitions showcase images by both nationally recognized and "undiscovered" regional artists. Related lectures and special programs take place during the year. Allow 1 hour.

600 S. Michigan Ave. ⓒ 312/663-5554. www.mocp.org. Free admission. Mon–Fri 10am–5pm (Thurs until 8pm); Sat 10am–5pm; Sun noon–5pm. Bus: 6, 146, or 151. Subway/El: Red Line to Harrison.

Spertus Museum   The Spertus Museum, an extension of the Spertus Institute of Jewish Studies, showcases intricately crafted and historic Jewish ceremonial objects, textiles, coins, paintings, and sculpture, tracing 5,000 years of Jewish heritage. In 2007, the museum moved to a new, contemporary building, with an angled glass facade that marks a welcome change from the solemn, solid structures surrounding it. Highlights of the building include a 400-seat theater for lectures and films; an interactive exhibit space designed for kids; and a kosher cafe operated by Chef Wolfgang Puck's catering company. Researchers can register to visit the Asher Library or study the Chicago Jewish Archives collection. The museum shop carries a large selection of art, books, music, videos, and contemporary and traditional Jewish ceremonial gifts. Allow 1 hour.

610 S. Michigan Ave. ⓒ 312/322-1747. www.spertus.org. Admission $7 adults; $5 seniors, students, and children. Free admission Tues 10am–noon and Thurs 3–7pm. Sun–Wed 10am–6pm; Thurs 10am–7pm; Fri 10am–3pm. Bus: 3, 4, 6, 145, 147, or 151. Subway/El: Red Line to Harrison, or Brown, Purple, Orange, or Green line to Adams. Validated parking in nearby lots.

⟮Value⟯ Museum Free Days

If you time your visit right, you can save yourself some admission fees—but not during prime tourist season. While some major museums offer free admission at specific times year-round, others schedule free days only during the slowest times of the year (usually late fall and the dead of winter); keep in mind that you will still have to pay for special exhibitions and films on free days. The good news? Some smaller museums never charge admission.

Monday: Adler Planetarium (Oct–Nov and Jan–Feb); Chicago History Museum; Museum of Science and Industry (mid-Sept through Nov and Jan–Feb); and Shedd Aquarium (Oct–Nov and Jan–Feb; Oceanarium admission extra).

Tuesday: Adler Planetarium (Oct–Nov and Jan–Feb); Museum of Contemporary Art; Museum of Science and Industry (mid-Sept through Nov and Jan–Feb); Shedd Aquarium (Oct–Nov and Jan–Feb; Oceanarium admission extra); and Spertus Museum (10am–noon).

Thursday: Art Institute of Chicago (5–8pm only, until 9pm Memorial Day–Labor Day); Chicago Children's Museum (5–8pm only); and Spertus Museum (3–7pm).

Sunday: DuSable Museum of African-American History.

Always Free: Chicago Cultural Center, Garfield Park Conservatory, David and Alfred Smart Museum of Art, Jane Addams Hull-House Museum, Lincoln Park Conservatory, Lincoln Park Zoo, National Museum of Mexican Art, Museum of Contemporary Photography, and Newberry Library.

⟨*Value*⟩ The Loop Tour Train

For a distinctive downtown view at an unbeatable price—free!—hop aboard the **Loop Tour Train,** a special elevated train that runs on Saturday from May through September. Docents from the Chicago Architecture Foundation point out notable buildings along the way and explain how the El shaped the city. Riders must pick tickets at the Chicago Cultural Center, 77 E. Randolph St., beginning at 10am on the day of the tour; tours leave at 11am, 11:40am, 12:20pm, and 1pm from the Randolph/Wabash El station. For more information, call ⟨✆⟩ **312/744-2400,** or visit www.cityofchicago.org/exploringchicago.

ELSEWHERE IN THE LOOP

For a map of these attractions (or this neighborhood), see p. 172.

Chicago Fed Money Museum   It's not worth a special trip (unless you're a monetary-policy megageek), but the visitor center at the Federal Reserve Bank of Chicago is worth a quick stop if you're wandering around the Loop. More than just the standard history-of-banking displays, the center has kid-friendly features such as a giant cube that holds a million dollars and an exhibit that lets you try detecting counterfeit bills. There's even a section where visitors can pretend to be Alan Greenspan for a moment; it shows how changes in interest rates affect the economy. Free guided tours begin at 1pm on weekdays. Allow a half-hour.

230 S. LaSalle St. (at Quincy St.). ⟨✆⟩ **312/322-2400.** www.chicagofed.org. Free admission. Mon–Fri 9am–4pm. Closed federal holidays. Bus: 134, 135, 136, or 156. Subway/El: Brown Line to Quincy/Wells.

Chicago Public Library/Harold Washington Library Center   A massive, hulking building that looks like an Italian Renaissance fortress, Chicago's main public library is the largest public library in the world. Named for the city's first and only African-American mayor, who died of a heart attack in 1987 at the beginning of his second term in office, the building fills an entire city block at State Street and Congress Parkway. The interior design has been criticized for feeling cold (you have to go up a few floors before you even see any books), but the stunning, 52-foot glass-domed **Winter Garden** ⟨✿⟩ on the top floor is worth a visit. On the second floor is another treasure: the vast Thomas Hughes Children's Library, which makes an excellent resting spot for families traveling with kids. The library also offers an interesting array of events and art exhibitions that are worth checking out. A 385-seat auditorium is the setting for a unique mix of dance and music performances, author talks, and children's programs. Want to check your e-mail? Stop by the third-floor Computer Commons, which has about 75 terminals available for public use. Allow a half-hour.

400 S. State St. ⟨✆⟩ **312/747-4300.** www.chipublib.org. Free admission. Mon–Thurs 9am–7pm; Fri–Sat 9am–5pm; Sun 1–5pm. Closed major holidays. Bus: 2, 6, 11, 29, 36, 62, 145, 146, 147, or 151. Subway/El: Red Line to Jackson/ State, or Brown Line to Van Buren/Library.

2 The Earth, the Sky & the Sea: The Big Three in the Grant Park Museum Campus

For a map of these attractions (or this neighborhood), see p. 172.

With terraced gardens and broad walkways, the Museum Campus at the southern end of Grant Park makes it easy for pedestrians to visit three of the city's most beloved

---

⟨Value⟩ Museums for Less

If you're planning on visiting lots of Chicago museums, you should invest in a CityPass, a prepaid ticket that gets you into the biggest attractions (the Art Institute, Field Museum of Natural History, Shedd Aquarium, Adler Planetarium, Museum of Science and Industry, and Hancock Observatory). The cost at press time was $50 for adults and $39 for children, which is about 50% cheaper than paying all the museums' individual admission fees. You can buy a CityPass at any of the museums listed above, or purchase one online before you get to town (www.citypass.net).

---

institutions: the natural history museum, aquarium, and planetarium. The campus is about a 15- to 20-minute walk from the Loop and is easy to reach by bus or subway (a free trolley runs from the Roosevelt Rd. El stop). To get to the Museum Campus from the Loop, head east across Grant Park on East Balbo Drive from South Michigan Avenue, and then trek south along the lakeshore path to the museums. Or, approach on the path that begins at 11th Street from South Michigan Avenue. Follow 11th to the walkway that spans the Metra tracks. Cross Columbus Drive, and then pick up the path that will take you under Lake Shore Drive and into the Museum Campus. The CTA no. 146 bus will take you from downtown to all three of these attractions. Call ℰ **836-7000** (from any city or suburban area code) for the stop locations and schedule.

A large indoor parking lot is accessible from Lake Shore Drive southbound; you can park there all day for $15. Be aware that there is no public parking during Chicago Bears games in the fall; Soldier Field is next to the Museum Campus, and football fans get first dibs on all the surrounding parking spaces.

Adler Planetarium and Astronomy Museum ✵✵   The building may be historic, but some of the attractions here will captivate the most jaded video-game addict. The first planetarium in the Western Hemisphere was founded by Sears, Roebuck and Co. executive Max Adler, who imported a Zeiss projector from Germany in 1930.

The good news for present-day visitors is that the planetarium has been updated since then. Your first stop should be the modern Sky Pavilion, where the don't-miss experience is the **StarRider Theater** ✵✵. Settle down under the massive dome, and you'll take a half-hour interactive virtual-reality trip through the Milky Way and into deep space, featuring a computer-generated 3-D-graphics projection system and controls in the armrest of each seat. Six high-resolution video projectors form a seamless image above your head—you'll feel as if you're literally floating in space. If you're looking for more entertainment, the **Sky Theater** shows movies with an astronomical bent. Recent shows have included *Secrets of Saturn* and *Mars Now!,* both of which are updated as new discoveries are made.

The planetarium's exhibition galleries feature a variety of displays and interactive activities. If you're only going to see one exhibit (and have kids in tow), check out **Shoot For the Moon** ✵✵, an exhibit on lunar exploration that's full of interactive stations (it also showcases the personal collection of astronaut Jim Lovell, captain of the infamous Apollo 13 mission, who now lives in the Chicago suburbs). Other exhibits include **Bringing the Heavens to Earth** ✵, which traces the ways different cultures have tried to make sense of astronomical phenomena, and **From the Night Sky to the**

Big Bang, which includes artifacts from the planetarium's extensive collection of astronomical instruments (although suitable for older children, these can get a bit boring for little ones unless they're real astronomy nuts).

The museum's cafe provides views of the lakefront and skyline. On the first Friday evening of the month, visitors can view dramatic close-ups of the moon, the planets, and distant galaxies through a closed-circuit monitor connected to the planetarium's Doane Observatory telescope.

Allow 2 hours, more if you want to see more than one show.

1300 S. Lake Shore Dr. ℂ 312/922-STAR. www.adlerplanetarium.org. Admission $10 adults, $8 seniors, $6 children 4–17, free for children 3 and under; admission including 1 show and audiotour $19 adults, $17 seniors, $15 children. Free admission Mon–Tues Oct–Nov and Jan–Feb. Memorial Day–Labor Day daily 9:30am–6pm; early Sept–late May daily 9:30am–4:30pm; 1st Fri of every month until 10pm. StarRider Theater and Sky Shows run throughout the day; call main number for current times. Bus: 12 or 146.

Field Museum of Natural History 𝔄𝔄𝔄 *(Kids* Is it any wonder that Steven Spielberg thought the Field Museum of Natural History was a suitable home turf for the intrepid archaeologist and adventurer hero of his Indiana Jones movies? Spread over the museum's 9 acres of floor space are scores of permanent and temporary exhibitions—some interactive but most requiring the old-fashion skills of observation and imagination.

Navigating all the disparate exhibits can be daunting, so start out in the grand Stanley Field Hall, which you enter from the north or south end. Standing proudly at the north side is the largest, most complete *Tyrannosaurus rex* fossil ever unearthed. The museum acquired the specimen—named **Sue** 𝔄𝔄𝔄 for the paleontologist who discovered it in South Dakota in 1990—for a cool $8.4 million after a high-stakes bidding war. The real skull is so heavy that a lighter copy had to be mounted on the skeleton; the actual one is on display nearby.

Families should head downstairs for two of the most popular kid-friendly exhibits. The pieces on display in ***Inside Ancient Egypt*** 𝔄𝔄 came to the museum in the early 1900s, after researchers in Saqqara, Egypt, excavated two of the original chambers from the tomb of Unis-ankh, son of the Fifth Dynasty ruler Pharaoh Unis. The *mastaba* (tomb) of Unis-ankh forms the core of a spellbinding exhibit that realistically depicts scenes from Egyptian funeral, religious, and other social practices. Visitors can explore aspects of the day-to-day world of ancient Egypt, viewing 23 actual mummies

---

⌒Tips Website Extras

Scanning the websites of museums and other attractions before you visit can enhance your trip when you get here. At the Field Museum of Natural History website (www.fieldmuseum.org), you can download an mp3 audiotour of the museum's permanent collection; you can also print out a Family Adventure Tour, which sends kids on a scavenger hunt throughout the museum. The **Millennium Park** mp3 audiotour (available at www.millenniumpark.org) includes interviews with the artists who created the park's eye-catching artwork. And if you're intimidated by the massive size of the **Museum of Science and Industry,** check out the website's Personal Planner, which will put together a customized itinerary based your family's interests (www.msichicago.org).

(*Tips* **Walker's Warning**

While Chicago is a great city to explore on foot, Lake Shore Drive is no place for pedestrians. People have been seriously injured and even killed attempting to dodge traffic on the busy road. Near Grant Park, cross only in crosswalks at Jackson Boulevard or Randolph, East Monroe, or East Balbo drives, or by using the underpass on the Museum Campus. North of the river, use underpasses or bridges at East Ohio Street, Chicago Avenue, Oak Street, and North Avenue.

---

and realistic burial scenes, a living marsh environment and canal works, the ancient royal barge, a religious shrine, and a reproduction of a typical marketplace of the period. Many of the exhibits allow hands-on interaction, and there are special activities for kids, such as making parchment from living papyrus plants.

Next to the Egypt exhibit, you'll find ***Underground Adventure*** ⊛⊛, a "total immersion environment" populated by giant robotic earwigs, centipedes, wolf spiders, and other subterranean critters. The Disneyesque exhibit is a big hit with kids, but— annoyingly—carries an extra admission charge ($7 on top of regular admission).

You might be tempted to skip the "peoples of the world" exhibits, but trust me, some are not only mind-opening but also great fun. ***Traveling the Pacific*** ⊛, hidden up on the second floor, is definitely worth a stop. Hundreds of artifacts from the museum's oceanic collection re-create scenes of island life in the South Pacific (there's even a full-scale model of a Maori meetinghouse). ***Africa*** ⊛, an assemblage of African artifacts and provocative interactive multimedia presentations, takes viewers to Senegal, a Cameroon palace, the wildlife-rich savanna, and on a "virtual" journey aboard a slave ship to the Americas. Native Chicagoans will quickly name two more signature highlights: the taxidermies of ***Bushman*** (a legendary lowland gorilla that made international headlines while at the city's Lincoln Park Zoo) and the ***Man-Eating Lions of Tsavo*** (the pair of male lions that munched nearly 140 British railway workers constructing a bridge in East Africa in 1898; their story is featured in the film *The Ghost and the Darkness*).

The museum books special traveling exhibits (recent blockbusters included shows on King Tut and ancient Pompeii), but be forewarned: The high-profile exhibits are usually crowded and—again—have an additional admission charge. A much better deal is a free tour of the museum highlights; tours begin daily at 11am and 2pm.

When you're ready to take a break, the Corner Bakery cafe, just off the main hall, serves food a cut above the usual museum victuals (to avoid lunchtime lines, pick up a premade salad or sandwich and head for the cash register). Families also flock to the McDonald's on the lower level. Allow 3 hours.

Roosevelt Rd. and Lake Shore Dr. ⓒ 312/922-9410. www.fieldmuseum.org. Admission $12 adults,; $7 seniors, students with ID and children 4–11; free for children 3 and under. Discounted admission Mon–Tues mid-Sept through Nov and Jan–Feb. Daily 9am–5pm. Closed Dec 25. Bus: 6, 10, 12, 130, or 146.

John G. Shedd Aquarium ⊛⊛⊛   The Shedd is one of the world's largest indoor aquarium, and houses thousands of river, lake, and sea denizens in standard aquarium tanks and elaborate new habitats within its octagon-shaped marble building. The only problem with the Shedd is its steep admission price ($23 for adults). You can keep your costs down by buying the "Aquarium Only" admission, but you'll miss some of the most stunning exhibits. A CityPass (see "Museums for Less," above) can also save you money if you visit enough of the other included attractions.

The first thing you'll see as you enter is the **Caribbean Coral Reef** ⍟. This 90,000-gallon circular tank occupies the Beaux Arts–style central rotunda, entertaining spectators who press up against the glass to ogle divers feeding nurse sharks, barracudas, stingrays, and a hawksbill sea turtle. A roving camera connected to video monitors on the tank's periphery gives visitors close-ups of the animals inside, but I'd recommend sticking around to catch one of the daily feedings, when a diver swims around the tank and (thanks to a microphone) talks about the species and their eating habits.

The exhibits surrounding the Caribbean coral reef re-create marine habitats around the world. The best is *Amazon Rising: Seasons of the River* ⍟, a rendering of the Amazon basin that showcases frogs and other animals as well as fish (although the sharp-toothed piranhas are pretty cool).

You'll pay extra to see the other Shedd highlights, but they're quite impressive, so I'd suggest shelling out for them if you plan to spend more than an hour here. The *Oceanarium* ⍟⍟⍟, with a wall of windows revealing the lake outside, replicates a Pacific Northwest coastal environment and creates the illusion of one uninterrupted expanse of sea. On a fixed performance schedule in a large pool flanked by an

The Pride of Prairie Avenue

Prairie Avenue, south of the Loop, was the city's first "Gold Coast," and its most famous address is **Glessner House,** a must-see for anyone interested in architectural history. The only surviving Chicago building designed by Boston architect Henry Hobson Richardson, the 1886 structure represented a dramatic shift from traditional Victorian architecture (and inspired a young Frank Lloyd Wright).

The imposing granite exterior gives the home a forbidding air. (Railway magnate George Pullman, who lived nearby, complained, "I do not know what I have ever done to have that thing staring me in the face every time I go out my door.") But step inside, and the home turns out to be a welcoming, cozy retreat, filled with Arts and Crafts furnishings. For an illustration of the Glessner House exterior, see "Richardsonian Romanesque (1870–1900)" on p. 12.

Visits to Glessner House are by guided tour only (they can also be combined with tours of the nearby **Clarke House Museum,** a Greek Revival home that's the oldest surviving house in the city). Tours begin at 1, 2, and 3pm Wednesday through Sunday (except major holidays); tours of the Clarke House are given at noon, 1, and 2pm. Tours are first-come, first-served, with no advance reservations except for groups of 10 or more.

1800 S. Prairie Ave. ⓒ **312/326-1480.** www.glessnerhouse.org. Admission $10 adults, $9 students and seniors, $5 children 5 to 12, free for children 4 and under; combination tickets for tours of the Glessner House and Clarke House cost $15 for adults, $12 student and seniors, and $8 for children. Bus: 1, 3, or 4 from Michigan Avenue at Jackson Boulevard (get off at 18th St.).

amphitheater, a crew of friendly trainers puts dolphins through their paces of leaping dives, breaches, and tail walking. Check out the Oceanarium schedule as soon as you get to the Shedd; seating can fill up quickly, so you'll want to get here early. If you're visiting during a summer weekend, you may also want to buy your Oceanarium ticket in advance to make sure you can catch a show that day. *Wild Reef—Sharks at Shedd* ✹✹ is a series of 26 connected habitats that house a Philippine coral reef patrolled by sharks and other predators. The floor-to-ceiling windows bring the toothy swimmers up close and personal (they even swim over your head at certain spots).

If you want a quality sit-down meal in a restaurant with a spectacular view of Lake Michigan, check out Soundings. There's also a family-friendly cafeteria.

Allow 2 to 3 hours.

1200 S. Lake Shore Dr. ⓒ 312/939-2438. www.sheddaquarium.org. All-Access Pass (to all exhibits) $23 adults, $16 seniors and children 3–11, free for children 2 and under; admission to aquarium and Wild Reef $18 adults, $14 seniors and children; aquarium only $8 adults, $6 seniors and children. Free admission to aquarium only Mon–Tues Oct–Nov and Jan–Feb. Memorial Day–Labor Day daily 9am–6pm; early Sept–late May Mon–Fri 9am–5pm, Sat–Sun 9am–6pm. Bus: 6 or 146.

3 North of the Loop: The Magnificent Mile & Beyond

For a map of these attractions (or this neighborhood), see p. 172.

Most of these sights are either on the Magnificent Mile (North Michigan Ave.) and its surrounding blocks or close by on the Near North Side.

The Hancock Observatory ✹✹   The Hancock isn't as famous as the Sears Tower, but for many locals, its bold tapered shape and steel cross-bracing exterior design represent the archetypal Chicago skyscraper. The Hancock Observatory delivers an excellent panorama of the city and an intimate view of nearby Lake Michigan and various shoreline residential areas. While the view from the top of Chicago's third-tallest building is enough to satisfy, high-tech additions have enhanced the experience. "Talking telescopes" have sound effects and narration in four languages, history walls illustrate the growth of the city, and the Skywalk open-air viewing deck allows visitors to feel the rush of the wind at 1,000 feet through a "screened porch." On a clear day, you can see portions of the three states surrounding this corner of Illinois (Michigan, Indiana, and Wisconsin), for a radius of 40 to 50 miles. The view up the North Side is particularly dramatic. It stretches from the nearby Oak Street and North Avenue beaches, along the green strip of Lincoln Park, to the line of high-rises tracing the shoreline that suddenly halt just below the boundary of the northern suburbs. A high-speed elevator carries passengers to the observatory in 40 seconds, and the entrance and observatory are accessible for people with disabilities. Allow 1 hour.

"Big John," as some locals call the building, also has a sleek restaurant, the Signature Room at the 95th, with an adjoining lounge. For about the same cost as the observatory, you can take in the views from the latter with a libation in hand.

94th floor, John Hancock Center, 875 N. Michigan Ave. (enter on Delaware St.). ⓒ 888/875-VIEW or 312/751-3681. www.hancock-observatory.com. Admission $11 adults, $8 seniors, $7 children 5–12, free for children 4 and under. Daily 9am–11pm. Bus: 145, 146, 147, or 151. Subway/El: Red Line to Chicago/State.

Museum of Contemporary Art ✹✹   Although the MCA is one of the largest contemporary art museums in the country, theaters and hallways seem to take up much of the space, so seeing the actual art won't take you long. The museum exhibits emphasize experimentation in a variety of media, including painting, sculpture, photography,

> **Fun Fact** **Rock Around the World**
>
> The impressive Gothic **Tribune Tower,** just north of the Chicago River on the east side of Michigan Avenue, is home to one of the country's media giants and the *Chicago Tribune* newspaper. It's also notable for an array of architectural fragments jutting out from the exterior. The newspaper's notoriously despotic publisher, Robert R. McCormick, started the collection shortly after the building's completion in 1925, gathering pieces during his world travels. *Tribune* correspondents then began supplying building fragments that they acquired on assignment. Each one now bears the name of the structure and country whence it came. There are 138 pieces in all, including chunks and shards from the Great Wall of China, the Taj Mahal, the White House, the Arc de Triomphe, the Berlin Wall, the Roman Colosseum, London's Houses of Parliament, the Great Pyramid of Cheops in Giza, Egypt, and the original tomb of Abraham Lincoln in Springfield, Illinois.

video and film, dance, music, and performance. The gloomy, imposing building, designed by Berlin's Josef Paul Kleihues, is a bit out of place between the lake and the historic Water Tower, but the interior spaces are more vibrant, with a sun-drenched two-story central corridor, elliptical staircases, and three floors of exhibition space. The MCA has tried to raise its national profile to the level of New York's Museum of Modern Art by booking major touring retrospectives of working artists such as Cindy Sherman and Chuck Close.

You can see the MCA's highlights in about an hour, although art lovers will want more time to wander (especially if a high-profile exhibit is in town). Your first stop should be the handsome barrel-vaulted galleries on the top floor, dedicated to pieces from the permanent collection. Visitors who'd like a little guidance with making sense of the rather challenging works can rent an audio tour or take a free tour (1 and 6pm Tues; 1pm Wed–Fri; noon, 1, 2, and 3pm Sat–Sun). In addition to a range of special activities and educational programming, including films, performances, and a lecture series in a 300-seat theater, the museum features Puck's at the MCA, a cafe operated by Wolfgang Puck of Spago restaurant fame, with seating that overlooks a 1-acre terraced sculpture garden. The store, with one-of-a-kind gift items, is worth a stop even if you don't make it into the museum. The museum's First-Friday program, featuring after-hours performances, live music, and food and drink, takes place on the first Friday of every month. Allow 1 to 2 hours.

220 E. Chicago Ave. (1 block east of Michigan Ave.). *(C)* 312/280-2660. www.mcachicago.org. Admission $10 adults, $6 seniors and students w/ID, free for children 12 and under. Free admission Tues. Tues 10am–8pm; Wed–Sun 10am–5pm. Closed Jan 1, Thanksgiving, and Dec 25. Bus: 3, 10, 66, 145, 146, or 151. Subway/El: Red Line to Chicago/State.

Navy Pier *☆ Kids*　Built during World War I, this 3,000-foot-long pier was a Navy training center for pilots during World War II. The military aura is long gone and replaced with a combination of carnival attractions, a food court, and boat dock, making it a bustling tourist mecca and a place for a fun stroll (if you don't mind the crowds). To get the best views back to the city, walk all the way down to the end.

Midway down the pier are the **Crystal Gardens** *☆*, with 70 full-size palm trees, dancing fountains, and other flora in a glass-enclosed atrium; a carousel and kiddie carnival rides; and a 15-story Ferris wheel, a replica of the original that made its debut at Chicago's 1893 World's Fair. The 50 acres of pier and lakefront property are also home to the **Chicago Children's Museum** (p. 211), a **3-D IMAX theater** (© **312/595-5629**), a small ice-skating rink, and the **Chicago Shakespeare Theatre** (p. 259). The shops tend to be bland and touristy, and dining options include a food court, an outpost of Lincoln Park's popular Charlie's Ale House, and the white-tablecloth seafood restaurant Riva. You'll also find a beer garden with live music; Joe's Be-Bop Cafe & Jazz Emporium, a Southern-style barbecue restaurant with live music; and Bubba Gump Shrimp Co. & Market, a casual family seafood joint. Summer is one long party at the pier, with fireworks on Wednesday and Saturday evenings.

The **Smith Museum of Stained Glass Windows** ☿☿ may sound incredibly dull, but decorative-art aficionados shouldn't miss this remarkable installation of more than 150 stained-glass windows set in illuminated display cases. Occupying an 800-foot-long expanse on the ground floor of Navy Pier, the free museum features works by Frank Lloyd Wright, Louis Sullivan, John LaFarge, and Louis Comfort Tiffany.

Navy Pier schedules a variety of conventions and trade shows, including an international art exposition in May, pro-tennis exhibitions, and a flower and garden show. There's something for everyone, but the commercialism might be too much for some. In that case, take the half-mile stroll to the end of the pier, east of the ballroom, where you can find a little respite and enjoy the wind, the waves, and the city view, which is the real delight of a place like this. Or, unwind in **Olive Park,** a small sylvan haven with a sliver of beach just north of Navy Pier.

You'll find more than half a dozen sailing vessels moored at the south dock, including a couple of dinner-cruise ships, the pristine white-masted tall ship *Windy,* and the 70-foot speedboats *Seadog I, II,* and *III.* In the summer months, water taxis speed between Navy Pier and other Chicago sights. For more specifics on sightseeing and dinner cruises, see "Lake & River Cruises," p. 213. Allow 1 hour.

600 E. Grand Ave. (at Lake Michigan). © **800/595-PIER** (outside 312 area code) or 312/595-PIER. www.navypier.com. Free admission. Summer Sun–Thurs 10am–10pm, Fri–Sat 10am–midnight; fall–spring Mon–Thurs 10am–8pm, Fri–Sat 10am–10pm, Sun 10am–7pm. Parking: $19/day weekdays; $23/day weekends. Lots fill quickly. Bus: 29, 65, 66, 120, or 121. Subway/El: Red Line to Grand/State; transfer to city bus or board a free pier trolley bus.

Newberry Library   The Newberry Library is a bibliophile's dream. Established in 1887 thanks to a bequest by Chicago merchant and financier Walter Loomis Newberry, the noncirculating research library contains many rare books and manuscripts (such as Shakespeare's first folio and Jefferson's copy of *The Federalist Papers*), housed in a comely five-story granite building. The library is also a major destination for genealogists digging at their roots, with holdings that are open free to the public (over the age of 16 with a photo ID). The collections include more than 1.5 million volumes and 75,000 maps, many of which are on display during an ongoing series of public exhibitions. For an overview, take a free 1-hour tour Thursday at 3pm or Saturday at 10:30am. The Newberry operates a fine bookstore and also sponsors a series of concerts (including those by its resident early-music ensemble, the Newberry Consort), lectures, and children's story hours throughout the year. One popular annual event is the **Bughouse Square debates** ☿. Held across the street in Washington Square Park, the debates re-create the fiery soapbox orations of the left-wing agitators in the 1930s and 1940s. Chicago's favorite son, Pulitzer Prize–winning oral historian Studs Terkel, often emcees the hullabaloo. Allow a half-hour.

60 W. Walton St. (at Dearborn Pkwy.). (📞) **312/943-9090**, or 312/255-3700 for programs. www.newberry.org. Reading room Tues–Thurs 10am–6pm; Fri–Sat 9am–5pm. Exhibit gallery Mon, Fri, and Sat 8:15am–5:30pm; Tues–Thurs 8:15am–7:30pm. Bus: 22, 36, 125, 145, 146, 147, or 151. Subway/El: Red Line to Chicago/State.

4 Lincoln Park Attractions

For a map of these attractions (or this neighborhood), see p. 172.

Lincoln Park is the city's largest park, and certainly one of the longest. Straight and narrow, the park begins at North Avenue and follows the shoreline of Lake Michigan north for several miles. Within its 1,200 acres are a world-class zoo, half a dozen beaches, a botanical conservatory, two excellent museums, a golf course, and the meadows, formal gardens, sporting fields, and tennis courts typical of urban parks. To get to the park, take bus no. 22, 145, 146, 147, 151, or 156.

The park, named after Abraham Lincoln, is home to the **statue of the standing Abraham Lincoln** (just north of the North Ave. and State St. intersection), one of the city's two Lincoln statues by Augustus Saint-Gaudens (the seated Lincoln is in Grant Park). Saint-Gaudens also designed the Bates Fountain near the conservatory.

Cafe Brauer   This landmark 1900 building is not technically open to the public, but an ice-cream parlor on the ground floor can get you entrance to see a fine example of Chicago's Prairie School of architecture. The Great Hall on the second floor, flanked by two curving loggias, is one of the city's most popular wedding-reception spots, so if you stop by on a weekend, chances are you can sneak a peek while the caterers are setting up. Even if you don't make it inside, Cafe Brauer is a nice stopping-off point during a walk around the park. Sit and sip a coffee, or rent a paddleboat at the edge of the lovely South Pond ($10 per half-hour). Best of all, though, is the picture-postcard view from the adjacent bridge spanning the pond of the John Hancock Center and neighboring skyscrapers beyond Lincoln Park's treetops. Allow a quarter-hour, longer for a paddleboat ride.

2021 Stockton Dr. (📞) **312/742-2400**. Daily 10am–5pm. Bus: 151 or 156.

Chicago History Museum (📷)   The Chicago History Museum at the southwestern tip of Lincoln Park is one of the city's oldest cultural institutions (founded in 1856), but it's reinvented itself for the 21st century. The main, must-see exhibit is *Chicago: Crossroads of America* (📷📷), which fills the museum's second floor. A survey of the city's history—from its founding as a frontier trading post to the riots at the 1968 Democratic Convention—it's filled with photos, artifacts, and newsreels that make the past come alive; surrounding galleries track the development of local sports teams, architecture, music, and art. Although the exhibit is geared toward families with older children (you can even download an mp3 audio tour for teenagers from the museum's website), little ones love the re-creation of an 1890s El station, where they can run inside the city's first elevated train. Another museum highlight is the hall of dioramas that re-create scenes from Chicago's past. Although they've been around for decades (and are decidedly low-tech), they're a fun way to trace the city's progression from a few small cabins to the grand World's Columbian Exposition of 1893. The museum's Costume and Textile Gallery showcases pieces from the museum's renowned collection of historic clothing; recent exhibitions included couture gowns by French designer Christian Dior and a survey of American quilts. The Children's Gallery on the ground floor has interactive exhibits for kids, including a giant table where you can experience the "Smells of Chicago" (my personal favorite).

The History Museum also presents a wide range of lectures, seminars, and tours, including walking tours of the surrounding neighborhood; check the museum's website for details, as the schedules change frequently. Allow 1 to 2 hours.

1601 N. Clark St. (at North Ave.). (C) 312/642-4600. www.chicagohistory.org. Admission $12 adults, $10 seniors and students, free for children 12 and under. Free admission Mon. Mon–Sat 9:30am–4:30pm (until 8pm Thurs); Sun noon–5pm. Research center Tues–Thurs 1–4pm; Fri 10am–4:30pm. Bus: 11, 22, 36, 72, 151, or 156.

Lincoln Park Conservatory ⟨ጽ⟩   Just beyond the zoo's northeast border is a lovely botanical garden housed in a soaring glass-domed structure. Inside are four great halls filled with thousands of plants. If you're visiting Chicago in the wintertime, I can't think of a better prescription for mood elevation than this lush haven of greenery. The Palm House features giant palms and rubber trees (including a 50-ft. fiddle-leaf rubber tree dating back to 1891); the Fernery nurtures plants that grow close to the forest floor; and the Tropical House is a shiny symphony of flowering trees, vines, and bamboo. The fourth environment is the Show House, where seasonal flower shows take place.

Even better than the plants inside, however, might be what lies outside the front doors. The expansive lawn, with its French garden and lovely fountain on the conservatory's south side, is one of the best places in town for an informal picnic (especially nice if you're visiting the zoo and want to avoid the congestion at its food concession venues).

The Lincoln Park Conservatory has a sister facility on the city's West Side, in Garfield Park, that is much more remarkable. In fact, the 2-acre **Garfield Park Conservatory,** 300 N. Central Park Ave. (ⓒ **312/746-5100**), designed by the great landscape architect Jens Jensen in 1907, is one of the largest gardens under glass in the world. It's open 365 days a year from 9am to 5pm. Unfortunately, a rather blighted neighborhood with a high crime rate surrounds the conservatory. If you want to see it, I recommend driving rather than using public transportation. Allow a half-hour for the Lincoln Park Conservatory.

Fullerton Ave. (at Stockton Dr.). (C) 312/742-7736. Free admission. Daily 9am–5pm. Bus: 73, 151, or 156.

Lincoln Park Zoo ⟨ጽጽጽ⟩ (Value)   One of the city's treasures, this family-friendly attraction is not only open 365 days a year, it's also free. Even if you don't have time for a complete tour of the various habitats, it's worth at least a quick stop during a stroll through Lincoln Park. The term "zoological gardens" truly fits here: Landmark Georgian Revival brick buildings and modern structures sit among gently rolling pathways, verdant lawns, and a kaleidoscopic profusion of flower gardens. The late Marlon Perkins, legendary host of the *Mutual of Omaha's Wild Kingdom* TV series, got his start here as the zoo's director, and filmed a pioneering TV show called *Zoo Parade* (*Wild Kingdom*'s predecessor) in the basement of the old Reptile House.

My favorite exhibit is the **Regenstein African Journey** ⟨ጽጽጽ⟩, a series of linked indoor and outdoor habitats that's home to elephants, giraffes, rhinos, and other large mammals; large glass-enclosed tanks allow visitors to go face-to-face with swimming pygmy hippos and (not for the faint of heart) a rocky ledge filled with Madagascar hissing cockroaches.

Your second stop should be the **Regenstein Center for African Apes** ⟨ጽጽ⟩. Lincoln Park Zoo has had remarkable success breeding gorillas and chimpanzees, and watching these ape families interact can be mesmerizing (and touching). *One caveat:* I've found the building incredibly noisy during weekend visits, so be prepared.

Moments **A Great View**

After a visit to Lincoln Park Zoo or the Peggy Notebaert Nature Museum, take a quick stroll on Fullerton Avenue to the bridge that runs over the lagoon (just before you get to Lake Shore Dr.). Standing on the south side of Fullerton Avenue, you'll have a great view of the Chicago skyline and Lincoln Park—an excellent backdrop for family souvenir photos. This path can get very crowded on summer weekends, so I suggest trying this photo op during the week.

Other exhibits worth a visit are the **Small Mammal–Reptile House,** which features a glass-enclosed walk-through ecosystem simulating river, savanna, and forest habitats, and the popular **Sea Lion Pool** in the center of the zoo, which is home to harbor seals, gray seals, and California sea lions (walk down the ramp and take a look at the underwater viewing area). If you're here for a while and need nourishment, the Park Place Café food court is a good option. The Mahon Theobold Pavilion features a sprawling indoor gift shop and a unique rooftop eatery called Big Cats Café that opens at 8am (1 hr. before the exhibits do) and serves fresh-baked muffins and scones, focaccia sandwiches, salads, and flatbreads. Allow 3 hours. For the adjoining children's zoo, see "Kid Stuff," p. 211.

2200 N. Cannon Dr. (at Fullerton Pkwy.). ⓒ **312/742-2000.** www.lpzoo.com. Free admission. Buildings daily 10am–5pm (Memorial Day–Labor Day until 6:30pm Sat–Sun). Grounds Memorial Day–Labor Day daily 9am–7pm; Apr–late May and early Sept–Oct daily 9am–6pm; Nov–Mar daily 9am–5pm. Parking $14 for up to 3 hours in on-site lot. Bus: 151 or 156.

Peggy Notebaert Nature Museum ⚘ *Kids* Built into the rise of an ancient sand dune—once the shoreline of Lake Michigan—this museum bills itself as "an environmental museum for the 21st century." While that sounds pretty dull, most of the exhibits are very hands-on, making this a good stop for active kids (most exhibits are designed for children rather than adults).

Shaded by huge cottonwoods and maples, the sand-colored exterior, with its horizontal lines composed of interlocking trapezoids, resembles a sand dune. Rooftop-level walkways give strollers a view of birds and other urban wildlife below, and paths wind through gardens planted with native Midwestern wildflowers and grasses. Inside, large windows create a dialogue between the outdoor environment and the indoor exhibits designed to illuminate it. My favorite exhibit by far is the ***Butterfly Haven*** ⚘⚘, a greenhouse habitat where about 25 Midwestern species of butterflies and moths carry on their complex life cycles (wander through as a riot of color flutters all around you). If you're traveling with little ones, I'd also recommend the **Extreme Green House** ⚘, a bungalow where kids can play while learning about environmentally friendly habits, and **RiverWorks,** a water play exhibit that gives children an excuse to splash around while building dams and maneuvering boats along a mini river. Allow 1 to 2 hours.

Fullerton Ave. and Cannon Dr. ⓒ **773/755-5100.** www.chias.org. Admission $7 adults, $5 seniors and students, $4 children 3–12, free for children 2 and under. Free admission Thurs. Mon–Fri 9am–4:30pm; Sat–Sun 10am–5pm. Closed Jan 1, Thanksgiving, and Dec 25. Bus: 151 or 156. Free trolley service from area CTA stations and parking garages Sat–Sun and holidays 10am–6pm Memorial Day–Labor Day. Visit the museum website for route information and schedule.

5 Exploring Hyde Park: The Museum of Science and Industry & More

Hyde Park, south of the loop, is the birthplace of atomic fission, home to the University of Chicago and the popular Museum of Science and Industry, and definitely worth a trip. You should allow at least half a day to explore the campus and neighborhood (one of Chicago's most successfully integrated) and a full day if you want to explore museums as well.

SOME HYDE PARK HISTORY   When Hyde Park was settled in 1850, it became Chicago's first suburb. A hundred years later, in the 1950s, it added another first to its impressive résumé, one that the current neighborhood is not particularly proud of: an urban-renewal plan. At the time, a certain amount of old commercial and housing stock—just the kind of buildings that would be prized today—was demolished rather than rehabilitated and replaced by projects and small shopping malls that actually make some corners of Hyde Park look more suburban, in the modern sense, than they really are.

What Hyde Park can be proud of is that, in racially balkanized Chicago, this neighborhood has found an alternative vision. As Southern blacks began to migrate to Chicago's South Side during World War I, many whites fled. But most whites here, especially those who wanted to stay near the university, chose integration as the only realistic strategy to preserve their neighborhood. The 2000 census proved that integration still works: About 40% of the residents are white and 37% are black; there is also a significant Asian population. Hyde Park is decidedly middle class, with pockets of affluence in Kenwood that reflect the days in the early 20th century when the well-to-do moved here to escape the decline of Prairie Avenue. The area's well-known black residents included the late Elijah Muhammad, and numerous Nation of Islam families continue to worship in a mosque, formerly a Greek Orthodox cathedral, that is one of the neighborhood's architectural landmarks. Surrounding this unusual enclave, however, are many marginal blocks where poverty and slum-housing abound. For all its nobility, Hyde Park's achievement in integration merely emphasizes that even more unwieldy than racial differences are socioeconomic ones.

The University of Chicago is widely hailed as one of the more intellectually exciting institutions of higher learning in the country, and has been home to some 73 Nobel laureates. The year the university opened its doors in 1892 was a big one for Hyde Park, but 1893 was even bigger. In that year, Chicago, chosen over other cities in a competitive international field, played host to the World's Columbian Exposition, commemorating the 400th anniversary of Columbus's arrival in America.

To create a fairground, the landscape architect Frederick Law Olmsted was enlisted to fill in the marshlands along Hyde Park's lakefront and link what was to become Jackson Park to existing Washington Park on the neighborhood's western boundary with a narrow concourse called the Midway Plaisance. On the resulting 650 acres—at a cost of $30 million—12 exhibit palaces, 57 buildings devoted to U.S. states and foreign governments, and dozens of smaller structures were constructed under the supervision of architect Daniel Burnham. Most of the buildings followed Burnham's preference for the Classical Revival style and white stucco exteriors. With the innovation of outdoor electric lighting, the sparkling result was the "White City," which attracted 27 million visitors in a single season, from May 1 to October 31, 1893. The exposition sponsors, in that brief time, had remarkably recovered their investment,

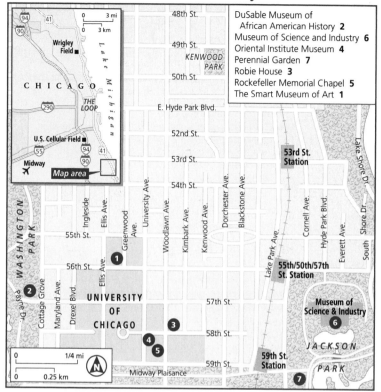

DuSable Museum of African American History **2**
Museum of Science and Industry **6**
Oriental Institute Museum **4**
Perennial Garden **7**
Robie House **3**
Rockefeller Memorial Chapel **5**
The Smart Museum of Art **1**

but within a few short years of the fair's closing, vandalism and fire destroyed most of its buildings. Only the Palace of Fine Arts, occupying the eastern tip of the midway, survives to this day, and it now houses the Museum of Science and Industry.

GETTING THERE From the Loop, the ride to Hyde Park on the **no. 6 Jeffrey Express bus** takes about 30 minutes. The bus originates on Wacker Drive, travels south along State Street, and ultimately follows Lake Shore Drive to Hyde Park. The bus runs daily from early morning to late evening, with departures about every 5 minutes on weekdays and every 10 minutes on weekends and holidays. The southbound express bus fare adds a surcharge of 25¢ to the normal fare of $2 (there's no surcharge if you use a CTA transit card). The **no. 1 local bus** originates at Union Station on Jackson Boulevard and Canal Street and takes about an hour.

For a faster trip, take the **Metra Electric train** on the South Chicago line, which goes from downtown to Hyde Park in about 15 minutes. Trains run every hour (more frequently during rush hour) Monday through Saturday from 5:15am to 12:50am, and every 30 to 90 minutes on Sunday and holidays from 5am to 12:55am. Downtown stations are at Randolph Street and Michigan Avenue, Van Buren Street and Michigan Avenue, and Roosevelt Road and Michigan Avenue (near the Museum Campus in Grant Park). Printed schedules are available at the stations. The fare is approximately $2 each way.

(*Fun Fact* **Did You Know?**

The world's first Ferris wheel was built on Hyde Park's midway during the World's Columbian Exposition in 1893. It was eventually dynamited and sold for scrap metal.

For CTA bus and Metra train information, call ℂ **836-7000** (from any city or suburban area code), or visit **www.transitchicago.com** or **www.metrarail.com**.

For taxis, dial ℂ **312/TAXI-CAB** (312/829-4222) for **Yellow Cab** or ℂ **312/ CHECKER** (312/243-2537) for **Checker.** The one-way fare from downtown is around $15 to $20.

A SUGGESTED ITINERARY A long 1-day itinerary for Hyde Park should include the following: a walk through the University of Chicago campus (including a stroll along the Midway Plaisance); a visit to the Museum of Science and Industry (for families), Frank Lloyd Wright's Robie House or one of the other local museums; and lunch or dinner in the neighborhood's commercial center.

THE TOP ATTRACTIONS

DuSable Museum of African-American History The DuSable Museum is a repository of the history, art, and artifacts pertaining to the African-American experience and culture. Named for Chicago's first permanent settler, Jean Baptiste Point du Sable, a French-Canadian of Haitian descent, it is admirable not so much for its collections and exhibits as for the inspiring story behind its existence. Founded in 1961 with a $10 charter and minimal capital, the museum began in the home of Dr. Margaret Burroughs, an art teacher at the city's DuSable High School. In 1973, as a result of a community-based campaign, the museum took up residence in its present building (a former parks administration facility and police lockup) on the eastern edge of Washington Park. With no major endowment to speak of, the DuSable Museum has managed to accumulate a respectable collection of more than 13,000 artifacts, books, photographs, art objects, and memorabilia. Its collection of paintings, drawings, and sculpture by African American and African artists is excellent.

In 1993, the DuSable Museum added a 25,000-square-foot wing named in honor of the city's first and only African-American mayor, Harold Washington. The permanent exhibit on Washington contains memorabilia and personal effects, and surveys important episodes in his political career. The museum also has a gift shop, a research library, and an extensive program of community-related events, such as a jazz and blues music series, poetry readings, film screenings, and other cultural events, all presented in a 466-seat auditorium. Allow 1 to 2 hours.

740 E. 56th Place. ℂ **773/947-0600.** www.dusablemuseum.org. Admission $3 adults, $2 students and seniors, $1 children 6–13, free for children 5 and under. Free admission Sun. Tues–Sat 10am–5pm; Sun noon–5pm. Closed major holidays. Bus: 6 or Metra Electric train to 57th St. and Lake Park Ave., and then a short cab ride.

Museum of Science and Industry ★★★ *(Kids* Even if you don't plan on spending the day in Hyde Park, you'll pass through the neighborhood on your way to one of Chicago's most popular tourist attractions. The massive Museum of Science and Industry is the granddaddy of interactive museums, with some 2,000 exhibits. Schedule at least 3 hours here; a comprehensive visit can take all day, especially if you catch an OMNIMAX movie.

While the museum is constantly adding new displays to cover the latest scientific breakthroughs, you shouldn't miss certain tried-and-true exhibits that have been here for years and epitomize the museum for Chicagoans. The **U-505** 🛈🛈🛈, a German submarine that was captured in 1944 and arrived at the museum 10 years later, brings home the claustrophobic reality of underwater naval life. The sub is displayed in a dramatic indoor arena with exhibits and newsreel footage that put the U-boat in historical context (a guided tour of the sub's interior costs $5 extra, but the exhibit is worth visiting even if you don't go inside). The full-scale **Coal Mine** 🛈🛈, which dates back to 1934, incorporates modern mining techniques into the exhibit—but the best part is the simulated trip down into a dark, mysterious mine. Get to these exhibits quickly after the museum opens because they attract amusement-park-length lines during the day.

Kids who love planes, trains, and automobiles shouldn't miss ***All Aboard the Silver Streak,*** a refurbished Burlington Pioneer Zephyr train with onboard interactive exhibits; the massive model-train exhibit that makes up ***The Great Train Story*** 🛈🛈; or ***Take Flight,*** an aviation exhibit featuring a full-size 727 airplane that revs up its engines and replays the voice recordings from a San Francisco–Chicago flight periodically throughout the day. ***Networld*** 🛈, which offers a flashy immersion in the Internet (with plenty of interactive screens), will entrance computer addicts. More low-tech—but fun for kids—are ***The Farm*** (where children can sit at the wheel of a giant combine) and the **chick hatchery** inside the exhibit ***Genetics: Decoding Life,*** where you can watch as tiny newborn chicks poke their way out of eggs. ***Enterprise*** 🛈 immerses minicapitalists in the goings-on of a virtual company and includes an entire automated toy-making assembly line. If you have really little ones (under age 5), head for the ***Idea Factory,*** which is filled with hands-on play equipment (admission is limited to a set number of kids, so pick up a free timed ticket in advance).

I hate to indulge in gender stereotypes, but girls (myself included) love **Colleen Moore's Fairy Castle** 🛈🛈, a lavishly decorated miniature palace filled with priceless treasures (yes, those are real diamonds and pearls in the chandeliers). The castle is hidden on the lower level. Also tucked away in an inconspicuous spot—along the Blue stairwell between the Main Floor and the Balcony—are the ***Human Body Slices,***

🛈 *Tips* Hyde Park Bites

When you're ready to take a break, Hyde Park has an eclectic selection of restaurants. As in any university town, you'll find plenty of affordable, student-friendly hangouts. The most famous University of Chicago gathering spot is **Jimmy's Woodlawn Tap,** 1172 E. 55th St. (📞 **773/643-5516;** p. 289). This 50-year-old bar and grill doesn't offer much in the way of atmosphere (and be prepared for cigarette smoke), but the hamburgers and sandwiches are cheap, and the person sitting next to you might just be a Nobel Prize–winning professor. Another casual spot near campus is **Medici,** 1327 E. 57th St. (📞 **773/667-7394**), where a few generations' worth of students have carved their names into the tables while chowing down on pizza, the house specialty. **Calypso Café,** 5211 S. Harper St., near the Metra train tracks (📞 **773/955-0229**), serves conch chowder, jerk chicken, and other Caribbean favorites in a bright, funky setting. A few blocks south you'll find **La Petite Folie,** 1504 E. 55th St. (📞 **773/493-1394**), a French bistro that offers a refined escape from student life.

actual slivers of human cadavers that are guaranteed to impress teenagers in search of something truly gross.

A major addition to the museum is the **Henry Crown Space Center** 𝕲𝕲, which documents the story of space exploration in copious detail, highlighted by a simulated space-shuttle experience through sight and sound at the center's five-story OMNI-MAX Theater. The theater offers double features on the weekends; call for show times.

When you've worked up an appetite, you can visit the museum's large food court or the old-fashion ice-cream parlor; there's also an excellent gift shop.

Although it's quite a distance from the rest of Chicago's tourist attractions, the museum is easy enough to reach without a car; your best options are the no. 6 Jeffrey Express bus and the Metra Electric train from downtown (the no. 10 bus runs from downtown to the museum's front entrance during the summer).

57th St. and Lake Shore Dr. 𝕮 **800/468-6674** outside the Chicago area, 773/684-1414, or TTY 773/684-3323. www. msichicago.org. Admission to museum only: $11 adults, $9 seniors, $7 children 3–11, free for children 2 and under. Free admission Mon–Tues mid-Sept through Nov and Jan–Feb. Combination museum and OMNIMAX Theater: $17 adults, $15 seniors, $12 children 3–11, free for children 2 and under on an adult's lap. Memorial Day–Labor Day Mon–Sat 9:30am–5:30pm, Sun 11am–5:30pm; early Sept–late May Mon–Sat 9:30am–4pm, Sun 11am–4pm. Closed Dec 25. Bus: 6 or Metra Electric train to 57th St. and Lake Park Ave.

Oriental Institute Museum 𝕲𝕲

Near the midpoint of the campus, a few blocks from Rockefeller Memorial Chapel, is the Oriental Institute, which houses one of the world's major collections of Near Eastern art. Although most of the galleries have been renovated within the last few years, this is still a very traditional museum: lots of glass cases and very few interactive exhibits (in other words, there's not much to interest young children). It won't take you long to see the highlights here, and a few impressive pieces make it worth a stop for history and art buffs.

Your first stop should be the **Egyptian Gallery** 𝕲𝕲, which showcases the finest objects among the museum's 35,000 Egyptian artifacts. At the center stands a monumental, 17-foot solid-quartzite statue of the boy king Tutankhamen; the largest Egyptian sculpture in the Western Hemisphere, it tips the scales at 6 tons. The surrounding exhibits, which document the life and beliefs of Egyptians from 5000 B.C. to the 8th century A.D., have a wonderfully accessible approach that emphasizes themes, not chronology. Among them are mummification (there are 14 mummies on display—five people and nine animals), kingship, society, and writing (including a deed for the sale of a house, a copy of the *Book of the Dead,* and a schoolboy's homework).

The Oriental Institute also houses important collections of artifacts from civilizations that once flourished in what are now Iran and Iraq. The highlight of the **Mesopotamian Gallery** 𝕲 is a massive 16-foot-tall sculpture of a winged bull with a human head, which once stood in the palace of Assyrian king Sargon II. The gallery also contains some of the earliest man-made tools ever excavated, along with many other pieces that have become one-of-a-kind since the destruction and looting of the National Museum in Baghdad in 2003. Artifacts from Persia, ancient Palestine, Israel, Anatolia, and Nubia fill other galleries.

The small but eclectic gift shop, called the Suq, stocks many unique items, including reproductions of pieces in the museum's collection. Allow 1 hour.

1155 E. 58th St. (at University Ave.). 𝕮 **773/702-9514**. http://oi.uchicago.edu. Free admission; suggested donation $5 adults, $2 children. Tues–Sat 10am–6pm (Wed until 8:30pm); Sun noon–6pm. Bus: 6 or Metra Electric train to 57th St. and Lake Park Ave.

Finds **More Frank Lloyd Wright Homes**

In addition to Robie House, several of Wright's earlier works, still privately owned, dot the streets of Hyde Park. They include the **Heller House**, 5132 S. Woodlawn Ave. (1897); the **Blossom House**, 1332 E. 49th St. (1882); and the **McArthur House**, 4852 S. Kenwood Ave. (1892). *Note:* These houses are not open to the public, so they should only be admired from the outside.

Robie House 🖈🖈   Frank Lloyd Wright designed this 20th-century American architectural masterpiece for Frederick Robie, a bicycle and motorcycle manufacturer. The home, which was completed in 1909, bears signs of Wright's Prairie School of design (an open layout and linear geometry of form), as well as exquisite leaded- and stained-glass doors and windows. It's also among the last of Wright's Prairie School–style homes: During its construction, he abandoned both his family and his Oak Park practice to follow other pursuits, most prominently the realization of his Taliesin home and studio in Spring Green, Wisconsin. Docents from Oak Park's Frank Lloyd Wright Home and Studio Foundation lead tours here, even though the house is undergoing a massive, 10-year restoration (the house is open throughout the process, but your photos may include some scaffolding). A Wright specialty bookshop is in the building's former three-car garage—which was highly unusual for the time in which it was built. Allow 1 hour per tour, plus time to browse the gift shop.

5757 S. Woodlawn Ave. (at 58th St.). ✆ **773/834-1847.** www.wrightplus.org. Admission $12 adults, $10 seniors and children 7–18, free for children 6 and under. Mon–Fri tours at 11am, 1, and 3pm; Sat–Sun every half-hour 11am–3:30pm. Bookshop daily 10am–5pm. Bus: 6 or Metra Electric train to 57th St. and Lake Park Ave.

Rockefeller Memorial Chapel   To call the Rockefeller Memorial Chapel a chapel is false modesty, even for a Rockefeller. When the university first opened its doors, the students sang the following ditty:

> *John D. Rockefeller, wonderful man is he*
> *Gives all his spare change to the U of C.*

John D. was a generous patron, indeed. He founded the university (in cooperation with the American Baptist Society), built the magnificent minicathedral that now bears his name, and shelled out an additional $35 million in donations over the course of his lifetime. Memorial Chapel, designed by Bertram Goodhue, an architect known for his ecclesiastical buildings—including the Cadet Chapel at West Point and New York City's St. Thomas Church—was dedicated in 1928.

In keeping with the rest of the campus, which is patterned after Oxford, the chapel is reminiscent of English Gothic structures; however, it was built from limestone using modern construction techniques. Its most outstanding features are the circular stained-glass window high above the main altar (the windows, in general, are among the largest of any church or cathedral anywhere) and the world's second-largest carillon, which John D. Rockefeller, Jr., donated in 1932 in memory of his mother Laura. The chapel's organ is nearly as impressive, with four manuals, 126 stops, and more than 10,000 pipes. Choir concerts, carillon performances, and other musical programs run throughout the year, usually for a small donation. Allow a half-hour.

5850 S. Woodlawn Ave. ✆ **773/702-2100.** http://rockefeller.uchicago.edu. Free admission. Daily 8am–4pm (except during religious services). Bus: 6.

The Smart Museum of Art 🅕 The University of Chicago's fine-arts museum looks rather modest, but it packs a lot of talent into a compact space. Its permanent collection of more than 7,000 paintings and sculptures spans Western and Eastern civilizations, ranging from classical antiquity to the present day. Bona fide treasures include ancient Greek vases, Chinese bronzes, and Old Master paintings; Frank Lloyd Wright furniture; Tiffany glass; sculptures by Degas, Matisse, and Rodin; and 20th-century paintings and sculptures by Mark Rothko, Arthur Dove, Diego Rivera, Henry Moore, and Chicago sculptor Richard Hunt. Built in 1974, the contemporary building doesn't really fit in with the campus's Gothic architecture, but its sculpture garden and outdoor seating area make a nice place for quiet contemplation. The museum also has a gift shop and cafe. Allow 1 hour.

5550 S. Greenwood Ave. (at E. 55th St.). 🕐 773/702-0200. http://smartmuseum.uchicago.edu. Free admission. Tues–Fri 10am–4pm (Thurs until 8pm); Sat–Sun 11am–5pm. Closed major holidays. Bus: 6.

EXPLORING THE UNIVERSITY OF CHICAGO

Walking around the Gothic spires of the University of Chicago campus is bound to conjure up images of the cloistered academic life. Allow about an hour to stroll through the grassy quads and dramatic stone buildings (if the weather's nice, do as the students do, and vegetate for a while on the grass). If you're visiting on a weekday, your first stop should be the university's **Visitors Information Desk** (🕐 773/702-9739) on the first floor of Ida Noyes Hall, 1212 E. 59th St., where you can pick up campus maps and get information on university events. The center is open Monday through Friday from 10am to 7pm. If you stop by on a weekend when the Visitors Information Desk is closed, you can get the scoop on campus events at the **Reynolds Clubhouse** student center (🕐 773/702-8787).

Start your tour at the **Henry Moore statue,** *Nuclear Energy,* on South Ellis Avenue between 56th and 57th streets. It's next to the Regenstein Library, which marks the site of the old Stagg Field where, on December 2, 1942, the world's first sustained nuclear reaction was achieved in a basement laboratory below the field. Then turn left and follow 57th Street until you reach the grand stone Hull Gate; walk straight to reach the main quad, or turn left through the column-lined arcade to reach **Hutchinson Court** (designed by John Olmsted, son of revered landscape designer Frederick Law Olmsted). The Reynolds Clubhouse, the university's main student center, is here; you can take a break at the C-Shop cafe or settle down at a table at Hutchinson Commons. The dining room and hangout right next to the cafe will bring to mind the grand dining halls of Oxford and Cambridge.

Other worthy spots on campus include the charming, intimate **Bond Chapel,** behind Swift Hall on the main quad, and the blocks-long **Midway Plaisance,** a wide stretch of green that was the site of carnival sideshow attractions during the World's Columbian Exposition in 1893 (ever since, the term "midway" has referred to carnivals in general).

The **Seminary Co-op Bookstore,** 5757 S. University Ave. (🕐 773/752-4381; www.semcoop.com), is a treasure trove of academic and scholarly books. Its selection of more than 100,000 titles has won it an international reputation as "the best bookstore west of Blackwell's in Oxford." It's open Monday through Friday from 8:30am to 9pm, Saturday from 10am to 6pm, and Sunday from noon to 6pm.

ENJOYING THE OUTDOORS IN HYDE PARK

Hyde Park is not only a haven for book lovers and culture aficionados; the community also has open-air attractions. Worthy outdoor environments near Lake Michigan include **Lake Shore Drive,** where many stately apartment houses follow the contour of the shoreline. A suitable locale for a quiet stroll during the day is **Promontory Point,** at 55th Street and Lake Michigan, a bulb of land that juts into the lake and offers a good view of Chicago to the north and the seasonally active 57th Street beach to the south.

Farther south, just below the Museum of Science and Industry, is **Wooded Island** in Jackson Park, the site of the Japanese Pavilion during the Columbian Exposition and today a lovely garden of meandering paths. In the **Perennial Garden** at 59th Street and Stony Island Avenue in Jackson Park, more than 180 varieties of flowering plants display a palette of colors that changes with the seasons.

KENWOOD HISTORIC DISTRICT

A fun side trip for architecture and history buffs is the Kenwood Historic District, just north of Hyde Park. The area originally developed as a suburb of Chicago, when local captains of industry (including Sears founder Julius Rosenwald) began building lavish mansions in the mid-1850s. The neighborhood's large lots and eclectic mix of architecture (everything from elaborate Italianate to Prairie-style homes) make it unique in Chicago, especially compared to the closely packed buildings in Hyde Park. Although many of the fine homes here became dilapidated after the South Side's "white flight" of the 1950s and '60s, a new generation of black and white middle-class homeowners has been lovingly renovating the one-of-a-kind houses. Today, the blocks between 47th and 51st streets (north-south) and Blackstone and Drexel boulevards (east-west) make for a wonderful walking tour, with broad, shady streets full of newly restored mansions.

6 More Museums

City Gallery   Along with the pumping station across the street, the Chicago Water Tower is one of only a handful of buildings to survive the Great Chicago Fire of 1871. It has long been a revered symbol of the city's resilience and fortitude, although today the building is dwarfed by the high-rise shopping centers and hotels of North Michigan Avenue. The Gothic-style limestone building is now an art gallery. The spiffed-up interior is intimate and sunny, and it's a convenient, quick pit stop of culture on your way to the Water Tower shopping center or the tourist information center across the street in the pumping station. Exhibits focus mostly on photography, usually featuring Chicago-based artists such as the fashion photographer Victor Skrebneski. Allow 15 minutes.

806 N. Michigan Ave. (between Chicago Ave. and Pearson St.). (C) **312/742-0808.** Free admission. Mon–Sat 10am–6:30pm; Sun 10am–5pm. Bus: 3, 145, 146, 147, or 151.

Historic Pullman 🦉🦉   Railway magnate George Pullman may have been a fabulously wealthy industrialist, but he fancied himself more enlightened than his 19th-century peers. So when it came time to build a new headquarters for his Pullman Palace Car Company, he dreamed of something more than the standard factory surrounded by tenements. Instead, he built a model community for his workers, a place where they could live in houses with indoor plumbing and abundant natural light—amenities almost unheard of for industrial workers in the 1880s. Pullman didn't do all this solely from the goodness of his heart: He hoped that the town, named after him, would attract the most skilled workers (who would be so happy that they wouldn't go on strike). As one of the first "factory towns," Pullman caused an international sensation and was seen as a model for other companies to follow. The happy workers that

Pullman envisioned did go on strike in 1894, however, frustrated by the company's control of every aspect of their lives.

Today the Pullman district makes a fascinating stop for anyone with a historical or architectural bent. While most of the homes remain private residences, a number of public buildings (including the lavish Hotel Florence, the imposing Clock Tower, and the two-story colonnaded Market Hall) still stand. You can walk through the area on your own (stop by the visitor center for a map), or take a guided a tour at 1:30pm on the first Sunday of the month from May through October ($5 adults, $4 seniors, $3 students). Allow 1½ hours for the guided tour.

11141 S. Cottage Grove Ave. (*C*) 773/785-8901. www.pullmanil.org. Visitor center Tues–Sun 11am–3pm. Free admission. Train: Metra Electric line to Pullman (111th St.), turn right on Cottage Grove Ave., and walk 1 block to the visitor center.

International Museum of Surgical Science *(F)* *(Finds)*   This unintentionally macabre shrine to medicine is my pick for the weirdest tourist attraction in town. Not for the faint of stomach, it occupies a historic 1917 Gold Coast mansion designed by the noted architect Howard Van Doren Shaw, who modeled it after Le Petit Trianon at Versailles. Displayed throughout its four floors are surgical instruments, paintings, and sculptures depicting the history of surgery and healing practices in Eastern and Western civilizations (it's run by the International College of Surgeons). The exhibits are old-fashioned (no interactive computer displays here), but that's part of the museum's odd appeal.

You'll look at your doctor in a whole new way after viewing the trepanned skulls excavated from an ancient tomb in Peru. The accompanying tools bored holes in patients' skulls, a horrific practice thought to release the evil spirits causing their illness (some skulls show signs of new bone growth, meaning that some lucky headache-sufferers actually survived the low-tech surgery). There are also battlefield amputation kits, a working iron-lung machine in the polio exhibit, and oddities such as a stethoscope designed to be transported inside a top hat. Other attractions include an apothecary shop and dentist's office (ca. 1900) re-created in a historic street exhibit, and the hyperbolically titled *Hall of Immortals,* a sculpture gallery depicting 12 historic figures in medicine from Hippocrates to Madame Curie. Allow 1 hour.

1524 N. Lake Shore Dr. (between Burton Place and North Ave.). (*C*) 312/642-6502. www.imss.org. Admission $8 adults, $4 seniors and students. Tues–Sat 10am–4pm; May–Sept Sun 10am–4pm. Closed major holidays. Bus: 151.

Intuit: The Center for Intuitive and Outsider Art   Chicago is home to an active community of collectors of "outsider art," a term attached to a group of unknown, unconventional artists who do their work without any formal training or connection to the mainstream art world. Often called folk or self-taught artists, they produce highly personal and idiosyncratic work using a range of media, from bottle caps to immense canvases. Intuit was founded in 1991 to bring attention to these artists through exhibitions and educational lectures. It's in the warehouse district northwest of the Loop, and has two galleries and a performance area. The museum offers a regular lecture series, and if you time your visit right, you might be here for one of the center's tours of a private local art collection. Allow 1 hour.

756 N. Milwaukee Ave. (at Chicago and Ogden aves.). (*C*) 312/243-9088. http://outsider.art.org. Free admission. Tues–Sat 11am–5pm (Thurs until 7:30pm). Bus: 56 or 66. Subway/El: Blue Line to Chicago.

Jane Addams Hull-House Museum   Three years after the 1886 Haymarket Riot, a young woman named Jane Addams bought a mansion on Halsted Street that had

been built in 1856 as a "country home" but was surrounded by the shanties of poor immigrants. Here, Addams and her co-worker, Ellen Gates Starr, launched the American settlement-house movement with the establishment of Hull House, an institution that endured on this site in Chicago until 1963. (It continues today as a decentralized social-service agency known as Hull House Association.) In that year, all but two of the settlement's 13 buildings, along with the entire residential neighborhood in its immediate vicinity, were demolished to make room for the University of Illinois at Chicago campus, which now owns the museum buildings. Of the original settlement, what remain today are the Hull-House Museum, the mansion itself, and the residents' dining hall, snuggled among the ultramodern, poured-concrete buildings of the university campus. Inside are the original furnishings, Jane Addams' office, and numerous settlement maps and photographs. Rotating exhibits re-create the history of the settlement and the work of its residents, showing how Addams was able to help transform the dismal streets around her into stable inner-city environments worth fighting over. Allow a half-hour.

University of Illinois at Chicago, 800 S. Halsted St. (at Polk St.). © 312/413-5353. www.uic.edu/jaddams/hull. Free admission. Tues–Fri 10am–4pm; Sun noon–5pm. Closed university holidays. Bus: 8. Subway/El: Blue Line to Halsted/University of Illinois.

McCormick Tribune Freedom Museum *Kids*   As you might guess from the name, the *Chicago Tribune* newspaper is the guiding force behind this celebration of the First Amendment. Thankfully, though, this is no corporate-PR stunt, but rather a thought-provoking overview of how freedom of speech impacts our daily life. Aimed predominantly at junior-high and high-school students, it includes the requisite high-tech bells and whistles aimed at jaded young attention spans (such as computer kiosks where you can listen to once-banned songs or take sides in a free speech debate), and during the week, you might be surrounded by loud school groups. But some of the exhibits—such as the stories of reporters who were jailed for telling the truth—are emotionally affecting, and it makes an easy stop during a walk along Michigan Avenue. Allow 1 hour.

445 N. Michigan Ave. (between Illinois St. and the Chicago River). © 312/222-4860. www.freedommuseum.us. Admission $5, children 5 and under free. Wed–Mon 10am–6pm. Closed Thanksgiving, Christmas, and New Year's Day. Subway/El: Red Line to Grand. Bus: 145, 146, 147, or 151.

National Museum of Mexican Art *★*   Chicago's vibrant Pilsen neighborhood, just southwest of the Loop, is home to one of the nation's largest Mexican-American communities. Ethnic pride emanates from every doorstep, taqueria, and bakery, and colorful murals splash across building exteriors and alleyways. This institution—the only Latino museum accredited by the American Association of Museums—may be the neighborhood's most prized possession. That's quite an accomplishment, given that it was founded in 1987 by a passel of public-school teachers who pooled $900 to get it started.

Exhibits showcase Mexican and Mexican-American visual and performing artists, often drawing on the permanent collection of more than 5,000 works, but the visiting artists, festival programming, and community participation make the museum really shine. Its Day of the Dead celebration, which runs for about 8 weeks beginning in September, is one of the most ambitious in the country. The Del Corazon Mexican Performing Arts Festival, held in the spring, features programs by local and international artists here and around town, and the Sor Juana Festival, presented in the fall, honors Mexican writer and pioneering feminist Sor Juana Ines de la Cruz with photography and painting exhibits, music and theater performances, and poetry readings by Latina women.

The museum is very family oriented, with educational workshops for kids and parents. It also has an excellent gift shop and stages a holiday market, featuring items from Mexico, on the first weekend in December. Allow 1 hour.

1852 W. 19th St. (a few blocks west of Ashland Ave.). ℂ 312/738-1503. www.nationalmuseumofmexicanart.org. Free admission. Tues–Sun 10am–5pm. Closed major holidays. Bus: 9. Subway/El: Blue Line to 18th St.

National Vietnam Veterans Art Museum ★★ *(Finds* This museum houses a stirring collection of art by Vietnam veterans, and is the only one of its kind in the world. After the war, many veterans made art as personal therapy, never expecting to show it to anyone, but in 1981 a small group began showing their work together in Chicago and in touring exhibitions. The collection has grown to more than 1,500 paintings, drawings, photographs, and sculptures from all over the world, including Vietnam. (Recently, the museum has also started hosting exhibits of work by veterans who have returned from Iraq.) Titles such as *We Regret to Inform You, Blood Spots on a Rice Paddy,* and *The Wound* give you an idea of the power of the images. Housed in a former warehouse in the Prairie Avenue district south of the Loop, the museum is modern and well organized. An installation suspended from the ceiling, ***Above & Beyond*** ★, comprises more than 58,000 dog tags with the names of the men and women who died in the war—it creates an emotional effect similar to that of the Wall in Washington, D.C. The complex also houses a small theater, cafe (open for breakfast and lunch), gift shop, and an outdoor plaza with a flagpole that has deliberately been left leaning because that's how veterans saw them in combat. Allow 1 hour.

1801 S. Indiana Ave. (at 18th St.). ℂ 312/326-0270. www.nvvam.org. Admission $10 adults, $7 seniors and students w/ID. Tues–Fri 11am–6pm; Sat 10am–5pm. Closed major holidays. Bus: 3 or 4.

Polish Museum of America One million people of Polish ancestry live in Chicago, giving the city the largest Polish population outside of Warsaw, so it's no surprise that the Polish Museum of America is here, in the neighborhood where many of the first immigrants settled. The museum has one of the most important collections of Polish art and historical materials outside Poland. (It is also the largest museum in the U.S. devoted exclusively to an ethnic group.) The museum's programs include rotating exhibitions, films, lectures, and concerts, and a permanent exhibit about Pope John Paul II. There's also a library with a large Polish-language collection, and archives where visitors can research genealogical history (call in advance if you want to look through those records). Allow a half-hour.

984 N. Milwaukee Ave. (at Augusta Blvd.). ℂ 773/384-3352. http://pma.prcua.org/homeen.html. Admission $5 adults, $4 students and seniors, $3 children 11 and under. Fri–Wed 11am–4pm. Subway/El: Blue Line to Division.

7 Exploring the 'Burbs
OAK PARK

Architecture and literary buffs alike make pilgrimages to Oak Park, a nearby suburb on the western border of the city that is easily accessible by car or train. Bookworms flock here to see the town where Ernest Hemingway was born and grew up, while others come to catch a glimpse of the Frank Lloyd Wright–designed homes that line the well-maintained streets.

Oak Park Attractions

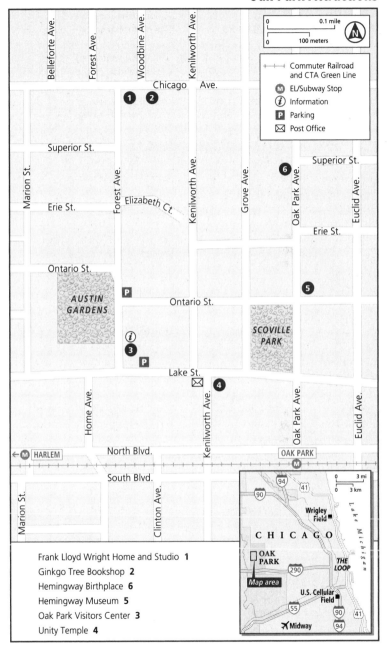

Frank Lloyd Wright Home and Studio **1**
Ginkgo Tree Bookshop **2**
Hemingway Birthplace **6**
Hemingway Museum **5**
Oak Park Visitors Center **3**
Unity Temple **4**

GETTING THERE

BY CAR   Oak Park is 10 miles due west of downtown Chicago. By car, take the Eisenhower Expressway (I-290) west to Harlem Avenue (Ill. 43) and exit north. Continue on Harlem north to Lake Street. Take a right on Lake Street and continue to Forest Avenue. Turn left here, and immediately on your right you'll see the **Oak Park Visitor Center** (see below).

BY PUBLIC TRANSPORTATION   Take the Green Line west to the Harlem stop, roughly a 25-minute ride from downtown. Exit the station onto Harlem Avenue, and proceed north to Lake Street. Take a right on Lake Street, follow it to Forest Avenue, and then turn left to the **Oak Park Visitor Center** (see below).

BY TOUR   The **Chicago Architecture Foundation** regularly runs guided tours from downtown Chicago to Oak Park. For details, see "Sightseeing Tours," p. 212.

VISITOR INFORMATION

The **Oak Park Visitor Center,** 158 Forest Ave. (© **888/OAK-PARK;** www.visitoak park.com), is open daily from 10am to 5pm April through October, and from 10am to 4pm November through March. Stop here for orientation, maps, and guidebooks. There's a city-operated parking lot next door. The heart of the historic district and the Frank Lloyd Wright Home and Studio are only a few blocks away.

An extensive tour of Oak Park's historic district leaves from the **Ginkgo Tree Bookshop,** 951 Chicago Ave., on weekends from 11am to 4pm on the hour (tour times are noon, 1pm, and 2pm Nov–Feb). The tour lasts 1 hour and costs $12 for adults, $10 for seniors and students ages 11 to 18, and $5 for children 4 to 10. If you can't make it to Oak Park on the weekend, you can follow a self-guided map and audiocassette tour of the historic district for the same price; the audio tour is available at the Ginkgo Tree Bookshop from 10am to 3:30pm. In addition to homes designed by Wright, you will see work by several of his disciples, as well as some charming examples of the Victorian styling that he so disdained. A more detailed map ($3 at the bookshop), *Architectural Guide Map of Oak Park and River Forest,* includes text and photos of all 80 sites of interest in Oak Park and neighboring River Forest.

THE WRIGHT STUFF

Frank Lloyd Wright Home and Studio ✸✸✸   For the first 20 years of Wright's career, this remarkable complex served first and foremost as the sanctuary where he designed and executed more than 130 of an extraordinary output of 430 completed buildings. The home began as a simple shingled cottage that the 22-year-old Wright built for his bride in 1889, but it became a living laboratory for his revolutionary reinvention of interior spaces. Wright remodeled the house constantly until 1911, when he moved out permanently (in 1909, he left his wife and six children and went off to Europe with the wife of one of his clients). During Wright's fertile early period, the house was Wright's showcase, but it also embraces many idiosyncratic features molded to his own needs rather than those of a client. With many add-ons—including a barrel-vaulted children's playroom and a studio with an octagonal balcony suspended by chains—the place has a certain whimsy that others might have found less livable. This was not an architect's masterpiece but rather the master's home, and visitors can savor every room in it for the view it reflects of the workings of a remarkable mind.

Tours cannot be booked in advance by phone, but a select number of tickets for each day can be reserved online. Allow 1 hour for the tour, more time if you want to browse in the bookshop.

Wright's Oak Park

Oak Park has the highest concentration of Frank Lloyd Wright–designed and –built houses or buildings anywhere. People come here to marvel at the work of a man who saw his life as a twofold mission: to wage a single-handed battle against excessively ornamental architecture (Victorian, in particular), and to create in its place a new form that would be at the same time functional, appropriate to its natural setting, and stimulating to the imagination.

Not everyone who comes to Oak Park shares Wright's architectural philosophy, but scholars and enthusiasts admire him for being consistently true to his vision, out of which emerged a unique and genuinely American architectural statement. The reason for Wright's success could stem from the fact that he was a living exemplar of a quintessential American type. In a deep sense, he embodied the ideal of the self-made and self-sufficient individual who had survived, even thrived, in the frontier society—qualities that he expressed in his almost-puritanical insistence that each spatial or structural form in his buildings serve some useful purpose. He was also an aesthete in Emersonian fashion, deriving his idea of beauty from natural environments, where apparent simplicity often belies a subtle complexity.

The three principal ingredients of a tour of Wright-designed structures in Oak Park are the **Frank Lloyd Wright Home and Studio Tour,** the **Unity Temple Tour,** and a **walking tour**—guided or self-guided—to view the exteriors of homes throughout the neighborhood that were built by the architect. Oak Park has 25 homes and buildings by Wright, constructed between 1892 and 1913, which constitute the core output of his Prairie School period.

951 Chicago Ave. ⓒ **708/848-1976.** www.wrightplus.org. Admission $12 adults, $10 seniors and students 11–18, $5 children 4–10; combined admission for Home and Studio tour and guided or self-guided historic district tour $20 adults, $10 seniors and students 11–18, $5 children 4–10. Admission to home and studio is by guided tour only; tours depart from bookshop Mon–Fri 11am, 1, and 3pm; Sat–Sun every 20 min. 11am–3:30pm. Closed Jan 1, last week in Jan, Thanksgiving, and Dec 25. Facilities for people with disabilities are limited; please call in advance.

Unity Temple ⓕ   After a fire destroyed its church around 1900, a Unitarian Universalist congregation asked one of its members, Frank Lloyd Wright, to design an affordable replacement. Using poured concrete with metal reinforcements—a necessity due to a small $40,000 budget—Wright created a building that on the outside seems as forbidding as a mausoleum but inside contains all the elements of the Prairie School that has made Wright's name immortal. Following the example of H. H. Richardson, Wright placed the building's main entrance on the side, behind an enclosure—a feature often employed in his houses as well—to create a sense of privacy and intimacy. Wright complained, furthermore, that the conventions of church architecture, such as the nave in the Gothic-style cathedral across the street, were overpowering. Of that particular church, he commented that he didn't feel a part of it.

Yet his vision in this regard was somewhat confused and contradictory. He wanted Unity Temple to be "democratic," but perhaps Wright was unable to subdue his own

---

Tips **The Wright Plus Tour**

Die-hard fans of the architect will want to be in town on the third Saturday in May for the annual Wright Plus Tour. The public can tour several Frank Lloyd Wright–designed homes and other notable Oak Park buildings, in both the Prairie School and Victorian styles, in addition to Wright's home, studio, and the Unity Temple. The tour includes 10 buildings in all. Tickets go on sale March 1 and can sell out by mid-April. Call the Frank Lloyd Wright Home and Studio (© **708/848-1976;** www.wrightplus.org) for details and ticket information.

---

personal hubris and hauteur in the creative process, for the ultimate effect of his chapel, and much of the building's interior, is grand and imperial. This is no simple meetinghouse; instead, its principal chapel looks like the chamber of the Roman Senate. Even so, the interior, with its unpredictable geometric arrangements and its decor reminiscent of Native American art, is no less beautiful.

Wright was a true hands-on, can-do person; he knew the materials he chose to use as intimately as the artisans who carried out his plans. He added pigment to the plaster (rather than the paint) to achieve a pale, natural effect. His use of wood trim and other decorative touches is still exciting to behold; his sensitivity to grain, tone, and placement was akin to that of an exceptionally gifted woodworker. His stunning, almost-minimalist use of form is what still sets him apart as a relevant and brilliant artist. Unity Temple still feels groundbreaking 100 years later—which Wright would consider the ultimate compliment. Allow a half-hour.

875 Lake St. © **708/383-8873.** http://unitytemple-utrf.org. Self-guided tours $8 adults; $6 seniors, children 6–12, and students w/ID; free for children 5 and under. Free guided tours weekends at 1, 2 and 3pm. Mon–Fri 10:30am–4:30pm; Sat–Sun 1–4pm. Church events can alter schedule; call in advance.

ON THE TRAIL OF HEMINGWAY

Hemingway Museum   Frank Lloyd Wright might be Oak Park's favorite son, but the town's most famous native son is Ernest Hemingway. Hemingway had no great love for Oak Park; he moved away right after high school and later referred to his hometown as a place of "wide lawns and narrow minds." But that hasn't stopped Oak Park from laying claim to the great American writer. A portion of the ground floor of this former church, now the Oak Park Arts Center, holds a small but interesting display of Hemingway memorabilia. A 6-minute video sheds considerable light on Hemingway's time in Oak Park, where he spent the first 18 years of his life, and covers his high school experiences particularly well.

The **Ernest Hemingway Birthplace Home** is 2 blocks north, at 339 N. Oak Park Ave. The lovely Queen Anne house—complete with wraparound porch and turret—was the home of Hemingway's maternal grandparents, and it's where the writer was born on July 21, 1899. Its connection to Hemingway is actually pretty tenuous—he spent most of his boyhood and high school years at 600 N. Kenilworth Ave., a few blocks away (that house is still privately owned)—but the birthplace has been carefully restored to replicate its appearance at the end of the 19th century, making this an appealing stop for fans of historic house tours (whether they're Hemingway fans or not). The hours are the same as the Hemingway Museum's. Allow 1 hour.

200 N. Oak Park Ave. © 708/848-2222. www.ehfop.org. Combined admission to Hemingway Museum and Ernest Hemingway Birthplace Home $7 adults, $5.50 seniors and children 5–12, free for children 4 and under. Sun–Fri 1–5pm; Sat 10am–5pm.

THE NORTH SHORE

Between Chicago and the state border of Wisconsin is one of the nation's most affluent residential areas, a swath of suburbia known as the North Shore. Although towns farther west like to co-opt the name for its prestige, the North Shore proper extends from Evanston, Chicago's nearest neighbor to the north, along the lakefront to tony Lake Forest, originally built as a resort for Chicago's aristocracy. Dotted with idyllic, picture-perfect towns such as Kenilworth, Glencoe, and Winnetka, this area has long attracted filmmakers such as Robert Redford, who filmed *Ordinary People* in Lake Forest, and the North Shore's own John Hughes, who shot most of his popular coming-of-age comedies (*Sixteen Candles, Ferris Bueller's Day Off, Home Alone,* and so on) here.

Although a Metra train line extends to Lake Forest and neighboring Lake Bluff, I highly recommend that you rent a car and drive north along **Sheridan Road,** which wends its leisurely way through many of these communities, past palatial homes and mansions designed in a startling array of architectural styles. Aside from Lake Shore Drive in Chicago, you won't find a more impressive stretch of roadway in the entire metropolitan area.

EXPLORING EVANSTON

Despite being frequented by Chicagoans, Evanston, the city's oldest suburb, retains an identity all its own. A unique hybrid of sensibilities, it manages to combine the tranquillity of suburban life with a highly cultured, urban charm. It's great fun to wander amid the shops and cafes in its downtown area or along funky Dempster Street at its southern end. The beautiful lakefront campus of **Northwestern University** (© 847/491-3741; www.northwestern.edu) is here, and many of its buildings—such as Alice Millar Chapel, with its sublime stained-glass facade, and the Mary and Leigh Block Gallery, a fine-arts haven that offers a top-notch collection and intriguing temporary exhibitions—are well worth several hours of exploration.

Evanston was also the home of Frances Willard, founder of the Women's Christian Temperance Union. **Willard House,** 1730 Chicago Ave. (© **847/328-7500**), is open to visitors on the first and third Sundays of every month from 1 to 4pm ($5 adults, $3 children under 13). Nine of the 17 rooms in this old Victorian "Rest Cottage" (as Willard called it) have been converted into a museum of period furnishings and temperance memorabilia. Among her personal effects is the bicycle she affectionately called "Gladys" and learned to ride late in life, in the process spurring women across the country to do the same. The headquarters of the WCTU is still on-site.

Another interesting house museum is the former **mansion of Charles Gates Dawes,** a wealthy financier who served as vice president under Calvin Coolidge and won the Nobel Peace Prize in 1925 for his smooth handling of German reparations on behalf of the League of Nations following World War I. It now houses the **Evanston History Center,** 225 Greenwood St. (© **847/475-3410;** www.evanston historical.org), which provides tours of this restored 100-plus-year-old landmark Fridays and Saturdays between 1pm and 3pm and Sundays between 1pm and 4pm ($5 adults, $3 seniors and children 6 to 18).

Tucked away in north Evanston, a few miles from the Northwestern campus, is the unusual and informative **Mitchell Museum of the American Indian,** 2600 Central Park Ave. (© **847/475-1030;** www.mitchellmuseum.org). The collection ranges from stoneware tools and weapons to the work of contemporary Native American artists. The museum is open Tuesday through Saturday from 10am to 5pm (Thurs until 8pm), and Sunday from noon to 4pm. It's closed on holidays and during the last 2 weeks of August. Admission is $5 for adults, $2.50 for seniors and children. Call in advance to arrange a volunteer-led tour.

For a bit of serenity, head to **Grosse Point Lighthouse and Maritime Museum,** 2601 Sheridan Rd. (✆ **847/328-6961;** www.grossepointlighthouse.net), a historic lighthouse built in 1873, when Lake Michigan still teemed with cargo-laden ships. Tours of the lighthouse, situated in a nature center, take place on weekends from June to September at 2, 3, and 4pm ($6 adults, $3 children 8–12; children under 8 not admitted for safety reasons). The adjacent Lighthouse Beach is a favorite spot for local families during the summer. If you're here between Memorial Day and Labor Day, you'll have to pay to frolic on the sand ($7 adults, $5 children 1–11), but it's a great place for a (free) stroll on a sunny spring or fall day.

OTHER AREA ATTRACTIONS

Bahá'í House of Worship   Up the road from Evanston in Wilmette is the most visited of all the sights in the northern suburbs, the Bahá'í House of Worship, an ethereal edifice that seems not of this earth. The gleaming white stone temple, designed by the French-Canadian Louis Bourgeois and completed in 1953, is essentially a soaring nine-sided 135-foot dome, draped in a delicate lacelike facade, that reveals the Eastern influence of the Bahá'í faith's native Iran. Surrounded by formal gardens, it is one of seven Bahá'í temples in the world, and the only one in the Western Hemisphere. The dome's latticework is even more beautiful as you gaze upward from the floor of the sanctuary, which, during the day, is flooded with light. Downstairs, displays in the visitor center explain the Bahá'í faith. Temple members offer informal tours of the building and exhibits to anyone who inquires. Allow a half-hour.

100 Linden Ave. (at Sheridan Rd.), Wilmette. ✆ 847/853-2300. www.bahai.us/bahai-temple. Free admission. Daily 7am–10pm; visitor center 10am–5pm (until 8pm May–Sept). From Chicago, take the El Red Line north to Howard St. Change for the Evanston train and go to the end of the line, Linden Ave. (Or, take the Purple/Evanston Express and stay on the same train all the way.) Turn right on Linden, and walk 2 blocks east. If you're driving, go north on the Outer Dr. (Lake Shore Dr.), which feeds into Sheridan Rd.

Chicago Botanic Garden 🦋🦋 (Value   Despite its name, the world-class Chicago Botanic Garden is 25 miles north of the city in the suburb of Glencoe. This 385-acre living preserve includes eight large lagoons and a variety of distinct botanical environments including the Illinois prairie, an English walled garden, and a three-island Japanese garden. Also on the grounds are a large fruit-and-vegetable garden, an "enabling garden" (which shows how gardening can be adapted for people with disabilities), and

---

(Moments **A Suburban Respite**

If you've made it to the Bahá'í temple, take a stroll across Sheridan Road to **Gilson Park** for a taste of north suburban life. Check out the sailors prepping their boats for a day cruise, families picnicking and playing Frisbee, and kids frolicking on the sandy beach. Access to the beach is restricted to local residents in the summer, but in the fall and spring, you're welcome to wander (just don't expect to take a dip in the frigid water).

a 100-acre old-growth oak woodland. If you're here in the summer, don't miss the extensive rose gardens (just follow the bridal parties who flock here to get their pictures taken). The Botanic Garden also has an exhibit hall, auditorium, museum, library, education greenhouses, outdoor pavilion, carillon, cafe, designated bike path, and garden shop. Carillon concerts take place at 7pm Monday evenings from late June through August; tours of the carillon are offered beforehand.

Every summer the Botanic Garden stages a special outdoor exhibition (one year giant animal-shaped topiaries stood in unexpected locations throughout the grounds; another year, model railroads wound through miniature versions of American national parks). Check the website or call for event schedules. Allow 3 hours.

1000 Lake-Cook Rd. (just east of Edens Expwy./I-94), Glencoe. © 847/835-5440. www.chicago-botanic.org. Free admission. Daily 8am–sunset. Tram tours Apr–Oct. Closed Dec 25. From Chicago, take Sheridan Rd. north along Lake Michigan or the Edens Expwy. (I-94) to Lake-Cook Rd. Parking $15/day.

Ravinia Festival 🌟🌟 *(Finds* Want to know where the natives get away from it all? Come summertime, you'll find us chilling on the lawn at Ravinia, the summer home of the highly regarded Chicago Symphony Orchestra in suburban Highland Park. The season runs from mid-June to Labor Day and includes far more than classical concerts: You can also catch pop acts, dance performances, operatic arias, and blues concerts. Tickets are available for the lawn and the covered pavilion, where you get a reserved seat and a view of the stage. The lawn is the real joy of Ravinia: sitting under the stars and a canopy of leafy branches while listening to music and indulging in an elaborate picnic (it's a local tradition to try to outdo everyone else by bringing candelabras and fine china). I've been here for everything from Beethoven symphonies to folksy singer-songwriters, and the setting has been magical every time. The lawn to the left of the stage is a popular place for families to spread out, but I'm partial to the tree-filled area on the right (the lights projected into the branches create a dramatic effect after the sun sets).

Don't let the distance from downtown discourage you from visiting, because an extremely convenient public-transportation system serves Ravinia. On concert nights, a special Ravinia Metra commuter train leaves at 5:50pm from the North Western train station at Madison and Canal streets (just west of the Loop). The train stops at the festival at 6:30pm, allowing plenty of time to enjoy a picnic before an 8 o'clock show. After the concert, trains wait right outside the gates to take commuters back to the city. The round-trip train fare is $5, a real bargain considering that traffic around the park can be brutal.

Dining options at the park range from the fine-dining restaurant **Mirabelle** (© 847/432-7550 for reservations) to prepacked picnic spreads from the **Gatehouse,** featuring gourmet items to go. For $10, you can rent a pair of lawn chairs and a table from booths set up near the park entrance. In case you're wondering about the weather conditions at concert time, dial Ravinia's Weather Line (© **847/433-5010**).

Green Bay and Lake-Cook roads, Highland Park. © 847/266-5100 or 312/RAVINIA. www.ravinia.org. Tickets: Pavilion $20–$75; lawn $10–$20. Most concerts are in the evening.

THE NORTH & NORTHWEST SUBURBS

The North Shore is only one slice of life north of Chicago. To its west lies a sprawling thicket of old and new suburbs, from the bucolic environs of equestrian-minded **Barrington** and its ring of smaller satellite communities in the far northwest, to near-northwest shopping mecca **Schaumburg,** home to the gigantic Woodfield Mall.

While Woodfield attracts a steady stream of dedicated shoppers—allowing it to tout its status as one of the top tourist destinations in Illinois—it's not that distinctive; you'll find most of the same stores at your local megamall back home.

A more pastoral option for visitors with time on their hands might be a day trip to the **historic village of Long Grove,** about 30 miles northwest of Chicago. Settled in the 1840s by German immigrants and pioneers traveling west from New England, Long Grove has assiduously preserved its old-fashion character. Set amid 500 acres of oak- and hickory-tree groves, the village maintains nearly 100 specialty stores, galleries, and restaurants, many of which are in former smithies, wheelwright barns, and century-old residences. (Don't skip the **Long Grove Confectionery Company,** a local institution.) By village ordinance, all new buildings constructed in the shopping district must conform to the architecture of the early 1900s. The village schedules several cultural and entertainment events, festivals, and art fairs throughout the year. The biggest and best is the annual **Strawberry Festival,** held during the last weekend in June. Call the village's information center or check the town's website (© **847/634-0888;** www.longgroveonline.com) for updates on coming events. To get there from the Chicago Loop, take the I-94 tollway north until it separates at I-90, another tollway that runs northwest. Follow I-90 until you reach Route 53, and drive north on 53 until it dead-ends at Lake-Cook Road. Take the west exit off 53, and follow Lake-Cook Road to Hicks Road. Turn right on Hicks Road and then left on Old McHenry Road, which will take you right into the center of town.

Arlington International Racecourse   With its gleaming-white, palatial, six-story grandstand and lush gardens, this racecourse is one of the most beautiful showcases for thoroughbred horse racing in the world. Its storied history stretches back to 1927, and such equine stars as Citation, Secretariat, and Cigar have graced the track. The annual Arlington Million (the sport's first million-dollar race, held in mid-Aug) attracts top jockeys, trainers, and horses and is part of the World Series Racing Championship, which includes the Breeders Cup races. Arlington's race days are thrilling to behold, with all of racing's time-honored pageantry on display—from the bugler in traditional dress to the parade of jockeys.

Arlington likes to say that it caters to families, and the ambience is more Disney than den of iniquity. "Family days" throughout the summer include live music and entertainment ranging from petting zoos to puppet shows.

2200 W. Euclid Ave., Arlington Heights. © 847/385-7500. www.arlingtonpark.com. May–Sept Wed–Sun gates open 11am, 1st post 1pm. No racing Oct–Apr. Admission $6 adults; $3–$6 for reserved seating. Take the Kennedy (I-94) Expwy. to the I-90 tollway, and exit north on Rte. 53. Follow 53 north to the Euclid exit. Or, take Metra train to Arlington Heights. Free parking.

THE WESTERN SUBURBS

So many corporations have taken to locating their offices beyond the city limits that today more people work in the suburbs than commute into Chicago. Much of the suburban sprawl in counties such as DuPage and Kane consists of seas of aluminum-sided houses that seem to sprout from cornfields overnight. But there are also some lovely older towns, such as upscale **Hinsdale** and, much farther west, the quaint tandem of **St. Charles** and **Geneva,** which lie across the Fox River from each other. Perhaps there is no more fitting symbol of this booming area than the city of **Naperville.** A historic, formerly rural community with a Main Street U.S.A. downtown district worthy of Norman Rockwell, Naperville has exploded from a population of about 30,000 residents in the early 1970s to approximately 140,000 today—which makes it the third-largest municipality in the state. Naperville maintains a collection of 19th-century buildings in an outdoor setting known as Naper Settlement, and its river walk is the envy of neighboring village councils. But much of its yesteryear charm seems to be disappearing bit by bit as new subdivisions and strip malls ooze forth across the prairie.

Brookfield Zoo 🐾🐾 *(Kids)*   Brookfield is the Chicago area's largest zoo. In contrast to Lincoln Park Zoo, Brookfield is spacious, spreading out over 216 acres and housing thousands of animals—camels, dolphins, giraffes, baboons, wolves, tigers, green sea turtles, Siberian tigers, snow leopards, and more—in naturalistic environments that put them side by side with other inhabitants of their regions. These creative indoor and outdoor settings, filled with activities to keep kids interested, are what set Brookfield apart.

Start out at *Habitat Africa!* 🐾🐾, a multiple-ecosystem exhibit that encompasses 30 acres—about the size of the entire Lincoln Park Zoo. Then wander through some of the buildings that allow you to see animals close up; my personal favorites are *Tropic World* 🐾, where you hang out at treetop level with monkeys, and *Australia House,* where fruit bats flit around your head. *The Living Coast* 🐾🐾 explores the west coast of Chile and Peru, and includes everything from a tank of plate-size moon jellies to a rocky shore where Humboldt penguins swim and nest as Inca terns and gray gulls fly freely overhead. *The Swamp* re-creates the bioregions of a southern cypress swamp and an Illinois river scene and discusses what people can do to protect wetlands. The dolphins at the *Seven Seas Panorama* 🐾🐾 put on an amazing show that has been a Brookfield Zoo fixture for years. If you go on a weekend, buy tickets to the dolphin show at least a couple of hours before the one you plan to attend, because they tend to sell out quickly.

The **Hamill Family Play Zoo** is a wonderful stop for kids. They not only get to pet animals but can also build habitats, learn how to plant a garden, and even play animal dress-up. The only catch: the separate admission fee ($3.50 adults, $2.50 children). Allow 3 hours.

First Ave. and 31st St., Brookfield. ⓒ **708/485-0263.** www.brookfieldzoo.org. Admission $10 adults, $6 seniors and children 3–11, free for children 2 and under. Parking $8. Free admission Tues and Thurs Oct–Feb. Memorial Day–Labor Day daily 9:30am–6pm (Sun until 7:30pm); fall–spring daily 10am–5pm. Bus: 304 or 311. Take the Stevenson (I-55) and Eisenhower (I-290) expressways 14 miles west of the Loop.

8 Kid Stuff

Chicago Children's Museum 🐾🐾 *(Kids)*   Located on tourist-filled Navy Pier, this museum is one of the most popular family attractions in the city. The building has areas especially for preschoolers as well as for children up to age 10, and several permanent exhibits allow kids a maximum of hands-on fun. *Dinosaur Expedition* re-creates an expedition to the Sahara, allowing kids to experience camp life, conduct scientific research, and dig for the bones of Suchomimus, a Saharan dinosaur discovered by Chicago paleontologist Paul Sereno (a full-scale model stands nearby). There's also a **three-level schooner** that children can board for a little climbing, from the crow's nest to the gangplank; *PlayMaze,* a toddler-scale cityscape with everything from a gas station to a city bus that children under 5 can touch and explore; and an **arts-and-crafts area** where visitors can create original artwork to take home. Allow 2 to 3 hours.

Navy Pier, 700 E. Grand Ave. © 312/527-1000. www.chichildrensmuseum.org. Admission $8 adults and children, $7 seniors. Free admission Thurs 5–8pm. Mon–Fri 10am–5pm (Thurs until 8pm); Sat 10am–8pm; Sun 10am–5pm. Closed Thanksgiving and Dec 25. Bus: 29, 65, or 66. Subway/El: Red Line to Grand; transfer to city bus or Navy Pier's free trolley bus.

Lincoln Park Pritzker Children's Zoo & Farm-in-the-Zoo ⛲ (Value (Kids   After hours of looking at animals from afar in the rest of Lincoln Park Zoo, kids can come here to get up close and personal. Unlike many other children's zoos, there are no baby animals at the **Pritzker Children's Zoo;** instead, the outdoor habitats feature wildlife of the North American woods, including wolves, beavers, and otters. Although there are a few interactive displays outside, most kids head inside to the Treetop Canopy Climbing Adventure, a 20-foot high wood-and-fabric tree (encased in soft safety netting) that kids can scramble up and down. There are also a few small padded play areas for little ones.

The **Farm-in-the-Zoo** ⛲ is a working reproduction of a Midwestern farm, complete with a white-picket-fenced barnyard, chicken coops, and demonstrations of butter churning and weaving. You'll also spot plenty of livestock, including cows, sheep, and pigs. Inside the Main Barn (filled with interactive exhibits), the main attraction is the huge John Deere tractor that kids can climb up into and pretend to drive. (Can you say "photo opportunity"?) Allow 1 hour.

2200 N. Cannon Dr. © 312/742-2000. www.lpzoo.com. Free admission. Daily 9am–5pm. Bus: 151 or 156.

Six Flags Great America ⛲ (Kids   One of the Midwest's biggest theme and amusement parks, Six Flags is midway between Chicago and Milwaukee on I-94 in Gurnee, Illinois. The park has more than 100 rides and attractions and is a favorite of rollercoaster devotees. There are a whopping 10 of them here, including the nausea-inducing Déjà Vu, where riders fly forward and backward over a twisting, looping inverted steel track, and Superman, where you speed along hanging headfirst (with your legs dangling). Other don't-miss rides for the strong of stomach include the Iron Wolf, where you do corkscrew turns and 360-degree loops while standing up, and the American Eagle, a classic wooden coaster. Because this place caters to families, you'll also find plenty to appeal to smaller visitors. The Looney Tunes National Park is full of kiddie rides with a cartoon theme; other worthwhile stops include the double-decker carousel and bumper cars. Hurricane Harbor, a massive water park with a giant wave pool, is fun on a hot day, but you risk heatstroke waiting in the long lines. Six Flags also has live shows, IMAX movies, and restaurants. If you take the trouble to get out here, allow a full day.

I-94 at Rte. 132 East, Gurnee. © 847/249-4636. www.sixflags.com. Admission (including unlimited rides, shows, and attractions) $55 adults, $35 children under 54 in. tall, free for children 3 and under. May daily 10am–7pm; June–Aug daily 10am–10pm; Sept Sat–Sun 10am–7pm. Parking $10. Take I-94 or I-294 West to Rte. 132 (Grand Ave.). Approximate driving time from Chicago city limits: 45 min.

9 Sightseeing Tours

If you're in town for a limited time, an organized tour may be the best way to get a quick overview of the city's highlights. Some tours—such as the boat cruises on Lake Michigan and the Chicago River—can give you a whole new perspective on the city's landscape. Because Chicago caters to sophisticated travelers from all over the world, many tours go beyond sightseeing to explore important historical and architectural landmarks in depth. These specialized tours can help you appreciate buildings or neighborhoods that you might otherwise have passed by without a second glance.

For information about touring Eli's bakery, which manufactures Chicago's most famous cheesecake, see the "Dessert Tour" box on p. 135.

CARRIAGE RIDES

Noble Horse ((C) **312/266-7878**) maintains the largest fleet of antique horse carriages in Chicago, stationed around the old Water Tower Square at the northwest corner of Chicago and Michigan avenues. Each of the drivers, outfitted in a black tie and top hat, has his or her own variation on the basic Magnificent Mile itinerary (you can also do tours of the lakefront, river, Lincoln Park, and Buckingham Fountain). The charge is $35 for each half-hour for up to four people. The coaches run year-round, with convertible coaches in the warm months and enclosed carriages furnished with wool blankets on bone-chilling nights. There are several other carriage operators, all of whom pick up riders in the vicinity.

ORIENTATION TOURS

Chicago Trolley Company   Chicago Trolley Company offers guided tours on a fleet of rubber-wheeled "San Francisco–style" trolleys that stop at a number of popular spots around the city, including Navy Pier, the Grant Park museums, the historic Water Tower, and the Sears Tower. You can stay on for the full 2-hour ride, or get on and off at each stop. The trolleys operate year-round, but winter visitors won't need to wear a snowsuit: The vehicles are enclosed and heated during the chilliest months. The same company also operates the **Chicago Double Decker Company,** which has a fleet of London-style red buses. The two-level buses follow the same route as the trolleys; if you buy an all-day pass, you can hop from bus to trolley at any point.

(C) **773/648-5000.** www.chicagotrolley.com. All-day hop-on, hop-off pass $25 adults, $20 seniors, $10 children 3–11; family package (2 adults, 2 children) $64. Apr–Oct daily 9am–6:30pm; Nov–Mar daily 9am–5pm.

Gray Line   Part of a worldwide bus-tour company, Gray Line Chicago offers professional tours in well-appointed buses. Excursions run 2 to 5 hours and feature highlights of downtown or various neighborhoods. For an additional fee, some tours include a cruise on Lake Michigan or a visit to the Sears Tower Skydeck.

27 E. Monroe St., Suite 515. (C) **800/621-4153** or 312/251-3107. www.grayline.com. Tours $20–$50.

LAKE & RIVER CRUISES

Chicago from the Lake   This company runs two types of 90-minute cruises: a tour of architecture along the Chicago River, and excursions that travel on the lake and river to explore the development of the city. The price includes coffee (Starbucks, no less), lemonade, cookies, and muffins. For tickets, call or stop by the company's ticket office on the lower level on the east end of River East Plaza. Advance reservations are recommended.

465 N. McClurg Ct., at the end of E. Illinois St. (C) **312/527-1977.** www.chicagoline.com. Tickets $32 adults, $30 seniors, $18 children 7–18, free for children 6 and under. May–Oct daily. Tours depart hourly 9am–4pm Memorial Day to Labor Day; every 2 hr. 10am–4pm May, Sept, and Oct.

Mystic Blue Cruises   A more casual alternative to fancy dinner cruises, this is promoted as more of a "fun" ship (that means DJs at night, although you'll have to put up with some kind of "live entertainment" no matter when you sail). Daily lunch and dinner excursions are available, as are midnight voyages on weekends. The same company offers more formal (and expensive) cruises aboard the ***Odyssey*** (www.odysseycruises. com) and motorboat rides on the 70-passenger ***Seadog*** (www.seadogcruises.com), if you really want to feel the water in your face.

Departing from Navy Pier. ✆ 877/299-7783. www.mysticbluecruises.com. Lunch cruise $32–$37; dinner cruise $60–$80; midday cruise $25; moonlight cruise $30. Cruises run year-round.

Shoreline Sightseeing ⟲   Shoreline launches 30-minute lake cruises every half-hour from its two dock locations at the Shedd Aquarium and Navy Pier. Shoreline has also gotten in on the popularity of architecture tours. Narrated by architectural guides, they cost more than regular tours. A **water taxi** also runs every half-hour between Navy Pier and the Sears Tower, Michigan Avenue, and the Shedd Aquarium. Tickets for the water taxi cost $3 to $13, depending how far you travel.

Departing from Navy Pier, Shedd Aquarium, and Buckingham Fountain in Grant Park. ✆ 312/222-9328. www.shoreline sightseeing.com. Tickets weekdays $14 adults, $13 seniors, $6 children 11 and under ($1 more per ticket on weekends); architectural tours $24 adults, $21 seniors, $12 children 11 and under ($2 more per ticket on weekends). May–Sept daily. Tours depart hourly 10am–5:30pm Memorial Day to Labor Day; every 30 min. 10am–4pm May and Sept.

The Spirit of Chicago   This luxury yacht offers a variety of wining-and-dining harbor cruises, from a lunch buffet to the "Moonlight Dance Party." This can be a fairly pricey night out if you go for the dinner package; the late-night moonlight cruises are a more affordable option for insomniacs.

Departing from Navy Pier. ✆ 866/211-3804. www.spiritcruises.com. Lunch cruise $40–$50; dinner cruise (seated) $80–$110; sunset and midnight cruises $32. Ask about children's rates. Year-round daily.

Wendella Sightseeing Boats ⟲   Wendella is the granddaddy of Chicago sightseeing operators. Started in 1935, it's run by the original owner's son, Bob Borgstrom, whose own two sons serve as captains. You won't find a more authoritative source on the Chicago River than Borgstrom.

Wendella operates a 1-hour tour along the Chicago River and a 1½-hour tour along the river and out onto Lake Michigan. (One of the most dramatic events during the boat tours is passing through the locks that separate the river from the lake.) Boats run from late April to early October. The 2-hour sunset tour runs Memorial Day to Labor Day starting at 7:45pm. Scheduling depends on the season and the weather, but cruises usually leave every hour during the summer.

Departing from Michigan Ave. and Wacker Dr. (north side of the river, at the Wrigley Building). ✆ 312/337-1446. www. wendellaboats.com. Tickets $22 adults, $20 seniors, $11 children 3–11, free for children 2 and under. Apr–Oct daily.

Windy ⟲⟲   One of the more breathtaking scenes on the lake is this tall ship approaching the docks at Navy Pier. The 148-foot four-masted schooner (and its new sister ship, the *Windy II*) sets sail for 90-minute cruises two to five times a day, both day and evening. The boats are at the whims of the wind, so every cruise charts a different course. Passengers are welcome to help raise and trim the sails and occasionally take turns at the ship's helm (with the captain standing close by). The boats are not accessible for people with disabilities.

Departing from Navy Pier. ✆ 312/595-5555. Tickets $27 adults, $20 seniors and children 11 and under. Tickets go on sale 1 hr. before the 1st sail of the day at the ticket office, on the dock at Navy Pier. Reservations (except for groups) are not accepted. Call for sailing times.

SPECIAL-INTEREST TOURS

Chicago Architecture Foundation ⟲⟲⟲   Chicago's architecture is world famous. Luckily, the Chicago Architecture Foundation offers first-rate guided tours to help visitors understand what makes this city's skyline so special. The foundation offers walking, bike, boat, and bus tours to more than 60 architectural sites and environments in and around Chicago, led by nearly 400 trained and enthusiastic docents (all volunteers). I highly recommend taking at least one CAF tour while you're in town—they help you look at (and appreciate) the city in a new way. Tours are available year-round but are scheduled less frequently in winter.

One of the CAF's most popular tours is the 1½-hour **Architecture River Cruise,** which glides along both the north and the south branches of the Chicago River. Although you can see the same 50 or so buildings by foot, traveling by water lets you enjoy the buildings from a unique perspective. The excellent docents also provide interesting historical details, as well as some fun facts (David Letterman once called the busts of the nation's retailing legends that face the Merchandise Mart the "Pez Hall of Fame"). The docents generally do a good job of making the cruise enjoyable for visitors with all levels of architectural knowledge. In addition to pointing out buildings—Marina City, the Civic Opera House, the Sears Tower—they approach the sites thematically, explaining, for example, how Chicagoans' use of and attitudes toward the river have changed over time.

Tours are $26 per person weekdays, $28 on weekends and holidays, and begin hourly every day June through October from 11am to 3pm (with more limited schedules in May and Nov). The trips are extremely popular, so purchase tickets in advance through **Ticketmaster** (📞 **312/902-1500;** www.ticketmaster.com), or avoid the service charge and buy tickets at one of the foundation's tour centers or from the boat launch on the southeast corner of Michigan Avenue and Wacker Drive.

If you want to squeeze a lot of sightseeing into a limited time, try **Highlights by Bus,** a 3½-hour overview tour that covers the Loop, Hyde Park—including a visit to the interior of Frank Lloyd Wright's Robie House—and the Gold Coast, plus several other historic districts. Tours start at 9:30am on Wednesday, Friday, Saturday, and Sunday April through November (Sat only Dec–Mar). Tickets are $38 per person.

A 4-hour bus tour of Frank Lloyd Wright sights in **Oak Park** ($40) is available on the first Saturday of the month from May to October. The tour includes walks through three neighborhoods and commentary on more than 25 houses—but does not take visitors inside Wright's home and studio. A separate 4-hour bus tour ($45), on Tuesday at 9:30am (June–Oct), takes Wright fans inside the master's home and Oak Park's Unity Temple.

If you prefer exploring on your own, the CAF offers a variety of guided walking tours. For first-time visitors, I highly recommend two tours for an excellent introduction to the dramatic architecture of the Loop. **Historic Skyscrapers** (daily 10am) covers buildings built between 1880 and 1940, including the Rookery and the Chicago Board of Trade; **Modern Skyscrapers** (daily 1pm) includes modern masterpieces by Mies van der Rohe and postmodern works by contemporary architects. The 2-hour tours cost $15 each for adults and $12 each for seniors and students.

The CAF also offers more than 50 **neighborhood tours,** visiting the Gold Coast, River North, Grant Park, Old Town, the Jackson Boulevard Historic District, and even Lincoln Park Zoo. Most cost $10 and last a couple of hours.

Departing from the Chicago ArchiCenter, 224 S. Michigan Ave.; a few tours leave from the John Hancock Center, 875 N. Michigan Ave. 📞 **312/922-3432,** or 312/922-TOUR for recorded information. www.architecture.org. Tickets for most walking tours $10–$15. Subway/El: Brown, Green, Purple, or Orange line to Adams, or Red Line to Jackson.

Finds **The Wright Stuff in the Gold Coast**

Architecture junkies may want to visit the **Charnley-Persky House,** 1365 N. Astor St., in the Gold Coast (© **312/915-0105** or 312/573-1365), designed by Frank Lloyd Wright and Louis Sullivan in 1891. Free 45-minute tours of the interior are given on Wednesday at noon. A 90-minute tour of the home and the surrounding neighborhood is offered Saturdays at 10am year-round ($10); an additional tour is given at 1pm April through November. Reservations are not accepted.

Untouchable Tours   The days of Al Capone are long gone, but Chicago's notorious past is still good for business, it seems, given the popularity of these "Gangster Tours." The 2-hour bus trip takes you to all of the city's old hoodlum hangouts from the Prohibition era, including O'Bannion's flower shop, the site of the St. Valentine's Day massacre. The focus is definitely more on entertainment than history (guides with names such as "Al Dente" and "Ice Pick" appear in costume and role-play their way through the tour), but the trip does give you a pretty thorough overview of the city.

Departs from the southeast corner of Clark and Ohio sts. © **773/881-1195**. www.gangstertour.com. $25 adults, $19 children. Tours depart Mon–Wed 10am; Thurs 10am and 1pm; Fri 10am, 1 and 7:30pm; Sat 10am, 1 and 5pm; Sun 10am and 1pm.

Chicago Supernatural Tours   An offbeat way to experience the real "spirit" of Chicago is to take a narrated bus tour of cemeteries, murder sites, Indian burial grounds, haunted pubs, and other spooky places. Richard Crowe, who bills himself as a "professional ghost hunter," spins ghost stories, legends, and lore on the 4-hour trip. Yes, there's plenty of shtick, but Crowe really knows his stuff, so you'll get an informative history lesson along the way. Reservations are required; Crowe's tours get especially popular around Halloween, so you'll definitely want to call ahead.

Crowe also leads 2-hour **supernatural boat excursions** from July through Labor Day weekend; the tour costs $25 per person and boards at 9:30pm at the Mercury boat dock at Michigan Avenue and Wacker Drive.

Departs from Goose Island Restaurant, 1800 N. Clybourn Ave. © **708/499-0300**. www.ghosttours.com. $39 per person. Tours offered once or twice a month Fri–Sat nights; call for exact schedule. Subway/El: Red Line to North/Clybourn and short walk.

NEIGHBORHOOD TOURS

It's a bit of a cliché to say that Chicago is a city of neighborhoods, but if you want to see what really makes the place special, that's where you have to go.

Sponsored by the city's Department of Cultural Affairs, **Chicago Neighborhood Tours** ⚐ (© **312/742-1190;** www.chgocitytours.com) are 4- to 5-hour narrated bus excursions to about a dozen diverse communities throughout the city. Departing at 10am from the Chicago Cultural Center, 77 E. Randolph St., every Saturday, the tours visit different neighborhoods, from Chinatown and historic Bronzeville on the South Side to the ethnic enclaves of Devon Avenue and Uptown on the North Side. Neighborhood representatives serve as guides and greeters along the way as tour participants visit area landmarks, murals, museums, and shopping districts. Tickets (including a light snack) are $25 for adults and $20 for seniors, students, and children

8 to 18. Tours do not run on major holidays (call first) or, usually, in January. Regularly available specialty tours include Literary Chicago; the Great Chicago Fire; Roots of Blues, Gospel & Jazz; Threads of Ireland; Jewish Legacy; and an Ethnic Cemetery tour. These tours, which generally run about 4 to 6 hours and include lunch, are more expensive ($50 adults, $45 seniors and children).

On Saturday mornings in the summer, the **Chicago History Museum** offers 2-hour walking tours of the neighborhoods surrounding the museum: the **Gold Coast, Old Town,** and **Lincoln Park.** Led by museum docents, they average about four per month June through August. Day and evening tours are available, and a few specialty walking tours are usually offered as well. Tours are $10 per person, and registration is recommended but not required. Tours depart from the museum at Clark Street and North Avenue, and light refreshments are served afterward. In the summer and fall, the museum also offers a few half-day trolley tours that cover unique themes or aspects of the metropolitan area's history. Led by historians and scholars, they take place in the city and surrounding areas ($40). Tours depart from the Chicago History Museum at Clark Street and North Avenue. Call ℭ **312/642-4600,** or visit the museum's website (www.chicagohistory.org) for schedules and to order tickets online.

Groups can arrange tours of Chicago's **"Black Metropolis,"** the name given to a South Side area of Bronzeville where African Americans created a flourishing business-and-artistic community after World War II. Contact **Tour Black Chicago** (ℭ 773/684-9034; www.tourblackchicago.com) for more information.

CEMETERY TOURS

Don't be scared away by the creepy connotations. Some of Chicago's cemeteries are as pretty as parks, and they offer a variety of intriguing monuments that are a virtual road into the city's history.

One of the best area cemeteries is **Graceland,** stretching along Clark Street in the Swedish neighborhood of Andersonville, where you can view the tombs and monuments of many Chicago notables. When Graceland was laid out in 1860, public parks were rare. The elaborate burial grounds that were constructed in many large American cities around that time had the dual purpose of relieving the congestion of the municipal cemeteries closer to town and providing pastoral recreational settings for the Sunday outings of the living. Indeed, cemeteries like Graceland were the precursors of such great municipal green spaces as Lincoln Park. Much of Lincoln Park, in fact, had been a public cemetery since Chicago's earliest times. (Many who once rested there were re-interred in Graceland when the building of Lincoln Park went forward.)

The **Chicago Architecture Foundation** (ℭ **312/922-TOUR;** www.architecture.org) offers walking tours of Graceland on select Sundays during August, September, and October. The tour costs $10 and lasts about 2 hours. Among the points of interest in these 121 beautifully landscaped acres are the Ryerson and Getty tombs, famous architectural monuments designed by Louis Sullivan. Sullivan himself rests here in the company of several of his distinguished colleagues: Daniel Burnham, Ludwig Mies van der Rohe, and Howard Van Doren Shaw. Chicago giants of industry and commerce buried at Graceland include Potter Palmer, Marshall Field, and George Pullman. The Chicago Architecture Foundation offers tours of other cemeteries including Rosehill Cemetery, suburban Lake Forest Cemetery, and Oak Woods Cemetery, the final resting place for many famous African-American figures, including Jesse Owens, Ida B. Wells, and Mayor Harold Washington.

10 Staying Active

Perhaps because winters can be brutal, Chicagoans take their summers seriously. In the warmer months, with the wide blue lake and the ample green parks, it's easy to think that the city is one big grown-up playground. Whether you prefer your activity in the water or on dry ground, you'll probably find it here. For information, contact the city's park district (© 312/742-PLAY; www.chicagoparkdistrict.com); for questions about the 29 miles of beaches and parks along Lake Michigan, call the park district's lakefront region office at © 312/747-2474.

Another handy resource is *Windy City Sports* (© 312/421-1551; www.windycity sports.com), a free monthly publication available at many retail shops, grocery stores, bars, and cafes.

BEACHES

Public beaches line Lake Michigan all the way up north into the suburbs and Wisconsin, and southeast through Indiana and into Michigan. The best known is **Oak Street Beach.** Its location, at the northern tip of the Magnificent Mile, creates some interesting sights as sun worshippers sporting swimsuits and carting coolers make their way down Michigan Avenue. The most popular is **North Avenue Beach,** about 6 blocks farther north, which has developed into a volleyball hot spot and recently rebuilt its landmark steamship-shaped beach house and added a Venice Beach–style outdoor gym; this is where the Lincoln Park singles come to play, check each other out, and fly by on bikes and in-line skates. **Hollywood-Ardmore Beach** (officially Kathy Osterman Beach), at the northern end of Lake Shore Drive, is a lovely crescent that's less congested and has steadily become more popular with gays who've moved up the lakefront from the Belmont Rocks, a longtime hangout. For more seclusion, try **Ohio Street Beach,** an intimate sliver of sand in tiny Olive Park, just north of Navy Pier, which, incredibly enough, remains largely ignored despite its central location. If you have a car, head up to **Montrose Beach,** a beautiful unsung treasure about midway between North Avenue Beach and Hollywood-Ardmore Beach (with plenty of free parking). Long popular with the city's Hispanic community, it has an expanse of beach mostly uninterrupted by piers or jetties, and a huge adjacent park with soccer fields, one big hill that's great for kite flying, and even a small bait shop where anglers can go before heading to a nearby long pier designated for fishing.

If you've brought the pooch along, you might want to take him for a dip at the **doggie beach** south of Addison Street, at about Hawthorne and Lake Shore Drive (although this minute spot aggravates some dog owners because it's in a harbor where the water is somewhat fouled by gas and oil from nearby boats). *A tip:* Try the south end of North Avenue Beach in early morning, before it opens to the public for the day. (Also consider that, in the off season, all beaches are fair game for dogs. The police won't hassle you, I promise.)

Beaches officially open with a full retinue of lifeguards on duty around June 20, though swimmers can wade into the chilly water from Memorial Day to Labor Day. Only the bravest souls venture into the water before July, when the temperature creeps up enough to make swimming an attractive proposition. Please take note that the entire lakefront is not beach, and don't go do anything stupid such as dive off the rocks.

BIKING

Biking is a great way to see the city, particularly along the lakefront bike path that extends for more than 18 miles. The stretch between Navy Pier and North Avenue Beach gets extremely crowded in the summer (you're jostling for space with in-line skaters, joggers, and dawdling pedestrians). If you're looking to pick up some speed, I recommend biking south (once you're past the Museum Campus, the trail is relatively wide open, and you can zip all the way to Hyde Park). If you want a more leisurely tour with people-watching potential, head north (through the crowds). After you pass Belmont Harbor, the traffic lets up a bit. Ride all the way to Hollywood Beach (where the lakefront trail ends) for a good but not exhausting workout.

To rent bikes, try **Bike Chicago** (www.bikechicago.com), which has locations at Navy Pier (© **312/595-9600**), North Avenue Beach (© **773/327-2706**), and Millennium Park (© **888/BIKE-WAY**). Open from 8am to 8pm May through October (weather permitting), Bike Chicago stocks mountain and touring bikes, kids' bikes, strollers, and—most fun of all—quadcycles, which are four-wheel contraptions equipped with a steering wheel and canopy that can accommodate four or five people. Rates for bikes start at $8.75 an hour, $34 a day, with helmets, pads, and locks included. If you'd like to cycle your way past some Chicago landmarks, guided tours are also available.

Both the park district (© **312/742-PLAY**) and the **Chicagoland Bicycle Federation** (© **312/42-PEDAL;** www.chibikefed.org) offer free maps that detail popular biking routes. The latter, which is the preeminent organization for cyclists in Chicago, sells a much larger, more extensive map ($6.95) that shows routes within a seven-county area. The federation sponsors a number of bike rides throughout the year, including the highly enjoyable **Boulevard Lakefront Tour,** held in mid-September, which follows the historic circle of boulevards that had their genesis in the Chicago Plan of 1909. It starts in Hyde Park at the University of Chicago campus.

A word of caution: Never head anywhere on the city's streets without first strapping on a helmet. Chicago Mayor Richard M. Daley, an avid cyclist, has tirelessly promoted the addition of designated bike lanes along many main thoroughfares, but most cabbies and drivers tend to ignore them. Bike with extreme caution on city streets (you can get a ticket for biking on the sidewalk), and stick to the lakefront path if you're not an expert rider. Locking your bike anywhere you go is a no-brainer.

GOLFING

For a major metropolis, Chicago has an impressive number of golf options within the city limits (not to mention many plush and pricey suburban courses). The closest you'll get to golfing downtown is **The Green at Grant Park** (© **312/642-7888;** www.thegreenonline.com), an 18-hole putting course on Monroe Street between Columbus Avenue and Lake Shore Drive, just east of Millennium Park. It's not exactly tournament-level play, but it's more challenging than miniature golf—and the setting can't be beat. The course is open daily from 10am to 10pm, and putters and golf balls are provided. Rates are $9 per round for adults, $6 for children under 13.

To warm up your swing, head to the **Diversey Driving Range,** 141 W. Diversey Pkwy. (© **312/742-7929**), in Lincoln Park just north of Diversey Harbor. This two-level range attracts all levels—from show-off heavy hitters to beginners—and is very popular on weekends with young singles who live in the surrounding apartment buildings. The price is right ($11 for a bucket of 100 balls), and the setting is pretty much perfect.

The Chicago Park District runs six golf courses in the city. One of the most popular is the 9-hole **Sydney Marovitz Course,** 3600 N. Lake Shore Dr. (at Waveland Ave.), which many Chicagoans simply call Waveland. Thanks to its picturesque lakefront location, it's always full on weekends, so make a reservation well in advance (and don't expect a quick game—this is where beginners come to practice). Another good bet—and usually less crowded—is the 18-hole course in **Jackson Park** on the South Side (63rd St. and Stoney Island Ave.). These city-run courses are open from mid-April through November; for information on greens fees, location, and hours, call the **Chicago Park District** golf office (© 312/245-0909; www.cpdgolf.com).

For information about suburban golf courses, visit the website of the **Chicago District Golf Association** (www.cdga.org).

ICE SKATING

The city's premier skating destination is the **McCormick-Tribune Ice Rink** at Millennium Park, 55 N. Michigan Ave. (© 312/742-5222). The location is pretty much perfect: You're skating in the shadows of grand skyscrapers and within view of the lake. The rink is open daily from 10am to 10pm November through March. Admission is free, and skate rentals are $7.

The park district runs dozens of other skating surfaces throughout the city, along the lakefront and in neighborhood parks. Call © 312/742-PLAY for locations. There's also a relatively small rink at **Navy Pier,** 600 E. Grand Ave. (© 312/595-PIER).

IN-LINE SKATING

The wheeled ones have been taking over Chicago's sidewalks, streets, and bike paths since the early 1990s. Numerous rental places have popped up, and several sporting-goods shops that sell in-line skates also rent them. Rentals generally include helmets and pads. **Bike Chicago,** with locations at Navy Pier (© 312/595-9600), North Avenue Beach (© 773/327-2706), and Millennium Park (© 888/BIKE-WAY), charges $8.75 an hour or $34 a day (8am–8pm). **Londo Mondo,** 1100 N. Dearborn St. (© 312/751-2794), on the Gold Coast, rents blades for $7 an hour or $20 a day.

The best route to skate is the lakefront trail that leads from Lincoln Park down to Oak Street Beach. Beware, though, that those same miles of trail are claimed by avid cyclists—I've seen plenty of collisions between 'bladers and bikers. Approach Chicago lakefront traffic as carefully as you would a major expressway.

SAILING

It seems a shame just to sit on the beach and watch all those beautiful sailboats gliding across the lake, so go on, get out there. **Chicago Sailing,** in Belmont Harbor (© 773/871-SAIL; www.chicagosailing.com), rents J-22 and J-30 boats from 9am to sunset, weather permitting, May through October. A J-22, which holds four or five adults, rents for $45 to $65 an hour; a J-30, which accommodates up to 10 people, costs $80 to $100 per hour. If you want to take the boat out without a skipper, you need to demonstrate your skills first (for an additional $15 fee). If you'd rather sit back and relax, you can charter a boat. Reservations are recommended.

SWIMMING

The Chicago Park District maintains about 30 indoor pools for lap swimming and general splashing around, but none is particularly convenient to downtown. The lakefront is open for swimming until 9:30pm Memorial Day to Labor Day in areas watched over by lifeguards (no swimming off the rocks, please). ***But be forewarned:***

The water is usually freezing. A good place for lake swimming is the water along the wall beginning at Ohio Street Beach, slightly northwest of Navy Pier. The Chicago Triathlon Club marks a course here each summer with a buoy at both the quarter- and half-mile distances. This popular swimming route follows the shoreline in a straight line. The water is fairly shallow. For more information, call the park district's beach and pool office (© **312/742-PLAY**).

WINDSURFING

Chicago's gusty breezes are welcomed by those windsurfing along the waves of Lake Michigan. This isn't the place for beginners, though: If you decide to give it a try, sign up for private lessons with **Windward Sports,** 3317 N. Clark St. (© **773/472-6868;** www.windwardsports.com). Classes ($50/hr.) are offered on weekends from May through August and usually fill up, so call for reservations as far in advance as possible.

11 In the Grandstand: Watching Chicago's Athletic Events

BASEBALL

Baseball is imprinted on the national consciousness as part of Chicago, not because of victorious dynasties but because of the opposite—the Black Sox scandal of 1919 and the perennially losing Cubs.

The **Chicago Cubs** haven't made a World Series appearance since 1945 and haven't been world champs since 1908, but that doesn't stop people from catching games at **Wrigley Field** ✸✸, with its ivy-covered outfield walls, its hand-operated scoreboard, its view of the shimmering lake from the upper deck, and its "W" or "L" flag announcing the outcome of the game to the unfortunates who couldn't attend. After all the strikes, temper tantrums, and other nonsense, Wrigley has managed to hold on to something like purity. Yes, Wrigley finally installed lights (it was the last major-league park to do so), but by agreement with the residential neighborhood, the Cubs still play most games in the daylight, as they should. Because Wrigley is small, just about every seat is decent.

No matter how the Cubs are doing, tickets ($15–$50) go fast; most weekend and night games sell out by Memorial Day. Your best bet is to hit a weekday game, or try your luck buying a ticket on game day outside the park (you'll often find some season-ticket holders looking to unload a few seats).

Wrigley Field, 1060 W. Addison St. (© **773/404-CUBS;** www.cubs.mlb.com), is easy to reach. Take the Red Line to the Addison stop, and you're there. Or take the no. 22 bus, which runs up Clark Street. To buy tickets in person, stop by the ticket windows at Wrigley Field, Monday through Friday from 9am to 6pm, Saturday from 9am to 4pm, and on game days. Call © **800/THE-CUBS** for tickets through **Tickets. com** (© **866/652-2827** outside of Illinois); you can also order online through the team website.

Despite their stunning World Series win in 2005, the **Chicago White Sox** still struggle to attract the same kind of loyalty (despite the fact that they regularly win more games than the Cubs). Longtime fans rue the day owner Jerry Reinsdorf (who is also majority owner of the Bulls) replaced admittedly dilapidated Comiskey Park with a concrete behemoth that lacks the yesteryear charm of its predecessor. That said, sightlines at the new stadium, **U.S. Cellular Field,** are spectacular from every seat (if you avoid the vertigo-inducing upper deck), and the park has every conceivable amenity, including above-average food concessions, shops, and plentiful restrooms.

⎛Moments⎞ Field of Dreams

Wrigley Field is one of the last old-time baseball stadiums in the country (no luxury boxes here!). For an intimate look at the historic ballpark, take one of the tours offered on various Saturdays throughout the summer; stops include the visitors' and home-team locker rooms, press box, behind-the-scenes security headquarters, and, yes, a walk around the field itself. Tours sell out, so buy tickets ($20) as far in advance as possible. Call ℂ **800/THE-CUBS,** or stop by the box office at 1060 W. Addison St.

The White Sox' endearing quality is the blue-collar aura with which so many Cubs-loathing Southsiders identify. Games rarely sell out—an effect, presumably, of Reinsdorf's sterile stadium and the blighted neighborhood that surrounds it. All of this makes it a bargain for bona fide baseball fans. Tickets cost $12 to $45 and are half-price on Monday.

U.S. Cellular Field is at 333 W. 35th St. (ℂ **312/674-1000;** www.whitesox.mlb.com), in the South Side neighborhood of Bridgeport. To get Sox tickets, call **Ticketmaster** (ℂ **866/SOX-GAME**), or visit the ticket office, open Monday through Friday from 10am to 6pm, Saturday and Sunday from 10am to 4pm, with extended hours on game days. To get to the ballpark by subway/El, take the Red Line to Sox/35th Street.

BASKETBALL

When it comes to basketball, Chicagoans still live in the past, associating the **Chicago Bulls** (ℂ **312/455-4000**) with the glory days of Michael Jordan and the never-ending championships of the 1990s. Although the team has rebounded somewhat from the dismal seasons following the departure of Jordan et al., the current players don't inspire the same city-wide excitement. The upside for visitors? The Bulls don't consistently sell out, which means you might be able to catch a game at the cavernous **United Center,** 1901 W. Madison St. (ℂ **312/455-4500;** www.chicagosports.com). Most tickets run $20 to $100 through **Ticketmaster** ℂ **312/559-1212**).

The **DePaul Blue Demons,** the local college team, are another good bet. They play mostly at the **Allstate Arena,** 6920 N. Mannheim Rd., Rosemont (ℂ **773/325-7526**), and sometimes at the United Center.

FOOTBALL

The **Chicago Bears** play at **Soldier Field,** Lake Shore Drive and 16th Street (ℂ **847/295-6600;** www.chicagobears.com), site of a controversial renovation that added what looks like a giant space ship on top of the original stadium's elegant colonnade. Architecturally, it's a disaster, but from a comfort perspective, the place is much improved—although that doesn't impress longtime fans who prided themselves on surviving blistering-cold game days and horrifying bathrooms. The Bears themselves have been inspiring high hopes—most recently, winning a trip to the Superbowl in 2007. But even during losing seasons, tickets are hard to come by (most are snapped up by season-ticket holders long before the season starts). If you plan ahead, individual tickets run $45 to $300; expensive seats are usually available through ticket brokers or online sites.

The **Northwestern Wildcats** play Big Ten college ball at **Ryan Field,** 1501 Central St., in nearby Evanston (© **847/491-CATS**).

HOCKEY

The **Chicago Blackhawks** have devoted, impassioned fans who work themselves into a frenzy with the first note of "The Star-Spangled Banner," but don't expect heroics that challenge the exploits of past Hawks legends such as Bobby Hull and Tony Esposito. Any player who turns into a star and, hence, earns the right to restructure his contract for a higher salary, is immediately traded by penny-pinching owner Bill Wirtz—derided by fans and local sportswriters as "Dollar Bill." The Blackhawks play at the **United Center,** 1901 W. Madison St. (© **312/455-7000;** www.chicagoblackhawks.com). Tickets cost $15 to $100.

For a more affordable and family-friendly experience, catch the semipro **Chicago Wolves** at Allstate Arena, 6920 N. Mannheim Rd., Rosemont (© **847/724-GOAL;** www.chicagowolves.com). The team has been consistently excellent over the past few years, and the games are geared toward all ages, with fireworks beforehand and plenty of on- and off-ice entertainment (tickets $13–$30).

HORSE RACING

Thoroughbreds race at **Arlington International Racecourse** (p. 210), 2200 W. Euclid Ave., Arlington Heights (© **847/385-7500;** www.arlingtonpark.com), and **Hawthorne Race Course,** 3501 S. Laramie Ave., Stickney (© **708/780-3700;** www.sportsmans park.com).

SOCCER

Chicago's Major League Soccer team, the **Chicago Fire,** plays at its own 20,000-seat stadium in suburban Bridgeview (about 12 miles southwest of downtown). The season runs from late May through October (© **888/MLS-FIRE;** http://chicago.fire.mlsnet.com). Games have a family feel, with plenty of activities for kids and affordable ticket prices ($15–$40).

9

Shopping

Forget Rodeo Drive or Fifth Avenue—Chicago is the country's original shopping center. As the United States expanded westward, catalogs from Chicago-based Sears and Montgomery Ward made clothes, books, and housewares accessible to even the most remote frontier towns. Department store magnate Marshall Field operated his namesake department store here, which opened in 1852, under the motto "Give the lady what she wants." Field pioneered many customer-service policies that are now standard, such as hassle-free returns.

Today Montgomery Ward is no more (and Marshall Field's has been taken over by Macy's), but downtown Chicago still draws hordes of shoppers (as anyone who's tried to walk quickly down Michigan Ave. on a busy summer Saturday can attest to). From the fine furniture showrooms at the imposing Merchandise Mart to the who's who of designer boutiques lining Oak Street and Michigan Avenue, the quality of stores in Chicago is top-notch. Because so many of the best are concentrated in one easy-to-walk area, the convenience of shopping in Chicago is unmatched.

This chapter concentrates on the Magnificent Mile, State Street, and several trendy neighborhoods, where you'll find one-of-a-kind shops and boutiques that make shopping here such an adventure.

SHOPPING HOURS As a general rule, store hours are 10am to 6 or 7pm Monday through Saturday, and noon to 6pm Sunday. Neighborhood stores tend to keep later hours, as do some of the stores along Michigan Avenue, which cater to after-work shoppers as well as tourists. Almost all stores have extended hours during the holiday season. Nearly all the stores in the Loop are open for daytime shopping only, generally from 9 or 10am to no later than 6pm Monday through Saturday. (The few remaining big downtown department stores have some selected evening hours.) Many Loop stores not on State Street are closed Saturday; on Sunday the Loop—except for a few restaurants, theaters, and cultural attractions—shuts down.

SALES TAX You might do a double take after checking the total on your purchase: At 9%, the state and local sales tax on nonfood items is one of the steepest in the country.

1 Shopping the Magnificent Mile

The nickname "Magnificent Mile"—hyperbole to some, an understatement to others—refers to the roughly mile-long stretch of North Michigan Avenue between Oak Street and the Chicago River.

The density of the area's first-rate shopping is, quite simply, unmatched. Even jaded shoppers from other worldly capitals are delighted at the ease and convenience of the

Magnificent Mile & Gold Coast Shopping

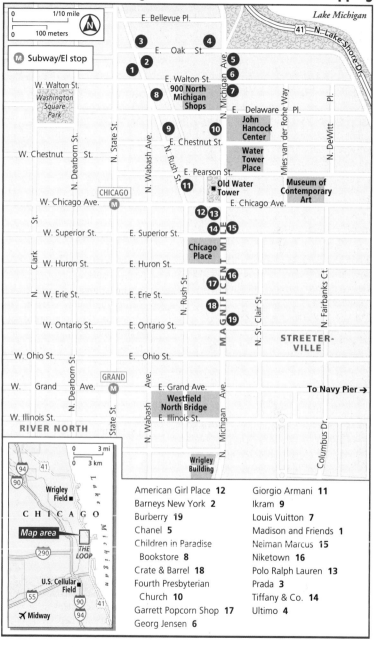

American Girl Place **12**
Barneys New York **2**
Burberry **19**
Chanel **5**
Children in Paradise
  Bookstore **8**
Crate & Barrel **18**
Fourth Presbyterian
  Church **10**
Garrett Popcorn Shop **17**
Georg Jensen **6**

Giorgio Armani **11**
Ikram **9**
Louis Vuitton **7**
Madison and Friends **1**
Neiman Marcus **15**
Niketown **16**
Polo Ralph Lauren **13**
Prada **3**
Tiffany & Co. **14**
Ultimo **4**

stores concentrated here. Taking into account that tony Oak Street (see below) is just around the corner, the overall area is a little like New York's Fifth Avenue and Beverly Hills's Rodeo Drive rolled into one. Whether your passion is Bulgari jewelry, Prada bags, or Salvatore Ferragamo footwear, you'll find it on this stretch of concrete. And don't think you're seeing everything by walking down the street: Michigan Avenue is home to several indoor, high-rise malls, where plenty more boutiques and restaurants are tucked away. Even if you're not the shop-till-you-drop type, it's worth a stroll because this stretch is, in many ways, the heart of the city, a place that bustles with life year-round (although it's especially crowded around Christmas and during the summer).

For the ultimate Mag Mile shopping adventure, start at one end of North Michigan Avenue and try to work your way to the other. Below I've listed some of the best-known shops on the avenue and nearby side streets.

A NORTH MICHIGAN AVENUE SHOPPER'S STROLL

This shopper's stroll begins at Oak Street at the northern end of the avenue and heads south toward the river. It just hits the highlights; you'll find much more to tempt your wallet as you meander from designer landmarks to well-known chain stores. (In general, this is not the place to pick up distinctive, one-of-a-kind items—other neighborhoods described later in this chapter cater more to shoppers searching for something unique). North Michigan Avenue's four vertical malls—each a major shopping destination in its own right—are discussed below under "The Magnificent Malls."

The parade of designer names begins at the intersection of Michigan Avenue and Oak Street, including a couple housed in The Drake Hotel, such as the legendary Danish silversmith **Georg Jensen,** 959 N. Michigan Ave. (✆ 312/642-9160), known for outstanding craftsmanship in sterling silver and gold, including earrings, brooches, watches, tie clips, and flatware; and **Chanel,** 935 N. Michigan Ave. (✆ 312/787-5500). One block south is another luxury emporium, the spacious **Louis Vuitton** store at 919 N. Michigan Ave. (✆ 312/944-2010), where you'll find trendy handbags and the company's distinctive monogrammed luggage.

On the other side of the street, opposite the dark, soaring Hancock Building, you'll find a quiet oasis that's worth a quick peek. The **Fourth Presbyterian Church,** 126 E. Chestnut St. (✆ 312/787-4570), looks like something out of an English country village, with a Gothic stone exterior and a peaceful, flower-filled courtyard (perfect for escaping the Mag Mile crowds for a few moments).

Giorgio Armani's sleek boutique, 800 N. Michigan Ave., in the Park Hyatt Hotel (✆ 312/573-4220), faces the small park next to the historic Water Tower. Across the street, a few doors west of Michigan Avenue, is one of Chicago's hottest family destinations: **American Girl Place,** at 111 E. Chicago Ave. (✆ 877/AG-PLACE). The three-story doll emporium attracts hordes of young girls (and parents) hooked on the popular mail-order company's line of historic character dolls. A stage show brings stories from the American Girl books to life, and the store's cafe is a nice spot for a special mother-daughter lunch or afternoon tea.

The next block of Michigan Avenue has a New York vibe, thanks to the world's largest **Polo Ralph Lauren,** 750 N. Michigan Ave. (✆ 312/280-1655), a four-floor, wood-paneled minimansion, and **Tiffany & Co.,** 730 N. Michigan Ave. (✆ 312/944-7500), with its signature clock, jewels, and tabletop accessories (if you want to get your hands on one of the coveted robin's-egg blue shopping bags without spending a fortune, the $80 sterling-silver key chains are the least expensive items in the store).

(*Moments* **Resting at Crate & Barrel**

Need a quick break during your shopping spree? The overstuffed couches on the third and fourth floors of Crate & Barrel practically beg to be tested out—and there are always at least a few weary shoppers slumped against the piles of pillows. Go ahead and rest awhile; the store's staff won't bug you. Make sure you stop by the terrace on the fourth floor for a bird's-eye view of Michigan Avenue, and enjoy a moment of contemplation before rejoining the hordes below.

A few doors south are **Neiman Marcus,** 737 N. Michigan Ave. (**(** **312/642-5900**), and at 669 N. Michigan Ave. (**(** **312/642-6363**), the hugely popular **Niketown,** a multilevel complex that helped pioneer the concept of retail as entertainment. Across the street, you'll probably see a line of people trailing out from the **Garrett Popcorn Shop,** 670 N. Michigan Ave. (**(** **312/944-2630**), a 50-year-old landmark. Join the locals in line and pick up some caramel corn for a quick sugar rush.

At the intersection of Michigan Avenue and Erie Street is the appropriately barrel-shaped **Crate & Barrel,** 646 N. Michigan Ave. (**(** **312/787-5900**). Crate & Barrel was started in Chicago, so this is the company's flagship location. Countless varieties of glassware, dishes, cookware, and kitchen gadgets for everyday use line the shelves. The top two floors are devoted to furniture.

Continuing south, you'll find **Burberry,** 633 N. Michigan Ave. (**(** **312/787-2500**), where the classic beige plaid shows up on chic purses, shoes, and bathing suits (if you're looking for luxury souvenirs, check out the collection of baby clothes and dog accessories).

THE MAGNIFICENT MALLS

Many of the Magnificent Mile's shops are hidden inside high-rise malls, most of which take up a whole city block. Here's a quick guide to what you'll find inside.

Chicago Place   This mall's main claim to fame is as the home of upscale retailer **Saks Fifth Avenue** (p. 243). The rest of the stores here are not as exclusive; in fact, the mall as a whole lacks a clear identity. You'll find a few home-decor and clothing stores here—but the main draw is the food court on the top floor (see box, "Lunch on the Mag Mile). 700 N. Michigan Ave. (between Superior and Huron sts.). **(** 312/642-4811. Subway/El: Red Line to Chicago.

900 North Michigan Shops   The most upscale of the Magnificent Mile's four vertical malls, 900 North Michigan (often called the Bloomingdale's building, for its most prominent tenant), avoids the tumult of Water Tower Place by appealing to a more well-heeled shopper. In addition to about 70 stores, there are a few good restaurants and a movie theater on the lower level.

The Chicago outpost of **Gucci** (ground floor; **(** **312/664-5504**) has the same hip attitude as the label's sexy clothing and much-in-demand purses. Also on the ground floor is **MaxMara** (**(** **312/475-9500**), the Italian women's fashion house known for elegantly constructed coats and separates (some of which will cost you about as much as a flight to Italy). Other goodies worth checking out include funky European footwear at **Charles David** (second floor; **(** **312/944-9013**), amazingly intricate

French glassware at **Lalique** (ground floor; ✆ 312/867-1787), and an eclectic selection of hats, mittens, scarves, and other accessories at **Glove Me Tender** (fifth floor; ✆ 312/664-4022), which should be your first stop if you're caught here during an unexpected cold spell. 900 N. Michigan Ave. (between Walton St. and Delaware Place). ✆ **312/915-3916.** Subway/El: Red Line to Chicago.

Water Tower Place   Water Tower was the first big indoor mall to open downtown (in 1975), and 30 years ago its glass elevators and shiny gold trim gave the place a glamorous air. These days the mall remains popular but doesn't have much to distinguish it from any other upscale shopping center. Water Tower is a magnet for suburban teenagers (just like your mall back home) and can get quite crowded during prime summer tourist season. Most of its stores are part of national chains (Ann Taylor, Victoria's Secret, and so on). The department stores anchoring the mall are the Mag Mile outpost of **Macy's** and a **Lord & Taylor** (see "Department Stores," in "Shopping A to Z," later in this chapter). One of Water Tower's best features is its funky food court, **foodlife** (p. 137). 835 N. Michigan Ave. (between Pearson and Chestnut sts.). ✆ 312/440-3166. Subway/El: Red Line to Chicago.

Westfield North Bridge   The anchor of this development is a four-story **Nordstrom** (p. 242). The rest of the mall is bright and open, thanks to high ceilings and a wide central walkway—but it can also feel somewhat deserted compared to the bustling street outside. The stores are a mix of clothing, jewelry, and bath-and-body shops (in a midrange to upscale price bracket). Distinctive stores that are worth checking out include the high-style chocolatier **Vosges Haut-Chocolat** on the second floor (p. 239) and the **LEGO** store on the third floor (✆ 312/494-0760), which features a mini re-creation of the Chicago skyline. The third-floor food court is a good stop for lunch, with a food station run by Tuscany, a local Italian restaurant, and other stands that offer Japanese tempura, grilled wraps, and Chicago-style hot dogs. 520 N. Michigan Ave. (between Grand Ave. and Illinois St.). ✆ 312/327-2300. Subway/El: Red Line to Grand.

CHIC SHOPPING ON NEARBY OAK STREET

Oak Street has long been a symbol of designer-label shopping; if a store has an Oak Street address, you can count on it being expensive. The shopping district itself is actually quite limited, taking up only 1 block at the northern tip of the Magnificent Mile (where Michigan Ave. ends and Lake Shore Dr. begins). While big-name designer boutiques such as Giorgio Armani and Louis Vuitton pride themselves on having a Michigan Avenue address, Oak Street features smaller, more personal shops

---

Tips Lunch on the Mag Mile

When I worked just off Michigan Avenue, my favorite spot for lunch was the food court on the eighth floor of Chicago Place. A bright, airy space with a fountain and palm trees, it's my pick for the best cheap eats in the area, especially if you're traveling with kids. The cuisine may be uninspired—food choices include Subway, Taco Bell, McDonald's—but the setting makes this a few steps above the average mall food court. If you're lucky, you can even snag one of the tables overlooking Michigan Avenue, the kind of view that costs big bucks at the city's luxury hotels.

Finds An Oak Street Bargain

Oak Street is not the place to come shopping for bargains—with one exception—**Bravco,** 43 E. Oak St. (✆ **312/943-4305**). This crowded, narrow drugstore seems out of place among the hip boutiques, but it's a popular spot among Chicago hairstylists and makeup artists. You'll find an excellent selection of professional hair and beauty products (including Aveda, Sebastian, and Bumble and Bumble) here for much less than they cost at salons. Even if you haven't heard of some of the brands, trust me, if Bravco carries them, they're hot.

(most of them high-priced). Since most of the stores are tucked into converted town houses, it also has a more tranquil feel than Michigan Avenue. It's well worth a stroll for people-watching: this is Main St. for Chicago socialites. Most of Oak Street is closed on Sunday, except during the holiday season.

Chicago's most high-profile clothing boutique, **Ultimo,** is right around the corner from Michigan Avenue; upscale and exclusive, it caters to the seriously fashionable (p. 241). Footwear fans can browse Italian shoemaker **Tod's,** best known for its luxuriously soft (and pricey) driving shoes (p. 247). Shoes, stationery, and handbags are available at **kate spade,** 101 E. Oak St. (✆ **312/654-8853**), along with the Jack Spade line of men's accessories. The priciest accessories on this very pricey block can likely be found at French luxury house **Hermès of Paris,** 110 E. Oak St. (✆ **312/787-8175**). Thread-count fanatics swear by the sheets from **Pratesi,** 67 E. Oak St. (✆ **312/943-8422**), and **Frette,** 41 E. Oak St. (✆ **312/649-3744**), both of which supply linens to top hotels (and where sheet sets cost more than what some people pay in rent).

Anchoring the western end of the block are two haute heavyweights, hip Italian designer **Prada,** 30 E. Oak St. (✆ **312/951-1113**), which offers three floors of sleek, postmodern fashions for men and women and plenty of the designer's signature handbags; and equally style-conscious **Barneys New York** (p. 241).

2 More Shopping Neighborhoods

STATE STREET & THE LOOP

Shopping in the Loop is mostly concentrated along State Street, from Randolph Street south to Congress Parkway (although there are stores sprinkled elsewhere, they're mostly places that cater to office workers: drugstores, sandwich shops, and chain clothing stores). State Street was Chicago's first great shopping district—by World War I, seven of the largest and most lavish department stores in the world were competing for shoppers' loyalties along this half-mile stretch. The area has been eclipsed by Michigan Avenue, and State Street is now lined with discount stores and fast-food outlets. However, one grand old department store makes it worth a visit: **Macy's at State Street** (formerly Marshall Field's), 111 N. State St., at Randolph Street (✆ **312/781-1000**). A city landmark and one of the largest department stores in the world, it occupies an entire city block and features the largest Tiffany glass mosaic dome in the U.S. If you're in Chicago between Thanksgiving and New Year's, Macy's has maintained a long-time Marshall Field's tradition: lavishly decorated holiday windows and lunch under the Great Tree in the store's restaurant, The Walnut Room.

> **Tips** **Point Zero**
>
> If the quick change from north to south in the Loop confuses you, keep in mind that in Chicago, point zero for the purpose of address numbering is the intersection of State and Madison streets.

The other stores along State Street are not particularly distinctive—the place still has a no-frills aura compared to Michigan Avenue—but it stays busy thanks to the thousands of office workers who stroll around during their lunch hour or after work. On weekends, the street is considerably more subdued.

RIVER NORTH

Since the 1960s, when the Chicago Imagists (painters Ed Paschke, Jim Nutt, and Roger Brown among them) attracted international attention with their shows at the Hyde Park Art Center, the city has been a fertile breeding ground for emerging artists and innovative art dealers. Today, the primary gallery district is concentrated in the River North neighborhood, where century-old, redbrick warehouses have been converted into lofty exhibition spaces. More recently, a new generation of gallery owners has set up shop in the rapidly gentrifying West Loop neighborhood, where you'll tend to find more cutting-edge work. The River North gallery district is an easy walk from many hotels; the West Loop may seem a little farther afield, but it's only a short cab ride from downtown (you can also take the bus, but I'd recommend a taxi at night).

The River North gallery season officially gets underway on the first Friday after Labor Day in September. Besides fall, another great time to visit the district is from mid-July through August, when the Chicago Art Dealers Association presents **Vision,** an annual lineup of programs tailored to the public. Early September also offers the annual **Around the Coyote** festival in Wicker Park/Bucktown (call © 773/342-6777 for information), when scores of artists open their studios to the public (the name refers to the now-departed Coyote Gallery, which used to stand at the corner of Damen and North aves.).

The *Chicago Reader,* a free weekly newspaper available at many stores, taverns, and cafes on the North Side, publishes a very comprehensive listing of current gallery exhibitions, as does the quarterly *Chicago Gallery News* (www.chicagogallerynews.com), which is available free at the city's three visitor information centers. Another good resource is the Chicago Art Dealers Association (© 312/649-0065; www.chicagoart dealers.org); the group's website has descriptions of all member galleries. For descriptions of the city's top galleries, see "Art Galleries" under "Shopping A to Z," below.

Along with its status as Chicago's primary art-gallery district, River North—the area west of the Magnificent Mile and north of the Chicago River—has attracted many interesting home-design shops concentrated on Wells Street from Kinzie Street to Chicago Avenue. My favorites include **Manifesto,** 755 N. Wells St., at Chicago Avenue (© 312/664-0733), which offers custom-designed furniture, as well as imports from Italy and elsewhere in Europe; **Mig & Tig,** 540 N. Wells St., at Ohio Street (© 312/644-8277), a charming furniture and decorative-accessories shop; and **Lightology,** 215 W. Chicago Ave., at Wells St. (© 312/944-1000), a massive lighting store that carries a mind-boggling array of funky lamps, chandeliers, and glowing orbs from more than 400 manufacturers (even if you have no intention of flying home with a stack of lamps in your luggage, it's fun to browse).

Looming above the Chicago River at the southern end of River North is the **Merchandise Mart,** the world's largest commercial building. The massive complex was built in 1930 by Marshall Field & Company and was bought in 1945 by Joseph P. Kennedy (JFK's dad); the Kennedy family ran the Mart until the late 1990s. Now the building houses mostly interior-design showrooms, which are open only to professional designers. One exception is Luxe Home, a collection of kitchen and bath showrooms on the first floor, all of which are open to the public (and worth a look for interior-design junkies). Public tours of the whole complex are offered once a week, usually on Fridays ($12 adults; 📞 **312/527-7762** for dates and reservations).

ARMITAGE AVENUE

Hovering between the North Side neighborhoods of Old Town and Lincoln Park, Armitage Avenue has emerged as a shopping destination in its own right, thanks to an influx of wealthy young professionals who have settled into historic town homes on the neighboring tree-lined streets. The main shopping district is concentrated between Halsted Street and Racine Avenue; I'd suggest starting at the Armitage El stop (Brown Line), working your way east to Halsted Street, and then wandering a few blocks north to Webster Street. As you stroll around, you'll get a good sense of the area's strong community spirit, with neighbors greeting each other and catching up on the street corners.

The shops and boutiques here are geared toward a sophisticated, well-heeled shopper and make for great browsing. (Most are suited for female shoppers—sorry, guys). You'll find trendy clothing boutiques, including that of local-gal-made-good **Cynthia Rowley** (808 W. Armitage Ave.; 📞 **773/528-6160**); jaw-droppingly beautiful home-decor stores; beauty emporiums (see the box, "Pamper Yourself," below); and one of my favorite impossible-to-classify gift shops, **Art Effect** (p. 243). Tiny **Multiple Choices,** 840 W. Armitage Ave. (📞 **773/477-4520**), is full of colorful ceramics and creative gifts (including Big Ten college board games such as "Wisconsinopoly"). The upscale pet accessories shop **Barker & Meowsky,** 1003 W. Armitage Ave. (📞 **773/868-0200**), has everything you need to spoil furry family members, including catnip cigars, doggy "sushi," and designer-inspired outfits.

Despite the area's upscale feel, you can snag bargains at some top-notch discount and consignment shops, including **Lori's Designer Shoes, McShane's Exchange,**

⌜Fun Fact Jewelers' Row

It's not quite as impressive as the Big Apple's diamond district, but Chicago's own "Jewelers' Row" is certainly worth a detour for rock hunters. Half a dozen high-rises along the Wabash Avenue El tracks in the heart of the Loop service the wholesale trade, but the one at 5 S. Wabash Ave. opens its doors to customers off the street. There's a mall-like retail space on the ground floor crammed with tiny booths manned by smooth-talking reps hawking their wares. You can grab a map here for a self-guided tour of the rest of the building's tenants. It's quite an experience because many of the booths are closet-size cubbyholes with hunched-over geezers who look as if they've been eyeballing solitaire and marquise cuts since the Roosevelt administration—Teddy, that is.

Finds Pamper Yourself

When all that Armitage Avenue shopping gets *too* exhausting, take a break at one of the beauty stores concentrated within a few blocks of each other on Halsted Street. **Endo-Exo Apothecary,** 2034 N. Halsted St. (© **773/525-0500**), lined with vintage wood cabinets, is a peaceful retreat that stocks a number of specialty skin-care and makeup lines; they'll even give you a complimentary makeover. The mood is more flashy and hip at **Fresh,** 2040 N. Halsted St. (© **773/404-9776**), where the sleek shelves are filled with skin treatments, at-home spa supplies, and their own line of cosmetics. To get really creative, visit the cozy **Aroma Workshop,** 2050 N. Halsted St. (© **773/871-1985**), where you can mix up your own custom-scented body lotions and perfumes. A few blocks south, you'll find all-natural soaps, creams, and bubble baths at the very fragrant **Lush** store, 859 W. Armitage Ave. (© **773/281-LUSH**), and skin-care products from the iconic New York apothecary **Kiehl's,** 907 W. Armitage Ave. (© **773/665-2515**).

Fox's, and **The Second Child** (see "Vintage Fashion/Resale Shops" under "Shopping A to Z," below).

LINCOLN PARK & LAKEVIEW

A few major north-south thoroughfares—Lincoln Avenue, Clark Street, and Broadway—are the main shopping streets in both Lincoln Park (south of Diversey Pkwy.) and Lakeview (north of Diversey). Most of the shops cater to young singles who live in the surrounding apartment buildings; you'll find plenty of minimart groceries, some clothing and shoe boutiques, and the occasional used-book store, but not much that's worth a special trip.

Radiating from the intersection of Belmont Avenue and Clark Street is a string of shops catering to rebellious kids on tour from their homes in the 'burbs (the Dunkin' Donuts on the corner is often referred to as "Punkin' Donuts" in their honor). One constant in the ever-changing youth culture has been the **Alley,** 3228 N. Clark St., at Belmont Avenue (© **773/883-1800**), an "alternative shopping complex" selling everything from plaster gargoyles to racks of leather jackets. It has separate shops specializing in condoms, cigars, and bondage wear. **Tragically Hip,** a storefront women's boutique, 931 W. Belmont Ave. (© **773/549-1500**), next to the Belmont El train stop, has outlasted many other similar purveyors of cutting-edge women's apparel.

You can get plugged into what the kids are reading at **Chicago Comics,** 3244 N. Clark St. (© **773/528-1983**), considered one of the best comics shops in the country. Besides the usual superhero titles, you'll find lots of European and Japanese comics, along with underground books and 'zines.

SOUTHPORT AVENUE

West of Lakeview, a few blocks from Wrigley Field, this residential area was considered up-and-coming about 10 years ago; now it's definitely arrived. The mix of restaurants, cool (but not *too* cool) clothing boutiques, and cafes appeals to the upscale urban families who have flocked to the area (watch out for strollers hogging the sidewalk). It's worth a look if you want to hang out in a neighborhood that's a little more laid-back than the Gold Coast or Wicker Park. Start at the Southport El stop on the Brown Line, and work your way north to Grace Street (round-trip, the walk will take you about half-an-hour—but allow more if you're doing some serious shopping or want to stop for lunch). Along the way you'll pass the historic **Music Box Theater** at 3733 N. Southport Ave. (© 773/871-6604), north of Addison Street, which shows independent films from around the world. Two clothing shops catering to hip young women with plenty of disposable income are **Krista K,** 3458 N. Southport Ave. (© 773/248-1967), and **Red Head Boutique,** 3450 N. Southport Ave. (© 773/325-9898), which both stock hot new designers that aren't widely available in Chicago. **Shane,** 3657 N. Southport Ave. (© 773/549-0179), and **Jake,** 3740 N. Southport Ave. (© 773/929-5253), carry more casual clothes for both men and women (think trendy T-shirts and specialty-label denim).

WICKER PARK/BUCKTOWN

The go-go gentrification of the Wicker Park/Bucktown area has been followed by not only a rash of restaurants and bars but also retailers with an artsy bent that reflect the neighborhood's bohemian spirit. Mixed in with old neighborhood businesses, such as discount furniture stores and religious-icon purveyors, is a proliferation of antique-furniture shops, too-cool-for-school clothing boutiques, and eclectic galleries and gift emporiums. Despite the hefty price tags in many of these shops, the neighborhood still feels gritty—so come here if you want to feel like you've gotten a real urban fix.

Start at the Damen El stop on the Blue Line, and walk north along Damen to Armitage Avenue to scope out the trendiest shops. If you've got time, some stores are also scattered along Milwaukee Avenue south of North Avenue.

The friendly modern-day Marco Polos at **Pagoda Red,** 1714 N. Damen Ave., second floor (© 773/235-1188), have imported beautiful (and expensive) antique furniture and art objects, including Chinese concubine beds, painted Tibetan cabinets, Burmese rolling water vessels, cast-iron lotus bowls, bronze Buddhas, and Chinese inspiration stones. The upscale bazaar **Embelezar,** 1639 N. Damen Ave. (© 773/645-9705), carries exotic merchandise from around the world, both old and new, including the famous Fortuny silk lamps—hand-painted in Venice at the only studio allowed to reproduce the original Fortuny designs. You'll find a well-edited selection of home accessories and jewelry at **Lille,** 1923 W. North Ave. (© 773/342-0563). The airy, white space looks like an art gallery, with pieces from internationally known designers (Lulu de Kwiatkowski handbags, Christian Tortu vases) alongside plenty of quirky objects.

Moments Taking a Break in Wicker Park

When you're ready to rest your weary self, settle down at a local coffeehouse and soak in Wicker Park's artsy vibe. **Earwax Café,** 1564 N. Milwaukee Ave. (© 773/772-4019), attracts the jaded and pierced set with a no-frills, slightly edgy atmosphere. **Filter,** across the street at 1585 N. Milwaukee Ave. (© 773/227-4850), is a little more welcoming; comfy couches fill the main dining room, which features paintings by local artists. Both cafes are near the bustling intersection of North, Milwaukee, and Damen avenues—the heart of Wicker Park—and draw a steady stream of locals. It's here you'll realize that Wicker Park is really just a small town—with cooler hair and funkier shoes.

WEST DIVISION STREET

Once home to just a few pioneering restaurants, Division Street is quickly being transformed from a desolate urban landscape to a hot shopping destination. It's a work in progress (you'll still find some boarded-up buildings among the cool boutiques), but for now this is what Wicker Park used to be: a place where rents are still cheap enough for eager young entrepreneurs. Start at the Division El stop on the Blue Line, and head west along Division; most stores are concentrated between Milwaukee Avenue and Damen Avenue (a round-trip walk will take about half-an-hour). Along the way, you'll stroll past eclectic clothing and shoe boutiques, bath-and-beauty shops, and home-decor stores such as **Porte Rouge,** 1911 W. Division St. (© 773/269-2800), which is filled with French antiques and housewares (they'll even offer you a complimentary cup of tea). The mix of people living here—from working-class Latino families to self-consciously edgy young singles—makes the local cafes great for people-watching.

3 Shopping A to Z

Chicago has shops selling just about anything you could want or need, be it functional or ornamental, whimsical or exotic. Although the following list only scratches the surface, it gives you an idea of the range of merchandise available. You'll find more shops in many of these categories, such as apparel and gifts, covered in the earlier sections of this chapter.

ANTIQUES

The greatest concentration of antiques businesses, from packed-to-the-rafters malls to idiosyncratic individual shops, can be found on Belmont Avenue west of Southport Avenue, or stretching north and south of Belmont Avenue along intersecting Lincoln Avenue. Here are a few others:

Architectural Artifacts, Inc. (R)(R) (Finds) Chicago has a handful of salvage specialists who cater to the design trades and retail customers seeking an unusual architectural piece for their homes. This one is the best and is well worth seeking out at its location next to the Metra train line in the far-northwest corner of the city's Lakeview neighborhood. Its brightly lit, well-organized, cavernous showroom features everything from original mantels and garden ornaments to vintage bathroom hardware and American and French Art Deco lighting fixtures. The store also has a museum on the lower level to display portions of historically significant buildings. 4325 N. Ravenswood Ave. (east of Damen Ave. and south of Montrose Ave.). © 773/348-0622. www.architecturalartifacts. com. Subway/El: Brown Line to Montrose.

Broadway Antique Market (R) Visiting Hollywood prop stylists and local interior designers flock here to find 20th-century antiques in near-perfect condition. In this two-level, 20,000-square-foot vintage megamart, you'll spot both pricey pieces (for example, an Arne Jacobsen egg chair) and affordable collectibles for less than $100 (Roseville pottery, Art Deco barware, Peter Max scarves). 6130 N. Broadway (half-mile north of Hollywood Ave. and Lake Shore Dr.). © 773/743-5444. www.bamchicago.com. Subway/El: Red Line to Granville.

Jay Robert's Antique Warehouse This mammoth River North space is within walking distance of downtown hotels, but you'll need comfortable shoes to explore all 50,000 square feet. The selection is wildly eclectic: fine furniture that includes fireplaces, stained glass, statues, tapestries, and an impressive selection of antique clocks in a variety of styles ranging from elaborate Victorian to sophisticated Art Deco. 149 W. Kinzie St. (at LaSalle St.). © 312/222-0167. www.jayroberts.com. Subway/El: Brown Line to Merchandise Mart.

Michael FitzSimmons Decorative Arts ⊛⊛   This shop is one of the top dealers anywhere for furniture and furnishings dating to the Arts and Crafts period, from Stickley chairs to antique British lamps. You'll also find top-notch reproductions, including William Morris wallpaper patterns. 311 W. Superior St. (between Franklin and Orleans sts.). © 312/787-0496. www.fitzdecarts.com. Subway/El: Brown Line to Chicago.

Modern Times   This shop specializes in the major designers of home furnishings from the 1930s to the 1960s—the sort of pieces that style-conscious shoppers buy to furnish their newly gentrified lofts. You'll also find lighting fixtures of all types and some jewelry. *Note:* The store is only open Friday through Sunday; weekdays by appointment only. 2100 W. Grand Ave. (at Damen Ave.). © 312/243-5706. www.moderntimes chicago.com. Subway/El: Blue Line to Division, then about a half-mile walk; or take a cab.

Salvage One ⊛   Like Architectural Artifacts (above), this sprawling space stocks everything but the kitchen sink—literally: There's an entire room filled with vintage sinks. You'll find hundreds of one-of-a-kind pieces for the home handyperson, including doors, mantels, tubs, stained glass, and antique chandeliers. 1840 W. Hubbard St. (at Damen Ave.). © 312/733-0098. www.salvageone.com. Bus: 65 (Grand Ave.).

ART GALLERIES

Most of the city's major art galleries are concentrated in two neighborhoods. The city's original gallery district is in River North, within easy walking distance of most downtown hotels. More recently, galleries have been opening in the converted loft buildings of the West Loop, which is best reached by taxi.

Alan Koppel Gallery   This expansive gallery showcases modern and contemporary works of art as well as French and Italian furniture from the '20s through the '50s (in a separate area). Koppel also specializes in 20th-century photography, so if you're hankering for something by Diane Arbus, Man Ray, or Walker Evans, this is the place to look. 210 W. Chicago Ave. (at Wells St.). © 312/640-0730. www.alankoppel.com. Subway/El: Brown or Red line to Chicago.

Aldo Castillo Gallery   Aldo Castillo left his native Nicaragua in 1976, shortly after the Sandinistas began their revolution against the Somoza regime. He arrived in Chicago in 1985 and, 8 years later, appalled at the lack of attention given to Latin American art, opened his eponymous gallery in Lakeview, moving to his present River North location in 1993. Castillo continues to promote a range of work by emerging artists and established masters from Latin America, Spain, and Portugal. 233 W. Huron St. (between Franklin and Wells sts.). © 312/337-2536. www.artaldo.com. Subway/El: Brown or Red line to Chicago.

Ann Nathan Gallery ⊛⊛   Ann Nathan, who started out as a collector, shows exciting (and sometimes outrageous) pieces in clay, wood, and metal—along with paintings, photographs, and "functional art" (pieces that blur the line between furniture and sculpture). Nathan's space in the center of the River North district is one of the most beautiful in the city. 212 W. Superior St. (at Wells St.). © 312/664-6622. www.annnathan gallery.com. Subway/El: Brown or Red line to Chicago.

Carl Hammer Gallery   A former schoolteacher and one of the most venerated dealers in Chicago, Carl Hammer touts his wares as "contemporary art and selected historical masterworks by American and European self-taught artists"—but it's the "self-taught" part that warrants emphasis. Hammer helped pioneer the field known as "outsider art," which has since become a white-hot commodity in the international art world. 740 N. Wells St. (at Superior St.). ℂ 312/266-8512. www.hammergallery.com. Subway/El: Brown or Red line to Chicago.

Catherine Edelman Gallery   One of Chicago's leading galleries in contemporary photography, Catherine Edelman represents a wide range of photographers, including well-known names such as Sally Mann. Across the street, **Stephen Daiter Gallery,** 311 W. Superior St. (ℂ 312/787-3350), also specializes in photography. 300 W. Superior St. (at Franklin St.). ℂ 312/266-2350. www.edelmangallery.com. Subway/El: Brown or Red line to Chicago.

Donald Young Gallery ⭐   Internationally renowned on the contemporary-art scene since the late 1970s, Donald Young returned to Chicago to much applause in 1999 after an 8-year residency in Seattle. His very dramatic West Loop gallery is a haven for critically acclaimed artists working in video, sculpture, photography, painting, and installation, including Anne Chu, Gary Hill, Martin Puryear, Bruce Nauman, Cristina Iglesias, Robert Mangold, and Charles Ray. 933 W. Washington St. (at Sangamon St.). ℂ 312/455-0100. www.donaldyoung.com. Bus: 20 (Madison).

Douglas Dawson Gallery ⭐   Offering a unique perspective to the Chicago art scene, Douglas Dawson specializes in ancient and historic ethnographic art—everything from tribal textiles to furniture, although a principal focus is African ceramics. The gallery's spectacular loft space in the West Loop looks like a museum. 400 N. Morgan St. (at Kinzie St.). ℂ 312/226-7975. www.douglasdawson.com. Bus: 65 (Grand).

G.R. N'Namdi Gallery   George N'Namdi founded his gallery, which specializes in African-American artists, 2 decades ago in the Detroit area. His son Jumaane operates this location (there's also another in New York). Artists they've helped bring to the attention of museums and art collectors include James Vanderzee, Al Loving, Edward Clark, and Robert Colescott. 110 N. Peoria St. (at Washington St.). ℂ 312/563-9240. www.grnnamdi.com. Bus: 20 (Madison).

Kavi Gupta Gallery   Owner Kavi Gupta is widely credited with kicking off the West Loop art scene when he developed this property as a home for new galleries. Gupta specializes in contemporary art by national and international emerging artists, so you never quite know what you're going to see here. Also worth checking out in the same building are the **Carrie Secrist Gallery** (ℂ 312/491-0917) and **Thomas McCormick Gallery** (ℂ 312/226-6800). 835 W. Washington St. (at Green St.). ℂ 312/432-0708. www.kavigupta.com. Bus: 20 (Madison).

Marx-Saunders Gallery   Chicago is home to two world-class galleries dealing in contemporary glass-art sculpture, conveniently located within steps of one another along Superior Street in River North. Marx-Saunders Gallery houses the city's largest showcase of glass art and features world-famous artists, past and present (William Morris, Mark Fowler, Therman Statom, and Hiroshi Yamano), as well as newcomers. Also worth a look for art-glass lovers is the nearby **Habatat Galleries Chicago,** 222 W. Superior St. (ℂ 312/440-0288). 230 W. Superior St. (between Franklin and Wells sts.). ℂ 312/573-1400. www.marxsaunders.com. Subway/El: Brown or Red line to Chicago.

Maya Polsky Gallery   Gallery owner Maya Polsky deals in international contemporary art and also represents some leading local artists, but she's best known for showcasing the contemporary and postrevolutionary art of Russia, including the work of such masters as Natalya Nesterova and Sergei Sherstiuk. 215 W. Superior St. (at Wells St.). © 312/440-0055. www.mayapolskygallery.com. Subway/El: Brown or Red line to Chicago.

Rhona Hoffman Gallery   The New York–born Rhona Hoffman maintains a high profile on the international contemporary-art scene. She launched her gallery in 1983 and, from the start, sought national and international artists, typically young and cutting-edge artists who weren't represented elsewhere in Chicago. Today she is the purveyor of such blue-chip players as Sol LeWitt and Jenny Holzer; she has also added young up-and-comers such as Dawoud Bey. 118 N. Peoria St. (between Randolph and Washington sts.). © 312/455-1990. www.rhoffmangallery.com. Bus: 20 (Madison).

Richard Gray Gallery ⚘   Richard Gray—whose gallery opened in 1963—is widely considered the dean of art dealers in Chicago. (He's served as president of the Art Dealers Association of America and been a longtime board member of the Art Institute of Chicago.) The gallery specializes in paintings, sculpture, and drawings by leading artists from the major movements in 20th-century American and European art (he also has a second location in New York). Gray and his son, Paul, who now runs the Chicago gallery, have shown the work of such luminaries as Pablo Picasso, Jean Dubuffet, Willem de Kooning, Alexander Calder, Claes Oldenburg, Joan Miró, and Henri Matisse. John Hancock Center, 875 N. Michigan Ave., Suite 2503 (between Delaware and Chestnut sts.). © 312/642-8877. www.richardgraygallery.com. Subway/El: Red Line to Chicago.

Zolla/Lieberman Gallery ⚘⚘   Bob Zolla and Roberta Lieberman kicked off the River North revival when they opened their gallery (considered the grande dame of the area) here in 1976. Today, Zolla/Lieberman, directed by Roberta's son William Lieberman, represents a wide range of artists, including sculptor Deborah Butterfield, installation artist Vernon Fisher, and painter Terence LaNoue. 325 W. Huron St. (at Orleans St.). © 312/944-1990. www.zollaliebermangallery.com. Subway/El: Brown Line to Chicago.

BOOKS

Abraham Lincoln Book Shop ⚘   This bookstore boasts one of the country's most outstanding collections of Lincolniana, from rare and antique books about the 16th president to collectible signatures, letters, and other documents illuminating the lives of other U.S. presidents and historical figures. The shop carries new historical and academic works, too. 357 W. Chicago Ave. (between Orleans and Sedgwick sts.). © 312/944-3085. Subway/El: Brown Line to Chicago.

Barnes & Noble   This two-level Gold Coast store comes complete with a cafe in case you get the munchies while perusing the miles of books. There's another store in Lincoln Park, at 659 W. Diversey Ave., 1 block west of Clark Street (© 773/871-9004), and one at 1441 W. Webster Ave., at Clybourn Avenue (© 773/871-3610). 1130 N. State St. (at Elm St.). © 312/280-8155. Subway/El: Red Line to Clark/Division.

Borders   You couldn't ask for a better location, right across from Water Tower Place. This place is like a mini department store, with books, magazines, CDs, and computer software spread over four floors, and a cafe with a view overlooking the Mag Mile. There's also a Borders in the Loop at 150 N. State St., at Randolph Street (© 312/606-0750), and one in Lincoln Park at 2817 N. Clark St., at Diversey Avenue (© 773/935-3909). 830 N. Michigan Ave. (at Pearson St.). © 312/573-0564. Subway/El: Red Line to Chicago.

Children in Paradise Bookstore ⟨Kids⟩   This is the largest store in town dedicated to children's books, with storytelling hours Tuesday and Wednesday and special events on Saturday. The personal service makes up for the somewhat limited selection. 909 N. Rush St. (between Delaware Place and Walton St.). © 312/951-5437. Subway/El: Red Line to Chicago.

Powell's Bookstore Used books, especially from scholarly and small Chicago presses, dog-eared paperbacks, and hardcover classics fill the shelves at this booklover's haven. There are also outlets in Lakeview at 2850 N. Lincoln Ave. (© **773/248-1444**), and Hyde Park at 1501 E. 57th St. (© **773/955-7780**). 828 S. Wabash Ave. (between 8th and 9th sts.). © 312/341-0748. Subway/El: Red Line to Harrison.

Prairie Avenue Bookshop ✸✸ This South Loop store does Chicago's architectural tradition proud with the city's finest stock of architecture, design, and technical books. 418 S. Wabash Ave. (between Congress Pkwy. and Van Buren St.). © 312/922-8311. Subway/El: Red Line to Jackson.

Seminary Co-op Bookstore A classic campus bookstore located near the University of Chicago, this shop has extensive philosophy and theology sections and is one of the premier academic bookstores in the country. 5757 S. University Ave. (between 57th and 58th sts.). © 773/752-4381. Bus: 69 (Jeffrey Express).

Unabridged Books This quintessential neighborhood bookseller in the area known as Boys Town has strong sections in gay and lesbian literature, travel, film, and sci-fi. 3251 N. Broadway (between Belmont Ave. and Addison St.). © 773/883-9119. Subway/El: Red Line to Addison.

Women & Children First *Kids* This feminist and children's bookstore holds the best selection in the city of titles for, by, and about women. But the shop is far from a male-free zone; the owners promote great independent fiction—by authors of both genders—making this a good place to discover books that have been overlooked by the bestseller lists. There's a section devoted to lesbian and gay books, and the store has a busy schedule of author appearances. 5233 N. Clark St. (between Foster and Bryn Mawr aves.). © 773/769-9299. Subway/El: Red Line to Berwyn.

CANDY, CHOCOLATES & PASTRIES

Bittersweet ✸✸ Run by Judy Contino, one of the city's top pastry chefs and bakers, this Lakeview cafe and shop is sought out by brides-to-be and trained palates who have a yen for gourmet cakes, cookies, tarts, and ladyfingers. The rich chocolate mousse cake, a specialty of the house, is out of this world. 1114 W. Belmont Ave. (between Seminary and Clifton aves.). © 773/929-1100. Subway/El: Red Line to Belmont.

Ethel's Chocolate Lounge A celebration of all things chocolate, this bright, candy-colored cafe has a distinctly feminine vibe; I have yet to see a group of guys huddling on one of the hot-pink couches. But what better way to catch up with a girlfriend than over a selection of gourmet truffles or a pot of hot chocolate? The chocolates are a tad pricy—more than a dollar per piece—but they run the range from espresso-flavored truffles to the "Etheltini" (a dark chocolate square spiked with vodka and dry vermouth). Ethel's also has locations inside the 900 N. Michigan Avenue mall (© 312/440-9747) and along the Armitage Avenue shopping strip, 819 W. Armitage Ave. (© 773/281-0029). 520 N. Michigan Ave. (inside the Westfield North Bridge mall). © 312/464-9330. www.ethelschocolate.com. Subway/El: Red Line to Grand.

Ghirardelli Chocolate Shop & Soda Fountain This Midwest outpost of the famed San Francisco chocolatier, just a half-block off the Mag Mile, gets swamped in the summer, so good thing they've got their soda-fountain assembly line down to a science.

Besides the incredible hot-fudge sundaes, there's a veritable mudslide of chocolate bars, hot-cocoa drink mixes, and chocolate-covered espresso beans to tempt your sweet tooth. 830 N. Michigan Ave. (between Michigan Ave. and Rush St.). (C) 312/337-9330. Subway/El: Red Line to Chicago.

Margie's Candies *Value*   This family-run candy and ice-cream shop hasn't changed much since it opened in 1921. It still offers some of the city's finest handmade fudge, whether it comes in a box or melted over a banana split served in a clamshell dish. The store is known for its turtles—chocolate-covered pecan and caramel clusters—and might be the only place in the city still selling rock candy on wooden sticks. 1960 N. Western Ave. (just north of Armitage Ave.). (C) 773/384-1035. Subway/El: Blue Line to Western.

Sweet Thang   If you're bopping around Wicker Park, don't miss Bernard Runo's Euro-style cafe for a tasty treat. Runo, a classically trained pastry chef who studied in France and has worked in the city's best hotel kitchens, imports most of the ingredients for his croissants, cookies, tarts, and other pastries from across the pond. The cafe has a laissez-faire atmosphere, with red distressed walls covered with abstract art and Parisian-style tables and chairs that are set outside in warm weather. 1921 W. North Ave. (at Winchester Ave.). (C) 773/772-4166. Subway/El: Blue Line to Damen.

Vosges Haut-Chocolat *Finds*   Chocolatier Katrina Markoff's exotic gourmet truffles—with fabulous names such as absinthe, mint julep, wink of the rabbit, woolloomooloo, and ambrosia—are made from premium Belgian chocolate and infused with rare spices, seasonings, and flowers from around the world. The store—which looks more like a modern art gallery than a chocolatier—includes a gourmet hot-chocolate bar, where you're welcome to sit and sip. Vosges also has a small store on trendy Armitage Avenue (951 W. Armitage Ave.; (C) 773/296-9866). 520 N. Michigan Ave. (in the Westfield North Bridge shopping center). (C) 312/644-9450. Subway/El: Red Line to Grand.

CLOTHING BOUTIQUES

In the not-so-distant past, local fashion addicts fled to the coasts to shop for cutting-edge designer duds. Those days are over. While over-the-top outrageousness doesn't sell here—this is the practical Midwest, after all—stylish Chicagoans now turn to local independent boutiques when they want to stay on top of the latest trends (without looking like fashion victims). Here are some of the best.

Apartment Number 9   Chicago men aren't renowned for their sense of style; most get by just fine with a wardrobe of baseball hats and sports-team T-shirts. But a few stores cater to hip young dudes, and this is the most stylish of the bunch. The clothing selection is trendy but not outrageous, with a good selection from menswear designers such as John Varvatos, Nicole Farhi, and Paul Smith, among other up-and-coming names. 1804 N. Damen Ave. (at Willow St.). (C) 773/395-2999. Subway/El: Blue Line to Damen.

Chasalla   More low-key than many of its Oak Street neighbors, this cozy, minimalist boutique specializes in men's and women's clothing from designers' younger, slightly more affordable labels, including Versace's Versus, D&G, Hugo Red Label, and Cinque. 70 E. Oak St. (between Rush St. and Michigan Ave.). (C) 312/640-1940. Subway/El: Red Line to Chicago.

Clever Alice   This River North shop attracts a clientele of stylish professional women who want polished looks. While the clothes here are body-conscious (including a good selection of hard-to-find European lines), the staff takes the time to help shoppers find pieces that fit and flatter. Don't miss the store's own clothing line, Alice in Oz. 750 N. Franklin St. (between Chicago Ave. and Superior St.). ℂ 312/587-8693. www.cleveralice.net. Subway/El: Brown Line to Chicago.

Ikram ⟨★★★⟩ Run by Ikram Goldman, a former saleswoman at well-known women's clothing store Ultimo (see below), this shop stocks all the big names, from Valentino to Yves St. Laurent—and whatever else *Vogue* has declared "hot" for the season. Tucked among the high-priced pieces are jewelry, stationery, and decorative accessories that give the place a personal touch. 873 Rush St. (between Delaware and Chestnut sts.). ℂ 312/587-1000. www.ikram.com. Subway/El: Red Line to Chicago.

p45 ⟨★⟩ You'll find a number of cool boutiques aimed at the younger crowd clustered along Damen Avenue in Bucktown, but this is the most cutting-edge, with a vibe that's funky rather than girly. A gold mine of urbane women's fashion, the dark, spare space is filled with a unique mix of hip national labels (Michelle Mason, Susana Monaco, Lauren Moffat) and local designers you've never heard of. If you're looking for something no one else at home will be wearing, this is the place to shop. 1643 N. Damen Ave. (between North and Wabansia aves.). ℂ 773/862-4523. www.p45.com. Subway/El: Blue Line to Damen.

Robin Richman You'll feel like you're poking through a big, antiques-filled closet as you browse around this tiny Bucktown storefront. The walls are adorned with balls of string, vintage diaries, and artful handmade wire hangers. While Richman carries a small assortment of men's and women's separates (mostly loose, unstructured pieces), the big draw here is her exquisite sweaters. 2108 N. Damen Ave. (at Dickens St.). ℂ 773/278-6150. Subway/El: Blue Line to Damen, and then a long walk (10 blocks) or a short cab ride.

Scoop NYC The newest hot spot for trendy young things with plenty of spending money is this loft-life space in Bucktown, the first Midwest outpost of the popular New York clothing boutique Scoop NYC. You'll find a mix of major fashion names (Marc Jacobs bags, Jimmy Choo shoes) along with the requisite selection of designer denim, flirty dresses, and seemingly simple T-shirts that will make you do a double-take when you check out the price tag. (The store stocks men's and kids' clothing, too.) Even if you're not planning on blowing your paycheck on a pair of artfully distressed jeans, it's fun to browse for a quick overview of the hot looks of the season, and the in-store cafe is a good place to people-watch while sipping a latte. 1702 N. Milwaukee Ave. (at Wabansia Ave.). ℂ 773/227-9930. www.scoopnyc.com. Subway/El: Blue Line to Damen.

Shopgirl ⟨★⟩ Lincoln Park 20- and 30-somethings flock to Shopgirl for the latest looks from trendy lines such as Blue Cult and Free People. It's a girly gathering place (pink walls, glittery chandeliers) with three-digit price tags, but it still has the feel of a neighborhood hangout, thanks to the friendly staff. The same owner runs a maternity store and kids' clothing shop across the street. 1206 W. Webster Ave. (at Racine Ave.). ℂ 773/935-7467. Subway/El: Red or Brown Line to Fullerton.

Tangerine You can't help but smile when you enter this cheery Bucktown shop. Huge windows fill the place with light, and the colorful clothing selection—from designers such as Tocca, Nanette Lepore, and Trina Turk—is feminine and fun. (You will, however, pay a fair amount for these cute looks—most pieces start at $100 and up.) The sales staff has an upbeat attitude to match. 1719 N. Damen Ave. (at Wabansia Ave.). ℂ 773/772-0505. Subway/El: Blue Line to Damen.

The T-Shirt Deli 👎👎 *(Finds* For a new twist on custom clothing, stop by this cozy Bucktown storefront, where you can order up your own personalized T-shirt creation. Browse through the entertaining books of vintage iron-on patches, and you'll find everything from '80s icons such as Mr. T to '70s-style "Foxy Lady" logos. Choose a design (or create your own message), and your shirt will be printed up while you wait. When it's done, the shirt is packaged in a paper bag with a side of potato chips—just like a real deli. 1739 N. Damen Ave. (between Willow St. and St. Paul Ave.). © 773/276-6266. www.tshirtdeli.com. Subway/El: Blue Line to Damen.

Ultimo 👎👎 The grande dame of local boutiques, Ultimo is known for carrying high-profile (and high-priced) designers, as well as up-and-coming names that have yet to show up in department stores. The store's warren of rooms, decked out in luxurious dark wood and red velvet, feels more like a spectacularly well-stocked private collection than a shop. Ultimo carries both women's and men's clothing, making it one of the rare spots fashion hounds of both genders can shop together. 114 E. Oak St. (between Michigan Ave. and Rush St.). © 312/787-1171. www.ultimo.com. Subway/El: Red Line to Chicago.

COLLECTIBLES

Quake Collectibles Off the beaten tourist path in the Lincoln Square neighborhood (northwest of downtown), this temple to all things kitschy includes an impressive vintage lunch-box collection and ample stacks of old fan magazines a la *Teen Beat,* with Shaun Cassidy tossing his feathered tresses. 4628 N. Lincoln Ave. (north of Wilson Ave.). © 773/878-4288. Subway/El: Brown Line to Western.

Quimby's The ultimate alternative newsstand, Quimby's stocks every kind of obscure periodical, from cutting-edge comics to 'zines "published" in some teenager's basement. Their book selection is also decadently different from your local Barnes & Noble; categories include "Conspiracy," "Politics & Revolution," and "Lowbrow Art." 1854 W. North Ave. (just east of Damen Ave.). © 773/342-0910. www.quimbys.com. Subway/El: Blue Line to Damen.

Uncle Fun 👎👎 *(Finds* Whenever I'm looking for a quirky Christmas stocking-stuffer or the perfect gag gift, I know Uncle Fun will come through for me (1950's-era toy robots for a sci-fi-geek friend? Check. And how about some 3-D Jesus postcards for a Catholic-school grad?) Bins and cubbyholes are stuffed full of the standard joke toys (rubber-chicken key chains and chattering wind-up teeth), but you'll also find every conceivable modern pop-culture artifact, from Jackson Five buttons to Speed Racer's Mach-Five model car. 1338 W. Belmont Ave. (1 block east of Southport Ave.). © 773/477-8223. www.unclefunchicago.com. Subway/El: Red or Brown line to Belmont.

DEPARTMENT STORES

Barneys New York The first Midwest outpost of Barneys has the same look and feel of the New York original: minimalist-chic decor, high-priced fashions, and a fair amount of attitude from the sales staff. That said, the store has a stellar—if high-priced—shoe selection, along with always-interesting home accessories and a fun-to-browse cosmetics area full of specialty beauty products. In Lincoln Park, not far from the Armitage Avenue shopping district, you'll find **Barneys Co-Op,** 2209–11 N. Halsted St., at Webster Street (© 773/248-0426), which features collections from younger, up-and-coming designers—and lots of denim. 25 E. Oak St. (at Rush St.). © 312/587-1700. www.barneys.com. Subway/El: Red Line to Chicago.

Bloomingdale's   Though not as large as the New York original, Chicago's Bloomingdale's appeals to stylish shoppers looking for just a bit of urban edge. The shoe department has a good range (with serious markdowns during semiannual sales), and a special section is devoted to souvenir Bloomingdale's logo merchandise. 900 N. Michigan Ave. (at Walton St.). ℂ 312/440-4460. www.bloomingdales.com. Subway/El: Red Line to Chicago.

Lord & Taylor   Lord & Taylor, one of two large department stores in Water Tower Place (see Macy's, below), carries about what you'd expect: women's, men's, and children's clothing and accessories. Overall, Lord & Taylor is a more affordable alternative to stores such as Bloomingdale's and Sak's Fifth Avenue, with styles geared to women a few sizes larger than waifish fashion models. The shoe department is worth checking out for its good selection and sales. Water Tower Place, 835 N. Michigan Ave. (between Chestnut and Pearson sts.). ℂ 312/787-7400. www.lordandtaylor.com. Subway/El: Red Line to Chicago.

Macy's 👁👁👁   When Macy's took over Marshall Field's—Chicago's best-known "hometown" department store—in 2006, there was much local hand-wringing about what the buyout meant for Field's grand State Street headquarters. Although Field's iconic green awnings and shopping bags have been replaced by Macy's more dreary black, the good news is that the store itself remains impressive; a testament to the days when shopping downtown was an eagerly anticipated event rather than a chore. This block-long store is second in size only to Macy's New York City flagship, and its impressive breadth of merchandise and historically significant interior make it a must-see for serious shoppers. A number of exclusive "miniboutiques" are scattered throughout the overwhelming space, including the 28 Shop, which stocks the latest from hot young designers; beauty stations where you can get a manicure and pick up exclusive products; and a gourmet food department developed by celebrity chef Charlie Trotter. The enormous shoe department is another highlight, with everything from killer high heels (at killer prices) and boots to sneakers and casual sandals.

The Water Tower store, 835 N. Michigan Ave. (ℂ 312/335-7700), is a scaled-down but respectable version of the State Street store. Its eight floors are actually much more manageable than the enormous flagship, and its merchandise selection is still vast (although this branch tends to focus on the more expensive brands). 111 N. State St. (at Randolph St.). ℂ 312/781-1000. www.macys.com. Subway/El: Red Line to Washington.

Neiman Marcus   Yes, you'll pay top dollar for designer names here—the store does, after all, need to live up to its Needless Mark-up moniker—but Neiman's has a broader price range than many of its critics care to admit. It also has some mighty good sales. The four-story store, a beautiful environment in its own right, sells cosmetics, shoes, furs, fine and fashion jewelry, and clothing. The top floor has a fun gourmet food department as well as a pretty home-accessories area. Neiman's has two restaurants: one relaxed, the other a little more formal. 737 N. Michigan Ave. (between Superior St. and Chicago Ave.). ℂ 312/642-5900. www.neimanmarcus.com. Subway/El: Red Line to Chicago.

Nordstrom   Nordstrom's spacious, airy design and trendy touches (wheatgrass growing by the escalators, funky music playing on the stereo system) gives it the feel of an upscale boutique rather than an overcrowded department store. The company's famed shoe department is large but not overwhelming; more impressive is the cosmetics department, where you'll find a wide array of smaller labels and an "open sell" environment (meaning you're encouraged to try on makeup without a salesperson hovering over you). In keeping with the store's famed focus on service, a concierge can check your coat, call a cab, or make restaurant reservations for you. 520 N. Michigan Ave., inside

Westfield North Bridge mall, 55 E. Grand Ave. (at Rush St.). (℃ **312/379-4300**. www.nordstrom.com. Subway/El: Red Line to Grand.

Saks Fifth Avenue   Saks Fifth Avenue might be best known for its designer collections—Valentino, Chloe, and Giorgio Armani, to name a few—but the store also does a decent job of buying more casual and less expensive merchandise. Still, the mood here can be somewhat chilly, and the high-fashion clothes on display seem geared toward the super-skinny. The men's department is located in a separate building across Michigan Avenue. Don't forget to visit the cosmetics department, where Saks is known, in particular, for its fragrance selection. Chicago Place, 700 N. Michigan Ave. (at Superior St.). (℃ **312/944-6500**. www.saksfifthavenue.com. Subway/El: Red Line to Chicago.

GOURMET FOOD

Fox & Obel 𝒜𝒜   The city's top gourmet market is a foodie paradise: from the wide selection of specialty cheeses to the mouth-watering display of desserts. Browsing the shelves is like taking a minitour through the best specialty foods from around the world (and I dare you to walk through the bakery section without buying a loaf of freshly baked bread). An easy walk to Navy Pier and the lakefront, it's a great place to pick up a picnic lunch or a bottle of wine and some chocolates to enjoy late-night in your hotel room. There's also an in-store cafe if you want to take a break while strolling around the Michigan Avenue area. 401 E. Illinois St. (at McClurg Ct.). (℃ **312/410-7301**. www.foxandobel.com. Subway/El: Red Line to Grand, and then 65 Grand bus.

Goddess & Grocer   This upscale version of a neighborhood deli stocks everything you need for a mouthwatering lunch or dinner on the go—from specialty sandwiches to chicken and pasta dishes to freshly baked cookies and brownies. The prepared foods are a few notches above the standard takeout spot (wild Alaskan salmon; wild mushroom risotto), and the staff can put together meals for any occasion, from a catered business lunch to a romantic evening picnic at Millennium Park. There's also a good selection of wine and prepackaged snacks. The same owners run another, smaller, outpost in Bucktown, 1646 N. Damen Ave, at North Ave. ((℃ **773/342-3200**). 25 E. Delaware St. (at Rush St.). (℃ **312/896-2600**. www.goddessandgrocer.com. Subway/El: Red Line to Chicago.

HOME DECOR & GIFTS

Art Effect 𝒜𝒜   Classifying this wonderfully eclectic Armitage Avenue shop is no easy task (the owners refer to it as a "modern day general store"). It's got everything from aromatherapy oils and kitchen mixing bowls designed by cookbook author Nigella Lawson to handcrafted jewelry and gag gifts, not to mention a whole room devoted to hippie-chic women's clothing. The merchandise has a definite female slant, with a vibe that's young and irreverent rather than fussy, but the laid-back, friendly sales staff makes everyone feel welcome. The wide, unpredictable selection makes this one of my favorite browsing spots in town. 934 W. Armitage Ave. (at Bissell St.). (℃ **773/929-3600**. www.arteffectchicago.com. Subway/El: Brown Line to Armitage.

Orange Skin 𝒜   It may look like an ultracool loft catering only to trendier-than-thou style experts, but don't be intimidated: Orange Skin is one of my favorite places to check out what's new in the world of modern interior design (and the staff is more welcoming than you might expect). From colored clear-plastic dining chairs to bowls made of welded steel wires, browsing here is a good way to gauge what's cool in the world of design. Visit the shop's lower level for smaller tabletop items that make good, one-of-a-kind gifts. 223 W. Erie St. (at Franklin St.). © **312/335-1033.** www.orangeskin.com. Subway/El: Brown Line to Chicago.

P.O.S.H. Love pieces with a past but can't afford fine antiques? This fun shop sells discontinued china patterns from a more elegant time gone by; recent selections included dishes used for first-class service on American Airlines and a tea service once used in an English country inn. If you're looking for a one-of-a-kind souvenir, they also produce a line of Chicago skyline dinnerware. 613 N. State St. (between Ontario and Ohio sts.). © **312/280-1602.** www.poshchicago.com. Subway/El: Red Line to Grand.

Sawbridge Studios Craftsmanship is the driving force behind this inviting River North shop. Exquisitely handcrafted furniture, tabletop accessories, lamps, mirrors, and paintings have a timeless quality; the pieces here are original enough to feel special but classic enough to look like family heirlooms rather than of-the-moment fads. 153 W. Ohio St. (between LaSalle and Wells sts.). © **312/828-0055.** www.sawbridge.com. Subway/El: Red Line to Grand, or Brown Line to Merchandise Mart.

Stitch 𝒦 *(Finds)* A favorite gift-shopping spot for savvy local fashion experts, Stitch stocks an almost unclassifiable mix of merchandise including candles, luggage, and bed linens. Unlike the stereotypical, overly cutesy "gift shoppe," the selection here is fresh and contemporary; whatever you buy here is pretty much guaranteed to be cool. 1723 N. Damen Ave. (at Wabansia St.). © **773/782-1570.** www.stitchchicago.com. Subway/El: Blue Line to Damen.

MUSIC

Dusty Groove America In 1996, using a rickety old PC, Rick Wojcik and John Schauer founded an online record store at **www.dustygroove.com**. Since then, the operation has expanded in both cyberspace and the real world. Dusty Groove covers a lot of ground, selling soul, funk, jazz, Brazilian, lounge, Latin, and hip-hop music on new and used vinyl and CDs. For the most part, selections are either rare, imported, or both. 1120 N. Ashland Ave. (1 block south of Division St.). © **773/342-5800.** www.dusty groove.com. Subway/El: Blue Line to Division.

Jazz Record Mart 𝒦𝒦 This is possibly the best jazz record store in the country. For novices, the "Killers Rack" displays albums that the store's owners consider essential to any jazz collection. Besides jazz, there are bins filled with blues, Latin, and "New Music." The albums are filed alphabetically and by category (vocals, big band, and so on), and there are a couple of turntables to help you spend wisely. Jazz Record Mart also features a stage and seating for 50, where local and national artists coming through town entertain with in-store performances. 27 E. Illinois St. (between Wabash Ave. and State St.). © **312/222-1467.** www.jazzrecordmart.com. Subway/El: Red Line to Grand.

New Sound Gospel Chicago is the birthplace of gospel music, and now, thanks to artists such as Kirk Franklin, it's also become big business. All the major labels have gospel music divisions, and this store on the city's far South Side is the best place in town to browse the full range of what's available. Not sure where to start? Ask the store's expert staff for advice—here, you'll find everything from gospel's greatest to groups with names such as Gospel Gangstaz. 10723 S. Halsted St. (at 107th St.). © **773/785-8001.** Subway/El: Red Line to 95th/Dan Ryan, then 108 Halsted bus to 107th St.

Reckless Records The best all-round local record store for music that the cool kids listen to, Reckless Records wins brownie points for its friendly and helpful staff. You'll find new and used CDs and albums in a variety of genres (psychedelic and progressive rock, punk, soul, and jazz) here, along with magazines and a small collection of DVDs. There are also locations in Wicker Park at 1532 N. Milwaukee Ave. (© 773/235-3727), and the Loop, 26 E. Madison St. (© 312/795-0878). 3157 N. Broadway (at Belmont Ave.). © 773/404-5080. www.reckless.com. Subway/El: Red or Brown line to Belmont.

PAPER & STATIONERY

All She Wrote   One of the many owner-operated specialty shops along Armitage Avenue, All She Wrote stocks a fun mix of cards and notepaper, all with a lighthearted, whimsical feel. 825 W. Armitage Ave. (1 block west of Halsted St.). © 773/529-0100. www.allshe wrote.com. Subway/El: Red Line to North/Clybourn.

Fly Paper *(Finds*   Located on a busy stretch of Southport Street in the Wrigleyville neighborhood, Fly Paper has one of the most offbeat and artsy selections of greeting cards in the city, as well as other novelty and gift items. **Paper Boy,** a 10-minute walk away at 1351 W. Belmont Ave. (© 773/388-8811), is under the same ownership and features a similarly eclectic collection. 3402 N. Southport Ave. (between Belmont Ave. and Addison St.). © 773/296-4359. Subway/El: Brown Line to Southport.

Paper Source   The acknowledged leader of stationery stores in Chicago, Paper Source is now expanding throughout the country (with locations from Boston to Beverly Hills). The store's claim to fame is its collection of handmade paper in a variety of colors and textures. You'll also find one-of-a-kind greeting cards and a large collection of rubber stamps for personalizing your own paper at home. The River North shop is the store's headquarters, but there's also a location in the trendy Armitage shopping district at 919 W. Armitage Ave. (© 773/525-7300). 232 W. Chicago Ave. (at Franklin St.). © 312/337-0798. www.paper-source.com. Subway/El: Red or Brown line to Chicago.

The Watermark   Chicago socialites come here to order their engraved invitations, but this stationery store also carries a good selection of handmade greeting cards for all occasions. 109 E. Oak St. (1 block from Michigan Ave.). © 312/337-5353. Subway/El: Red Line to Clark/Division.

SALONS & SPAS

Art + Science   This Lincoln Park spot, just steps from the Armitage Avenue shopping strip, may look a little intimidating from outside, but the ambience inside is welcoming. Stylists can get as creative as you want, but most clients here are young professional women who want the same basic cut as everyone else. There's also another location in Wicker Park at 1552 N. Milwaukee Ave. (© 773/227-HAIR). 1971 N. Halsted St. (at Armitage Ave.). © 312/787-HAIR. www.artandsciencesalon.com. Subway/El: Brown Line to Armitage.

Charles Ifergan   Charles Ifergan, one of the city's top salons, caters to the ladies-who-lunch, and his rates, which vary according to the seniority of the stylist, are relatively high. But if you're a little daring, you can get a cut for the price of the tip on Tuesday and Wednesday evenings when junior stylists do their thing gratis—under the watchful eye of Monsieur Ifergan (call © 312/640-7444 between 10am and 4pm to make an appointment for that night). 106 E. Oak St. (between Michigan Ave. and Rush St.). © 312/642-4484. www.charlesifergan.com. Subway/El: Red Line to Chicago.

Kiva Day Spa   Kiva is the city's reigning "super spa," and is named for the round ceremonial space used by Native Americans seeking to quiet, cleanse, and relax the spirit. The two-floor, 6,000-square-foot space offers spa, salon, nutrition, and apothecary services, and a nutritional-juice-and-snack bar in a setting that evokes its namesake inspiration. The round first-floor salon is equipped with a massive granite circular counter surrounded by hair-care, facial, and aromatherapy products and body massage oils. Water Tower Place, entrance at 196 E. Pearson St (at Mies van der Rohe Way). ⓒ 312/840-8120. www.premierspacollection.com. Subway/El: Red Line to Chicago.

Mon Ami Coiffeur   Sure, you can get a haircut at this popular Gold Coast salon, but Mon Ami also has some of the very best colorists in town. Resident makeup artist Diane Ayala is known for her magic touch with eyebrow shaping (as well as her custom cosmetics line). 65 E. Oak St. (between Rush St. and Michigan Ave.). ⓒ 312/943-4555. Subway/El: Red Line to Clark/Division.

Salon Buzz   This hip hair parlor, operated by wizardly stylist Andreas Zafiriadis (who has wielded his scissors in Paris, Greece, New York, and California), is the choice for young women in creative professions. 1 E. Delaware Place (at State St.). ⓒ 312/943-5454. Subway/El: Red Line to Chicago.

Spa Space ⓡⓡ *Finds*   Located in the up-and-coming West Loop, this trendy spa offers the latest skin-care treatments in a stylishly modern building that feels like a boutique hotel. The gender-neutral decor and specialized menu of guy-friendly treatments (including a massage designed for golfers) has given this spa a far larger male clientele than other local spots. 161 N. Canal St. (at Randolph St.). ⓒ 312/943-5454. www.spaspace.com. Subway/El: Green Line to Clinton.

Tiffani Kim Institute   Occupying a modern three-story building in the heart of River North's art-gallery district, the Tiffani Kim Institute has to be seen to be believed. This sanctuary for women provides salon, spa, wellness, and cosmetic surgery treatments—not to mention a fashion and bridal boutique. Treatments include such faves as a detox seaweed body wrap, Asian ear candling, acupuncture and Chinese herbal medicine, and the "Serenity Stone Massage," a Tiffani Kim specialty in which smooth stones are warmed in a thermal unit to 135°F (57°C) and then used as tools in a Swedish-style massage. 310 W. Superior St. (between Franklin and Orleans sts.). ⓒ 312/943-8777. www.tiffanikiminstitute.com. Subway/El: Red or Brown line to Chicago.

Truefitt & Hill ⓡ *Finds*   Women have their pick of hair and beauty salons, but men don't often come across a place like Truefitt & Hill, the local outpost of a British barbershop listed in the *Guinness Book of World Records* as the oldest barbershop in the world. You'll pay a steep price for a haircut here (about $50), but the old-world atmosphere is dead-on, from the bow-tied barbers to the antique chairs. Services include lather shaves, manicures, massages, and shoeshines. Up front, the apothecary sells imported English shaving implements and toiletries. 900 N. Michigan Ave. shopping center (between Walton St. and Delaware Place), 6th floor. ⓒ 312/337-2525. www.truefittandhill.com. Subway/El: Red Line to Chicago.

Urban Oasis *Finds*   After a long day of sightseeing, try a soothing massage in this spa's subdued, Zen-like atmosphere. The ritual begins with a steam or rain shower in a private changing room followed by the spa treatment you elect—various forms of massage (including a couples' massage, in which you learn to do it yourself), an aromatherapy wrap, or an exfoliating treatment. Fruit, juices, or herbal teas are offered on completion. There's also another location in a burgeoning retail district a few blocks south of the Armitage Avenue shopping strip at 939 W. North Ave. (ⓒ 773/640-0001). 12 W. Maple St., 3rd floor (between Dearborn and State sts.). ⓒ 312/587-3500. www.urbanoasis.biz. Subway/El: Red Line to Clark/Division.

SHOES & BAGS

Alternatives   This locally owned shoe-store chain offers far more than Doc Marten wannabe designs; you'll find cutting-edge styles for men and women that are more affordable than you'd find in designer boutiques. 942 Rush St. (at Delaware St.). © 312/266-1545. www.altshoes.com. Subway/El: Red Line to Chicago.

1154 Lill Studio ⚡ *Finds*   Purse-a-holics and wannabe designers will find fashion heaven at this custom-handbag shop. Pick a style (which includes everything from evening purses to diaper bags), and then browse the huge selection of fabrics to create your own custom interior and exterior. Your finished creation can be picked up in a few weeks or shipped to your home. Not feeling particularly creative? There's also a selection of premade bags. Personal handbag parties can be arranged for groups of five or more. 904 W. Armitage Ave. (at Fremont St.). © 773/477-LILL. Subway/El: Brown line to Armitage.

G'Bani   On the corner of Oak and State streets, this funky, European-style boutique caters to men and women unfulfilled by designs made for the masses. The owner, a former fashion buyer for several high-style stores abroad, sells upscale clothing and shoes skewed toward fit fashionistas in their 20s through their 40s. Expect high style, not comfort; towering heels are the norm here. 949 N. State St. (between Oak St. and Walton Place). © 312/440-1718. Subway/El: Red Line to Chicago.

Lori's Designer Shoes ⚡⚡ *Value*   Lori's looks like a local version of Payless Shoes (shoeboxes stacked on the floor and women surrounded by piles of heels and boots), but the designer names on most of those shoes prove that this is a step above your typical discount store. A mecca for the shoe-obsessed, Lori's stocks all the latest styles, at prices that average 10% to 30% below department-store rates. 824 W. Armitage Ave. (between Sheffield Ave. and Halsted St.). © 773/281-5655. www.lorisdesignershoes.com. Subway/El: Brown Line to Armitage.

Stuart Weitzman   Strappy high-heeled sandals from this shoe seller make regular appearances on the red carpet at the Academy Awards and other A-list celebrity events. Go to Stuart Weitzman for shoes that make a dramatic impression—on your feet and on your wallet. You'll find lots of special-occasion heels here, as well as some lovely knee-high boots. 900 N. Michigan Ave. (between Walton St. and Delaware Place), 1st floor. © 312/943-5760. www.stuartweitzman.com. Subway/El: Red Line to Chicago.

Tod's   Characterized by detailed workmanship and top-quality materials, this upscale Italian footwear line is known for its moccasin-style driving shoes, but the shop also stocks high-heeled sandals, ballerina-style flats, mules in various colors, plus their fabulous trademark handbags. 121 E. Oak St. (between Michigan Ave. and Rush St.). © 312/943-0070. www.tods.com. Subway/El: Red Line to Chicago.

SOUVENIRS & MAPS

ArchiCenter Shop ⚡⚡⚡   Stop here for the coolest gifts in town. This bright, sleek shop is part of the Chicago Architecture Foundation, so everything in stock—including photography books, tour guides, stationery, and kids' toys—has a definite sense of style. Whether you're in the market for a $900 reproduction of a vase from Frank Lloyd Wright's Robie House or more affordable black-and-white photos of the city skyline, it's well worth a visit. 224 S. Michigan Ave. (at Jackson St.). © 312/922-3432, ext. 241. www.architecture.org. Subway/El: Red Line to Jackson.

Chicago Tribune Store   Yes, you'll find plenty of newspaper-logo T-shirts and Cubs hats here (the Tribune Company owns the team), but this shop, located on the ground floor of the newspaper offices, also has a great collection of books. You can also order reproductions of past *Tribune* front pages or color prints of photos from the newspaper's archives. 435 N. Michigan Ave. (at Hubbard St.). © 312/222-3080. Subway/El: Red Line to Grand.

City of Chicago Store   Located in the Water Works Visitor Center right off Michigan Avenue, this is a convenient stop for Chicago-related souvenirs and gifts, including truly one-of-a-kind pieces of retired municipal equipment (although the parking meters we've seen for sale here might be a little hard to stuff in your suitcase). 163 E. Pearson St. (at Michigan Ave.). © 312/742-8811. Subway/El: Red Line to Chicago.

The Savvy Traveller   This Loop specialty store carries just about everything a traveler might need, from guidebooks and maps to rain gear and portable games. 310 S. Michigan Ave. (between Van Buren St. and Jackson Blvd.). © 312/913-9800. www.thesavvytraveller. com. Subway/El: Red Line to Jackson.

SPORTING GOODS

Momentum   This store takes running seriously, but you don't have to be a marathoner to shop here. The knowledgeable sales staff takes the time to find the shoe that's right for you, no matter what your fitness level. The store also stocks running apparel and accessories as well as swimwear. 2001 N. Clybourn Ave. (between North and Fullerton aves.). © 773/525-7866. www.momentumchicago.com. Subway/El: Brown Line to Armitage.

Niketown *(Overrated*   When Niketown opened almost 10 years ago, it was truly something new: a store that felt more like a funky sports museum than a place hawking running shoes. These days, however, Niketown is no longer unique to Chicago (it's sprung up in cities from Atlanta to Honolulu), and the store's celebration of athletes can't cover up the fact that the ultimate goal is to sell expensive shoes. But the crowds keep streaming in to snatch up products pitched by Niketown's patron saints Michael Jordan and Tiger Woods. 669 N. Michigan Ave. (between Huron and Erie sts.). © 312/642-6363. http://niketown.nike.com. Subway/El: Red Line to Grand.

Sports Authority   The largest sporting-goods store in the city, Sports Authority offers seven floors of merchandise, from running apparel to camping gear. Sports fans will be in heaven in the first- and fifth-floor team merchandise departments, where Cubs, Bulls, and Sox jerseys abound. Cement handprints of local sports celebs dot the outside of the building; step inside to check out the prints from Michael Jordan and White Sox slugger Frank Thomas. 620 N. LaSalle St. (at Ontario St.). © 312/337-6151. www. sportsauthority.com. Subway/El: Red Line to Grand.

TOYS & CHILDREN'S CLOTHING

Fantasy Costumes *(Finds*   Not exactly a toy store, this sprawling costume shop (covering an entire city block) is nonetheless devoted to make-believe and is just as fun. The store stocks more than a million items, including 800 styles of masks (priced $1–$200) and all the accessories and makeup needed to complete any costume. There's also a full-service wig salon here. 4065 N. Milwaukee Ave. (west of Cicero Ave.). © 773/777-0222. www.fantasycostumes.com. Subway/El: Blue Line to Irving Park.

Grow   For a look at the future of baby style, trek out to this trendy boutique in the up-and-coming West Division Street neighborhood. The bright, open space showcases streamlined, ultramodern kids' furniture (such as bubble-shaped high chairs that would look right at home on *The Jetsons*), as well as clothing made of organic fabrics.

Sure, many of the environmentally friendly products on display are out of most parents' price range, but families that have had their fill of plastic kiddy gear will have fun browsing here. 1943 W. Division St. (at Damen Ave.). 🕐 **773/489-0009.** Subway/El: Blue Line to Division.

Little Strummer ⚘   This compact store is located in the Old Town School of Folk Music, which offers music classes for children, and stocks every kind of mini-instrument imaginable, from accordions and guitars to wind chimes and music boxes. There's also a good selection of music-related games and kids' CDs. 909 W. Armitage Ave. (at Halsted St.). 🕐 **773/751-3410.** Subway/El: Brown Line to Armitage.

Madison & Friends   Clothing for kids that's both cute and wearable is the specialty here, from baby-size leather bomber jackets to yoga pants for toddlers. A separate back room caters to older kids and tweens—including a staggering array of jeans. 940 N. Rush St. (at Oak St.). 🕐 **312/642-6403.** www.madisonandfriends.com. Subway/El: Red Line to Chicago.

Psycho Baby   The opening of this everything-for-baby shop was the definitive sign that Bucktown had gentrified. The prices may sometimes cause a double take ($60 for shoes that your kid will outgrow in 3 months), but the creative selection and happy vibe make it fun for browsing. 1630 N. Damen Ave. (1 block north of North Ave.). 🕐 **773/772-2815.** www.psychobabyonline.com. Subway/El: Blue Line to Damen.

VINTAGE FASHION/RESALE SHOPS

Beatnix   This solid vintage store, good for day-to-day and dress-up items, also carries a huge selection of old tuxes. Both men's and women's apparel are available. 3400 N. Halsted St. (at Roscoe St.). 🕐 **773/281-6933.** Subway/El: Red Line to Addison.

The Daisy Shop ⚘   A significant step up from your standard vintage store, The Daisy Shop specializes in couture fashions. These designer duds come from the closets of the city's most stylish socialites and carry appropriately hefty price tags. Even so, paying hundreds of dollars for a pristine Chanel suit or Louis Vuitton bag can still be considered a bargain, and well-dressed women from around the world stop by here in search of the perfect one-of-a-kind item. 67 E. Oak St. (between Michigan Ave. and Rush St.). 🕐 **312/943-8880.** Subway/El: Brown Line to Sedgwick.

Fox's   This no-frills shop near Armitage Avenue offers designer clothing at a steep discount. The downside: Most clothing labels are cut out, so you might not know exactly which A-list name you're buying, but the last time I was here, I heard a woman telling a friend that she'd seen the same clothes in Saks, a sure sign that Fox's stays up-to-date with the fashion pulse. 2150 N. Halsted St. (at Dickens St.). 🕐 **773/281-0700.** Subway/El: Brown Line to Armitage.

McShane's Exchange ⚘⚘ (Finds)   This consignment shop has a selection that's a few steps above the standard thrift store, and for designer bargains, it can't be beat. The store expands back through a series of cramped rooms, with clothes organized by color, making it easy to scope out the perfect black dress. The longer a piece stays in stock, the lower the price drops—and I've done plenty of double takes at the price tags here: Calvin Klein coats, Prada sweaters, and Armani jackets all going for well under $100. If that's not tempting enough, you'll also find barely used shoes and purses. McShane's has another location with a similar selection at 1141 W. Webster St. (🕐 773/525-0211). 815 W. Armitage Ave. (at Halsted St.). 🕐 **773/525-0282.** www.mcshanesexchange.com. Subway/El: Brown Line to Armitage.

The Second Child (Kids)   This self-described "upscale children's resale boutique" may not look all that upscale—it's basically one long, dark room on the second floor of an

Armitage Avenue town house—but take a look at the labels on these kids' clothes (Ralph Lauren, Lilly Pulitzer, and the like), and you'll see that they come from very fashionable closets. There's also a nice—if limited—selection of maternity clothes. 954 W. Armitage Ave. (between Bissell St. and Sheffield Ave.). ✆ 773/883-0880. Subway/El: Brown Line to Armitage.

WINE & LIQUOR

Binny's Beverage Depot *(Value)*   This River North purveyor of fermented libations is housed in a delightfully no-frills warehouse space and offers an enormous selection of wine, beer, and spirits—often at discounted prices. Binny's has a second, smaller location at 3000 N. Clark St. (✆ 773/935-9400). 213 W. Grand Ave. (at Wells St.). ✆ 312/332-0012. www.binnys.com. Subway/El: Red Line to Grand.

House of Glunz *(Finds)*   Not only is this Chicago's oldest wine shop, but it's also the oldest in the Midwest, with an inventory of 1,500 wines dating back to 1811. The shop periodically cracks open a few of its vintage wines for special wine-tasting events, but not all the selections here are rare or expensive. There's a stock of modern wines from California and Europe, and the knowledgeable owners are able to steer you to the right bottle to fit your budget. 1206 N. Wells St. (at Division St.). ✆ 312/642-3000. www.houseofglunz.com. Subway/El: Brown Line to Sedgwick.

Sam's Wines & Spirits   Believe it or not, this football-field-size warehouse store evolved from a modest packaged-goods store. Today, the family-owned operation is the best-stocked wine and spirits merchant in the city and offers pleasant, friendly service. It also features a superb cheese selection in the on-site Epicurean shop. 1720 N. Marcey St. (near Sheffield and Clybourn aves.). ✆ 800/777-9137 or 312/664-4394. www.samswine.com. Subway/El: Red Line to North/Clybourn.

10

Chicago After Dark

Chicago's bustling energy isn't confined to daylight hours. The city offers loads of after-hours entertainment, all with a distinctly low-key, Midwestern flavor.

The inviting atmosphere at both the Chicago Symphony Orchestra and the Lyric Opera of Chicago is appealing to culture vultures, while Broadway buffs can choose between big-league theaters such as Steppenwolf and Goodman and the scrappy storefront companies springing up around the city. The theater scene here was built by performers who valued gritty realism and a communal work ethic, and that down-to-earth energy is still very much present. Music and nightclub haunts are scattered throughout the city, but Chicago's thriving music scene is concentrated in Lincoln Park, Lakeview, and Wicker Park, where clubs are devoted to everything from jazz and blues to alternative rock and reggae.

While the city has its share of see-and-be-seen spots, Chicagoans in general are not obsessed with getting into the latest hot club; we'd much rather hang out with our buddies at a neighborhood bar. To join us, you only have to pick a residential area and wander. You don't have to go far to find a tavern filled with locals, a pool table, and maybe even a dartboard.

For up-to-date entertainment listings, check the local newspapers and magazines, particularly the "At Play" (Thursday) and "On the Town" (Friday) sections of the *Chicago Tribune* and the "Weekend Plus" (Friday) section of the *Chicago Sun-Times;* the weekly magazine *Time Out Chicago,* which has excellent comprehensive listings; and the *Chicago Reader* or *New City,* two free weekly tabloids with extensive listings. The *Tribune's* entertainment-oriented website, **www.metromix. com**; the *Reader's* website, **www.chicago reader.com**; and the local Citysearch website, **http://chicago.citysearch.com**, are also excellent sources of information, with lots of opinionated reviews.

1 The Performing Arts

Chicago is a regular stop on the big-name entertainment circuit, whether it's the national tour of Broadway shows such as *Wicked* or pop music acts such as U2 or the Dave Matthews Band (both of whom sell out multiple nights at stadiums when they come to town). High-profile shows including Monty Python's *Spamalot* and Mel Brooks's stage version of *The Producers* had their first runs here before moving on to New York.

Thanks to extensive renovation efforts, performers have some impressive venues where they can strut their stuff. The **Auditorium Theatre,** 50 E. Congress Pkwy., between Michigan and Wabash avenues (© **312/922-2110;** www.auditoriumtheatre. org), is my pick for the most beautiful theater in Chicago—and it's a certified national landmark, too. Built in 1889 by Louis Sullivan and Dankmar Adler, this grand hall schedules mostly musicals and dance performances. Even if you don't catch a show here, stop by for a tour (for more details, see p. 179).

The city's other great historic theaters are concentrated in the North Loop. The **Ford Center for the Performing Arts/Oriental Theater,** 24 W. Randolph St., and the **Cadillac Palace Theater,** 151 W. Randolph St., book major touring shows and are well worth a visit for arts buffs. The Oriental's fantastical Asian look includes elaborate carvings almost everywhere you look; dragons, elephants, and griffins peer down at the audience from the gilded ceiling. The Palace features a profusion of Italian marble surfaces and columns, gold-leaf accents a la Versailles, huge decorative mirrors, and crystal chandeliers. (If you'd like to get a look at these historic theaters for a fraction of the standard ticket price, guided tours of both start at 11am Sat and cost $10 per person; meet in the Oriental lobby.) The **LaSalle Bank Theatre** (formerly the Schubert Theatre), 18 W. Monroe St., was built in 1906 as a home for vaudeville; today it books mostly big-name musicals and sometimes comedy performers. For show schedules at all three theaters, call ℂ 312/977-1700, or visit www.broadwayinchicago.com.

The **Chicago Theatre,** 175 N. State St., at Lake Street (ℂ **312/443-1130**), is a 1920s music palace reborn as an all-purpose entertainment venue, playing host to pop acts, magicians, stand-up comedians, and more. **Arie Crown Theater,** in the McCormick Place convention center at 23rd Street and Lake Shore Drive (ℂ **312/791-6190**), books musicals and pop acts; a renovation has improved previously terrible acoustics (Elton John once interrupted a performance to complain about the sound), but this is still a massive, somewhat impersonal hall. Since all these theaters are quite large, the cheaper seats are in nosebleed territory.

Symphony Center, 220 S. Michigan Ave., between Adams Street and Jackson Boulevard (ℂ **312/294-3000**), is the building that encompasses Orchestra Hall, home of the Chicago Symphony Orchestra (CSO). Expanded and renovated a few years back, the building now holds a six-story sky-lit arcade, recital spaces, and the fine-dining restaurant Rhapsody (p. 119). While the CSO is the main attraction, the Symphony Center schedules a series of piano recitals, classical and chamber music concerts, a family matinee series, and the occasional jazz or pop artist.

Chicago has a few other major venues for traveling shows, but they are not as convenient for visitors. The **Rosemont Theatre,** 5400 River Rd. in Rosemont, near O'Hare Airport (ℂ **847/671-5100**), is a top suburban stop for musicals and concerts. The **North Shore Center for the Performing Arts in Skokie,** 9501 Skokie Blvd. in the northern suburb of Skokie (ℂ **847/673-6300**), is home to the well-respected Northlight Theater, the Skokie Valley Symphony Orchestra, and a series of touring acts, including comics, dance troupes, and children's programs.

⌐Tips Finding a Better Seat

Most of Chicago's grand old theaters have balconies that go way, way up toward the ceiling—and if you're stuck in the cheap seats, you'll be straining to see what's happening onstage. While theaters are very strict about checking tickets when you arrive, the ushers relax during intermission, so scope out empty seats during the first act, and then move down to better (and much pricier) spots for the rest of the show.

The Loop After Dark

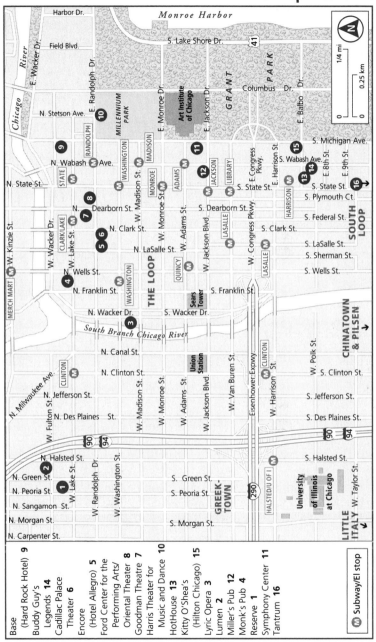

Base
(Hard Rock Hotel) **9**

Buddy Guy's
Legends **14**

Cadillac Palace
Theater **6**

Encore
(Hotel Allegro) **5**

Ford Center for the
Performing Arts/
Oriental Theater **8**

Goodman Theatre **7**

Harris Theater for
Music and Dance **10**

HotHouse **13**

Kitty O'Shea's
(Hilton Chicago) **15**

Lyric Opera **3**

Lumen **2**

Miller's Pub **12**

Monk's Pub **4**

Reserve **1**

Symphony Center **11**

Tantrum **16**

Ⓜ Subway/El stop

CLASSICAL MUSIC

For current listings of classical music concerts and opera, check with the **Chicago Dance and Music Alliance** (© 312/987-1123; www.chicagoperformances.org).

Chicago Symphony Orchestra ★★ The Chicago Symphony Orchestra is considered among the best in the world; a legacy of the late maestro Sir Georg Solti, who captured a record-breaking 31 Grammy awards for his CSO recordings and showcased the orchestra at other major musical capitals during frequent international tours. Recently departed musical director Daniel Barenboim—a talented conductor and piano prodigy who left the CSO after the 2005–06 season—proved a worthy successor. (Currently, interim leadership is in place in the form of Bernard Haitink, the CSO's principal conductor; and Pierre Boulez, the CSO's conductor emeritus.) Under Barenboim, the orchestra added more modern works into their repertoire, but crowd-pleasing favorites by Beethoven or Brahms are performed regularly as well.

Like many other orchestras around the country, the CSO has tried to diversify its programming to attract younger audiences. The "Symphony Center Presents" series has recently included some of the top jazz, world beat, Latin, and cabaret artists in the world. Although demand is high, good seats for concerts—turned in by subscribers who can't make it—often become available on concert days. Call Symphony Center, or stop by the box office to check availability.

Summertime visitors have an opportunity to hear a CSO performance at the delightful **Ravinia Festival** ★★ (© 847/266-5100) in suburban Highland Park, led by music director Christoph Eschenbach. (For more information, see p. 209.)

The highly regarded **Civic Orchestra of Chicago,** the CSO's training orchestra since 1919, presents free programs at Orchestra Hall. The **Chicago Symphony Chorus** also performs there. Orchestra Hall in Symphony Center, 220 S. Michigan Ave. © 312/294-3000. www.cso.org. Tickets $25–$110; box seats $185. Subway/El: Red Line to Jackson.

Grant Park Symphony and Chorus (Value One of the city's best cultural bargains, this music festival offers a series of free outdoor classical music concerts from June through August. The symphony, along with well-known visiting musicians and singers, performs in the Frank Gehry–designed Pritzker Music Pavilion in Millennium Park. Featuring Gehry's signature sinuous lines, the pavilion is surrounded by dramatic ribbons of curved steel. The Grant Park Symphony not only looks better than ever, it sounds great, too—thanks to a state-of-the-art sound system. Concerts are held Wednesday, Friday, and Saturday, with most performances beginning at 6:30pm (7:30pm on Sat). Seats in the front of the pavilion are reserved for subscribers, but the back rows are available on a first-come, first-served basis. There's also plenty of lawn seating, so bring a blanket and enjoy a picnic dinner. Pritzker Music Pavilion, Michigan Ave. and Randolph St. © 312/742-7638. www.grantparkmusicfestival.com. Subway/El: Red Line to Washington/State; or Brown, Orange, or Green line to Randolph/Wabash.

ADDITIONAL OFFERINGS

The **Apollo Chorus of Chicago** (© 312/427-5620; www.apollochorus.org) is best known for its annual holiday-season performance of Handel's *Messiah* at Orchestra Hall. Founded in 1872, 1 year after the Great Chicago Fire, the oldest all-volunteer civic chorus in the country began life as an all-male group and now includes women. Concerts take place throughout the year at various venues.

The **Chicago Chamber Musicians** (© 312/225-5226; www.chicagochamber music.org), a 14-member ensemble drawn from performers from the CSO and

Northwestern and DePaul universities, presents chamber music concerts at various locales around the city. The season runs September through May, and you can always find the CCM performing free noontime concerts on the first Monday of the month (except Sept and Mar) at the Chicago Cultural Center. The **Chicago String Quartet** is affiliated with the group.

The **Chicago Sinfonietta** (© 312/236-3681; www.chicagosinfonietta.org), with its racially diverse 45-member orchestra and a wide-ranging repertoire, seeks to broaden the audience for classical music. In the past the group has followed a Beethoven piano concerto with a piece featuring a steel drum. Playing about 10 times a year at Orchestra Hall and other venues, the group often takes a multimedia approach to its multicultural mission, collaborating with dance troupes, visual artists, museums (such as slide shows depicting art from the Art Institute and the National Museum of Mexican Art), rock bands, and gospel choirs.

Music of the Baroque (© 312/551-1414; www.baroque.org) is a small orchestra and chorus that pulls members from both the CSO and the Lyric Opera orchestra, and features professional singers from across the country. The ensemble performs the music of the 16th, 17th, and 18th centuries, in (appropriately) Gothic church settings in various neighborhoods. The group has made several recordings and has introduced works by Mozart and Monteverdi to Chicago audiences.

OPERA

Lyric Opera of Chicago ✹✹   One of the top American opera companies, the Lyric attracts the very best singers in the world for its lavish productions. Talented musicians and performers satisfy opera devotees, while newcomers are often swept away by all the grandeur (English supertitles make it easy to follow the action). Opening night in September remains the quasi-official kickoff of the Chicago social season, but don't be scared off by the snooty factor; audiences here are relatively casual (to the dismay of all those opera snobs). The company has a strong commitment to new American works (the Metropolitan Opera picked up the Lyric's production of *A View from the Bridge,* based on the Arthur Miller play).

The Lyric Opera performs in the handsome 3,563-seat Art Deco Civic Opera House, the second-largest opera house in the country, built in 1929. If you're sitting in one of the upper balconies, you'll definitely want to bring binoculars (if you're nice, the regulars sitting nearby may lend you theirs). There's only one problem with catching a show at the Lyric: The season, which runs through early March, sells out way in advance. Single tickets are sometimes available a few months in advance. Your other option is to call the day of a performance, when you can sometimes buy tickets that subscribers have turned in.

If you're in town in February or March, you can check out the theater by taking a tour (offered only during those months; call © 312/827-5685). The opera has an adjunct, the Lyric Opera Center for American Artists, which in spring and summer performs in smaller venues around town. Civic Opera House, Madison St. and Wacker Dr. © 312/332-2244. www.lyricopera.org. Tickets $31–$187. Subway/El: Brown Line to Washington.

Chicago Opera Theater   The "other" opera company in town, Chicago Opera Theater doesn't get all the big names, but it does make opera accessible to a wider audience with an emphasis on American composers and performers who sing in English. It also helps that tickets are less expensive and more plentiful than the Lyric Opera's. The company performs three operas a year (Mar–May), which usually run the gamut from classical tragedies by Handel to 20th-century satirical works. No matter what the bill, the talent and production values are top-notch (a recent production of two 20th-century Czech operas featured English text by playwright Tony Kushner and sets by illustrator Maurice Sendak). Chicago Opera Theater also runs a family opera program. Harris Theater for Music and Dance, 205 E. Randolph Dr. © 312/704-8414. www.chicago operatheater.org. Tickets $35–$120 adults, half-price for children and students. Subway/El: Red Line to Washington/State.

DANCE

Chicago's dance scene is lively, but unfortunately it doesn't attract the same crowds as our theaters or music performances. Some resident dance troupes have international reputations, but they spend much of their time touring to support themselves. Dance performances in Chicago tend to occur in spurts throughout the year, with visiting companies such as the American Ballet Theatre and the Dance Theater of Harlem stopping in Chicago for limited engagements. Depending on the timing of your visit, you may have a choice of dance performances—or there may be none at all. Dance lovers should schedule their visit for November, when the annual **"Dance Chicago"** festival (© 773/989-0698; www.dancechicago.com) is held at the Athenaeum Theatre, 2936 N. Southport Ave., on the North Side. Featuring performances and workshops from the city's best-known dance companies and countless smaller groups, it's a great chance to check out the range of local dance talent.

The major Chicago dance troupes perform at the **Harris Theater for Music and Dance,** 205 E. Randolph St. (© 312/334-7777), in Millennium Park. The 1,500-seat theater feels fairly stark and impersonal—the gray concrete lobby could be mistaken for a parking garage—but the sightlines are great, thanks to the stadium-style seating. Most of the troupes listed below perform there. For complete information on local dance performances, check the Chicago Dance and Music Alliance information line at © 312/987-1123, or visit **www.chicagoperformances.org**.

Another phenomenon that has enlivened the local scene is the scintillating **Chicago Human Rhythm Project** (© 773/281-1825; www.chicagotap.com), an annual tap-dance festival and nonprofit foundation created in 1990. The organization brings together tap and percussive dancers from around the world for a series of workshops and outreach programs in July and August at locations throughout the city and suburbs.

Ballet Chicago   The company, under the artistic direction of former New York City Ballet dancer Daniel Duell, is known mostly for its training classes but performs one full-length story ballet a year, usually in April or May. The group is notable for its specialty: the ballets of Balanchine. Office: 218 S. Wabash Ave. © 312/251-8838. www.ballet chicago.org. Tickets $12–$30.

The Dance Center–Columbia College Chicago *Finds*   Columbia College, a liberal arts institution specializing in the arts and media, has been growing by leaps and bounds in recent years. Its Dance Center—the hub of Chicago's modern-dance milieu—features an intimate "black box" 275-seat performance space with stadium seating and marvelous sightlines. The center schedules at least a dozen performances a year by both international and national touring groups and homegrown choreographers. 1306 S. Michigan Ave. © 312/344-8300. www2.colum.edu/cps/dancecenter. Tickets $18–$26. Bus: 151. Subway/El: Red Line to Roosevelt.

Hubbard Street Dance Chicago ✸   If you're going to see just one dance performance while you're in town, make it a Hubbard Street one. Chicago's best-known dance troupe mixes jazz, modern, ballet, and theater dance into an exhilarating experience. Sometimes whimsical, sometimes romantic, the crowd-pleasing 22-member ensemble incorporates a range of dance traditions, from Kevin O'Day to Twyla Tharp (who has choreographed pieces exclusively for Hubbard Street). Although the troupe spends most of the year touring, it has regular 2- to 3-week Chicago engagements in the fall and spring. In the summer, the dancers often perform at Ravinia, the Chicago Symphony Orchestra's lovely outdoor pavilion in suburban Highland Park (p. 209). Office: 1147 W. Jackson Blvd. *(C)* 312/850-9744. www.hubbardstreetdance.com. Tickets $20–$75.

Joffrey Ballet of Chicago *(R)*   While this major classical company concentrates on touring, the Joffrey schedules about 6 weeks of performances a year in its hometown. Led by co-founder and artistic director Gerald Arpino, the company is committed to the classic works of the 20th century. Its repertoire extends from the ballets of Arpino, Robert Joffrey, Balanchine, and Jerome Robbins to the cutting-edge works of Alonzo King and Chicago choreographer Randy Duncan. The Joffrey continues to draw crowds with its popular rock ballet, *Billboards,* which is set to the music of Prince and tours internationally. The company is usually in town in the spring (Mar or Apr), fall (Sept or Oct), and December, when it stages a popular rendition of the holiday favorite *The Nutcracker.* Office: 70 E. Lake St. *(C)* 312/739-0120. www.joffrey.com. Tickets $25–$130.

Muntu Dance Theatre of Chicago   The tribal costumes, drumming, and energetic moves of this widely touring group, which focuses on both traditional and contemporary African and African-American dance, are always a hit with audiences. The company performs at the Harris Theater for Music and Dance in December and the spring (Apr or May). Office: 6800 S. Wentworth Ave. *(C)* 773/602-1135. www.muntu.com. Tickets $25–$50.

River North Dance Company   Chicago can be a brutal testing ground for start-up dance companies, which have to struggle to find performance space and grab publicity. But the odds didn't buckle the well-oiled knees of the River North Dance Company. This talented jazz dance ensemble performs programs of short, Broadway-style numbers by established and emerging choreographers. They perform periodically at the Harris Theater for Music and Dance, but you never know where they'll pop up next; check their website or call for information on upcoming shows. Office: 1016 N. Dearborn St. *(C)* 312/944-2888. www.rivernorthchicago.com. Tickets $25–$30.

THEATER

Ever since the Steppenwolf Theatre Company burst onto the national radar in the late '70s and early '80s with in-your-face productions of Sam Shepard's *True West* and Lanford Wilson's *Balm in Gilead,* Chicago has been known as a theater town. As Broadway produced bloated, big-budget musicals with plenty of special effects but little soul, Chicago theater troupes gained respect for their risk-taking and no-holds-barred emotional style. Some of Broadway's most acclaimed dramas in recent years (the Goodman Theatre's revival of *Death of a Salesman* and Steppenwolf's *The Grapes of Wrath,* to name a few) hatched on Chicago stages. With more than 200 theaters, Chicago might have dozens of productions playing on any given weekend—and seeing a show here is on my must-do list for all visitors.

The city's theaters have produced a number of legendary comedic actors, including comic-turned-director Mike Nichols *(The Graduate, Postcards from the Edge, Primary Colors),* as well as fine dramatic actors and playwrights. David Mamet, one of America's greatest playwrights and an acclaimed film director and screenwriter, grew up in

Chicago's South Shore steel-mill neighborhood and honed his craft with the former St. Nicholas Players, which included actor William H. Macy *(Fargo, Boogie Nights)*.

The thespian soil here must be fertile. Tinseltown and TV have lured away such talents as John Malkovich, Joan Allen, Dennis Franz, George Wendt, John and Joan Cusack, Aidan Quinn, Anne Heche, and Lili Taylor. But even as emerging talent leave for higher paychecks, a new pool of fresh faces is always waiting to take over. This constant renewal keeps the city's theatrical scene invigorated with new ideas and energy. Many of the smaller theater companies place great emphasis on communal work: Everyone takes part in putting on a production, from writing the script to building the sets. These companies perform in tiny, none-too-impressive venues, but their enthusiasm and commitment are inspiring. Who knows, the group you see performing in some storefront theater today could be the Steppenwolf of tomorrow.

The listings below represent only a fraction of the city's theater offerings. For a complete listing of current productions playing, check the comprehensive listings in the two free weeklies, the *Reader* (which reviews just about every show in town) and *New City;* the weekly *Time Out Chicago;* or the Friday sections of the two dailies. The website of the **League of Chicago Theatres** (www.chicagoplays.com) also lists all theater productions playing in the area.

GETTING TICKETS

To order tickets for many plays and events, call the **Ticketmaster Arts Line** (② 312/ 902-1500), a centralized phone-reservation system that allows you to charge full-price tickets (with an additional service charge) for productions at more than 50 Chicago theaters. Individual box offices also take credit card orders by phone, and many of the smaller theaters will reserve seats for you with a simple request under your name left on the answering machine. For hard-to-get tickets, try **Chicago Ticket Exchange** (② 312/902-1888; www.chicagoticketexchange.com) or **Gold Coast Tickets** (② 800/ 889-9100; www.goldcoasttickets.com).

About Face Theatre   About Face Theatre takes its mission seriously: to promote the creation of new works that examine gay and lesbian themes and experiences. While that often makes for a night of thought-provoking theater, the fare isn't always heavy with social-justice issues. One of the group's big hits was a very campy musical version of *Xena: Warrior Princess.* Performances are in the upstairs studio at Steppenwolf Theatre (see below). Office: 1222 W. Wilson Ave. ② 773/784-8565. www.aboutfacetheatre.com. Tickets $20–$40.

American Theater Company   Its mission is to produce stories that ask the question: "What does it mean to be an American?" With that broad mandate, the company generally focuses on serious American dramas (Mamet's *American Buffalo,* for instance, and works by Sam Shepherd and Thornton Wilder), but comical and even musical fare shows up on the schedule from time to time. Recent literary adaptations have included *Catch-22* and *Working,* based on the book by veteran Chicago writer Studs Terkel. 1909 W. Byron St. (2 blocks south of Irving Park Rd. at Lincoln Ave.). ② 773/929-1031. www.atcweb.org. Tickets $20–$35. Subway/El: Brown Line to Irving Park.

Bailiwick Repertory Theatre   Bailiwick gets my vote as the most eclectic theater in the city. Its three stages showcase works both dramatic and light-hearted, some produced by Bailiwick, others by smaller, scrappier start-up troupes. Each year, the theater produces a main-stage series of classics and musicals, the Director's Festival of one-act plays by fresh local talents (in June), and gay- and lesbian-oriented shows during the Pride Performance series, which generally runs over 20 weeks from mid-May

Value Half-Price Theater Tickets

For half-price tickets on the day of the show, drop by one of the **Hot Tix** ticket centers (© **312/977-1755;** www.hottix.org), located in the Loop at 72 E. Randolph St. (between Wabash and Michigan aves.); at the Water Works Visitor Center, 163 E. Pearson St.; in Lincoln Park at Tower Records, 2301 N. Clark St.; and in several suburban locations. All branches are open Tuesday through Saturday 10am to 6pm, Sunday noon to 5pm; on Friday you can also purchase tickets for weekend performances. Hot Tix also offers advance-purchase tickets at full price. Tickets are not sold over the phone. The website lists what's on sale for that day beginning at 10am.

In addition, a few theaters offer last-minute discounts on leftover seats. **Steppenwolf Theatre Company** often has $20 tickets available beginning at 11am on the day of a performance; stop by Audience Services at the theater. Also, half-price tickets become available 1 hr. before the show; call or stop by the box office, or visit www.steppenwolf.org. The "Tix at Six" program at the **Goodman Theatre** offers half-price day-of-show tickets; many of them are excellent seats returned by subscribers. Tickets go on sale at the box office at 6pm for evening performances, noon for matinees.

to early October. This is also one of the few companies to stage performances for deaf audiences, performing new spins on classics such as Thornton Wilder's *Our Town* with casts of hearing and hearing-impaired actors. The company's children's theater program produces an original musical for kids each spring. 1229 W. Belmont Ave. (at Racine Ave.). © **773/883-1090.** www.bailiwick.org. Tickets $20–$35. Subway/El: Red or Brown line to Belmont.

Briar Street Theatre *Kids*   The Briar Street Theatre has been the "Blue Man theater" since the fall of 1997. The avant-garde New York City performance phenomenon known as **Blue Man Group** has transformed the 625-seat theater, beginning with the lobby, which is now a jumble of tubes, wires, and things approximating computer innards. The show—which mixes percussion, performance art, mime, and rock 'n' roll—has become an immensely popular permanent fixture on the Chicago theater scene. (Note to those with sensitive ears: It can also get pretty loud.) The three strangely endearing performers, whose faces and heads are covered in latex and blue paint, know how to get the audience involved. Your first decision: Do you want the "splatter" or the "nonsplatter" seats? (The former necessitates the donning of a plastic sheet.) Although the show is a great pick for older children, it's not recommended for kids under 5 years old. 3133 N. Halsted St. (at Briar St.). © **773/348-4000.** www.blueman.com. Tickets $49–$59. Subway/El: Red or Brown line to Belmont.

Chicago Shakespeare Theatre *Finds*   This group's home on Navy Pier is a visually stunning, state-of-the-art jewel. The centerpiece of the glass-box complex, which rises seven stories, is a 525-seat courtyard-style theater patterned loosely after the Swan Theater in Stratford-upon-Avon. The complex also houses a 180-seat studio theater, an English-style pub, and lobbies with commanding views of Lake Michigan and the Chicago skyline. But what keeps subscribers coming back is the talented company of actors, including some of the finest Shakespeare performers in the country.

The main theater presents three plays a year, almost always by the Bard; founder and artistic director Barbara Gaines usually directs one show. Chicago Shakespeare also books special short-run performances and events, such as a recent production of *Hamlet* by acclaimed British director Peter Brook. Shakespeare Theatre subscribers are loyal, so snagging tickets can be a challenge; reserve well in advance if possible. If you have a choice of seats, avoid the upper balcony; the tall chairs are uncomfortable, and you have to lean way over the railing to see all the action onstage—definitely not recommended for anyone with a fear of heights. 800 E. Grand Ave. ℂ 312/595-5600. www.chicago shakes.com. Tickets $40–$67. Subway/El: Red Line to Grand, and then bus 29 to Navy Pier. Discounted parking in attached garage.

Court Theatre *(Finds)*   Given its affiliation with the University of Chicago, it should come as no surprise that this theater knows its way around the classics, from Molière to Ibsen. The productions here, however, are far from stuffy academic exercises: the vibrant, energetic takes on well-known works draw some of the finest actors in the city. In recent years, Court's eclectic season have included at least one musical (*Man of La Mancha* and *Raisin,* based on Lorraine Hansberry's *A Raisin in the Sun*), as well as plays by modern masters such as August Wilson and Tom Stoppard. It's a bit of trek to get here from downtown (I'd recommend a cab at night), but no matter what show is playing when you're in town, it's well worth the trip for theater lovers. 5535 S. Ellis Ave. (at 55th St.). ℂ 773/753-4472. www.courttheatre.org. Tickets $26–$50. Metra train: 57th St.

ETA Creative Arts Foundation   Since 1971, this theater has been staging original or seldom-seen dramatic works by African-American writers from Chicago and beyond. Along with **Black Ensemble Theater** (which performs at the Uptown Center Hull House, 4520 N. Beacon St.; ℂ 773/769-4451; www.blackensembletheater. org), this is one of the best African-American theater troupes in the city. The company stages six plays a year in its 200-seat theater, including works geared toward children that are performed on Saturday afternoons. 7558 S. Chicago Ave. (at 76th St.). ℂ 773/752-3955. www.etacreativearts.org. Tickets $25. Subway/El: Red Line to 69th St., transfer to bus 30.

Factory Theater   This irreverent young troupe offers the quintessential low-budget Chicago theater experience. The group specializes in original works written by the ensemble, many of which aim at a young, nontheatrical crowd (you're encouraged to bring your own beer and drink it during the late-night shows). The company's biggest hit—which it stages off and on throughout the year—is the raunchy trailer-park potboiler *White Trash Wedding and a Funeral;* it's hilarious, tacky fun, but not for those with delicate sensibilities. Lately, the Factory has been trying out serious dramatic works as well. 3504 N. Elston Ave. ℂ 312/409-3247. www.thefactorytheater.com. Tickets $15–$20. Subway/El: Red Line to Addison, then bus 152 (Addison St.).

Goodman Theatre *(★★)*   The Goodman, under artistic director Robert Falls, is the dean of legitimate theaters in Chicago. The theater produces both original productions—such as Horton Foote's *The Young Man from Atlanta* before it went to Broadway—and familiar standards, including everything from Shakespeare to musicals. Its acclaimed revival of Arthur Miller's *Death of a Salesman,* starring Brian Dennehy, not only made it to the Broadway stage in 1999 but also won four Tonys—more than any other production that year. The theater has nurtured the talents of solo artists such as John Leguizamo, and played host to such acclaimed actors as Denzel Washington, William Hurt, Sigourney Weaver, Chita Rivera, and Rip Torn. Productions at the

Goodman are always solid; you may not see anything revolutionary, but you'll get some of the best actors in the city and top-notch production values.

The Goodman's custom-designed home in the North Loop is a rehab of the historic Harris and Selwyn theaters, a pair of rococo former movie houses, but the renovation retained none of the historic bric-a-brac; the new structure has a modern, minimalist feel (the side of the building glows with different colors in the evenings). The centerpiece is the 830-seat limestone-and-glass Albert Ivar Goodman Theatre. Connected to the main theater is a cylindrical, glass-walled building that houses retail operations, the 400-seat Owen Theatre, and the restaurant Petterino's (p. 118).

Every December, the Goodman stages a production of *A Christmas Carol,* which draws families from throughout the Chicago area and beyond. If you're in town then, it's great fun, but buy your tickets in advance, because many performances sell out. 170 N. Dearborn St. ⓒ 312/443-3800. www.goodman-theatre.org. Tickets $10–$68. Subway/El: Red Line to Washington/State or Lake/State; Brown or Orange line to Clark/Lake.

The House Theatre *(Finds* If you're looking for the up-and-coming stars of Chicago theater, keep your eyes on the House. This group of young actors takes on big themes (Harry Houdini and his obsession with death; the space-age tales of Ray Bradbury) and turns them into nonstop spectacles of drama, music, and comedy. Despite the usual budget constraints, the sets and special effects are impressive—as is the troupe's energy, imagination, and humor. The House has only been around for about 5 years, but the buzz on this group is definitely picking up (so come see them while their tickets remain ultra-affordable). Office: 4700 N. Ravenswood Ave. ⓒ 773/251-2195. www.thehouse theatre.com. Tickets $17–$22. Performances: The Viaduct, 3111 N. Western Ave. Subway/El: Red Line to Belmont, then bus 77 (Belmont Ave.).

Lookingglass Theatre Company *ⓖ* A rising star on the Chicago theatrical scene, Lookingglass produces original shows and unusual literary adaptations in a highly physical and visually imaginative style. (Its location in the Water Tower Pumping Station—just off Michigan Avenue and within walking distance of many downtown hotels—makes it especially visitor-friendly.) The company, founded more than a decade ago by graduates of Northwestern University (including *Friend* David Schwimmer), stages several shows each year. Recent offerings included *Metamorphoses,* a sublime and humorous modern recasting of Ovid's myths that became a hit in New York, and *Lookingglass Alice,* an acrobatic retelling of *Alice in Wonderland.* Ensemble member Mary Zimmerman—who directed *Metamorphoses*—has built a national reputation for her creative interpretations of literature, so if she's directing a show while you're in town, don't miss it. Schwimmer also appears here occasionally, as either an actor or director. Lookingglass shows emphasize visual effects as much as they do acting, whether it's having performers wade through a giant shallow pool or take to the sky on trapeze. 821 N. Michigan Ave. (at Chicago Ave.). ⓒ 312/337-0665. www.lookingglasstheatre. org. Tickets $25–$55. Subway/El: Red Line to Chicago.

Neo-Futurists *(Finds* A fixture on Chicago's late-night theater scene, the Neo-Futurists have been doing their hit *Too Much Light Makes the Baby Go Blind* since 1988 (it's now the longest-running show in Chicago). The setting—a cramped room above a funeral home—isn't much, but the gimmick is irresistible: Every night the performers stage a new collection of "30 plays in 60 minutes." The "plays" vary from a 3-minute comedy sketch to a lightning-quick wordless tableau; the mood veers from laugh-out-loud silly to emotionally touching. The show starts at 11:30pm on weekends; get there about an hour ahead, because seats are first-come, first-served, and they do sell out. The late-night curtain attracts a younger crowd, but I've taken 60-something relatives who have had a great time (unlike many improv comedy troupes, the Neo-Futurists don't rely on raunchy or gross-out humor). Admission is random: Theatergoers pay $7 plus the roll of a six-sided die. If you want to feel that you've experienced edgy, low-budget theater—but still want to be entertained—this is the place to go. 5153 N. Ashland Ave. (at Foster Ave.). ℂ 773/275-5255. www.neofuturists.org. Tickets $8–$13. Subway/El: Red Line to Berwyn.

Pegasus Players Performing in a rented college auditorium in the gritty North Side neighborhood of Uptown, Pegasus Players specializes in the kind of intellectually demanding fare that bigger mainstream theaters are afraid to risk. A few years ago, Pegasus scored a coup, convincing Stephen Sondheim to let the performers stage the U.S. premiere of his first musical, the little-known *Saturday Night.* Challenging musicals aren't the theater's only Herculean efforts. Pegasus Players has also mounted rarely produced dramatic works such as Robert Schenkkan's 1992 Pulitzer Prize–winning *The Kentucky Cycle,* a 6-hour nine-play marathon. The group prides itself on picking shows that highlight social issues. O'Rourke Performing Arts Center, Truman College, 1145 W. Wilson Ave. ℂ 773/878-9761. www.pegasusplayers.org. Tickets $15–$25. Subway/El: Red Line to Wilson.

Redmoon Theater *(Finds* Redmoon Theater might well be the most intriguing and visionary theater company in Chicago. Founded in 1990, the company produces "spectacle theater" involving masks, objects, and an international range of puppetry styles in indoor and outdoor venues around town. Utterly hypnotic, highly acrobatic and visceral, and using minimal narration, Redmoon's adaptations of Melville's *Moby Dick,* Mary Shelley's *Frankenstein,* Victor Hugo's *The Hunchback of Notre Dame,* and *Rachel's Love,* an original work based on Jewish folktales, were revelations that earned the company an ardent and burgeoning following. Every September, Redmoon presents an annual "spectacle," transforming a public park into a site for performance art, larger-than-life puppet shows, and dramatic visual effects. Office: 1438 W. Kinzie St. ℂ 312/850-8440. www.redmoon.org. Tickets $18–$22.

Steppenwolf Theatre Company Once a pioneer of bare-bones guerilla theater, Steppenwolf has moved firmly into the mainstream with a state-of-the-art theater and production budgets to rival those in any big city. The company has garnered many national awards and has launched the careers of several respected and well-known actors, including John Malkovich, Gary Sinise, Joan Allen, John Mahoney (of *Frasier*), and Laurie Metcalf (of *Roseanne*). Famous for pioneering the edgy, "rock 'n' roll," spleen-venting style of Chicago acting in the 1970s and '80s—characterized by such incendiary tours de force as Sam Shepard's *True West,* Lanford Wilson's *Balm in Gilead,* Lyle Kessler's *Orphans,* and an adaptation of John Steinbeck's *The Grapes of Wrath*—Steppenwolf lately has become a victim of its own success. No longer a scrappy storefront theater, it now stages world premieres by emerging playwrights, revivals of classics, and adaptations of well-known literary works. While the acting is always high caliber, shows can be hit-or-miss, and unlike in the early days, you're not guaranteed a thrilling experience.

Under artistic director Martha Lavey, Steppenwolf has drawn upon its star power, bringing back big names to perform or direct from time to time. But don't come here expecting to see John Malkovich or Joan Allen on stage; most of the big-name actors are too busy with their movie careers. Struggling troupes sometimes perform at Steppenwolf's smaller studio theater, which stages more experimental fare. Tickets $20 to

$65. Tickets ($20) go on sale at Audience Services at 11am the day of a performance; rush tickets (subject to availability; main stage half price, studio $10) go on sale 1 hr. before performance. 1650 N. Halsted St. (at North Ave.). ℂ 312/335-1650. www.steppenwolf.org. Subway/El: Red Line to North/Clybourn.

Theater on the Lake *(Value)*   What a great way to see two of the city's signature strengths: a sublime skyline view from the water's edge, and an evening of off-Loop Chicago theater. This Prairie School–style theater has mounted theatrical productions along the lake for half a century, but in recent years, the park district has hit upon a perfect programming gimmick. Each week a different independent theater company gets to strut its stuff, usually restaging a play they performed earlier in the year. Performances run from June into August on Wednesday to Sunday evenings, and some shows do sell out, so it pays to reserve in advance. At intermission, you can walk out the back door and look south to the city lights. If it's a cool night, bring a sweater, because the screened-in theater is open to the night air (allowing the noise of traffic on Lake Shore Dr. to intrude somewhat, too). And a warning for those hot summer nights: the building is not air-conditioned. Fullerton Ave. and Lake Shore Dr. ℂ 312/742-7994. Tickets $18. Bus: 151 (Sheridan).

Trap Door Theatre   Trap Door is emblematic of the streetwise, no-holds-barred brand of off-Loop theater. A risk-taking, emotionally high-voltage company that has somehow stayed afloat (despite performing in a converted garage hidden behind a Bucktown restaurant), Trap Door concentrates on plays with a social or political bent. Many tend to be original works or decidedly noncommercial, provocative pieces by rarely produced cerebral artists, many of them European. (A few years ago, the show *AmeriKafka,* inspired by writer Franz Kafka and his visit to a performance by a Yiddish theater troupe, even featured a brief X-rated puppet show.) Prepare to be challenged: Theater doesn't get any more up close and personal than this. 1655 W. Cortland St. (1 block west of Ashland Ave.). ℂ 773/384-0494. www.trapdoortheatre.com. Tickets $15–$20. Subway/El: Blue Line to Division.

Victory Gardens Theater *(Finds)*   Victory Gardens is one of the few pioneers of off-Loop theater that has survived from the 1970s. The company was rewarded for its unswerving commitment to developing playwrights with a Tony Award for regional theater in 2001—a real coup for a relatively small theater. The five or six productions presented each season are new works, many developed through a series of workshops. The plays tend to be accessible stories about real people and real situations—nothing

---

(Tips **Theater for All**

Visitors with disabilities will find that some local theaters go the extra mile to make their performances accessible. The Steppenwolf, Goodman, and Lookingglass theaters offer sign-language interpretation for deaf patrons and audio-described performances for visually impaired audiences. Bailiwick Repertory runs a regular series of plays featuring deaf actors. Victory Gardens Theater, which has a long-standing commitment to accessible theater, schedules special performances customized for audiences with different disabilities throughout the year. The theater even offers deaf patrons special glasses that project captions of dialogue onto the frame of the glasses.

too experimental. Even though most shows don't feature nationally known actors, the casts are always first-rate, and the plays usually leave you with something to think about (or passionately discuss) on the way home.

Victory Gardens stages shows at its main stage inside the former Biograph movie theater (known in Chicago lore as the place where the FBI gunned down bank robber John Dillinger in 1934). Smaller independent companies such as Shattered Globe and Remy Bumppo play on four smaller stages at the Victory Gardens Greenhouse Theater, 2257 N. Lincoln Ave., a few blocks south. 2433 N. Lincoln Ave. (1 block north of Fullerton Ave.). ✆ 773/871-3000. www.victorygardens.org. Tickets $30–$45. Subway/El: Red or Brown line to Fullerton.

2 Comedy & Improv

In the mid-1970s, the nation was introduced to Chicago's brand of comedy through the skit-comedy show *Saturday Night Live*. Back then, John Belushi and Bill Murray were among the latest brood to hatch from the number-one incubator of Chicago-style humor, Second City. Since then, two generations of American comics, from Mike Nichols and Robert Klein to Mike Myers and Tina Fey, have honed their skills in Chicago before making it big in film and TV. Chicago continues to nurture young comics, affording them the chance to learn the tricks of improvisational comedy at Second City, the ImprovOlympic, and numerous other comedy and improv outlets.

ComedySportz *(Kids* Most improv-comedy shows aren't exactly family-friendly, but ComedySportz does away with the barlike atmosphere and R-rated topics to deliver shows that are funny for the whole family. Chicago's only all-ages professional improv troupe sets two groups of five comedians against each other to compete for audience applause. "It isn't *about* sports—it *is* a sport," is the tagline here. Kids 10 and older are welcome at shows, held Thursday and Friday at 8pm, and Saturday at 6, 8, and 10pm. Offices: 5100 N. Ravenswood Ave. ✆ 773/549-8080. www.comedysportzchicago.com. Performances are held at the Chicago Center for the Performing Arts, 777 N. Green St. Tickets $19. El: Blue Line to Chicago, bus 66 and 8.

iO *(Finds* The iO improv troupe was founded in 1981 by the late, great, and inexplicably unsung Del Close, an improv pioneer who branched off from his more mainstream counterparts at Second City to pursue an unorthodox methodology (the letters "iO" stand for "ImprovOlympic," the group's original name). A legendary iconoclast, the colorful Close developed a long-form improv technique known as "The Harold." It eschewed the traditional sketch format in favor of more conceptual comedy scenes: The audience suggests a theme for the evening, then a series of skits, monologues, and songs are built around it. Second City, whose vignette-blackout-vignette format had grown weary, has since co-opted the method.

iO offers a nightclub setting for a variety of unscripted nightly performances, from free-form pieces to shows loosely based on concepts such as *Star Trek* or dating. Like all improv, it's a gamble: It could be a big laugh, or the amateur performers could go down in flames. Monday is an off night for most other clubs in town, and iO takes advantage with a show called the Armando Diaz Experience, an all-star improv night that teams up some of the best improvisers in Chicago, from Second City and elsewhere. Besides Mike Myers, successful alums include the late Chris Farley, Tim Meadows, Andy Dick, and Conan O'Brien's former *Late Night* sidekick, Andy Richter. 3541 N. Clark St. (at Addison St.). ✆ 773/880-0199. www.iochicago.net. Tickets $5–$14. Subway/El: Red Line to Addison.

The Magnificent Mile, the Gold Coast & River North After Dark

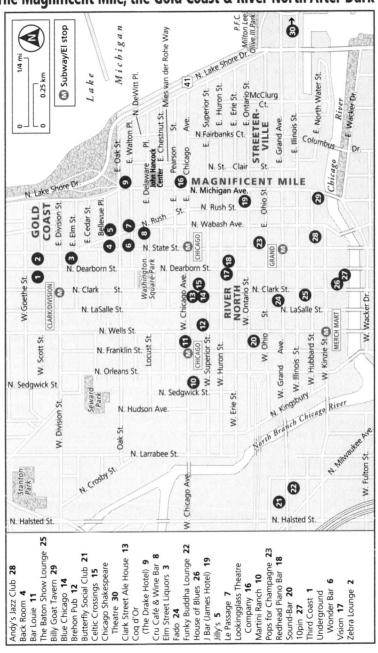

Andy's Jazz Club **28**
Back Room **4**
The Baton Show Lounge **25**
Billy Goat Tavern **29**
Blue Chicago **14**
Brehon Pub **12**
Butterfly Social Club **21**
Celtic Crossings **15**
Chicago Shakespeare
  Theatre **30**
Clark Street Ale House **13**
Coq d'Or
  (The Drake Hotel) **9**
Cru Café & Wine Bar **8**
Elm Street Liquors **3**
Fado **24**
Funky Buddha Lounge **22**
House of Blues **26**
J Bar (James Hotel) **19**
Jilly's **5**
Le Passage **7**
Lookingglass Theatre
  Company **16**
Martini Ranch **10**
Pops for Champagne **23**
Redhead Piano Bar **18**
Sound-Bar **20**
10pin **27**
Third Coast **1**
Underground
  Wonder Bar **6**
Vision **17**
Zebra Lounge **2**

Second City   For nearly 50 years, Second City has been the top comedy club in Chicago and the most famous of its kind in the country. Photos of famous graduates line the lobby walls and include Elaine May, John Belushi, and recent *Saturday Night Live* cast members Tina Fey, Horatio Sanz, and Rachel Dratch.

Today's Second City is a veritable factory of improv, with shows on two stages (the storied main stage and the smaller Second City ETC) and a hugely popular training school. The main-stage ensembles change frequently, and the shows can swing wildly back and forth on the hilarity meter. In recent years, the club has adopted the long-form improvisational program pioneered by iO (ImprovOlympic; see above listing), which has brought much better reviews. Check the theater reviews in the *Reader,* a free local weekly, for an opinion on the current offering. To sample the Second City experience, catch the free postshow improv session (it gets going around 10:30pm); no ticket is necessary if you skip the main show (except Fri). 1616 N. Wells St. (in the Pipers Alley complex at North Ave.). (©) **877/778-4707** or 312/337-3992. www.secondcity.com. Tickets $8–$25. Subway/El: Brown Line to Sedgwick.

Zanie's Comedy Club   Just down the street from Second City in Old Town is Zanie's, one of the few traditional comedy clubs left in Chicago. Zanie's often draws

---

An Escape from the Multiplex

Chicago has a fine selection of movie theaters, but even the so-called art houses show mostly the same films that you'd be able to catch back home (or eventually on cable). But three local movie houses cater to cinema buffs with original programming. The **Gene Siskel Film Center,** 164 N. State St. ((©) **312/846-2600**; www.siskelfilmcenter.org; subway/El: Red Line to Washington or Brown Line to Randolph), named after the well-known *Chicago Tribune* film critic who died in 1999, is part of the School of the Art Institute of Chicago. The center schedules an eclectic selection of film series in two theaters, including lectures and discussions with filmmakers. The Film Center often shows foreign films that are not released commercially in the U.S.

The **Music Box Theatre,** 3733 N. Southport Ave. ((©) **773/871-6604**; www. musicboxtheatre.com; subway/El: Brown Line to Southport), is a movie palace on a human scale. Opened in 1929, it was meant to re-create the feeling of an Italian courtyard; a faux-marble loggia and towers cover the walls. The Music Box books an eclectic selection of foreign and independent American films—everything from Polish filmmaker Krzysztof Kieslowski's epic *Decalogue* to a sing-along version of *The Sound of Music.* (I saw the Vincent Price cult favorite, *House of Wax,* complete with 3-D glasses, here.)

Facets MultiMedia, 1517 W. Fullerton Ave. ((©) **773/281-4114**; www.facets. org; subway/El: Red or Brown line to Fullerton), a nonprofit group that screens independent film and video from around the world, is for the die-hard cinematic thrill-seeker. The group also mounts a Children's Film Festival (Oct–Nov) and the Chicago Latino Film Festival (Apr–May), and rents its impressive collection of classic, hard-to-find films on video and DVD by mail.

its headliners straight off *The Late Show with David Letterman* and *The Tonight Show,* and it's a regular stop for nationally known comedians. Stand-up routines are the usual fare, played to packed, appreciative houses. Inquire about smoke-free shows. Patrons must be 21 or older. 1548 N. Wells St. (between North Ave. and Schiller St.). (C) **312/337-4027.** www.chicago.zanies.com. Tickets $22 plus 2-drink minimum, more for big-name performers. Subway/El: Brown Line to Sedgwick.

3 The Music Scene

JAZZ

In the first great wave of black migration from the South just after World War I, jazz journeyed from the Storyville section of New Orleans to Chicago. Jelly Roll Morton and Louis Armstrong made Chicago a jazz hot spot in the 1920s, and their music lives on in a whole new generation of talent. Chicago jazz is known for its collaborative spirit and a certain degree of risk-taking—which you can experience at a number of lively clubs.

Andy's Jazz Club   Casual and comfortable, Andy's, a full restaurant and bar, is popular with both the hard-core and the neophyte jazz enthusiast. It's the only place in town where you can hear jazz nearly all day long, with sets beginning at noon, 5pm, and 9pm on weekdays; Saturday at 6 and 9:30pm; or Sunday at 5 and 7pm. The midday performances are the perfect setting for a nontraditional business lunch; it's also a good spot to grab a late-night bite (on weekends, the kitchen stays open until 1am). 11 E. Hubbard St. (between State St. and Wabash Ave.). (C) **312/642-6805.** www.andysjazzclub.com. Cover $5–$20. Subway/El: Red Line to Grand.

Back Room   One of the vestiges of the celebrated old Rush Street, the Back Room still packs a well-dressed crowd into an intimate candlelit spot at the back of a long gangway. The tuxedoed doorman offers patrons a seat on the main floor or in the balcony overlooking the stage. Jazz quartets and trios perform four times a night. 1007 N. Rush St. (between Oak St. and Bellevue Place). (C) **312/751-2433.** www.backroomchicago.com. Cover $8–$12 plus 2-drink minimum. Subway/El: Red Line to Chicago.

Green Dolphin Street 𝕶   An old garage on the north branch of the Chicago River was transformed, Cinderella-like, into this sexy, retro, 1940s-style nightclub and restaurant. The beautiful, well-appointed crowd shows up here to smoke stogies from the humidor, lap up martinis, and take in the scene (there's also a fine-dining restaurant whose patrons can move on to jazz after dinner without paying the cover charge). Green Dolphin books jazz in all its permutations, from big band to Latin. The main room is closed Monday. 2200 N. Ashland Ave. (at Webster Ave.). (C) **773/395-0066.** www.jazzitup. com. Cover $7–$20. Subway/El: Brown Line to Armitage or Red Line to Fullerton, and then a 10-min. cab ride.

Green Mill 𝕶 *Finds*   Green Mill, in the heart of Uptown, is "Old Chicago" down to its rafters. It became a popular watering hole during the 1920s and 1930s, when regulars included Al Capone, Sophie Tucker (the Last of the Red Hot Mamas), and Al Jolson, and today it retains its speakeasy flavor. On Sunday night, the Green Mill plays host to the **Uptown Poetry Slam,** when poets vie for the open mic to roast and ridicule each other's work. Most nights, however, jazz is on the menu, beginning around 9pm and winding down just before closing at 4am (5am Sat). Regular performers include vocalist Kurt Elling, who performs standards and some of his own songs with a quartet, and chanteuse Patricia Barber (they're both worth seeing). The Green Mill is a Chicago treasure and not to be missed. Get there early to claim one of

Lincoln Park & Wrigleyville After Dark

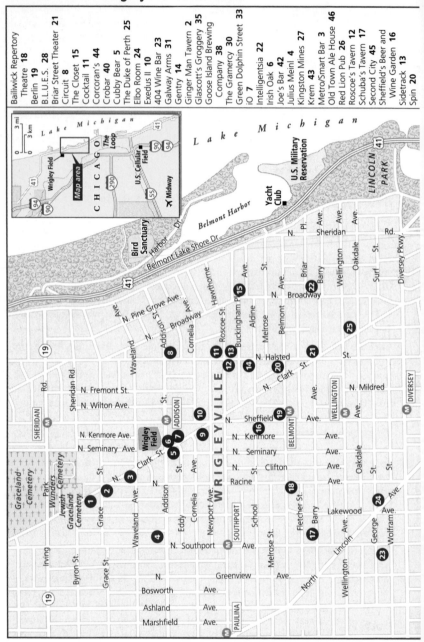

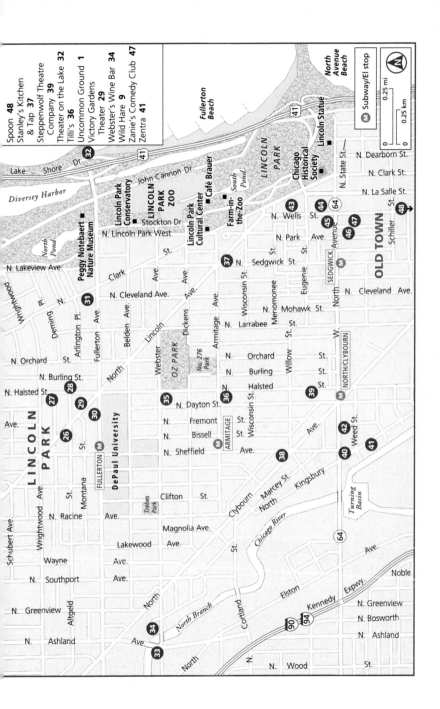

Spoon **48**
Stanley's Kitchen
  & Tap **37**
Steppenwolf Theatre
  Company **39**
Theater on the Lake **32**
Tilli's **36**
Uncommon Ground **1**
Victory Gardens
  Theater **29**
Webster's Wine Bar **34**
Wild Hare **9**
Zanie's Comedy Club **47**
Zentra **41**

Ⓜ Subway/El stop

Ⓐ

0.25 mi
0.25 km

*North
Avenue
Beach*

*Fullerton
Beach*

Lake Shore Dr.

Diversey Harbor

John Cannon Dr.

Lincoln Park Conservatory

LINCOLN PARK ZOO

Café Brauer

*South
Pond*

Farm-in-
the-Zoo

*North
Pond*

Peggy Notebaert
Nature Museum

Lincoln Park Cultural Center

N. Lincoln Park West

Stockton Dr.

LINCOLN
PARK

Chicago
Historical
Society

Lincoln Statue

N. Dearborn St.
N. Clark St.
N. La Salle St.
N. State St.

N. Lakeview Ave.

Clark

N. Cleveland Ave.

N. Wells St.
N. Park Ave.

Sedgwick St.

Eugenie St.

SEDGWICK Ⓜ

OLD TOWN

Schiller

N. Cleveland Ave.

Wrightwood

Deming

Pl.
N.

Arlington Pl.

Fullerton Ave.

Belden Ave.

Lincoln

Webster

OZ PARK

No. 276
Park

Dickens

Armitage

Ave.

Wisconsin St.

Menomonee St.

N. Larrabee

Mohawk St.

N. Orchard St.

N. Burling St.

N. Halsted St.

North

Ave.

N. Orchard St.
N. Burling St.
N. Halsted St.

Willow St.

NORTH/CLYBOURN Ⓜ

LINCOLN
PARK

Ave.

St.

Montana

FULLERTON Ⓜ

DePaul University

N. Racine Ave.

N. Dayton St.

N. Fremont St.

N. Bissell St.

N. Sheffield Ave.

ARMITAGE Ⓜ

Wisconsin St.

Clifton St.

Magnolia Ave.

Lakewood Ave.

Wayne Ave.

N. Southport Ave.

N. Greenview

Altgeld

N. Ashland Ave.

Schubert Ave.

Wrightwood Ave.

*Trebes
Park*

North

North Branch

Chicago River

Clybourn

Marcey St.

Kingsbury

*Turning
Basin*

Weed St.

Ave.

Cortland

Elston

Kennedy Expwy.

Noble

N. Greenview
N. Bosworth
N. Ashland

N. Wood St.

27
28
29
30
31
32
33
34
35
36
37
38
39
40
41
42
43
44
45
46
47
48
64
90
94

269

the plush velvet booths. 4802 N. Broadway (at Lawrence Ave.). © 773/878-5552. Cover $6–$15. Subway/El: Red Line to Lawrence.

Pops for Champagne *(Finds)*   A civilized, elegant way to enjoy jazz, the Pops champagne bar is one of the prettiest rooms in the city, and its River North location makes it a convenient walk from most downtown hotels. Live jazz—mostly small-combo piano music—is presented 7 nights a week, beginning at 8:30pm Sunday through Thursday, and 9pm on Friday and Saturday. While you're here, it's pretty much required that you sample one of the club's 100 varieties of bubbly. 601 N. State St. (at Ohio St.). © 312/266-POPS. www.popsforchampagne.com. Cover $5–$10 Tues–Sat; no cover Sun–Mon. Subway/El: Red Line to Grand.

BLUES

If Chicagoans were asked to pick one musical style to represent their city, most of us would start singing the blues. Thanks in part to the presence of the influential Chess Records, Chicago became a hub of blues activity after World War II, with musicians such as Muddy Waters, Howlin' Wolf, and Buddy Guy recording and performing here. Chicago helped usher in the era of "electric blues"—low-tech soulful singing melded with the rock sensibility of electric guitars. Blues-influenced rock musicians (the Rolling Stones and Led Zeppelin, for example) made Chicago a regular pilgrimage spot. Today, the blues has become yet another tourist attraction, especially for international visitors, but the quality and variety of blues acts is still impressive. Hardcore blues fans shouldn't miss the annual (free) **Blues Fest,** held along the lakefront in Grant Park in early June. See the "Chicago Calendar of Events" in chapter 3 for more on the festival.

Blue Chicago   Blue Chicago pays homage to female blues belters with a strong lineup of the best women vocalists around. The 1940s-style brick-walled room, decorated with original artwork of Chicago blues vignettes, is open Monday through Saturday, with music beginning at 9pm. Admission allows you to club-hop between this venue and a second location, open Tuesday through Sunday, at 536 N. Clark St. Next door, at 534 N. Clark St., is the Blue Chicago Store, which sells blues-related clothing, merchandise, and artwork. 736 N. Clark St. (between Chicago Ave. and Superior St.). © 312/642-6261. www.bluechicago.com. Cover $8–$10. Subway/El: Red or Brown line to Chicago.

B.L.U.E.S.   On the Halsted strip, look for B.L.U.E.S.—the name says it all. This is a small joint for the serious aficionado—if you've got claustrophobia, this isn't the place for you. On the upside, the cozy space makes every performance personal; you won't miss a single move of the musicians standing onstage only yards away. Shows start at 9:30pm nightly. 2519 N. Halsted St. (between Wrightwood and Fullerton aves.). © 773/528-1012. www.chicagobluesbar.com. Cover $5–$10. Subway/El: Red or Brown line to Fullerton.

Buddy Guy's Legends *(Finds)*   A legend himself, gifted guitarist Buddy Guy runs one of the most popular and comfortable clubs in town. Blues paraphernalia, from a Koko Taylor dress to a Muddy Waters tour jacket, decorates the walls of this club near the South Loop. You may catch Buddy onstage when he's in town. (Or, if you're lucky, one of his high-profile friends, such as Mick Jagger, will stop by for an impromptu jam session.) The kitchen serves good Louisiana-style soul food and barbecue. 754 S. Wabash Ave. (between Balbo Dr. and Eighth St.). © 312/427-0333. www.buddyguys.com. Cover $10–$15. Subway/El: Red Line to Harrison.

Kingston Mines ✸   Chicago's premier blues bar, Kingston Mines, is where musicians congregate after their own gigs to jam and socialize. Celebs have been known to drop by when they're in town shooting movies, but most nights the crowd includes a big contingent of conventioneers looking for a rockin' night on the town. But don't worry about the tourist factor—everyone's here to have a good time, and the energy is infectious. The nightly show begins at 9:30pm, with two bands on two stages, and goes until 4am (5am Sat). The late-night kitchen serves up burgers and ribs. 2548 N. Halsted St. (between Wrightwood and Fullerton aves.). ✆ **773/477-4646.** www.kingstonmines.com. Cover $10–$15. Subway/El: Red or Brown line to Fullerton.

Rosa's Lounge ✸   Rosa's is strictly a neighborhood hangout, but it has live blues every night and all the atmosphere required to fuel its heartfelt lamentations. Mama Rosa and her son, Tony Mangiullo, run a homey, lovable spot that, despite its somewhat distant location, is decidedly one of the best joints in town for spirited, authentic Chicago blues. (Because of its off-the-beaten-track location, it attracts local fans rather than tourists.) Rosa's also sponsors a blues cruise on Lake Michigan every summer. The doors open at 8pm, and the show starts around 9:30pm Tuesday through Saturday. 3420 W. Armitage Ave. (at Kimball Ave.). ✆ **773/342-0452.** www.rosaslounge.com. Cover $5–$12. Subway/El: Blue Line to Logan Sq., and then a short cab ride.

Underground Wonder Bar   This intimate club on the Near North Side only gets better as the night wears on (it's open until 4am Sun–Fri, until 5am Sat). Although I've listed it under blues clubs, it's one of the most eclectic live-music spots in town; you'll hear jazz trios, folk singers, and R&B vocalists playing the quirky, compact, and, yep, below-street-level room early in the evening. Things really heat up when co-owner Lonie Walker and her Big Bad Ass Company Band take the stage at 11pm on Friday and Saturday, playing a raucous blues-rock mix. Stick around until the wee hours, which is when the fun really begins—musicians stop by after gigs at other clubs to improvise a final set. The kitchen serves Tex-Mex and other chow late. 10 E. Walton St. (at State St.). ✆ **312/266-7761.** www.undergroundwonderbar.com. Cover $8–$15. Subway/El: Red Line to Chicago.

ROCK (BASICALLY)

In the early 1990s, Chicago's burgeoning alternative-rock scene produced such national names as the Smashing Pumpkins, Liz Phair, Veruca Salt, Urge Overkill, and Material Issue. Although the city's moment of pop hipness quickly faded (as did most of the aforementioned artists), the live music scene has continued to thrive. Most Chicago bands concentrate on keeping it real, happy to perform at small local clubs and not obsessing (at least openly) about getting a record contract. The city is a regular stop for touring bands, from big stadium acts to smaller up-and-coming groups. Scan the *Reader, New City,* or *Time Out Chicago* to see who's playing where.

The biggest rock acts tend to play at the local indoor stadiums: The **United Center** (✆ **312/455-4500;** www.unitedcenter.com), home of the Bulls and Blackhawks, and **Allstate Arena** (✆ **847/635-6601;** www.allstatearena.com), in Rosemont near O'Hare Airport. During the summer, you'll also find the big names at the outdoor **First Midwest Bank Amphitheatre** (✆ **708/614-1616;** www.livenation.com/venue/getVenue/venueId/785), inconveniently located in the suburb of Tinley Park, about an hour outside the city, and cursed with pretty bad acoustics.

You can catch rock acts at local venues with a lot more character. The **Riviera Theatre,** 4746 N. Racine Ave. (✆ **773/275-6800**), is a relic of the Uptown neighborhood's swinging days in the 1920s, '30s, and '40s. A former movie palace, it retains the original ornate ceiling, balcony, and lighting fixtures, but it has definitely gotten grimy with age (head upstairs to avoid the crowd that rushes toward the stage during shows). The **Aragon Ballroom,** a few blocks away at 1106 W. Lawrence Ave. (© 773/561-9500; www.aragon.com; subway/El: Red Line to Lawrence), was once an elegant big-band dance hall; the worn Moorish-castle decor and twinkling-star ceiling now give the place a seedy charm. A former vaudeville house is now the **Vic Theatre,** 3145 N. Sheffield Ave. (© 773/472-0366; www.victheatre.com; subway/El: Red or Brown line to Fullerton), a midsize venue that features up-and-coming acts (get there early to snag one of the lower balcony rows).

More sedate audiences love the **Park West,** 322 W. Armitage Ave. (© 773/929-5959; www.parkwestchicago.com; subway/El: Brown Line to Armitage, or bus no. 22 [Clark St.]), both for its excellent sound system and its cabaret-style seating (no mosh pit here). For tickets to most shows at all these venues, you're stuck going through the service-fee-grabbing **Ticketmaster** (© 312/559-1212).

Here are some bars and clubs that book live music most nights of the week.

Abbey Pub   Irish brogues abound at this barnlike gathering place for indie-rock, folk-pop, and other hard-to-classify acts. It's tucked away in a residential neighborhood—far from the usual tourist haunts—so you're pretty much guaranteed to be surrounded by locals. Besides Guinness and other Emerald Isle beers on tap, there's a full menu. Traditional Irish music sessions are held Sunday night. 3420 W. Grace St. (at Elston Ave.). © 773/478-4408. www.abbeypub.com. Cover $6–$20. Subway/El: Brown Line to Irving Park, and then a 10-min. cab ride.

Cubby Bear   Across from Wrigley Field, Cubby Bear is a showcase for new rock bands and an occasional offbeat act, and draws in a scrub-faced postcollegiate crowd. Concerts are staged on weekends and many Wednesday nights. Otherwise, there are always billiards, darts, and other distractions. 1059 W. Addison St. (at Clark St.). © 773/327-1662. www.cubbybear.com. Cover $5–$10 on band nights, more for special shows. Subway/El: Red Line to Addison.

Double Door *Finds*   This club has capitalized on the Wicker Park/Bucktown neighborhood's ascendance as a breeding ground for rock and alternative music. Owned by the proprietors of Metro (see below), the club has some of the better acoustics and sightlines in the city and attracts buzz bands and unknowns to its stage. When you need to escape the noise, there's a lounge-type area with pool tables in the basement. 1572 N. Milwaukee Ave. (at North Ave.). © 773/489-3160. www.doubledoor.com. Tickets $5–$20. Subway/El: Blue Line to Damen.

Elbo Room *Value*   Upstairs, Elbo Room looks like any other low-key Lincoln Park watering hole, but in the basement you'll find delightfully schizophrenic live music: rockabilly, hip-hop, soul, funk, and more. The subterranean setting is cozy and brings the bands up close and personal, but when the place gets packed, you might not see much of the onstage action. 2871 N. Lincoln Ave. (at George St.). © 773/549-5549. www.elboroomchicago.com. Cover $5–$10. Subway/El: Brown Line to Diversey.

The Empty Bottle   This alternative-rock club in the Ukrainian Village neighborhood is a haven for young arty scenesters drawn here for camaraderie, obscure bands, and cheap beer. Offerings are eclectic, with experimental jazz on Wednesday, and other nights given over to a DJ's underground improvisations. The Wednesday night Jazz Series showcases a wide range of musicians, some with international reputations.

1035 N. Western Ave. (between Division St. and Augusta Blvd.). ℂ 773/276-3600. www.emptybottle.com. Cover $8–$20. Subway/El: Blue Line to Western, and then bus 49.

House of Blues   The largest location in a national chain of music venues, the House of Blues could more appropriately be called the House of Pop. Although it's decorated with Mississippi Delta folk art, the bands that play here tend to be rock groups, '80s novelty acts, and the occasional hip-hop or reggae performer. This is a great place to see a show—concerts are in a theater that re-creates a gilded European opera house (minus the seats), and the stage views are pretty good no matter where you stand. A restaurant also serves lunch and dinner with hometown blues accompaniment. The popular **Sunday gospel brunch,** offering a Southern-style buffet, brings a different Chicago gospel choir to the stage each week; the three weekly "services" often sell out, so get tickets in advance. 329 N. Dearborn St. (at Kinzie St.). ℂ 312/923-2000 for general information, or 312/923-2020 for concert information. www.hob.com. Tickets usually $15–$45. Subway/El: Red Line to Grand.

Joe's Bar   Part sports bar, part music venue, Joe's Bar is a vast, warehouse-size space with the spirit of a quirky neighborhood tavern. There's live music Wednesday through Sunday, with local and national bands playing everything from rock to reggae. Gimmicks abound, such as the popular summer "Doggy Happy Hour" on the patio. Joe's can get smoky when it's crowded, but the scenery—lots of attractive people in their 20s—makes up for it. *Another bonus:* Because there are so many bar areas, you won't have to wait long to get a drink. 940 W. Weed St. (at North Ave.). ℂ 312/337-3486. Live music cover $3–$20. Subway/El: Red Line to North/Clybourn.

Martyrs' *(Finds* Dedicated to the memories of such late great rock and blues performers as Jimi Hendrix and Janis Joplin (who are immortalized on the mural facing the stage), Martyrs' presents a variety of local bands and the occasional performance by national touring acts. On the first Wednesday of the month, catch the popular Tributasaurus, a note-perfect rock tribute band that "becomes" a different rock legend every month. The low tables, high ceiling, and huge windows make Martyrs' one of the best places to catch a rock-'n'-roll show. 3855 N. Lincoln Ave. (between Berenice Ave. and Irving Park Rd.). ℂ 773/404-9494. www.martyrslive.com. Cover $5–$15. Subway/El: Brown Line to Addison.

Metro ⭐   Metro is located in an old auditorium and is Chicago's premier venue for live alternative and rock acts on the verge of breaking into the big time. There's not much in the way of atmosphere—it's basically a big black room with a stage—but the place has an impressive history. Everybody who is anybody played here when they were starting out, including REM, Pearl Jam, and local heroes the Smashing Pumpkins. Newer "alternative" bands that are getting attention from MTV and radio stations show up at Metro eventually. The subterranean Smart Bar—at the same location—is a dance club open 7 nights a week (you can get in free if you've seen a concert that night at Metro). Some shows are all-ages, but most require concertgoers to be at least 21. Tickets are sold in person through the adjoining **Metro Store** (sans service charges), or by phone through Ticketmaster. 3730 N. Clark St. (at Racine Ave.). ℂ 773/549-0203 or 312/559-1212 for Ticketmaster orders. www.metrochicago.com. Tickets $8–$25. Subway/El: Red Line to Sheridan.

Phyllis' Musical Inn   Typical of the borderline dive-y neighborhood bars that used to be scattered around Wicker Park—before rampant gentrification brought hip lounges and overpriced martinis—Phyllis' is a small, generally uncrowded club that books live rock music (sometimes jazz and blues) 4 to 5 nights a week. The bookers encourage musicians to perform original songs, so you won't find any Grateful Dead cover bands here. 1800 W. Division St. (at Wood St.). ② 773/486-9862. Cover $3–$5. Subway/El: Blue Line to Division.

COUNTRY, FOLK & ETHNIC MUSIC

Exedus II   Like its flashier neighbor, the Wild Hare (see below), Exedus offers nightly reggae shows; the specialty here is Jamaican dancehall, performed live or by DJs. Although this small storefront tavern gets smoky and crowded, the music's good and the attitude of the international crowd is laid back. In general, it's more authentic than the competition, which tends to draw more of the frat-party element. 3477 N. Clark St. (between Newport Ave. and Roscoe St.). ② 773/348-3998. www.exeduslounge.com. Cover usually under $10. Subway/El: Red Line to Addison.

The Hideout *(Value*   This friendly tavern's OLD STYLE BEER sign shines like a beacon, guiding roots-music fans through the grimy industrial neighborhood that surrounds it. The owners' beer-can collection and some eclectic "celebrity" memorabilia are on display in the front room. In back, local musicians play country, rock, and bluesy tunes on a small stage backed by an impressive stuffed sailfish. It's no-frills, all right, but the Hideout also books some of the best lineups of folk and "alt country" bands in the city, including Jeff Tweedy (of Wilco), Kelly Hogan, and the New Duncan Imperials. 1354 W. Wabansia Ave. (between Elston Ave. and Throop St.). ② 773/227-4433. www.hideout chicago.com. Cover usually $5–$10. Subway/El: Blue Line to Damen.

HotHouse *(Finds*   This "Center for International Performance and Exhibition" schedules some of the most eclectic programming in the city, attracting well-known jazz and avant-garde musicians from around the world. When the heavy hitters aren't booked, you'll see anything from local musicians improvising on "invented instruments" to Japanese blues singers. 31 E. Balbo Dr. (at S. Wabash Ave.). ② 312/362-9707. www.hothouse.net. Cover $10–$25. Subway/El: Red Line to Harrison.

Old Town School of Folk Music *(Finds*   Country, folk, bluegrass, Latin, Celtic— the Old Town School of Folk Music covers a spectrum of indigenous musical forms. Best known as a training center offering a slate of music classes, the school also plays host to everyone from the legendary Pete Seeger to bluegrass phenom Alison Krauss. The school's home, in a former 1930s library, is the world's largest facility dedicated to the preservation and presentation of traditional and contemporary folk music. The Old Town School also houses an art gallery showcasing exhibitions of works by local, national, and international artists; a music store offering an exquisite selection of instruments, sheet music, and hard-to-find recordings; and a cafe. In midsummer it sponsors the popular Folk and Roots outdoor music festival. The school maintains another retail store and offers children's classes at its first location, 909 W. Armitage Ave. 4544 N. Lincoln Ave. (between Wilson and Montrose aves.). ② 773/728-6000. www.oldtownschool. org. Tickets $10–$25. Subway/El: Brown Line to Western.

Schubas Tavern *(Finds*   Country and folk singer-songwriters have found a home in this divine little concert hall in a former Schlitz tavern. It's a friendly and intimate place, best experienced from one of the wooden booths ringing the room. There's music 7 nights a week, and Schubas occasionally books big-name performers such as John Hiatt and Train. You'll also find a bar up front and an attached restaurant, Harmony Grill, where you can grab a pretty good burger and fries after the show. 3159 N. Southport Ave. (at Belmont Ave.). ② 773/525-2508. www.schubas.com. Tickets $10–$20. Subway/El: Red or Brown line to Belmont.

Wild Hare   Number one on Chicago's reggae charts is the Wild Hare, in the shadow of Wrigley Field. After 20 years in business (an eternity in the nightclub world), this spot has kept up with the times by adding a state-of-the-art sound and video systems. Owner Zeleke Gessesse, who has toured with Ziggy Marley and the Melody Makers, books top acts such as Burning Spear and Yellow Man; he also nurtures local talent. With a Red Stripe in hand, you might even forget that it's 20 degrees outside. 3530 N. Clark St. (between Addison and Roscoe sts.). ✆ 773/327-4273. www.wildharereggae.com. Cover $7–$15. Subway/El: Red Line to Addison.

CABARETS & PIANO BARS

The Baton Show Lounge   Catch the city's long-running revue of female impersonators at this River North lounge, which has been showcasing fabulous "gals" in outrageous getups for more than 30 years. Shows are Wednesday through Sunday at 8:30p and 10:30pm, and 12:30am. This is a very popular spot for bachelorette outings, so be prepared for groups of rowdy women. 436 N. Clark St. (between Hubbard and Illinois sts.). ✆ 312/644-5269. www.thebatonshowlounge.com. Cover $10–$14 plus 2-drink minimum. Subway/El: Red Line to Grand.

Coq d'Or   Whether you're huddled close around the piano or hanging back on the red Naugahyde banquettes, this old-time, clubby haunt in the historic Drake hotel offers an intimate evening of song stylings (it's one of the only downtown hotel lounges that still offers live music). The Coq d'Or claims to be the second bar in Chicago to serve drinks after the repeal of Prohibition in 1933—and the place hasn't changed much since then. In The Drake Hotel, 140 E. Walton St. (at Michigan Ave.). ✆ 312/787-2200. Subway/El: Red Line to Chicago/State.

Davenport's Piano Bar & Cabaret *Finds*   The youthful hipster haunt of Wicker Park isn't the first place you'd expect to find a tried-and-true piano bar and cabaret venue, but Davenport's does its best to revive a fading art form. Owner Bill Davenport and his partners transformed a single-story storefront into an intimate, chic gem that provides a much-needed showcase for Chicago-bred talent, with a sprinkling of visiting performers from New York and L.A. The piano bar in front is flashier than the subdued cabaret in back, featuring a singing waitstaff, blue velvet banquettes, funky lighting fixtures, and a hand-painted mural-topped bar. The cabaret's sound equipment is first-rate. 1383 N. Milwaukee Ave. (just south of North Ave.). ✆ 773/278-1830. http://davenportspianobar.com. Cover $10–$20. Subway/El: Blue Line to Damen.

Jilly's   Named for Frank Sinatra's former manager, Jilly's has a retro feel that's timeless, not dated. Music and a lively buzz from the patrons spill into the street during warm weather, and pianists and trios play the dark room decorated with photos of the Rat Pack, Steve and Eydie, and the like. The eclectic crowd includes everyone from wealthy Gold Coast residents to young singles catching up after work. 1007 N. Rush St. (at Oak St.). ✆ 312/664-1001. Subway/El: Red Line to Chicago.

Redhead Piano Bar   The Redhead attracts a well-heeled, sharp-dressed Gold Coast clientele with its classic, old-time lounge vibe. Yesteryear memorabilia—movie-star glamour shots, playbills, and old sheet music—covers the walls, and the drink list focuses on single-malt scotch and other premium liquors rather than flavored martinis (the crowd teeming around the piano is a throwback as well). Suggested attire is "business casual," so don't show up wearing shorts and gym shoes. 16 W. Ontario St. ✆ 312/640-1000. Subway/El: Red Line to Grand.

Zebra Lounge *(Finds* The most wonderfully quirky piano bar in town, Zebra Lounge has a loyal following despite (or maybe because of) the campy decor. Just as you would expect, black-and-white stripes are the unifying element at this dark, shoe-box-size Gold Coast spot, furnished with black vinyl booths, a small mirrored bar, and zebra kitsch galore. Bar lore has it that the Zebra Lounge opened December 5, 1933— the day Prohibition ended. Since then, it has passed through numerous owners, but the name, a tribute to a long-forgotten tavern in New York, has remained. For the past quarter-century, it has been a raucous piano bar, attracting a multigenerational crowd of regulars. The place is relatively mellow early in the evening, though it can get packed late into the night on weekends. 1220 N. State Pkwy. (between Division and Goethe sts.). *©* 312/642-5140. Subway/El: Red Line to Clark/Division.

4 The Club Scene

Chicago is the hallowed ground where house music was hatched in the 1980s, so it's no surprise to find that it's also home to several vast, industrial-style dance clubs with pounding music and a mostly under-30 crowd. Some spots specialize in a single type of music, while others offer an ever-changing mix of rhythms and beats that follow the latest DJ-driven trend. Many clubs attract a different clientele on each day of the week (Sun night, for example, is gay-friendly at many of the clubs listed below), so check the club's website to get an idea of each night's vibe. Given the fickle nature of clubgoers, some places listed below might have disappeared by the time you read this, but there is an impressive list of longtime survivors—clubs that have lasted more than a decade but continue to draw loyal crowds.

Berlin One of the more enduring dance floors in Chicago, Berlin is primarily gay during the week but draws dance hounds of all stripes on weekends and for special theme nights (disco the last Wed of every month, Prince music the last Sun of the month). It has a reputation for outrageousness and creativity, making it prime ground for people-watching. The space isn't much—basically a square room with a bar along one side—but the no-frills dance floor is packed late into the evening. The owners are no dummies: The cover charge applies only on Friday and Saturday after midnight, which is about an hour earlier than you ought to show up. (For more, see "The Gay & Lesbian Scene," p. 290.) 954 W. Belmont Ave. (at Sheffield Ave.). *©* 773/348-4975. www.berlinchicago.com. Cover $3–$5. Subway/El: Red or Brown line to Belmont.

Crobar A veteran of Chicago's late-night scene, Crobar has managed to stay hip since 1991; it's even expanded to locations in New York City and Miami. The warehouse-gone-glam look and thumping sound system give the space a quintessential dance-club feel, and the booth-lined balcony overlooking the huge dance floor is a good spot for people-watching. If you're especially gorgeous—or free-spending—you might make it into the glass-encased VIP room. The soundtrack is mostly hip-hop and house, and the weekend DJs have a strong local following, so you might be fighting for prime dance space. The crowd is fairly mixed racially and age-wise and mostly attitude-free. 1543 N. Kingsbury St. (at North Ave.). *©* 312/266-1900. www.crobar.com. Cover $20 on weekends. Subway/El: Red Line to North/Clybourn.

Funky Buddha Lounge A bit off the beaten path, west of the River North gallery district, this club blends in with its industrial surroundings—even the whimsical Buddha sculpture on the heavy steel front door is a rusted husk. Inside is a different scene altogether: low red lighting, seductive dens with black-leather and faux leopard-skin sofas, lots of candles, and antique light fixtures salvaged from an old church. The DJs are among the best in the city, flooding the nice-size dance floor with everything from hip-hop, bhangra, and funk to African, soul, and underground house. The crowd is just as eclectic as the music—everything from yuppies and after-dinner hipsters to die-hard clubhoppers and barely legal wannabes. Hugely popular Thursday nights pack in the young, mostly white club kids; Friday and Saturday feature a cool, eclectic crowd decked out in funky gear. The bus runs to this area, but take a cab at night. 728 W. Grand Ave. ℂ 312/666-1695. www.funkybuddha.com. Cover $10–$30. Bus: 65 (Grand Ave.).

Le Passage The Gold Coast's swankiest nightclub fits all the prerequisites for chic exclusivity, starting with the semihidden entrance at the end of a narrow (but well-lit) alleyway just steps from Oak Street's Prada and Barneys New York stores. You descend a long flight of stairs into an environment filled with gilded furnishings and exquisite decor imported from France; to gain access, you must pass muster with the gatekeepers staffing the velvet rope. The beautiful, the rich, and the designer-suited come here for the loungy aesthetic. The soundtrack mixes R&B, soul, hip-hop, house, funk, and acid jazz. Another highlight is the stellar French fusion menu and the late-night eats such as mini-cheeseburgers and fries, served well into the wee hours. The place teems on Friday and Saturday nights; Thursday night caters to local fashion-industry folk, with occasional runway shows. Stop by the Yow Bar—a legendary local bartender who inspired the Tiki cocktails—but don't expect him to pay a visit. However, celebs and big-name athletes have been known to spend an evening mingling in the roped-off VIP area. 1 Oak Place (between Rush and State sts). ℂ 312/255-0022. www.lepassage.tv. Cover $20. Subway/El: Red Line to Chicago.

Rednofive Taking its name from the ubiquitous dye used in food products, Red-nofive is no fake, thanks to its sleek design and tight lineup of local DJs spinning a sonic deluge of progressive and abstract house music, hip-hop, and pop, sometimes accompanied by a percussionist on drums. The dark, underground feel attracts club-bers who are serious about their music; you don't have to dress to impress, but you probably won't make it past the doorman in shorts and sneakers. This club tends to attract a diverse, scantily clad crowd that wants to dance and hang out till 4 or 5 am. The bi-level space offers lounge seating and a clubby vibe—with an elevated VIP area—but devoted dance fans will throw down just about anywhere. 440 N. Halsted St. (at Hubbard St.). ℂ 312/733-6699. www.rednofive.com. Cover $10–$20. Subway/El: Green Line to Clinton.

Reserve No longer just a neighborhood rife with restaurants, the West Loop has also become a hot nightlife destination, thanks to its anchor, Reserve nightclub. The bi-level club became so popular for its ultra-exclusive VIP offerings that it took over as *the* place to rub elbows with visiting celebs, music artists, and athletes alike. Even under-the-radar high rollers splurge here on the bottle service (call ahead to book a table, as they often fill up on weekends.) You can settle in downstairs for a more low-key lounge vibe, or head up to the 5,000-square-foot club to join the throngs of scen-esters who can't seem to get enough of the mashed-up music spun nightly. But nothing draws in the crowds like spinner-to-the-stars DJ AM's occasional Thursday night appearances. 858 W. Lake St. (at Green St.). ℂ 312/455-1111. www.reserve-chicago.com. Cover $20 on weekends. Subway/El: Green Line to Clinton.

Smart Bar A long-established name on the dance circuit, Smart Bar, tucked in the basement below the rock club Metro (p. 273), spins the latest musical forms from underground house and punk to ethereal and gothic. The scene starts late, and the dancing denizens vary widely depending on which bands are playing upstairs (concertgoers get free admission to the Smart Bar). The no-frills club, which has stayed in business (amazingly) for almost a quarter-century, attracts a diverse and edgy crowd, and that's part of the appeal. This is an established Chicago spot where clubbers can come as they are, and you'll see a range of fashion. Smart Bar stays open until 5am on weekends. No cover before 11pm during the week. 3730 N. Clark St. (at Racine Ave.). © 773/549-4140. www.smartbarchicago.com. Cover $10–$15 (free with show at Metro). Subway/El: Red Line to Addison.

Sound-Bar   DJs are the stars at this multilevel, high-tech dance club, which prides itself on booking top international nightlife names. The look is industrial chic, with silver banquettes, frosted-glass walls, and stainless-steel accents; holographic images and laser lights flash across the massive central dance floor. The crowd tends to be young and club-savvy on weeknights, with a little more diversity on weekends. (Dress

---

Tips Late-Night Bites

Chicago's not much of a late-night dining town; most restaurants shut down by 10 or 11pm, leaving night owls with the munchies out of luck. But if you know where to go, you can still get a decent meal past midnight. Here are a few spots that serve real food until real late:

In the Loop, your best—and practically only—choice is **Miller's Pub** (p. 280), 134 S. Wabash Ave. (© 312/645-5377), which offers hearty American comfort food until 2am daily. Many late-night visitors to this historic watering hole and restaurant are out-of-towners staying at neighboring hotels.

In River North, food is available until 4am at **Bar Louie** (p. 281), 226 W. Chicago Ave. (© 312/337-3313). The menu is a step above mozzarella sticks and other standard bar food: Focaccia sandwiches, vegetarian wraps, and salads are among the highlights.

After a night out, Wicker Park and Bucktown residents stop by **Northside Café** (p. 168), 1635 N. Damen Ave. (© 773/384-3555), for sandwiches and salads served until 2am (3am Sat). In nice weather, the front patio is the place to be for prime people-watching.

The bright, welcoming atmosphere at **Clarke's Pancake House**, 2441 N. Lincoln Ave. (© 773/472-3505), is a dose of fresh air after an evening spent in dark Lincoln Park bars. Yes, there are pancakes on the menu, as well as plenty of other creative breakfast choices, including mixed skillets of veggies, meat, and potatoes. If you need to satisfy a *really* late-night craving, Clarke's is open 24 hours.

When the Lincoln Park bars shut down at 2am, the action moves to the **Wieners Circle**, 2622 N. Clark St. (© 773/477-7444). This hot-dog stand is strictly no-frills: You shout your order across the drunken crowd, and the only spots to sit are a few picnic tables out front. Open until 4am during the week and 6am on weekends, the Wieners Circle is the center of predawn life in Lincoln Park—and I know people who swear that the greasy cheese-topped fries are the perfect hangover prevention.

well if you want to make it past the bouncers.) While there's a fair amount of posing, overall this crowd comes for the music, which includes electronic dance, trance, and house. Saturday night resident DJ John Curley is a longtime local club fixture with an encyclopedic house repertoire; if you want a primer on Chicago house, this is a good place to start. 226 W. Ontario St. (at Franklin St.). ℂ 312/787-4480. www.sound-bar.com. Cover $10–$20. Subway/El: Red Line to Grand, or Brown Line to Merchandise Mart.

Transit Carved out of a warehouse space beneath the elevated train tracks just west of the hip Randolph Street restaurant row, Transit is an excellent no-nonsense dance club that doesn't trick itself out with a wacky theme. Its 10,000 square feet feature a sleek, boldly colored geometric interior with modern, minimalist furniture. The postindustrial metal staircases surrounding the large dance-floor area lead to a VIP room, the tiny Light Bar, and another VIP space named the Chandelier Room. The bone-rattling, state-of-the-art sound system and DJs—spinning progressive dance, remixed hip-hop, and R&B—don't disappoint the die-hard dance fans. Come wearing your best club attire. 1431 W. Lake St. ℂ 312/491-8600. www.transitnightclubchicago.com. Cover $15–$20. Subway/El: Green Line to Ashland.

Vision The spot now known as Vision has been through several name and decor changes, but it keeps plugging away, taking advantage of a tourist-friendly location not far from Michigan Avenue. Stretching over four levels, Vision caters to the current club trend of providing different environments in different spaces. The dance floor—thumping with house, trance, progressive, and hip-hop—fills the first floor; upper floors offer plenty of nooks and crannies for groups to sit and chat. Vision prides itself on offering some of the best turntable talent in the city—the club's owners even bring in internationally known DJs. 640 N. Dearborn St. (at Ontario St.). ℂ 312/266-2114. www.visionnightclub.com. Cover $10–$25. Subway/El: Red Line to Grand/State.

Zentra Club-hoppers often make Middle Eastern and Moroccan-flavored Zentra, which stays open into the wee hours, their last stop of the night. A large four-room space, Zentra banks on the current trend of East meets West, with exotic Moroccan textiles, thick drapes, Indian silks, red lanterns, funky chrome fixtures, and even "Hookah Girls" proffering hits on pipes packed with fruity tobacco blends. There are two floors, each catering to different sounds of resident and guest DJs. Upstairs entertains those who want to move to progressive dance and techno sounds, while downstairs has DJs spinning mostly house and hip-hop. Zentra attracts an eclectic mix of patrons who come to soak in the exotic vibes, do some people-watching, and simply have fun dancing. In the summer, an outdoor deck puts a funky spin on the beer-garden concept. There is no dress code, but feel free to dress up—you'll see a bit of everything here. 923 W. Weed St. (just south of North Ave. at Clybourn Ave.). ℂ 312/787-0400. http://zentranightclub.com. Cover $15–$20. Subway/El: Red Line to North/Clybourn.

5 The Bar & Cafe Scene

If you want to soak up the atmosphere of a neighborhood tavern or sports bar, it's best to venture beyond downtown into the surrounding neighborhoods. Lincoln Park, Wrigleyville, and Bucktown/Wicker Park have well-established nightlife zones that abound with bright, upscale neighborhood bars. You'll also find numerous dives and no-frills "corner taps" in the blue-collar neighborhoods.

As for hotel nightlife, virtually every hotel in Chicago has a cocktail lounge or piano bar and, in some cases, more than one distinct environment where you can take an aperitif before dinner or watch an evening of entertainment. The piano bars at The Drake Hotel and the Ambassador East Hotel's Pump Room are standouts.

BARS
THE LOOP & VICINITY

Lumen   The gimmick at this newer spot, which occupies a former meat-packing facility in the West Loop, is light, particularly the overhead LED display, which changes color throughout the night. The 5,000-square-foot space features concrete, stainless steel, and bamboo in its design, along with the aforementioned light specta-cle, which is coordinated with its powerful sound system. There's no VIP list, which gives it an everyman kind of feel, and means minimal line-waiting out front. 839 W. Fulton Market, at Halsted St. ℂ 312/733-2222. Subway/El: Green Line to Clinton.

Miller's Pub ☆   A true Loop landmark, Miller's has been serving up after-work cocktails to downtown office workers for more than 50 years; it's one of the few places in the area that offers bar service until the early morning hours. There's a full dinner menu, too. Autographed photos of movie stars and sports figures cover the walls; while some might be unrecognizable to younger patrons, they testify to the pub's long-standing tradition of friendly hospitality. 134 S. Wabash Ave. (between Jackson Blvd. and Adams St.). ℂ 312/645-5377. Subway/El: Red Line to Jackson.

Monk's Pub   This is a joint you'd walk by without even knowing it's there. But once inside you'll delight in a comfortable, expansive, divey yet clean German–Old English hodgepodge of a place with lots of beer varieties and decent pub food, including a long list of burgers. In business since 1969, Monk's is a no-nonsense peanut-shells-on-the-floor kind of bar where downtown workers blow off steam during the week amid shelves of old books and wooden barrels in the rafters. 205 W. Lake St. (between Randolph St. and the Chicago River). ℂ 312/357-6665. www.mmonks.com. Subway/El: Brown Line to Clark/Lake.

Tantrum   Don't worry—you won't see folks pitching a fit at this stylish South Loop bar. (The owners came up with the name after being pushed to the limit of their

---

Finds Hotel Hopping

Forget the stereotypical bland hotel bar filled with drunken conventioneers. In downtown Chicago, some of the most distinctive watering holes are in hotel lobbies. In the Loop, the coolest happy-hour spot is **Encore** in the Hotel Allegro, 171 W. Randolph St. (ℂ 312/236-0123), where the spiral-shaped bar, purple velvet upholstery, and silver accents create a futuristic feel. Things heat up later in the evening at **Base,** the bar in the Hard Rock Hotel, 230 N. Michigan Ave. (ℂ 312/345-1000). The look is sleek—lots of black and gray—and the music (live acts or a DJ) is always good. You'll find the beautiful people hanging out at the tiny **Whiskey Sky,** on the top floor of the W Chicago Lakeshore hotel, 644 N. Lakeshore Dr. (ℂ 312/943-9200). There's not much seating and the decor is minimal, but the views—of both the surrounding skyline and the gorgeous staff—are terrific. At the Sofitel Chicago Water Tower, **Le Bar,** 20 E. Chestnut St. (ℂ 312/324-4000), is a popular after-work hangout with a low-lit, intimate vibe. If you prefer to stick to tradition, **Kitty O'Shea's,** 720 S. Michigan Ave. (ℂ 312/294-6860), is an authentically appointed Irish pub inside the Hilton Chicago—a genuine Irish bartender will even pour your Guinness.

patience while trying to get their liquor license.) Located in the heart of the rapidly gentrifying South Loop, it's a good destination for anyone staying in a Loop hotel and searching for a casually cool cocktail lounge. The centerpiece of the spacious, airy main room is a long mahogany bar. Sip the signature Tantrum martini (Stoli orange mixed with orange juice), and enjoy a civilized conversation—the pleasantly diverse jukebox pumps out everything from smooth jazz to rap metal, but never at an ear-shattering volume, which is just how the hip, professional crowd likes it. 1023 S. State St. (at 11th St.). © 312/939-9160. Subway/El: Red Line to Roosevelt.

NEAR THE MAGNIFICENT MILE

Billy Goat Tavern *(Value* Hidden below the Wrigley Building is this storied Chicago hole-in-the-wall, a longtime hangout for newspaper reporters over the years, evidenced by the yellowed clippings and memorabilia papering the walls. The "cheeze-borger, cheezeborger" served at the grill inspired the famous *Saturday Night Live* sketch. Despite all the press, the Goat has endured the hype without sacrificing a thing (including its vintage decor, which pretty much epitomizes the term "dive bar"). 430 N. Michigan Ave. © 312/222-1525. Subway/El: Red Line to Grand/State.

Cru Café and Wine Bar *(Finds* A couple of blocks west of the Mag Mile, Cru draws both discriminating oenophiles and curious tourists with its sleek interior of gold-painted surfaces, a zebra-wood bar, hip light fixtures, and 400-plus wine list. Comfortable and loungy, the cafe also serves a lunch, dinner, and late-night menu of seafood, soups and salads, quiche, caviar, sandwiches, and desserts. A 40-seat alfresco seating area is available in warm weather. 888 N. Wabash Ave. © 312/337-4078. Subway/El: Red Line to Chicago.

Elm Street Liquors In a neighborhood often teeming with tourists, this lounge for locals exudes an urban but laid-back style with its anything-goes attitude. Dressing to impress here means an old-school T-shirt and Chuck Taylors (leave the striped button-down at home, boys). The music is familiar, and the drinks are forward-thinking, boasting champagne cocktails rather than the ubiquitous martinis found at every other nightspot in Chicago. We especially like that you don't have to pay a cover charge to enjoy the party. 12 W. Elm St. (at State St.). © 312/337-3200. Subway/El: Red Line to Clark/Division.

Signature Lounge For the price of a trip to the John Hancock tower observatory ($11, two floors below), you can drink in the view and a cocktail at this lofty lounge. The views are fabulous (especially at sunset), though you'll probably be surrounded by other tourists. It's open until 1am Sunday through Thursday and until 2am on the weekends. 96th floor, John Hancock Center, 875 N. Michigan Ave. © 312/787-7230. Subway/El: Red Line to Chicago.

RIVER NORTH & VICINITY

Bar Louie A slightly more upscale take on the neighborhood-bar concept, Bar Louie has built its reputation on better-than-average bar food and a creative selection of beers and cocktails. Professionals gather here after work; their restaurant and club equivalents stop by between 1 and 3am. Bar Louie isn't doing anything revolutionary, but its friendly service and approachable atmosphere make it a popular spot for locals who want a casual night out. In the past few years, outposts have also appeared in the West Loop (123 N. Halsted St.; © 312/207-0500), Lincoln Park (1800 N. Lincoln Ave.; © 312/337-9800), Lakeview (3545 N. Clark St.; © 773/296-2500), and

Bucktown (1704 N. Damen Ave.; © **773/645-7500**). 226 W. Chicago Ave. (between Franklin and Wells sts.). © 312/337-3313. Subway/El: Red or Brown line to Chicago.

Brehon Pub   Big front windows, a high tin ceiling, and a great antique back bar lend charm to this little neighborhood bar in (often) tourist-packed River North. Brehon regulars hang out weeknights after work and even at lunchtime, when the tavern serves sandwiches and soup. In the 1970s, the *Sun-Times* newspaper set up this spot as a phony bar (appropriately named the Mirage) and used it in a "sting" operation to expose city corruption. 731 N. Wells St. (at Superior St.). © 312/642-1071. Subway/El: Red or Brown line to Chicago.

Butterfly Social Club   At last, a nightclub that Al Gore can appreciate. This environmentally friendly lounge features treehouse-like nooks, organic juices in drinks, and is smoke-free (fittingly, it opened on Earth Day in 2007). It uses solar power for some of its electrical needs, and incorporates recycled and natural materials into its design, such as "trees" made from mud, sand, clay and straw. DJs spin upbeat world music that thumps through speakers made of recycled wood. 722 W. Grand Ave. (between Union Ave. and Halsted St.). © 312/666-1695. Bus: 65 (Grand Ave.).

Celtic Crossings   Drop in on a Sunday evening for the bar's weekly traditional Irish jam session, and you're sure to hear an authentic brogue. There's no television in this quaint pub, just a decent jukebox stocked with Irish and American favorites, delicious pints of Guinness (the best in Chicago, claim many Irish expats), and a cozy fireplace. 751 N. Clark St. (between Superior St. and Chicago Ave.). © 312/337-1005. Subway/El: Red or Brown line to Chicago.

Clark Street Ale House *Finds*   A handsome, convivial tavern and a popular after-work spot for white- and blue-collar types alike, Clark Street Ale House features a large open space filled with high tables and a long cherrywood bar along one wall. Better than the atmosphere are the 95 varieties of beer, a large majority of them from American microbreweries. The bar also offers a wide selection of scotches and cognacs. 742 N. Clark St. © 312/642-9253. Subway/El: Red or Brown line to Chicago.

Fado   The crowds have abated somewhat since Fado opened a few years back, but this sprawling, multilevel theme-park facsimile of an Irish pub still lures the masses on most nights. Bursting with woodwork, stone, and double-barreled Guinness taps (all of it imported from Ireland), Fado has several themed rooms, each designed to evoke a particular Irish pub style—country cottage and Victorian Dublin, for instance. The pub fare is above par. 100 W. Grand Ave. © 312/836-0066. Subway/El: Red Line to Grand.

J Bar   Yes, this lounge is just off the lobby of the James Hotel, but it's no conventioneer hangout. The low-slung leather couches, seating cubes, and flickering votive candles give it the look of an upscale urban club, and its laid-back vibe has made it a gathering place for stylish locals in their 20s and 30s. The drinks have as sense of style, too (the house martini blends blue raspberry vodka and elderflower cordial and is served in a glass coated with a raspberry-candy shell). One drawback: you have to call and reserve a table if you want to be guaranteed a place to sit into the late-night hours. 610 N. Rush St. (at Wabash Ave.) © 312/660-7200. Subway/El: Red Line to Grand.

Martini Ranch   Staying in a Magnificent Mile hotel and looking for a late-night libation? Martini Ranch serves 40 different versions of its namesake cocktail until 4am during the week, attracting bar and nightlife insiders—and a fair share of insomniacs. The Western theme is subtle (paintings of Roy Rogers and other cowpoke art) and the seating is minimal (come early to snag one of the four red booths), but fans swear by the chocolate martini, and the pop-rock soundtrack keeps the energy level high. If the crowded bar scene is too much, chill out at the pool table in the back room, or settle down at one of the tables in the heated beer garden. 311 W. Chicago Ave. (at Orleans St.). ℭ 312/335-9500. Subway/El: Red or Brown line to Chicago.

Rockit Bar & Grill   The same guys who created the swanky late-night scene at Le Passage (see listing in "The Club Scene," above) took things down a notch with this roadhouse-chic restaurant and late-night hangout, which was designed by Oprah's sidekick, Nate Berkus (see restaurant listing on p. 148). The buzzing upstairs bar area is where clean-cut professionals in their 20s and 30s go to flirt or catch up with friends—there are some pool tables, but posing attractively seems to be the main recreational activity here. Expect to be among the nose-pressers cooling your heels outside if you don't arrive early enough. 22 W. Hubbard St. (between State and Dearborn sts.). ℭ 312/645-6000. Subway/El: Red Line to Grand.

10pin   A modern interpretation of the classic bowling alley, this lounge is tucked away under the Marina Towers complex on the Chicago River. Everything feels bright and new (even the rental shoes), and there's a full menu of designer beers and upscale snacks (gourmet pizzas, smoked salmon, specialty martinis). A giant video screen overlooks the 24 bowling lanes, and a top-notch sound system gives the place a nightclubby vibe. You don't *have* to bowl—the bar area is a casual, welcoming place to hang out—but I'd certainly recommend giving it a try. 330 N. State St. (between Kinzie St. and the Chicago River). ℭ 312/644-0300. www.10pinchicago.com. Subway/El: Red Line to Grand or Brown Line to Merchandise Mart.

RUSH & DIVISION STREETS
Around Rush Street are what a bygone era called singles bars—although the only singles that tend to head here now are suburbanites, out-of-towners, and barely legal partiers. Rush Street's glory days may be long gone, but there are still a few vestiges of the old times on nearby Division Street, which overflows with party-hearty spots that attract a loud, frat-party element. They include **Shenanigan's House of Beer,** 16 W. Division St. (ℭ **312/642-2344**); **Butch McGuire's,** 20 W. Division St. (ℭ **312/337-9080**); the **Lodge,** 21 W. Division St. (ℭ **312/642-4406**); and **Mother's,** 26 W. Division St. (ℭ **312/642-7251**). Many of these bars offer discounts for women, as loud pitchmen in front of each establishment will be happy to tell any attractive ladies who pass by.

OLD TOWN
The center of nightlife in Old Town is Wells Street, home to Second City and Zanies Comedy Club, as well as a string of reliable restaurants and bars, many of which have been in business for decades. You're not going to find many trendy spots in Old Town; the nightlife here tends toward neighborhood pubs and casual restaurants, filled mostly with a late-20s and 30-something crowd.

Corcoran's   Owned by the same family for more than 30 years, this is one of Old Town's favorite local hangouts, and it makes a good stop before or after a show at Second City, which is located right across the street. The cozy, wood-lined interior and hearty pub food (bangers and mash, shepherd's pie, fish and chips) will put you right at ease. In nice weather, check out the beer garden in back, which offers a tranquil retreat from the city traffic. 1615 N. Wells St. (at North Ave.). ℭ 312/440-0885. Subway/El: Brown Line to Sedgwick.

Goose Island Brewing Company *(Finds)* On the western fringes of Old Town, the best-known brewpub in the city features its own Honker's Ale on tap, as well as several other beers produced here and at an off-site distillery. Ask for a tasting menu to try them all, or show up on any Tuesday when they give out free samples of the newest weekly release at 6pm. Goose Island has the added benefit of a casual full-service restaurant with more than just bar food (see restaurant listing on p. 159). A $5 brewery tour (including a beer sample) starts Sunday at 3pm. Goose Island has an outpost in Wrigleyville at 3535 N. Clark St. (© 773/832-9040). 1800 N. Clybourn Ave. (at Sheffield Ave.). © 312/915-0071. Subway/El: Red Line to North/Clybourn.

Krem A 33-foot "bed" is the highlight of this see-and-be-seen, subterranean Lincoln Park haunt. Part club, part small-plates restaurant, Krem is a "dine and disco" spot filled with white furniture that glows in a blue light. It has also jumped on the bottle service bandwagon; regulars can even reserve their own liquor storage lockers. There is no cover charge, but drink prices approach those of downtown clubs. Dinner is served until 11pm, desserts until midnight. 1750 N. Clark St. (at Eugenie St.). © 312/932-1750. Bus: 22 (Clark St.).

Old Town Ale House This was one of Old Town's legendary saloons until the ironic college kids discovered it. A dingy neighborhood hangout since the late 1950s with a fading mural that captures the likenesses of a class of regulars from the early 1970s, the place was cleaned up in 2006 and lost much of its old charm. Gone are the days when John Belushi commandeered the pinball machines or old-timers outnumbered kids in their 20s. If drinking with kids doesn't bother you, put some quarters in the jukebox, which is filled with an eclectic selection of crooner tunes, and just hang out. 219 W. North Ave. (at Wells St.). © 312/944-7020. Subway/El: Brown Line to Sedgwick.

Spoon The closest Old Town has to a trendy nightspot, this bar and restaurant pulls in an attractive, professional crowd on weekend evenings. The modern, loftlike space would be right at home in the River North neighborhood, but it's a novelty in tradition-bound Old Town. Although Spoon attracts loud groups of singles on weekends, weeknights are a little less frenzied, and locals are able to sip their Mucho Mango martinis in peace. 1240 N. Wells St. (at Division St.). © 312/642-5522. Subway/El: Red Line to Clark/Division.

Stanley's Kitchen & Tap Staying true to the neighborhood bar formula, Stanley's has built its long-standing reputation on providing a comfortable atmosphere and good food for its loyal patrons. Stanley's has a Southern-roadhouse-inspired vibe and home-style cooking, and is a great place to catch a game. It also boasts one of the most popular Sunday nights in the city, with live-band karaoke that often attracts musicians passing through town (Kid Rock gave an impromptu performance once) and a host of athletes such as the Chicago Blackhawks hockey team. People also come for the Sunday buffet and Bloody Mary bar—and let's not overlook the free mashed potatoes offered every night at midnight. 1970 N. Lincoln Avenue (at Armitage Ave.). © 312/642-0007. Bus: 22 (Clark St.).

LINCOLN PARK

Lincoln Park, with its high concentration of apartment-dwelling singles, is one of the busiest nightlife destinations in Chicago. Prime real estate is at a premium in this residential neighborhood, so you won't find many warehouse-size dance clubs here; most of the action is at pubs and bars. Concentrations of in-spots run along Halsted Street and Lincoln Avenue.

The Duke of Perth   This traditional Scottish pub serves one of the city's best selections of single-malt scotch, plus baskets of fish and chips ($9.25 all-you-can-eat special Wed and Fri). The outdoor beer garden is especially inviting on warm summer nights. 2913 N. Clark St. (at Wellington Ave.). © 773/477-1741. Subway/El: Brown Line to Diversey.

Galway Arms   The large heated front patio, which is open from St. Patrick's Day through late fall, sets this Irish bar apart from all the other pubs in town. Indoors, the quaint, cozy dining rooms with fireplaces attract a fairly sophisticated crowd. *Another bonus:* the smoke-free upstairs bar area. There's live music Thursday through Sunday. 2442 N. Clark St. (at Arlington). © 773/472-5555. Subway/El: Red or Brown line to Fullerton.

Glascott's Groggery   At the top of any self-respecting Lincoln Park yuppie's list of meeting places is Glascott's, an Irish pub that has been in the same family since it opened in 1937. You'll see groups of guys stopping in after their weekly basketball game, couples coming in after dinner to catch up with their friends, and singles hoping to hook up with old college buddies and meet new friends. 2158 N. Halsted St. (at Webster Ave.). © 773/281-1205. Subway/El: Brown Line to Armitage.

The Gramercy   In a previous life, this space held the influential live-music club Lounge Ax. Now the ghosts of punks past have been exorcised with the building's transformation into the upscale Gramercy, an oasis of sophistication in a neighborhood of frat bars. The decor may appear high-end at first—an all-white interior with vinyl-covered booths and streams of water trickling down behind the bar—but the place is attitude-free: no dress code, no cover, and no obvious pickup lines at the bar. People come here to hang out and talk—and they can actually hear what their companions are saying. 2438 N. Lincoln Ave. (at Fullerton Ave.). © 773/477-8880. Subway/El: Red or Brown line to Fullerton.

Red Lion Pub *(Finds)*   An English pub in the heart of Lincoln Park, the Red Lion is a comfortable neighborhood place with a mix of old and young DePaul students, actors, and Anglophiles who feel right at home among the Union Jacks and photos of Churchill. And if you're looking for atmosphere, the British owner even claims the place is haunted. 2446 N. Lincoln Ave. (between Fullerton and Wrightwood aves.). © 773/348-2695. Subway/El: Red or Brown line to Fullerton.

Tilli's   A favorite gathering spot for good-looking 20- and 30-somethings, Tilli's is an upscale version of the neighborhood bar. In nice weather, the entire front opens to the street; when it's chilly, try to snag a table near the brick fireplace in the main dining room. You can snack on appetizers or order dinner, but the main attraction is the front room, where everyone people-watches around the bar. 1952 N. Halsted St. (at Armitage St.). © 773/325-0044. Subway/El: Brown Line to Armitage.

Webster's Wine Bar   It's a bit off the beaten track—on the western fringe of Lincoln Park—but the low-lit, sophisticated decor makes Webster's a good alternative to the usual beer blast. The waitstaff can help you choose from a list of dozens of wines by the bottle or glass, or you can hone your taste buds with a flight of several wines. There's also a tapas-style menu for noshing. Step back into the library area to light up a cigar and recline on the couch. 1480 W. Webster Ave. (between Clybourn and Ashland aves.). © 773/868-0608. Subway/El: Red or Brown line to Fullerton, and then a short cab ride.

WRIGLEYVILLE, LAKEVIEW & THE NORTH SIDE

Real estate in Wrigleyville and Lakeview is a tad less expensive than in Lincoln Park, so the nightlife scene here skews a little younger. You'll find a mostly postcollegiate crowd partying on Clark Street across from Wrigley Field (especially after games in the summer). But head away from the ball field, and you'll discover some more eclectic choices.

Chicago Brauhaus Lincoln Square—a few miles northwest of Wrigley Field—used to be the heart of Chicago's German community. Although not much of that tradition remains, a few old world-style delis and European shops (including a terrific old-fashioned apothecary) dot Lincoln Avenue from Wilson to Lawrence avenues. For a dose of Oktoberfest at any time of year, stop into the Brauhaus. German bands perform on weekends, when the older crowd puts the youngsters to shame on the dance floor. The Erdinger, Spaten, and BBK flow freely, and the kitchen serves up big plates of 'wurst, schnitzel, and sauerkraut. 4732 N. Lincoln Ave. (between Leland and Lawrence aves.). ✆ 773/784-4444. Subway/El: Brown Line to Western.

404 Wine Bar One of the most inviting bars in the city, 404 Wine Bar makes you feel as if you've been invited to a party in a private home (it adjoins Jack's, a standard sports-and-beer spot; make sure you go in the entrance on the left side of the building). Tables and soft leather couches fill a series of cozy, low-lit rooms; the laid-back vibe attracts groups of friends and couples rather than on-the-prowl singles. The wine list features more than 100 labels from around the world, all fairly reasonably priced. Order by the bottle, glass, or flight (the selection changes every 2 weeks). In the summer, tables are set up in an outdoor courtyard; in the winter, fireplaces fill the rooms with a warm glow. 2852 N. Southport Ave. (at George St.). ✆ 773/404-5886. Subway/El: Brown Line to Wellington.

Ginger Man Tavern Ginger Man definitely plays against type in a row of predictable sports bars across the street from Wrigley Field. On game days the earthy bar has been known to crank classical music in an attempt to calm drunken fans—or at least shoo them away. Pool tables (free on Sun) are always busy with slightly bohemian neighborhood 20-somethings, who have more than 80 beers to choose from. 3740 N. Clark St. (at Racine Ave.). ✆ 773/549-2050. Subway/El: Red Line to Addison.

Irish Oak *Finds* Owned and staffed by folks from the Old Sod, this is one of the city's nicest Irish bars. The handsome woodwork and collection of antiques give the tavern a mellow, laid-back feel. Irish bands perform once in a while on weekends. There are plenty of whiskeys, stouts, and ales to sip, and the kitchen offers shepherd's pie and other Irish fare. 3511 N. Clark St. (between Cornelia Ave. and Addison St.). ✆ 773/935-6669. Subway/El: Red Line to Addison.

Sheffield's Beer and Wine Garden A popular neighborhood gathering spot for years, the main claim to fame at Sheffield's is the large beer garden, where you can order off an extensive menu of BBQ dishes. The bar boasts a selection of more than 80 beers, including one featured "bad beer" of the month. Sheffield's can get jammed with a young, loud crowd, but the attitude is welcoming—there always seems to be room to squeeze in one more person. 3258 N. Sheffield Ave. (between Belmont Ave. and Roscoe St.). ✆ 773/281-4989. Subway/El: Red or Brown line to Belmont.

WICKER PARK & BUCKTOWN

For an alternative scene, head over to Wicker Park and Bucktown, where slackers and some adventurous yuppies populate bars dotting the streets near the confluence of North, Damen, and Milwaukee avenues. Don't dress up if you want to blend in: A casually bohemian getup and low-key attitude are all you need. While you can reach

Wicker Park/Bucktown After Dark

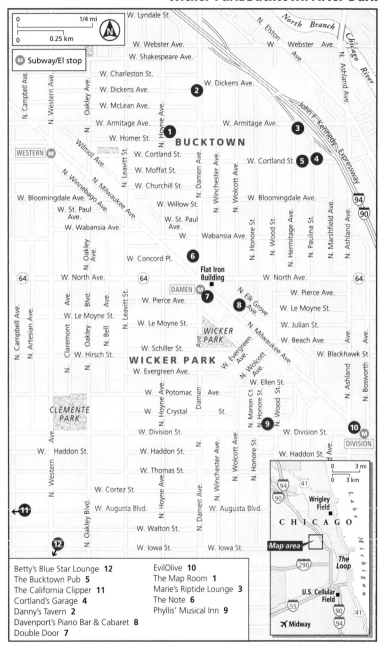

Betty's Blue Star Lounge **12**
The Bucktown Pub **5**
The California Clipper **11**
Cortland's Garage **4**
Danny's Tavern **2**
Davenport's Piano Bar & Cabaret **8**
Double Door **7**

EvilOlive **10**
The Map Room **1**
Marie's Riptide Lounge **3**
The Note **6**
Phyllis' Musical Inn **9**

most of these places relatively easily by public transportation, I recommend taking a cab at night—the surrounding neighborhoods are what I'd call "transitional."

Betty's Blue Star Lounge   Wicker Park scene makers have turned Betty's, an unpretentious, low-key neighborhood tavern just south of Wicker Park in Ukrainian Village, into a trendy late-night destination. Part local watering hole, part biker bar, it's your typical pool-table-and-darts joint earlier in the evening, but Thursday through Saturday the bar transforms into a jam-packed venue for local bands and DJs. The action is in the back room, equipped with a stellar sound system and lots of mirrors. 1600 W. Grand Ave. ⓒ 312/243-8778. Bus: 65 (Grand Ave.).

The Bucktown Pub *Value*   The owners' collection of groovy 1960s and '70s rock-'n'-roll posters and cartoon art is phenomenal. However, most Bucktown patrons are more interested in nursing their pints of imported and domestic microbrews than in gawking at the walls. Other Wicker Park/Bucktown bars try to come off as low-key; this is the real thing, where attitude is firmly discouraged at the door. The psychedelic- and glam-rock-filled jukebox keeps toes tapping, and competition on the skittle-bowling machine can get quite fierce. Credit cards not accepted. 1658 W. Cortland St. (at Hermitage Ave.). ⓒ 773/394-9898. Subway/El: Blue Line to Damen.

The California Clipper   A bit off the beaten path in Humboldt Park (just south of Wicker Park), the Clipper is well worth seeking out. For the past couple of years, this beautifully restored 1940s tavern, with its gorgeous Art Deco bar and red walls bathed in dim light, has been colonized on the weekends by the young and terminally restless. Friday and Saturday nights feature live music, mostly rockabilly and "country swing." 1002 N. California Ave. ⓒ 773/384-2547. www.californiaclipper.com. Subway/El: Blue Line to Damen.

Cortland's Garage   This cozy spot in Bucktown is unpretentious and cleanly designed, with a retractable garage door in front and exposed brick walls inside featuring black-and-white photos of garage scenes. DJs spin records from an elevated booth in the corner Thursday through Saturday nights. Although there's music other nights of the week, it's mostly a place to hang out rather than catch the latest hip band. 1645 W. Cortland St. (between Ashland and Hermitage aves.). ⓒ 773/862-7877. Subway/El: Blue Line to Damen.

Danny's Tavern   Located off the beaten Milwaukee/Damen path, Danny's has become the neighborhood hangout of choice for Bucktown's original angry young men and women, the ones who complain that an influx of yuppies is ruining the area. Just finding Danny's takes insider knowledge: The only sign out front flashes SCHLITZ in neon red. Inside, votive candles on the tables provide dim lighting; head to the back room to grab a seat on the leather couches and chairs. Once there, you can revel in the fact that you're hanging with the cool kids—just don't let them know you're a tourist. 1951 W. Dickens Ave. (at Damen Ave.). ⓒ 773/489-6457. Subway/El: Blue Line to Damen.

EvilOlive   That's right, it's a palindrome, and the palindromes don't end with the name of this 4am bar (5am on Saturdays); they're also scribbled on the wall ("If I had a hi-fi") and printed on the drink menu (try a "Dr. Awkward"). Hand-stuffed olives are a specialty here, too, both in drinks and on plates. The place has an upscale rock club feel, with oversize booths, a pool table, a photo booth, and projected movies. A DJ is perched on the second floor spinning rock and hip-hop well into the wee hours. 15551 W. Division St. (at Ashland Ave.). ⓒ 773/235-9100. http://fourchicago.com. Subway/El: Blue Line to Division.

The Map Room ✵ *(Finds* Hundreds of travel books and guides line the shelves of this globe-trotter's tavern. Peruse that tome on Fuji or Antarctica while sipping a pint of one of the 20-odd draft beers. The Map Room's equally impressive selection of bottled brews makes this place popular with beer geeks as well as the tattered-passport crew. Tuesday is theme night, featuring the food, music, and spirits of a certain country, accompanied by a slide show and tales from a recent visitor. 1949 N. Hoyne Ave. (at Armitage Ave.). 🕿 773/252-7636. Subway/El: Blue Line to Damen.

Marie's Riptide Lounge Nothing here looks as though it has been updated since the 1960s (owner Marie is long past retirement age), but personal touches and the retro cool of the place have made it a hip stop on the late-night circuit. A jukebox stocked with campy oldies, a curious low-tech duck-hunting "video" game, and the occasional blast of black light make Marie's a hoot. The owner takes great pains to decorate the interior of the little bar for each holiday season (the wintertime "snow-covered" bar is not to be missed.) 1745 W. Armitage Ave. (at Hermitage Ave.). 🕿 773/278-7317. Subway/El: Blue Line to Damen.

The Note Located in the historic Flat Iron Building, The Note is a great after-hours bar with the right after-hours music: a jukebox exclusively devoted to blues and jazz. On weekends this Wicker Park bar is packed until closing time (4am; 5am Sat) with a cross section of club crawlers who make this their last stop of the night. Rock and funk bands play earlier in the evening; when the late-night crowd shows up, the DJ spins hip-hop, salsa, and soul. It has pool tables, too. 1565 N. Milwaukee Ave. (at North Ave.). 🕿 773/489-0011. Live music cover $5–$7. Subway/El: Blue Line to Damen.

HYDE PARK

Jimmy's Woodlawn Tap *(Value* One of the few places to hang in Hyde Park, Jimmy's survived redevelopment in the 1960s that erased what was once a busy strip of bars. Namesake Jimmy, who worked behind the bar into his 80s, died in 1999, and the Woodlawn Tap almost went with him. The bar holds a sentimental spot in many Hyde Parkers' hearts, and they came together to support the place even as it battled complicated city ordinances under new management. Even though Woodlawn Tap is the place's official name, it will forever be "Jimmy's" to generations of U of C students. 1172 E. 55th St. (at Woodlawn Ave.). 🕿 773/643-5516. Metra train to 57th St. stop.

Seven Ten Lanes Seven Ten has a retro feel, and covers all the bases: burgers and sandwiches, a good selection of beers on tap, a room to shoot pool, and eight lanes of bowling. It's definitely a step up from the usual scruffy college tavern. 1055 E. 55th St. 🕿 773/347-2695. Metra train to 57th St. stop.

CAFES

Café Jumping Bean A great little cafe in the heart of Pilsen, just southwest of the Loop, the Jumping Bean is ideal for taking in this vibrant Mexican-American neighborhood. It serves the usual espresso drinks, muffins, and pastries, but it also offers decent salads, cheesecakes, natural vegetable and fruit juices, and—best of all—a tantalizing selection of *liquados,* Mexican drinks made with milk, sugar, ice, and fresh fruit (try the mango). The artistic doings outside, characterized by colorful outdoor murals, spill over into the cafe, which features rotating exhibitions of paintings and hand-painted tables by local artists. The place even schedules live flamenco music and poetry readings in Spanish. Everyone is welcome, from families with little kids to the loft-dwelling artists who've lately infiltrated Pilsen. 1439 W. 18th St. (2 blocks east of Ashland Ave.). © 312/455-0019. Subway/El: Blue Line to 18th St.

Intelligentsia   A down-to-earth San Francisco married couple set up this coffee-roasting operation in the heart of Lakeview. A French roaster dominates the cafe, and the owners also make their own herbal and black teas. Warm drinks are served in handsome cups nearly too big to get your hands around, and tea sippers receive their own pots and brew timers. Sit at the window or in an Adirondack chair on the sidewalk, or decamp to the homey back seating area. 3123 N. Broadway (between Belmont Ave. and Diversey Pkwy.). © 773/348-8058. Subway/El: Red Line to Addison.

Julius Meinl ✯   Austria's premier coffee roaster chose Chicago—and, even more mysteriously, a location near Wrigley Field—for its first U.S. outpost. The result is a mix of Austrian style (upholstered banquettes, white marble tables, newspapers hanging on wicker frames) and American cheeriness (lots of natural light, smiling waitstaff, smoke-free air). The excellent coffee and hot chocolate are served European-style on small silver platters with a glass of water on the side, but it's the desserts that keep the regulars coming back. Try the apple strudel or millennium torte (glazed with apricot jam and chocolate ganache), and for a moment you'll swear you're in Vienna. 3601 N. Southport Ave. (at Addison St.). © 773/868-1857. Subway/El: Brown Line to Southport.

Third Coast ✯   Just steps from the raucous frat-boy atmosphere of Division Street is this laid-back, classic, independent coffeehouse. The below-ground space is a little shabby, but it attracts an eclectic mix of office workers, students, and neighborhood regulars. The full menu is available late, and the drinks run the gamut from lattes to cocktails. There's often some kind of folk music on weekends. 1260 N. Dearborn St. (north of Division St.). © 312/649-0730. Subway/El: Red Line to Clark/Division.

Uncommon Ground ✯✯   When you're looking for refuge from Cubs game days and party nights in Wrigleyville, Uncommon Ground offers a dose of laid-back, vaguely bohemian civility. Just off busy Clark Street, the cafe has a fireplace in winter (when the cafe's bowl—yes, bowl—of hot chocolate is a sight for cold eyes) and a spacious sidewalk operation in more temperate months. Breakfast is served all day, plus there's a full lunch and dinner menu. Music figures strongly; the late Jeff Buckley and ex-Bangle Susanna Hoffs are among those who've played the place. Open until 2am daily. 1214 W. Grace St. (at Clark St.). © 773/929-3680. Subway/El: Red Line to Addison.

6 The Gay & Lesbian Scene

Most of Chicago's gay bars are conveniently clustered on a stretch of North Halsted Street in Lakeview (in what's known as Boys Town), making it easy to sample many of them in a breezy walk. Men's bars predominate—few places in town cater exclusively to lesbians—but a few gay bars get a mix of men and women. A couple of helpful free resources are the weekly entertainment guide *Nightspots* and the club rag *Gab.* The bars and clubs recommended below don't charge a cover unless otherwise noted.

Berlin   Step into this frenetic Lakeview danceteria, and you're immediately swept into the mood. The disco tunes pulse, the clubby crowd chatters, and the lighting bathes everyone in a cool reddish glow. Special nights are dedicated to disco, amateur drag, and 1980s new wave; male dancers perform some nights. Don't bother showing up before midnight; the club stays open until 4am Friday and 5am Saturday. 954 W.

Belmont Ave. (east of Sheffield Ave.). ℂ **773/348-4975.** www.berlinchicago.com. Cover after midnight Fri–Sat $5. Subway/El: Red or Brown line to Belmont.

Big Chicks *(Finds* One of the more eclectic bars in the city, Big Chicks is a magnet for the artsy goateed set (perhaps a bit weary of the bars on Halsted Street), some lesbians, a smattering of straights, and random locals from the surrounding rough-hewn neighborhood (the bar's motto is "Never a Cover, Never an Attitude"). They come for owner Michelle Fire's superb art collection, the midnight shots, and the free buffet on Sunday afternoon. There is also dancing on weekends. The same owner also runs the restaurant next door, **Tweet,** 5020 N. Sheridan Rd. (ℂ **773/728-5576**), which offers a menu of mostly organic American comfort food; it has become a popular gay-friendly weekend brunch spot. 5024 N. Sheridan Rd. (between Argyle St. and Foster Ave.). ℂ **773/728-5511.** www.bigchicks.com. Subway/El: Red Line to Berwyn.

Circuit It has all the necessary nightclub elements: flashing lights, a killer sound system, the biggest dance floor in Boys Town, and plenty of eye candy. Open 'til 4am on weekends, Circuit attracts a hard-partying, minimally dressed crowd after all the other local bars have closed. Friday is "girls' night." 3641 N. Halsted St. (at Addison St.). ℂ **773/325-2233.** www.circuitclub.com. $5–$10 cover. Subway/El: Red Line to Addison.

The Closet The Closet is an unpretentious neighborhood spot with a loud and constant loop of music videos (and sports, when the game matters) that draws mostly lesbian regulars, although gay men and straights show up, too. The space is not much bigger than a closet, which makes it easy to get up close and personal with other partiers. There's also a small dance floor that's usually packed on weekends. Open until 4am every night, 5am on Saturday. 3325 N. Broadway (at Buckingham St.). ℂ **773/477-8533.** Subway/El: Red or Brown line to Belmont.

Cocktail This corner spot, less frenzied than its neighbors, is more of a friendly hangout than a cruising scene; it's easy to converse and watch the passing parade from big picture windows. This is one of the few places on the street where both men and women congregate. 3359 N. Halsted St. (at Roscoe St.). ℂ **773/477-1420.** Subway/El: Red or Brown line to Belmont.

Crew Crew is a gay-friendly sports bar, where local softball leagues stop by for a drink after the game. Up to eight pro games play on multiple TVs, and there's a full menu of sandwiches, salads, and shareable appetizer plates. Located in the residential neighborhood of Uptown, a few miles north of the main Halsted Street strip, Crew attracts a crowd that's more interested in hanging out than hooking up. 4804 N. Broadway (at Lawrence St.). ℂ **773/784-CREW.** www.worldsgreatestbar.com. Subway/El: Red Line to Lawrence.

Gentry This gay cabaret in River North has been around since 1983, so expect to see plenty of regulars. The piano bar attracts out-of-town headliners along with some quirky local favorites. There's also a Boys Town branch at 3320 N. Halsted St. (ℂ **773/348-1053**). 440 N. State St. (between Illinois and Hubbard sts.). ℂ **312/836-0933.** Subway/El: Red Line to Grand.

Roscoe's Tavern *(Finds* The picture windows facing Halsted make Roscoe's, a gay neighborhood bar in business since 1987, an especially welcoming place. It has a large antiques-filled front bar, an outdoor patio, a pool table, and a large dance floor. The 20- and 30-something crowd is friendly and laid-back—except on weekends when the dance floor is hopping. The cafe serves sandwiches and salads. 3356 N. Halsted St. (at Roscoe St.). ℂ **773/281-3355.** Cover after 10pm Sat $4. Subway/El: Red or Brown line to Belmont.

Sidetrack *(Finds)*   If you make it to Roscoe's, you'll no doubt end up at Sidetrack. The popular bars are across the street from each other, and there's a constant flow of feet between the two. Sidetrack is a sleek video bar where TV monitors are never out of your field of vision, nor are the preppy professional patrons. Don't miss Show Tunes Night on Sunday, Monday, and Friday, when the whole place sings along to Broadway and MGM musical favorites. 3349 N. Halsted St. (at Roscoe St.). ℂ 773/477-9189. Subway/El: Red or Brown line to Belmont.

Spin   This dance club attracts one of Halsted Street's most eclectic crowds, a mix of pretty boys, nerds, tough guys, and the occasional drag queen. The video bar in front houses pool tables and plays a steady stream of dance-friendly music videos. The club thumps with house music. Spin keeps regulars coming back with daily theme parties, featuring everything from Friday-night shower contests to cheap drinks. 800 W. Belmont Ave. (at Halsted St.). ℂ 773/327-7711. www.spin-nightclub.com. Cover $5 Sat. Subway/El: Red or Brown line to Belmont.

Appendix:
Chicago in Depth

1 History 101

By virtue of its location, Chicago became the great engine of America's westward expansion. The patch of land where Chicago stands straddles a key point along an inland water route linking Canada, via Lake Erie, to New Orleans and the Gulf of Mexico by way of the Mississippi River.

The French, busy expanding their own territory in North America throughout the 17th and 18th centuries, were the first Europeans to survey the topography of the future Chicago. The French policy in North America was simple—to gradually settle the Mississippi Valley and the Northwest Territory (modern Ohio, Indiana, Michigan, Illinois, Wisconsin, and Minnesota). The policy relied on an alliance between religion and commerce: The French sought a monopoly over the fur trade with the Native American tribes, whose pacification and loyalty they attempted to ensure by converting them to Catholicism.

The team of Jacques Marquette, a Jesuit missionary, and Louis Joliet, an explorer, personified this policy. In 1673 the pair found a short portage between two critically placed rivers, the Illinois and the Des Plaines. One was connected to the Mississippi, and the other, via the Chicago River, led to Lake Michigan and onward to Montreal and Quebec.

Chicago owes its existence to this strategic 1½-mile portage trail, which the Native Americans had blazed in their travels over centuries of moving throughout this territory. Marquette was on the most familiar terms with the Native Americans, who helped him make his way over the well-established paths of their ancestral lands. The Native Americans did not anticipate the European settlers' hunger for such prime real estate.

FIRST SETTLEMENT
Over the next 100 years, the French used this waterway to spread their American

Dateline

- **1673** French explorers Marquette and Joliet discover portage at Chicago linking the Great Lakes region with the Mississippi River valley.
- **1779** Afro-French-Canadian trapper Jean Baptiste Point du Sable establishes a trading post on the north bank of the Chicago River. A settlement follows 2 years later.
- **1794** Gen. "Mad" Anthony Wayne defeats the British in the Battle of Fallen Timbers; England finally cedes disputed Illinois Territory to the young American Republic by treaty a year later.
- **1818** Illinois is admitted to the Union as the 21st state.
- **1833** Town of Chicago is officially incorporated, with about 300 residents.
- **1837** Chicago is incorporated as a city, with about 4,000 residents.
- **1847** *Chicago Tribune* begins publishing.
- **1848** The 96-mile Illinois and Michigan Canal opens, linking the Great Lakes with the Mississippi River.
- **1860** Republican National Convention in Chicago nominates Abraham Lincoln for the presidency.
- **1865** After Lincoln's assassination, his body lies in state at the Chicago Courthouse.

continues

empire from Canada to Mobile, Alabama. Yet the first recorded settlement in Chicago, a trading post built by a French Canadian of Haitian descent, Jean Baptiste Point du Sable, did not appear until 1781. By this time, the British had already conquered the territory, part of the spoils of 70 years of intermittent warfare that cost the French most of their North American holdings. After the American War of Independence, the Illinois Territory was wrested from British and Native American control in a campaign led by the Revolutionary War hero Gen. "Mad" Anthony Wayne. The campaign ended with a 1795 treaty ceding the land around the mouth of the Chicago River to the United States.

Between du Sable's day and 1833, when Chicago was officially founded, the land by the mouth of the Chicago River served as a military outpost that guarded the strategic passage and provided security for a few trappers and a trading post. The military base, Fort Dearborn, which stood on the south side of what is now the Michigan Avenue Bridge, was first garrisoned in 1803.

At first the settlement grew slowly, impeded by continued Native American efforts to drive the new Americans from the Illinois Territory. During the War of 1812, inhabitants abandoned Fort Dearborn, and many were slain during the evacuation. But before long, the trappers drifted back; by 1816, the military, too, had returned.

Conflict diminished after that, but even as a civil engineer plotted the building lots of the early town as late as 1830, periodic raids continued, ceasing only with the defeat of Chief Black Hawk in 1832. A year later, the settlement of 300-plus inhabitants was officially incorporated under the name Chicago, said to derive from a Native American word referring to the powerful odors of the abundant wild vegetation (most likely onions) in the marshlands surrounding the riverbanks.

COMMERCE & INDUSTRY

Land speculation began immediately, and Chicago was carved piecemeal and sold off to finance the Illinois and Michigan Canal, which would eliminate the narrow land portage and fulfill the long-standing vision of connecting the two great waterways. Commercial activity quickly followed. Chicago grew in size and wealth, shipping grain and livestock to the Eastern markets and lumber to the prairies of the West. Ironically, by the time the Illinois and Michigan Canal was completed in 1848, the railroad had arrived, and the water route that gave Chicago its raison d'être was rapidly becoming obsolete.

More than 125,000 mourners pay their respects. Chicago stockyards are founded.

- **1870** City's population numbers almost 300,000, making it perhaps the fastest-growing metropolis in history.

- **1871** Great Chicago Fire burns large sections of the city; rebuilding begins while the ashes are still warm.

- **1882** The 10-story Montauk Building, the world's first skyscraper, is erected.

- **1885** William Le Baron Jenney's nine-story Home Insurance Building, the world's first steel-frame skyscraper, is built.

- **1886** Bomb explodes during a political rally near Haymarket Square, causing a riot in which eight policemen and four civilians are killed and almost 100 are wounded. Eight labor leaders and socialist-anarchists are later convicted in one of the country's most controversial trials. Four are eventually hanged.

- **1892** The city's first elevated train goes into operation.

- **1893** Completely recovered from the Great Fire, Chicago stages its first World's Fair, the World's Columbian Exposition. The world's first Ferris wheel is a big draw.

- **1894** Led by Eugene V. Debs, members of the American Railway Union hold a massive strike against the Pullman

Boxcars, not boats, became the principal mode of transportation throughout the region. The combination of the railroad, the emergence of local manufacturing, and, later, the Civil War caused Chicago to grow wildly.

The most revolutionary product of the era sprang from the mind of Chicago inventor Cyrus McCormick, whose reaper filled in for the farmhands who now labored on the nation's battlefields. Local merchants not only thrived on the contraband trade in cotton but also secured lucrative contracts from the federal government to provide the army with tents, uniforms, saddles, harnesses, lumber, bread, and meat. By 1870, Chicago's population had grown to 300,000, a thousand times greater than its original population, in just 37 years since incorporation.

THE GREAT FIRE

A year later, the city lay in ashes. The Great Chicago Fire of 1871 began on the southwest side of the city on October 8. Legend places its exact origin in the O'Leary shed on DeKoven Street, although most historians have exonerated the long-blamed bovine that locals speculate started the blaze by kicking over a lantern. The fire jumped the river and continued north through the night and the following day, when it was checked by the use of gunpowder on the South Side and rainfall to the north and west. The fire took 300 lives, destroyed 18,000 buildings, and left 90,000 homeless.

The city began to rebuild as soon as the rubble was cleared. By 1873, the city's downtown business and financial district was up and running again, and 2 decades later Chicago had sufficiently recovered to stage the 1893 World's Columbian Exposition commemorating the 400th anniversary of the discovery of America.

The Great Fire gave an unprecedented boost to the professional and artistic development of the nation's architects. Drawn by the unlimited opportunities to build, they gravitated to the city in droves, and the city raised a homegrown crop of architects. Chicago's reputation as an American Athens, packed with monumental and decorative buildings, is a direct by-product of the disastrous fire that nearly brought the city to ruin.

In the meantime, as many immigrants forsook the uncultivated farmland of the prairie to join Chicago's labor pool, the city's population continued to grow. Chicago still shipped meat and agricultural commodities around the nation and the world, and the city was rapidly becoming a mighty industrial center, creating finished goods, particularly for the markets of the ever-expanding Western settlements.

Palace Car Company; President Grover Cleveland calls in federal troops after 2 months, ending the strike.
- **1900** The flow of the Chicago River is reversed to end the dumping of sewage into Lake Michigan.
- **1905** Wobblies, or Industrial Workers of the World (IWW), founded in Chicago. Robert S. Abbott founds the *Chicago Defender*, which becomes the nation's premier African-American newspaper.
- **1908** The Chicago Cubs win their second World Series. They haven't won one since!
- **1917** The Chicago White Sox win their first World Series.
- **1919** "Black Sox" bribery scandal perpetrated by eight White Sox players.
- **1920–33** During Prohibition, Chicago becomes a "wide-open town"; rival mobs battle violently throughout the city for control of distribution and sale of illegal alcohol.
- **1924** University of Chicago students Nathan Leopold and Richard Loeb murder 14-year-old Bobby Franks. They are defended by famed attorney Clarence Darrow and are found guilty, but spared the death penalty, in the "Trial of the Century."

continues

Chicago & the Great Black Migration

From 1915 to 1960, hundreds of thousands of black Southerners poured into Chicago, trying to escape segregation and seeking economic freedom and opportunity. The "Great Black Migration" radically transformed Chicago, both politically and culturally, from an Irish-run city of recent European immigrants into one in which no group had a majority and no politician—white or black—could ever take the black vote for granted. Unfortunately, the sudden change gave rise to many of the disparities that still plague the city, but it also promoted an environment in which many black men and women could rise from poverty to prominence.

From 1910 to 1920, Chicago's black population almost tripled, from 44,000 to 109,000; from 1920 to 1930, it more than doubled, to 234,000. The Great Depression slowed the migration to a crawl, but the boom resumed when World War II revived the economy, causing the black population to skyrocket to 492,000 by 1950. The postwar expansion and the decline of Southern sharecropping caused the black population to nearly double again, to 813,000, by 1960.

Unfortunately, Chicago was not the paradise that many blacks envisioned. Segregation was almost as bad here as it was down South, and most blacks were confined to a narrow "Black Belt" of overcrowded apartment buildings on the South Side. But the new migrants made the best of their situation, and for a time in the 1930s and '40s, the Black Belt—dubbed "Bronzeville" or the "Black Metropolis" by the community's boosters—thrived as a cultural, musical, religious, and educational mecca.

Some of the Southern migrants who made names for themselves in Chicago included black separatist and Nation of Islam founder Elijah Muhammed; New Orleans–born jazz pioneers "Jelly Roll" Morton, King Oliver, and Louis Armstrong; *Native Son* author Richard Wright; John H. Johnson, publisher of *Ebony* and *Jet* magazines and one of Chicago's wealthiest residents; and blues musicians Willie Dixon, Muddy Waters, and Howlin' Wolf.

- **1929** On St. Valentine's Day, Al Capone's gang murders seven members of rival George "Bugs" Moran's crew in a Clark Street garage.
- **1931** Al Capone finally goes to jail, not for bootlegging or murder but for tax evasion.
- **1932** Franklin Delano Roosevelt is nominated for the presidency by the Democratic National Convention, held at Chicago Stadium (since demolished).
- **1933** Chicago Mayor Anton Cermak, on a political trip to Miami, is shot and killed during an attempt on president-elect FDR's life.
- **1933–34** Chicago plays host to its second World's Fair, "A Century of Progress." The biggest attraction is fan dancer Sally Rand, who wears only two large ostrich feathers.
- **1934** Police gun down bank robber and "Public Enemy Number One" John Dillinger outside the Biograph Theater.
- **1942** Scientists, led by Enrico Fermi, create the world's first nuclear chain reaction under Stagg Field at the University of Chicago.
- **1945** The Chicago Cubs make their most recent appearance in the World Series—and lose to Detroit.
- **1953** Chicago native Hugh Hefner starts publishing *Playboy* (the original Playboy

When open-housing legislation enabled blacks to live in any neighborhood, the flight of many Bronzeville residents to less crowded areas took a toll on the community. Through the 1950s, almost a third of the housing became vacant, and by the 1960s, the great social experiment of urban renewal through wholesale land clearance and the creation of large tracts of public housing gutted the once-thriving neighborhood.

Community and civic leaders now appear committed to restoring the neighborhood to a semblance of its former glory. Landmark status has been secured for several historic buildings in Bronzeville, including the Liberty Life/Supreme Insurance Company, 3501 S. King Dr., the first African-American-owned insurance company in the northern United States, and the Eighth Regiment Armory, which, when completed in 1915, was the only armory in the U.S. controlled by an African-American regiment. The former home of the legendary Chess Records at 2120 S. Michigan Ave.—where Howlin' Wolf, Chuck Berry, and Bo Diddley gave birth to the blues and helped define rock 'n' roll—now houses a museum and music education center. Willie Dixon's widow, Marie Dixon, set up the **Blues Heaven Foundation** (✆ **312/808-1286**) with assistance from John Mellencamp. Along Dr. Martin Luther King Jr. Drive, between 24th and 35th streets, several public-art installations celebrate Bronzeville's heritage. The most poignant is sculptor Alison Saar's Great Northern Migration bronze monument, at King Drive and 26th Street, depicting a suitcase-toting African-American traveler standing atop a mound of worn shoe soles.

For tours of Bronzeville, contact the Chicago Office of Tourism's **Chicago Neighborhood Tours** (✆ **312/742-1190**; www.chgocitytours.com); **Tour Black Chicago** (✆ **312/332-2323**; www.tourblackchicago.com); or the **Black Metropolis Convention and Tourism Council** (✆ **773/548-2579**).

Mansion was in Chicago's Gold Coast neighborhood).

- **1955** Richard J. Daley begins term as mayor; he is widely regarded as the "last of the big-city bosses."
- **1959** Chicago White Sox make a World Series appearance and lose to Los Angeles.
- **1966** Civil rights leader Martin Luther King, Jr., moves to Chicago to lead a fair housing campaign.
- **1968** After King's assassination, much of the West Side burns during heavy rioting. Anti–Vietnam War protests in conjunction with the Democratic National Convention end in police riot and a "shoot to kill" order by Mayor Richard J. Daley.
- **1969** Fred Hampton and Mark Clark are killed in a police raid on the West Side headquarters of the radical Black Panther party.
- **1974** The 1,454-foot Sears Tower, the tallest building in the world, is completed.
- **1976** Mayor Daley dies in office.
- **1979** Jane Byrne becomes the first woman elected mayor of Chicago.
- **1983** Harold Washington becomes the first African-American mayor of Chicago.
- **1986** The Chicago Bears win their only Super Bowl.

continues

THE CRADLE OF TRADE UNIONISM

Chicago never seemed to outgrow its frontier rawness. Greed, profiteering, exploitation, and corruption were as critical to its growth as hard work, ingenuity, and civic pride. The spirit of reform arose most powerfully from the ranks of the working classes, whose lives were plagued by poverty and disease, despite the city's prosperity. When the sleeping giant of labor awakened in Chicago, it did so with a militancy and commitment that would inspire the union movement throughout the nation.

By the 1890s, many of Chicago's workers were already organized into the American Federation of Labor. The Pullman Strike of 1894 united black and white railway workers for the first time in a common struggle for higher wages and workplace rights. The Industrial Workers of the World, or the Wobblies, which embraced for a time so many great voices of American labor—Eugene V. Debs, Big Bill Haywood, and Helen Gurley Flynn—was founded in Chicago in 1905.

AN AFRICAN-AMERICAN CAPITAL

The major change in Chicago in the 20th century, however, stems from the enormous growth of the city's African-American population. Coincident with the beginning of World War I, Chicago became the destination for thousands of blacks leaving the Deep South. Most settled on the South Side. With the exception of Hyde Park, which absorbed the black population into an integrated middle-class neighborhood, Chicago gained a reputation as the most segregated city in the U.S. Today, although increased black representation in local politics and other institutions has eased some tensions, the city remains far more geographically segregated than most of its urban peers.

THE CHICAGO MACHINE

While Chicago was becoming a center of industry, transportation, and finance, and a beacon of labor reform, it was also becoming a powerhouse in national politics. Between 1860 and 1968, Chicago was the site of 14 Republican and 10 Democratic presidential nominating conventions. (Some even point to the conventions as the source of Chicago's "Windy City" nickname, laying the blame on a politician who was full of hot air.) The first of the conventions gave the country Abraham Lincoln; the 1968 convention saw the so-called Days of Rage, a police riot against demonstrators who had camped out in Grant Park to protest the Vietnam War. As TV cameras rolled, the

- **1987** Mayor Washington dies in office.
- **1989** Richard M. Daley, the son of the long-serving mayor, is elected mayor.
- **1994** Chicago is host to portions of soccer's World Cup, including the opening ceremonies.
- **1996** The city patches up its turbulent political history by serving as the site of the Democratic National Convention, its first national political gathering in 3 decades.
- **1999** Michael Jordan, arguably the best basketball player ever, retires (for the second time) after leading the Chicago Bulls to six NBA championships in the previous 8 years.
- **2000** The Goodman Theatre opens its new $46-million theater complex in the Loop, completing the revitalization of a downtown theater district.
- **2001** Chicago's second airport, Midway, opens a new $800-million terminal, attracting new airlines and giving travelers more options for Chicago flights.
- **2004** Millennium Park, Chicago's largest public-works project in decades, opens at the north end of Grant Park.
- **2005** The Chicago White Sox win their second World Series.

demonstrators chanted, "The whole world is watching."

And it was; many politicos blame Mayor Richard J. Daley for Hubert Humphrey's defeat in the general election. (Maybe it was a wash; some also say that Daley stole the 1960 election for Kennedy.)

A few words about (the original) Mayor Daley: He did not invent the political machine, but he certainly perfected it. Daley understood that as long as the leaders of every ethnic and special-interest group had their share of the spoils, he could retain ultimate power. His reach extended well beyond Chicago's borders; he controlled members of Congress, and every 4 years he delivered a solid Democratic vote in the November elections. Since his death in 1976, the machine has never been the same.

Today, Daley's son, Richard M., holds his father's former office, but he doesn't control the Cook County machine. Mayor Richard M. Daley has abandoned his late father's power base of solid white working-class Bridgeport for the newly developed (some would say yuppie) Central Station neighborhood just south of the Loop. The baby boomer appears to be finding himself, but many in the city still enjoy calling him—with more than a hint of condescension—"Richie."

The city has ongoing problems. With roughly 2.8 million people total, Chicago has nearly equal numbers of black and white residents—a rarity among today's urban areas—but the residential districts continue to be some of the most segregated in the country. Families are trying to cope with the school system, which has been undergoing major restructuring, but its outlook is still dismal. In 1995, the federal government seized control of the city's public housing, pledging to replace dangerous high-rises with smaller complexes in mixed-income neighborhoods. It is a long-term goal, but authorities have been gradually tearing down the notorious apartment buildings of Cabrini Green, where then-mayor Jane Byrne moved briefly to show her support for the crime-victimized residents.

Index

See also Accommodations and Restaurant indexes, below.

FROMMER'S® COMPLETE TRAVEL GUIDES

Alaska
Amalfi Coast
American Southwest
Amsterdam
Argentina & Chile
Arizona
Atlanta
Australia
Austria
Bahamas
Barcelona
Beijing
Belgium, Holland & Luxembourg
Belize
Bermuda
Boston
Brazil
British Columbia & the Canadian
  Rockies
Brussels & Bruges
Budapest & the Best of Hungary
Buenos Aires
Calgary
California
Canada
Cancún, Cozumel & the Yucatán
Cape Cod, Nantucket & Martha's
  Vineyard
Caribbean
Caribbean Ports of Call
Carolinas & Georgia
Chicago
China
Colorado
Costa Rica
Croatia
Cuba
Denmark
Denver, Boulder & Colorado Springs
Edinburgh & Glasgow
England
Europe
Europe by Rail
Florence, Tuscany & Umbria

Florida
France
Germany
Greece
Greek Islands
Hawaii
Hong Kong
Honolulu, Waikiki & Oahu
India
Ireland
Israel
Italy
Jamaica
Japan
Kauai
Las Vegas
London
Los Angeles
Los Cabos & Baja
Madrid
Maine Coast
Maryland & Delaware
Maui
Mexico
Montana & Wyoming
Montréal & Québec City
Moscow & St. Petersburg
Munich & the Bavarian Alps
Nashville & Memphis
New England
Newfoundland & Labrador
New Mexico
New Orleans
New York City
New York State
New Zealand
Northern Italy
Norway
Nova Scotia, New Brunswick &
  Prince Edward Island
Oregon
Paris
Peru
Philadelphia & the Amish Country

Portugal
Prague & the Best of the Czech
  Republic
Provence & the Riviera
Puerto Rico
Rome
San Antonio & Austin
San Diego
San Francisco
Santa Fe, Taos & Albuquerque
Scandinavia
Scotland
Seattle
Seville, Granada & the Best of
  Andalusia
Shanghai
Sicily
Singapore & Malaysia
South Africa
South America
South Florida
South Pacific
Southeast Asia
Spain
Sweden
Switzerland
Tahiti & French Polynesia
Texas
Thailand
Tokyo
Toronto
Turkey
USA
Utah
Vancouver & Victoria
Vermont, New Hampshire & Maine
Vienna & the Danube Valley
Vietnam
Virgin Islands
Virginia
Walt Disney World® & Orlando
Washington, D.C.
Washington State

FROMMER'S® DAY BY DAY GUIDES

Amsterdam
Chicago
Florence & Tuscany

London
New York City
Paris

Rome
San Francisco
Venice

PAULINE FROMMER'S GUIDES! SEE MORE. SPEND LESS.

Hawaii

Italy

New York City

FROMMER'S® PORTABLE GUIDES

Acapulco, Ixtapa & Zihuatanejo
Amsterdam
Aruba
Australia's Great Barrier Reef
Bahamas
Big Island of Hawaii
Boston
California Wine Country
Cancún
Cayman Islands
Charleston
Chicago
Dominican Republic

Dublin
Florence
Las Vegas
Las Vegas for Non-Gamblers
London
Maui
Nantucket & Martha's Vineyard
New Orleans
New York City
Paris
Portland
Puerto Rico
Puerto Vallarta, Manzanillo &
  Guadalajara

Rio de Janeiro
San Diego
San Francisco
Savannah
St. Martin, Sint Maarten, Anguila &
  St. Bart's
Turks & Caicos
Vancouver
Venice
Virgin Islands
Washington, D.C.
Whistler

FROMMER'S® CRUISE GUIDES

Alaska Cruises & Ports of Call

Cruises & Ports of Call

European Cruises & Ports of Call

FROMMER'S® NATIONAL PARK GUIDES

Algonquin Provincial Park
Banff & Jasper
Grand Canyon

National Parks of the American West
Rocky Mountain
Yellowstone & Grand Teton

Yosemite and Sequoia & Kings
 Canyon
Zion & Bryce Canyon

FROMMER'S® MEMORABLE WALKS

London
New York

Paris
Rome

San Francisco

FROMMER'S® WITH KIDS GUIDES

Chicago
Hawaii
Las Vegas
London

National Parks
New York City
San Francisco

Toronto
Walt Disney World® & Orlando
Washington, D.C.

SUZY GERSHMAN'S BORN TO SHOP GUIDES

France
Hong Kong, Shanghai & Beijing
Italy

London
New York

Paris
San Francisco

FROMMER'S® IRREVERENT GUIDES

Amsterdam
Boston
Chicago
Las Vegas

London
Los Angeles
Manhattan
Paris

Rome
San Francisco
Walt Disney World®
Washington, D.C.

FROMMER'S® BEST-LOVED DRIVING TOURS

Austria
Britain
California
France

Germany
Ireland
Italy
New England

Northern Italy
Scotland
Spain
Tuscany & Umbria

THE UNOFFICIAL GUIDES®

Adventure Travel in Alaska
Beyond Disney
California with Kids
Central Italy
Chicago
Cruises
Disneyland®
England
Florida
Florida with Kids

Hawaii
Ireland
Las Vegas
London
Maui
Mexico's Best Beach Resorts
Mini Mickey
New Orleans
New York City

Paris
San Francisco
South Florida including Miami &
 the Keys
Walt Disney World®
Walt Disney World® for
 Grown-ups
Walt Disney World® with Kids
Washington, D.C.

SPECIAL-INTEREST TITLES

Athens Past & Present
Best Places to Raise Your Family
Cities Ranked & Rated
500 Places to Take Your Kids Before They Grow Up
Frommer's Best Day Trips from London
Frommer's Best RV & Tent Campgrounds
 in the U.S.A.

Frommer's Exploring America by RV
Frommer's NYC Free & Dirt Cheap
Frommer's Road Atlas Europe
Frommer's Road Atlas Ireland
Great Escapes From NYC Without Wheels
Retirement Places Rated

FROMMER'S® PHRASEFINDER DICTIONARY GUIDES

French

Italian

Spanish

— I don't speak sign language.

A hotel can close for all kinds of reasons.
Our Guarantee ensures that if your hotel's undergoing construction, we'll let you know in advance. In fact, we cover your entire travel experience. See www.travelocity.com/guarantee for details.

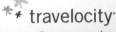

travelocity
You'll never roam alone.

There's a parking lot where my ocean view should be.

 À la place de la vue sur l'océan, me voilà avec une vue sur un parking.

 Anstatt Meerblick habe ich Sicht auf einen Parkplatz.

 Al posto della vista sull'oceano c'è un parcheggio.

 No tengo vista al mar porque hay un parque de estacionamiento.

 Há um parque de estacionamento onde deveria estar a minha vista do oceano

 Ett parkeringsområde har byggts på den plats där min utsikt över oceanen borde vara.

 Er ligt een parkeerterrein waar mijn zee-uitzicht zou moeten zijn.

 هنالك موقف للسيارات مكان ما وجب ان يكون المنظر الخلاب المطل على المحيط .

 眼前に広がる紺碧の海・・・じゃない。窓の外は駐車場！

 停车场的位置应该是我的海景所在。

I'm fluent in pig latin.

Hotel mishaps aren't bound by geography.
Neither is our Guarantee. It covers your entire travel experience,
including the price. So if you don't get the ocean view you booked,
we'll work with our travel partners to make it right, right away. See
www.travelocity.com/guarantee for details.